Anti-Discrimination Law

The International Library of Essays in Law and Legal Theory

Schools

Natural Law, Vols I & II *John Finnis*
Justice *Thomas Morawetz*
Law and Economics, Vols I & II *Jules Coleman and Jeffrey Lange*
Critical Legal Studies *James Boyle*
Marxian Legal Theory *Csaba Varga*
Legal Reasoning, Vols I & II *Aulis Aarnio and Neil MacCormick*
Legal Positivism *Mario Jori*
American Legal Theory *Robert Summers*
Law and Language *Fred Schauer*
Sociological Theories of Law *Kahei Rokumoto*
Rights *Carlos Nino*
Law and Psychology *Martin Levine*
Feminist Legal Theory *Frances Olsen*

Areas

Criminal Law *Thomas Morawetz*
Tort Law *Ernest Weinrib*
Contract Law, Vols I & II *Larry Alexander*
Anti-Discrimination Law *Christopher McCrudden*
Consumer Law *Iain Ramsay*
International Law *Martti Koskenniemi*
Property Law *Elizabeth Mensch and Alan Freeman*
Constitutional Law *Mark Tushnet*
Procedure, Vol I *Denis Galligan*
Evidence and Proof, Vol II *William Twining and Alex Stein*
Administrative Law *Denis Galligan*
Family Law *Harry Krause*
Welfare Law *Peter Robson*
Medicine and the Law *Bernard Dickens*
Commercial Law *Ross Cranston*
Child Law *Harry Krause*
Communications Law *David Goldberg*
Environmental Law *Michael Blumm*
Conflict of Laws *Richard Fentiman*
Law and Religion *Wojciech Sadurski*

Legal Cultures

Comparative Legal Cultures *Csaba Varga*
Law and Anthropology *Peter Sack*
Hindu Law and Legal Theory *Ved Nanda*
Islamic Law and Legal Theory *Ian Edge*
Chinese Law and Legal Theory *Michael Palmer*
Japanese Law and Legal Theory *Kiochiro Fujikura*
The Common Law and Legal Theory *A W Brian Simpson*
Law and Development *Anthony Carty*
Jewish Law and Legal Theory *Martin Golding*
Legal Education *Martin Levine*

Anti-Discrimination Law

Edited by

Christopher McCrudden

Lincoln College, Oxford

NEW YORK UNIVERSITY PRESS
REFERENCE COLLECTION

First published in the U.S.A. in 1991 by
NEW YORK UNIVERSITY PRESS
Washington Square
New York NY 10003

Library of Congress Cataloging-in-Publication Data
Anti-discrimination law / edited by Chris McCrudden.
p. cm. – (The International library of essays in law and legal theory)
A selection of articles originally published in legal periodicals between 1976–1989.
"A New York University Press reference collection."
Includes bibliographical references and index.
ISBN 0-8147-5466-X (cloth)
1. Minorities–Legal status, laws, etc. 2. Discrimination.
3. Discrimination–United States. I. McCrudden, Christopher.
II. Series.
K3242.Z9A57 1991
346.01'3–dc20
[342.613] 91-17394
CIP

Contents

PART V ECONOMIC AND MARKET-BASED PERSPECTIVES

Acknowledgements

The editor and publishers wish to thank the following for permission to use copyright material.

Basil Blackwell for essay: Nicola Lacey (1987), 'Legislation Against Sex Discrimination', *Journal of Law and Society*, **14**, pp.411–21.

Harvard Law Review Association for essays: Abram (1986), 'Affirmative Action: Fair Shakers and Social Engineers', *Harvard Law Review*, **99**, pp.1312–326 and Paul Brest (1976), 'In Defence of the Anti-discrimination Principle', *Harvard Law Review*, **90**, pp.1–54 and Crenshaw (1988), 'Race Reform and Retrenchment: Transformation and Legitimation in Anti-Discrimination Law', *Harvard Law Review*, **101**, pp.1331–387 and Westen (1982), 'The Empty Idea of Equality', *Harvard Law Review*, **95**, pp.537–96. Copyright © by the Harvard Law Review Association.

Harvard Law School for essay: R. Delgado (1987), 'The Ethereal Scholar: Does Critical Legal Studies Have What Minorities Want?', *Harvard Civil Rights – Civil Liberties Law Review*, **22**, pp.301–22.

Oxford University Press for essay: John B. Gardner (1989), 'Liberals and Unlawful Discrimination', *Oxford Journal of Legal Studies*, **9**, pp.1–22. Reprinted by permission of Oxford University Press.

Princeton University Press for essay: Owen Fiss (1976), 'Groups and the Equal Protection Clause', *Philosophy and Public Affairs*, **5**, pp.141–77.

The University of Chicago Law Review for essay: Richard A. Posner (1989), 'An Economic Analysis of Sex Discrimination Laws', *University of Chicago Law Review*, **56**, pp. 1311–335.

The University of Chicago Press for essays: Mary Becker [1987], 'Prince Charming: Abstract Equality', *Supreme Court Review*, pp.201–47 and Richard Fallon and Paul Weiler (1984), '*Firefighters* v. *Stotts*: Conflicting Models of Racial Justice', *Supreme Court Review*, pp.1–68.

University of Minnesota Law Review for essay: Alan Freeman (1978), 'Legitimizing Racial Discrimination Through Anti-Discrimination Law', *Minnesota Law Review*, **62**, pp. 1049–119.

Every effort has been made to trace all the copyright holders, but if any have been inadvertently overlooked the publishers will be pleased to make the necessary arrangement at the first opportunity.

Series Preface

The International Library of Law and Legal Theory is designed to provide important research materials in an accessible form. Each volume contains essays of central theoretical importance in its subject area. The series as a whole makes available an extensive range of valuable material which will be of considerable interest to those involved in the research, teaching and study of law.

The series has been divided into three sections. The Schools section is intended to represent the main distinctive approaches and topics of special concern to groups of scholars. The Areas section takes in the main branches of law with an emphasis on essays which present analytical and theoretical insights of broad application. The section on Legal Cultures makes available the distinctive legal theories of different level traditions and takes up topics of general comparative and developmental concern.

I have been delighted and impressed by the way in which the editors of the individual volumes have set about the difficult task of selecting, ordering and presenting essays from the immense quantity of academic legal writing published in journals throughout the world. Editors were asked to pick out those essays from law, philosophy and social science journals which they consider to be fundamental for the understanding of law, as seen from the perspective of a particular approach or sphere of legal interest. This is not an easy task and many difficult decisions have had to be made in order to ensure that a representative sample of the best journal essays available takes account of the scope of each topic or school.

I should like to express my thanks to all the volume editors for their willing participation and scholarly judgement. The interest and enthusiasm which the project has generated is well illustrated by the fact that an original projection of 12 volumes drawn up in 1989 has now become a list of some 60 volumes. I must also acknowledge the vision, persistence and constant cheerfulness of John Irwin and the marvellous work done by Mrs Margaret O'Reilly and Mrs Sonia Bridgman.

TOM D. CAMPBELL
Series Editor
The Faculty of Law
The Australian National University

Introduction*

The Aims of the Introduction

Anti-discrimination law is a relatively recent phenomenon. Nevertheless, the theoretical literature surrounding it is remarkably rich and diverse in its approach. The amount of literature published in English on anti-discrimination law is such that there are substantial difficulties in selecting the few which this volume can accommodate. The choice of which essays to include and discuss is not only difficult because of the sheer weight of available material, it is also seen as implying a political stance and has indeed itself become the subject of controversy in the literature (Delgado, 1984). At the outset, it can be said that the selection does not purport to establish a canon of the 'best' or 'classic' essays, although a number included must surely fall into that category. It does aim, however, to provide a selection which reflects a number of the major theoretical approaches which have been taken to anti-discrimination law: 'process' versus 'results' approaches, 'liberal' critiques, 'left' critiques, 'feminist' critiques, and 'economic' and 'market-based' critiques. Fortunately, the general approaches taken in the essays are not so well-defined as to be mutually exclusive, and a number of themes can be identified which cross the somewhat hazy boundaries of the sections. This introduction will consider some of these major cross-cutting themes.

The essays are a selection taken from legal periodicals. The essays selected, and their general arrangement, aim to provide an adequate introduction to the major themes. The volume does not purport to be a selection of readings from all available sources, such as full length book treatments, of which a number of particular importance have been published (Bell, 1980; Edwards, 1987; Fullinwider, 1980; Glazer, 1975; Goldman, 1979; Gross, 1978; Kirp, et al., 1986; MacKinnon, 1979, 1987; O'Donovan and Szyszczak, 1988; O'Donovan, 1985; Rhode, 1989); in general it has also avoided including essays which may be found in other collections of essays (Cohen, et al., 1977; Feinberg, 1969; Guest and Milne, 1985; Phillips, 1987), though an exception has been made in the case of the important essay by Fiss (1976).

I

The Beginnings of Modern Anti-discrimination Law

This section aims to sketch out the scope of anti-discrimination law and to discuss briefly a number of major legal developments of which readers unfamiliar with the area need to

---

* I would like to thank John Gardner, Nicola Lacey, Joseph Raz, Michael Rosen and Rob Wintemute, who read an earlier draft of this introduction and made many helpful and perceptive comments.

be aware before approaching the theoretical essays which this volume contains.[1] Although legal protection of minorities, their aspirations and conditions of life developed in international law particularly during the 19th and the first part of the 20th Centuries, contemporary anti-discrimination law is largely a product of domestic jurisdictions after the Second World War and, for a considerable period of time, of the domestic law of one country in particular: the United States of America.

Gross discrimination against black Americans became institutionalized in American law and custom soon after the enfranchisement of the slaves in the mid-19th Century, despite the constitutional and statutory protections provided after the American Civil War. There were sustained attempts in the United States during the 1920s and 1930s to use legal means to counter this. Until after the Second World War, however, the success of such an approach was patchy and agonizingly slow, with little sustained conceptual or theoretical underpinning (Cover, 1982). After the Second World War, however, anti-discrimination law developed at a speed and intensity which quickly built up a sophisticated legal and conceptual basis, even if its effects were slow to be seen by those discriminated against.

American anti-discrimination law developed on three different levels. The first was in the United States Supreme Court. The United States Constitution provided a number of protections enacted after the Civil War, in particular the 14th Amendment. This Amendment, especially the Equal Protection Clause, was developed by the United States Supreme Court as a powerful anti-discrimination standard against government-sponsored race discrimination. The 1954 decision by the Supreme Court in *Brown* v. *Board of Education* [2] (in which a state law which segregated schools on the basis of race was held unconstitutional) heralded a sustained attempt by the Supreme Court to provide a constitutional basis for eradicating racial discrimination and segregation (Black, 1960).

Second, various Presidents of the United States, from Franklin D. Roosevelt on, used the legal powers of their office to develop anti-discrimination requirements. In particular, from the entry of the United States into the Second World War, increasing numbers of those contracting with the federal government were required to adhere to various non-discrimination requirements regarding the treatment of black workers. This technique of using the contracting power of the government to achieve social change became known as 'contract compliance'.

Third, increasing numbers of state legislatures enacted legislation prohibiting racial discrimination, in particular in employment. These state 'fair employment practice' laws often had the common pattern of establishing an independent regulatory commission to oversee the enforcement of the legislation, for example, by receiving and resolving individual complaints. At the federal level anti-discrimination legislation was more delayed but, from the beginning of the 1960s, increasing numbers of anti-discrimination measures were passed, covering public accommodation, education, employment, voting, and housing. One of the most widely litigated statutes involved employment discrimination. Known as Title VII of the Civil Rights Act of 1964 (later amended in 1972), it provides (with the Equal Protection Clause) the basis for much of the doctrinal development of anti-discrimination in the United States, and it is frequently referred to in the essays included in this volume. From the mid-1960s, legislation enacted by Congress after the Civil War under the authority of the 14th Amendment was resuscitated by the federal courts and this too strengthened further the statutory basis for federal intervention.

The 'Proliferation of the Protectorate'

So far this introduction has concentrated mainly on those legal developments in the United States which prohibited discrimination on the grounds of race or colour. One of the most important developments from the 1960s, however, was what has been referred to by Fiss (1974) as the 'proliferation of the protectorate', that is the extension of the coverage of anti-discrimination law beyond the original prohibition of discrimination on the basis of race or colour.

The extent to which grounds other than race should come within the purview of anti-discrimination law has been the subject of considerable debate. The most common, and now most firmly accepted, extension of the 'protectorate' relates to gender. In 1963 the United States statutory requirement of equal pay for the same or similar work, irrespective of sex, was enacted. In 1964 the prohibition of race discrimination in employment was extended to include sex discrimination in the Civil Rights Act 1964. Increasingly, too, there has been litigation to extend the coverage of the Equal Protection Clause to prohibit government-sponsored sex discrimination, on the analogy of the use of the 14th Amendment against race discrimination, and this has met with some success from the early 1970s. Since then other grounds have increasingly been offered on the analogy of race and gender as also properly included in the coverage of anti-discrimination law and legislation. Litigation and political pressure has been used to try to extend protection on the basis of age, sexual orientation, disability, religion, ethnic or national origin, nationality, marital status and wealth, with some successes and some failures.

The Export of American Anti-discrimination Law

Thus far, the development of anti-discrimination law has been discussed as a largely American phenomenon. From the 1960s onwards, however, anti-discrimination became one of the more successful ideological exports of the United States, and anti-discrimination law developed significantly in other countries, often influenced by developments in American law. No comparable survey of these non-American developments is possible here, but since a number of the essays included draw on relevant United Kingdom developments, it will be appropriate to draw attention to these in particular. There have been three Acts prohibiting racial discrimination in Britain, in 1965, 1968 and most recently in 1976, with the last constituting the current legislative basis for intervention.

Sex discrimination was made unlawful in the Equal Pay Act 1970 and the Sex Discrimination Act 1975. Subsequent to the enactment of this domestic law, the law of the European Communities grew rapidly, extending the rudimentary prohibition of sex discrimination in pay, and prohibiting sex discrimination in working conditions and social security as well. Numerous changes have been made to the domestic legislation of a number of members of the European Community both to accommodate European legislative developments and judgments by the European Court of Justice interpreting this legislation. European law, for example, necessitated the amendment of the British equal pay legislation in the Equal Pay (Amendment) Regulations 1983, to permit complaints that equal pay was not being provided to women in circumstances where they were doing work of 'equal value' to a man (or vice versa). In addition, there have been important amendments in the Sex Discrimination Act 1986, the Sex Discrimination

(Amendment) Order 1988, the Employment Act 1989 and the Social Security Acts of 1980, 1986 and 1990.

In Northern Ireland, there have been three pieces of anti-discrimination legislation, in addition to equivalent sex discrimination provisions to those discussed above, dealing with religious discrimination. In the first, under the Northern Ireland Constitution Act 1973, government bodies and any local legislative assembly were prohibited from discriminating on grounds of religious belief or political opinion. In the Fair Employment Act 1976, the prohibition against discrimination was extended to make discrimination in most employment relationships unlawful and legislation in 1989 strengthened those restrictions.

II

This then is the basic constitutional and legislative structure of which readers of the essays included in this volume will need to be aware. But appreciation of some of the legal debates and terminology within these jurisdictions will allow an even fuller understanding of the debates in this theoretical literature. Having identified the sources of anti-discrimination law in the United Kingdom and the United States, it is necessary to appreciate something of the contours and shape of the territory.

Meaning of Discrimination

This introduction has assumed thus far that the meaning of the concepts of 'discrimination' and 'anti-discrimination' is unproblematic. But the meaning of these key concepts has been anything but free from doubt. Courts and legislatures have grappled with these concepts for some considerable time. The law on the issue is exceedingly complex and no definitive description is possible here. Indeed, one of the central issues debated in the essays is exactly the question of what the definition of discrimination ought to be.

One of the most basic questions raised in the debate over the meaning of discrimination is whether it is synonymous with action motivated by prejudice: treating a person with a particular characteristic less favourably than others because of a feeling of dislike or hostility towards persons with that characteristic. This popular conception of discrimination is the one which came to be most easily accepted as the problem which anti-discrimination law should aim to eradicate. But whether anti-discrimination law should seek to prevent action motivated by factors other than prejudice of this type has been controversial. Courts have interpreted 'non-discrimination' as prohibiting actions grounded in a discriminatory 'intent', but the meaning of what constitutes such an intent has proven a frequent source of debate and dispute (Jencks, 1983; Note, 1982; Strauss, 1986, 1989; Willborn, 1986a). Is it, for example, sex discrimination to dismiss a pregnant woman on grounds of her pregnancy (Lacey, 1986)?

More controversial still has been the extension of the meaning of discrimination to cover actions which, although not intentionally discriminatory, have that effect in practice (Bartholet, 1982; Blumrosen, 1975; Fiss, 1971, 1974; Gold, 1985; Lerner, 1979; McCrudden, 1982). The prohibition of practices which have the effect of disproportionately disadvantaging a particular group defined by race or sex, yet which cannot be justified by other countervailing considerations has variously been identified as the 'disparate impact' theory of discrimination, the 'effects' test, or 'indirect' discrimination. It was first developed by the United States Supreme Court in the important 1971 case of *Griggs* v. *Duke Power Company* [3], interpreting Title VII of the Civil Rights Act 1964, and this approach has been followed in United Kingdom statutes, and European Community law.[4] Attempts to have the Supreme Court recognize such an approach to discrimination in interpreting the Equal Protection Clause were unsuccessful, however, and in the 1976 case of *Washington* v. *Davis*,[5] the Supreme Court held to an 'intent'-based approach to the idea of discrimination in the constitutional context, whilst retaining an 'effects' test in the statutory context. Since then, United States Supreme Court cases have interpreted even the statutorily based effects test more and more narrowly.[6]

Scope of Remedies and Affirmative Action

So too the scope of appropriate legal remedies for discrimination has been controversial (Gewirtz, 1983, 1986). Should remedies attempt to provide a monetary substitute for a lost opportunity, or should they attempt to require a re-run of the occasion, minus the discrimination? Should remedies seek to compensate only those involved in the litigation as parties, or should they also address others in a like situation, but not parties to the litigation? Should the aim of remedies be to deter others from engaging in prohibited conduct, or to aim to bring about change only in relationships between the parties before the specific court?

Affirmative action has long been one of the central issues around which debate over the appropriate scope of remedies has flowed (Cohen, et al., 1977; Edwards, 1987; Fullinwider, 1980; Glazer, 1975; Goldman, 1979; Gross, 1978; Heaney, 1985; McCrudden, 1986a). In this context, affirmative action (the equivalent term in Britain is 'positive action') means action designed to secure the increased representation of previously under-represented groups such as women or ethnic minorities. In the United States, beginning in the late 1960s, affirmative action was increasingly used both compulsorily and voluntarily to achieve these objectives, especially in the spheres of education and employment. The legal issues surrounding affirmative action have been complex but in summary two major groups of issues can be isolated:

i To what extent can a tribunal, court or regulatory agency order a respondent to take affirmative action as part of a legal remedy designed to offset proven discrimination?
ii To what extent may an employer or a university, for example, take such action voluntarily? In particular, to what extent is the employer or university constrained in taking such action by its effect on third parties? May someone who is not employed or not admitted to a university successfully argue that he or she has been unlawfully discriminated against where the reason for their non-employment or non-admission is that another person has been admitted or employed in their place as part of an affirmative action programme?

In the United States, in particular, these questions have been the subject of continuous litigation.[7] In other countries, too, the debate over the extent of appropriate affirmative action has been sustained, in particular in India (Galanter, 1962, 1984) and Northern Ireland (Standing Advisory Commission on Human Rights, 1987).

Judges have taken varying positions on the justifiability of affirmative action in general and of its different variants. Both supporters and opponents of affirmative action have drawn support for their positions from a variety of different types of argument. Some have argued that it is justified (or not justified) on grounds of social utility, others on grounds of distributive justice, others on grounds of compensation for past discrimination, others on grounds of need. The role and justification of affirmative action is a central issue in the essays which follow.

Comparable Worth and Work of Equal Value

Although in a number of respects the United Kingdom has looked to the United States for inspiration on questions of anti-discrimination law, in one respect it has gone substantially beyond the United States. As we have seen, the United Kingdom adopted equal pay for work of equal value due to pressure from European Community law (McCrudden, 1986b, Willborn, 1989). One of the major aims of 'equal value' is to allow women in traditionally 'women's work' to argue that their work is undervalued in comparison with traditionally 'men's work'. The meaning, scope and justification of this development has remained highly controversial despite the incorporation of this concept into United Kingdom law, as it has in the United States where the equivalent concept of comparable worth is not incorporated, except in a comparatively few states (Paul, 1989; Rhode, 1989; Weiler, 1986; Willborn, 1986b). Some of the debates involve questions similar to those which arise in the context of the 'effects' definition of discrimination; others are more similar to debates over affirmative action. Yet further issues arise from the perceived difficulty of how to assess 'undervaluation' of jobs, what role job evaluation should play in doing so, how much such undervaluation (if such there is) is a function of gender discrimination, and to what extent the operation of a freely functioning labour market should provide a defence where undervaluation is established.

III

The essays included in this volume aim to make sense of these developments. They are all concerned to argue for a particular approach which they think should be taken to these basic issues. They are, in that sense, normative. However in doing so they start from varying standpoints and often concentrate on different specific concerns. In the rest of this introduction, the essays and their varying approaches are introduced.

'Process' versus 'Results'

One of the most common distinctions in the theoretical literature is between those who take a 'process' approach to anti-discrimination law, and those who take a 'results' approach. Brest (1976), for example, advances a view of anti-discrimination law which emphasizes that it seeks to prohibit 'race-dependent decisions that disadvantage the members of minority groups' (Brest, 1976, p. 2). Disadvantage is not in itself sufficient to justify intervention unless it is brought about by decisions which are 'race dependent'. Brest's approach has been widely influential in the United States and beyond as will be seen in the essays included in this volume, finding echoes (if not support) in various other essays. There are notable similarities between Brest's theorising and the 'individual justice' model of Fallon and Weiler (1984), the 'harm principle' approach identified by Gardner (1989), the 'perpetrator perspective' of Freeman (1978) and the 'fair shaker' approach of Abram (1986). At the risk of oversimplifying, these approaches are generally consistent with a view that the aim of anti-discrimination law is to secure the reduction of discrimination by eliminating from the processes decision making those illegitimate considerations based on race or gender which have harmful consequences for individuals. These approaches concentrate on cleansing the process of decision-making, and are not concerned with the result, except as an indicator of a flawed process. They are also markedly individualistic in their orientation: concentrating on securing fairness for the individual. They are also generally expressed in universal and symmetrical terms: blacks and whites (or men and women) are equally protected. They reflect respect for efficiency, merit and achievement, and given the limited degree of intervention permitted, they preserve and possibly enhance the operation of the market. They are 'manageable' in that their aims can be stated with some degree of certainty, and their application does not depend on extensive factual enquiries and judgments (see also Lewis, 1988; Reynolds, 1984).

Such approaches have been criticized as deeply flawed. Fiss (1976), Westen (1982a), Gardner (1989), Freeman (1978) and Lacey (1987) all view these approaches as deficient. Various arguments tend to recur. These approaches are said to misconceive the deep structure of racial discrimination. Race and sex discrimination are as often institutional as individual. The problem is misconceived as being one of intention rather than effect. These approaches are said not to take adequately into account the surrounding and reinforcing nature of racial or gender disadvantage, and concentrate only on particular actions in assessing whether there should be legal intervention, ignoring the wider picture (see also Marshall, 1984).

Out of these criticisms come various alternative approaches. Fiss's 'group disadvantaging' principle has been influential as the starting point for many who seek such an alternative. Fiss (1976) interprets the Equal Protection Clause as properly concerned with the results of decision-making and as seeking to redistribute resources from the group of advantaged white Americans to the group of disadvantaged black Americans. Echoes of this approach are to be found in the 'group justice' model identified by Fallon and Weiler (1984), in the 'redistributive' approach of Gardner (1989), in the 'victim perspective' of Freeman (1978) and in Abram's 'social engineers' (1986). Common to these approaches is a view that the aim of anti-discrimination law should be to fix on the outcomes of the decision-making processes. The basic aim is the improvement of the relative position of blacks or women, whether to redress past subordination and discrimination, or out of a concern for distributive justice at the present time (McCrudden, 1985). The approaches tend to be redistributive and to be concerned with the relative position of groups or classes, rather than individuals. As Fallon and Weiler write: 'The triggering incident for rectification may often be the statutory violation of a particular employer, but the deep underlying wrongs are social and historical more than those of a contemporary particular violator' (1984, p. 31). These approaches depend on a recognition of social classes or groups. The principle is often expressed in asymmetrical terms as focusing on the betterment of minority groups or women and are less concerned with symmetrical protection for white males.

These approaches too have been subject to criticism, represented in this volume by Brest (1976), Fallon and Weiler (1984) to some extent, and Abram (1986) in particular. Some criticisms relate to the open-endedness and unmanageability of the principles espoused. They have been criticized for elevating concern for groups above concern for individuals, for their asymmetrical tendency, and for the lack of emphasis given to (if not actual hostility towards) efficiency, merit and individual achievement. Other criticisms have focused on the implications these approaches have for remedies. In particular, these approaches have been said to take insufficient account of the extent to which the burden of helping racial minority groups or women falls on third parties who may be 'innocent' of past wrong-doing, who may have gained no benefit from discrimination against these groups in the past, and who comprise some of the least advantaged sections of the community in terms of their economic circumstances.

The essays by Brest (1976), Fiss (1976), and Fallon and Weiler (1984) thus provide both an introduction to a number of the issues with which the subsequent essays are concerned, and contrasting arguments as to how they should be approached. In retrospect, however, they may be thought to represent also the high point of agreement as to what the central theoretical debates surrounding anti-discrimination law should be about. Since the mid-1970s, a range of perspectives has emerged which has challenged the map of the terrain provided by the 'process' versus 'results' debate. The essays following those in the first section attempt to illustrate these contrasting perspectives. The essays have been divided into four further sections reflecting the basic, if loose, political orientations commonly found in the theoretical anti-discrimination law literature. These categories are not put forward as examples of coherent 'schools' of political thought, but as indications of some shared perspectives between the authors included in the section. Before turning to these essays, however, there is one further theme emerging from the essays in the first section to which attention should be drawn.

'Anti-discrimination': an End in Itself or a Mediating Principle?

Brest's essay tends to treat the 'anti-discrimination' principle as a unique principle, one worth supporting in its own right, and one which is attempting to advance a goal which is different from other goals such as justice or equality. It is, however, a limited principle and it is limited by the unique goal which it is advancing. Other essays (for example, Fiss, 1974) have tended explicitly or implicitly to regard the anti-discrimination principle in a similarly limited light but have for that reason proposed alternatives. What we should be aiming for, according to this argument, is not anti-discrimination but some other goal, because the anti-discrimination principle is so limited in its scope, or because it is antithetical to the goal preferred by these authors.

Yet others, however, explicitly or implicitly, appear to regard the anti-discrimination principle as only a partial translation of another principle, such as equality. From this perspective, the anti-discrimination principle is often regarded as open-ended or ambiguous or standardless, and thus needing to be interpreted in the light of the other principle on which it is based. If the anti-discrimination principle is to be given content this meta-principle needs to be articulated. In this view the anti-discrimination principle is in reality a principle which mediates between the meta-principle and the resolution of specific problems. Debate among those who hold this view tends to involve the question of what the appropriate meta-principle is which gives the anti-discrimination principle its content and its limits. There appears to be no shortage of alternatives put forward: equality, liberty, justice and community have all been suggested on occasion. Equality, however, has often proven one of the more popular bases on which the anti-discrimination principle is seen to rest.

Liberal Critiques, Rights Discourse and Consequentialist Arguments

The essays by Westen (1982a) and Gardner (1989) have been included in a section on 'liberal' perspectives because both situate themselves in that tradition of political discussion. These essays are close in political orientation to those in the first section. While both tend to eschew the use of 'equality' as the basis for justifying anti-discrimination law, it seems clear that both share the general concerns of the authors in the first section while rejecting the way in which those concerns are articulated. Both bring different perspectives to bear from within the liberal tradition. While Westen (1982a) seeks to undermine the argument that equality is the basis, without proposing what specific content the rights protected should have, Gardner argues for a specific approach.

Westen (1982a), seeks to free the debate on the underlying justifications for anti-discrimination law from the egalitarian basis on which it is so often assumed to rest. The concept of equality, he argues, is an 'empty vessel with no substantive moral content of its own' (1982a, p. 547). The entitlements that are mistakenly attributed to the idea of equality all derive from external substantive 'rights', that is 'claims that can justly be made by or on behalf of an individual or group of individuals to some condition or power'. The task of articulating what these rights are or should be is one which can and should be conducted without reference to the principle of equality. Westen's essay helps us to focus on two of the most controversial aspects of anti-discrimination theory: what role should notions of 'equality' play, and what weight should be given to 'rights' discourse. His rejection of equality has occasioned considerable debate (Burton, 1982; Greenawalt, 1983; Karst, 1983; Westen, 1982b).

But no simple answers are provided by looking at anti-discrimination law through rights-tinted spectacles either, for there are a variety of issues which are controversial within this tradition, even accepting the general rights-based approach. One issue is *whose* rights are in question. To what extent does the provider of goods, services or benefits have rights? Can we say that an employer, for example, should have a right of free choice as to how to select his or her employees, and if not, why not (Posner, 1989)? Why should an employer not have a right to choose employees on the same basis as he or she chooses his or her friends?

A second issue is the extent to which things other than individuals may be thought to be the *possessor* of rights. Some have argued, for example, that *groups* have rights, not only in the sense that the collection of individuals comprising the group have individual rights, but also in the sense that the group itself has rights, *qua* group. This has sometimes been used to support affirmative action and reverse discrimination policies, for example, on the basis that such policies are reparations to a group whose rights have previously been overridden (Bittker, 1973; Matsuda, 1987).

A third issue is the question, rights to *what*? One of the most influential recent arguments has been that developed by Dworkin (1985) who has argued that individuals have a right to 'equal concern and respect', and this has been seen as supporting an anti-discrimination principle. However, liberals who also support affirmative action and reverse discrimination in principle for reasons of general welfare, as does Dworkin (see also Fullinwider, 1980), have been put on the defensive by the argument that affirmative action violates the rights of, or is unjust to, those whites or males who are dispreferred in favour of a black or female applicant (Goldman, 1979). Supporting affirmative action seems to involve a violation of rights for reasons having nothing to do with the support of rights.

Dworkin (1985) attempts to resolve this apparent dilemma by arguing that the white male's rights are not in fact being overridden, because there is no right not to be treated adversely by reason of race or gender as such, only a right to be accorded equal concern and respect. Such a person is being accorded such equal concern and respect even though he is dispreferred. Given that the white male's rights are not being overridden, decisions based on the welfare of the society in general are permitted. Nagel (1979) argues that although such policies are not required by justice, they are not seriously unjust either, because the system from which they depart is already unjust.

A 'rights' approach therefore raises one important set of debates within the liberal tradition, but another set of arguments of a 'consequentialist' type is also to be found within the liberal tradition. Arguments of this type typically justify or contest actions on the basis of whether they promote good results. Utilitarian arguments in favour of affirmative action such as Dworkin's are one example. Others argue in favour of anti-discrimination law on the basis that discrimination is distributive *in*justice and the law is thus justified in terms of requiring distribution of resources on 'appropriate' criteria. What are considered 'appropriate' has, however, been vigorously contested. Some argue for a principle of distribution which favours the least well-off, while others argue in favour of a principle of equality in distribution, and so on.

The debate between Brest (1976) and Fiss (1976) may usefully be seen in part as involving both a debate between a 'rights' approach and a 'consequentialist' approach, and between different 'consequentialist' approaches. For Gardner (1989), the principle of 'autonomy' espoused by Raz (1986) serves to explain what anti-discrimination law seeks to achieve more coherently than either Brest's approach (which he regards as based on the 'harm principle') or Fiss's approach (which he regards as based on a principle of 'distributive justice'). In doing so this principle of autonomy better 'subsumes and consolidates' orthodox liberal principle (Gardner, 1989, p. 18) and better explains developments in British anti-discrimination law. In emphasising autonomy as the firmest basis for anti-discrimination law, Gardner enables us to focus on the controversial role which 'choice' can and should play in this area of law, an issue which reverberates through many of the contributions (see also Posner, 1989; Schultz, 1990).

'Left' Critiques, 'Community' and the Role of Informality

The essays by Freeman (1978), Delgado (1987) and Crenshaw (1988) reflect a long standing debate within the broadly 'left' political tradition on the role and function of reformist law (see for example, Sivanandan, 1976). The essays included are part of that debate but also, more specifically, they arise out of a more recent American development: the growth of the Critical Legal Studies movement. The rejection of 'rights' and 'legalism' is a consistent theme in much of the literature associated with this development. Hostility to 'rights discourse' focuses in particular on the extent to which rights are said to emphasise atomistic individualism and undermine 'community', the extent to which rights discourse shifts discussion away from responsibilities and duties, and the extent to which rights are formal and abrasive rather than accommodating and informal (Karst, 1984).

Thus, of the two dominant approaches identified in the previous section ('rights' and 'consequentialist' approaches), there is an explicit rejection of the first and, among some, a preference for the second. However, the variety of consequentialist arguments drawn on appears much wider than the traditional utilitarian and distributive justice arguments discussed above. In particular, some writers appear to be arguing that the good which should be promoted is one which does not necessarily address the well-being of the individual, but rather the well-being of the 'community', conceived as encompassing, but going beyond, the interests of the individuals which make it up.

However, a third approach, differing from both rights approaches and from consequentialist approaches, seems to be identifiable in some of the literature associated with 'left' critiques. This third approach may be termed a 'duty'-based approach. Under this approach, anti-discrimination law is justified not because it supports rights, nor because it secures distributive justice, but rather because it enforces duties. The way in which anti-discrimination law is conceptualised is that the employer, for example, is described as having the duty not to discriminate, or (more positively) a duty to provide equality of opportunity, rather than the employee having a right not to be discriminated against.

This is not the place to explain and analyse the development and content of other features of Critical Legal Studies, but suffice it to say that a number of other features associated with that movement are reflected in the Freeman (1978) essay. Law serves, in his view, largely 'to legitimize the existing social structure and, especially, class relations' (Freeman, 1978, p. 1051). Neither the legal system nor the courts appear to be anything other than nominally autonomous of this existing social and class structure. What autonomy they do have is in order to make the operation of the legal system seem credible, to serve the function of legitimating the status quo. The role of the courts is the manipulation of doctrine to that end.

> The doctrine cannot legitimize unless it is convincing, but it cannot be convincing in the context of anti-discrimination law unless it holds out a promise of liberation. Simultaneously, the doctrine must refrain from delivering on the promise if it is to serve its function of merely legitimizing. And finally, the doctrine must occasionally offer at least illusions of reconciliation and resolution, lest it collapse in obvious self-contradiction (Freeman, 1978, p. 1052).

The 'perpetrator perspective' is seen by Freeman as the dominant judicial interpretation of American anti-discrimination law. There have been alternative interpretations which have offered more hope of making the quest for racial justice possible, but these have proven illusory; though the courts have adopted the more far reaching 'victim perspective', preservation of the class structure 'compels' its rejection (Freeman, 1982).

In subsequent essays by Freeman (1981, 1982, 1988), further elements of this argument are articulated, though they are also implicit in the essay in this volume. Anti-discrimination laws were adopted, it is said, because it was in the interests of the American ruling classes to do so, in part for internal economic reasons, and in part to justify the United States to the world, to avoid embarrassment and to stablize its position (Freeman, 1981, p. 1894). Without challenging the class structure, a credible measure of tangible progress will not be possible to any great extent. The movement for greater justice for American minorities 'has been compromised by the implicit limitations associated with reliance on rights and the legalism of formal equality' (Freeman, 1988, p. 335).

Over time, the Freeman essays and the arguments they explicitly or implicitly espoused became relative orthodoxy within the Critical Legal Studies movement, so far as the analysis of race discrimination law was concerned. This appears to have happened partly due to their incorporation of so many Critical Legal Studies themes, and partly because so few other contributions within that movement sought to theorize about race discrimination law. More recently, however, there has been a heated debate within that movement which has sought to challenge this orthodoxy. The essays by Delgado (1987) and Crenshaw (1988) are representative of the issues on which the Freeman approach has been most consistently challenged from within a 'left' perspective.

Delgado (1987) argues that analyses such as Freeman's contain features 'that repel and in fact threaten minorities' (Delgado, 1987, p. 303). There are a number of such elements but he considers the disparagement of legal rules and rights to be particularly worrying. Much of the misfit between the 'CLS program' and minority aspirations, he argues, is due to scholars such as Freeman opting for 'consciously informal processes that rely on good will, inter-subjective understanding and community' (Freeman, 1988, p. 315). In a later essay Delgado (1988) argues that rights (and the formality that goes with them) are indispensable for the empowerment they provide to otherwise unprotected persons and groups. Whites, who have little to lose, may feel free to gamble by exchanging relative security for the promises of power-sharing and the benefits of community. For minorities to embrace the informality espoused in Critical Legal Studies rhetoric is to risk losing the very rights that constitute the only means of securing, and protecting their hard won gains.

Crenshaw's essay echoes this argument of Delgado's. She argues also that Critical Legal Studies authors disregard the 'transformative potential' that liberalism and rights consciousness in fact offer (Crenshaw, 1988, p. 1357). Where she advances the discussion is in her sensitive treatment of the dilemma that the oppressed face when engaging in the process of reform by using legal methods: the problem of how to take advantage of the transformative potential which anti-discrimination law offers, without at the same time becoming powerless to go beyond the limited vision from which it has emerged.

From these essays, three major themes emerge: the function and place of rights discourse (see also Horwitz, 1988), the role of the communitarian arguments in the context of anti-discrimination law (see also Karst, 1980; McCrudden, 1986c; Rhode, 1989), and the extent of the transformative potential which anti-discrimination law is able to offer (Fitzpatrick, 1987; Freedman, 1983; Lacey, 1987; Lustgarten, 1986, 1987). As with the other themes identified previously however, these themes are not restricted to the essays discussed in this section. To take but one theme: Gardner, for example, seems clearly attracted by elements of a communitarian perspective, and this is further developed in a subsequent essay (Gardner, in press).

'Feminist' Critiques, Comparisons, Differences and the Role of the Private

Just as the Critical Legal Studies movement is more of a tendency than a coherent school, and thus presents no single perspective on anti-discrimination law, so too there is no single 'feminist' perspective (Rhode, 1989). The essays by Lacey (1987) and Becker (1987) reflect some of the contours of these debates, with Becker in particular seeking to articulate and assess the different perspectives within feminist debate, including the influential work of Mackinnon (1979, see also 1987).

There is some degree of overlap between the concerns of some feminists and those who write from a left perspective (Rhode, 1990). So, although Lacey (1987) raises doubts about the British anti-discrimination legislation from a feminist perspective, her concern with the perceived individualistic nature of these laws reflects concerns similar to those of Freeman

(1978, 1981, 1982, 1988) writing of race discrimination law in the United States. So too, her view that anti-discrimination law can play only a minor part in a 'genuinely feminist political strategy' (Lacey, 1987, p. 412), while reflecting a significant tendency within feminism, reflects the scepticism about legal reform measures which we have earlier identified as 'left' concerns more generally. Nor is her view that the symmetrical protection of both men and women under anti-discrimination law mistakes the nature of the problem particularly feminist, echoing as it does a similar view articulated by many in the context of race discrimination law.

What is perhaps the most importantly different idea is her criticism of anti-discrimination law as establishing an idea of discrimination as *comparative* treatment between men and women (see also O'Donovan and Szyszczak, 1988; Wildman, 1984). This is a damaging conception of discrimination, Lacey argues, since it creates the norm of male treatment as the appropriate norm. This has, however, given rise to legal problems in contexts where the comparison is weak, non-existent or regarded as inappropriate. This has particularly been the case in the context of discrimination against pregnant women on the basis of their pregnancy. Is such discrimination sex discrimination? Courts have had difficulties bringing such discrimination within the ambit of sex discrimination law in part because the condition of pregnancy seems so special as not to be comparable to other conditions to which men are prone, and thus to give rise to problems of comparison of treatment between men and women. If pregnancy is incomparable, then how can discrimination against pregnant women be less favourable treatment of women than men?

The more recent attempt to extend the ambit of anti-discrimination law to cover 'equal pay for work of equal value', or 'comparable worth' has been seen by Rhode (1989) as raising similar problems. In part the resistance to the acceptability of such a legal claim has been due to the perceived inappropriateness or inherent difficulties of comparing the worth or value of dissimilar jobs, and thus the difficulties of fitting it within the comparative mode of traditional anti-discrimination law. Yet 'discrimination' seems to necessitate some degree of comparison between the treatment accorded the preferred person and the treatment accorded the dispreferred person; we discriminate between x and y, and thus some comparative element seems inevitable. If so, the question at issue is whether requiring a comparison inevitably requires male norms to be accepted as the appropriate standard.

But the problem of how to deal with issues such as pregnancy has sparked a debate which goes well beyond the apparently technical issue of the extent of the need for a comparison in anti-discrimination law. In attempting to grapple with the problem of pregnancy discrimination, many feminists have given the question of whether anti-discrimination law is founded on a principle of equality a new twist (see for example, Law, 1984). A number of feminists have argued that equality between men and women is the goal and that departures from this principle (by, for example, giving specifically pregnancy-related leave from employment) are unacceptable (Williams, 1982). Others have argued that strict equality is not the goal and the law should at least seek to accommodate differences, if not actively welcome, encourage and celebrate such differences (Finley, 1986; Minow, 1987; Wolgast, 1980). The debate has ranged considerably beyond the pregnancy question. The extent to which there are differences between men and women that are other than socially constructed has, for example, generated heated controversy.

Attempting to deal with the issue of pregnancy and child care within the potential scope of anti-discrimination policy also raises the issue of how far anti-discrimination law should penetrate into the 'private' sphere of relationships. The issue of the depth of intervention of anti-discrimination law has long been the subject of considerable debate. In particular, how far beyond the prohibition of government sponsored discrimination should the law seek to go? Should legislation make 'private' (that is, non-governmental) employers liable for discrimination? Few now contest that it should (though see the discussion by Posner, 1989). Should associations such as businessmen's clubs or schools not established by government be prohibited from discriminating? Probably, yes. But should law seek to enter into the 'private' realm of family life (O'Donovan, 1985). Here again, we see a degree of overlap between the perspectives of some writing from a Critical Legal Studies perspective and some feminists. For some in both groups the distinction between the 'private' sphere (where intervention should be limited and mostly prohibited) and the 'public' sphere (where intervention is desirable) is unacceptable, both in theory and in practice. Rooting out conditions of dominance and oppression in the home is, on this argument, a necessary precondition for justice in the public sphere (Powers, 1979), though there remains a substantial degree of uneasiness and ambivalence as to how far such intervention should be permitted.

One of the other effects of attempting to deal with the pregnancy issue within the context of anti-discrimination law has been to lead some to reconsider what they see as the domination of anti-discrimination law by an approach which may be inappropriate for tackling the concerns of women, due to its historical roots in tackling race discrimination (Chafe, 1977; Kay, 1985; Littleton, 1987; Note, 1981; Wasserstrom, 1977). Analogising sex to race discrimination clearly gave both political and legal weight to the development of a legal prohibition against sex discrimination (Karst, 1984). A recurring concern, however, is that the analogy is flawed in so far as race discrimination law seems to be aiming at access by minority groups to institutions and economic resources on the same basis as whites. A concern of some feminists is that sex discrimination law should only be seeking equal access on some occasions, while on others it should be seeking to change the institutions themselves, the better to accommodate women's needs and perspectives (Freedman, 1983). To that extent it is attempting to achieve a different goal than that of traditional race discrimination law, and attempting to analogize race and sex discrimination law is inappropriate (Note, 1981). It is worth noticing, however, that Gardner (1989), for example, argues for a role for race discrimination law which is not so limited and which aims for the accommodation of the needs and choices of minority groups in ways which appear to parallel the arguments of some feminists regarding the appropriate function of sex discrimination law (see also Ackerman, 1985; Fong, 1978; Minow, 1985; Modood, 1988).

Becker's essay (1987) considers the arguments of a number of the participants in these debates. She concludes that formal equality not only can effect only limited change but that for some women further movement towards formal equality is positively harmful. Yet no acceptable alternative general standard has so far been articulated, and she questions whether one can be. For she argues that '[w]omen are not a homogeneous group with homogeneous values, concerns, and interests' (Becker, 1987, p. 247). In this conclusion there are echoes of a number of other essays discussing minority groups and anti-discrimination law. Freeman (1978) and Fiss (1976), for example, argue that class interests should not be missed out of the analysis of how to tackle discrimination against black Americans. But the issue of the homogeneity of the group protected has been seen to be particularly important in the context of women, perhaps because of the differences of wealth and interest which separate working class from professional women, and women homemakers with children from single unmarried working women.

'Economic' and 'Market Based' Critiques, Efficiency and Freedom

Posner (1989) also draws attention to the heterogeneity of women as an economic class and argues that due to this and their interdependence with men, laws aimed at combating sex discrimination are more likely to benefit particular groups of women rather than women as a whole. Posner's contribution is linked with that by Abram (1986) because they both reflect some concerns which have gained considerable political strength in the United States and Britain, in particular since the late 1970s. These include the need to protect the operation of the market system (see also Sowell, 1983), a concern to advance efficiency and individual choice (see also Kirp, et al. 1986), and the desirability of recognising merit and individual achievement (Fallon, 1980).

Posner's concern in the essay included in this collection, and in an earlier essay (Posner, 1987), is to point to the trade off between advancing equality and advancing efficiency. He attempts to identify, through micro-economic analysis, the economic properties of the laws and doctrines relating to sex discrimination in employment. Posner distinguishes between legal intervention to remove discrimination in two situations:

a intervention where no competitive market exists, such as in monopsonistic labour markets or in government employment, and
b intervention where there is a competitive labour market in existence.

Though his conclusions are tentative he argues that overriding individual preferences and outlawing some types of discrimination which are nevertheless 'efficient' (such as relying on generalizations on the basis of sex which do in fact predict relevant job-related attributes) diminishes overall social welfare where there is a competitive market. By reducing the overall efficiency of the economy, effective enforcement of such laws would harm women in general. To the extent that such laws are ineffectively enforced, the costs of enforcement and administration are dead weight losses. Although his conclusions on these issues have been vigorously contested (Donohue, 1986, 1987, 1989), the benefit of Posner's analysis is in forcing attention on the costs of anti-discrimination laws and more closely requiring the identification of what the benefits may be, and the circumstances in which legal intervention is necessary to achieve them (see also Fiss, 1971), rather than relying on market forces.

Reliance on the 'free market' is also a central theme in Abram's (1986) essay. He distinguishes between two approaches to anti-discrimination law. On the one hand are 'fair shakers' who are preoccupied with 'equality of opportunity'. The notion of 'equality of opportunity' is one with a long and controversial content (Campbell, 1974; Hepple, 1990; Williams, 1969). Abram's definition is that it consists in

> an equality to be reached by the elimination of discriminatory barriers that denied the individual the opportunity to exercise his franchise effectively, to compete for housing and employment, and to use public accommodations (Abram, 1986, p. 1312).

This is the view he subscribes to. On the other hand are 'social engineers' who are preoccupied with equality of results. For them, the 'only way to measure equality is in terms of... representation, and... it is the government's role to bring about proportional representation in short order' (p. 1313). This is the approach he opposes (see also Glazer, 1975).

He presents a considerable range of arguments in favour of the former and against the latter, but a conception of the role of law in the free market similar to that of Posner (1989) seems central to his concerns. Intervention is justified to eliminate discriminatory barriers that deny individuals the opportunity to compete, that is to participate in the market. Such a role for law is 'consistent with our meritocratic view of the relevant differences between individuals – a view through which our society rewards the individual for attainment...' (Abram, 1986, p. 1315–6). Occupational and professional standards should enable the 'best available' candidates for jobs to be hired (Abram, 1986, p. 1320). Not only is the social engineering approach unjustified in seeking to go beyond these goals, it is also dangerous because it threatens the operation of this system by politicizing the process of selection and distribution. In the absence of the 'neutral decision-making' of the free market, the process 'must inevitably degenerate into a crude political struggle between groups seeking favored status' (Abram, 1986, p. 1321). Societies that have departed from such neutral decision-making have suffered a history 'not of liberation but of crippling oppression' (Abram, 1986, p. 1322). Nor, echoing Posner's argument, is a 'social engineering' approach likely to deliver the higher standard of living for disadvantaged groups desired because of the overall decrease in the efficiency of the economy.

The essays drawing on economic and market-based critiques are, not surprisingly, ones which cast an empirically attuned eye on a number of theoretical issues, but they are not alone in this. A number of the other contributors draw from empirical observations to support their arguments. However, one of the limitations in this volume is that the rich and diverse empirical literature on the operation of anti-discrimination law is scarcely touched on, and those interested in these issues may wish to follow them up elsewhere for more systematic treatments (see for example, McCrudden, et al., 1991).

Issues of Legal Process

Although there have been significant developments in enforcement, adjudication and litigation which have influenced the theoretical arguments put forward in the essays included in this volume, and on occasion these developments are adverted to and their influence assessed explicitly, for the most part they remain as background assumptions. We have seen above that three main institutions have been adopted for enforcement purposes: litigation, enforcement by a regulatory agency, and contract compliance. Within these general institutional categories, however, there is a considerable range of types of institutional competence, style and role. Apparently similar institutions may operate very differently in different countries due to tradition and constitutional structure. So too within particular jurisdictions, enforcement institutions are subject to change and adaptation over time. Institutions may adapt over time and pursue different goals from those with which they were originally most closely associated. In the United States, in particular, the practice of anti-discrimination litigation in the federal courts has developed in significant ways over the last fifty years.

Litigation has become increasingly directed at restructuring institutions in addition to resolving individual grievances, and techniques of 'structural' and 'public law' litigation have developed which in turn have had effects on doctrinal development and on theoretical debate (Chayes, 1976; Fiss, 1979). Statistics have become increasingly important as an element of identifying potential violation of the anti-discrimination laws, proving discrimination in court, devising remedies, and disciplining the carrying out of affirmative action programmes. The development of the class action, the growth of public interest law firms which sought to use litigation to further the interests of the disadvantaged, the development of expanded remedies which necessitated continuing supervision by courts, are all examples of an expanded role for the courts and the judiciary in the United States which has been one of the more controversial elements in the development of anti-discrimination law. Such issues as the legitimacy of judicial (rather than legislative) establishment of standards, the competence of the judicial process in handling attempts at achieving widespread change, the potential adaptability of enforcement institutions in coping with the stresses of such a role, the proper balance between settlement and litigation, have all been central questions. A full treatment of these issues lies beyond the scope of either this introduction or this volume, but it is nevertheless important to bear in mind that many of these legal process questions may lie below the surface of concerns of authors whether American or not (see Hepple, 1983; McCrudden, 1983).

Notes

1 Neither this introduction nor this volume provides, however, a comprehensive or up-to-date analysis of the twists and turns of anti-discrimination law doctrine. The issues of legal doctrine raised in this introduction are those which have a particular resonance in the articles which follow, and they are discussed in general terms without giving attention to the different nuances of judicial decision or statutory provisions over time or between jurisdictions. For these, other studies must be consulted.
2 *Brown* v. *Board of Education*, 394 U.S. 294 (1954).
3 *Griggs* v. *Duke Power Co.*, 401 U.S. 424 (1971).
4 *Bilka Kaufhaus GmbH* v. *Weber von Harz* [1987] ICR 110, (1986) ECR 1607 (ECJ), *Rinner Kuhn* v. *FWW Spezial-Gebaudereiningung GmbH and Co.* [1989] IRLR 493 (ECJ), and *Kowalska* v. *Freie Und Hansesstadt Hamburg* [1990] IRLR 447 (ECJ).
5 *Washington* v. *Davis*, 426 U.S. 229 (1976).
6 *Watson* v. *Fort Worth Bank & Trust*, 108 S. Ct. 2777 (1988); *Wards Cove Packing Co.* v. *Atonio*, 109 S. Ct. 2115 (1989).
7 See, for example, *University of California Regents* v. *Bakke*, 438 U.S. 265 (1978); *United Steelworkers of America* v. *Weber*, 443 U.S. 192 (1979); *Fullilove* v. *Klutznick*, 448 U.S. 448 (1980); *Firefighters Local Union No. 1784* v. *Stotts*, 467 U.S. 561 (1984); *Wygant* v. *Jackson Board of Education*, 476 U.S. 267 (1986).

Bibliography

Abram, M. (1986), 'Affirmative Action: Fair Shakers and Social Engineers', *Harvard Law Review*, **99**, 1312–1326.

Ackerman, B. (1985), 'Beyond Carolene Products', *Harvard Law Review*, **98**, 713.

Bartholet, E. (1982), 'Application of Title VII to Jobs in High Places', *Harvard Law Review*, **95**, 945.

Becker, M. [1987], 'Prince Charming: Abstract Equality', *Supreme Court Review*, 201.

Bell, D. (1980), *Race, Racism and American Law*, 2nd ed. Little Brown, Boston.

Bittker, B. (1973), *The Case for Black Reparations*, Random House, New York.
Black, C. (1960), 'The Lawfulness of the Segregation Decisions', *Yale Law Journal*, **69**, 421.
Blumrosen, A. (1975), 'Strangers in Paradise: *Griggs* v. *Duke Power Co.* and the Concept of Employment Discrimination', *Michigan Law Review*, **71**, 59.
Brest, P. (1976), 'In Defense of the Anti-discrimination Principle', *Harvard Law Review*, **90**, 1.
Burton, (1982), 'Comment on "Empty Ideas: Logical Positivist Analyses of Equality and Rules"', *Yale Law Journal*, **91**, 1136.
Campbell, T. (1974), 'Equality of Opportunity', *Proceedings of the Aristotelian Society*, **75**, 51.
Chafe, W.H. (1977), *Women and Equality: Changing Patterns in American Culture*, NY, OUP.
Chayes, A. (1976), 'The Role of the Judge in Public Law Litigation', *Harvard Law Review*, **89**, 1281.
Cohen, M., Nagel, T. and Scanlon, T., (eds) (1977), *Equality and Preferential Treatment*, Princeton U.P., Princeton.
Cover, R. (1982), 'The Origins of Judicial Activism in the Protection of Minorities', *Yale Law Journal*, **91**, 1287.
Crenshaw, K.W. (1988), 'Race Reform and Retrenchment: Transformation and Legitimation in Anti-Discrimination Law', *Harvard Law Review*, **101**, 1331.
Delgado, R. (1987), 'The Ethereal Scholar: Does Critical Legal Studies Have What Minorities Want?', *Harvard Civil Rights – Civil Liberties Law Review*, **22**, 301–322.
Delgado, R. (1988), 'Critical Legal Studies and the Realities of Race – Does the Fundamental Contradiction Have a Corollary', *Harvard Civil Rights – Civil Liberties Law Review*, **23**, 407.
Delgado, R. (1984), 'The Imperial Scholar: Reflections on a Review of Civil Rights Literature', *University of Pennsylvania Law Review*, **132**, 561.
Donohue, J. (1987), 'Further Thoughts on Employment Discrimination Legislation: A Reply to Judge Posner', *University of Pennsylvania Law Review*, **136**, 523–551.
Donohue, J. (1986), 'Is Title VII Efficient?', *University of Pennsylvania Law Review*, **134**, 1411.
Donohue, J. (1989), 'Prohibiting Sex Discrimination in the Workplace: An Economic Perspective', *University of Chicago Law Review*, **56**, 1337.
Dworkin, R. (1985), *A Matter of Principle*, Harvard U.P., Cambridge, Mass.
Edwards, J. (1987), *Positive Discrimination, Social Justice, and Social Policy: Moral Scrutiny of a Policy Practice*, Tavistock Publications, London.
Fallon, R.H., and Weiler, P. [1984], '*Firefighters* v. *Stotts*: Conflicting Models of Racial Justice', *Supreme Court Review*, 1.
Fallon, R.H., (1980), 'To Each According to His Ability, From None According to His Race: the Concept of Merit in the Law of Antidiscrimination', *Boston University Law Review*, **60**, 815.
Feinberg, J. (ed.) (1969), *Moral Concepts*, OUP.
Finley, L. (1986), 'Transcending Equality Theory: A Way Out of the Maternity and the Workplace Debate', *Columbia Law Review*, **86**, 1118.
Fiss, O. (1971), 'A Theory of Fair Employment Laws', *University of Chicago Law Review*, **38**, 235.
Fiss, O. (1976), 'Groups and the Equal Protection Clause', *Philosophy and Public Affairs*, **5**, 141.
Fiss, O. (1974), 'The Fate of an Idea Whose Time Has Come: Anti-Discrimination Law in the Second Decade After *Brown* v. *Board of Education*', *University of Chicago Law Review*, **41**, 742.
Fiss, O. (1979), 'The Forms of Justice', *Harvard Law Review*, **93**, 1.
Fitzpatrick, P. (1987), 'Racism and the Innocence of Law', in Fitzpatrick, P. and Hunt, A., *Critical Legal Studies*, Blackwell.
Fong, (1978), 'Cultural Pluralism', *Harvard Civil Rights – Civil Liberties Law Review*, **13**, 133.
Freedman, A. (1983), 'Sex Equality, Sex Differences and the Supreme Court', *Yale Law Journal*, **92**, 913.
Freeman, A. (1978), 'Legitimating Racial Discrimination Through Anti-Discrimination Law', *Minnesota Law Review*, **62**, 1049.
Freeman, A. (1982), 'Antidiscrimination Law: A Critical Review' in Kairys, D. (ed.), *The Politics of Law*, 96.
Freeman, A. (1981), 'Book Review, Race and Class: The Dilemma of Liberal Reform', *Yale Law Journal*, **90**, 1880.
Freeman, A. (1988), 'Racism, Rights and the Quest for Equality of Opportunity: A Critical Legal Esay', *Harvard Civil Rights – Civil Liberties Law Review*, **23**, 295.

Fullinwider, R.K. (1980), *The Reverse Discrimination Controversy: A Moral and Legal Analysis*, Rowman and Littlefield, New Jersey.
Galanter, M. (1962), 'Equality and "Protective Discrimination" in India', *Rutgers Law Review*, **16**, 42.
Galanter, M. (1984), *Competing Equalities: Law and the Backward Classes in India*, University of California Press, California.
Gardner, J. (1989), 'Liberals and Unlawful Discrimination', *Oxford Journal of Legal Studies*, **9**, 1.
Gardner, J. (1991), 'Private Activities and Personal Autonomy', in Hepple, B., and Szyszczak, E., *Discrimination: The Limits of Law?*, Mansell, London, in press.
Gewirtz, P. (1986), 'Choice in the Transition: School Desegregation and the Corrective Ideal', *Columbia Law Review*, **86**, 728.
Gewirtz, P. (1983), 'Remedies and Resistance', *Yale Law Journal*, **92**, 585.
Glazer, N. (1975), *Affirmative Discrimination*, Basic Books, New York.
Gold, M.E. (1985), 'Griggs' Folly: An Essay on the Theory, Problems and Origin of the Adverse Impact Definition of Employment Discrimination and a Recommendation for Reform', *Industrial Relations Law Journal*, **7**, 429.
Goldman, A. (1979), *Justice and Reverse Discrimination*, Princeton U.P., Princeton.
Greenawalt, K. (1983), 'How Empty is the Idea of Equality?', *Columbia Law Review*, **83**, 1167.
Gross, B.R. (1978), *Discrimination in Reverse*, New York U.P., New York.
Guest, S., and Milne, A. (eds) (1985), *Equality and Discrimination: Essays in Freedom and Justice*, Stuttgart, Frank Steiner Verlag.
Heaney, G.W. (1985), 'Busing, Timetables, Goals and Ratios: Tombstones of Equal Opportunity', *Minnesota Law Review*, **69**, 735.
Hepple, B. (1990), 'Discrimination and Equality of Opportunity: Northern Ireland Lessons', *Oxford Journal of Legal Studies*, **10**, 408.
Hepple, B. [1983], 'Judging Equal Rights', *Current Legal Problems*, 71.
Horwitz, M. (1988), 'Rights', *Harvard Civil Rights – Civil Liberties Law Review*, **23**, 393.
Jencks, C. (1983), 'Discrimination and Thomas Sowell', *New York Review of Books*, March 3, 33.
Karst, K. (1980), 'Equality and Community: Lessons from the Civil Rights Era', *Notre Dame Lawyer*, **56**, 183.
Karst, K. (1983), 'Why Equality Matters', *Georgia Law Review*, **17**, 245.
Karst, K. (1984), 'Woman's Constitution', *Duke Law Journal*, 447.
Kay, H.H. [1985], 'Models of Equality', *University of Illinois Law Review*, 39.
Kirp, D.L., Youdof, M.G., and Franks, M.S. (1986), *Gender Justice*, U. Chicago Press, Chicago.
Lacey, N. (1986), 'Note: Dismissal by reason of pregnancy', *Industrial Law Journal*, **15**, 43.
Lacey, N. (1987), 'Legislation Against Sex Discrimination', *Journal of Law and Society*, **14**, 411.
Law, S. (1984), 'Rethinking Sex and the Constitution', *University of Pennsylvania Law Review*, **132**.
Lerner, B. (1979), 'Employment Discrimination: Adverse Impact, Validity and Equality', *Supreme Court Review*, 17.
Lewis, R. (1988), *Anti-Racism: A Mania Exposed*, Quartet, London.
Littleton, C. (1987), 'Reconstructing Sexual Equality', *California Law Review*, **75**, 1279.
Lustgarten, L. (1987), 'Racial Inequality and the Limits of Law', in Jenkins, R., and Solomos, J., *Racism and Equal Opportunity Policies in the 1980s*, Cambridge U.P.
Lustgarten, L. (1986), 'Racial Inequality and the Limits of Law', *Modern Law Review*, **49**, 68–85.
MacKinnon, C.A. (1979), *Sexual Harassment of Working Women*, Yale U.P., New Haven.
MacKinnon, C.A. (1987), *Feminism Unmodified*, Harvard U.P., Cambridge, Mass, 32–45.
Marshall, B. (1984), 'A Comment on the Non-discrimination Principle in a "Nation of Minorities"', *Yale Law Journal*, **93**, 1006.
Matsuda, M.J. (1987), 'Looking to the Bottom: Critical Legal Studies and Reparations', *Harvard Civil Rights – Civil Liberties Law Review*, **22**, 323.
McCrudden, C. (1983), 'Anti-discrimination Goals and the Legal Process', in Young, K., and Glazer, N. (eds), *Ethnic Pluralism and Public Policy*, Policy Studies Institute, London.
McCrudden, C. (1985), 'Changing Notions of Discrimination', in Guest, S., and Milne, A., *Equality and Discrimination: Essays in Freedom and Justice*, 83, Stuttgart, Steiner Verlag Wiesbaden GmbH.
McCrudden, C. (1986) (1986c), 'Community and Discrimination', in Bell, J. and Eekelaar, J. (eds),

Oxford Essays in Jurisprudence, OUP, 3rd. edition.
McCrudden, C. (1986) (1986b), 'Comparable Worth: A Common Dilemma', *Yale Journal of International Law*, **11**, 396.
McCrudden, C. (1982), 'Institutional Discrimination', *Oxford Journal of Legal Studies*, **2**, 303.
McCrudden, C. (1986) (1986a), 'Rethinking Positive Action', *Industrial Law Journal*, **15**, 219.
McCrudden, C., Smith, D., and Brown, C. (1991), *Racial Justice at Work*, Policy Studies Institute, London.
Minow, M. (1987), 'The Supreme Court 1986 Term Forward: Justice Engendered', *Harvard Law Review*, **101**, 10.
Minow, M. (1985), 'Learning to Live with the Dilemma of Difference: Bilingual and Special Education', *Law and Contemporary Problems*, **48**, 157.
Modood, T. (1988), '"Black" Racial Equality and Asian Identity', *New Community*, 397.
Nagel, T. (1979), *Mortal Questions*, Cambridge U.P., Cambridge.
Note (1982), 'Making the Violation Fit the Remedy: The Intent Standard and Equal Protection Law', *Yale Law Journal*, **92**, 328.
Note (1981), 'Towards a Redefinition of Sexual Equality', *Harvard Law Review*, **95**, 487.
O'Donovan C. and Szyszczak, E. (1988), *Equality and Sex Discrimination Law*, Blackwells, Oxford.
O'Donovan, C. (1985), *Sexual Divisions in Law*, Weidenfeld, London.
Paul, E.F. (1989), *Equality and Gender: The Comparable Worth Debate*, Transaction Publishers, New Brunswick and Oxford.
Phillips, A. (ed.) (1987), *Feminism and Equality*, Blackwells, Oxford.
Posner, R. (1989), 'An Economic Analysis of Sex Discrimination Laws', *University of Chicago Law Review*, **56**, 1311–1335.
Posner, R. (1987), 'The Efficiency and the Efficacy of Title VII', *University of Pennsylvania Law Review*, **136**, 513.
Powers, [1979], 'Sex Segregation and the Ambivalent Directions of Sex Discrimination Law', *Wisconsin Law Review*, 55.
Raz, J. (1986), *The Morality of Freedom*, Oxford, OUP.
Reynolds, B. (1984), 'Individualism v. Group Rights: The Legacy of Brown', *Yale Law Journal*, **93**, 995.
Rhode, D.L. (1990), 'Feminist Critical Theories', *Stanford Law Review*, **42**, 617.
Rhode, D.L. (1989), *Justice and Gender: Sex Discrimination and the Law*, Harvard U.P., Cambridge Mass.
Schultz, V. (1990), 'Telling Stories About Women and Work: Judicial Interpretations of Sex Segregation in the Workplace in Title VII Cases Raising the Lack of Interest Argument', *Harvard Law Review*, **103**, 1749.
Sivanandan, A. (1976), 'Race, Class and the State: The Black Experience in Britain', *Race and Class*, **XVII**, 347.
Sowell, T. (1983), *Markets and Minorities*, Basic Books, New York.
Standing Advisory Commission on Human Rights (1987), *Religious and Political Discrimination and Equality of Opportunity in Northern Ireland, Report on Fair Employment*, Cm 237, HMSO, London.
Strauss, D.A. (1989), 'Discriminatory Intent and the Taming of Brown', *University of Chicago Law Review*, **56**, 935.
Strauss, D.A. [1986], 'The Myth of Colorblindness', *The Supreme Court Review*, 99.
Wasserstrom, R. (1977), 'Racism, Sexism and Preferential Treatment: An Approach to the Topic', *University of California Los Angeles Law Review*, **24**, 581–622.
Weiler, P. (1986), 'The Wages of Sex', *Harvard Law Review*, **99**, 1728.
Westen, P. (1982) (1982a), 'The Empty Idea of Equality', *Harvard Law Review*, **95**, 537.
Westen, P. (1982) (1982b), 'On "Confusing Ideas": Reply', *Yale Law Journal*, **91**, 1153.
Wildman, S.M. (1984), 'The Legitimation of Sex Discrimination: A Critical Response to Supreme Court Jurisprudence', *Oregon Law Review*, **63**, 265.
Willborn, S.L. (1986) (1986a), 'Theories of Employment Discrimination in the United Kingdom and the United States', *Boston College International and Comparative Law Review*, **9**, 243.
Willborn, S.L. (1989), *A Secretary and A Cook: Challenging Women's Wages in the Courts of the United States and Great Britain*, ILR Press, Ithaca.

Willborn, S.L. (1986) (1986b), 'Equal Pay for Work of Equal Value: Comparable Worth in the United Kingdom', *American Journal of Comparative Law*, **34**, 415.
Williams, B. (1969), 'The Idea of Equality' in Feinberg J. (ed.), *Moral Concepts*, OUP.
Williams, W. (1982), 'The Equality Crisis: Some Reflections on Culture, Courts and Feminism', *Women's Rights Law Reporter*, **7**, 175.
Wolgast, E.H. (1980), *Equality and the Rights of Women*, Cornell U.P., Ithaca and London.

Part I
Process versus Results Approaches

[1]

VOLUME 90 NOVEMBER 1976 NUMBER 1

HARVARD LAW REVIEW

THE SUPREME COURT 1975 TERM

FOREWORD: IN DEFENSE OF THE ANTIDISCRIMINATION PRINCIPLE

*Paul Brest**

BY THE "antidiscrimination principle" I mean the general principle disfavoring classifications and other decisions and practices that depend on the race (or ethnic origin) of the parties affected.[1]

A century after the Civil War, our nation was committed to the antidiscrimination principle. Of the Reconstruction amendments, only the fifteenth explicitly embodied it.[2] In the Civil Rights Act of 1866, however, Congress read the antidiscrimination principle into the thirteenth amendment;[3] and the Supreme Court has construed the amorphous language of the equal protection clause of the fourteenth amendment to hold that racial classifications are "constitutionally suspect" and subject to "the most rigid scrutiny."[4] The antidiscrimination principle lies at the core of most state and federal civil rights legislation, including the Civil Rights Act of 1964,[5] the Voting Rights Act of 1965,[6] and the Fair Housing Act of 1968.[7]

---

* Professor of Law, Stanford University. A.B., Swarthmore College, 1962; LL.B. Harvard Law School, 1965.

That this article contains fewer egregious errors than earlier drafts is due to Iris Brest and the following colleagues here and elsewhere: Lawrence Alexander, William Cohen, Richard Danzig, Walter Dellinger, David Engel, Owen Fiss, Lawrence Friedman, Thomas Grey, Sanford Levinson, David Kirp, Michael Piore, and Peter Temin. Doubtless there would be still fewer errors had I heeded even more of their advice. I am also grateful to Robert Garcia, who worked as my research assistant during the summer of 1976.

[1] For the moment, I leave open whether the antidiscrimination principle disfavors so-called "benign" race-dependent practices — practices designed to benefit, and that seem in fact to benefit, the members of traditionally disadvantaged minorities.

[2] "The right of citizens of the United States to vote shall not be denied or abridged by the United States or by any State on account of race, color, or previous condition of servitude." U.S. CONST. amend. XV, § 1.

[3] Civil Rights Act of 1866, ch. 31, § 1, 14 Stat. 27 (codified at 42 U.S.C. §§ 1981–82 (1970)).

[4] McLaughlin v. Florida, 379 U.S. 184, 192 (1964); Bolling v. Sharpe, 347 U.S. 497, 499 (1954).

[5] 42 U.S.C. §§ 2000a to 2000h–6 (1970).

[6] 42 U.S.C. §§ 1971, 1973 to 1973bb–4 (1970).

[7] 42 U.S.C. §§ 3601–31 (1970).

The heart of the antidiscrimination principle is its prohibitions of race-dependent decisions that disadvantage the members of minority groups. *Brown v. Board of Education* [8] settled that the principle applies to racial segregation as well as to other forms of differential treatment, correcting the Court's earlier approval of the pernicious notion of "separate but equal." [9] The first order of business in the era following *Brown* was to halt the ongoing, pervasive, and often overt practices of discriminatory exclusion of blacks from schools, voting booths, jobs, restaurants, housing, and the like. The Court expanded the concept of "state action" under the fourteenth amendment,[10] and then in effect construed the thirteenth amendment to prohibit a broad range of private discrimination [11] — just as Congress began to use its power over interstate commerce to achieve similar results.[12] By the late 1960's, the civil rights enforcement effort had eliminated the most flagrant practices. Covert discrimination continued to flourish, however, and the very successes of the '60's dispelled any notions that blacks would quickly become integrated into the economic and social life of the nation.

The policy of the 1960's provided common ground for persons having divergent aims. Disappointment with its results exposed latent differences and eroded the coalition that had been responsible for much of the earlier progress in civil rights. Some former members of the coalition have urged that the antidiscrimination principle be replaced by the independent goal of assuring that no minority racial group is — for any reason — appreciably worse off than the rest of society. Among those who still profess to adhere to the antidiscrimination principle, many support sweeping measures, including race-conscious ones, designed to prevent ongoing discrimination, to eliminate the effects of past discrimination, and otherwise to benefit racial minorities. Others argue that these measures are excessively costly, that they impose unjust burdens on nonminority persons, and that the antidiscrimination principle forbids race-consciousness even for benign purposes. Some advocates of civil rights have come to doubt the desirability of widespread busing for school desegregation. The

---

[8] 347 U.S. 483 (1954).

[9] *See* Plessy v. Ferguson, 163 U.S. 537 (1896).

[10] *See, e.g.*, Burton v. Wilmington Parking Auth., 365 U.S. 715 (1961); Reitman v. Mulkey, 387 U.S. 369 (1967).

[11] *See* Jones v. Alfred H. Mayer Co., 392 U.S. 409 (1968) (applying 42 U.S.C. § 1982 to private housing discrimination). Last Term, in Runyon v. McCrary, 96 S. Ct. 2586 (1976), the Court applied the companion provision, 42 U.S.C. § 1981 (1970), to prohibit racial discrimination by a private school.

[12] *See* Civil Rights Act of 1964, 42 U.S.C. §§ 2000a to 2000h-6 (1970); Fair Housing Act of 1968, 42U.S.C. §§ 3601-31 (1970).

university professoriate, once a faithful member of the coalition, has often responded grudgingly to government-induced affirmative action programs. And such former allies as the Anti-Defamation League and the NAACP Legal Defense and Educational Fund filed *amicus curiae* briefs on opposite sides in *DeFunis v. Odegaard*,[13] a case involving the constitutionality of racially preferred admissions to a law school.

A glance at last Term's decisions — even those tending toward restraint — indicates how far national policy has moved from a narrow conception of the antidiscrimination principle. *Hills v. Gautreaux*[14] affirmed a decision requiring that government agencies remedy their past discriminatory selection of public housing sites by consciously locating future projects in predominantly white neighborhoods. *Pasadena City Board of Education v. Spangler*[15] held that after four years under a court-ordered plan requiring cross-district busing to assure that no school had more than fifty percent minority students, the school board need not continue to reassign students on the basis of race to compensate for demographic changes. Although the decision was for the defendants, it cast no doubt on the propriety of race-conscious desegregation orders, a concept that the Court has explicitly approved in other recent decisions.[16]

The Department of Justice and lower courts have construed the Voting Rights Act of 1965 to require that political districting decisions be color-conscious to assure that the voting strength of racial minorities is not diluted.[17] The issue in *Beer v. United States*[18] was whether a redistricting of the City Council of New Orleans complied with the Act. Although the Court's decision upholding the plan may reflect a concern with the broad implications of this result-oriented interpretation of the Act,[19] the case turned on a technicality and did not call the interpretation into question.

Franks v. Bowman Transportation Co.[20] held that an applicant, discriminatorily denied a job, was entitled to instatement with full seniority retroactive to the date that his original application was rejected. *McDonald v. Santa Fe Trail Transportation*

[13] 416 U.S. 312 (1974).

[14] 96 S. Ct. 1538 (1976).

[15] 96 S. Ct. 2697 (1976).

[16] *E.g.*, Swann v. Charlotte-Mecklenburg Bd. of Educ., 402 U.S. 1 (1971).

[17] *See* Georgia v. United States, 411 U.S. 526 (1973); Allen v. State Bd. of Educ., 393 U.S. 544 (1969).

[18] 96 S. Ct. 1357 (1976).

[19] *See also* City of Richmond v. United States, 422 U.S. 358 (1975).

[20] 96 S. Ct. 1251 (1976).

Co.[21] held that the 1866 and 1964 civil rights acts protected white as well as black employees against racially discriminatory disciplinary discharges. Although the remedy in *Franks* impinges upon the interests of incumbents whose seniority is subordinated to that of the discriminatees, it is essentially within the antidiscrimination paradigm; [22] and *McDonald* affirms a general principle of color-blindness. Lurking in the background of both decisions, however, is the issue of racially preferential remedies for minority applicants who do not claim to be victims of a particular employer's past discrimination,[23] as well as the problem, avoided several Terms before in *DeFunis v. Odegaard*,[24] of the preferential admission of minority students to institutions of higher learning.[25]

Finally, in *Washington v. Davis*,[26] which may be last Term's most significant civil rights decision, the Court refused to incorporate into the Constitution the far-reaching rule of *Griggs v. Duke Power Co.*,[27] which construed Title VII of the Civil Rights Act of 1964 to invalidate employment tests that disproportionately disadvantage the members of racial minorities (and women) unless the tests are demonstrably related to job performance. Although *Davis* may weaken the standards for test-validation developed by courts and the EEOC, it did not question the soundness of *Griggs* as statutory doctrine. But the Court explicitly disapproved of a general constitutional doctrine of "racially disproportionate impact," developed by some lower federal courts, which disfavors even color-blind decisions that disproportionately disadvantage the members of racial minorities.[28]

Of the civil rights issues that have emerged during the past decade, two of the most controversial and important involve the propriety of granting racial preferences to traditionally disadvantaged minorities and the operational relevance of the fact that a color-blind practice has a disproportionate adverse impact on the

---

[21] 96 S. Ct. 2574 (1976).

[22] *See* pp. 37–39 *infra*.

[23] *See* pp. 39–43 *infra*.

[24] 416 U.S. 312 (1974).

[25] Since the close of the 1975 Term, in Bakke v. Regents of the Univ. of Cal., 45 U.S.L.W. 2179 (Cal. Sept. 16, 1976), the Supreme Court of California struck down a state medical school's preferential admissions program in a sweeping opinion that bodes ill for the programs of all other California institutions. *See also* Flanagan v. President and Directors of Georgetown College, 44 U.S.L.W. 2067 (D.D.C. July 25, 1976) (financial aid program according automatic preference to minority applicants held to violate Title VI of the Civil Rights Act of 1964). *But see* Alevy v. Downstate Medical Center, 348 N.E.2d 537, 384 N.Y.S.2d 82 (1976).

[26] 96 S. Ct. 2040 (1976), *noted* p. 114 *infra*.

[27] 401 U.S. 424 (1971).

[28] *See* pp. 23–26 *infra*.

members of a racial minority group. Any attempt to resolve these issues must begin by examining the rationales for, and parameters of, the antidiscrimination principle. Part I attempts this task, and concludes by considering the application of the antidiscrimination principle to "benign" race-conscious practices.

By definition the antidiscrimination principle applies only to race-dependent decisions and their effects. Part II examines the rationales for the contrasting doctrine of "racially disproportionate impact" which the Court disapproved in *Washington v. Davis*.[29] We shall see that, although this doctrine may be used to implement the antidiscrimination principle, it may also serve quite different objectives.

My "defense" of the antidiscrimination principle is that it prevents and rectifies racial injustices without subordinating other important values. At the risk of stating the obvious, the antidiscrimination principle is not the only principle of justice that should guide policymaking. For example, I believe that governments should assure that people are not denied fundamental needs because of their poverty and, more generally, should promote greater equalization in the distribution of wealth among individuals. To adopt the antidiscrimination principle as the exclusive principle of *racial* justice surely does not preclude adopting these or other principles concerned with *economic* justice.

Throughout this essay I use the word "race" as a shorthand for race and ethnic origin. However, the antidiscrimination principle can be and has been extended to encompass a variety of other traits, including alienage, illegitimacy, and sex. By limiting my concern to race-dependent decisions I do not imply that the antidiscrimination principle should not be so extended; but the inquiries necessary to evaluate such extensions lie beyond the scope of this essay.

I. The Antidiscrimination Principle

The antidiscrimination principle rests on fundamental moral values that are widely shared in our society. Although the text and legislative history of laws that incorporate this principle can inform our understanding of it, the principle itself is at least as likely to inform our interpretations of the laws. This is especially true with respect to the equal protection clause of the fourteenth amendment. The text and history of the clause are vague and ambiguous and cannot, in any event, infuse the antidiscrimination principle with moral force or justify its extension to novel circumstances and new beneficiaries. Therefore, the argument of this

[29] 96 S. Ct. 2040 (1976).

section does not ultimately turn on authority, but on whether it comports with the reader's reflective understanding of the antidiscrimination principle.

Stated most simply, the antidiscrimination principle disfavors race-dependent decisions and conduct — at least when they selectively disadvantage the members of a minority group. By race-dependent, I mean decisions and conduct (hereafter, simply decisions) that would have been different but for the race of those benefited or disadvantaged by them. Race-dependent decisions may take several forms, including overt racial classifications on the face of statutes and covert decisions by officials.

A. Rationales for the Antidiscrimination Principle

The antidiscrimination principle guards against certain defects in the *process* by which race-dependent decisions are made and also against certain harmful *results* of race-dependent decisions. Restricting the principle to a unitary purpose vitiates its moral force and requires the use of sophisticated reasoning to explain applications that seem self-evident.

1. Defects of Process. — The antidiscrimination principle is designed to prevent both irrational and unfair infliction of injury.

Race-dependent decisions are irrational insofar as they reflect the assumption that members of one race are less worthy than other people. Not all such decisions are necessarily irrational, however. For example, if black laborers tend to be absent from work more often than their white counterparts—for whatever reason—it is not irrational for an employer to prefer white applicants for the job.[30] If Americans of Japanese ancestry were more prone to disloyalty than Caucasians during World War II, it was not irrational for the United States government to take special precautions against sabotage and espionage by them.[31] Regulations and decisions based on statistical generalizations are commonplace in all developed societies and essential to their functioning. And it is often rational for decisionmakers to rely on weak and even dubious generalizations. Consider, for example, a fire department's or airline's policy against employing overweight per-

---

[30] *See generally* L. THUROW, GENERATING INEQUALITY 170–77 (1975); Fiss, *A Theory of Fair Employment Laws*, 38 U. CHI. L. REV. 235, 239, 257 (1971).

[31] *See* Hirabayashi v. United States, 320 U.S. 81 (1943); Korematsu v. United States, 323 U.S. 214 (1944). Consider also the rationality of a regulation requiring that blacks but not Caucasians be tested for sickle-cell anemia, *see* S.F. Chronicle, July 3, 1976, at 2, col. 5, and of a police practice of "stopping and questioning a Negro carrying a suitcase late at night in a white neighborhood," J. WILSON, VARIETIES OF POLICE BEHAVIOR 295 (1968).

sonnel, based on the rather slight probability that they will suffer a heart attack while on duty.

In short, the mere fact that most blacks are industrious and most Japanese-Americans loyal does not make the employer's or the Government's decision irrational. Indeed, if all race-dependent decisions were irrational, there would be no need for an antidiscrimination principle, for it would suffice to apply the widely held moral, constitutional, and practical principle that forbids treating persons irrationally.[32] The antidiscrimination principle fills a special need because — as even a glance at history indicates — race-dependent decisions that are rational and purport to be based solely on legitimate considerations are likely in fact to rest on assumptions of the differential worth of racial groups or on the related phenomenon of racially selective sympathy and indifference.

Mr. Justice Black focused on the first of these dangers in *Korematsu v. United States*,[33] the case in which the Government sought to justify its policy of interning Japanese-Americans, and in which the Court first enunciated the modern "suspect classification" doctrine. He wrote for the majority:

> [A]ll legal restrictions which curtail the civil rights of a single racial group are immediately suspect . . . . [C]ourts must subject them to the most rigid scrutiny. Pressing public necessity may sometimes justify the existence of such restrictions; racial antagonism never can.[34]

Mr. Justice Black chose the word "suspect" advisedly.[35] For, although a court often cannot ascertain the true motives underlying a decision, our history and traditions provide strong reasons to suspect that racial classifications ultimately rest on assumptions of the differential worth of racial groups. These racial value judgments appear in forms besides "racial antagonism" — for example in paternalistic assumptions of racial inferiority.

By the phenomenon of racially selective sympathy and indifference I mean the unconscious failure to extend to a minority

[32] *See, e.g.*, F.S. Royster Guano Co. v. Virginia, 253 U.S. 412, 415 (1920). *See generally* P. Brest, Processes of Constitutional Decisionmaking 558–63 (1975).

[33] 323 U.S. 214 (1944).

[34] *Id.* at 216.

[35] My colleague John Kaplan, an expert on civil rights law, believes that Mr. Justice Black meant nothing more than "disfavored" and that his use of the word "suspect" was happenstance. My colleague Richard Danzig, an expert on Mr. Justice Black, says that the Justice took pains to use ordinary language in ordinary ways, and most probably meant to convey the special implications of the word. On the issue of the meaning of "suspect," Professor Kaplan, despite his many fine qualities of character and intellect, is simply in error.

the same recognition of humanity, and hence the same sympathy and care, given as a matter of course to one's own group.[36]

Although racially selective sympathy and indifference (hereafter, just indifference) is an inevitable consequence of attributing intrinsic value to membership in a racial group, it may also result from a desire to enhance our own power and esteem by enhancing the power and esteem of members of groups to which we belong. And it may also result — often unconsciously — from our tendency to sympathize most readily with those who seem most like ourselves. Whatever its cause, decisions that reflect this phenomenon, like those reflecting overt racial hostility, are unfair; for by hypothesis, they are decisions disadvantaging minority persons that would not be made under the identical circumstances if they disadvantaged members of the dominant group. The unequal treatment could be justified only if one group were in fact more worthy than the other. This justification failing, such treatment violates the cardinal rule of fairness — the Golden Rule.[37]

2. Harmful Results. — A second and independent rationale for the antidiscrimination principle is the prevention of the harms which may result from race-dependent decisions. Often, the most obvious harm is the denial of the opportunity to secure a desired benefit — a job, a night's lodging at a motel, a vote. But this does not completely describe the consequences of race-dependent decisionmaking. Decisions based on assumptions of intrinsic worth and selective indifference inflict psychological injury by stigmatizing their victims as inferior. Moreover, because acts of discrimination tend to occur in pervasive patterns, their victims suffer especially frustrating, cumulative and debilitating injuries.

The prevention of stigmatic harm played a major role in *Strauder v. West Virginia*,[38] the first race discrimination case to reach the Supreme Court after the Civil War. On alternative grounds, the Court struck down a state law excluding blacks from juries. Although the first ground was the black defendant's right to a jury composed of a cross-section of the community, the second involved the rights of the members of the black community them-

[36] *Cf.* Ely, *The Wages of Crying Wolf: A Comment on* Roe v. Wade, 82 YALE L.J. 920, 933–34 n.85 (1973). *See also* Ely, *The Unconstitutionality of Reverse Racial Discrimination*, 41 U. CHI. L. REV. 723 (1974).

[37] *Cf.* I KANT, GROUNDWORK OF THE METAPHYSICS OF MORALS *421 (3d ed. H. Paton trans. 1956) (Kant's categorical imperative) ("Act only on that maxim through which you can at the same time will that it should become a universal law."); J. ROUSSEAU, 4 CORRESPONDENCE GENERALE 827 (1924–34) ("All the preferences of friendship are thefts committed against the human race and the fatherland. Men are all our brothers, they should all be our friends.").

[38] 100 U.S. 303 (1880).

selves. Mr. Justice Strong reasoned that the fourteenth amendment protects Negroes "from legal discriminations, implying their inferiority in civil society," and held that the West Virginia statute was "practically a brand upon them . . . , an assertion of their inferiority."[39] Dissenting in *Plessy v. Ferguson*,[40] Mr. Justice Harlan likewise observed that the segregation of railway passengers was a "badge of servitude" because it proceeded "on the ground that colored citizens are . . . inferior and degraded."[41]

Similarly, the essence of *Brown v. Board of Education*[42] lay in Chief Justice Warren's observation that the segregation of black public school pupils "generates a feeling of inferiority as to their status in the community that may affect their hearts and minds in a way unlikely ever to be undone."[43] As Charles L. Black noted, the Court could not properly have ignored "a plain fact about the society of the United States — the fact that the social meaning of segregation is the putting of the Negro in a position of walled-off inferiority — or the other equally plain fact that such treatment is hurtful to human beings."[44]

Recognition of the stigmatic injury inflicted by discrimination explains applications of the antidiscrimination principle where the material harm seems slight or problematic. For example, it fully explains the harmfulness of de jure school segregation without the need to invoke controversial social science evidence concerning the effects of segregation on achievement, interracial attitudes, and the like,[45] and thus explains the Supreme Court's casual extension of *Brown* to prohibit the segregation of public beaches, parks, golf courses and buses.[46] It also explains how present practices

---

[39] *Id.* at 308. *See also* Peters v. Kiff, 407 U.S. 493, 499–500 (1972).

[40] 163 U.S. 537 (1896).

[41] *Id.* at 560, 562 (Harlan, J., dissenting).

[42] 347 U.S. 483 (1954).

[43] *Id.* at 494.

[44] Black, *The Lawfulness of the Segregation Decisions*, 69 YALE L.J. 421, 427 (1960). *See also* Cahn, *Jurisprudence*, 30 N.Y.U.L. REV. 150, 158–59 (1955):

> As is observed in the ancient Babylonian Talmud, to shame and degrade a fellow-creature is to commit a kind of psychic mayhem upon him. Like an assailant's knife, humiliation slashes his self-respect and human dignity. He grows pale, the blood rushes from his face just as though it had been shed. That is why we are accustomed to say he feels "wounded." . . .
>
> So one speaks in terms of the most familiar and universally accepted standards of right and wrong when one remarks (1) that racial segregation under government auspices inevitably inflicts humiliation, and (2) that official humiliation of innocent, law-abiding citizens is psychologically injurious and morally evil. . . . The cruelty is obvious and evident.

[45] *See* pp. 45–46 & notes 207–10 *infra*.

[46] *See, e.g.*, Muir v. Louisville Park Theatrical Ass'n, 347 U.S. 971 (1954); Mayor of Baltimore v. Dawson, 350 U.S. 877 (1955); Holmes v. City of Atlanta, 350 U.S. 879 (1955); Gayle v. Browder, 352 U.S. 903 (1956).

that are racially neutral may nonetheless perpetuate the harms of past de jure segregation.[47]

Racial generalizations usually inflict psychic injury whether or not they are in fact premised on assumptions of differential moral worth. Although all of us recognize that institutional decisions must depend on generalizations based on objective characteristics of persons and things rather than on individualized judgments, we nonetheless tend to feel unfairly treated when disadvantaged by a generalization that is not true as applied to us. Generalizations based on immutable personal traits such as race or sex are especially frustrating because we can do nothing to escape their operation. These generalizations are still more pernicious, for they are often premised on the supposed correlation between the inherited characteristic and the undesirable voluntary behavior of those who possess the characteristic [48] — for example, blacks are less industrious, trustworthy or clean than whites. Because the behavior is voluntary, and hence the proper object of moral condemnation, individuals as to whom the generalization is inaccurate may justifiably feel that the decisionmaker has passed moral judgment on them.

The psychological injury inflicted by generalizations based on race is compounded by the frustrating and cumulative nature of their material injuries. Racial generalizations are pervasive and have traditionally operated in the same direction — to the disadvantage of members of the minority group. A person who is denied one opportunity because he or she is short or overweight will find other opportunities, for in our society height and weight do not often serve as the bases for generalizations determining who will receive benefits. By contrast, at least until very recently, a black was not denied *an* opportunity because of his or her race, but denied virtually *all* desirable opportunities. As door after door is shut in one's face, the individual acts of discrimination combine into a systematic and grossly inequitable frustration of opportunity.

The cumulative disadvantage caused by the use of race as a proxy even for legitimate characteristics provides an independent ground for disfavoring nonbenign race-dependent decisions regardless of the integrity of the process by which they were made. To the unprejudiced employer who would prefer white applicants to blacks solely for reasons of efficiency, the antidiscrimination principle says in effect: "If you were the only one to do this, we would permit you to make efficient generalizations based on race. But so many other firms might employ similar generalizations that

[47] *See* pp. 35–36 *infra*.

[48] I am indebted to Professor Lawrence A. Alexander for this point.

black individuals would suffer great cumulative harms. And, in the absence of an overriding justification, this cannot be permitted."

I have argued that the prevention of stigmatic and cumulative harms, as well as concerns for process, support the antidiscrimination principle. Individuals may, however, be stigmatized by *non*-race-dependent practices that *appear* to be discriminatory, and may also suffer cumulative disabilities from various non-race-dependent practices. Whereas the process rationales for the antidiscrimination principle apply only to race-dependent decisions, the result-oriented rationales seem to disfavor all practices that produce these harms and thus to support a doctrine broader than the antidiscrimination principle.

Nonetheless, these practices cannot automatically be presumed invalid. Race correlates so weakly with the legitimate characteristics for which it might be used as a proxy that, even if race-dependent decisions are sometimes rational, society loses little if they are presumptively forbidden. By contrast, a presumption prohibiting all decisions that stigmatize or cumulatively disadvantage particular individuals would affect an enormously wide range of practices important to the efficient operation of a complex industrial society. (Furthermore, a general doctrine disfavoring harmful results could not be administered by the judiciary.) Therefore, the law has tended to reflect the result-oriented concerns of the antidiscrimination principle, not by operating directly to scrutinize results, but by disfavoring particular classifying traits that tend to be especially harmful and have little social utility. This approach, as well as suspected defects of process, underlies the expansion of the antidiscrimination principle beyond race to encompass decisions based on ethnic and national origin,[49] alienage,[50] illegitimacy [51] and sex.[52] It also explains the occasional use of the cognate notion of "conclusive presumptions" [53] to disfavor other classificatory traits.

Practices that produce cumulative harms of the nature described above should not be confused with practices that ad-

---

[49] *See, e.g.*, Hernandez v. Texas, 347 U.S. 475 (1954); Korematsu v. United States, 323 U.S. 214 (1944).

[50] *See, e.g.*, *In re* Griffiths, 413 U.S. 717 (1973); Sugarman v. Dougall, 413 U.S. 634 (1973); Graham v. Richardson, 403 U.S. 365 (1971).

[51] *See, e.g.*, Levy v. Louisiana, 391 U.S. 68 (1968); Glona v. American Guar. & Liab. Ins. Co., 391 U.S. 73 (1968).

[52] *See, e.g.*, Weinberger v. Wiesenfeld, 420 U.S. 636 (1975); Frontiero v. Richardson, 411 U.S. 677 (1973); Reed v. Reed, 404 U.S. 71 (1971).

[53] *See, e.g.*, Cleveland Bd. of Educ. v. LaFleur, 414 U.S. 632 (1974); Vlandis v. Kline, 412 U.S. 441 (1971). *See also* Carrington v. Rash, 380 U.S. 89 (1965).

versely affect disproportionately more of the members of one racial group than of another. The concept of cumulative disability developed in this section is concerned with a harm that may befall *individuals* who are systematically denied benefits because of a particular trait they possess. The fact that a practice has a racially disproportionate impact does not entail or imply that it imposes a cumulative disability on any individuals. If a non-race-dependent practice does inflict a cumulative disability on individuals, it should be disfavored only for that reason, and not because of the race of those affected. For example, intelligence tests may disproportionately disadvantage members of a racial minority, and widespread use of such tests may cumulatively disadvantage individuals who consistently score low on them. But the result-oriented argument of this section justifies disfavoring intelligence tests (if at all), only because of their cumulative impact on the low scorers, the large majority of whom surely belong to the dominant racial group however it is defined.

B. *Modes of Race-Dependent Decisionmaking*

The paradigm race-dependent decision is a statute that in terms classifies people by race. But race-dependent decisions can take other forms as well.

1. *Racially Motivated Administrative Decisions.* — A decisionmaker who is not authorized to take race into account may nonetheless do so. As early as 1886, in *Yick Wo v. Hopkins*,[54] the Supreme Court held that discriminatory administration of an ordinance, nondiscriminatory on its face, violates the equal protection clause. In that case, the San Francisco Board of Supervisors had systematically denied laundry permits to two hundred Chinese applicants because of their race. But even an isolated racially-motivated decision violates the antidiscrimination principle. The unfairness to an individual affected by an isolated decision is no smaller; and although decisions whose racial motives are well-concealed cannot cause stigmatic harm, even covert acts of discrimination may often be recognized or suspected and will thus inflict psychological injury.

A person aggrieved by a racially-motivated decision need not allege and prove that she would have gained a particular benefit — say, a job — but for her race. If she does establish this, she is entitled to the benefit or to compensation for its loss. But it suffices to show that, because of her race, she was denied an *equal opportunity* to enjoy the benefit — the opportunity to be

[54] 118 U.S. 356 (1886).

considered under the employer's nonracial criteria.[55] Proof of this does not usually entitle the complainant to the job, but only to have the decisionmaker reconsider her application under the proper criteria.[56]

As the employment example suggests, race-dependent decisions may be manifested by inaction as well as action. The inaction may sometimes be less evident, as where a school district decides *not* to construct a new school or not to alter existing attendance zones in order to avoid integration. In terms of the antidiscrimination principle, however, these are not different from decisions *to* construct a school or to alter zones for the same purpose.[57]

2. *Racially-Motivated Regulations.* — Does the antidiscrimination principle apply to a regulation that does not in terms classify on the basis of race but which was adopted for race-dependent motives? For example, does the antidiscrimination principle prohibit a legislature from adopting a stringent voting test for the purpose of disfranchising blacks, or prohibit a board of education from initiating a testing and tracking system in order to segregate minorities?

This issue sometimes is confused with the quite different one of whether courts or other agencies charged with administering the antidiscrimination principle can effectively enforce it in this context. But institutional issues aside — as they are at least when legislators consider their own motives for supporting a proposed measure[58] — the rationales for the antidiscrimination principle apply fully to race-dependent decisions that produce regulations and other laws not discriminatory on their faces.

Such a law may or may not inflict stigmatic injury, depending on whether its discriminatory purpose is known by the community. But the law is in any event unfair in the same way as an individualized act of discrimination. If a state adopts a voting literacy test in order to disfranchise black voters, a person who fails the test is denied a benefit only because the legislature gave positive weight to the impermissible factor of racial prejudice.[59] The decision is not less unfair because the legislature did not single

---

[55] *See, e.g.*, McDonnell Douglas Corp. v. Green, 411 U.S. 792 (1973). *Cf.* Flanagan v. President and Directors of Georgetown College, 44 U.S.L.W. 2067 (D.D.C. July 25, 1976).

[56] *Cf.* United States v. Sheet Metal Workers Local 36, 416 F.2d 123 (8th Cir. 1969); Bakke v. Regents of the Univ. of Cal., 45 U.S.L.W. 2179 (Cal. Sept. 16, 1976).

[57] *See, e.g.*, Hart v. Community School Bd. of Educ., 512 F.2d 37 (2d Cir. 1975).

[58] *See generally* Brest, *The Conscientious Legislator's Guide to Constitutional Interpretation*, 27 STAN. L. REV. 585 (1975).

[59] *Id.* at 589–90.

out particular blacks for discriminatory treatment, or because it injures some whites as well. Nor is the law rescued by the possibility that the legislature *might* have adopted it for entirely legitimate reasons. This is like the claim by an employer who has discriminatorily refused to consider a minority applicant that he or she might have turned out to be unqualified anyway. Perhaps the applicant would turn out to be unqualified and perhaps the legislature would adopt the literacy test for legitimate reasons. But neither the decisionmaker nor a reviewing court can know this until the decision is made without taking race into account.

3. Racially Selective Indifference. — Race-dependent decisions need not be race-conscious, but may reflect unconscious racially selective indifference.[60] Such indifference violates the antidiscrimination principle when its effect is to deny benefits to minority persons, or impose burdens on them, which would not be denied or imposed if they were white.

Imagine, for example, a white welfare worker who sincerely believes that he is not prejudiced, but who nonetheless consistently exercises discretion to grant more relief to white families than to similarly situated black families because he identifies more readily with the plight of one than the other. Or imagine a personnel manager who, though believing that she is not prejudiced, feels more comfortable with whites than with blacks and therefore usually selects whites from among otherwise equally qualified applicants. These decisions, though unselfconscious, are not essentially different from the Board of Supervisors' decisions granting and denying laundry permits in *Yick Wo v. Hopkins*.[61] They are unfair. They are also stigmatic, for to show less empathy for people because of their race is to treat them as less human because of their race.

Unconscious racially selective indifference may also be a causal factor in the adoption or retention of practices that are not overtly race-dependent. For example, Mr. Justice Marshall suggested in *Furman v. Georgia* [62] that the death penalty is tolerated only because its burden falls mostly on members of minority groups and the poor — "the forlorn, easily forgotten members of society" [63] — toward whom the majority is indifferent because of their race or status. One can easily imagine a school district resting content with an inefficient assignment scheme that results in segregation, which it would abandon if the scheme produced substantial racial mixing; or a union retaining admission require-

---

[60] *See* pp. 7–8 *supra*.

[61] 118 U.S. 356 (1886); *see* p. 12 *supra*.

[62] 408 U.S. 238 (1972).

[63] *Id.* at 366 (Marshall, J., concurring).

ments that favor whites, which it would abandon if they resulted in a large influx of minorities. Practices that are neutral on their face but are retained only because of racially selective indifference violate the antidiscrimination principle.

C. Permissible Race-Dependent Decisions

1. The Strict Scrutiny of Suspect Classifications. — It follows from the central rationale for the antidiscrimination principle that all decisions based on judgments of racial value and racially selective indifference are absolutely forbidden. But even a race-dependent decision that disadvantages minorities may be based on entirely legitimate grounds. This might be true, for example, of the Government's decision to intern Japanese-Americans because of their supposed disloyalty. Under what circumstances, if any, should such decisions be permitted?

The answer cannot be deduced from the antidiscrimination principle, but depends on the accomodation of the objective of preventing discrimination with other concerns. A flat prohibition of race-dependent decisions provides as much assurance as possible against discrimination, but at the cost of precluding what may be thought to be desirable uses of race — for example, the temporary segregation of prisoners during a race riot, or the integration of a de facto or formerly de jure segregated school system. A case-by-case approach, though sensitive to all of the interests at stake, invites discriminatory abuses.

The Court has taken an alternative approach in adjudication under the equal protection clause: race-dependent decisions — at least those that are not obviously benign — are forbidden unless they are necessary to promote important or "compelling" objectives.[64] This so-called "strict scrutiny" or "suspect classification" standard serves as a proxy for a direct (and problematic) inquiry into the integrity of the decisionmaking process: as the legitimate reasons for race-dependent decisions increase, so does the likelihood that they were not made for illegitimate reasons. The standard also guards against the stigmatic and cumulative harms of race-dependent decisions by permitting them only in extraordinary circumstances.[65]

[64] *E.g.*, Korematsu v. United States, 323 U.S. 214 (1944); McLaughlin v. Florida, 379 U.S. 184 (1964).

[65] Some commentators have asserted that concerns for the integrity of the decisionmaking process are fully satisfied by a requirement that a race-dependent decision be necessary to achieve a *legitimate* objective, without regard to whether the objective is compelling or important. *See, e.g.*, Ely, *The Unconstitutionality of Reverse Racial Discrimination*, 41 U. CHI. L. REV. 723, 727 n.26 (1974); Fiss, *Groups and the Equal Protection Clause,* 5 J. PHIL. & PUB. AFF. 107, 116–17 (1976); Comment, *Mental Illness: A Suspect Classification?*, 83 YALE L.J. 1237, 1251 (1974). But the requirement of a compelling objective is a prophylactic against improperly made decisions.

2. *Benign Decisions.* — The suspect classification standard was developed in response to traditional practices of racial discrimination when race-dependent decisions were seldom designed to benefit the members of disadvantaged minorities. The past decade has seen a significant increase in benignly motivated race-dependent practices, and their reconciliation with the antidiscrimination principle has become a matter of controversy.[66]

Does the antidiscrimination principle disfavor race-dependent means for achieving ends such as preventing discrimination, remedying past discrimination, improving race relations, and ameliorating the status of traditionally disadvantaged minorities? To make the discussion more concrete, consider the effects of the following policies, adopted by white decisionmakers, upon whites and blacks. A school board remedies de facto segregation by assigning and busing pupils so that the racial proportion in each school approximately reflects the racial composition of the district.[67] A firm preferentially employs black applicants in order to compensate for past discrimination against blacks. A legislature gerrymanders the lines of a political district to assure that blacks can elect a representative.[68] A housing authority locates a low income project in a white neighborhood and sets both a minimum and maximum quota for black families, the maximum being short of a supposed "tipping point" at which whites will flee.[69] A university or professional school preferentially admits black applicants to increase the diversity of the school and increase the number of blacks in high status occupations and professions.[70]

From the point of view of the white individuals affected, it is highly improbable that decisions such as these are premised on assumptions that blacks are superior to whites or on the selective

[66] *See, e.g.*, Ely, *supra* note 65; Greenawalt, *Judicial Scrutiny of "Benign" Racial Preference in Law School Admissions*, 75 COLUM. L. REV. 559, 565 n.51 (1975); Posner, *The DeFunis Case and the Constitutionality of Preferential Treatment of Racial Minorities*, 1974 SUP. CT. REV. 1; Sandalow, *Racial Preferences in Higher Education: Political Responsibility and the Judicial Role*, 42 U. CHI. L. REV. 653 (1975). For an earlier and prescient discussion of the issues, see Kaplan, *Equal Justice in an Unequal World: Equality for the Negro — The Problem of Special Treatment*, 61 NW. L. REV. 363 (1966).

[67] In dictum in Swann v. Charlotte-Mecklenburg Board of Education, 402 U.S. 1, 16 (1971), the Court stated that a school district could voluntarily remedy de facto segregation.

[68] *See* Note, *Compensatory Racial Reapportionment*, 25 STAN. L. REV. 84 (1972).

[69] *See* Ackerman, *Integration for Subsidized Housing and the Question of Racial Occupancy Controls*, 26 STAN. L. REV. 245 (1974).

[70] *Compare* Bakke v. Regents of the Univ. of Cal., 45 U.S.L.W. 2179 (Cal. Sept. 16, 1976), *with* Alevy v. Downstate Medical Center, 348 N.E.2d 537, 384 N.Y.S.2d 82 (1976).

indifference of white decisionmakers to the humanity or aspirations of whites compared to blacks. With respect to results, each of these decisions may effectively deprive white individuals of a desired benefit — attendance at a neighborhood school, a place in a university, a job, a strong voice in the electoral process, an apartment. Yet in none of these cases is stigmatic injury likely to accompany the deprivation. Moreover, only preferential admissions and employment policies present any likelihood of cumulative disadvantage to whites based on race or of the frustration of being denied benefits because of an unchangeable trait. But, though reasonable people may differ, I doubt that "reverse discrimination" is likely to become so pervasive at any occupational level in our white-dominated society as to cause cumulative harms or frustrations approaching the magnitude of those inflicted by the malign discrimination to which the antidiscrimination principle fully responds. (It bears emphasis, however, that the antidiscrimination principle is not the only policy or principle of fairness that may be implicated by benign race-dependent practices. For example, even if preferential admissions or hiring programs do not violate the principle, their objectives may be misconceived, they may be premised on erroneous factual assumptions, and they may reflect an improper accommodation of the competing equities of the parties affected. Preferential practices may be constitutional, but as Charles Curtis remarked in a different context, "to call a statute constitutional is no more of a compliment than it is to say that it is not intolerable." [71])

So far I have focused on race-dependent decisions that benefit a disadvantaged minority at the expense of the society at large. But one can imagine a decision that, though benign with respect to one minority, involves prejudice against another "discrete and insular" [72] minority group and inflicts discriminatory injuries upon its members. The mere fact that a political gerrymander designed to aid blacks diminishes the voting power of a neighboring Jewish community does not trigger the antidiscrimination principle.[73] But if the circumstances suggest that the decision was motivated by anti-Semitic prejudice, it should be treated like any other nonbenign race-dependent decision.

A more subtle problem of this sort may arise in choosing among the beneficiaries of a preferential hiring or university admissions program. Because such programs may serve several

---

[71] Curtis, *A Modern Supreme Court in a Modern World*, 4 VAND. L. REV. 427, 433 (1951).

[72] *See* United States v. Carolene Products Co., 304 U.S. 144, 152–53 n.4 (1938).

[73] *Cf.* United Jewish Organizations v. Wilson, 510 F.2d 512 (2d Cir.), *cert. granted sub nom.* United Jewish Organizations v. Carey, 423 U.S. 945 (1975).

purposes, including the amelioration of race-specific harms,[74] and because the need for and likely success of the programs turn on speculative empirical assumptions and may vary from one geographic region to another, the selection of beneficiaries allows the exercise of considerable discretion. Between a self-serving preference (which, of course, violates the antidiscrimination principle) and a preference for the most disadvantaged and needy minorities, there lies an amorphous middle range. One can imagine hypothetical situations in which the choice among disadvantaged beneficiaries violates the antidiscrimination principle — for example, where a group is excluded from a preferential program because its members are regarded as hopelessly inferior. But a more realistic problem is likely to arise if an arguably eligible group is not included because it is not sufficiently large, visible, vocal, powerful, or disruptive. Although noninclusion based on indifference to the plight of such a group may fit the phrase "racially selective indifference," this is not the same phenomenon discussed above; [75] for the majority decisionmakers do not show less sympathy for the nonincluded group than for the remainder of the majority. Noninclusion under these circumstances is not racially stigmatic. And, though members of the nonincluded group may be in competition with those receiving preferences, it seems unlikely that a pattern of preferential schemes would be so pervasive and tight as to systematically frustrate the opportunities of members of the nonincluded group.

Can apparently benign practices actually injure their supposed beneficiaries in ways cognizable by the antidiscrimination principle? It is conceivable, but not likely, that school desegregation and preferential employment and admissions policies might reflect assumptions that minorities are innately inferior and therefore in need of special aid. It is somewhat more likely that school desegregation may inflict stigmatic harm and reinforce feelings of differential worth in children of both races; [76] that preferential admissions programs may foster the white community's belief that all minority students are preferentially admitted and, perhaps, graduated; [77] and that preferential employment programs may induce or encourage white racial animus.[78]

---

[74] *See* pp. 45–48 *infra*.

[75] *See* pp. 14–15 *supra*.

[76] *See* N. St. John, School Desegregation Outcomes for Children chs. 2, 3 (1975); Epps, *The Impact of School Desegregation on Aspirations, Self-Concepts and Other Aspects of Personality*, 39 L. & Contemp. Prob. 300 (1975); Goodman, *De Facto School Segregation: A Constitutional and Empirical Analysis*, 60 Calif. L. Rev. 275, 336 (1972).

[77] *See* Foster, *Race and Truth at Harvard*, New Republic, July 17, 1976, at 16.

[78] *See generally* N. Glazer, Affirmative Discrimination, ch. 5 (1975).

If, as I have argued, the antidiscrimination principle is concerned with harmful effects as well as invidious motives, these dangers cannot be ignored. Nonetheless, where the objective and immediate effect are to benefit minority persons, it seems inappropriate to subject the practice to the demanding criteria of the suspect classification standard. It should suffice for a policymaker to conclude that the probable benefits outweigh the harms, that the benefits cannot readily be gained by other than race-dependent means, and that the program is designed to minimize its possible adverse consequences.[79]

Greater difficulties arise where a benign program disadvantages some minority persons to benefit others of the same group and to achieve long-run goals at the expense of immediate gains. Maximum integration quotas for schools and public housing, designed to avert white flight, are paradigm examples. Not only may such quotas deny desired benefits to minorities because of their race, but the justification for the quotas conveys the stigmatic message that whites cannot tolerate too many minority persons. From the extrinsic evidence, an observer cannot tell whether the decisionmaker condones the white attitudes or just acknowledges that they cannot be changed in the short run; whether the policy panders to white prejudice or is truly designed to promote a stable, integrated environment. Indeed, decisionmakers may find it difficult to separate these factors in their own minds.

This problem has received the most judicial attention in the context of school desegregation. In the typical case, a school board, found to have engaged in a longstanding practice of de jure segregation, argues that whites will flee the system if it fully integrates the schools. Because the district is affirmatively obligated to eliminate all vestiges of de jure segregation,[80] and because its past conduct provides scant assurance that its present motives are benign, the Supreme Court has given short shrift to this contention. In *Monroe v. Board of Commissioners*,[81] the Court refused to approve a provision, neutral on its face, that in effect permitted whites to transfer out of a desegregated school. Mr. Justice Brennan wrote:

> We are frankly told . . . that without the transfer option it is apprehended that white students will flee the school system altogether. "But it should go without saying that the vitality of these constitutional principles cannot be allowed to yield simply because of disagreement with them." [82]

[79] *Cf.* Greenawalt, *supra* note 66, at 565–79.

[80] Green v. County School Bd., 391 U.S. 430 (1968).

[81] 391 U.S. 450 (1968).

[82] *Id.* at 459 (citing Brown v. Board of Educ., 349 U.S. 294 (1955) (Brown II)).

In a subsequent decision the Court held that a de jure segregated city-county system could not be divided into separate systems to avoid white flight.[83]

Some lower federal courts have read *Monroe* to preclude any consideration of white flight in formulating desegregation decrees.[84] However, other courts have explicitly limited the scope of desegregation in order to achieve "an acceptable racial balance without aggravating conditions that produce a self-defeating exodus of the middle class white and black."[85] Surely a court should avoid issuing self-defeating orders. But in view of the potential stigma inflicted by a desegregation quota designed to prevent white flight, it should be permitted only if the evidence indicates persuasively that any alternative would in fact be counterproductive.

The Court of Appeals for the Second Circuit adopted this standard with respect to limiting the admission of minority families to public housing units, holding that racial occupancy restrictions were permissible only when the alternative "would lead to a substantial increase in the overall nonwhite population in the community, precipitating a trend toward ultimate ghettoization of the entire community."[86] But Judge Mansfield's opinion for the court emphasized:

> Absent convincing evidence that a color-blind [policy] . . . would almost surely lead to eventual destruction of the racial integration that presently exists in the community, the Authority's denial of housing to a family because of its race could, whether or not labelled a "benign" quota, constitute a form of unlawful racial discrimination in violation of the family's constitutional rights. For these reasons the burden on the Authority is a heavy one.[87]

In view of the stigma of rejection because of one's race and the likelihood that a racial quota will exacerbate the cumulative disadvantage imposed by still-pervasive patterns of malign housing discrimination, I doubt whether the objective of residential integration is so overriding as to justify this means of achieving it under any circumstances.

---

[83] United States v. Scotland Neck City Bd. of Educ., 407 U.S. 484 (1972).

[84] *See* Morgan v. Kerrigan, 523 F.2d 917 (1st Cir. 1975); United States v. Board of School Comm'rs, 503 F.2d 68 (7th Cir. 1974). *Cf.* Brunson v. Board of Trustees, 429 F.2d 820 (4th Cir. 1970).

[85] Bradley v. Milliken, 402 F. Supp. 1096, 1130 (E.D. Mich. 1975). *See also* Calhoun v. Cook, 522 F.2d 717 (5th Cir. 1975); Higgins v. Board of Educ., 508 F.2d 779, 794 (6th Cir. 1974).

[86] Otero v. New York City Housing Authority, 484 F.2d 1122, 1135 (2d Cir. 1973).

[87] *Id.* at 1136.

If my analysis of benign race-dependent practices is basically correct, they should be disfavored and avoided where other means can achieve the same ends, but they should not automatically be subject to the extraordinary demands of the suspect classification standard. A court or other decisionmaker confronted with an apparently benign race-dependent practice should assess the extent to which it in fact implicates the antidiscrimination principle, by determining whether it seems to reflect assumptions of racial inferiority or selective indifference and whether it seems likely to inflict stigmatic injury or add to cumulative harms. These inquiries will usually focus on the supposed beneficiaries of the practice. But it is not inconceivable that a race-dependent practice may sometimes affect others — especially those in competition with the beneficiaries — in a manner that implicates the antidiscrimination principle.

This proposal for a variable standard of judicial review of race-dependent decisions is open to criticism from two sides. On the one hand, those who favor a single, color-blind equal protection standard might contend that it allows too much room for operation of the judges' personal values. Indeed, Richard A. Posner has argued:

> The exception [for benign discrimination] is inadmissible, because it requires the court not only to consider whether there is discrimination but to decide whether the discrimination harms or hurts a particular racial group, and to weigh the competing claims of different racial groups, and the additional inquiries rob the principle of its precision and objectivity. . . . The antidiscrimination principle is not only more objective, but more compelling, when it is divorced from empirical inquiries into the effects of particular forms of discrimination on the affected groups. The necessary inquiries are intractable and would leave the field open to slippery conjecture.[88]

Although I share Professor Posner's concerns about judicial capacities, the institutional problems seem more tractable than he implies and do not, in any event, justify prohibiting other agencies from adopting legitimate and possibly important social policies. Most benign race-dependent practices do not require a court "to weigh the competing claims of different racial groups," for a practice that is benign as to one group typically does not selectively disadvantage the members of another under circumstances evidencing a violation of the antidiscrimination principle as to them. If it does, the practice is subject to the "compelling interest" standard — a standard that places so heavy a weight on one side that the outcome of the balance is virtually a fore-

[88] Posner, *supra* note 66, at 24.

gone conclusion. The fact remains that even where no competing racial group is involved, the court may have to engage in the highly intuitive process of identifying and weighing the harms and benefits of race-dependent decisions. But the costs of judicial subjectivity strike me as far smaller than those of a rule prohibiting all race-dependent decisions, including, for example, voluntarily-adopted or remedially-imposed school desegregation programs.

On the other hand, it may be thought that even if the antidiscrimination principle itself is properly concerned to prevent the harmful results of race-dependent decisions as well as decisions based on judgments of comparative racial worth and selective indifference,[89] *judicial review* of the decisions of other institutions is justified only by defects of process and therefore may be concerned only with them. There are two responses. First, even apparently benign race-dependent decisions may reflect these defects of process. More fundamentally, judicial review guards against failures of process besides improper motivation. As Alexander M. Bickel noted, "many actions of government have two aspects: their immediate, necessarily intended, practical effects, and their perhaps unintended or unappreciated bearing on values we hold to have more general and permanent interest." [90] I shall not rehearse Professor Bickel's eloquent argument that the judiciary plays a special role as "the pronouncer and guardian of such values." [91] But especially in a period of crisis, when policymakers are most likely to act hastily and least likely to consider the long-range implications of their policies, the judiciary provides what Mr. Justice Stone called the opportunity for "the sober second thought." [92] And there are few issues that presently demand the judiciary's studied reflection more than those considered in this essay.

II. Racially Disproportionate Impact

Race-dependent decisions typically produce a racially dis proportionate impact — a disproportion between the number of blacks and whites on the voting rolls, in an employer's work force, on a jury, or in a school. Because race-dependent decisions are so often concealed, racially disproportionate impact has customarily been offered as evidence that ostensibly nondiscriminatory

---

[89] *See* pp. 8–12 *supra*.

[90] A. Bickel, The Least Dangerous Branch 24 (1962).

[91] *Id.*

[92] Stone, *The Common Law in the United States*, 50 Harv. L. Rev. 4, 25 (1936), *quoted in* A. Bickel, *supra* note 90, at 26.

decisions are in fact race-dependent.[93] A complainant who demonstrates a strong pattern that does not seem explicable by nonracial factors or chance, may be deemed to have established a "prima facie case" that the respondent has engaged in race-dependent decisionmaking. The respondent may rebut the prima facie case by various means, including direct testimony about how the challenged decisions were in fact made, evidence that the decisionmaking process was incapable of taking race into account, or proof that other variables persuasively account for the disproportionate impact.[94] If the respondent fails, the anti-discrimination principle comes into play and, under the general equal protection clause standard, the practice will be upheld only if it is necessary to promote a compelling interest.

A number of recent judicial decisions have subjected official acts and practices to the "compelling interest" test, without finding that they were race-dependent, solely on the ground that they produced a racially disproportionate impact. For example, in *United States v. Black Jack*,[95] the Court of Appeals for the Eighth Circuit struck down an ordinance that prohibited the construction of new multiple-family dwellings, on the ground that it effectively excluded black families from a white suburb of St. Louis, Missouri. Judge Heaney wrote:

> To establish a prima facie case of racial discrimination, the plaintiff need prove no more than that the conduct of the defendant actually or predictably results in racial discrimination; in other words, that it has a discriminatory effect . . . . The plaintiff need make no showing whatsoever that the action resulting in racial discrimination in housing was racially motivated . . . . Effect, and not motivation, is the touchstone, in part because clever men may easily conceal their motivations, but more importantly, because . . . "we now firmly recognize that the arbitrary quality of thoughtlessness can be as disastrous and unfair to private rights and the public interest as the perversity of a willful scheme.". . .
>
> Once the plaintiff has established a prima facie case by demonstrating racially discriminatory effect, the burden shifts to the

[93] *See* Yick Wo v. Hopkins, 118 U.S. 356 (1886); p. 12 *supra*.

[94] *See, e.g.*, Alexander v. Louisiana, 405 U.S. 625 (1972) (juries); United States v. Real Estate Dev. Corp., 347 F. Supp. 776, 782 (N.D. Miss. 1972) (housing). *See generally* Bogen & Falcon, *The Use of Racial Statistics in Fair Housing Cases*, 34 MD. L. REV. 59 (1974); Montlack, *Using Statistical Evidence to Enforce the Laws Against Discrimination*, 22 CLEV. ST. L. REV. 259 (1973); Note, *Beyond the Prima Facie Case in Employment Discrimination Law: Statistical Proof and Rebuttal*, 89 HARV. L. REV. 387 (1975).

[95] 508 F.2d 1179 (8th Cir. 1974).

governmental defendant to demonstrate that its conduct was necessary to promote a compelling governmental interest.[96]

Although *Black Jack* was decided under the Fair Housing Act of 1968, this racially disproportionate impact doctrine has been applied to a variety of actions arising under the Constitution. Courts have invalidated similar zoning regulations,[97] and held that public housing authorities are affirmatively obligated to promote integration.[98] On essentially the same theory, the Court of Appeals for the Fifth Circuit discarded what it termed "the anodyne dichotomy of classical de facto and de jure segregation." [99] Reasoning that "regardless of motive, the children that suffer from segregation suffer the same deprivation of educational opportunity that *Brown* condemns," [100] the court wrote that "[d]iscriminatory motive and purpose . . . are not necessary ingredients of constitutional violations in the field of public education," [101] and held that school districts could not assign Mexican-American children to neighborhood schools in ethnically segregated neighborhoods.[102] A number of courts have also invoked the disproportionate impact doctrine to incorporate the employment test validation rule of *Griggs v. Duke Power Co.*[103] into the equal protection clause.[104]

Last Term, in *Washington v. Davis*,[105] an action challenging the verbal ability test required of applicants by the District of Columbia Police Department, the Supreme Court held that the Constitution does not incorporate the *Griggs* rule and, more

[96] *Id.* at 1184–85 (quoting Hobson v. Hansen, 269 F. Supp. 401, 497 (D.D.C. 1967) (Wright, J.), *aff'd sub nom.* Smuck v. Hobson, 408 F.2d 175 (D.C. Cir. 1969) (en banc)).

[97] *E.g.*, Metropolitan Hous. Dev. Corp. v. Village of Arlington Heights, 517 F.2d 409 (7th Cir. 1975), *cert. granted*, 423 U.S. 1030 (1975); Kennedy Park Homes Ass'n v. City of Lackawana, 436 F.2d 108 (2d Cir. 1970), *cert. denied*, 401 U.S. 1010 (1970). *See generally* Comment, *Applying the Title VII Prima Facie Case to Title VIII Litigation*, 11 HARV. C.R.-C.L. L. REV. 128 (1976).

[98] *E.g.*, Otero v. New York City Hous. Auth., 484 F.2d 1122 (2d Cir. 1973).

[99] Cisneros v. Corpus Christi Independent School Dist., 467 F.2d 142, 148 (5th Cir. 1972), *cert. denied*, 413 U.S. 920 (1973).

[100] *Id.* at 150.

[101] *Id.* at 149.

[102] In Keyes v. School Dist. No. 1, 413 U.S. 189 (1973), the Supreme Court reaffirmed the distinction between de jure and de facto segregation. The Fifth Circuit responded in United States v. Texas Educ. Agency, 532 F.2d 380 (5th Cir. 1976), by recasting its doctrine to create an irrebuttable presumption that a school district segregated in fact is intentionally segregated; it invoked the torts maxim that a person intends the natural and foreseeable consequences of his actions.

[103] 401 U.S. 424 (1971); *see* p. 32 *infra*.

[104] *E.g.*, Bridgeport Guardians v. Bridgeport Civil Serv. Comm'n, 482 F.2d 1333 (2d Cir. 1973); Castro v. Beecher, 459 F.2d 725 (1st Cir. 1972).

[105] 96 S. Ct. 2040 (1976).

broadly, that only official conduct having a "discriminatory purpose" violates the equal protection clause. An unusual footnote specifically cited and disapproved of a number of lower court decisions — including some of those mentioned above — that had invoked the disproportionate impact doctrine to hold unconstitutional various official acts and practices.[106]

Writing for the Court, Mr. Justice White noted that, although disproportionate impact may sometimes be evidence of purposeful discrimination, "[s]tanding alone, it does not trigger the rule . . . that racial classifications are to be subjected to the strictest scrutiny and justifiable only by the weightiest of considerations."[107] He found this conclusion supported by precedent,[108] and also by substantive policy:

> A rule that a statute designed to serve neutral ends is nevertheless invalid, absent compelling justification, if in practice it benefits or burdens one race more than another would be far reaching and would raise serious questions about, and perhaps invalidate, a whole range of tax, welfare, public service, regulatory, and licensing statutes that may be more burdensome to the poor and to the average black than to the more affluent white.[109]

Turning to the test administered by the police department — one designed and widely used by the United States Civil Service Commission — Mr. Justice White found nothing to "warrant the conclusion that it is a purposeful device to discriminate against Negroes,"[110] and observed that it seemed reasonably related to the legitimate objective of upgrading the communicative skills of department personnel. The test therefore was not unconstitutional. Because the complainants had also challenged the test under a local statute that in effect incorporated Title VII doctrine, the Court finally examined the test under the *Griggs* standards and upheld it.[111]

---

[106] *Id.* at 2050 n.12.

[107] *Id.* at 2049.

[108] *Id.* at 2047–48.

[109] *Id.* at 2051–52. *See also* Jefferson v. Hackney, 406 U.S. 535 (1972).

[110] 96 S. Ct. at 2051.

[111] The Court apparently applied the usual due process "rational relation" standard. *See, e.g.*, Williamson v. Lee Optical Co., 348 U.S. 483 (1955).

Mr. Justice Stewart did not join the portion of the Court's opinion upholding the verbal ability test under *Griggs*. 96 S. Ct. at 2054. Mr. Justice Brennan's dissent, joined by Mr. Justice Marshall, focused on this aspect of the decision, arguing that the Court had significantly weakened the validation criteria developed under Title VII. *Id.* at 2057. The dissenters did not address the constitutional issue. In a concurring opinion, Mr. Justice Stevens reserved his opinion on the merits of the cases disapproved in the Court's footnote, and cautioned "that the line between discriminatory purpose and discriminatory impact is not nearly as bright, and perhaps not quite as critical, as the reader of the Court's opinion

Davis reflects both the centrality of race-dependence to the equal protection clause and the judicial unmanageability of a general rule requiring an extraordinary justification for practices that produce racially disproportionate effects. The following discussion identifies and evaluates five possible rationales for the disproportionate impact doctrine. The first three are rooted in the antidiscrimination principle and involve remedies for present, past, and future discrimination. I believe that the disproportionate impact doctrine can continue to play a useful role, for courts as well as for legislatures, in enforcing the antidiscrimination principle. The fourth rationale is concerned with remedying "race-specific harms" produced by disproportionate impact. Although legislatures may properly ameliorate race-specific harms, I argue that the Constitution provides no basis for judicial intervention. The fifth rationale embodies a theory that accords moral status to groups and holds that it is intrinsically unjust for one racial group to be appreciably worse off than others. I believe that this theory is fundamentally misconceived and should not serve as the basis of policymaking by any institution.

A. Suspected Race-Dependency

Federal courts have used the disproportionate impact doctrine to avoid the unique difficulties of dealing with discriminatory intent or motive. The Supreme Court focused on these difficulties several years ago in *Palmer v. Thompson*,[112] a decision that inadvertently contributed to the growth of the disproportionate impact doctrine.

In *Palmer* the Court denied relief against the Jackson, Mississippi, City Council's decision to close the municipal swimming pools, in the face of overwhelming evidence that they were closed solely to avoid desegregating them.[113] In a sweeping opinion for a closely divided Court, Mr. Justice Black emphasized the "hazards of declaring a law unconstitutional because of the motivations of its sponsors." [114] The Justice conceded that some of the Court's precedent "may suggest that the motive or purpose

might assume." *Id.* at 2054. In voting to sustain the challenged test "on a ground narrower than the Court describes," *id.*, Mr. Justice Stevens emphasized that there was not enough evidence of disproportionate impact "to overcome the presumption that a test which is this widely used by the Federal Government is in fact neutral in its effect as well as its 'purpose' as that term is used in constitutional adjudication." *Id.* at 2055.

[112] 403 U.S. 217 (1971).

[113] The evidence is summarized in Mr. Justice White's dissenting opinion, 403 U.S. at 246–54.

[114] 403 U.S. at 224.

behind a law is relevant to its constitutionality," [115] but he reanalyzed two major decisions — *Griffin v. County School Board* [116] and *Gomillion v. Lightfoot* [117] — to conclude that they turned "on the actual effect of the enactments, not upon the motivation which led the States to behave as they did." [118]

Mr. Justice Black rewrote history. The Court's entire line of civil rights precedent, beginning in 1879 with *Strauder v. West Virginia*,[119] explicitly turns on the race-dependence of the practices invalidated. And the language of *Griffin* and *Gomillion* — decisions rendered at a time when the antidiscrimination principle had no acknowledged competitors — belies his reinterpretations. *Griffin* authorized enjoining the county from closing its public school system in the face of an order to desegregate. The Court emphasized that the schools were closed "for one reason, and one reason only: to ensure . . . that white and colored children in Prince Edward County would not, under any circumstances, go to the same school. Whatever nonracial grounds might support a State's allowing a county to abandon public schools, the object must be a constitutional one . . . ." [120] In *Gomillion*, the Alabama legislature had altered the shape of the city of Tuskegee from a square to what Mr. Justice Frankfurter described as "an uncouth twenty-eight-sided figure," [121] with the effect of removing all but a handful of black voters, but not a single white voter, from the city limits. The Court sustained an action to set aside the change, finding these facts "tantamount for all practical purposes to a mathematical demonstration, that the legislation is solely concerned with segregating white and colored voters by fencing Negro citizens out of town . . . . " [122]

One effect of *Palmer v. Thompson* was to induce lower courts to conceal decisions based on discriminatory motivation in the guise of disproportionate impact. For example, in *Hawkins v. Town of Shaw*,[123] one of the decisions explicitly disapproved in *Washington v. Davis*,[124] the record showed gross racial disparities in the provision of municipal services funded from general revenues.[125] The district court nonetheless found that the town had

[115] *Id.* at 225.

[116] 377 U.S. 218 (1964).

[117] 364 U.S. 339 (1960).

[118] 403 U.S. at 225.

[119] 100 U.S. 303 (1880).

[120] 377 U.S. at 231.

[121] 364 U.S. at 340.

[122] *Id.* at 341.

[123] 437 F.2d 1286 (1971), *aff'd on rehearing en banc*, 461 F.2d 1171 (5th Cir. 1972).

[124] 96 S. Ct. 2040, 2050 & n.12 (1976).

[125] 437 F.2d at 1288.

not allocated municipal services according to race and denied relief.[126] The panel reversed on the ground that "no compelling state interests can possibly justify the discriminatory *results* of Shaw's administration of municipal services," [127] and the Fifth Circuit sitting en banc reaffirmed the panel's decision on that ground.[128] Judge Wisdom concurred specially, emphasizing that the judgment was not based "even in part on proof of motive, purpose, or intent. To imply that proof of motive, purpose, or intent is necessary to establish a basis for relief . . . is to misstate the clear and unambiguous law on the subject." [129] He cited *Palmer*, *Griffin*, and *Gomillion* among other cases.[130]

Since *Palmer*, the Court has again acknowledged the importance of discriminatory motivation. *Keyes v. School District No. 1* [131] held that the Denver schools were unlawfully segregated as a result of race-dependent decisions by the school board, noting that "the differentiating factor between *de jure* segregation and so-called *de facto* segregation . . . is *purpose* or *intent* to segregate." [132] And in *Washington v. Davis*, Mr. Justice White — author of the chief dissenting opinion in *Palmer* — briefly reviewed the precedents to conclude: "To the extent that *Palmer* suggests a generally applicable proposition that legislative purpose is irrelevant in constitutional adjudication, our prior cases . . . are to the contrary. . . ." [133] Thus — if *Keyes* did not suffice — *Davis* not only undermines the disproportionate impact doctrine but explicitly revives the antidiscrimination principle and the legitimacy of judicial inquiry into purpose, intent, or motive.

This does not entirely obviate the problems implicit in *Palmer v. Thompson*, however. Mr. Justice Black was correct that it often is difficult to determine whether a decision was discriminatorily motivated.[134] If courts may grant relief only when plaintiffs have made a clear case on the record, many instances will remain where race-dependent decisions are strongly suspected but cannot be proved. Although this is not essentially different from the difficulty facing the proponents in most litigation seeking to

[126] 303 F. Supp. 1162, 1168 (N.D. Miss. 1969).

[127] 437 F.2d at 1292.

[128] 461 F.2d 1171, 1172–73 (5th Cir. 1972).

[129] *Id.* at 1174.

[130] *Id.*

[131] 413 U.S. 189 (1973).

[132] *Id.* at 208.

[133] 96 S. Ct. at 2050 n.11.

[134] For discussions of this and other difficulties presented by judicial review of motivation, *see* Brest, Palmer v. Thompson: *An Approach to the Problem of Unconstitutional Legislative Motive*, 1971 SUP. CT. REV. 95; Ely, *Legislative and Administrative Motivation in Constitutional Law*, 79 YALE L.J. 1205 (1970).

overturn government policies, it is especially troubling in the race area. The accumulation of suspected but unproved race-dependent conduct, such as decisions to zone out low income housing, may systematically deprive minorities of important benefits. And the very existence of a state of affairs which "everyone knows" is based on racial discrimination but no one will remedy is demoralizing and stigmatic.

The disproportionate impact doctrine thus acts as a safeguard against improper race-dependent decisions. But for the reasons suggested by Mr. Justice White's parade of horribles in *Washington v. Davis*,[135] the doctrine cannot reasonably be applied across the board. If disproportionate impact is to remain a useful device, it must be used selectively and perhaps be modified to create rebuttable rather than conclusive presumptions of discriminatory intent. Some decisions and regulations concerning school segregation and employment discrimination provide examples of such modified uses of the doctrine.

In several school desegregation cases involving districts not formerly segregated by statutory mandate, federal courts have invoked the torts maxim that a person "intends the natural and foreseeable consequences of his actions" [136] to create a presumption that a school district that is segregated in fact is intentionally segregated.[137] In the absence of other evidence of segregative intent, the school district may rebut the presumption by showing, for example, that it has consistently adhered to a policy of assigning children to neighborhood schools located on neutrally-selected sites.[138] This shifting of the burden of proof is justified on two grounds. First, the school district enjoys far better access than the plaintiffs to the true reasons underlying the myriad of decisions that determine the extent of school segregation — decisions concerning such matters as the drawing of attendance zone lines, the location and size of new schools, and the closing of old ones. Second, despite indications of support for some degree of school integration,[139] it is reasonable to assume that school boards

[135] 96 S. Ct. at 2051–52, *quoted at* p. 25 *supra*.

[136] *See, e.g.*, United States v. Texas Educ. Agency, 532 F.2d 380, 388 (5th Cir. 1976), *citing* W. Prosser, Handbook of the Law of Torts § 8, at 31 (4th ed. 1971).

[137] *See, e.g.*, United States v. School Dist., 521 F.2d 530, 535–36 (8th Cir. 1975); Morgan v. Kerrigan, 509 F.2d 580, 593–94 (1st Cir. 1974); Oliver v. Michigan State Bd. of Educ., 508 F.2d 178, 182 (6th Cir. 1974).

[138] *E.g.*, Higgins v. Board of Educ., 508 F.2d 779, 791 (6th Cir. 1974); Diaz v. San Jose Unified School Dist., 412 F. Supp. 310, 335 (N.D. Cal. 1975).

[139] A Harris Poll of October, 1975, indicated that Americans approve of the desegregation of public schools 56% to 35%, but are opposed to busing as a means of achieving racial balance 75% to 20%. N.Y. Times, Oct. 5, 1975, at 59, col. 5. The Gallup Poll of the same month indicated that white parents in both the North and South were increasingly in favor of school integration, a turnabout in their

throughout the nation tend to reflect the desires of many white constituents to avoid having their children attend schools with too high a proportion of minority students.

A substantial discrepancy between the proportion of qualified available minorities in a community and the proportion on an employer's workforce or in a particular job or department has long been taken as evidence that the employer discriminates. Such evidence may serve both as the basis for an initial finding that the employer has violated the antidiscrimination principle, and as a basis for finding that it has not complied with an order to cease and desist discriminating.[140]

Some federal agencies have incorporated this evidentiary principle directly into a prophylactic remedy and, without making prior findings of discrimination, require a grantee or contractor to take affirmative measures to assure that minorities are represented in its workforce in the proportion that they would be in the absence of discrimination.[141]

If a hiring goal is based on an accurate assessment of the proportion of qualified and available minorities in the community, or underestimates their number; if the employer's compliance is based on a large sample; and if the effect of noncompliance is only to place on the employer the burden of proving that it has not discriminated, then an employer can theoretically comply by using color-blind employment procedures. In reality, the threat of sanctions or even the hassle of an enforcement proceeding may induce an employer to be color-conscious to the extent of assuring that it meets the goal. If the agency has overestimated the proportion of qualified minorities; if compliance is based on a small sample; or if the employer may not justify its failure to meet a quota, the employment process is almost certain to be race-dependent, and the employer may prefer some minority applicants to equally or better qualified whites.

Hiring goals provide an efficient alternative to case-by-case adjudication as a means of enforcing the antidiscrimination principle — a means potentially so effective as to outweigh the possible costs of color-conscious decisionmaking. But an agency charged with setting the goals must do so with sensitivity. It may be predisposed to err on the side of stringency to guard against violations of the antidiscrimination principle. But, although the setting of too high a goal may not violate the antidis-

attitudes since the polling organization first measured such views in 1963. *Id.*, Oct. 12, 1975, at 67, col. 4.

[140] *See* Fiss, *supra* note 30, at 263–81.

[141] *See, e.g.*, 35 C.F.R. §§ 60–2.10 to 60–2.11 (1975) (Office of Federal Contract Compliance).

crimination principle,[142] it may nonetheless work individual unfairness upon nonminority applicants as well as hinder the employer's performance of its legitimate functions.

B. *The Effects of Past and Remote Discrimination*

The effects of discrimination may attenuate over time or be submerged in superseding events. But the injuries inflicted by discrimination can place its victims at a disadvantage in a variety of future endeavors, and discrimination can also perpetuate itself by altering the social environment to harm new generations of victims. Discrimination often works its injuries through practices, not themselves race-dependent, implemented by institutions that have not themselves discriminated. Past and remote discrimination often manifest themselves in racially disproportionate impact, and the antidiscrimination principle may therefore support its amelioration or elimination.

1. The Causal Connection. — The Voting Rights Act of 1965 [143] suspends literacy and other tests as a precondition to voting in all jurisdictions subject to the Act's coverage formula — a formula aimed at states and subdivisions where voting discrimination was most prevalent.[144] To reinstate a test, or otherwise modify voting procedures, a jurisdiction must prove to the satisfaction of the Attorney General or the United States District Court for the District of Columbia that it has not abridged the franchise on account of race for the five preceding years and that the proposed change "does not have the purpose and will not have the effect of denying or abridging the right to vote on account of race or color. . . ." [145] In *Gaston County v. United States* [146] the Supreme Court read the Act broadly to eliminate even indirect effects of past discrimination. In a suit by a South Carolina county to reinstate its literacy test, the Court assumed that the test had been administered impartially and that the county's purposes were nondiscriminatory, but held that the test would nonetheless have the impermissible effect of disadvantaging black adults who as children may have attended the county's segregated and inferior schools. Mr. Justice Harlan wrote:

> It is only reasonable to infer that among black children compelled to endure a segregated and inferior education, fewer will achieve

[142] *See* pp. 16–18 *supra*.

[143] 42 U.S.C. §§ 1971, 1973 to 1973bb-4 (1970).

[144] As originally adopted, the Act applied to any state or subdivision which maintained a voting "test or device" and in which less than 50% of its voting age residents were registered on November 1, 1964 or voted in the November, 1964 presidential election. 42 U.S.C. § 1973b(b) (1970).

[145] 42 U.S.C. § 1973c (1970).

[146] 395 U.S. 285 (1969).

> any given degree of literacy than will their better-educated white contemporaries. And on the Government's showing, it was certainly proper to infer that Gaston County's inferior Negro schools provided many of its Negro residents with a subliterate education, and gave many others little inducement to enter or remain in school . . . . "Impartial" administration of the literacy test today would serve only to perpetuate these inequities in a different form.[147]

The Supreme Court relied on *Gaston County* in its innovative decision in *Griggs v. Duke Power Co.*,[148] which interpreted Title VII of the Civil Rights Act of 1964 [149] to prohibit tests and other criteria for employment that disproportionately exclude minority applicants unless the criteria are shown to bear a demonstrable relationship to successful performance of the jobs for which they are used. Writing for a unanimous Court, Chief Justice Burger assumed that the defendant's requirements of a high school diploma and passing scores on two tests were adopted without discriminatory intent, but responded that past discrimination by other institutions might account for the disproportionate failure of blacks to satisfy the requirements.[150] The Court has since asserted that "*Griggs* was rightly concerned that childhood deficiencies in the education and background of minority citizens, resulting from forces beyond their control, not be allowed to work a cumulative and invidious burden on such citizens for the remainder of their lives." [151]

These voting and employment remedies are overbroad. The tests are suspended or invalidated for all persons, not just for minority applicants, and even with respect to minorities, not all racially disproportionate impact can be attributed to past and remote discrimination: culture and social environment play major roles in shaping people's motivations, habits, and skills, and the values voluntarily held by different social groups conduce to differing extents to success on tests and jobs in any society.[152] Nonetheless, it seems obvious that, were it not for past discrimination, more members of some minority groups would satisfy voting and employment requirements. The federal doctrines are overbroad both for administrative reasons [153] and because, in addition to remedying the effects of past discrimination, they may prevent

---

[147] *Id.* at 295–97.

[148] 401 U.S. 424 (1971).

[149] 42 U.S.C. § 2000e (1970).

[150] 401 U.S. at 430.

[151] McDonnell Douglas Corp. v. Green, 411 U.S. 792, 806 (1973).

[152] See ETHNICITY 11–15 (N. Glazer & D. Moynihan eds. 1975). H. GUTMAN, WORK, CULTURE AND SOCIETY IN INDUSTRIALIZING AMERICA (1975).

[153] *See generally* Fiss, Gaston County v. United States: *Fruition of the Freezing Principle*, 1969 SUP. CT. REV. 379, 382–401.

future discrimination,[154] and perhaps ameliorate race-specific harms.[155]

The causal connection between past discrimination and present states of affairs has also received the Court's attention in school segregation litigation. *Green v. County School Board*[156] involved a small Virginia school district which, like many rural areas, was not residentially segregated. The district had only two schools, which were de jure segregated — first pursuant to state law, later by local practice. In 1965, in order to remain eligible for federal financial aid, the school board adopted a "freedom of choice" plan of desegregation, which required each pupil to choose which school to attend each year. After three years under the plan, fifteen percent of the black pupils attended the formerly all-white school; no whites attended the all-black school.

A unanimous Court held that the freedom of choice plan was inadequate under these circumstances. Mr. Justice Brennan wrote that formerly de jure segregated school systems were "charged with the affirmative duty to take whatever steps might be necessary to convert to a unitary system in which racial discrimination would be eliminated root and branch" — "a system without a 'white' school and a 'Negro' school, but just schools."[157] Freedom of choice was " 'only a means to a constitutionally required end — the abolition of the system of segregation and its effects.' "[158]

In *Green* the causal connection between past discrimination and the current racial composition of the schools was as clear as such matters ever can be. It is not plausible, and the school board did not try to argue, that the county school system would have been substantially segregated in 1968 had children never been assigned by race. In this respect, *Green* was the Court's last easy school desegregation case. Freedom of choice was generally abandoned and replaced by the conventional and far more efficient method of assigning pupils to schools near their homes. But, though this produced considerable desegregation in rural districts, it left many metropolitan schools substantially segregated. At least superficially, they now seemed segregated because of segregated residential patterns rather than the past practices of school boards.

In *Swann v. Charlotte-Mecklenburg Board of Education*,[159]

---

[154] *See, e.g.*, Davis v. Schnell, 81 F. Supp. 872 (S.D. Ala. 1949), *aff'd per curiam*, 336 U.S. 933 (1949), *discussed in* Fiss, *supra* note 153, at 387–88; pp. 43–44 *infra*.

[155] *See* pp. 44–48 *infra*.

[156] 391 U.S. 430 (1968).

[157] *Id.* at 437–38, 442.

[158] *Id.* at 440, *quoting* Bowman v. County School Bd., 382 F.2d 326, 333 (4th Cir. 1967) (Sobeloff, J., concurring).

[159] 402 U.S. 1 (1971).

however, the Court extended *Green* to formerly de jure segregated urban school districts, and upheld an order requiring the assignment of pupils so that the racial composition of each school approximated the composition of the system as a whole. Chief Justice Burger's brief discussion of the link between past de jure segregation and the present state of affairs suggested that " '[r]acially neutral' assignment plans . . . may fail to counteract the continuing effects of past school segregation resulting from discriminatory location of school sites or distortion of school size in order to achieve or maintain an artificial racial separation": [160]

> People gravitate toward school facilities . . . . In addition to the classic pattern of building schools specifically intended for Negro or white students, school authorities have sometimes, since *Brown*, closed schools which appeared likely to become racially mixed through changes in neighborhood residential patterns. This was sometimes accompanied by building new schools in the areas of white suburban expansion farthest from Negro population centers in order to maintain the separation of the races with a minimum departure from the formal principles of "neighborhood zoning." Such a policy . . . may well promote segregated residential patterns which, when combined with "neighborhood zoning," further lock the school system into the mold of separation of the races.[161]

It is doubtful that the processes described by the Chief Justice account for much of the segregation in Charlotte and other metropolitan areas. Whether or not an order to integrate the schools might properly have been premised on residential segregation caused by agencies other than the school board, the Court explicitly disavowed deciding the case on that theory.[162] If *Swann* is truly based on the school district's prior history of de jure segregation, the most plausible justification for the decision lies in the possibility, discussed immediately below, that affirmative steps were necessary to counteract the continuing psychological effect of the past designation of schools as "white" or "black." [163]

---

[160] *Id.* at 28.

[161] *Id.* at 20–21.

[162] *Id.* at 23.

[163] *Swann* concluded with the observation that "[n]either school authorities nor district courts are constitutionally required to make year-by-year adjustments of the racial composition of student bodies once the affirmative duty to desegregate has been accomplished and racial discrimination through official action is eliminated from the system." 402 U.S. at 31–32. Last Term in Pasadena City Board of Education v. Spangler, 96 S. Ct. 2697 (1976), the Court held that absent proof that resegregation was caused by the school district's actions or by the judicial decree itself, a federal court lacked authority to readjust the racial composition of schools that had operated for four years under a desegregation decree.

2. *The Continuing Harm.* — When an act of discrimination denies its victim a benefit (*e.g.*, the right to vote), a finding that the present state of affairs (the disproportionately small number of blacks registered to vote) was caused by past discrimination is tantamount to a determination that past discrimination inflicts present injuries. However, some acts of discrimination may inflict their main or sole injury, not by denying a benefit, but by stigmatizing the victim. Assuming that this is true of school segregation (where exhaustive analyses by social scientists have not yielded a consensus that adventitious or de facto segregation inflicts race-specific harms) does the stigmatic harm of past de jure segregation continue into the present, or is the Court's attempt to design "a decree which will so far as possible eliminate the effects of past [segregation]" [164] simply a quest for the abstract ideal of restoring a hypothetical status quo ante?

In this respect, *Green v. County School Board* is again a relatively easy case. For in a formerly de jure segregated district with no residential segregation, where it is apparent that any conventional assignment scheme would integrate the schools, the theoretical possibilities of freedom of choice do not obscure the clear message that the schools are presently segregated because school officials intended them to be so. Even if the present school board is indifferent to the racial consequences of its policy,[165] the clarity of the causal relationship between past discrimination and the present state of affairs carries the stigmatic harm forward in time. Aside from the practical constraints on the exercise of choice,[166] a pupil's freedom to choose what school to attend cannot remove the stigma so long as his choice is between attending a school that is all-black because of past de jure segregation, and being an outsider at a school, white not only in composition but by longstanding tradition also rooted in de jure segregation.

Swann is harder to justify in these terms. Because the metropolitan school system assigned children by geographic zones it cannot be so readily apparent to the community that today's segregated schools resulted from yesterday's de jure school segregation, rather than from residential patterns. (After all, the Court itself established the connection only by presuming it.) Still, the insult of past discriminatory acts may have persisted. Until only

[164] Green v. County School Bd., 391 U.S. 430, 438 n.4 (1968) (quoting Louisiana v. United States, 380 U.S. 145, 154 (1695)).

[165] Freedom of choice plans were so inefficient that the only plausible reason for retaining them was to avoid desegregating the schools. Inaction for this reason is a present violation of the antidiscrimination principle. *See* p. 13 *supra*.

[166] *See* U.S. COMM'N ON CIVIL RIGHTS, SURVEY OF SCHOOL DESEGREGATION IN THE SOUTHERN AND BORDER STATES, 1965–66, at 51–52 (1966); U.S. COMM'N ON CIVIL RIGHTS, SOUTHERN SCHOOL DESEGREGATION, 1966–67, at 88 (1967).

a few years before the decision in *Swann*, the school district was segregated de jure, and it is possible that the community still viewed the "white" and "black" schools as so designated by official policy rather than having come about adventitiously. Just as the Court resolved all doubts about the causal link between past and present segregation against the known wrongdoer, so may it have resolved doubts about the persistence of stigmatic injury.

3. The Benefits and Costs of Eliminating Racially Disproportionate Impact. — All other things being equal, racially disproportionate impact should be eliminated to the extent that it inflicts injuries attributable to past discrimination. But remedies for disproportionate impact may impose heavy costs on institutions and individuals, and cannot be tailored narrowly to compensate all those and only those whose present situation is the result of past discrimination.

The voting test suspension remedies have been relatively uncontroversial because they do not frustrate the legitimate expectations of third parties or prefer the intended beneficiaries to others similarly situated; they are not thought to impose undue costs on the institutions they affect; and they may produce social gains independent of racial justice, such as facilitating political participation by all citizens. The employment test invalidation remedies have been more controversial largely because of the costs they impose on employers.[167] Massive busing remedies for school segregation have also been controversial because of the costs they impose on school districts, individual children, and families, and because of doubts about the benefits of integration.[168]

The remainder of this section examines racially preferential employment remedies that are based on the theory that the disproportionate absence of minority employees from particular industries, firms, and occupations is caused by past and remote violations of the antidiscrimination principle. It ignores questions of statutory construction, and focuses instead on the fundamental problems of policy and equity that inhere in preferential remedies.

Like programs for the preferential admission of minorities to institutions of higher education, preferential employment remedies implicate the interests of two groups of third parties: the *dispreferred* — persons in direct competition with the beneficiary so that his or her gain is their loss; and the *nonpreferred* — persons who, though not immediately affected by the remedy, may be equally entitled to its benefits. Before turning to racially prefer-

---

[167] *See, e.g.*, Wall St. J., Sept. 3, 1975, at 1, col. 8.

[168] *See, e.g.*, N. Glazer, Affirmative Discrimination ch. 3 (1975); L. Graglia, Disaster by Decree (1976).

ential remedies as such, it is useful to consider the equities of dispreferred persons in the conventional case where an identifiable victim of an employer's discrimination seeks specific relief against the employer.

(*a*) *Relief for Identifiable Victims of Discrimination.* — Even the most conventional and undisputed specific remedy — an order requiring the employer to accord an identifiable discriminatee priority for the next vacancy — adversely affects another applicant for the vacancy who would otherwise have gotten the job. The law's traditional indifference to the competitor's equities is partly explained by the view that he has no "right" to the job and that no reasonable expectations will be frustrated by denying it to him. Additionally, the prior act of discrimination is treated as giving the discriminatee a special claim against the employer — like a priority in bankruptcy — to which all others are subordinated. Moreover, the remedy may be premised on a model of the employment market in which, if the employer had not discriminated in the first instance, no vacancy would exist.[169]

Concern for the equities of third parties emerges when their reasonable expectations are frustrated by remedies for past discrimination. Last Term, in *Franks v. Bowman Transportation Co.*,[170] a divided Court held that individuals whom the defendant had discriminatorily denied positions as over-the-road truck drivers were not only entitled to priority consideration for vacancies but, if hired, were presumptively entitled to full seniority benefits retroactive to the date of their initial job applications. The decision rested on the theory that Title VII seeks to restore " 'persons aggrieved by the consequences and effects of the unlawful employment practice . . . to a position where they would have been were it not for the unlawful discrimination.' " [171] Observing that seniority determines the order of layoff and recall of employees, as well as job assignments and vacation and pension benefits, Mr. Justice Brennan reasoned that without an award of seniority, a discriminatee "will perpetually remain subordinate to persons who, but for the illegal discrimination, would have been in respect to entitlement to these benefits his inferiors." [172]

In separate opinions, Chief Justice Burger, and Mr. Justice Powell joined by Mr. Justice Rehnquist, agreed that the retro-

---

[169] This model treats employment applicants as waiting in a queue for vacancies. If the discriminatee had been hired originally, the current vacancy would go to the applicant who was hired in the discriminatee's place rather than to the discriminatee's present competitor. To the extent that the model bears any resemblance to reality, it describes a larger employment market than a single firm.

[170] 96 S. Ct. 1251 (1976).

[171] *Id.* at 1264.

[172] 96 S. Ct. at 1265–66.

active award of *benefit*-type seniority, such as accrued entitlements to vacations and pensions, was often appropriate. Mr. Justice Powell wrote that "[b]enefit-type seniority, like back pay, serves to work complete equity by penalizing the wrongdoer [*i.e.*, the employer] economically at the same time that it tends to make whole the one who was wronged."[173] By contrast, a retroactive award of *competitive*-type seniority — priority in the order of layoff and recall and in bidding jobs — "usually does not directly affect the employer at all," but "directly implicate[s] the rights and expectations of perfectly innocent employees."[174] For this reason, he argued, a court should not presumptively award competitive-type seniority, but should weigh the competing equities in each case. Chief Justice Burger doubted that retroactive competitive-type seniority was ever equitable.[175]

Certainly, the doctrine approved by the Court — the so-called "rightful place" doctrine[176] — may impose substantial costs on third parties, for regardless of what an incumbent's position might have been in the absence of discrimination, to find herself suddenly demoted through no fault of her own must come as a severe blow both psychologically and materially (to the extent that she relied on accrued seniority in making investments and expenditures and foregoing other job opportunities). Nonetheless, as between entirely denying retroactive competitive-type seniority or imposing its full costs on incumbent employees, the latter better comports with my own intuitions of equity.[177] The Court's holding may, moreover, deter future discrimination by unions which, as in *Franks*, are often complicit in, if not the moving force behind, an employer's discrimination.[178]

The situation in *Franks* need not, however, be treated as a zero-sum game between incumbent employees and victims of an employer's discrimination. Money damages assessed against an employer who has engaged in discrimination can compensate the victims of past discrimination, or compensate incumbents for the loss of accrued seniority,[179] while imposing the costs on the wrong-

---

[173] *Id.* at 1275 (Powell, J., concurring in part and dissenting in part).

[174] *Id.* at 1275–76.

[175] *Id.* at 1272.

[176] *See* Note, *Last Hired, First Fired Layoffs and Title VII*, 88 HARV. L. REV. 1544, 1553 (1975).

[177] For a suggestion of equitable means for allocating the costs between these parties, see Summers & Love, *Work Sharing as an Alternative to Layoffs by Seniority: Title VII Remedies in Recession*, 124 U. PA. L. REV. 893 (1976).

[178] *See, e.g.*, UNITED STATES CIVIL RIGHTS COMM'N, THE CHALLENGE AHEAD: EQUAL OPPORTUNITY IN REFERRAL UNIONS (1976); W. GOULD, BLACK WORKERS in WHITE UNIONS (forthcoming 1976).

[179] The present capitalized value of foregone seniority can be estimated and

doer and deterring its future discrimination. The Court has previously recognized the appropriateness of money damages in Title VII actions,[180] and both the Court's and Chief Justice's passing references to this possibility [181] suggest that the Court may be open to judicial remedies designed to allocate the costs of discrimination in a more equitable manner.[182]

(*b*) *Racially Preferential Treatment.* — Cases like *Franks* [183] do not present problems of racially preferential remedies. The beneficiaries receive a preference not because they are minorities, but because the employer discriminated against them; they are entitled to a priority not over whites alone, but over all incumbents, including any minorities, hired during the relevant period. By contrast, hiring quotas and the protection of recently hired minority workers against layoffs under the "last hired, first fired" rule are indifferent to whether the preferred individuals were victims of the employer's discrimination and thus present more difficult issues of fairness.

Many lower courts have ordered hiring quotas to remedy past discrimination or — more typically — to remedy the racially disproportionate effect of an employer's or union's use of nonvali-

---

reduced to a money judgment. *See generally* Briefs for Local 682, JAW, United States, and EEOC as Amicus Curiae, Franks v. Bowman Transp. Co., 96 S. Ct. 1251 (1976). A court may also order a company to retain incumbents who otherwise would be laid off, *see, e.g.*, Watkins v. United Steelworkers Local 2369, 369 F. Supp. 1221 (E.D. La. 1974), *rev'd on other grounds*, 516 F.2d 41 (5th Cir. 1975).

[180] Albemarle Paper Co. v. Moody, 422 U.S. 405 (1975).

[181] 96 S. Ct. at 1270 n.38, 1272.

[182] *But see* EEOC v. Local 638, Sheet Metal Workers, 532 F.2d 821 (2d Cir. 1976). In refusing to award backpay to "a class of individuals whose claims are too speculative for adjudication: . . . those who never applied to [the unions] because of their well-deserved reputation for discrimination," the court observed:

> We are aware that . . . we [recently] indicated that retroactive or constructive seniority could be granted to female police officers who could prove that they had been deterred from applying for jobs in the police department because of its discriminatory practices, relief arguably broader than that granted here. However, the remedy . . . [of] retroactive seniority [is] far less drastic for a defendant to be required to bear than back pay.

Id. at 833 n.6. But retroactive seniority is "less drastic" for the defendant only because its full burden falls on incumbent employees. To do justice in this complex area, a court must not ignore their claims.

[183] Several courts have extended the "rightful place" doctrine approved in *Franks* to grant retroactive competitive-type seniority to minority individuals who were deterred by an employer's or labor organization's known discriminatory policy from even applying for a job or for membership in a union. *See, e.g.*, Acha v. Beame, 531 F.2d 648 (2d Cir. 1976); United States v. Sheet Metal Workers Local 36, 416 F.2d 123 (8th Cir. 1969). So long as relief is limited to persons who can establish with reasonable certainty that they would have sought and obtained the position on the date to which seniority is made retroactive, the competing equities are not qualitatively different from those in *Franks*. As the certainty diminishes, however, the relative equities of incumbents increase.

dated tests and criteria.[184] In *Vulcan Society v. Civil Service Commission*,[185] for example, the Second Circuit, having invalidated the eligibility examination for the New York City Fire Department, permitted the city to continue to employ applicants who had passed the invalid exam while it developed a new one, but required the department to hire at least one minority who had passed the examination for every three nonminorities. Since the individuals injured by the exam were those who had failed it, they received no benefit from this interim quota remedy. Similarly, in *Carter v. Gallagher*,[186] after invalidating various requirements for employment by the Minneapolis Fire Department, the Court of Appeals for the Eighth Circuit went on to order that "one out of every three persons hired by the Fire Department . . . be a minority individual who qualifies until at least 20 minority persons have been so hired." [187] Although the Court recognized that the beneficiaries of the decree were unlikely to include individuals injured by the department's past practices, it wrote that "as a method of presently eliminating the effects of past racial discriminatory practices and . . . making meaningful in the immediate future the constitutional guarantees against racial discrimination, more than a token representation should be afforded." [188]

In contrast to the hiring quota decisions, appellate courts have consistently refused to order the preferential retention of minority employees in slack periods. The Fifth Circuit's decision in *Watkins v. United Steel Workers Local 2369* [189] is typical. A manufacturing plant with a long history of discrimination began hiring blacks in the 1960's, and by 1971 one-eighth of its workforce was black. For economic reasons the plant then began to reduce its work force, laying off employees (pursuant to the terms of a collective bargaining agreement) in reverse order of seniority and therefore laying off almost all of the blacks. The district court ordered the company to reinstate enough black employees to achieve its 1971 racial proportion and thereafter to allocate layoffs among black and white employees in accordance with that proportion and to recall one black for every white recalled.[190] The Court of Appeals reversed, holding that

> regardless of an earlier history of employment discrimination, when present hiring practices are nondiscriminatory and have

[184] Many of the cases are gathered in Slate, *Preferential Relief in Employment Discrimination Cases*, 5 LOY. CHI. L.J. 315 (1974).

[185] 490 F.2d 387 (2d Cir. 1973).

[186] 452 F.2d 315 (8th Cir. 1971) (en banc), *cert. denied*, 406 U.S. 950 (1972).

[187] *Id.* at 331.

[188] *Id.*

[189] 369 F. Supp. 1221 (E.D. La. 1974), *rev'd*, 516 F.2d 41 (5th Cir. 1975).

[190] 516 F.2d at 44.

> been for over ten years, an employer's use of a long-established seniority system for determining who will be laid-off, and who will be rehired, adopted without intent to discriminate, is not a violation of Title VII or [42 U.S.C.] § 1981, even though the use of the seniority system results in the discharge of more blacks than whites to the point of eliminating blacks from the work force, where the individual employees who suffer layoff under the system have not themselves been the subject of prior employment discrimination.[191]

The different judicial attitudes toward racially preferential hiring quotas and preferential protection from reverse discrimination may reflect the degree to which the two remedies frustrate the reasonable expectations of dispreferred parties,[192] as well as distinctions implicit in Title VII.[193] For present purposes, however, I shall not distinguish between the two remedies, which have in common the characteristic that the dispreferred white is not subordinated to an identifiable victim of discrimination holding a claim against the employer, but to a minority individual who was most likely *not* injured by this employer. In either case, if the racial preference is to be treated as compensation to its beneficiary for past discrimination, the traditional requirement of mutuality between wrongdoer and beneficiary must be satisfied or dispensed with.

There are two possible solutions to the problem of mutuality. One, which I shall discuss below, asserts that compensation is due the racial *group* and, for want of a better alternative, may be paid to any member of the group.[194] The other asserts that the employer should not be viewed as an isolated actor, but as one part of a network of institutions that have discriminated against minorities — including other employers, schools, realtors, and national, state and local governments. Even if the beneficiary of a preferential remedy adopted by a particular firm was never injured by that firm, she suffered discrimination at the hands of others; the beneficiaries of other preferential programs will include the victims of that firm's discrimination, and so on. More broadly, even if the beneficiary is a young person just entering the labor market who has not directly suffered employment discrimination, she may have been discriminated against by other institutions, such as schools, or have indirectly suffered from discrimination against her forebears and other members of her

[191] *Id.* at 44–45.

[192] *See, e.g.*, Kirkland v. New York State Dept. of Correctional Services, 520 F.2d 420, 429 (2d. Cir. 1975); Bridgeport Guardians, Inc. v. Bridgeport Civil Service Comm'n, 482 F.2d 1333, 1341 (2d Cir. 1973).

[193] *See generally* Note, *supra* note 176.

[194] *See* pp. 50–52 *infra*.

race. Past discrimination of various sorts is reflected in the disproportionate unemployment and underemployment of minorities, and preferential hiring can ameliorate its effects.

This analysis recasts a preferential hiring or layoff scheme as a general program for compensating minorities for past discrimination. Even if the minority beneficiary's claim were superior to that of the dispreferred applicant or employee, imposing the full costs of the program on the latter (who typically is not much better off than the beneficiary) runs against the grain of most enlightened social welfare policies. My doubts about the analysis are more fundamental, however, and would also apply to a program of "black reparations" [195] funded from general revenues. I believe that an individual's moral claim to compensation loses force as the nature, extent, and consequences of the wrongs inflicted become harder to identify and as the wrongs recede into the past. Not only does the image blur as the focus shifts from a specific claim based on an identifiable act to encompass amorphous wrongs, but new kinds of claims enter the field of vision. For racial discrimination is hardly the only injury that our society has inflicted on its members. The minority's claim to compensation for past discrimination must now share the field with the claims of all persons whose present position is the result of economic exploitation and other social injustices.

Indeed, as claims to compensation based on the past injustices of human institutions become attenuated, they begin to compete with claims based on the vagaries of fate, and thus become indistinguishable from demands for greater distributive justice among all individuals. If we are to compensate people for the adverse effects of their environments there is no reason to distinguish among the causes of the environments. One major function of compensation is to remedy the upset or outrage occasioned by the wrongdoer's frustration of the victim's justified expectations — to remedy the loss of the anticipated enjoyment of benefits possessed or reasonably expected. But a person cannot, in this sense, "expect" to be brought up from the start in an environment different from the one in which he or she was in fact raised.

The poor nonpreferred white and the black beneficiary of a preferential program are like two children raised as brothers in an impoverished household. It is later discovered that one or the other is probably the heir to a small fortune, which is given to the one with the more likely claim, the other taking nothing. All parties concerned would regard the occurrence as a windfall, and certainly not based on desert. So too is a preference premised on

[195] *See, e.g.*, B. Bittker, The Case for Black Reparations (1973); Hughes, *Reparations for Blacks?*, 43 N.Y.U.L. Rev. 1063 (1968).

a greater probability that the minority's situation is the result of past injury.

It may be thought that these doubts about the propriety of preferential treatment as a remedy for generalized past discrimination confuse what Professor Boris Bittker calls "vertical equity, i.e., justice as between one income group and another" with "horizontal equity, i.e., justice within each income group." [196] He writes:

> If Jones and Smith both earn $5,000 a year but Smith has been prevented by society from earning $6,000 a year, his complaint is not adequately answered by telling him that when society is ready to help persons at the $5,000 level, he and Jones will share equally in public assistance. . . . [A] program of black reparations . . . is a remedy for injustice, not a poverty program, and its objective would not be achieved by increasing public assistance or welfare benefits for everyone at the bottom of the economic ladder.[197]

Certainly, the paradigm model of compensatory justice is not concerned with issues of equity between the victim of a wrong and others who are similarly situated for different reasons; but only with equity between the wrongdoer and the victim, whose claim has priority over most other beneficial uses of the wrongdoer's resources. But the thrust of the preceding discussion is that a general preferential treatment or reparations program moves well beyond this paradigm to a point where the distinction between compensatory and distributive justice becomes untenable.

C. Preventing Future Remote Discrimination

The disproportionate absence of minorities from certain positions — whether or not itself the result of racial discrimination — may conduce to discrimination in other areas. Such a link underlies the special legislative and judicial concern to protect the political power of minorities. In *Katzenbach v. Morgan*,[198] in sustaining section 4(e) of the Voting Rights Act of 1965, which exempts persons educated through sixth grade in Puerto Rican schools from English literacy tests, Mr. Justice Brennan wrote for the Court:

> The practical effect of § 4(e) is to prohibit New York from denying the right to vote to large segments of its Puerto Rican community. Congress has thus prohibited the State from denying to that community the right that is "preservative of all

---

[196] B. Bittker, *supra* note 195, at 133–34.

[197] *Id.* at 134.

[198] 384 U.S. 641 (1966).

> rights." . . . This enhanced political power will be helpful in gaining nondiscriminatory treatment in public services for the entire Puerto Rican community. Section 4(e) thereby enables the Puerto Rican minority better to obtain "perfect equality of civil rights and the equal protection of the laws." [199]

The provisions of the Voting Rights Act that suspend literacy tests and require voting material to be provided in the native language of certain "language minorities" [200] also serve this objective.

The Supreme Court's constitutional doctrine concerning multimember legislative districts seems responsive to similar concerns. A 1966 opinion indicated that constitutional problems would arise if "designedly or otherwise, a multi-member constituency apportionment scheme . . . operate[d] to minimize or cancel out the voting strength of racial or political elements of the voting population." [201] In *White v. Regester*,[202] a unanimous Court struck down two multimember districts in Texas, on the ground that black and Mexican-American minorities were effectively excluded from political processes. Mr. Justice White's opinion assigned plaintiffs a heavy burden, but not one requiring proof of discriminatory intent:

> [I]t is not enough that the racial group allegedly discriminated against has not had legislative seats in proportion to its voting potential. The plaintiffs' burden is to produce evidence to support findings that the political processes leading to nomination and election were not equally open to participation by the group in question — that its members had less opportunity than did other residents in the district to participate in the political processes and to elect legislators of their choice.[203]

The Court did not imply that the multimember districts had been discriminatorily designed. It noted, however, that both counties involved had histories of discrimination in the provision of public services and that in one the major political organization had intentionally excluded minorities.

D. Race-Specific Harms

The disproportionate disadvantage or exclusion, or the segregation, of the members of a racial minority may give rise to in-

[199] *Id.* at 652–53 (footnote omitted).

[200] 42 U.S.C. §§ 1973aa–1a(b) (1970).

[201] Burns v. Richardson, 384 U.S. 73, 88 (1966). In Whitcomb v. Chavis, 403 U.S. 124 (1971), the Court scrutinized, but upheld, multimember districts in Marion County, Indiana.

[202] 412 U.S. 755 (1973).

[203] *Id.* at 765–66.

dividual and social costs produced solely because of the race of the people affected — costs that would not arise from the identical practices if their impact was random with respect to race. These "race-specific harms" can result from practices that are not race-dependent.

The disproportionate absence of minorities from juries is an example. The principle that juries should represent a cross-section of the community reflects a belief that jurors from different racial, ethnic, and socioeconomic groups tend to have different viewpoints which affect their perceptions of fact and exercise of discretion, and that the system will function most accurately and fairly if a variety of viewpoints is brought to bear on the decision.[204] For this reason, although it would be impossible to assure the proportional representation of the many relevant social groups on jury panels, some legislatures and courts have taken measures to assure that salient groups are not systematically underrepresented.[205] The Court of Appeals for the Fifth Circuit has held that states must design their procedures for the selection of criminal juries toward this end, and has invalidated procedures — regardless of whether they were racially motivated — that disproportionately exclude blacks.[206]

In contrast to the disproportionate exclusion of minorities from juries, which arguably violates the sixth and seventh amendment requirements that juries represent cross-sections of the community, other putative race-specific harms do not violate definite constitutional provisions. This is true, for example, of the harms that may result from de facto segregation and from the depressed socioeconomic status of certain minorities.

School segregation, whatever its cause, has been said to reduce the self-esteem, aspirations, motivations, and achievement of black children and to encourage racial fears, hostility, and prejudice.[207] But although these hypotheses have been tested in

---

[204] *See, e.g.*, Taylor v. Louisiana, 419 U.S. 522, 526–30 (1975).

[205] *See, e.g.*, Federal Jury Selection and Service Act of 1968, 28 U.S.C. § 1861 (1970); United States v. Lewis, 472 F.2d 252 (3d Cir. 1973); United States v. Dellinger, 472 F.2d 340 (7th Cir. 1972), *cert. denied*, 410 U.S. 970 (1973); United States v. Guzman, 468 F.2d 1245 (2d Cir. 1972), *cert denied*, 410 U.S. 937 (1973); United States v. Hyde, 448 F.2d 815, 830 (5th Cir. 1971), *cert. denied*, 404 U.S. 1058 (1972); United States v. Bennett, 445 F.2d 638 (9th Cir. 1971), *cert. denied*, 404 U.S. 1023 (1972); United States v. Parker, 428 F.2d 488 (9th Cir.), *cert. denied*, 400 U.S. 910 (1970); United States v. Dangler, 422 F.2d 344 (5th Cir. 1970); United States v. Arnett, 342 F. Supp. 1255 (D. Mass. 1970).

[206] Labat v. Bennett, 365 F.2d 698 (5th Cir. 1966) (systematic exclusion of "daily wage earners"), *cert. denied*, 386 U.S. 991 (1967).

[207] For reviews of the literature, see, *e.g.*, N. St. John, School Desegregation Outcomes for Children (1975); On Equality of Educational Opportunity (F. Mosteller & D. Moynihan eds. 1972); Goodman, *De Facto School Segregation: A*

hundreds of studies, none has been established or disproved to the satisfaction of disinterested social scientists.[208] Some students of the subject have concluded that the effects of school segregation and integration are situation-specific, and that, while a thoughtfully designed integrated environment may be highly advantageous, the mere mixing of children of different races without more may accomplish nothing or even be counter-productive.[209] Because cultural, rather than genetic, characteristics of race are salient, and because race and class co-vary in so many situations, harms that appear to be race-specific may in fact be class-specific. Thus, there has been a continuing controversy over the extent to which any positive educational effects of integration derive from the mixture of black and white, rather than lower- and middle-class children.[210] Nonetheless, commentators have argued [211] and some courts have held [212] that de facto school segregation must be prohibited because it causes race-specific harms.

Whether, apart from its educational effects, the disproportionately low socio-economic status of certain minority groups inflicts race-specific injuries on their members has also been controversial. Advocates of programs for racially preferential employment and admissions to universities and professional schools have suggested [213] that improvement in the status and income of some members of an impoverished minority community produces external benefits, increasing the wealth, status, and power of the community as a whole; that minorities in high status occupations

---

Constitutional and Empirical Analysis, 60 CALIF. L. REV. 275, 400–35 (1972); Weinberg, *The Relationship Between School Desegregation and Academic Achievement: A Review of the Research*, 39 L. & CONTEMP. PROB. 241 (1975); Cohen, *The Effects of Desegregation on Race Relations*, *id.* at 271; Epps, *Impact of School Desegregation on Aspirations, Self-Concepts, and Other Aspects of Personality*, *id.* at 300.

[208] *See* note 207 *supra*.

[209] *See, e.g.*, Cohen, *supra* note 207; Orfield, *How to Make Desegregation Work: The Adaptation of Schools to Their Newly Integrated Student Bodies*, 39 L. & CONTEMP. PROB. 314 (1975).

[210] *Compare* J. COLEMAN, ET AL., EQUALITY OF EDUCATIONAL OPPORTUNITY 307–08 (1966), *with* 1 U.S. COMM'N ON CIVIL RIGHTS, RACIAL ISOLATION IN THE PUBLIC SCHOOLS 113–14 (1967).

[211] *See, e.g.*, Fiss, *Racial Imbalance in the Public Schools: The Constitutional Concepts*, 78 HARV. L. REV. 564 (1965).

[212] *See, e.g.*, Cisneros v. Corpus Christi Independent School Dist., 467 F.2d 142 (5th Cir. 1972), *cert. denied*, 413 U.S. 920 (1973); United States v. Texas Educ. Agency, 532 F.2d 380 (5th Cir. 1976) (irrebuttable presumption that segregation is intentional); Crawford v. Board of Educ., 130 Cal. Rptr. 724 (1976).

[213] Much of the written discussion has focused on the external benefits of preferential admissions of minority applicants to institutions of higher education. *See, e.g.*, R. O'NEIL, DISCRIMINATING AGAINST DISCRIMINATION (1975); Sandalow, *supra* note 66, at 682–92 (1975). Cf. Fiss, *supra* note 65, at 147–56.

have access to others in positions of power and are thus able to provide their communities with a variety of benefits that depend on "knowing the right people" — a bank loan for a small business enterprise, a new school or park, or a zoning variance; that the very presence of minorities in traditionally white occupations, associations, and unions may undermine stereotypes that perpetuate prejudice, and provide minorities with the leverage to prevent discrimination against others of their group; that successful minority individuals may provide necessary role models for youths who would not otherwise aspire to professional careers; and perhaps even that minorities regularly employed in lower level occupations may serve as role models for learning industrial discipline and bring needed stability to a socially disorganized culture of poverty.

The existence, degree, and nature of these and most other race-specific harms arguably produced by non-race-dependent practices are seldom self-evident. The independent significance of race, as distinguished from poverty, will likely remain unknown for the immediate future. Assuming, however, that significant race-specific harms do exist, by what authority may they be ameliorated?

Much race-specific harm in contemporary American society may be traceable to present or past violations of the antidiscrimination principle. It seems improbable that most lower-class, isolated, and intradependent minority communities would possess these vulnerable characteristics to nearly the same degree were it not for longstanding and pervasive patterns of discrimination. The antidiscrimination principle provides sufficient authority for ameliorating race-specific harms to the extent that they depend on conditions caused by discrimination.[214]

An institution enjoying more or less plenary policymaking authority may remedy race-specific harms that are *not* traceable to violations of the antidiscrimination principle, just as it may remedy any number of other kinds of injuries wholly unrelated to race. For example, a school board might focus on the special needs of minority children today, and deal with blind and retarded children a decade later — as claims come to its attention through interest groups, social upheavals, personal experience, and the like. But where the very authority of the judiciary is based on its ability to expound and apply general principles, it cannot act on such an ad hoc basis. Apart from the antidiscrimination principle, does there exist a coherent principle that requires remedy of race-specific harms but not other equally severe injuries — a principle,

[214] The amelioration of race-specific harms attributable to past discrimination is, however, subject to economic and equitable constraints of the sort considered in connection with remedies for past discrimination generally. *See* pp. 36–43 *supra*.

for example, under which a school district must spend $X to prevent Y amount of race-specific harm by integrating the schools, but need not spend the same amount of money to prevent the same amount of harm to mentally or physically handicapped children or to white children from impoverished environments?

To be sure, race-specific harms may produce serious individual and social costs. But these costs seem neither different in kind nor of a greater order of magnitude to the individuals affected than many others that might be ameliorated by changing school assignment schemes, employment criteria, and the like. Mark G. Yudof has suggested a possible distinction in what he terms the "universalist ethic." [215] Its basic premise is that a "stable, just society, without violence, alienation, and social discord, must be an integrated society. Segregation of the races in public institutions, employment, and housing will inevitably lead to conflict and the destruction of democratic values and institutions." [216] But, as Professor Yudof concedes, the universalist ethic not only depends on complex and nonobvious empirical assumptions, but is ideologically controversial: "[i]t does not rest on the consent of the minorities, and it faces a resurgent 'community consciousness.' " [217] The universalist ethic does not seem so obviously right or widely held, as compared to competing ethics, that it can properly be read into the Constitution.

E. Justice for Racial Groups

The most pernicious feature of racial prejudice and discrimination is their underlying premise that members of some racial groups are less worthy than members of others. The antidiscrimination principle holds that this assumption is fallacious because race has no moral salience. For administrative purposes, some remedies for racial discrimination are triggered by disproportionate racial impact or treat persons according to membership in racial groups; but group membership is always a proxy for the individual's right not to be discriminated against. Similarly, remedies for race-specific harms recognize the sociological consequences of group identification and affiliation only to assure justice for individual members.

In contrast to the theories considered so far, some commentators have suggested that racial groups should be treated as moral entities, holding rights as groups to distributive and compensatory justice. The distributive theory assumes the moral permissibility

[215] Yudof, *Equal Educational Opportunity and the Courts*, 51 TEXAS L. REV. 411, 456–64 (1973).

[216] *Id.* at 457.

[217] *Id.*

of unequal distributions of welfare among individuals, but holds that it is at least prima facie unjust for one racial or ethnic group to be substantially worse off than others. Like many individual-oriented theories of distributive justice, a group theory is essentially indifferent to the history that led to the unequal distribution. For example, Owen M. Fiss proposes a noncompensatory, purely redistributive principle — a "group disadvantaging principle" — that requires relief for any group that constitutes a "perpetual underclass." He argues that "[t]he redistributive strategy could give expression to an ethical view against caste, one that would make it undesirable for any social group to occupy a position of subordination for any extended period of time." [218] Similarly, Vernon Van Dyke suggests that John Rawls' principles of individual equality [219] might be expanded to encompass distributive justice among social groups.[220]

The arguments supporting the theories of group distributive justice are difficult to discern. Professor Fiss states that his "group disadvantaging principle" is justified primarily by its intuitive correctness: "visions about how society should be structured may be as irreducible as visions about how individuals should be treated — for example, with dignity." [221] Professor Van Dyke notes that many nations recognize the rights of groups based on race, language, religion, and national origin, and that some political theories accord groups moral and political rights as entities. He concludes that "[g]roups in fact have status and rights of an intermediate level between the individual and the state, and it is imperative for a theory of justice to take this fact into account." [222]

If a society can be said to have an underlying political theory, ours has not been a theory of organic groups but of liberalism, focusing on the rights of individuals, including rights of distributive justice. Of course, we recognize the sociological fact that people desire to affiliate and associate with others who share common interests or characteristics. The religion and association clauses of the first amendment are responsive to such desires. But though groups and associations may benefit incidentally from these guarantees, the amendment is designed to protect the individual's freedom to associate. We grant rights to associations or treat them as fictitious persons only to protect the rights of their individual members and for other instrumental purposes.

[218] *Fiss*, supra note 65, at 151.

[219] J. Rawls, A Theory of Justice (1971).

[220] Van Dyke, *Justice as Fairness: For Groups?*, 69 Am. Pol. Sci. Rev. 607 (1975).

[221] Fiss, *supra* note 65, at 151.

[222] Van Dyke, *supra* note 220, at 614.

Otherwise, the rights of associations and groups are no greater than the sum of those of their members. Indeed, under our received — albeit philosophically inadequate — metaphor of the social contract, the state itself does not enjoy rights greater than those of its citizens.

To say that we generally embrace the liberal tradition is, of course, no response to the claim that we should modify the theory and restructure our institutions accordingly. But without derogating from competing political traditions, they have implications that vie with, if they are not inconsistent with, principles that we hold fundamental — including the antidiscrimination principle, which attributes no moral significance to membership in racial groups, and notions of individual autonomy. Moreover, although the practices of nations — including our own — often fall short of their aspirations, most societies in which power is formally allocated among racial and national groups are strikingly oppressive, unequal, and unstable.[223] In view of all of this, it seems reasonable to place the burden on proponents of a theory of group racial justice to show that it is morally tenable and consistent with other values that we cherish. To my knowledge, this has not yet been done.

Several commentators, who concede that racial groups have no intrinsic moral salience, assert that they acquire moral rights once the members of a group have suffered racial discrimination. For example, Paul W. Taylor argues that the group as a moral entity is in effect "*created* by the original unjust practice":

> The principle of compensatory justice is that in order to restore the balance of justice when an injustice has been committed to a group of persons, some form of compensation must be made to the group. Thus if there has been an established social practice . . . of treating any member of a certain class of persons in a certain way on the ground that they have characteristic C and if this practice has involved the doing of an injustice to C-persons, then the principle of compensatory justice requires that C-persons as such be compensated in some way . . . . [E]ven if the individual C-person who now enjoys the favourable compensatory treatment was not himself one of those who suffered injustice as a result of the past social practice, he nevertheless has a right (based on his being a member of the class of C-persons) to receive the benefits extended to all C-persons as such.[224]

Michael D. Bayles asserts:

> [T]here need be no contradiction involved in claiming that being

[223] *See, e.g.*, A. Rabushka & K. Shepsle, Politics in Plural Societies (1972).

[224] Taylor, *Reverse Discrimination and Compensatory Justice*, 33 Analysis 177, 179 (1973).

> black is both morally irrelevant for discriminating against people and morally relevant in discriminating in favour of people to provide reparations . . . . One may hold that people have an obligation to give reparations to groups they have wronged. By using the characteristic of being black as an identifying characteristic to discriminate against people, a person has wronged the group, blacks. He thus has an obligation to make reparations to the group. Since the obligation is to the group, no specific individual has a right to reparation. However, since the group is not an organized one like a state, church, or corporation, the only way to provide reparations to the group is to provide them to members of the group.[225]

A similar view may be implicit in some judicial decisions requiring employers and unions to adopt hiring and admission quotas to compensate for their past discrimination, even though the remedies are not likely to benefit the victims.[226] For example, in upholding the validity of hiring "goals," the Second Circuit seems to treat minority persons as fungible:

> [W]here the imbalance is directly caused by past discriminatory practices it is readily apparent that if the rights of minority members had not been violated, many more of them would enjoy those rights than presently do so and that the ratio of minority members enjoying such rights would be higher. . . . The effects of such past violation of the minority's rights cannot be eliminated merely by prohibiting future discrimination, since this would be illusory and inadequate as a remedy. Affirmative action is essential . . . to place eligible minority members in the position which the minority would have enjoyed if it had not been the victim of discrimination.[227]

Of course, an act of discrimination against an individual can indirectly inflict material and psychological injury on others of the same race. But even if preferential treatment were thought an appropriate remedy for such harms, this is not the argument made by Bayles and Taylor. Their view is that an act of discrimination is a wrong to the "group," and that (at least where the immediate victim has not been compensated) redress is appropriately made to any member of the group regardless of his or her personal injuries. In effect, the member receives compensation as a representative of the group.

The notion that the treatment of individuals as a group for malign purposes requires their treatment as a group for benign compensatory purposes has the superficial appeal of all such sym-

---

[225] Bayles, *Reparations to Wronged Groups*, 33 ANALYSIS 182, 183 (1973).

[226] *See* pp. 39–41 *supra*.

[227] Rios v. Steamfitters Local 638, 501 F.2d 622, 631–32 (2d Cir. 1974).

metries. But, unless one adopts a notion of group rights such as that examined and rejected above, the fact is that most injuries of discrimination — even indirect or secondary ones — were inflicted on particular persons and only they are entitled to compensation.[228] Where discrimination has undermined the unity or culture of a group, it may be appropriate to characterize the injury as one to the group; but the appropriate remedy then is one that reestablishes the group, an end that is not promoted by the fiction of treating individual members as its agents.[229]

I have argued that neither the Constitution nor sound moral or political theory disfavors practices that disproportionately injure the members of racial minorities unless the disproportionate impact reflects or conduces to violations of the antidiscrimination principle. I have also argued that, although agencies exercising plenary policymaking authority may ameliorate race-specific harms, no principle provides an a priori basis for according these harms priority over the many others that can befall individuals in our society. It remains to be explained why these conclusions strike some thoughtful people as counterintuitive. There are at least two possible explanations.

First, racial discrimination — especially against blacks — is so longstanding and pervasive in our society that most instances of racially-disproportionate impact may seem to be the products of discrimination, and the disproportionate impact doctrine may therefore seem equivalent to the antidiscrimination principle. Although I am skeptical about the invariable truth of this complex assumption, I agree that disproportionate impact may often reflect discrimination. Indeed, part of my "defense" of the antidiscrimination principle is based on its ability to respond to a variety of forms of discrimination and to remedy past and remote dscrimination. But the theme of Part II is that disproportionate impact has no constitutional or moral life of its own apart from the antidiscrimination principle.

A second explanation for the intuitive appeal of the racially disproportionate impact doctrine lies in its superficial resemblance to doctrines concerned with ameliorating conditions of poverty. These include the constitutional doctrine requiring governments to assure that no one must forego certain "fundamental interests"

---

[228] *Cf.* Appendix B, "West German Reparations to Nazi Victims," in B. BITTKER, *supra* note 195, at 177–91.

[229] I am indebted to Professor Robert Simon of Hamilton College for this point. Reparations paid by Germany to the State of Israel, though largely designed to compensate for the costs of resettling victims of Nazi persecution, *see* B. BITTKER, *supra* note 195, at 78, may have served this function.

—for example, voting [230] and an adequate criminal defense [231] — because of poverty. If this doctrine is characterized as disfavoring non-wealth-dependent practices that disproportionately injure the poor, it provides an apparent analogy to non-race-dependent practices that disproportionately injure the members of racial minorities. But this misconceives the fundamental interest doctrine, which is not concerned with disproportionate impact on poor persons, but with the denial of important benefits to individuals who cannot afford to pay for them. This doctrine, and more general theories of distributive justice, are not ultimately concerned with "the poor" as a class, but with individuals who lack adequate resources. Race is, at best, a weak proxy for need; there are more direct and accurate ways of identifying needy people.

III. Conclusion: The Judicial Role

The antidiscrimination principle remains the vital force behind contemporary civil rights policy. Even for Congress and the states, which enjoy broad authority to remedy race-specific harms and other social injustices, it provides the primary rationale for programs designed to achieve racial equality. For the federal judiciary, whose constitutional authority is circumscribed by the relatively narrow mandate of the equal protection clause of the fourteenth amendment, the antidiscrimination principle is the only coherent source of civil rights policy independent of congressional legislation.

Between the end of Reconstruction and the mid-1960's the federal judiciary served as the major protector of civil rights. Within the past dozen years, however, Congress and the federal executive have assumed substantial responsibility for civil rights enforcement and many public and private institutions have voluntarily adopted remedial measures. What role should the courts continue to play in supervising the remedial and enforcement efforts of other agencies, and in independently protecting civil rights?

Judicial supervision of other agencies' efforts to remedy racial injustices should be rather limited. Although the constitutionality of "reverse discrimination" is not the only issue that may come before the courts, it is currently the most controversial one. Under the approach proposed in this essay, all or most preferential employment and admissions programs would survive constitu-

[230] *See* Harper v. Virginia Bd. of Elections, 383 U.S. 663 (1966); Kramer v. Union Free School Dist. No. 15, 395 U.S. 621 (1969).

[231] *See* Griffin v. Illinois, 351 U.S. 12 (1956); Douglas v. California, 372 U.S. 353 (1963).

tional scrutiny.[232] It is a truism — only because it is true — that a practice may be unwise or even unfair and yet not be unconstitutional.[233]

By contrast, the courts should continue to enforce the equal protection clause aggressively against traditional forms of discrimination. To be sure, courts are more severely limited by institutional constraints than are most other policymaking agencies. In fashioning their own remedies courts must be extraordinarily sensitive to interests besides those protected by the antidiscrimination principle, including ones that lie beyond its purview, in supervising the remedial efforts of others. But the tenacious persistence of racial injustice does not permit the federal judiciary to cease its bold and creative enforcement of the antidiscrimination principle.

---

[232] The major federal civil rights statutes, such as 42 U.S.C. §§ 1981 & 1982, and Titles VI and VII of the Civil Rights Act of 1964, are sufficiently open-textured to permit interpretations consistent with the proposed equal protection standard. *Cf.* McDonald v. Santa Fe Trail Transp. Co., 96 S. Ct. 2574, 2578 n.8 (1976).

[233] However, decisions sustaining preferential programs will almost surely be seen as "legitimating" them. *See* A. BICKEL, *supra* note 90, at 29–33, 129–32.

[2]

OWEN M. FISS

Groups and the Equal Protection Clause

This is an essay about the structure and limitations of the antidiscrimination principle, the principle that controls the interpretation of the Equal Protection Clause. To understand the importance of that principle in constitutional adjudication a distinction must first be drawn between two different modes of interpretation.

Under one mode the constitutional text is taken pure—the primary decisional touchstone is the actual language of the Constitution. The text of the Constitution is viewed as providing an intelligible rule of decision and that text, rather than any gloss, is the primary referent; at most, disagreement may arise as to how much weight should be given to one or two words and what the words mean. This is a plausible —arguable, though far from persuasive—approach to the Free Speech Clause. It is the approach associated with Justice Black.

The second mode of constitutional interpretation deemphasizes the text. Primary reliance is instead placed on a set of principles—which I call *mediating* because they "stand between" the courts and the Constitution—to give meaning and content to an ideal embodied in the text. These principles are offered as a paraphrase of the

The original version of this paper was presented at a conference held in June 1975 at the Institute for Advanced Study, Princeton, N.J., and sponsored by the Alfred P. Sloan Foundation. The paper also benefited from a discussion at the Society for Ethical and Legal Philosophy in October 1975, and from criticism from students in two seminars of mine at the Yale Law School, one in the spring of 1975 and the other (taught with my colleague Bruce Ackerman) in the fall of 1975.

particular textual provision, but in truth the relationship is much more fundamental. They give the provision its only meaning as a guide for decision. So much so, that over time one often loses sight of the artificial status of these principles—they are not "part of" the Constitution, but instead only a judicial gloss, open to revaluation and redefinition in a way that the text of the Constitution is not.

The Equal Protection Clause has generally been viewed in this second way. The words—no state shall "deny to any person within its jurisdiction the equal protection of the laws"—do not state an intelligible rule of decision. In that sense the text has no meaning. The Clause contains the word "equal" and thereby gives constitutional status to the ideal of equality, but that ideal is capable of a wide range of meanings. This ambiguity has created the need for a mediating principle, and the one chosen by courts and commentators is the antidiscrimination principle. When asked what the Equal Protection Clause means, an informed lawyer—even one committed to Justice Black's textual approach to the First Amendment—does not repeat the words of the Clause—a denial of equal protection. Instead, he is likely to respond that the Clause prohibits discrimination.

One purpose of this essay is simply to underscore the fact that the antidiscrimination principle is not the Equal Protection Clause, that it is nothing more than a mediating principle. I want to bring to an end the identification of the Clause with the antidiscrimination principle. But I also have larger ambitions. I want to suggest that the antidiscrimination principle embodies a very limited conception of equality, one that is highly individualistic and confined to assessing the rationality of means. I also want to outline another mediating principle—the group-disadvantaging principle—one that has as good, if not better, claim to represent the ideal of equality, one that takes a fuller account of social reality, and one that more clearly focuses the issues that must be decided in equal protection cases.

I. The Structure of the Antidiscrimination Principle

The construction of the antidiscrimination principle proceeds in three steps. The first is to reduce the ideal of equality to the principle of equal treatment—similar things should be treated similarly. The

109 *Groups and the Equal Protection Clause*

second step is to take account of the fact that even the just state must make distinctions, must treat some things differently from others; for example, even the most noncontroversial criminal statute distinguishes between people on the basis of their conduct. Recognition of the inevitability and indeed the justice of some line-drawing makes the central task of equal protection theory one of determining which lines or distinctions are permissible. Not all discriminations can be prohibited; the word "to discriminate," once divested of its emotional connotation, simply means to distinguish or to draw a line. The mediating principle of the Equal Protection Clause therefore must be one that prohibits only "arbitrary"[1] discrimination. The Clause does not itself tell us which distinctions are arbitrary, and as the third step in this process a general method is posited for determining the rationality and thus the permissibility of the lines drawn. The method chosen by the Supreme Court, and the one that generally goes under the rubric of the antidiscrimination principle, has two facets: (a) the identity of the discrimination is determined by the criterion upon which it is based, and (b) the discrimination is arbitrary if the criterion upon which it is based is unrelated to the state purpose.

To illustrate this method of determining whether a discrimination is arbitrary, let us suppose the state wishes to pick the best employees or students for a limited number of openings. That process inevitably involves choices. The state must discriminate. Assume also that the choice is made on the basis of performance on a written test designed to pick the most productive workers or the most brilliant students. The state would then be making an academic discrimination. Presumably it would not be arbitrary since the criterion is related to the state

1. Sometimes the word "invidious" is used interchangeably with "arbitrary" to describe the universe of impermissible discriminations, though with little attention to the special connotations of the word "invidious"–"tending to cause ill will, animosity, or resentment." Professor Karst, in a valuable article, reveals a sensitivity to the difference between the two terms. "Invidious Discrimination: Justice Douglas and the Return of the 'Natural-Law–Due Process Formula' " 16 *U.C.L.A. L. Rev.* 716, 732–734 (1969). He, however, uses the term "invidious discrimination" in a conclusory sense, devoid of descriptive meaning. The term is used "to describe the Court's ultimate conclusion on the question of a violation of equal protection." Ibid., p. 740 fn. 110.

purpose. This would be true even if it turned out that the only applicants selected happened to be white. But suppose the criterion for selection is color: the state grants the position to whites and denies it to blacks, on the basis of their color. That would make the discrimination a racial one and arbitrary because the criterion is not related to the state purpose of selecting the most brilliant students or most productive employees.

In this example, the racial criterion has been deemed arbitrary because it is not related to the state purpose. But Tussman and tenBroek, in their now classic article of the late 1940s,[2] pointed out that un-

2. "The Equal Protection of the Laws," 37 *Calif. L. Rev.* 341 (1949) (hereafter cited as Tussman and tenBroek). Tussman and tenBroek saw three principles, not one, governing the application of the Equal Protection Clause. The one I am describing under the rubric of the antidiscrimination principle was called the "reasonable classification" principle. They also spoke of a principle opposing "discriminatory legislation" and a third guarantee, one of "substantive equal protection." By the latter they meant that certain "rights" (analogous to those that were previously protected by the doctrine of "substantive due process") were to be protected by the Equal Protection Clause; these rights could not be interfered with even though the interference was even-handed. They sought to explain *Shelley v. Kraemer* on the basis of this principle—the enforcement of a racial restrictive covenant was not a form of unequal treatment, but rather an interference with the "right" of a willing seller to sell to a willing buyer. They sought to justify the use of the Equal Protection Clause as "a sanctuary" for these "rights," not because they have any connection to equality, but because, in their words, the Clause "was placed in our Constitution as the culmination of the greatest humanitarian movement in our history." Ibid., p. 364. This doctrine has received little formal recognition by the Court in the past twenty-five years. At most, strands of this doctrine are reflected in the fundamental-right trigger of the strict scrutiny branch of the antidiscrimination principle; in that instance the "right" is used to determine the appropriate degree of fit. On the other hand, what Tussman and tenBroek referred to as the ban on "discriminatory legislation," is completely integrated within what I call the antidiscrimination principle. For Tussman and tenBroek the ban on "discriminatory legislation" was a "criticism of legislative purpose," a "demand for purity of motive." Ibid., pp. 357, 358. Certain legislative purposes, such as the subordination of blacks, were denied to the state altogether, and thus it was irrelevant that the fit might have been perfect between the criterion (or classification) and the (forbidden) purpose. They were not especially clear as to which purposes were forbidden—they spoke in terms of "bias," "prejudice," "hostility," and "antagonism." They also recognized that the word "discrimination" could also be used in the sense that it is being used here (that is, as a term to describe the reasonable classification doctrine), but they failed to integrate the two senses of the word. Ibid., p. 358 fn. 35.

relatedness is not a dichotomous quality. In most cases it is not a question of whether the criterion and end are related or unrelated, but a question of how well they are related. A criterion may be deemed arbitrary even if it is related to the purpose, but only poorly so. Tussman and tenBroek explained that, given the purpose, a criterion could be ill-suited in two different ways: it could be overinclusive (it picked out more persons than it should) or underinclusive (it excluded persons that it should not). These evils can be described, to use the jargon of contemporary commentators, as ill-fit.[3]

This is the core idea—the foundational concept—of the antidiscrimination principle, one of means-end rationality. But it must also be recognized that the principle contemplates a series of additional inquiries that yield a superstructure. First, the principle requires that the court identify the underlying criterion. This means that a distinction must be drawn between the stated criterion and the *real* criterion. If the challenge is to a statute in all its applications, then the stated criterion may be taken at face value. But if the challenge is to the statute as applied, or to administrative action, then there is no reason why the stated criterion should be treated as the real criterion. The administrator may say he is selecting students on the basis of academic performance, when in fact he is ignoring their test scores, and making his decision on the basis of race.

Second, the court must identify the state's purpose and determine whether it is legitimate. For example, suppose the state's purpose is to subordinate blacks rather than to choose the best students or employees. Then the color black would be well-suited for determining

3. Tussman and tenBroek did not use the term "ill-fit." They did, however, make the points about over- and underinclusiveness (words they actually used and introduced into legal discourse) by the use of diagrams: *P* is the universe of person that *should* be selected given the purpose, and *C* is the universe of person *actually* selected by the criterion. The diagram where *P* is a subset of *C* is used by them to represent overinclusiveness and the diagram where *C* is a subset of *P* is used to represent underinclusiveness. The term "fit" is suggested by these diagrams, and perhaps for that reason is used by the contemporary commentators, such as, Ely, "The Constitutionality of Reverse Racial Discrimination," 41 *U. Chi. L. Rev.* 723, 727 fn. 26 (1974) (hereafter cited as Ely), and is now part of ordinary constitutional parlance.

who should be excluded from the state colleges or jobs, and under a test consisting exclusively of means-end rationality, this use of the racial criterion would be permissible. The Equal Protection Clause would thereby be transformed into a minor protection against state carelessness, permitting intervention only when it was plain that the state did not know how best to achieve its ends.[4] Accordingly, it seemed necessary to go beyond the concept of ill-fit, and the anti-discrimination principle has been modified so as to require that the state purpose against which the criterion is to be measured be legitimate (or permissible).

This account of the inquiry into purpose suggests two steps: first, identifying the state purpose and second, determining whether the purpose is legitimate. But if the court need not take the state's professed purpose as that against which the criterion is to be measured, then the two steps collapse into one. The court fixes the state's purpose by the process of imagination: only legitimate purposes would be imagined, and the judge's mind would scan the universe of legitimate purposes until he identified the legitimate state purpose that was best served by the criterion, the one that left the smallest margins of over- and underinclusiveness. The universe of imaginable purposes would not contain those purposes disavowed by the state, and the disavowal could occur implicitly, for example, it could be implied by the overall statutory framework of the state.[5]

Some have argued that the criterion should be measured against the *stated* purpose. Such a restriction might enhance the invalidating power of the Equal Protection Clause, for it was always assumed—perhaps out of simple fairness—that the process of imagination would yield the best purpose, the one most favorable to the state. This restriction would also reduce judicial maneuverability. And some have further hypothesized that a stated-purpose requirement would invigorate the political process—for "it would encourage the airing and critique of those reasons [justifying the legislative means] in

4. See generally, Note, "Legislative Purpose, Rationality, and Equal Protection," 82 *Yale L. J.* 123 (1972).

5. See, for example, Eisenstadt v. Baird, 405 U.S. 438 (1972).

the state's political process."[6] This hypothesis seems to me to posit a somewhat naive conception of the state political process and what might invigorate it. But more importantly, the restriction is inconsistent with judicial practice in other areas (such as determining whether legislation is authorized by the enumerated powers), and it would be hard to apply. The state rarely identifies its purpose with any degree of precision, and the restriction would be virtually meaningless if, as one proponent of this idea has suggested, "A state court's or attorney general office's description of purpose should be acceptable."[7] For these reasons, the stated-purpose requirement has not taken root, and probably should not be viewed as an important or permanent feature of the antidiscrimination principle.

A third set of auxiliary concepts is responsive to two facts—that the critical inquiry of ill-suitedness, as modulated by Tussman and tenBroek, is one of degree and that some margin of over- and underinclusiveness can always be discovered. Standards must therefore be set for determining how poor the relationship must be between criterion and purpose before it is deemed arbitrary—or to use the jargon of the contemporary commentators, how tight a fit must there be? The doctrines of "suspect classification" and "fundamental right" seek to answer this question. They are essentially standards for determining the requisite degree of fit. In contrast to the more permissive standard called "mere rational relationship" or "minimum scrutiny," which tolerates broad margins of over- and underinclusiveness, these doctrines trigger a strict scrutiny, one that demands a tight fit. If the criterion is "suspect" (the exemplar being race) or the "right" affected "fundamental" (the exemplar being the right to vote)[8] there has to be a very tight fit—any degree of avoidable over-

6. Gunther, "Foreword: In Search of Evolving Doctrine on a Changing Court: A Model for a Newer Equal Protection," 86 *Harv. L. Rev.* 1, 47 (1972) (hereafter cited as Gunther). See also Greenawalt, "Judicial Scrutiny of 'Benign' Racial Preference in Law School Admissions," 75 *Colum. L. Rev.* 559, 600 (1975) (hereafter cited as Greenawalt).

7. Gunther, p. 47.

8. See, for example, Carrington v. Rash, 380 U.S. 89 (1965) (denying the right to vote to those serving in the armed forces). As originally conceived, the

inclusiveness or underinclusiveness would be deemed "too much."[9] The use of the term "avoidable" gives the state an out: ill-fit would be accepted if there is no closer-fitting way of satisfying its purpose. Assuming a legitimate purpose and no better alternative, the discriminatory criterion, however "suspect," would seem necessary, and so acceptable under the Equal Protection Clause.

The strict-scrutiny branch of the antidiscrimination principle has necessitated the establishment of methods for determining which criteria are "suspect" and which rights are "fundamental." It has also required, as the fourth feature of the superstructure, the introduction of defensive doctrines—those that allow for the validation of laws and practices that would otherwise seem invalid. There is no analytic reason why these defensive doctrines cannot be applied in the minimum-scrutiny context (and on some occasions they have been); the point is simply that there is less need for them there. In the minimum-scrutiny context, the impulse toward validation could easily be accommodated in the judgment that the margins of over- and underinclusiveness are not "excessive." In the strict-scrutiny

"fundamental right" did not have to be of constitutional stature. The constitutional status of the right to vote is shrouded in controversy, but strict scrutiny seems also to have been applied to laws restricting rights clearly of nonconstitutional stature, such as the right to procreate. Skinner v. Oklahoma, 316 U.S. 535 (1952). In 1973, a majority of the Supreme Court said the right had to be of constitutional stature—though in order to pay respects to precedent—they acknowledged that the constitutional right may be an *implicit* one. San Antonio Ind. School District v. Rodriguez, 411 U.S. 1 (1973). It might also be noted that both triggers of strict scrutiny—suspect classification and fundamental right—might be present at the same time (for example, a state denying some ethnic group the right to procreate). The operative significance of this double trigger is not clear. One trigger alone may be sufficient to result in the invalidation of the law, and in that instance the second one would be superfluous—merely frosting on the cake.

9. In these cases it is often difficult to describe the discrimination as "arbitrary" within the ordinary meaning of that word. But one loses sight of the need to make that judgment. The concept of arbitrariness enters only in the establishment of the general method, as a foundational concept, and other factors account for the additional tiers. For an awareness of how the suspect-classification branch of the antidiscrimination principle causes this departure from the rationality test, see Justice Harlan's dissent in Harper v. Virginia Bd. of Elections, 383 U.S. 663, 682 n. 3 (1966).

context, on the other hand, that method of avoidance is not available since, by definition, any margin of over- or underinclusiveness is "excessive."

One defensive doctrine permits the state to take one step at a time. It is a defense aimed at excusing underinclusiveness. For example, assume there is a literacy requirement for voting at time-1. Later, at time-2, the state decides to pass a law establishing that the completion of the sixth grade in a school where subjects are taught primarily in English or Spanish (including schools in Puerto Rico or Mexico) is sufficient proof of literacy. An individual who completed the sixth grade in France (or Poland) complains that the change wrought by the new law is underinclusive—given the purpose of the state, there is no reason why he should not be included. The state might defend on the ground that it is simply taking one step at a time, and the defense has been allowed.[10]

Such a defense obviously has the capacity for completely undermining the complaint of underinclusiveness—each instance of underinclusiveness might be explained as an instance in which the legislature chose to take one step at a time. Tussman and tenBroek, fully aware of this risk, sought to limit the defense by drawing a distinction between the reasons that explained why the state took only one step at a time. If the reach of the law was confined because of *administrative* considerations (for example, additional complications would be introduced) as opposed to *political* considerations (for example, the sponsors could not muster enough votes for extending the law to others), then the one-step-at-a-time defense was allowable. The Supreme Court, on the other hand, has on at least one occasion sought to use the concept of "reform" as the limiting one: the state is allowed to take one step at a time on when the law is a "reform" measure—a law that improves (rather than worsens) the status quo.

Another defensive doctrine requires the court to rank the legitimate

10. See Katzenbach v. Morgan, 384 U.S. 641 (1966) (involving American-flag schools). In Williamson v. Lee Optical Co., 348 U.S. 483, 489 (1955), the Court said, "The reform may take one step at a time, addressing itself to the phase of the problem which seems most acute to the legislative mind."

purposes of the state–to make a distinction between ordinary and special state purposes. Hence, the concept of "a compelling state interest": the achievement of such an interest or purpose is so important that it excuses imperfect means. This doctrine seems to have its roots in the *Japanese Relocation Cases*, where the Supreme Court permitted the use of a racial or national-origin criterion (clearly a suspect one) for determining who should be relocated and otherwise confined.[11] The state purpose–self-preservation of the nation in time of war–was deemed to be of sufficient importance to excuse the overinclusiveness (not all Japanese were security risks) and underinclusiveness (those of German origin might be as much of a security risk).

This appeal to a compelling state interest must be carefully delineated. In the *Japanese Relocation Cases*, the concept was used defensively, to excuse what would otherwise be impermissible, and there was no doubt that the evil to be excused was ill-fit–over- and underinclusiveness. It was not part of a general balancing test. A minor debate has broken out recently, however, as to whether the exclusive focus must remain on ill-fit, or whether there can be, in a case where there is admittedly a perfect fit between means and ends, a "weighing of ends"–a balancing of the harm to the individuals subjected to the law and the good to be achieved.[12] Professor Brest poses the issue in his hypothetical: "How should a court treat a school principal's decision, based solely on aesthetics, to have black and white students sit on opposite sides of the stage at the graduation ceremony?"[13]

11. Korematsu v. United States, 323 U.S. 214 (1944) (relocation); See also Hirabayashi v. United States, 320 U.S. 81 (1943) (curfew).

12. Compare, for example, Ely, p. 727 fn. 26 ("I have argued that, rhetoric to the contrary notwithstanding, special scrutiny in the suspect classification context has in fact consisted not in weighing ends but rather in insisting that the classification in issue fit a constitutionally permissible state goal with greater precision than any available alternative.") with Greenawalt, p. 565 fn. 41 ("It is clear, however, that in some suspect classification cases, the Court has weighed ends, even though it has not been explicit about what it is doing.").

13. *Processes of Constitutional Decisionmaking* (Boston, 1975), p. 489. The oddity of the example is important: it is testimony of how far one must go to find a situation in which complaint of ill-fit could not be made, and thus it reveals the potential reach of the antidiscrimination principle, even as a means focused tool. It is always possible to find ill-fit. I might also add that the

117 *Groups and the Equal Protection Clause*

There is little doubt in my mind as to how a court would or should decide the case: the practice is a violation of the Equal Protection Clause. But that is not the issue. The issue is whether it is possible to get to that result (or get there as easily as one should) from the antidiscrimination principle—taken as the mediating principle of the Equal Protection Clause. I think not. If the court finds a state purpose that does not allow the slightest degree of over- or under-inclusiveness, as is indeed suggested by Professor Brest's hypothetical, then the statute or practice would be valid under the antidiscrimination principle. This would be true even though the criterion is "suspect," for example, race. It would not be permissible, within the structure of the antidiscrimination principle, to decide the question by "balancing" or "weighing" the harm done by the state practice (for example, blacks are stigmatized) against the (noncompelling) interests to be served by the state practice (for example, aesthetic satisfaction). The antidiscrimination principle—as I understand it, as Tussman and tenBroek designed it, and as the Supreme Court has generally used it—is a theory about ill-fit, not about the balance of advantage.[14]

---

example is meant only to reveal the structure of the antidiscrimination principle and it can fulfill that purpose even if it is an unlikely case.

14. I realize it is difficult to document this assertion (or perhaps any assertion about a so-called mediating principle). The meaning of the word "discrimination" as gleaned from ordinary usage or the dictionaries is hardly decisive. The word merely requires that a distinction be involved in the analysis—perhaps be the trigger of scrutiny. It does not set the limit or terms of scrutiny. Nor is there an authoritative (official) text to which I can point and say, here is the full and definitive statement of the antidiscrimination principle. Even if there were, one might contend (as those who take opposite sides in the issue do) that the rhetoric is not decisive—what is important is not what the courts say, but what they do. But let me say by way of defense that it is important to be clear about what is at stake—I am only trying to construct a prototype for purposes of analysis and exposition. I will ultimately contend that this prototype is too limited, and seek to supplement it. Of course, it might be contended that my conception of the antidiscrimination principle is too narrow and that the supplemental principle could be viewed as only a slight modification of what I call the antidiscrimination principle, for example, that it might be called "antidiscrimination principle 2." The force of that contention depends on the degree of resemblance—whether the supplemental principle is a close relative of the antidiscrimination principle or rather the member of a new

II. The Appeal of the Antidiscrimination Principle

Antidiscrimination has been the predominant interpretation of the Equal Protection Clause. The examples I have given are cast primarily in terms of race, but the principle also controls cases that do not involve race. It is the general interpretation of the Equal Protection Clause; and indeed it is viewed as having preemptive effect—if the state statute or practice passes the means-end test, then it does not violate the Clause. There have been exceptions, but they have been criticized precisely because they were departures from the principle. It was the substantive character of the one-man, one-vote standard of *Reynolds v. Sims*[15] that prompted Justice Harlan's strong dissent. The standard criticism of that decision invokes the antidiscrimination principle, which would have allowed distinctions among voters if, for example, those differences in treatment were related to legitimate interests, such as preserving the integrity of government subdivisions.

Why, it might fairly be asked, has the antidiscrimination principle been given this position of preeminence? The Equal Protection Clause may need some mediating principle, but why this one? An answer couched in terms of text and history does not suffice. The antidiscrimination principle is not compelled or even suggested by the language of the Clause. That language stands in sharp contrast to that of the Fifteenth Amendment, which does speak in terms of discrimination—the right to vote shall not be denied on account of race. Nor is the antidiscrimination interpretation securely rooted in the legislative history of the Clause. The debates preceding the adoption of the Equal Protection Clause, as best I have been able to deter-

family altogether. To decide that issue it is important to understand the intellectual roots of what might be deemed the primary version of the antidiscrimination principle, and there is no dispute that the version focusing on means—the one that conceives of the evil as ill-fit and does not weigh ends—is the primary one. At the very most commentators such as Brest or Greenawalt argue that the principle should be extended far enough to embrace a weighing of ends, and concede that it is predominantly expressive of a conception of means-end rationality.

15. 377 U.S. 533, 615–624 (1964). See also Justice Harlan's dissent in Harper v. Virginia Bd. of Elections, 383 U.S. 663, 682 (1966).

119 *Groups and the Equal Protection Clause*

mine, do not justify this choice.[16] Nor is there any reason to believe that antidiscrimination was chosen by the Court as *the* interpretation because of some special view of the legislative history. Yet, even with history and text aside, it is important to note that the predominance of the antidiscrimination principle can in large part be traced to considerations that are particularly appealing to a court.

First, the antidiscrimination principle embodies a conception of equality that roughly corresponds to the conception of equality governing the judicial process. When we speak of "equal justice" we have in mind a norm prohibiting the adjudicator from taking into account certain irrelevant characteristics of the litigants—their race, wealth, and so on. That is the message conveyed by the blindfold on the icon of justice. The antidiscrimination principle also invokes the metaphor of blindness—as in "color blindness."[17] The overarching

16. The materials which have been examined, including the debates on the Fourteenth Amendment itself, are not revealing, and obviously not decisive on an intended mediating principle. See, for example, H. Flack, *The Adoption of the Fourteenth Amendment* (Gloucester, Mass., 1908); Frank & Munro, "The Original Understanding of 'Equal Protection of the Laws,'" 50 *Colum. L. Rev.* 131 (1950); J. James, *The Framing of the Fourteenth Amendment* (1956); J. tenBroek, *Equal Under Law* (New York, 1965). In all fairness I should report that tenBroek's research led him to conclude that "equal" was of secondary importance to "protection" in the Fourteenth Amendment. He wrote, "It was because the protection of the laws was denied to some men that the word 'equal' was used. The word 'full' would have done as well." tenBroek, p. 237. I have not examined the history of all the civil rights debates during the Thirty-ninth Congress. As secondary sources on these debates, see C. Fairman, *Oliver Wendell Holmes Devise History of The Supreme Court, Volume VI, Reconstruction and Reunion 1864–1888*, part one (New York, 1971), pp. 1117–1300; Bickel, "The Original Understanding and the Segregation Decision," 69 *Harv. L. Rev.* 1 (1955); and Casper, "Jones v. Mayer: Clio, Bemused and Confused Muse," 1968 *Sup. Ct. Rev.* 89. But the provisions of the Civil Rights Act of 1866 which are still with us, 42 U.S.C. 1981 and 1982, do not speak in terms of discrimination. Instead, they say all persons "shall have the same right . . . as is enjoyed by white citizens. . . ."

17. This metaphor first surfaced in Justice Harlan's dissent in Plessy v. Ferguson, 163 U.S. 537, 559 (1896) ("our Constitution is color-blind"). The metaphor was suggested by the attorney for the blacks, Albion W. Tourgee, and he—clever lawyer that he must have been—understood why this metaphor would be appealing to a judge. Page 19 of Tourgee's brief in *Plessy* reads: "Justice is pictured blind and her daughter, the Law, ought at least to be color-blind."

obligation is to treat similar persons similarly, declaring certain individual characteristics—such as color—irrelevant.

It is natural for the Justices to seize upon the ideal of their craft in setting norms to govern others. Their craft sets limits to their horizons, it influences their choice among the many meanings of equality. This limit on vision may have been reinforced by the fact that some of the early equal protection cases challenged exclusionary conduct occurring in the course of the judicial process.[18] Moreover, the words "protection of the laws" in the Clause may have led the Justices to think primarily of the administration of justice, and the concept of equality that governs judicial activity in general (equal justice). At some point in history the word "equal" shifts its location so as to deemphasize the word "protection"—it becomes understood that the Clause guarantees "the protection of equal laws," rather than just the "equal protection of the laws"; but the implications of the original version still linger.[19]

Second, the antidiscrimination principle seems to further another supposed norm of the craft—value neutrality—that the judges not substitute their preferences for those of the people. The antidiscrimination principle seems to respond to an aspiration for a "mechanical jurisprudence"—to use Roscoe Pound's phrase—by making the predicate of intervention appear technocratic. The antidiscrimination principle seems to ask no more of the judiciary than that it engage in what might at first seem to be the near mathematical task of determining whether there is, in Tussman and tenBroek's terms, "overinclusiveness" or "underinclusiveness," or, in the terms of the contemporary commentators, whether there is the right "fit" between means and ends. The terms used have an attractively quantitative ring. They make the task of judicial judgment appear to involve as little discretion as when a salesman advises a customer whether a pair of shoes fit. Moreover, under the antidiscrimination principle, whatever judgment there is would seem to be one about means, not

18. For example, Strauder v. West Virginia, 100 U.S. 303 (1880); Virginia v. Rives, 100 U.S. 313 (1880) (both involve the exclusion of blacks from the jury).

19. Tussman and tenBroek, p. 342.

ends, thereby insulating judges from the charge of substituting their judgments for that of the legislature. The court could invalidate state action without passing on the merit or importance of the end—a task, it might be argued, that is especially committed to the more representative branches of government.[20]

The belief that the countermajoritarian objection to judicial review can be avoided by a "mechanical jurisprudence" is false. The entitlement of the judiciary to intervene is no less controversial because only the means are being attacked. They too have been chosen by the people. And there is, in any event, nothing mechanical about the antidiscrimination principle. The promise of value neutrality is only an illusion. On the explicit level, the court must determine whether the state end is legitimate, which classifications are suspect, which rights are fundamental, which legitimate state interests are compelling, and whether the occasion is a proper one for invoking the one-step-at-a-time defense. On the implicit level, the preferences of the judge enter the judicial process when he formulates the imaginable state purposes and chooses among them, and also when he decides whether the criterion is sufficiently ill-suited to warrant invalidation—whether the right degree of fit is present. In contrast to the case of shoes, the concept of fit here has no quantitative content. It only sounds quantitative—as do the words "how much" when used to describe the intensity of affection.

A third explanation for the predominance of the antidiscrimination principle may be found in another supposed ideal of the law—objectivity. In this instance the aspiration is for rules with three characteristics: (a) the rules can be stated with some sharpness or certainty; (b) they are not heavily dependent on factual inquiries or judgments of degree; and (c) they are not time-bound. Rules of this sort are thought to be more "manageable"[21] and to conform to some abstract view about the necessary attributes of "legal rules"—a view

20. See Gunther, pp. 21, 23, 28, 43, who echoes the sentiment expressed in Justice Jackson's concurrence in Railway Express Agency v. New York, 336 U.S. 106, 111–13 (1949). Professor Gunther makes the argument as part of his plea to abandon the fundamental-right branch of the strict-scrutiny inquiry, and thus to make the antidiscrimination principle more focused on means.

21. Gunther, p. 24.

likely to be shared by those seeking a "mechanical jurisprudence" and value-neutrality. I once again doubt the validity of the supposed ideal of objectivity,[22] but it cannot be denied that the antidiscrimination principle makes some contribution toward the satisfaction of this ideal, perhaps to a greater degree than toward the ideal of value-neutrality. With the possible exception of the inquiries necessary to identify the true criterion, an inquiry that need be taken only when administrative action is being challenged, the antidiscrimination principle is not especially fact-oriented. More often than not, over- and underinclusiveness is established, not by a presentation of evidence, but rather by the process of imagination–imagining whether, given the state purpose, other persons might be included within the coverage of the statute or whether people who were included might properly have been excluded. Little turns on the actual numbers involved. Moreover, although uncertainty and gradations of degree may be introduced by certain of the critical judgments required by the principle, for example, judgments about which purposes are legitimate and what is the requisite degree of fit, it is entirely possible that these judgments could be made with a high degree of generality. Once the Supreme Court spoke to an issue–for example, once the Court declared a certain criterion (such as race) to be suspect–a flat rule would emerge (no racial discrimination) that could easily be applied by the lower courts. Indeed, when the antidiscrimination principle was adopted by the legislative branch, and made the central regulatory device of the Civil Rights Acts of 1964 and 1968, it was expressed in a form that satisfied the objectivist ideal. The statutes specified the criteria (such as race, sex, religion, and national origin) that could not be the basis of discrimination.[23]

22. Fiss, "The Jurisprudence of Busing," 39 *Law & Contemp. Prob.* 194 (1975).

23. Some statutes make exceptions for certain criteria: under the Civil Rights Act of 1968, religion is a permissible criterion for allocating housing owned by a religious society, and under the Civil Rights Act of 1964 discrimination on the basis of sex is permitted in employment when sex is a "bona fide occupational criterion." Moreover, the courts have permitted the remedial use of a criterion that seemed to be flatly forbidden (for example, color-conscious

123 *Groups and the Equal Protection Clause*

Fourth, the appeal of the antidiscrimination principle may derive from the fact that it appears highly individualistic. The method for determining the permissibility of classifications does not rely, so Tussman and tenBroek proclaim, on the concept of a "natural class" (where "natural" refers not to the biological origins of the class, but rather to the fact that it is not formally created by the law in question). They acknowledge that a judgment about the arbitrariness of a classification might conceivably depend on whether it "coincides with" social groupings deemed appropriate; in that instance, the central inquiry in an equal protection case would be "whether, in defining a class, the legislature has carved the universe at a natural joint."[24] Tussman and tenBroek sought to avoid that inquiry, an inquiry they declared to be "fruitless," and did so by making the permissibility of the classification turn exclusively on the relation of means to end. Hence, the antidiscrimination principle would seem individualistic in a negative sense—it is not in any way dependent on a recognition of social classes or groups. Indeed, that is why means-end rationality is such an attractive concept: it avoids the need of making any statement about the basic societal units.

To some degree this appearance is misleading. The foundational concept—means-end rationality—is individualistic. It is not dependent on the recognition of social groups. On the other hand, elements of groupism appear as one moves up the superstructure. For one thing, the recognition and protection of social groups may be required to determine which state purposes are legitimate, or even to rank state purposes to apply the compelling state-interest doctrine. The paradigm of a state purpose that is illegitimate is couched in terms of a group: "The desire to keep blacks in a position of subordination is an illegitimate state purpose." And the standard of illegitimacy is constructed by attributing what might be viewed as a group-oriented

employment is often decreed to correct the effects of past discrimination)—a judicial improvisation that has been ratified by Congress in the course of reenactments (Equal Employment Opportunity Act of 1972). From this perspective, despite the striking difference in language, the civil rights statutes have been treated as mini-equal protection clauses.

24. Tussman and tenBroek, p. 346.

purpose to the Equal Protection Clause—to protect blacks from hostile state action.[25] Admittedly the paradigm of a "compelling state interest" is not often expressed in group terms. That doctrine emerged in the *Japanese Relocation Cases* of the 1940s and there the state interest deemed "compelling" was "self-preservation of a nation at a time of war." But, as Justice Brennan recently perceived, the concept of a compelling state interest might be stretched to embrace the protection of certain groups. In the context of a statute that embodied a classification favoring women, he wrote: "I agree that, in providing a special benefit for a needy segment of society long the victim of purposeful discrimination and neglect, the statute serves the compelling state interest of achieving equality for such groups."[26]

The suspect-classification doctrine also affords some recognition to the role or importance of social groups or natural classes. This is apparent from the original and classic statement of the doctrine by Justice Black: "It should be noted, to begin with, that all legal restrictions which curtail the civil rights of a single racial group are immediately suspect."[27] Tussman and tenBroek, intent on keeping groups out of their account of the Equal Protection Clause, quoted this passage of Justice Black but were then careful to add that "suspect classification" should not be thought of as coextensive with a "single racial group." The obvious next question is whether there are any "suspect classifications" that do not identify a natural class or social group. To this, they simply replied, "[A]n attempt at an exhaustive listing of suspect classifications would be pointless. It suffices to say that this is of necessity a rather loose category."[28] In the last twenty-

25. I think this might—to be somewhat cynical—explain why Tussman and tenBroek tried to talk in terms of two different principles—that of "reasonable classification" and that of "discriminatory legislation"—even though they perceived the interconnections between the principles and the fact that they might be embraced with one principle—what I have called the antidiscrimination principle.

26. Kahn v. Shevin, 416 U.S. 351, 358–59 (1974) (dissenting opinion, joined by Justice Marshall). I suspect that group recognition might also enter through deciding when to honor the one-step-at-a-time defense. See *Katzenbach v. Morgan*, referred to fn. 10 above, another opinion written by Justice Brennan.

27. Korematsu v. United States, 323 U.S. 214, 216 (1944).

28. Tussman and tenBroek, p. 356.

125 *Groups and the Equal Protection Clause*

five years, the category has been kept "loose"; but the important fact to note is that almost all of the serious candidates for the status of suspect classification are those that coincide with what might be conceived of as natural classes—for example, blacks, Chicanos, women, and maybe the poor. Moreover, although Tussman and tenBroek did not even try to explain why certain classifications were suspect, it is not at all clear to me that an adequate explanation can be given that does not recognize the role and importance of social groups.

Some might explain the suspectness of race, to use the exemplar of a suspect classification, in terms of the special history of the Equal Protection Clause.[29] But that explanation does not altogether avoid the reference to groups, for it may be contended that the Clause was not intended to ban the racial classification but rather to protect blacks—as a group—from hostile state action. And in any event, that explanation might be too confining. It anchors the category of suspect classification in historical fact, without room for the kind of generality expected of constitutional doctrines, a generality that might be sufficient to embrace new situations (for example, the demand of women that sex be treated as a suspect classification).[30] Others might seek to explain the suspectness of race solely on the grounds of immutability.[31] That would avoid the reference to groups, but would be an inadequate explanation for it would also render suspect such classifications as "height," "good hearing," "good eyesight," or "intelligence"—a result the antidiscrimination theorist would no doubt deny. A final explanation for the suspectness of race that might avoid the reference to groups, and that indeed does have a connection with the foundational concept of means-end rationality, asserts that race is "generally . . . irrelevant to any legitimate public

29. In his dissent in Harper v. Virginia Bd. of Elections, 383 U.S. 663, 682, fn. 3 (1966), Justice Harlan argued that "insofar as that clause may embody a particular value in addition to rationality, the historical origins of the Civil War Amendments might attribute to racial equality this special status."

30. See Getman, The Emerging Constitutional Principle of Sexual Equality, 1972 *Sup. Ct. Rev.* 157.

31. See, for example, Frontiero v. Richardson, 411 U.S. 677, 686 (1973).

purpose."[32] This would make the individualism of the antidiscrimination strategy pure. But I fail to understand how a claim about general practices (race is generally unrelated) can yield a special standard about the degree of fit (or relatedness) to be required—and that is precisely the function of the suspect-classification doctrine—to trigger strict scrutiny, making any avoidable over- or underinclusiveness impermissible.

Once again, what we are left with is an illusion—that the antidiscrimination principle need not depend on the recognition of "natural classes." This illusion of individualism can be maintained only by ignoring or failing to justify some of the key elements of the antidiscrimination strategy—elements that might be deemed part of the superstructure, but are nonetheless esssential for they have made us willing to live with that strategy.

Wholly apart from this question of whether all the elements of the antidiscrimination principle—the superstructure as well as the foundation—are explicable on individualistic premises, it should be noted that the antidiscrimination principle furthers the ideal of individualism more subtly by making classification the focus of the Equal Protection Clause. Classification is the triggering mechanism and the object of inquiry. To be sure, not all classifications are prohibited, only those that are imprecise. Yet the demand for greater and greater precision in classification has the inevitable effect of disqualifying one classification after another, and that demand is consistent with, and indeed furthers the ideal of treating people as "individuals"—recognizing each

32. "Developments in the Law—Equal Protection," 82 *Harv. L. Rev.* 1065, 1108 (1969). In response to this explanation, Professor Ely argues, "The fact that a characteristic is irrelevant in almost all legal contexts (as most characteristics are) need not imply that there is anything wrong in seizing upon it in the rare context where it does make a difference.[39]" But this response seems to confuse the suspect-classification doctrine with the forbidden-classification doctrine—an absolute ban on all racial classification. This is seen most clearly by noting that Ely's fn. 39 refers to that portion of the Tussman and tenBroek article that eschews the forbidden-classification doctrine (for the reason he articulates) not to the portion of their article that deals with the suspect classification doctrine. It should be noted that Professor Ely's explanation for the suspectness of race, the we-they theory discussed below, is a theory cast in group terms—it seeks to explain legislative motivation in terms of group membership.

person's unique position in time and space, his unique combination of talent, ability and character, and his particular conduct. The pervasiveness of this ideal in society cannot be denied, nor is it likely that judges would be insensitive to it.

The tie between individualism and the antidiscrimination principle may also stem from the fact that it yields a highly individualized conception of rights. Under the antidiscrimination principle, the constitutional flaw inheres in the structure of the statute or the conduct of the administrator, not in its impact on any group or class. Any individual who happens to be burdened by a statute or practice, or any individual excluded from the benefits, can complain of the wrong. True, other persons—namely all those within the legal classification—can make a similar complaint; and in a sense the individual is making the claim as part of a group or class (the legal class). But, the individual's entitlement to relief is not dependent on the interests or desires of others similarly subject to or excluded from the statute or practice.

Such an individualized conception of rights coincides with one strong view of what we mean by a "constitutional right"—the vindication turns on the judgment of the tribunal, not upon the views or action of third parties. Institutional considerations also make the individualized conception of rights appealing. The Equal Protection Clause is primarily enforced through litigation, and it is especially difficult to fit the vindication of group rights into the mold of the law suit. There is no way of making certain that the plaintiff is the appropriate representative of the group, and even more, there is no mechanism for resolving intraclass conflicts—differences among the members of a group as to what is in their best interest.[33]

33. Such differences frequently arise and they are not in any way resolved by the class action device. That procedural device (viewed from the plaintiff's side) only legitimizes the concept of the self-appointed representative, and then seeks to erect safeguards—such as notice—to limit, as far as possible the risk of abuse arising from this power of self-appointment. But the factors that tend to legitimize the mechanism of self-appointment also tend to undermine the effectiveness of the safeguards—each individual stands to gain so little. When the stakes are small it does not make sense for an individual to start a law suit, and for the very same reason it does not make sense for the individual to respond to the notice in order to scrutinize the adequacy of his self-appointed

Finally, under the antidiscrimination principle, equal protection rights are not only individualized, but also universalized and this is another source of its appeal. Everyone is protected. There may be a limitation on the laws brought within its sweep—they must contain a discrimination or classification. But once a distinction among persons is made by a state statute or practice, that measure can be tested by anyone who happens to be burdened by it. Even the suspect-classification doctrine can be construed in universalistic terms—any racial classification, whether black, yellow, or white, is suspect. In contrast, a mediating principle that is, for example, built on the concept of social groups might not be so universal in scope, since it is conceivable that some individual adversely affected by the state might not be a member of one of the protected groups.

The universalizing tendency of the antidiscrimination principle no doubt accounts for its popular appeal—no person seems to be given more protection than another. This universalizing tendency also appeals to a court. It relieves the judiciary of the burden of deciding who will receive the protection (in the jurisdictional sense) of a constitutional provision and then explaining why some are left out. It also creates a strategic advantage for the court—it enables the court to use the Equal Protection Clause to fill some of the gaps created by the (temporary?) retirement of substantive due process. The antidiscrimination principle can be used just as comfortably to challenge a statute that draws a distinction between opticians and optometrists or one that draws a distinction between filled milk and margarine as it can be used to challenge a statute that draws a distinction between whites and blacks.[34] The result may be different, but that

representative. And without such a response, there is no reliable way of judging the adequacy of representation. There is an adversarial void—neither the defendant nor the self-appointed representative has an interest in challenging the adequacy. Indeed, from the defendants' perspective the best representative is an inadequate one (at least if adequacy is judged from the perspective of effectiveness).

34. See, for example, Williamson v. Lee Optical Co., 348 U.S. 483 (1955). It is striking that Tussman and tenBroek built their "reasonable classification" principle (which I call the antidiscrimination principle) almost entirely out of the business regulation cases—the traditional province of substantive due process. This can be explained in part by the fact that at least up until 1949,

is not due to any fundamental shift of theory, but only to a difference in the degree of fit required.

III. The Limitations of the Antidiscrimination Principle

The appeal of the antidiscrimination principle may be unfounded. The ideals served by the principle may not have any intrinsic merit, or the connection between those ideals and the principle may be nothing more than an illusion. As we have seen, the antidiscrimination principle may be criticized on this level. But I believe the criticism runs deeper. The antidiscrimination principle has structural limitations that prevent it from adequately resolving or even addressing certain central claims of equality now being advanced. For these claims the antidiscrimination principle either provides no framework of analysis or, even worse, provides the wrong one. Conceivably, the principle might be adjusted by making certain structural modifications; and indeed, on occasion, over the last twenty-five years, that has occurred, though on an ad hoc and incremental basis, and at the expense of severing the principle from its theoretical foundations and widening the gap between the principle and the ideals it is supposed to serve.

The Permissibility of Preferential Treatment

One shortcoming of the antidiscrimination principle relates to the problem of preferential treatment for blacks. This is a difficult issue, but the antidiscrimination principle makes it more difficult than it is: the permissibility of preferential treatment is tied to the permissibility of hostile treatment against blacks. The antidiscrimination principle does not formally acknowledge social groups, such as blacks; nor does it offer any special dispensation for conduct that benefits a disadvantaged group. It only knows criteria or classifications; and the color black is as much a racial criterion as the color white. The regime it introduces is a symmetrical one of "color blindness," making the criterion of color, any color, presumptively impermissible. Reverse

this was the principal use of the Equal Protection Clause. Their formulation was bound by the prior practice, just as mine is bound by the intervening twenty-five years' experience—where the Clause was principally used as a means of protecting the racial minority.

discrimination, so the argument is made, is a form of discrimination and is equally arbitrary since it is based on race.

The defense of preferential treatment under the antidiscrimination regime begins with the search for a purpose that the racial criterion (the color black) would fit perfectly. This is not an easy undertaking. To illustrate the difficulty, let us assume that the policy at issue is one preferring blacks for admission to law school.[35] The first impulse is to identify the purpose as one of increasing the number of black lawyers. Surely if that is the purpose, there is a perfect fit between criterion and purpose—no margins of over- or underinclusiveness. But what appears at first to be a purpose seems to be nothing more than a restatement of the practice. Why does the state want to increase the number of black lawyers? The answer to this question yields what may more properly be deemed a purpose.

An answer cast in terms of the self-interest of the class or in terms of the preferences of those in power (for example, they happen to like blacks) would not be adequate. These answers would not yield a legitimate state purpose. But a number of purposes would be served by the preferential treatment that could be deemed permissible. Here are some examples: to elevate the status of a perpetual underclass by giving certain members of the group positions of power and prestige (on the theory that the elevation of the group will enhance the self-image and aspirations of all members of the group); to insulate the minority from future hostile action by strategically placing members of the group in positions of power; to diversify the student body intellectually and culturally and thereby enrich the educational experience of all; or, finally, to atone for past wrongs to the group. The difficulty with each of these purposes is, however, that once the perspective shifts from groups to individuals, as the antidiscrimination principle requires, the margins of under- and/or overinclusiveness become apparent and indeed pronounced. The fit between criterion (black) and purpose is not perfect—perhaps just as imperfect as the fit between the criterion and purpose when

35. DeFunis v. Odegaard, 416 U.S. 312 (1974). See also two symposia, "DeFunis: The Road Not Taken," 60 *Va. L. Rev.* 917 (1974), and "DeFunis Symposium," 75 *Colum. L. Rev.* 483 (1975).

the action is hostile. The overinclusiveness stems from the fact that there are blacks who are not entitled to the preferential treatment if any of these were the state purpose (the common example is the upper class black, who arguably did not suffer past discrimination and/or independently of the preferential admission to the law school, would be a "success"). The underinclusiveness stems from the fact that there are other persons who are not black and who are nevertheless as entitled to preferential treatment as blacks if the state purpose is what I have imagined (for example, Chicanos, Orientals, the poor).

The next move in the defense of preferential treatment under the antidiscrimination principle is to discover ways of tolerating these margins of ill-fit. The defense of the overinclusion is likely to be couched in terms of administrative convenience.[36] True, not all blacks are entitled to the preferential treatment, but it would be exceedingly difficult and costly to try to pick out those not deserving the preferential treatment, and the costs would not be worth the gains. Administrative convenience may also be used to justify the underinclusion, particularly as it relates to the poor. It would be difficult, so the argument runs, to pick out those nonblacks who have the same social or economic status as blacks and thus, under the stipulated purposes, are as deserving of preferential treatment as blacks. Blackness is an easy criterion to work with, and although there may be mistakes, they are small compared to the costs inherent in the use of alternative criteria ("poor" or "low socioeconomic status"). The difficulty with this administrative convenience argument is that it is standard practice to reject such a defense when whites rather than blacks are the preferred race. Why should this defense be accepted in one context and not another?

Professor Ely's we-they analysis (see fn. 3) might be thought to be responsive to this dilemma. He argues that when the dominant group (whites) use the racial criterion for conferring benefits on the minority (preferential treatment for blacks), there is less reason to be suspicious than when they use the racial criterion for conferring benefits on their

36. See Nickel, "Preferential Policies in Hiring and Admissions: A Jurisprudential Approach," 75 *Colum. L. Rev.* 534, 550–53 (1975).

own class (preferential treatment for whites). When benefits are conferred by one class upon its own members, the risk is high that the arguments about administrative convenience are a sham: it is like voting oneself a pay raise. The risk is high that you would believe any argument in favor of the decision, irrespective of the merits. But when a sacrifice is involved, so the argument continues, as when members of one group (we) confer a benefit on another group (they) at its own (our) expense, then there is less reason to be suspicious of the arguments used to defend that action.

I have some difficulty with the psychological model upon which the we-they analysis rests. It is incomplete. The only motivational factor reflected is self-interest (elaborated in terms of group membership). But, of course, as seems particularly true in the case of preferential admission of blacks to law school, there may be other motivational factors that make arguments about administrative convenience especially suspect. The body making the decision may tend to overvalue arguments about administrative convenience out of a feeling of guilt or fear (for example, of disruption in the university) and there may be little to check those impulses since the costs of the preferential policy are primarily borne by "others" (not the professors or administrators who decide upon the admission policy but by some of the rejected nonblack applicants—not the superstars, but rather by those who are at the end of the meritocratic queue).[37]

The principal difficulty with this we-they analysis is not, however, the incompleteness of the psychological model; for it is conceivable this could be corrected. Rather the principal difficulty stems from what this model (or perhaps any model focusing on the psychology of the discriminators) yields. As Professor Ely acknowledges, the we-they analysis can only provide grounds for (asymmetrical) suspicion, and yet that does not seem sufficient.[38] For even if suspicion turns

37. Burt, "Helping Suspect Groups Disappear" (unpublished manuscript, 1975); Greenawalt, pp. 573–74.

38. I think Ely went wrong in reading the suspect-classification doctrine too weakly. When the Supreme Court and commentators, such as Tussman and tenBroek, spoke of suspect classification, they were trying to express a substantive, not just an evidentiary judgment—that in the generality of cases certain kinds of classification will be invalid. The suspect-classification doc-

133 *Groups and the Equal Protection Clause*

out to be wrong, and the argument of administrative convenience is determined to have merit, to be sincere and well-founded, the argument would still be rejected as a justification for ill-fit when preferential treatment is being conferred on whites.

For example, imagine it is the 1940s, the state electorate is predominantly white and the state legislature directs the law school to adopt a preferential admission policy in favor of whites.[39] Assume also that this policy is justified on the ground that whites are better prepared academically (given the dual school system) and that the state wishes to have the most brilliant persons as members of the bar. Color is used because of administrative convenience. Under the we-they analysis, there is reason to be suspicious about this explanation of the use of race; the policy in effect serves the class interest of whites and it is likely that the white legislators (or administrators) will undervalue the costs to the blacks of an imprecise fit and mistakenly believe only the "negative myths" about blacks. But it would seem to me that even if that suspicion were refuted, even if it were (somehow) demonstrated that the argument about administrative convenience was sincere and well-founded and in some sense accurate, the result would still be unacceptable under the Equal Protection Clause. Those who are committed to the antidiscrimination principle can reach this result only by insisting that the arguments of administrative convenience are no defense to ill-fit, even assuming that they are sincere and well-founded. It is that move, above all, that plays into the hands of those who wish to attack preferential treatment in favor of blacks: why, they will ask, should administrative convenience be

---

trine was simply a way of avoiding a flat no-exception per se rule—a doctrine of forbidden classifications (no racial classifications at all). When it rejected the forbidden-classification doctrine, the Court may have been looking ahead to the problem of preferential treatment and for that reason rejected the forbidden-classification doctrine. But the discussion of this issue in Tussman and ten-Broek, and the fact that the doctrine originates in the *Japanese Relocation Cases*, leads me to other explanations: a forbidden-classification doctrine would be hard to reconcile with the generality of the language of the Equal Protection Clause; and it would have tied the hands of the legislators and administrators too much, precluding the use of the classification in even extraordinary instances—such as those involving the relocation of the Japanese.

39. See Sweatt v. Painter, 339 U.S. 629 (1950).

allowed to justify ill-fit when the state action is beneficial to the minority but not when it is hostile to the minority?

The we-they analysis cannot resolve this dilemma because it is only an evidentiary, and not a substantive, approach. There are, however, two other strategies employed within the context of the antidiscrimination principle to justify preferential treatment, and these do seem more substantive. One such strategy shifts the definition of the harm —classifications should not be judged in terms of the means-end relationship (fit), but rather in terms of whether they stigmatize.[40] An exclusionary classification aimed at blacks stigmatizes them in a way that preferential treatment does not stigmatize whites; administrative convenience cannot justify or offset the stigmatizing harm caused by the exclusionary policy, and the nonstigmatizing preferential policy does not call for a justification (or if it calls for one, it need be only a weak one, for which administrative convenience will suffice). I am willing to assume that the preferential policy does not stigmatize the rejected applicants,[41] and yet this strategy still seems unsatisfactory. It moves beyond the structure of the antidiscrimination principle in that (a) the evil becomes stigma rather than ill-fit, and (b) it contemplates a weighing of ends—a judgment as to whether the state interest is of sufficient importance to offset the harm. A connection with the original antidiscrimination principle remains: the trigger remains the same—classification. But that seems to be a trivial connection. The tie with the foundational concept—means-end rationality—is severed. And once this step is taken, it is hard to confine the modification. It is difficult to explain why classification should be the only trigger for the Equal Protection Clause and, even if it is, why that Clause should be concerned only with stigmatic harm (or why stigmatic harm alone is capable of overriding a defense of administrative convenience). The rejected white applicant may not be stigma-

40. See Brest, "Palmer v. Thompson: An Approach to the Problem of Unconstitutional Legislative Motive," 1971 *Sup. Ct. Rev.* 95, 116 fn. 109; and Brest, *Processes of Constitutional Decisionmaking* (Boston, 1975), p. 481. See also Greenawalt, p. 566.

41. Fiss, "School Desegregation: The Uncertain Path of the Law," 4 *Philosophy & Public Affairs* 3, 13 (1974). Some have argued that a preferential admissions policy stigmatizes the blacks admitted under it. See Burt, fn. 37 above.

tized, but he is being harmed in other ways; and there is nothing in the theory underlying the antidiscrimination principle that suggests why nonstigmatic harm should be given a subordinate (or weaker) status. And if it is not given that subordinate status, then we are back to the same dilemma of symmetry: why reject administrative convenience in one context and not in the other?

The final move in defense of preferential treatment under the antidiscrimination principle is to invoke one or both of the standard defenses. The charge of underinclusiveness might be defended on the one-step-at-a-time theory—this time the law school helps blacks, next time Chicanos, and so on. This would be considered a "reform" measure, while the exclusionary policy would only be a "regression." The defense of compelling state interest may also be deployed: the purposes served by the preferential admission program are especially desirable or important, while those served by the exclusionary one (having the bar consist of the academically superior) are ordinary.[42] The upshot of both defenses is that the ill-fit (the over- and underinclusiveness) is excused in one case (the preference for blacks) but not in the other (the exclusion of blacks).

The problem with both these defensive moves is that they are devoid of any theoretical foundations. In the ultimate analysis, they are resolution by fiat; for the antidiscrimination principle does not supply any basis or standards for determining what is "reform" and what is "regression," what is an "ordinary" state purpose, and what is a "special" one. These distinctions can only be made if the court has some notion of what is "good" or "desirable," only if the court identifies certain substantive ends as those to be favored under the Equal Protection Clause. As an intellectual feat this may be possible but not within the confines of the antidiscrimination principle. That principle

42. Greenawalt, pp. 574–79, distinguishes between a "compelling interest" and a "substantial interest." He argues, "Because benign racial classifications are less 'suspect,' however, a 'substantial' public interest should be enough to support them." Karst and Horowitz, on the other hand, contend that racial classifications "must be tested against the exacting standard of the 'compelling state interest' formula." "Affirmative Action and Equal Protection," 60 *Va. L. Rev.* 955, 965 (1974).

disclaims any reliance on substantive ends.[43] Indeed that is thought to be a primary source of its appeal.

In my judgment, the preferential and exclusionary policies should be viewed quite differently under the Equal Protection Clause. Indeed, it would be one of the strangest and cruelest ironies to interpret that Clause in such a way that linked–in some tight, inextricable fashion–the judgments about the preferential and exclusionary policies. This dilemma can only be avoided if the applicable mediating principle of the Clause is clearly and explicitly asymmetrical, one that talks about substantive ends, and not fit, and one that recognizes the existence and importance of groups, not just individuals. Only then will it be possible to believe that when we reject the claim against preferential treatment for blacks we are not at the same time undermining the constitutional basis for protecting them. Of course, even if the antidiscrimination principle were not the predominant interpretation of the Clause, it might still be possible to formulate a claim against preferential treatment. The element of individual unfairness to the rejected applicants inherent in preferential treatment could be considered a cost in evaluating the state action in the same way as a loss of liberty or a dignitary harm might be. The failure of the state to include other disadvantaged groups, such as the Chicanos, might also become significant. But the impenetrable barrier posed by the seemingly symmetrical antidiscrimination principle would be gone. The stakes would not be so high.

Nondiscriminatory State Action

The antidiscrimination principle has created several gaps in the coverage of the Equal Protection Clause. The principle purports to be universalistic in terms of the persons protected, and yet it turns out to be far from universalistic in terms of the state practices proscribed. The gaps in coverage arise from the fact that not all objectionable state conduct is discriminatory. Discrimination involves a choice among persons and, as I said, an antidiscrimination principle operates by prohibiting government from making that choice arbitrarily. But there are

43. It might also be noted that this disclaimer is also inconsistent with the legitimate purpose limitation.

government enactments or practices where no choice is made among persons and of these it does not make sense to ask whether there is "arbitrary" discrimination. I am not complaining of the fact that the antidiscrimination principle leaves standing state conduct that should be invalidated; but rather that it provides no frame of reference for assessing certain types of state conduct and for that reason is incomplete.

This gap in part accounts for the difficulty the Supreme Court has had with some of the classic state action cases. One such case is *Shelley v. Kraemer*.[44] The Court there invalidated a state policy of enforcing racially restrictive covenants, and although that result seems right, on an analytic level *Shelley v. Kraemer* is generally deemed to be an extraordinarily difficult case—the Finnegans Wake of constitutional law.[45] The difficult question was not, in my judgment, whether the state judges who enforced the restrictive covenant were acting as representatives of the "state." True, that issue was discussed by the Court, but it hardly seemed of any moment. Rather the troublesome question arose in trying to determine whether the state's action was the kind of "action" prohibited by the Equal Protection Clause. The Clause was viewed as prohibiting (racial) discrimination, and only that. The state asserted that its policy was not in any way discriminatory—restrictive covenants would be enforced against blacks and whites alike.

The basis of the Court's rejection of this defense remains a mystery to me to this day. Only a couple of sentences in the opinion purport to be responsive. In one the Court mentions the factual assertions of plaintiffs that, by and large, these racially restrictive covenants are used against blacks, rather than whites. The Court seemed willing to assume the truthfulness of this assertion as a factual matter, but it was hesitant to conclude much from it. That seemed a sound instinct, provided the Court was confined to the antidiscrimination principle and wanted to invalidate the policy, rather than its application; as long as the state stands ready to, and in fact would, enforce

44. 334 U.S. 1 (1948).

45. Kurland, "Foreward: Equal in Origin and Equal in Title to the Legislative and Executive Branches of the Government," 78 *Harv. L. Rev.* 143, 148 (1964).

a racially restrictive covenant against whites this state policy cannot itself be deemed a form of racial discrimination. The other response is the well-known passage of *Shelley v. Kraemer* declaring that the Equal Protection Clause protects individual rights.[46] But I fail to see why this is responsive to the state's defense—there is no discrimination by the state. The more appropriate response to the state would be to reject its premise as to the kind of state action prohibited by the Clause. Why, I would ask, must the action of the state be discriminatory before it is deemed a violation of the Equal Protection Clause?

Recently, the Court was faced with another state action case that presented a similar problem and, given the faulty frame of reference, the result was not so fortuitous. In *Moose Lodge*,[47] Pennsylvania granted a liquor license to a private club that discriminated on the basis of race. The club refused to serve blacks. The liquor license did not confer monopoly power but it was of great benefit to the club and, even more importantly, it had the effect of limiting the places available in the locality for blacks to purchase liquor. Only a limited number of liquor licenses were made available in each area, and a license was required before liquor could be sold. Once again, the defense of the state was that it did not discriminate on the basis of race: the state did not exclude blacks from the Lodge, nor did it grant the license because the Lodge was discriminating on racial

46. The text reads: "The rights created by the first section of the Fourteenth Amendment are, by its terms, guaranteed to the individual. The rights established are personal rights." 334 U.S., at 22. A clever lawyer might have asserted that the discrimination was not between whites and blacks, but rather between two classes of sellers—those who sell land burdened with a restrictive covenant and those who sell unencumbered land. But if that were the challenged distinction, we have moved beyond the realm of suspect classifications and thus might have to operate under a minimum scrutiny inquiry. The Court did not seem willing to operate at that level; for them it was a racial case—a wrong to blacks. It is interesting to note that Tussman and tenBroek did not see *Shelley v. Kraemer* as resting on the "reasonable classification" (or antidiscrimination) principle. They did not view the case as a racial one, but rather as a matter of "substantive due process"—interference with the liberty to sell—though recognizing, given the bad taste left by that doctrine, that it might have to be called "substantive equal protection." Tussman and tenBroek, at 362; see fn. 2 above.

47. Moose Lodge No. 107 v. Irvis, 407 U.S. 163 (1972).

grounds. The state simply regarded the admission practice of the club as an irrelevance. The Court thought it had to link the state with the discriminatory refusal to serve. According to Justice Rhenquist, the black was claiming that "the refusal to serve him was 'state action' for the purposes of the Equal Protection Clause."[48] Of course, under this formulation the black could not win, and relief was in fact denied.[49]

Both the result of *Moose Lodge* and the mode of analysis seem wrong. The Equal Protection Clause does not govern the behavior of private clubs, but it does govern the conduct of the state. The state was not discriminating, racially or otherwise, but it was engaging in conduct—the conferral of liquor licenses (without regard to admission policies)—and that action could be evaluated in terms of the Equal Protection Clause. Moose Lodge may be free to discriminate, but that does not make it correct for the state to confer a scarce franchise on the club, thereby foreclosing opportunities to blacks. It was the premise of the Court that the only kind of action denied the state is discriminatory action that prevented it from focusing on this foreclosure of opportunities to blacks.

In the state action cases such as *Shelley v. Kraemer* and *Moose Lodge* there were clearly acts of discrimination—the restrictive covenant itself or the refusal of the club to serve blacks. Those discriminatory acts were not performed by the state, and the Court saw the question as whether the discriminatory acts could be *imputed* to the state.[50] In another group of cases, also put beyond the Equal

48. 407 U.S., at 165.

49. With a nod toward *Shelley v. Kraemer*, the Court prohibited the state from directing the club to comply with the national Supreme Lodge rules, which embodied the racial policy. The local was allowed to make up its own mind.

50. I think this imputation occurs in the Proposition 14 case, Reitman v. Mulkey, 387 U.S. 369 (1967). The Court thought it had to impute the discrimination (the refusal to sell) to the state, and it tried to create the linkage by saying that Proposition 14 had the effect of "encouraging" the discrimination. This conceptualization probably prevented the Court from relying on the rationale linked to Charles Black's name, "Foreword: 'State Action,' Equal Protection and California's Proposition 14," 81 *Harv. L. Rev.* 69 (1967) (an additional obstacle was created for blacks in their effort to obtain protective legislation).

Protection Clause by the antidiscrimination interpretation, there was no clear act of discrimination, racial or otherwise, that could easily be imputed to the state. The acts in question clearly belonged to the state, but they were not discriminatory. The antidiscrimination principle left the Court even more at sea. Here I have in mind the on-off decisions of government—the decision whether or not to have a public facility, such as a swimming pool[51] or a public housing project.[52]

The principal challenge to these decisions focused attention on the basis for the decision—why did the town close the swimming pools? Why did the town refuse to build a public housing project? These questions *seem* similar to the inquiry required by an antidiscrimination principle, but that appearance is misleading. The kind of decision most amenable to an antidiscrimination analysis is one choosing among persons, a state decision, for example, about who shall be admitted to the swimming pool or the public housing project. With decisions of that sort, the why-question asks for an identification of the *criterion* of selection: why were these individuals and not others allowed into the swimming pool or the housing project? Answer: because of their race. Once identified, the criterion of selection could be judged under the antidiscrimination principle in terms of its relatedness to the state purpose. With an on-off decision, such as a decision whether or not to provide a public service, the why-question asks, not for the criterion, but for the *motive* or *purpose* itself: why did the town close the swimming pool? Answer: in order to save money or to prevent integration. Why did the town refuse to build a public housing project? Answer: in order to save money or in order to limit the number of poor persons in the community. Accordingly, in this context there is no criterion of selection that can be evaluated for its relatedness.[53] Guided by the antidiscrimination principle, and

51. Palmer v. Thompson, 403 U.S. 217 (1971).

52. James v. Valtierra, 402 U.S. 137 (1971).

53. In some situations, it may be able to reformulate the on-off decision as a choice among various public activities: why did the town decide to close the swimming pool rather than stop the buses. That why-question does yield a criterion of selection, but a different type of one—not an individual trait (such as race or performance on a test), but rather communal goals (to promote full employment). And it is the former type of criterion of selection that permits a court

141 *Groups and the Equal Protection Clause*

that alone, one hardly knows where to begin in analyzing these governmental decisions, and I think that accounts for the difficulty the Court has experienced with them. One might conclude that these decisions are not invalid, or that relief should not be provided because it is impossible to fashion an appropriate judicial remedy. But the difficulty with the antidiscrimination interpretation is that it puts these on-off decisions beyond purview of the Equal Protection Clause.

The Problem of Facially Innocent Criteria

The classic state action cases and those cases involving on-off decisions reveal the inability of the antidiscrimination principle to deal adequately with state conduct that does not discriminate among persons. Another problem area arises from state conduct that does in fact discriminate among persons, but not on the basis of a suspect criterion. The discrimination is based on a criterion that seems innocent on its face and yet nonetheless has the effect of disadvantaging blacks (or other minorities). For example, when the state purports to choose employees or college students on the basis of performance on standardized tests, and it turns out that the only persons admitted or hired are white.

As originally conceived—both by Tussman and tenBroek and by the Supreme Court in the important formative period of the 1940s and 1950s—the antidiscrimination principle promised to evolve a small, finite list of suspect criteria, such as race, religion, national origin, wealth, sex. These would be presumptively impermissible. The great bulk of other criteria may ultimately be deemed arbitrary in some particular instances because of ill-fit, but they would be presumptively valid. For these criteria—which I call *facially innocent*—the mere rational-relation test would suffice, and the probability would be very high that the statute or administrative action incorporating or utilizing such criteria would be sustained.

---

to ask the foundational question of the antidiscrimination principle—one of over- and underinclusiveness of persons. The reader should consult Professor Brest's article on *Palmer v. Thompson* (see fn. 40 above), for he views the motivational analysis as a much closer relative of the antidiscrimination analysis than I would.

In some instances the presumption of validity may be dissolved, and the contrary presumption created, through the use of the concept of the *real* criterion. The plaintiffs can charge cheating: while the state says that it is selecting on the basis of an innocent criterion (such as performance on a written test), in truth the selection is being made on the basis of a suspect criterion (race). The substantiation of this charge confronts the plaintiffs with enormous evidentiary burdens. No one can be expected to admit to charges of cheating, and rarely is the result so striking (for example, the twenty-eight-sided voting district of *Gomillion v. Lightfoot*[54] or no blacks on the work force) as to permit only one inference—discrimination on the basis of a suspect criterion. But if the charge could be substantiated (perhaps with an assist from the reallocation of the burdens of proofs when the criterion had almost the same effect as a suspect one), then there would be no problem of using the strict-scrutiny branch of the antidiscrimination principle: the real criterion, as opposed to the stated criterion, is a suspect one, and there the court should insist upon a very tight fit between purpose and criterion. The troublesome cases arise, however, when the charge of cheating cannot be substantiated, where, for example, the court finds that in truth the jobs were allocated or students selected on the basis of academic performance. What then?

One possible response is, of course, to apply the mere rational-relation test and validate the practice: there is certainly some connection between the state's purposes and these criteria. The fit may not be perfect, but perfection is not required. But the courts have balked. They have been troubled by the fact that the practice is particularly injurious to a disadvantaged group and for that reason have scrutinized state conduct with the greatest of care. The judicial inclination is all toward invalidation.[55] This impulse seems correct as

54. 364 U.S. 339 (1960).

55. See, for example, Lau v. Nichols, 414 U.S. 563 (1974); Keyes v. School Dist. No. 1, Denver, Colo., 413 U.S. 189 (1973); Swann v. Charlotte-Mecklenburg Board of Education, 402 U.S. 1 (1971); Griggs v. Duke Power Co., 401 U.S. 424 (1971); Gaston County v. United States, 395 U.S. 285 (1969). Some of these cases, such as *Griggs*, involve civil rights statutes. The language and legislative history of those statutes generally restrain rather than encourage the judicial inclination. The Court may have been responding to the fact that

a matter of substantive justice, and yet it is difficult to reconcile treatment of the facially innocent criteria with the original, modest conception of the antidiscrimination principle.

One response—that which emerged most clearly during the mid-1960s phase of the Warren Court[56]—was to postulate a second trigger for strict scrutiny—impingement of a fundamental right. This, of course, constituted a radical modification of the antidiscrimination principle, for it introduced a ranking of ends or interests, and it meant that the antidiscrimination principle could no longer be justified exclusively in terms of means-end rationality. The pretense of value-neutrality could not be easily maintained. That is why Tussman and tenBroek did not anticipate the doctrine,[57] and why Professor Gunther, who wrote in the early days of the Burger Court, and who appears committed to returning the Equal Protection Clause to its former glory as a means-focused inquiry, disavows the fundamental-right trigger of the strict-scrutiny inquiry.[58] But even if this modification of the antidiscrimination principle were accepted, and ends were ranked and weighed, the problem of justifying the judicial treatment of facially innocent criteria that especially disadvantaged blacks could not be solved. Admittedly in some instances, the criteria in fact invalidated impinged on what might be considered a fundamental interest; the literacy test for voting might be such an instance.[59] On the other hand, the striking fact is that the Supreme Court has afforded strict scrutiny to facially innocent criteria that do not im-

legislative revision is easier when a statute is being construed, though my impression is that civil rights statutes soon become minimum guarantees not open to the ordinary legislative processes of revision, and thus have the same degree of permanence as a constitution.

56. See Note, "Developments in the Law—Equal Protection," 82 *Harv. L. Rev.* 1065, 1120, 1127 (1969), which was written at the peak of the fundamental-right development, codified the development and was thereby instrumental in legitimating it.

57. See fn. 2 above.

58. Gunther, p. 24. Professor Gunther retains the suspect classification branch of the traditional equal protection analysis.

59. Gaston County v. United States, 395 U.S. 285 (1969). In that case, however, the Court did not seek to explain its decisions in terms of a fundamental interest, and this is not surprising since the opinion was written by Justice Harlan. See fn. 8 above.

pinge on fundamental interests—for example, test scores as a criterion for jobs[60] and residence as a criterion for assignment to schools.[61] Although "jobs" and "schools" might in some view be deemed fundamental, certainly as important as the right to procreate, one of the first rights deemed "fundamental," this extension of the fundamental-right test would make what might first have seemed to be an exception much greater than the rule.

A second, and seemingly more modest way of rationalizing the judicial treatment of facially innocent criteria, is to introduce the concept of past discrimination. Strict scrutiny should be given, so the argument runs, to state conduct that perpetuates the effects of earlier conduct (it might be state or private) that was based on the use of a suspect classification. Conduct that perpetuates the effects of past (suspect-criterion) discrimination is as presumptively invalid as the present use of suspect criteria. An objective civil service test is presumptively impermissible whenever it perpetuates the past discrimination of the dual school system (the dual school system put the blacks at a competitive disadvantage and the test perpetuates that disadvantage). The use of geographic proximity is an impermissible criterion of school assignment whenever it perpetuates the past discrimination of the dual school system. The racial assignments of that school system led to the present residential segregation and account for the location and size of the school buildings, and both of these factors in turn explain why the use of geographic proximity as a criterion of assignment results in segregated patterns of school attendance today.

A ban on "the perpetuation of past arbitrary discrimination" looks like a close cousin of the ban on "arbitrary discrimination." But this tie can only be maintained at great expense to important institutional

60. Griggs v. Duke Power Co., 401 U.S. 424 (1971). Although that case involved a statutory discrimination claim (Title VII of the Civil Rights Act of 1964), recent cases illustrate use of the same principle outside the statutory context, e.g. Bridgeport Guardians, Inc. v. Bridgeport Civil Serv. Comm'n., 482 F. 2d 1333 (2d Cir. 1973), cert. denied 421 U.S. 991 (1975); Carter v. Gallagher, 452 F. 2d 315, 327 (8th Cir. 1972), cert. denied, 406 U.S. 950 (1972).

61. Keyes v. School Dist. No. 1, Denver, Colo., 413 U.S. 189 (1973). But see Milliken v. Bradley, 418 U.S. 717 (1974).

values—those that cluster around the ideal of objectivity, an ideal the antidiscrimination principle is supposed to serve. A true inquiry into past discrimination necessitates evidentiary judgments that are likely to strain the judicial system—consume scarce resources and yield unsatisfying results. It would require the courts to construct causal connections that span significant periods of time, periods greater than those permitted under any general statute of limitations (a common device used to prevent the judiciary from undertaking inquiries where the evidence is likely to be stale, fragmentary, and generally unreliable). The difficulties of these backward-looking inquiries are compounded because the court must invariably deal with aggregate behavior, not just a single transaction; it must determine the causal explanation for the residential patterns of an entire community, or the skill levels of all the black applicants.

There are techniques for reducing these strains. The court can create presumptions to limit the evidentiary inquiries or dispense with the need for a showing of identity between victim and beneficiary, or between past perpetrator and present cost-bearer. But these techniques have their own costs. The use of presumptions involves the court in fictionalizing and thereby impairing its credibility. And, more importantly, once the connections between victim and beneficiary and between past perpetrator and present cost-bearer are severed, we have ceased talking about the perpetuation of past discrimination in any individualized sense. The past discrimination that we are talking about is of a more global character—for example, that the group were slaves for one century and subject to Jim Crow laws for another. The ethical significance of this global past discrimination cannot be denied; it gives the group an identity and might explain why we are especially concerned with its welfare. But at the same time it should be understood that once we start talking of global past discrimination, the link between the proposed anti-past-discrimination principle and the original antidiscrimination principle becomes highly attenuated. We have embarked on another journey altogether, one that is decidedly not individualistic—and, as a result, one important source of appeal of the antidiscrimination principle is lost.

The third move designed to deal with the problem of facially innocent criteria—the introduction of the concept of de facto discrimination (or discriminatory effect)—does not focus on the past. Instead it shifts the trigger for strict scrutiny from the *criterion* of selection to the *result* of the selection process, and the result is stated in terms of a *group* rather than an individual. What triggers the strict scrutiny is not the criterion of selection itself, but rather the result—the fact that a minority group has been especially hurt. (This special hurt is sometimes described as a "differential impact.")

This concept of de facto discrimination also involves a basic modification of the antidiscrimination principle. The trigger is no longer classification, but rather group-impact. This modification deeply threatens two goals allegedly served by the antidiscrimination principle—objectivity and individualism.[62] Of course, even with group-impact as the trigger, it is still possible to ask the ultimate question of the antidiscrimination principle—are there (excessive) margins of over- and underinclusiveness? But the modification does reveal the basic poverty of antidiscrimination theory. It makes me acutely aware of the failure to explain (a) why this finite list of criteria deemed suspect should ever trigger the demand for stricter scrutiny and (b) why scrutiny should be confined to determining the fit of the criterion and purpose. The concern with the result reveals to me that what is ultimately at issue is the welfare of certain disadvantaged groups, not just the use of a criterion, and if that is at issue, there is no reason why the judicial intervention on behalf of that group should be limited to an inquiry as to the degree of fit between a criterion and a purpose.

62. And that is why Professor Goodman, upon becoming aware of this fact, believes he has discovered the decisive argument against a theory of de facto discrimination: "These and countless other de facto discriminations would be disallowed by a rule condemning, or requiring special justification for, all state action disproportionately harmful to members of minority groups. The objection to such a rule is not solely one of practicality, but also one of principle. It is the individual, not the group, to whom the equal protection of laws is guaranteed.[102]" See "De Facto School Segregation: A Constitutional and Empirical Analysis," 60 *Calif. L. Rev.* 275, 300–301 (1972). Goodman's fn. 102 does not elaborate, but only refers the reader to the mystifying sentence of *Shelley v. Kraemer* quoted above in fn. 46.

147 *Groups and the Equal Protection Clause*

IV. The Group-Disadvantaging Principle

The Shift from Classification to Class: Integrating the Concept of a Disadvantaged Group into the Law

In attempting to formulate another theory of equal protection, I have viewed the Clause primarily, but not exclusively, as a protection for blacks. In part, this perspective stems from the original intent—the fact that the Clause was viewed as a means of safeguarding blacks from hostile state action. The Equal Protection Clause (following the circumlocution of the slave-clauses in the antebellum Constitution)[63] uses the word "person," rather than "blacks." The generality of the word chosen to describe those protected enables other groups to invoke its protection; and I am willing to admit that was also probably intended. But this generality of coverage does not preclude a theory of primary reference—that blacks were the intended primary beneficiaries, that it was a concern for their welfare that prompted the Clause.

It is not only original intent that explains my starting point. It is also the way the courts have used the Clause. The most intense degree of protection has in fact been given to blacks; they have received a degree of protection that no other group has received. They are the wards of the Equal Protection Clause, and any new theory formulated should reflect this practice. I am also willing to speculate that, as a matter of psychological fact, race provides the paradigm for judicial decision. I suspect that in those cases in which a claim of strict

63. At least three clauses in the Constitution refer to slaves without using the word "slave," though the circumlocution in fact is so transparent as to be mystifying. The Slave Trade Clause provides, "The Migration or Importation of such Persons as any of the States now existing shall think proper to admit, shall not be prohibited by the Congress prior to the Year one thousand eight hundred and eight, but a Tax or duty may be imposed on such Importation, not exceeding ten dollars for each Person." (Article I, section 9, clause 1). See also Article I, section 2, clause 3 ("three-fifths of all other Persons") and Article IV, section 2, clause 3 ("Person held to Service or Labour"). The issue of circumlocution was debated in the original convention in connection with the Slave Trade Clause, some arguing that the generality of the word "persons" would have unintended effects—impliedly creating national power over immigration. For the discussion during the Constitutional Convention see Farrand, 2 *Records of the Federal Convention* 415 & fn. 8 (1937).

scrutiny has been or reasonably could have been made, it is commonplace for a judge to reason about an equal protection case by thinking about the meaning of the Clause in the racial context and by comparing the case before him to a comparable one in the racial area. Moreover, the limitations or inadequacies of the antidiscrimination principle surface most sharply when it is used to evaluate state practices affecting blacks.

Starting from this perspective, a distinctively racial one, it strikes me as odd to build a general interpretation of the Equal Protection Clause, as Tussman and tenBroek did, on the rejection of the idea that there are natural classes, that is, groups that have an identity and existence wholly apart from the challenged state statute or practice. There are natural classes, or social groups, in American society and blacks are such a group. Blacks are viewed as a group; they view themselves as a group; their identity is in large part determined by membership in the group; their social status is linked to the status of the group; and much of our action, institutional and personal, is based on these perspectives.

I use the term "group" to refer to a social group, and for me, a social group is more than a collection of individuals, all of whom, to use a polar example, happen to arrive at the same street corner at the same moment. A social group, as I use the term, has two other characteristics. (1) It is an *entity* (though not one that has a physical body). This means that the group has a distinct existence apart from its members, and also that it has an identity. It makes sense to talk about the group (at various points of time) and know that you are talking about the same group. You can talk about the group without reference to the particular individuals who happen to be its members at any one moment. (2) There is also a condition of *interdependence*. The identity and well-being of the members of the group and the identity and well-being of the group are linked. Members of the group identify themselves—explain who they are—by reference to their membership in the group; and their well-being or status is in part determined by the well-being or status of the group. That is why the free blacks of the antebellum period—the Dred Scotts—were not really free, and could never be so long as the institution of Negro slavery still existed.[64] Similarly, the well-being and status of the group is determined by reference to the well-being and status of the members of the group. The emancipation of one slave—the presence of one Frederick Douglass—may not substantially alter the well-being or status of the group; but if there were enough Frederick Douglasses, or if most blacks had his status, then surely the status of blacks as a social group would be altered. That is why the free black posed such a threat to the institution of slavery. Moreover, the identity and existence of the group as a discrete entity is in part determined by whether individuals identify themselves by membership in the group. If enough individuals cease to identify themselves in terms of their membership in a particular group (as occurs in the process of assimilation), then the very identity and separate existence of the group—as a distinct entity—will come to an end.

I would be the first to admit that working with the concept of a group is problematic, much more so than working with the concept of an individual or criterion.[65] It is "messy." For example, in some in-

64. On the plight of the free blacks, see I. Berlin, *Slaves Without Masters: The Free Negro in the Antebellum South* (New York, 1974); J. Franklin, *From Slavery to Freedom*, 3d ed. (New York, 1967); Dred Scott v. Sandford, 60 U.S. (19 How.) 393 (1857).

65. For a sensitive discussion of all the difficulties of working with the concept of groups, see B. Bittker, *The Case for Black Reparations* (New York, 1973), particularly Chapters 8, 9, and 10. It should be noted that the peculiar remedial context of that discussion—the payment of money—accentuates the difficulties; some of these difficulties may be modulated in the injunctive context, where less turns on individual errors of classification. For an earlier legal literature on groupism, see Reisman, "Democracy and Defamation: Control of Group Libel," 42 *Colum. L. Rev.* 727 (1942); Pekelis, "Full Equality in a Free Society: A Program for Jewish Action," in *Law and Social Action*, ed. M. Konvitz (Ithaca, N.Y., 1950), pp. 187, 218. The comparative literature includes Marc Galanter's work on India, "Equality and 'Protective Discrimination' in India," 16 *Rutgers L. Rev.* 421 (1962) and "The Problem of Group Membership: Some Reflections on the Judicial View of Indian Society," 4 *J. of the Indian L. Institute* 331 (1962). For a discussion of the role of groups in John Rawls' work, *A Theory of Justice*, see R. Nozick, *Anarchy, State, and Utopia* (New York, 1974), p. 190; Van Dyke, "Justice as Fairness: For Groups?" 69 *Am. Pol. Sci. Rev.* 607 (1975). And for the recent sociological and psychological literature see R. Dahrendorf, *Class and Class Conflict in Industrial Society* (Stanford, Calif., 1959); M. Gordon, *Assimilation in American Life* (New York, 1964); *Ethnicity*, ed. N. Glazer and D. Moynihan (Cambridge, Mass., 1975); R. Sennett and J. Cobb, *The Hidden Injuries of Class* (New York, 1972).

stances, it may be exceedingly difficult to determine whether particular individuals are members of the group; or whether a particular collection of persons constitutes a social group. I will also admit that my definition of a social group, and in particular the condition of interdependence, compounds rather than reduces, these classificatory disputes. But these disputes do not demonstrate the illegitimacy of this category of social entity nor deny the validity or importance of the idea. They only blur the edges. Similarly, the present reality of the social groups should not be obscured by a commitment to the ideal of a "classless society" or the individualistic ethic—the ideal of treating people as individuals rather than as members of groups. Even if the Equal Protection Clause is viewed as the means for furthering or achieving these individualistic ideals (and I am not sure why it should be), there is no reason why the Clause—as an instrument for bringing about the "good society"—must be construed as though it is itself governed by that ideal or why it should be assumed that the "good society" had been achieved in 1868, or is so now.

The conception of blacks as a social group is only the first step in constructing a mediating principle. We must also realize they are a very special type of social group. They have two other characteristics as a group that are critical in understanding the function and reach of the Equal Protection Clause. One is that blacks are very badly off, probably our worst-off class (in terms of material well-being second only to the American Indians), and in addition they have occupied the lowest rung for several centuries. In a sense, they are America's perpetual underclass. It is both of these characteristics—the relative position of the group and the duration of the position—that make efforts to improve the status of the group defensible. This redistribution may be rooted in a theory of compensation—blacks as a group were *put* in that position by others and the redistributive measures are *owed* to the group as a form of compensation. The debt would be viewed as owed by society, once again viewed as a collectivity.[66]

66. See generally Bayles, "Reparations to Wronged Groups," 33 *Analysis* 177 (1973); Cowan, "Inverse Discrimination," 33 *Analysis* 10 (1972); Shiner, "Individuals, Groups and Inverse Discrimination," 33 *Analysis* 182 (1973); Taylor, "Reverse Discrimination and Compensatory Justice," 33 *Analysis* 185

151 *Groups and the Equal Protection Clause*

But a redistributive strategy need not rest on this idea of compensation, it need not be backward looking (though past discrimination might be relevant for *explaining* the identity and status of blacks as a social group). The redistributive strategy could give expression to an ethical view against caste, one that would make it undesirable for any social group to occupy a position of subordination for any extended period of time.[67] What, it might be asked, is the justification for that vision? I am not certain whether it is appropriate to ask this question, to push the inquiry a step further and search for the justification of that ethic; visions about how society should be structured may be as irreducible as visions about how individuals should be treated–for example, with dignity. But if this second order inquiry is appropriate, a variety of justifications can be offered and they need not incorporate the notion of compensation. Changes in the hierarchical structure of society–the elimination of caste–might be justified as a means of (a) preserving social peace; (b) maintaining the community as a community, that is, as one cohesive whole; or (c) permitting the fullest development of the individual members of the subordinated group who otherwise might look upon the low status of the group as placing a ceiling on their aspirations and achievements.

It is not just the socioeconomic status of blacks as a group that explains their special position in equal protection theory. It is also their political status. The power of blacks in the political arena is

(1973); Sher, "Justifying Reverse Discrimination in Employment," 4 *Philosophy & Public Affairs* 159 (1975).

67. The critical temporal issue is one of duration, not whether the subordination has taken place in the past or in the future. The past has only an evidentiary relevance; it enables us to make judgments about how long the group will occupy the position of subordination. If the group has occupied the position of subordination for the last two centuries, certainly it is likely they will occupy that position for a long time in the future unless remedial steps are taken. On the other hand, if we were somehow assured that notwithstanding past history the subordination will end tomorrow, there would be no occasion for redistributive strategy on this group's behalf. Similarly, if we are told that today a period of perpetual subordination is about to begin for another group, we should be as concerned with the status of that group as we are with the blacks.

severely limited. For the last two centuries the political power of this group was circumscribed in most direct fashion—disenfranchisement. The electoral strength of blacks was not equal to their numbers. That has changed following the massive enfranchisement of the Voting Rights Act of 1965, but structural limitations on the political power of blacks still persist.[68] These limitations arise from three different sources, which can act either alternatively or cumulatively and which, in any event, are all interrelated. One source of weakness is their numbers, the fact that they are a numerical minority; the second is their economic status, their position as the perpetual underclass; and the third is that, as a "discrete and insular" minority, they are the object of "prejudice"—that is, the subject of fear, hatred, and distaste that make it particularly difficult for them to form coalitions with others (such as the white poor) and that make it advantageous for the dominant political parties to hurt them—to use them as a scapegoat.[69]

Recently, in some localities, such as large cities, the weakness of the group derived from their number has been eliminated; indeed in certain of these localities blacks may no longer be in the minority. The blacks may have a majority of a city council, or there may even be a black mayor. It would be wrong, however, to generalize from these situations. They are the exception, not the rule, and therefore should not control the formulation of a general theory of the Equal

68. For the time being, I put to one side the problems of dilution (districting that divides the group) or submersion (including the group in a larger universe through the technique of multi-member districts) since I do not have a full sense of either the prevalence of these practices or their constitutionality. See Witcomb v. Chavis, 403 U.S. 124 (1971); White v. Regester, 412 U.S. 755 (1973); Richmond v. United States, 422 U.S. 358 (1975); United Jewish Organizations of Williamsburgh v. Wilson, 510 F.2d 512 (2d Cir. 1975), cert. granted, CCH Sup. Ct. Bull. (Nov. 11, 1975) (No. 75–104, 1975 Term).

69. The quoted words are from Justice Stone's fn. 4 in United States v. Carolene Prods. Co., 304 U.S. 144, 152–53 (1938), which in part reads: "Nor need we enquire . . . whether prejudice against discrete and insular minorities may be a special condition, which tends seriously to curtail the operation of those political processes ordinarily to be relied upon to protect minorities, and which may call for a correspondingly more searching judicial inquiry." For a stimulating and illuminating discussion of the footnote, see Ball, "Judicial Protection of Powerless Minorities," 59 *Iowa L. Rev.* 1059 (1974).

Protection Clause. Moreover, these black-dominated political agencies —the black city council or the black mayor—must be placed in context. One facet of their context is the white domination of those extra-political agencies such as the banks, factories, and police, that severely circumscribe the power of the formal political agencies. Another facet is the persistent white domination of the national political agencies, such as the Congress and presidency, agencies that have become the critical loci of political power in American society.

Hence, despite recent demographic shifts in several large cities, I think it appropriate to view blacks as a group that is relatively powerless in the political arena and in my judgment that political status of the group justifies a special judicial solicitude on their behalf. When the product of a political process is a law that hurts blacks, the usual countermajoritarian objection to judicial invalidation—the objection that denies those "nine men" the right to substitute their view for that of "the people"—has little force. For the judiciary could be viewed as amplifying the voice of the powerless minority; the judiciary is attempting to rectify the injustice of the political process as a method of adjusting competing claims. The need for this rectification turns on whether the law is deemed one that harms blacks—a judgment that is admittedly hard to make when the perspective becomes a group one, for that requires the aggregation of interests and viewpoints, many of which are in conflict. It is important to emphasize, however, that the need for this rectification does not turn on whether the law embodies a classification, racial or otherwise; it is sufficient if the state law simply has the *effect* of hurting blacks. Nor should the rectification, once triggered by a harmful law, be confined to questions of fit—the judicial responsibility is more extensive than simply one of guarding against the risk of imprecise classifications by the political agencies. The relative powerlessness of blacks also requires that the judiciary strictly scrutinize the choice of ends; for it is just as likely that the interests of blacks as a group will not be adequately taken into account in choosing ends or goals. Maximizing goals such as reducing transportation costs (a goal that might account for the neighborhood-school plan) or having the most brilliant law students (a goal that might account for requiring a 650 on the LSAT) are constitutionally permissible goals in the sense that there is no substantive constitutional provision (or implied purpose lying behind some provision) that deny them to the state. On the other hand, these maximizing goals are obviously not in any sense constitutionally compelled goals and there is a chance–a most substantial one–that they would not be chosen as *the* goals (without any modification) if the interests of the blacks as a group were adequately taken into account–if the goal-choosers paid sufficient attention to the special needs, desires, and views of this powerless group.

The injustice of the political process must be corrected, and perhaps as a last resort, that task falls to the judiciary. But this claim does not yield any basis for specifying what the corrected process would look like, or what the court should say when it amplifies the voice of the powerless minority. A just political process would be one in which blacks would have "more" of a voice than they in fact do, but not necessarily one in which they would "win." In a sense there is a remedial lacuna; a pure process claim cannot determine substantive outcomes. (At the very most, it could yield those substantive outcomes that would tend to enhance the position of this group in the political process–such as favoring an increase in the numbers of black lawyers given the pivotal role lawyers play in the political process or favoring electoral districting that enhances the power of blacks as a group.) But this processual theory focusing on the relative powerlessness of blacks in the political arena need not stand alone. The substantive standards can be supplied by the other critical characteristics of this social group–perpetual subordination. The political status of the group justifies the institutional allocations–our willingness to allow those "nine men" to substitute their judgment (about ends as well as means) for that of "the people." The socioeconomic position of the group supplies an additional reason for the judicial activism and also determines the content of the intervention–improvement of the status of that group.

I would therefore argue that blacks should be viewed as having three characteristics that are relevant in the formulation of equal protection theory: (a) they are a social group; (b) the group has been in a position of perpetual subordination; and (c) the political power of the group is severely circumscribed. Blacks are what might be called a specially disadvantaged group, and I would view the Equal Protection Clause as a protection for such groups. Blacks are the prototype of the protected group, but they are not the only group entitled to protection. There are other social groups, even as I have used the term, and if these groups have the same characteristics as blacks —perpetual subordination and circumscribed political power—they should be considered specially disadvantaged and receive the same degree of protection. What the Equal Protection Clause protects is specially disadvantaged groups, not just blacks. A concern for equal treatment and the word "person" appearing in the Clause permit and probably require this generality of coverage.

Some of these specially disadvantaged groups can be defined in terms of characteristics that do not have biological roots and that are not immutable; the Clause might protect certain language groups and aliens. Moreover, in passing upon a claim to be considered a specially disadvantaged group, the court may treat one of the characteristics entitling blacks to that status as a sufficient but not a necessary condition; indeed the court may even develop variable standards of protection[70]—it may tolerate disadvantaging practices that would not be tolerated if the group was a "pure" specially disadvantaged group. Jews or women might be entitled to less protection than American Indians, though nonetheless entitled to some protection. Finally, these judicial judgments may be time-bound. Through the process of assimilation the group may cease to exist, or even if the group continues to retain its identity, its socioeconomic and political positions may so improve so as to bring to an end its status as specially disadvantaged.[71]

70. Compare Justice Marshall's variable approach in San Antonio Ind. School Dist. v. Rodriguez, 411 U.S. 1, 70 (1973).

71. Talcott Parsons commented on the changing status of Chinese and Japanese in the United States in "Some Theoretical Considerations on the Nature and Trends of Change of Ethnicity," in *Ethnicity*, ed. N. Glazer and D. Moynihan (Cambridge, Mass., 1975), pp. 73–74. On the claim that the socioeconomic status of blacks has changed, see Wattenberg & Scammon, "Black Progress and Liberal Rhetoric," 55 *Commentary* 35 (1973) and "Letters, An Exchange on Black Progress: Ben J. Wattenberg and Richard M. Scammon and Critics," 56 *Commentary* 20 (1973).

All this means that the courts will have some leeway in identifying the groups protected by the Equal Protection Clause. I think, however, it would be a mistake to use this flexibility to extend the protection to what might be considered artificial classes, those created by a classification or criterion embodied in a state practice or statute, for example, those classes created by tax categories (those having incomes between $27,000 and $30,000, or between $8,000 and $10,-000) or licensing statutes (the manufacturers of filled milk).[72] By definition those classes do not have an independent social identity and existence, or if they do, the condition of interdependence is lacking. It is difficult, if not impossible, to make an assessment of their socioeconomic status or of their political power (other than that they have just lost a legislative battle). And, if this is true, neither redistribution nor stringent judicial intervention on their behalf can be justified. It is not that such arguments are unpersuasive, but that they are almost unintelligible. Thus, in only one sense should the group-disadvantaging strategy be viewed as conducive to "more equality": it will get more for fewer. It will get more for the specially disadvantaged groups but will not provide any protection for artificial classes, those solely created by statute or a state practice. Of course, this loss may be more formal than real. Artificial classes constitute part of the universe that the antidiscrimination principle *purports* to protect, but in truth almost never does protect given the permissibility of the minimum-scrutiny inquiry.

72. What about those with income under $4,000? To some extent Justice Powell addresses this issue in his opinion in San Antonio Ind. School District v. Rodriguez, 411 U.S. 1 (1973) and he there employs a concept of social group similar to the one articulated in this essay. See also Michelman, "Forward: On Protecting the Poor Through the Fourteenth Amendment," 83 *Harv. L. Rev.* 7 (1969), suggesting the inappropriateness of using an antidiscrimination theory in this context, and attempting to shift the mode of analysis (which may take the courts beyond the Equal Protection Clause) to "just wants" and "minimum needs." For further development of this theme, see also Michelman, "In Pursuit of Constitutional Welfare Rights: One view of Rawls' Theory of Justice," 121 *U. Pa. L. Rev.* 962 (1973). On the increasing saliency of primordial rather than economic (or "class") categories, see Bell, "Ethnicity and Social Change," in *Ethnicity*, ed. N. Glazer and D. Moynihan (Cambridge, Mass., 1975), p. 141.

157 *Groups and the Equal Protection Clause*

The Nature of the Prohibited Action

The Concept of a Group-Disadvantaging Practice. Some state laws or practices may just be a mistake—they make all groups and all persons worse off, and equally so. These do not seem to be the concern of a constitutional provision cast in terms of equality. Equality is a relativistic idea. The concern should be with those laws or practices that particularly hurt a disadvantaged group. Such laws might enhance the welfare of society (or the better-off classes), or leave it the same; what is critical, however, is that the state law or practice aggravates (or perpetuates?) the subordinate position of a specially disadvantaged group. This is what the Equal Protection Clause prohibits.

Implicit in this formulation of the prohibition of the Equal Protection Clause is a view that certain state practices may be harmful to the members of a specially disadvantaged group, and yet not impair or threaten or aggravate the status or position of the group. For example, it is conceivable that a sales tax is harmful to blacks, and yet, due to several factors—such as the diffuseness of the impact[73] and the nature of the deprivation—it need not be viewed as a practice that aggravates the subordinate status of blacks as a group. What is needed in order to bring a state practice within the equal protection ban is a theory of status-harm, one that shows how the challenged practice has this effect on the status of the group.

It is from this perspective—one of a proscription against status-harm—that discriminatory state action should be viewed. Such action is one form of state conduct that impairs the status of a specially disadvantaged group. The Equal Protection Clause prohibits the state, for example, from using race as the criterion of admission to a swimming pool or a public housing project because that practice tends to aggravate the subordinate position of blacks by excluding them from a state facility. The same is true for the dual school system—the practice of assigning students to schools (or other public facilities) on the basis of race in order to segregate them. Once again,

73. Goodman, fn. 62 above, p. 306.

this state action is prohibited by the Equal Protection Clause because it aggravates the subordinate position of blacks, not because the classification is "unrelated" or only "poorly related" to a (permissible) state purpose.

I acknowledge that in these examples the state action may also be viewed as "arbitrary discrimination." Yet it is important to emphasize that "arbitrary discrimination" is the species, not the genus. Discrimination, arbitrary or otherwise, is only one form—one form among many—of conduct that disadvantages a group. There may be group-disadvantaging conduct that is not discriminatory. This would be true of state conduct that seemed beyond the reach of the Equal Protection Clause under the antidiscrimination principle because it embodied no discrimination, racial or otherwise; for example, the state policies of enforcing all racially restrictive covenants, allocating the scarce supply of liquor licenses without regard to whether the recipients will serve blacks, closing a municipal swimming pool or other public facilities in order to avoid integration, and refusing to build a public housing project in order to limit the number of poor blacks in the community. Similarly, conduct that did discriminate but on the basis of criteria innocent on their face, such as performance on a standardized test for employment or college admission, or geographic proximity for student assignment, could be evaluated from the perspective of whether it had the effect of impairing the status of a specially disadvantaged group. There would be no need to attempt to force them into the "arbitrary discrimination" pigeonhole. The need, instead, would be to formulate a theory that linked the practice and the status of the group. To be sure, such a theory may be highly problematic; for it might well require something more than a statistical showing that by and large the practice hurts blacks more than any other group (the differential impact). To take one central example, in the context of determining whether it is permissible to use performance on a standardized test as an employment criterion, a full theory of status-harm might have to include an assessment of (a) the status (determined on several scales such as income and prestige) of the job itself (professor vs. street cleaner), (b) the public visibility of the position (a judge vs. a chemist), (c) the diffuseness

159 *Groups and the Equal Protection Clause*

of the exclusionary impact (whether blacks are the predominant group excluded), and (d) the strength of the reasons justifying the use of the criterion (how accurate a test was it and how significant were the differences).

Admittedly, racially discriminatory conduct need not be viewed from this perspective—as a species of the genus of group-disadvantaging conduct. It could be viewed as the member of another genus, that of unfair treatment: what is wrong, it may be argued, with using race as the criterion for admission to a swimming pool or a public housing project is that it is a form of unfair treatment—an individual is being judged (for the purpose of allocating the scarce resource) on the basis of an irrelevant characteristic. The problem, however, is one of double membership: arbitrary discrimination is a member of the genus of unfair treatment as well as that of group-disadvantaging conduct. Double membership is possible because of an area of overlap of the two genuses (unfair treatment and group-disadvantaging conduct), though to be sure, the genuses are not coextensive, nor is one embraced by the other.

This analytic distinction between the two genuses is important. It preserves the possibility that conduct may be unfair and yet not a group-disadvantaging practice. Preferential treatment in favor of one of the specially disadvantaged groups would be an instance of such conduct. The white applicant who is rejected because of the preference for blacks may have been treated unfairly—may claim that he is being treated unfairly because he is being judged on the basis of an inappropriate criterion (not being black) and because the costs of a social policy are being localized on him.[74] The individual unfairness to the rejected nondisadvantaged applicant is relevant in assessing the justification of the state's refusal to institute the practice of preferential treatment; it might be relevant in fashioning a remedy, or it might even give rise to the violation of another constitutional provision, such as the Due Process Clause. But I do wish to deny that unfair treatment—such as being judged on the basis of an inappropriate criterion—is the domain of the Equal Protection Clause—

74. For elaboration of this point see my article, "School Desegregation: The Uncertain Path of the Law," 4 *Philosophy & Public Affairs* 3, 7–11 (1974).

even though such unfair treatment may be viewed from the individual perspective as a form of unequal treatment. As a protection for specially disadvantaged groups, the Equal Protection Clause should be viewed as a prohibition against group-disadvantaging practices, not unfair treatment.

Even if the claim of individual unfairness is put to one side, and the Equal Protection Clause is viewed as a protection for specially disadvantaged groups, a state policy of preferential treatment for blacks may be nonetheless constitutionally vulnerable. For one thing, it remains to be seen whether this policy in fact improves the position of the disadvantaged group. A preferential law-school admission program for blacks, to take a familiar example, may be justified on the ground that it gives positions of power, prestige, and influence to members of the racial group, positions that they would not otherwise attain in the immediate future, and that the acquisition of those positions will be an advantage to both the individual blacks admitted and, more importantly, to the group. The theory is that an increase in the number of black lawyers will disperse members of the racial group through the higher economic and social strata, raise aspirations of all members of the group, and create a self-generating protective device for the group—providing some members of the group with the power and leverage needed to protect the group from hostile attacks in the future. The status of the group will be improved. This is the theory, but, of course, these assertions of group-benefit are not totally free from doubt; indeed, some might raise the claim of counterproductivity—a regime of preferential treatment casts doubt upon the ability of all members of the group for it gives expression to the belief that the group would not succeed on its own.

If the court truly believed that a state policy—even if called "benign" —impaired the status of blacks then the policy would be invalid. But I doubt whether anyone believes that preferential admissions to law schools for blacks impairs the status of the group; those who argue that the policy is counterproductive today do so for the more limited purpose of casting doubt on the truth of the assertions supporting the policy. They wish to make the factual assertions on behalf of the policy open to controversy. And if that is so, it is important to delineate the role of the court in such a dispute. The dispute is simply over the constitutional permissibility of the preferential policy, and from that perspective the question for the court is whether there is *some rational basis* for legislators and administrators believing that a preferential policy would benefit the group. The appropriate standard for viewing a policy that appears to the court to benefit a specially disadvantaged group should be a rational-basis standard. The judicial activism authorized by the Equal Protection Clause is, under the group-disadvantaging principle, asymmetrical.

Another possible objection to a preferential admission policy under the group-disadvantaging principle seeks to expand the universe of beneficiaries—the relevant group preferred should not be blacks, but rather the poor. The resolution of this objection might be thought to call for a judicial inquiry into what are the "true" groups in American society today—an inquiry into what group identifications are the most important to the individual, either on a psychological, political, economic, or sociological level, or which ones should be encouraged.[75] However, once again, I believe that the judicial inquiry should be a much more modest one. The court should ask whether there is any rational basis for the legislator or administrator choosing the group delineation that it did. There would be little doubt that an antipoverty strategy—an admission policy preferring the poor—would be constitutionally permissible. But that is not the issue. This particular objection to preferential treatment for blacks—the one that demands the preferred group be the poor rather than blacks—seeks to make an antipoverty strategy the only constitutionally permissible redistributive strategy. It is this constitutional strait jacket that I find is troubling and without basis in the Equal Protection Clause.

The fact that some individual blacks may identify themselves in terms of their economic position ("poor") does not deny—at least today—the reality of the racial identification—that these individuals also identify themselves as blacks or that blacks are a social group. To acknowledge the multiplicity of group identifications is not to embrace a reductionism that denies the reality of some of the groups. Nor can the reductionism be justified on the ground that the preferential

75. Bell, fn. 72 above.

policy seeks to improve the socioeconomic status of blacks. The focus on blacks (as opposed to persons who happen to have the same economic status) should be viewed as a matter of legislative or administrative perogative—a question of setting priorities. The plight of the poor may be bad, but, so the legislator or administrator should be allowed to say, not as bad as that of the blacks.[76] Such a judgment about the urgency of the situation of blacks may be rooted in two considerations. The first is the caste quality of the blacks' low status—the fact that blacks have occupied the lowest socioeconomic rung in America for at least two centuries and will continue to do so unless redistributive measures are instituted. True, we may have always had and perhaps will always have people called "the poor," but that is to confuse a stratum with the occupant of a stratum. The second consideration is that blacks face disabilities not encountered by the poor (even conceived of as a group). These disabilities manifest themselves in all spheres of life—economic, social, and political—and derive from the fact that the individuals are members of the racial group. These are disabilities that do not saddle persons who are poor. Indeed, in order to elevate themselves, the white poor have incentives to disassociate themselves from the blacks and to accentuate the racial distinction. They have incentives to make blackness the lowest status, for of necessity it is a status into which they cannot fall.[77]

Similarly, there are reasons—good ones, though not necessarily compelling—for the legislators or administrators to treat blacks as a single group without trying to sort out the "rich blacks," without trying to fractionate the group. One reason is administrative convenience—the likely number of rich blacks are so few, and the costs of the mechanisms needed to identify them are so high, that the sorting is not worth the effort. Under the antidiscrimination principle, the central evil was one of loose fit and all arguments of administrative convenience were suspect; but under the group-disadvantaging principle, imprecision is not itself a constitutional vice. Imprecision can be

76. See the penetrating article of Duncan, "Inheritance of Poverty or Inheritance of Race?" in *On Understanding Poverty: Perspectives from the Social Sciences*, ed. Moynihan (New York, 1968).

77. Parsons, fn. 71 above, p. 77.

163 *Groups and the Equal Protection Clause*

tolerated when the state law or practice seeks to improve the position of a disadvantaged group and is in fact related to that end. Moreover, wholly apart from considerations of administrative convenience, the decision not to exclude the rich black (even once identified) can be justified. The argument is not that rich blacks as individuals are as "entitled" (in the compensatory sense) to as much of an assist as persons who are poor (though that may entirely be possible, for even though these individuals are rich, they are still black and being black may have been as severe a disadvantage in our society as being poor, if not greater). Rather, the claim is that the preference of the rich blacks may be justified in terms of improving the position of the group. Even if the blacks preferred happen to be rich, a benefit abounds to the group as a whole. Members of that group have obtained these positions of power, prestige, and influence that they otherwise might not have and to that extent the status of that group is improved. On the other hand, it is not clear that preferring a poor person confers a benefit on the poor conceived as a group—the preferred individual merely leaves the group; and even if there were group benefits entailed in a preference for the poor, certainly legislators or administrators are entitled to rank the improvement of blacks as a group as a social goal of first importance, more important than elevating the poor conceived of as a social group.

Finally, the preferential admission program for blacks (or any other single disadvantaged group) may be thought vulnerable because of its impact on other disadvantaged groups, whether they be American Indians, Chicanos, or perhaps even the poor, the poor black, or the poor black women (if these latter categories can be considered discrete disadvantaged social groups). The adverse impact on these groups arises in a two-step fashion and is ultimately traceable to the fact of scarcity: starting with a fixed number of openings, the preference for blacks lessens the number of places available to the members of these other groups. What is given to one group cannot be given to another.

There are several lines of response to this particular objection. One might argue, for example, that the nonpreferred group is not as badly off as the preferred group (for example, Chicanos are not as badly off as blacks). Another might emphasize the indirect quality of the exclusion (exclusion occurs because blacks are preferred and the places are limited), a factor that has an important bearing on the question whether the preferential treatment gives rise to a status-harm to the nonpreferred disadvantaged group. Preferring blacks may limit the number of places open to other disadvantaged groups, but it is not clear that it impairs their status. Finally, the objection might be answered by invoking the standard defense to underinclusion—one step at a time. Under the antidiscrimination principle, this defense was troubling because it seemed to threaten the claim of underinclusiveness; the defense could be raised to every instance of underinclusiveness. With the group-disadvantaging principle, no particular importance is attached to the claim of underinclusiveness itself, and thus the defense is less threatening; and in any event, it is conceivable that substantive standards could be developed to limit the defense and to thereby maintain as much pressure on the political agencies to remain responsive to the demands of all specially disadvantaged groups.

Having identified these possible lines of defense to this particular objection to preferential treatment for blacks, I do not want to obscure its force. The harm to other disadvantaged groups that arises from the fact of scarcity would be a significant point of constitutional vulnerability for a restricted preferential policy. It invokes the prohibition against group-disadvantaging practices and in responding to this objection, unlike the others, no help can be derived from the asymmetrical quality of judicial activism. The claim is that specially disadvantaged groups are being hurt, and the group-disadvantaging principle requires the court to be particularly attentive to such claims. But perhaps it is correct that a *restricted* preferential policy should be constitutionally vulnerable; and that it should be vulnerable precisely for this reason—because of its impact on other disadvantaged groups rather than because of its impact on the dominant group—the rejected white males. This is more than a purely analytic point, for it indicates what must be done to save the policy constitutionally—extend it to those specially disadvantaged groups that are as entitled to the preferential treatment as blacks.

The Accommodation of Considerations of Total Welfare. The overriding concern is with the status of the specially disadvantaged groups, and any state practice which aggravates their subordinate position would be presumptively invalid. There is, however, an element of restraint, and that arises from the fact that certain group-disadvantaging practices further interests of the polity as a whole, some of which are material (for example, increased productivity) and others nonmaterial (for instance, increased individual liberty). There must be some accommodation of other such competing interests. I doubt, for example, whether the Equal Protection Clause should be construed so stringently as to deny the state the right to insist upon certain minimum levels of proficiency or competence for its employees or students, even if such insistence were to aggravate (or at least perpetuate) the subordinate position of blacks. The problem, of course, is that if too large a role is allowed these considerations of total welfare, the protectionist edge of the Equal Protection Clause would be severely dulled: the state could always defend against an equal protection claim on the ground that, even though a disadvantaged group is especially harmed, total welfare is being maximized.

Two analytic tools must be introduced in order to avoid this dilemma. The first is the concept of a nonallowable interest. An example would be the interest of whites to keep blacks in a subordinate position. That interest should be given no weight in determining whether the group-disadvantaging practice is justified. In that sense it has no normative weight, although account of it might have to be taken out of sheer necessity. It *should* not be taken into consideration, but it might *have to be* because the court has no choice. For example, the resistance to the busing decree may be so intense as to be expressed in open rebellion, and in that case the court might have to proceed more slowly.[78] Resistance is an obstacle to be reckoned with, though there are limits to what can be done.

The concept of a nonallowable interest corresponds roughly to the concept of an illegitimate state purpose under the antidiscrimination

78. See Hart v. Community School Board No. 21, 383 F. Supp. 699 (E.D.N.Y. 1974); Cooper v. Aaron, 358 U.S. 1, 16-17 (1958); Buchanan v. Warley, 245 U.S. 60, 81 (1917).

principle. The difference relates not so much to the content of what is allowed or illegitimate; rather the standard for legitimacy or allowability is directly anchored in the governing principle. The antidiscrimination principle talks in terms of fit, in terms of over- and underinclusiveness, and such a principle can provide no standard for determining the legitimacy of state purposes; the antidiscrimination principle had to go beyond itself, and in that sense is incomplete, not in itself fully intelligible. The group-disadvantaging principle, on the other hand, does itself provide a standard of legitimacy or allowability. Interests should not be allowed when they would effectively give the dominant group a veto power over the elevation of the specially disadvantaged group. Such a veto would be inconsistent with what I perceive to be the very purpose of the Equal Protection Clause and with the notion of a constitutional restraint.

The second analytic tool that must be introduced to prevent the weighing process from degenerating into no-protection is the concept of a compelling benefit. This concept structures the relationship between the harm to the group's status and the benefit to the polity. If some compelling benefit is to be obtained by the practice or statute, either because of the importance of the interest served or the size of the benefit, the practice will be permitted, notwithstanding the status-harm to the specially disadvantaged group. The required benefit is linked to the harm: the more severe the disadvantage, the more compelling the benefit must be. But in linking the two, it is important to emphasize that the harm caused the disadvantaged class by the practice need not be greater than the benefit to the polity. That is why, in thinking of the Equal Protection Clause as a redistributional device, the balancing metaphor seems inapt: relief would be granted even if the harm to the group were less than the benefit to society. The more appropriate metaphor would be one that conceives of the status-harm to the disadvantaged group as the trigger of the remedial effort with the legitimate interests of the polity serving as the restraining force. The restraint starts once the benefit is greater than the harm, but only when it reached a certain quantity and intensity—denoted by the term "compelling"—would the remedial effort be brought to a halt.

167 *Groups and the Equal Protection Clause*

In the first instance the concept of compelling benefit will require the court to ask if there are alternative ways available to society for furthering its interests, and whether these alternatives are less harmful to the disadvantaged group. If so, the practice will be invalidated, for the state practice is not, in the ordinary meaning of that word, compelled. If, however, there are no alternatives that are less disadvantaging, then the court must move to a second order inquiry: it must gauge the status-harm to the disadvantaged group and the benefit to society and, in the final analysis, determine whether the benefit is of a compelling quality.

It might be noted that the first step of this inquiry is similar to that required by the strict-scrutiny branch of the antidiscrimination principle: strict scrutiny requires a search for better alternatives. But the difference is four-fold. First, we have an explanation for the strictness of the scrutiny, and one that is contained within the principle—the scrutiny is stringent because the status of an already subordinated group is being threatened. Under the antidiscrimination principle, the strictness of the scrutiny depends on a judgment about which interests are fundamental and which criteria are suspect; and although it might be possible to explain and justify those choices, the explanation would take the court far beyond the foundational concept of the antidiscrimination principle—means-end rationality—and thus transform the antidiscrimination principle so as to make it inconsistent with the ideals it is supposed to serve. Second, the action that triggers the inquiry differs. Under the group-disadvantaging principle, it is harm to a specially disadvantaged group, not the use of a criterion (somehow) deemed "suspect" or impingement on an interest deemed "fundamental." Third, there is a difference in the standard of what is a "better" alternative. Under the group-disadvantaging principle the alternative is judged not in terms of fit (reduction of under- and overinclusiveness) but rather in terms of its status-harm to the disadvantaged group. Fourth, the inquiry goes on to a second level if there is no better alternative. Under the antidiscrimination principle, the inquiry stops once it is determined there is no closer fitting or more precise criterion; the statute or practice is validated. But under the group-disadvantaging principle, even if the judge determines there is no less harmful way of satisfying the purpose, he must still gauge the harm to the group and the benefit to society. He must determine whether the benefit to society is so important or so great as to make the status-harm to the specially disadvantaged group tolerable—an inquiry that has no meaning under the antidiscrimination principle, and one that is inconsistent with the assurance that the principle exclusively rests on the modest conception of means-end rationality.

The State Action Requirement. I identified the state action requirement of the Fourteenth Amendment as one of the persistent sources of difficulty with the antidiscrimination principle. The problem to me, seemed to me to stem not so much from the "state" component, but from the "action" component, or more specifically, from the requirement that the "action" be a form of forbidden "discrimination." This artificial conception of the requisite "action" prevented the courts from tracing the effects of the state law or practice on the status of various disadvantaged groups in society, such as the blacks. Under the group-disadvantaging principle, however, this artificial limitation is eliminated.

In removing this limitation I do not mean to suggest an abandonment of the traditional view that the prohibition of the Equal Protection Clause applies only to the conduct—the laws and practices—of the state. Due account has been taken of this view. It is the state that is prohibited from aggravating the subordinate position of specially disadvantaged groups. There is a state action requirement. The most troublesome question that is likely to arise is whether state "inaction" shall be treated as "action." Should the failure of the state to *initiate* redistributive measures on behalf of specially disadvantaged groups—to counteract the inequalities imposed by private activity—be viewed as a practice that aggravates the position of subordination and thus as a violation of the Equal Protection Clause? As a purely analytic matter, it is possible to answer that question in the affirmative. But, on the other hand, there are three factors that argue for a negative answer, for preserving the distinction between action and inaction.

One is a concern for the text. Professor Black has argued that the words "denial" and "protection" suggest to him an affirmative obligation, an obligation to throw a life preserver.[79] On the other hand, without the distinction between action and inaction, the words "state" and "laws" in the Clause would become superfluous. The line between individual action and governmental action would be obliterated; the Clause would oblige the state to enact laws counteracting private group-disadvantaging practices and thus, in that sense, private action would be covered by the Clause.

The conception of constitutional prohibitions as restraints on the use of governmental power is a second factor that suggests that the distinction between action and inaction be preserved. This negative conception has historical roots. I suspect that this is probably how the framers viewed their task in drafting the first section of the Fourteenth Amendment (in contrast to those provisions of the Constitution establishing the structure of government). I also think the negative conception would be the one most consistent with the goal—of some undeniable validity—to minimize intervention by the judiciary (the agency primarily entrusted to enforce the Equal Protection Clause). If inaction were viewed as action, the intervention by the judiciary would be enormously increased, if not endless. This degree of intervention might be at odds with our democratic traditions, even tempered by a concern for minority rights, and it might push the judiciary beyond the limits of its competence. There is some awkwardness in having the judiciary act as the primary redistributive agency, in large part because it does not set its own agenda and thus cannot rationally order its priorities: should it be bread rather than housing?[80] A court must depend on the choices set by the litigators and I suspect that the resulting pattern of decision would tend to over emphasize those redistributive measures connected to the criminal process (for example, providing free transcripts on appeal). The criminal defendant always has the incentive to litigate, and society facilitates that proclivity by subsidizing litigation costs.

The problems of fashioning an appropriate remedy also bear on

79. Black, fn. 50 above, p. 73.

80. See Winter, "Poverty, Economic Equality and the Equal Protection Clause," 1972 *Sup. Ct. Rev.* 41, 89.

the action/inaction issue. Of course, even if the state action limitation is taken seriously, and the distinction between action and inaction preserved, acute remedial problems can arise. It is these factors, above all, that might persuade a court not to intervene when, for example, a town decides to close the swimming pool or to close its public schools in order to avoid integration. I have little doubt that such action disadvantages blacks, and yet the difficulty of fashioning an effective decree may be so great as to lead the court to deny injunctive (though perhaps not declaratory) relief. These negative decisions of the state come very close to no decision (the pure state inaction category), but once the line is crossed, and the court moves from action to inaction, these problems of fashioning an effective remedy are compounded.[81] The court would have to imagine a universe of possible measures that might be taken (by the legislature) on behalf of the disadvantaged group, make a choice among the permissible ones, compel its enactment, and then police the police.[82] This is not an impossible task but it is exceedingly treacherous, and perhaps further reason for limiting the group-disadvantaging principle to actions of the state.

V. The Choice of Principle

In many situations it will not make a great deal of difference whether the court operates under the antidiscrimination principle or the group-disadvantaging one. An example of such a situation—which I would like to call "first-order"—would be one in which the state excludes blacks from public institutions. In these first-order situations, which were the focus of judicial attention up to the late 1940s, and the following decade or two, the same result is likely to flow from either

81. It is hard to know on which side of the line to place a decision not to enter a field all together, for example, not to build public housing. See James v. Valtierra, 402 U.S. 137 (1971).

82. In addition to enjoining the legislature and compelling the enactment of an ameliorative measure, a court could act negatively. For example, instead of ordering the state legislature to enact a law prohibiting operators of public accommodation from refusing to serve individuals because of their race, it could overturn to trespass convictions of those who were not served because of their race.

171 *Groups and the Equal Protection Clause*

principle. I would still prefer the group-disadvantaging principle on the ground of frankness—it more accurately captures the intellectual process that should go on in the mind of the judge. It is nevertheless hard to believe much turns on the choice of principle.

Today, however, we find ourselves beyond these first-order situations. A new situation arises when the court is confronted with challenges to nondiscriminatory state action (such as conferring liquor licenses without regard to admission practices or closing public facilities) and with challenges to the state use of facially innocent criteria (such as test performance for allocating jobs or college places). With these second-order situations, there is more than frankness to recommend the group-disadvantaging principle. I believe this principle will frame matters in such a way as to expose the real issues and thus be more likely to lead to the correct decision—invalidation of those state practices that aggravate the subordinate position of the specially disadvantaged groups. It is, of course, possible that under the antidiscrimination principle a court willing to stretch and strain could reach the same result as it would under the group-disadvantaging principle; but that seems either to be a fortuity, or to require such a modification of the antidiscrimination principle—as evidenced by the "past discrimination," "de facto discrimination," or "fundamental right" offshoots—as to deprive the principle of any intellectual coherence and transform it into something it was never intended to be. In these situations, the group-disadvantaging principle should be preferred because it has a degree of coherence and completeness that can never be achieved with the antidiscrimination principle.

There is, to be sure, a third-order situation—as exemplified by state preferential treatment of blacks. In this instance more turns on the choice of principle than frankness, increased likelihood of the right result, or formal elegance. With these third-order problems there is a genuine conflict of principles. The antidiscrimination principle, with its individualistic, means-focused, and symmetrical character, would tend toward prohibiting such preferential treatment; the group-disadvantaging principle, on the other hand, would tend toward permitting it (and indeed might even provide the foundation for the fourth-order claim that may lie around the corner—that of requiring the preferential treatment). I believe this conflict should be resolved in favor of the group-disadvantaging principle but conceivably that this preference need not be one that has preemptive effect (all the way back down the scale). The antidiscrimination principle has coexisted with at least one other equal protection principle, the numerical-equality-of-persons principle of *Reynolds v. Sims*; and, similarly, the group-disadvantaging principle can coexist with other principles.[83] If that be so, then the group-disadvantaging principle can be viewed as a supplemental one: the use of the principle becomes more important as one moves from the first order to the second and then on to the third; and when one arrives at the third order, a hierarchy of the principles must be constructed; and when there is a conflict of principles, the principle of first priority takes precedence. I would argue that in this hierarchy the group-disadvantaging principle should be the one of first priority, should be placed ahead of the antidiscrimination principle. But I would be the first to acknowledge that this choice is not an easy one.

Part of the difficulty of making the choice stems from the fact that the usual material of judicial decisions—legislative history and text—provides no guidance. History indicates that the Clause was extended

83. If the group-disadvantaging principle did have a preemptive effect (all the way down the scale), it would knock-out the antidiscrimination principle as it now exists, that is, with its elaborate superstructure. It might, nevertheless, be possible to find a place in the Constitution—either in the Equal Protection Clause or perhaps more appropriately in the Due Process Clause—for a stripped-down version of the antidiscrimination principle—that is, simply a guarantee of means-end rationality. A law that bore no relation (or very little relation to) an end would be thought "arbitrary." (It might even be possible to append to this basic guarantee of means-end rationality a requirement that the end be constitutionally permissible, though the standard of permissibility would derive from other provisions, such as the First Amendment, rather than the Equal Protection Clause itself—now viewed as a protection for specially disadvantaged groups.) This basic guarantee of means-end rationality would sometimes enable a court to invalidate a state law that, for example, curtailed in a strikingly underinclusive way the speaking privilege of some particular individual or individuals who are not members of a disadvantaged group. The court could reach that result under a means-end test without passing on the general validity of the particular end chosen (for example, to prevent incitement), as it might have to if exclusive reliance were placed on a substantive constitutional provision (such as the First Amendment).

173 *Groups and the Equal Protection Clause*

to protect blacks. But it does not tell us whether blacks were to be viewed as a group or as individuals, nor does it say much about the intensity or degree of protection that is to be afforded. Similarly the text does little more than give the ideal of equality constitutional status and circumscribe it with a state action requirement. It is hard to believe that the use of the word "person" was intended to foreclose the recognition of the importance and status of groups. In essence, the text clothes the court with the authority to give specific meaning to the ideal of equality—to choose among the various subgoals contained within the ideal. A judge must become a natural lawyer out of default. The ethical issue is whether the position of perpetual subordination is going to be brought to an end for our disadvantaged groups, and if so, at what speed and at what cost.

The antidiscrimination principle roughly corresponds to the lay concept of equal treatment, and some might argue that the antidiscrimination principle should be given priority (and perhaps preemptive effect) because equal treatment is a more widely accepted goal of personal and social action (or more in accord with traditional American values, such as individualism). But this argument seems wrong, even if the informal Gallup Poll came out as imagined. It is not the job of the oracle to tell people—whether it be persons on the street or critical moralists—what they already believe.

For one thing, the public morality may be only an echo: the concept of equal treatment may be the more widely accepted subgoal of the ideal of equality because it more nearly accords with the concept of equality previously propounded by the Supreme Court and because it is the one embodied in the law. The Equal Protection Clause provides the Court with a textual platform from which it can make pronouncements as to the meaning of equality; it shapes the ideal. There pronouncements are viewed as authoritative, part of the "law," and play an important—though by no means decisive—role in shaping popular morality.[84] Law is a determinant, not just an instrument, of

84. The impact of *Brown v. Board of Education* on popular morality, especially of those growing up in the 1950s and 1960s, is ample testimony of this phenomenon. So is the wait in the spring of 1974 for the Supreme Court's decision in *DeFunis*. More seemed to be at stake than a directive against the University of Washington Law School, or for that matter all other state schools.

equality. Of course, this relationship between law (viewed as pronouncement rather than directive) and popular morality does not deny the existence of the latter; an echo is still a sound. But it does mean that the group-disadvantaging principle may also be widely accepted once it too is propounded to be the chosen strategy of the Supreme Court, once the judiciary says that this principle and the concept of equal status has an important claim to the constitutional ideal of equality.

Moreover, deference to the prevailing popular morality seems particularly inappropriate when what is being construed is a constitutional protection for minorities. Our commitment to democracy might dictate a reference to the people for the adoption and amendment of the Constitution, but once those processes are complete, a second reference to the electorate to elaborate the content of the ideal embodied in the Constitution seems inconsistent with the very idea of a constitutional restraint. This is particularly true of one that was in large part intended to protect a racial minority. All constitutional restraints are to be countermajoritarian, and this one particularly so.

It might be contended that the priority between the two principles should be set, not on the basis of text, history, or a rough sense of popular morality, but rather on the basis of certain institutional values —which strategy would best further the ideals of the craft. As we have seen, the predominance of the antidiscrimination strategy could in part be explained in terms of its supposed institutional advantages, objectivity and value-neutrality. Supposedly, judges will not be called on to make judgments about ends. The lines that emerge will be sharp. The decisions of the courts will not be heavily steeped in factual inquiries. In contrast, under the group-disadvantaging interpretation, the courts must deal with highly speculative entities, social groups. Subtle factual inquiries are required as to the contours and status of the group and the impact of a challenged practice on the group. Invariably value judgments would have to be made as to the costs and benefits of the practice to the disadvantaged group and to the polity.

People looked to the Court for some guidance in the solution of an intractable moral problem, and this guidance was supposed to emerge from the Court's decision on the meaning of the Equal Protection Clause.

I am willing to assume that the group-disadvantaging strategy will strain the resources, the imagination and even the patience of the judiciary. From the perspective of "mechanical jurisprudence" the group-disadvantaging principle offers no advantages. But I doubt whether these institutional considerations ought to be the bases for the choice between principles. For one thing, as we saw, this image of what judicial life will be under the antidiscrimination principle—no value judgments, sharp lines and no factual judgments—is largely illusory. The court must make determinations about whether the purpose served by the classification is "legitimate," which classifications are "suspect," what rights are "fundamental," what purposes are special or ordinary, whether it is permissible to take one step at a time, and whether the "fit" is sufficient. The quantitative ring to the terms "fit," "overinclusion," and "underinclusion" is decidedly an illusion. Moreover, once the antidiscrimination strategy is modified to embrace "the perpetuation of past discriminations" or "de facto discrimination," as I believe it must, the factual inquiries become overwhelming and the value judgments used (for example, in determining which effects of past discrimination are to be eliminated) become commonplace.

In any event, even if it can (somehow) be demonstrated that the antidiscrimination principle is more conducive to the traditional ideals of the craft, it still remains to be seen why these ideals—the ideals of "mechanical jurisprudence"—should be preserved at all[85] or at least at the expense of substantive results deemed just. It is understandable why judges will choose that strategy most in accord with the ideal of their craft but that hardly makes it just, nor, for the self-conscious judge, inevitable. The redistributive aims served by the group-disadvantaging principle—the elevation of at least one group that has spent two centuries in this country in a position of subordination—may simply override these supposed institutional advantages.

Finally, even if these institutional arguments provide a basis for preferring the antidiscrimination principle, it must be remembered that at best they dictate a choice of the judicial strategy. These arguments cannot be used by all. A sharp line should be drawn between the principles governing the judicial process and those that govern

85. This view is elaborated in the article referred to in fn. 22 above.

nonjudicial processes, some legislative, some private. This is one sense in which law and morals should be separated. For the institutional considerations have little relevance for those who do not act as judges, but nonetheless must struggle with the task of giving meaning to the ideal of equality—for example, citizens deciding upon admissions policies to a law school and legislators acting under Section 5 of the Fourteenth Amendment. Nor should these institutional considerations be allowed to operate subsilentio in nonjudicial spheres, a danger created when the citizenry gives excessive deference to the judicial pronouncement as to the meaning of equality—when sight is lost of the reason for the choice of strategy, and the citizenry defers to judicial pronouncement as to the meaning of "equality" simply because it is "The Law," or even worse, "The Constitution."

The roots of such excessive deference are deep. It may reflect the psychological need for an authoritative agency to decide questions of individual morality. The need becomes particularly acute when, as is true here, the ethical questions become more difficult, the arguments on each side more balanced, and when it is not just a conflict between liberty and equality, but in essence a conflict between two important senses of equality—equal treatment and equal status. Moreover, when what is demanded is a nationwide morality, one that could subordinate the morality of a particular region, as has been true in racial matters, the Supreme Court is particularly well positioned to perform the function of such an authoritative decision-making agency. The impact of judicial pronouncement on positive morality may also be traced to the strategic position of lawyers in our society, as managers of important nonlegal institutions and as formulators of opinion. The Court is "their" institution and they are bound to look to it in formulating their conception of equality.[86]

But whatever the reasons for this deference, and regardless of how understandable it might be, what strikes me as important is that we should become increasingly aware of the role of judicial pronounce-

86. Indeed a person committed to the Court as a legal institution—because of constitutional structure or results in particular cases—might be willing or even desirous to have the Court's sphere of influence broadened as a means of buttressing or fortifying its legal position.

ment in translating the ideal of equality, the nature of the choices the courts have made, and the explanation for the choices. We should become aware of the fact that the antidiscrimination principle is not inevitable and, indeed, that its predominance may be traceable to institutional values that have little relevance for individual morality or legislative policy. At best they explain the choice of judicial strategy. This increased consciousness does not necessarily mean that the group-disadvantaging principle must be adopted as a matter of individual morality or legislative policy. Indeed considerations that might have given little weight in determining what should be the correct interpretation of the Equal Protection Clause–such as the consideration of individual fairness–may play a larger role in determining what is right for a citizen or legislator. Old dilemmas may appear in new guises.

[3]

RICHARD H. FALLON, JR.

PAUL C. WEILER

FIREFIGHTERS v. STOTTS: CONFLICTING MODELS OF RACIAL JUSTICE

I. INTRODUCTION

In *Memphis Firefighters v. Stotts*,[1] the Supreme Court finally addressed the question whether a judge may impose racial quotas as a remedy for employment discrimination. The issue arose in the especially troublesome context of layoffs and demotions, in which the Court was asked to "allocate the burdens of recession and fiscal austerity"[2] between senior white and junior black employees. The Court might have confined its inquiry to this particularly thorny problem. But the majority elected a broader basis—one that re-

---

Richard H. Fallon, Jr. is Assistant Professor of Law, and Paul C. Weiler is Professor of Law, Harvard Law School.

AUTHORS' NOTE: We are grateful to Charles Fried, Andrew Kaufman, Martha Minow, and Lloyd Weinreb, who read earlier drafts and offered helpful criticisms and suggestions, and to research assistants Florrie Darwin, Glenn Fine, Judith Starr, and David Webbert.

[1] 104 S.Ct. 2576 (1984).

[2] *Id.* at 2591 (O'Connor, J., concurring). During the recession of the early eighties, the unemployment rate leaped from 6 percent at the beginning of 1980 to 11 percent by the end of 1982, the highest point since the Great Depression of the 1930s, while black unemployment rose from 11 percent to 19 percent. ECONOMIC REPORT OF THE PRESIDENT 259 (1984). As a result, the relative economic position of black workers, which had steadily improved from the mid-sixties to the end of the seventies with the help of Title VII of the 1964 Civil Rights Act, not only flattened out but actually dipped in the early eighties. For example, the ratio of black male median wage and salary income to white, which had risen from 59.4 percent in 1966 to 68.4 percent by 1979, receded to 65.8 percent by 1982. See CURRENT POPULATION REPORTS, SERIES P-60, MONEY INCOME OF HOUSEHOLDS, FAMILIES AND PERSONS IN THE UNITED STATES 166 (1982).

0-226-46437-7/85/1984-0062$01.00

quired a stark choice between two antithetical visions of racial justice.

On one side of *Stotts* was a phalanx of civil rights organizations, defending a group-based approach to current racial issues. Their Model of Group Justice argues that discrimination has had harmful effects on blacks as a group, not merely on the victims of particular discriminatory acts, and that group-based remedies—racial quotas[3] —ought therefore to be upheld. Aspiring to economic equality for blacks and minorities, the Model of Group Justice had gained increasing acceptance as a thesis for executive, legislative, and judicial action during the 1970s. But the approach has always been controversial. The Reagan administration was eager to contest it in *Stotts*, and to return to the philosophy of color blindness that had initially inspired the American civil rights movement.[4] The government argued that only proved victims of discrimination should benefit from judicial remedies, and that individually innocent whites could not be "dispreferred"[5] in order to create group preferences for minorities. A majority of the Court[6] opted for this "individual justice" approach, or at least endorsed its prescribed limitations on judicial remedies.[7] For the civil rights movement, *Stotts* represents perhaps its biggest defeat[8] in litigation under Title VII of the 1964

[3] In this area, perhaps no choice of vocabulary is entirely neutral. As the NEW YORK TIMES reported recently, "It sometimes seems almost everybody likes 'affirmative action,' nobody likes 'reverse discrimination,' and hardly anybody likes 'quotas.'" July 24, 1984, A16, col. 3. Because the word "quotas" may have negative connotations, we shall more frequently use other terms. See note 10 *infra*.

[4] The position of the Solicitor General was mirrored in the amicus brief of the AFL-CIO, the bitter opponent of Reagan policies on almost every other front, but here seeking to preserve its seniority rights against judicial erosion. Within the Jewish community, the Anti-Defamation League argued that racial preferences could never be ordered under the Title VII, while the brief of the American Jewish Congress defended color-conscious remedies, though only as a last resort.

[5] See Brest, *The Supreme Court 1975 Term—Foreword, In Defense of the Antidiscrimination Principle*, 90 HARV. L. REV. 1, 36 (1976).

[6] Justice White's majority opinion was joined by Chief Justice Burger and by Justices Powell, Rehnquist, and O'Connor. Justice O'Connor also wrote a separate concurring opinion. Justice Stevens concurred in the judgment, but solely on an interpretation of a consent decree entered by the parties. Unlike the majority, he offered no judgment as to permissible judicial remedies for proven statutory violations. Justice Blackmun wrote a dissent, which was joined by Justices Brennan and Marshall.

[7] Seemingly untouched by *Stotts*, and entirely unmentioned by the majority, was the Court's previous holding in United Steel Workers v. Weber, 443 U.S. 193 (1979), that voluntarily adopted racial quotas are permissible under Title VII.

[8] Solicitor General Rex Lee characterized the decision as a "slam dunk," "perhaps one of the greatest decisions of all time!"

Civil Rights Act.[9] It may also signal a judicial attitude of broader import for the future of "affirmative discrimination."[10]

II. THE STOTTS CASE

A. THE FACTS

Firefighters v. Stotts involved a clash between black firefighters, hired by the City of Memphis under a consent decree,[11] and white workers with seniority rights under their labor agreement. The consent decree established racial hiring and promotion goals within the fire department in a class action alleging race discrimination by the City.[12] *Stotts* arose in the spring of 1981, when fiscal difficulties

---

[9] Pub. L. No. 88-352, 78 Stat. 253–66 (current version at 42 U.S.C. 2000e-15–2000C-17 (1982)).

[10] We take the term from GLAZER, AFFIRMATIVE DISCRIMINATION: ETHNIC INEQUALITY AND PUBLIC POLICY (1975). By "affirmative discrimination" we mean to refer to two forms of racial preferences: (i) judicially mandated "quotas" or "race-conscious remedies" prescribed at the end of a lawsuit as a remedy for past unlawful employment practices; and (ii) "voluntarily" adopted racial preferences, often called programs of "affirmative action," undertaken by employers outside the context of a lawsuit. Two reasons make "affirmative discrimination" our most frequent terminological choice in this article. First, the questions of morality and policy are largely the same in cases of voluntary and of judicially mandated racial preferences. "Affirmative discrimination" conveniently encompasses both. Second, this term may carry fewer connotations, either positive or negative, than its alternatives. Many of the questions surrounding affirmative discrimination are extraordinarily difficult, both legally and morally, and we do not wish our choice of terminology to prejudice the weighing of arguments. We assume "affirmative discrimination," as most of the more contentious terms (such as "quota" and "reverse discrimination"), to imply the following: the implementation of racial preferences, not merely to break ties between equally qualified candidates, but at least sometimes to prescribe the selection of a candidate who otherwise appears less qualified than his or her rivals; the conferral of preferences on minority candidates who have not proven that they personally are the victims of illegal conduct by the employer or agency extending the preference; and the use of numerical targets or goals to determine the number of minority candidates to be hired based on the racial preferences.

[11] There were two proceedings resulting in two consent decrees affecting the Memphis Fire Department. The first lawsuit, brought by the Federal government challenging the City's overall employment practices, ended with a 1974 consent decree (with no admission of liability) which, inter alia, established the long-term goal of a racially proportionate work force in the fire department, to be pursued through an interim target of 50 percent new black hirees. The second suit was a class action by the respondent Carl Stotts (later consolidated with an individual suit by Jones) attacking the hiring and promotion practices in the fire department alone. This was settled by a 1980 consent decree, which reiterated the long-term employment goal and the 50 percent annual hiring target and added a 20 percent promotion target. It also contained a directive that eighteen named blacks be given immediate promotions.

[12] Although there had never been any judicial finding of illegal discrimination or any such admission by the City, the district judge was prepared to take judicial notice of discriminatory employment practices within the fire department. The supporting evidence contained in the record strongly indicated purposeful discrimination prior to passage of the 1964 Civil

moved the City to commence a program of layoffs.[13] The City's established personnel policy, detailed in a memorandum of understanding with the firefighters' union, prescribed that lay-offs would occur on a last-hired, first-fired schedule.[14] But when the City proposed to proceed on this basis, the burden threatened to fall primarily on blacks hired under the consent decree.[15] The class represented by Stotts sought an injunction against their discharges. Relying on the consent decree, the district judge forbade the City to apply its seniority policy in a way that would reduce the proportional representation of blacks in the fire department.[16] The City understood this ruling to authorize the dismissal of senior white firefighters, and the fire department acted accordingly in executing its layoffs.

Stotts exhibited many characteristic features of class litigation involving patterns and practices of employment discrimination: the historic exclusion and continuing underrepresentation of blacks

---

Rights Act. (In the period 1950–63, the department hired no blacks in any year except 1955.) Following the enactment of federal antidiscrimination legislation, the City's performance improved somewhat. (From 1964 to 1971, 7 percent of new firefighters were black.) Once the Act was made applicable to public employers such as Memphis, the recruitment of black firefighters jumped sharply. (From March 1972 through November 1974, roughly 10 percent of new firefighters were black in a region where one-third the labor market was black.)

[13] Initially the City projected that it would need to lay off about forty out of approximately 1,500 fire department personnel.

[14] The memorandum was probably not an enforceable contract under Tennessee law. See Fulenwider v. Firefighters Ass'n Local Union 1784, 649 S.W.2d 268 (Tenn. 1982). Regardless of the enforceability of the memorandum, however, the City had adopted and maintained a seniority system reflecting its terms.

[15] Application of a "last-hired, first-fired" policy would have produced a layoff of twenty-five white privates (out of 497) and fifteen blacks (out of eighty-five), all the latter to be drawn from the eighteen new hirees under the 1980 decree, as well as the demotion of fourteen of the eighteen named blacks who had been promoted under that decree. This would have reduced black employment in the fire department from an 11 percent to a 10 percent share.

[16] The district court actually entered three orders: (i) a temporary restraining order on May 4, 1981, barring any layoffs or demotions of blacks at all; (ii) an interim injunction on May 18, 1981, which prohibited the layoff or demotion of blacks if, and to the extent that, this would reduce their existing share of employment in the fire department and its various job classifications; and (iii) an order on June 25, 1981, which apparently approved the City's plan to lay off senior whites to the extent necessary to maintain black representation within the department. There was a sharp disagreement between the parties and within the Supreme Court about the precise import of these judicial directives. Justice White's majority opinion characterized the orders as issuing "an injunction requiring white employees to be laid off, when the otherwise applicable seniority system would have called for the layoff of black employees with less seniority." 104 S.Ct. at 2585 (footnotes omitted). Justice Blackmun interpreted the injunction as doing no more than preventing "the city from conducting layoffs in accordance with its seniority systems insofar as it will decrease the percentage of black," but not requiring "the city to lay off any white employees at all." *Id.* at 2602.

within the fire department; the institution of multiple suits and the entry of consent decrees, establishing racially defined hiring goals; significant improvements in black employment, though far less than proportionate representation; and, in the context of fiscally mandated layoffs, a collision between the aspirations of the consent decree and the seniority interests of incumbent whites. In other respects, however, *Stotts* was a rather unprepossessing candidate for a momentous legal engagement. Because of changes in the City's layoff schedule, only three additional whites were laid off by the fire department, and these three were recalled less than a month later.[17] Moreover, it was a curiosity of *Stotts* that all six of the firefighters actually affected by the judicial order—the three "senior" whites who were laid off and the three "junior" blacks who were retained—were all hired on the same day, less than two years earlier. The reason the blacks ranked below the whites on the seniority list was that the first letter in their last names came later in the alphabet, and the Memphis seniority system used alphabetical priority as its tie-breaking criterion.[18]

B. A PRELIMINARY ISSUE: MOOTNESS

The peculiar features of *Stotts* furnished plausible arguments that the case was moot.[19] Because the laid-off firefighters had long since

---

[17] They each lost roughly $1,200.00 in back pay, less unemployment insurance benefits. By the spring of 1983, the City's financial position had improved sufficiently that sixty-three new firefighters had been recruited, thus effectively insulating all the white firefighters affected by the 1981 injunction from any future layoffs that might be contemplated.

[18] If the Court had wanted to address the seniority layoffs issue in a situation that did exhibit its true human implications, there was no shortage of candidates. The City of Boston, for example, was confronted in the early eighties with much more serious fiscal problems than Memphis's, resulting in the layoff of 1,300 Boston schoolteachers. A federal judicial order analogous to that in *Stotts* forbade any reduction in the minority share of school employment, with the result that tenured white teachers with up to fifteen years of service were laid off, while the school board continued to hire new black teachers. See Morgan v. O'Bryant, 671 F.2d 23 (1st Cir. 1982). Three years later, there are still over 400 white teachers laid off in Boston, for all intents and purposes having lost their jobs in the cause of racial integration. Yet not once but twice the Supreme Court has refused to accept the Boston Teachers case for review. (We are indebted to Steven Kautner, who is studying the post-layoff experience of the Boston schoolteachers, for providing us with information about the scope and aftermath of the layoff.)

[19] When the Court granted certiorari in June 1983, it already had been apprised by the parties of the facts supporting an argument of mootness. Curiously, in the light of the serious mootness issue, the Court granted certiorari in *Stotts* on the same day that it cited a mootness question in declining to decide an already argued case presenting essentially the same legal issue. In Boston Firefighters v. Boston Chapter, NAACP 103 S.Ct. 2076 (1983), several hundred white firefighters and police officers had been laid off, while junior blacks were

been recalled to work, the controversy had abated.[20] Furthermore, as Justice Blackmun argued in dissent, the judgment under review was only a temporary restraining order, addressed to the layoffs scheduled for June, 1981. It was by no means certain that the order would apply to future layoffs.[21] But the Court dismissed these objections. The majority found that the district court's orders had either effected or reflected a judicial modification in the underlying consent decree that would restrain the City from laying off junior blacks on future occasions.[22] The Court also concluded that white employees, adversely affected by the layoffs, might have rightful claims against the city for lost seniority and back pay, and that the City could be constrained from satisfying these claims so long as the injunction remained unmodified.

Although its analysis was by no means free of difficulty,[23] the majority did not stray indefensibly beyond the bounds of mootness doctrine in finding *Stotts* fit for decision. The contours of justiciabil-

retained in order to preserve the level of black employment that had been achieved under an earlier hiring decree. The layoffs were ended unexpectedly by state legislation that provided the City of Boston with additional funds, on condition that the City recall all the laid-off police and firefighters and undertake not to lay them off in the future. Though all these facts were apparent in the record when the Boston case was accepted for review, the Court, after oral argument, decided to return the matter to the First Circuit for a judgment whether the case was moot. Following its mootness decision in *Stotts*, the Supreme Court vacated the Court of Appeals's ruling that the Boston case was moot and remanded the case for further consideration in the light of *Stotts*. 104 S.Ct. 3576 (1984).

[20] 104 S.Ct. at 2596–2600 (Blackmun, J., dissenting).

[21] It was very clear indeed that the order could have no effect on future layoffs if the Supreme Court simply vacated it—the usual practice with temporary injunctions governing specific disputes already concluded. United States v. Munsingwear, Inc., 340 U.S. 36, 39 (1950).

[22] 104 S.Ct. at 2583.

[23] *Id.* at 2584. With respect to back pay, at least, there are two difficulties with the Court's argument. First, the Court assumed that the temporary injunction might have an effect on future negotiations or litigation between the City and the "senior" whites who had been laid off. But the City and the senior whites were aligned on the same side of the suit in the Supreme Court. A hypothetical future controversy between these *Stotts* allies seems a strange basis on which to find that a live dispute existed between either or both of those two parties and a class of black firefighters, the adverse parties in *Stotts*, who presumably would have no role in any future back pay litigation between the union and the City. See *id.* at 2597–2600 (Blackmun, J., dissenting). Second, under principles articulated by the Court in the previous Term, the temporary injunction need not have prevented recovery by the disadvantaged white firefighters. See W. R. Grace & Co. v. Local Union 759, 103 S.Ct. 2177 (1983); see also Note, 97 HARV. L. REV. 70, 269–78 (1983).

ity contain a widely recognized,[24] if often lamented, flexibility,[25] and there was some precedential support for the Court's conclusion that the case remained live for decision.[26] In this context, two facts seem worthy of comment. First, eager to reach the merits, the usual apostles of judicial restraint held the case justiciable, while more "liberal" Justices protested that the case was unfit for the exercise of judicial power.[27] Second, this Term's resolution followed a pattern exhibited before in cases presenting hard issues of racial justice: a dubious decision not to decide one case[28] was followed by an equally doubtful conclusion that a later case, presenting the same but now more "percolated" issue, was fit for judicial resolution.[29] The sequence does not seem coincidental. According to one celebrated argument, justiciability doctrines perform an important

---

[24] See, *e.g.*, Varat, *Variable Justiciability and The Duke Power Case*, 58 TEX. L. REV. 273, 278–79, 319–27 (1980).

[25] The Court itself has occasionally recognized that there is an element of "flexibility" in mootness doctrine, see, *e.g.*, United States Parole Comm'n v. Geraghty, 445 U.S. 388, 400 (1980); Franks v. Bowman Transp. Co., 424 U.S. 747, 752–57 & n.8 (1976). Mootness issues generally arise only in cases in which an issue is framed by facts adequate to inform and delimit a judicial decision. Moreover, in *Stotts* the submissions of the parties and the amici afforded the Court all the benefits of adverse argument as a device to clarify legal issues. When these functional requisites of justiciability are satisfied, it is not improper for the Court to be guided in part by policy considerations as to the desirability of resolving a particular dispute. See Fallon, *Of Justiciability, Remedies and Public Law Litigation: Notes on the Jurisprudence of Lyons*, 59 N.Y.U. L. REV. 1 (1984).

[26] See Super Tire Engineering Co. v. McCorkle 122–25 (1974). Other cases, however, pointed as strongly to an opposite conclusion. See, *e.g.*, University of Texas v. Caminisch, 451 U.S. 390 (1981).

[27] Illustrative of the reversal of characteristic positions is a comparison of *Stotts* with two recent and important standing decisions, City of Los Angeles v. Lyons, 103 S.Ct. 1660 (1983), and Valley Forge Christian College v. Americans United for Separation of Church and State, Inc., 454 U.S. 464 (1982). Holding both the earlier cases nonjusticiable were five-member majorities consisting of Chief Justice Burger and Justices White, Powell, Rehnquist, and O'Connor. In *Stotts*, these same five joined in Justice White's opinion holding *Stotts* not moot and thus fit for judicial decision. By contrast, the three Justices who argued that *Stotts* should be dismissed as moot (Brennan, Marshall, and Blackmun) all would have applied loose tests and upheld justiciability in *Lyons* and *Valley Forge*. Only Justice Stevens prevented the *Stotts* line-up from being an exact reversal of those in *Lyons* and *Valley Forge*: he found all three cases to satisfy the justiciability requirements of Article III.

[28] See note 19 *supra*.

[29] Compare DeFunis v. Odegaard, 416 U.S. 312 (1974), which the Court held moot, with Regents of the Univ. of California v. Bakke, 438 U.S. 265 (1978), in which the Court chose to overlook a difficult standing problem. For a general discussion of the Court's use of "avoidance" techniques in a substantive domain fraught with "ambivalence," see Mishkin, *The Uses of Ambivalence: Reflections on the Supreme Court and the Constitutionality of Affirmative Action*, 131 U. PA. L. REV. 907 (1983).

function in allowing the Supreme Court to pick its time and its case for decision.[30]

C. A SUBSIDIARY ISSUE: CONSENT DECREES

In forbidding the City to engage in seniority-based layoffs, the district judge acted pursuant to a consent decree. As commonly occurs in Title VII litigation, the decree contained no admission of illegal discrimination, and it established guidelines only for the City's hiring and promotion practices, without reference to layoffs. But the decree did authorize the district judge to issue any "further orders . . . necessary or appropriate to effectuate the purposes of this decree."[31] In addition, federal courts ordinarily retain their traditional equitable power to modify consent decrees in adaptation to changed conditions.[32] But the *Stotts* majority denied that the district court's preliminary injunction could be justified on either basis. First, the majority found that the parties had not intended to authorize judicial modification of the City's seniority system.[33] As to the scope of the district court's equitable powers, a question of more general importance was presented, and Justice Stevens's concurring opinion would have put the decision solely on this ground: he would have enforced a strict standard for the identification of "changed circumstances" needed to authorize judicial modification of a consent decree.[34] But the Court did not treat this as an independent question. Linking the district court's equitable powers with the statutory basis for the plaintiffs' cause of action, the majority held that neither a consent decree nor a judicial modification could provide relief that would not have been available had plaintiffs

[30] See BICKEL, THE LEAST DANGEROUS BRANCH 205 (1962); *cf.* Mishkin, note 29 *supra;* but see Gunther, *The Subtle Vices of the "Passive Virtues"—a Comment on Principle and Expediency in Judicial Review*, 64 COLUM. L. REV. 1 (1964).

[31] 104 S.Ct. at 2581 (quoting Stotts v. Memphis Fire Dept., 679 F.2d at 578 (app.).

[32] The Court took the approach that "the 'scope of a consent decree must be discerned within its four corners.'" 104 S.Ct. at 2586 (quoting United States v. Armour & Co., 402 U.S. 673, 681–82 (1971)). It is unclear whether the Court, in citing this familiar maxim, meant to disapprove of the view that the four-corners rule generally should be applied less restrictively in civil rights class actions than in other types of litigation. See Massachusetts Association for Retarded Citizens v. King, 668 F.2d 602, 607–08 (1st Cir. 1981) (noting that consent decrees in public law litigation may require "more flexible interpretation").

[33] 104 S.Ct. at 2586.

[34] See 104 S.Ct. at 2594–95 (Stevens, J., concurring in the judgment).

prevailed at trial.[35] And, the Supreme Court found, the plaintiffs' legal theory, even if proved, would not have justified a judicially mandated interference with bona fide seniority rights.[36]

D. THE LAW OF JUDICIAL REMEDIES

Assuming that relief under a consent decree may not exceed what could be imposed as a judicial remedy for proved discrimination, the Supreme Court easily fit *Stotts* into its existing Title VII jurisprudence. In *Teamsters v. United States*,[37] the Court had held that competitive seniority—seniority giving one employee actual or potential preferences over others—could be awarded only to the individual victims of past discrimination. Relying on § 703(h) of Title VII,[38] which confers express protection on bona fide seniority systems, *Teamsters* found that "mere membership in the disadvantaged class is insufficient to warrant a seniority award."[39] *Stotts* extended the logic of *Teamsters* to consent decrees. By overriding the seniority rights of white employees, the district court had effectively given "competitive seniority" benefits to "junior" blacks. And because the black beneficiaries were not proved victims of past discrimination,[40] the Court found that the district court's *Stotts* decision conflicted with *Teamsters*.[41] This decision will make more

---

[35] Justice Stevens characterized the Court's discussion of Title VII as "wholly advisory." *Id.* at 2594.

[36] 104 S.Ct. at 2587–88.

[37] 431 U.S. 324 (1977).

[38] 42 U.S.C. 2000e–2h: "Notwithstanding any other provision of this subchapter, it shall not be an unlawful employment practice for an employer to apply different standards of compensation, or different terms, conditions, or privileges of employment pursuant to a bona fide seniority or merits system . . . provided that such differences are not the result of an intention to discriminate because of race, color, religion, sex, or national origin . . ."

[39] 104 S.Ct. at 2588.

[40] In entering the consent decree, the City had acknowledged no wrongdoing whatsoever.

[41] Even in connection with the seniority issue, while *Teamsters* held that 703(h) precludes any individual right to an award of full constructive seniority for blacks who cannot show that they were the actual victims of their employer's discrimination, Justice Blackmun correctly noted that that case did not address the rather different question of whether it might be appropriate and equitable for a court temporarily to override seniority rights in certain layoff situations in pursuit of the objective of eliminating discrimination against blacks as a group. 104 S.Ct. at 2608 (Blackmun, J., dissenting). Moreover, *Stotts*, unlike *Teamsters*, directly implicated the Title VII policy favoring settlement of disputed issues. See, *e.g.*, Ford Motor Co. v. EEOC, 458 U.S. 219 (1982); Carson v. American Brands, Inc., 450 U.S. 79, 88 n.14 (1981).

difficult the settlement of Title VII seniority issues without resort to trial.

The *Teamsters* rationale was adequate to dispose of the case. The majority apparently decided, however, that it might as well resolve as much legal debate as possible. Consistent with the views urged by the litigants,[42] the Court found a link between the remedial policies governing seniority awards and those applicable to hiring and promotion remedies. It was, said the Court, a general "policy of Title VII" to provide "make-whole relief only to those who have been actual victims of illegal discrimination."[43] The Court thus introduced a broad proposition, unnecessary to resolution of the seniority dispute, that the positive benefit of Title VII remedies could not be afforded to blacks who had not been proved to be personal victims of the employer's discrimination.

Here the majority plainly slid into dictum. But dictum from the Supreme Court is not just so many words, even if it is something less than the law. Among its other effects, the *Stotts* majority's discussion throws into doubt the validity of a large body of law, currently applicable throughout the United States, holding that hiring quotas may be an appropriate remedy for proved violations of Title VII.[44]

III. The Contending Models

The *Stotts* majority adopted the resolutely individualistic approach of what we call the Model of Individual Justice. Writing for three dissenting Justices, Justice Blackmun presented a highly sympathetic statement of the contending group justice position. As we turn to a deeper examination of these alternative views, we concern ourselves less with the legislative history of Title VII than with broader concerns of morality and public policy in civil rights law. We do so for a variety of reasons. First, the surrounding moral

[42] Each of the briefs submitted to the Court in *Stotts*, as in *Boston Firefighters* the year before, took the position either that it favored race-conscious remedies, in which case it was ready to override seniority rights so that this kind of remedy could operate in layoffs, or it insisted on the integrity of the seniority rights, in which case it disapproved of racial preferences in any context.

[43] 104 S.Ct. at 2588–89.

[44] The courts of appeals are unanimous on this point. For a collection of cases, see *id.* at 2606 n.10 (Blackmun, J., dissenting).

debate, bifurcated into individual and group approaches, consistently colors judicial readings of Title VII and its legislative history, and also of the Equal Protection Clause of the Fourteenth Amendment. In this area, moral and policy arguments could not be unrelated to jurisprudence. Second, the implications of the moral and policy debate are not confined to judicial orders. Crucially important are the "voluntary" affirmative action programs of private employers, which were upheld as legal by the Supreme Court's 1980 decision in *United Steel Workers v. Weber*,[45] and the incentive to undertake such programs that is provided by Executive Order 11246,[46] which covers a substantial proportion of the national work force.[47] Subject to executive revision, the current Ex-

---

[45] 443 U.S. 193 (1979).

[46] Exec. Order No. 11246, 3 C.F.R. 339 (1964-64 comp.), reprinted in 42 U.S.C. 2000e (1982). Issued by President Johnson in 1965 and still in force as amended, Executive Order 11246 built on an unbroken tradition dating back to 1941 of executive orders imposing nondiscrimination obligations on federal contractors. See generally Contractors Ass'n v. Secretary of Labor, 442 F.2d 159, 168–71 (3rd Cir. 1971) (reviewing progenitors of Order 11246). The current Order applies to all nonexempt federal contracts, subcontracts of federal contracts, and federally assisted construction contracts, Exec. Order No. 11246, supra at § 202(7), 301. The major regulatory exemption from the Order is for contracts and subcontracts not exceeding $10,000. 41 C.F.R. § 60-1.5(a)(1) (1983). The key substantive element of the Executive Order is the requirement that contractors take "affirmative action" to ensure the nondiscriminatory treatment of job applicants and employees. Exec. Order No. 11246, supra at § 202(1). The Regulations specify that nonconstruction contractors with fifty or more employees and a contract of $50,000 or more must develop a "result-oriented" written affirmative action compliance program. 41 C.F.R. § 60-2,1, 2.10. This program includes a sophisticated "utilization analysis" designed to determine whether there are fewer minorities in any job group than would reasonably be expected by their availability. *Id.* § 60-2.11. If "underutilization" is discovered in any job group, the employer must establish and in good faith seek to fulfill goals and timetables "to achieve prompt and full utilization of minorities at all levels and segments of the workplace." *Id.* § 60-2.1, 2.10, 2.12, 2.15. Construction contractors are required to make a good faith effort to meet the goals and timetables for minority employment set for the local region by the governing administrative agency, the Labor Department Office of Federal Contract Compliance Programs. *Id.* § 60-4.6. The present nationwide goal is for immediate minority utilization equal to the percentage of minorities in the local labor force. 45 Fed. Reg. 65979, 65903 (1980). The affirmative action obligations for nonconstruction and construction contractors apply without regard to whether the contractor has discriminated in the past. The Executive Order also provides for a wide range of penalties for noncompliance, including cancellation of the contract and ineligibility for all future federal contracts. Exec. Order No. 11246, *supra*, § 202(2), 209.

[47] As many as two-thirds of the jobs in the national labor market may be in firms affected by the Executive Order. See LEONARD, THE IMPACT OF AFFIRMATIVE ACTION 133 (1983); *cf.* Rousea, *Enforcing a Clear Mandate*, 7 J. INTERGROUP REL. 4 (1979) (one-third). Smith & Welch, *Affirmative Action and Labor Markets*, 2 J. LABOR ECON. 269, 280–83 (1984), report statistics showing that from 1970 to 1980, all the improvement in black employment in private sector firms subject to EEOC reporting requirements under Title VII actually took place in federal contractors subject to Executive Order 11246. LEONARD, *supra*, has demonstrated the causal effect of the incentives generated under the Executive Order. From 1974

ecutive Order establishes a highly controversial set of affirmative action requirements. There are politically powerful forces, capable of forcing the issue into the national political agenda, that would have this powerful vehicle for color-conscious distribution of jobs meet the same fate as did the judicial order in *Stotts*. Third, while *Stotts* dealt with and was constrained by Title VII, there are other statutes that prohibit discrimination by both public and private employers.[48] These statutory provisions forbid only intentional discrimination,[49] a legal condition not established in *Stotts*. But when the issue of remedies for intentional discrimination does arise, the Court will not be able to rely on the special language and legislative history of Title VII. It will need to formulate a judicial definition of the appropriate scope of remedial policy.[50]

A. THE MODEL OF INDIVIDUAL JUSTICE

At the center of the Model of Individual Justice[51] is the antidiscrimination principle—"the general principle disfavoring classifica-

through 1980, the fact of being subject to federal contract compliance (rather than Title VII alone) increased the initial black share of employment with contractors by 17% for males and 15% for females. *Id.* at 120. In view of the federal contractors' share of the overall labor market, this implies that the Executive Order increased the total demand for black male workers by 12% and for female blacks by 10%. *Id.* at 120. The broad dicta of *Stotts* conceivably could have legal implications for Executive Order 11246. If Title VII expresses a congressional decision to limit racial remedies to the proved individual victims of employment discrimination, the Executive Order's affirmative action requirements could be vulnerable to judicial invalidation as incompatible with the statute. See *Weber*, 443 U.S. at 209 n.9 (leaving open whether affirmative action efforts to comply with Executive Order 11246 could be incompatible with Title VII).

[48] See 42 U.S.C. 1981 and 42 U.S.C. 1983.

[49] See Washington v. Davis, 426 U.S. 229 (1976); General Building Contractors Assn. v. Pennsylvania, 457 U.S. 375 (1982).

[50] A case presenting this issue, NAACP Detroit Branch v. Detroit Police Officers Ass'n, 35 Fair Empl. Prac. Cas. (BNA) 631 (D. Mich. 1984), has arisen from a factual situation similar to that in Memphis. The Detroit police force recruited large numbers of black police officers in the 1970s to remedy earlier discrimination in hiring. But the City's fiscal problems required major layoffs in 1979 and 1980, and the application of a seniority provision in the City's collective agreement meant that the burden fell disproportionately on black officers. In this context, the district court held that layoffs in order of seniority amounted to intentional discrimination, forbidden under both the Fourteenth Amendment and § 1983. It ordered the recall of all the black police officers who wished to return. *Id.* at 641. Interestingly, the district court also ordered the City not to lay off any senior white police officers pending a further inquiry into the nature and force of their contractual rights.

[51] Judicial opinions reflecting the principles of the Model of Individual Justice, and exhibiting elements that we have used to define it, include Arizona Governing Comm. v. Norris, 103 S.Ct. 3492, 3498 (1983) (opinion of Marshall, J.); Connecticut v. Teal, 457 U.S. 440, 453–54 (1982); Fullilove v. Klutznick, 448 U.S. 448, 522–27 (1980) (Stewart, J., dissenting);

tions and other decisions and practices that depend on the race (or ethnic origin) of the parties affected."[52] Because racial classifications have been used historically to deny the moral worth of human beings, and because race is almost never relevant to any morally permissible purpose, this model holds that race-based decision making ought to be prohibited.[53] But the Model of Individual Justice does not represent simply an ad hoc rejection of racial bias. On the contrary, within this model the antidiscrimination principle derives strength from its location in a cluster of conventional moral values. However vague, these values all reflect a view of individual human beings, each entitled to respect and concern, as the fundamental elements of the moral and legal universe.[54] Within this value scheme, the ideal of human equality represents an important article of moral faith.[55] But equally important are values—reflecting respect for individual autonomy, merit, and achievement—that may foster distributive inequalities.[56] Although welfare statutes may establish the minimal requirements of social justice, above that floor the Model of Individual Justice recognizes the right of individual human beings to reap the benefits of their own hard work and personal talents.

Regents of the Univ. of California v. Bakke, 438 U.S. 265, 289–90, 293, 299, 307, 318 (1979) (opinion of Powell, J., announcing the judgment of the Court); Franks v. Bowman Transp. Co., 424 U.S. 747, 780–81 (1976) (Burger, C.J., concurring in part and dissenting in part); DeFunis v. Odegaard, 416 U.S. 312, 343 (1974) (Douglas, J., dissenting). Among the commentators, see notes 53–65 *infra* and accompanying text.

[52] Brest, note 5 *supra*, at 1.

[53] In Alexander Bickel's frequently quoted words, the Model of Individual Justice affirms that the "lesson of the great decisions of the Supreme Court and the lesson of contemporary history have been the same for at least a generation: discrimination on the basis of race is illegal, immoral, unconstitutional, inherently wrong, and destructive of democratic society." Bickel, The Morality of Consent 133 (1975).

[54] See, *e.g.*, Regents of the Univ. of California v. Bakke, 438 U.S. 265 (opinion of Powell, J., announcing the judgment of this Court); Reynolds, *Individualism v. Group Rights: The Legacy of Brown*, 93 Yale L.J. 995, 1003 (1984).

[55] See H.R. Rep. No. 914, 88th Cong., 1st Sess. (1963), at 30, reprinted in EEOC, Legislative History of Titles VII and XI of Civil Rights Acts of 1964, at 2151: "Aside from the political and economic considerations, however, we believe in the creation of job equality because it is the right thing to do. We believe in the dignity of man. He is born with certain inalienable rights. His uniqueness is such that we refuse to treat him as if his rights and well-being are bargainable. All vestiges of inequality based solely on race must be removed in order to preserve our democratic society, to maintain our country's leadership and enhance mankind."

[56] See Reynolds, note 54 *supra*, at 1004; Meltzer, *The Weber Case: The Judicial Abrogation of the Antidiscrimination Standard in Employment*, 47 U. Chi. L. Rev. 423, 424 (1980); see generally Fallon, *To Each according to His Ability, From None according to His Race: The Concept of Merit in the Law of Antidiscrimination*, 60 B.U. L. Rev. 815, 840–43 (1980).

Beyond prohibition of race-based decision making, the Model of Individual Justice assumes that the allocation of people to jobs should be left to the relatively free functioning of the labor market. At least three values—which themselves may stand in an interesting state of tension—commend this approach. First, the market provides an arena for individual liberty in economic action. Liberty is a good in itself. Second, a market based on free exchange serves the economic aim of allocating persons to the jobs in which they will be most productive. There is accordingly a social welfare justification. Third, on the whole the market rewards merit, effort, and productivity. These virtues deserve cultivation, partly as intrinsically valuable, partly as instrumentally useful to the national community.

The Model of Individual Justice recognizes no exception to the antidiscrimination principle for the "benign" quotas of affirmative discrimination. Where a wrong is done, the Model of Individual Justice prescribes that the wrongdoer must correct it. But the model views the aim of legal remedies as the compensation of victims, not the achievement of any particular pattern of distribution across racial classes. For government to prescribe race as a basis for employment decisions would be thoroughly wrong. Racial quotas would interfere unduly with the liberty of the employer to select the best available employee and would undermine the moral and economic values supporting rewards to individual merit.[57] Moreover, racial quotas predictably would visit the burdens of "reverse discrimination" on innocent whites—an independent moral wrong not justifiable for reasons of policy or convenience.[58]

Reflecting in general the views of the early champions of the American civil rights movement,[59] the Model of Individual Justice finds recurrent expression in both the language and the legislative history of Title VII.[60] First, the protections of Title VII are framed

---

[57] See BICKEL, note 53 *supra*, at 133–34.

[58] See Franks v. Bowman Transp. Co., 424 U.S. 747, 780–81 (1976) (Burger, C.J., concurring in part and dissenting in part); Brest, note 5 *supra*, at 39–43.

[59] See, *e.g.*, Reynolds, note 54 *supra*, at 999–1001 (quoting, among others, Jack Greenberg, Hubert Humphrey, Martin Luther King, Jr., and Roy Wilkins). In *Stotts*, the majority relied on quotations from legislative proponents of Title VII, including Senators Humphrey, Clark, and Case. See 104 S.Ct. at 2589–90.

[60] See, *e.g.*, *Developments in the Law—Employment Discrimination and Title VII of the Civil Rights Act of 1964*, 84 HARV. L. REV. 1109, 1166 (1971).

directly and specifically to safeguard the "individual."[61] Though animated by concern for "the plight of the Negro in our economy,"[62] the statute establishes a general right, benefiting nonminority as well as minority, to be free from discrimination on the basis of race, sex, or national origin.[63] Second, beyond the antidiscrimination strictures, Congress seemingly meant Title VII to effect no fundamental change in the operation of the employment market. Title VII gives expression to the traditional value of equality of opportunity, defined formally to bar the exclusion of talented persons based solely on race. With this exception, the market was intended to continue as the principal determinant of employment opportunities and the resulting distributive outcomes.[64] Third, by purifying the market by preventing hiring based on characteristics presumptively unrelated to efficiency, Title VII conforms with the Model of Individual Justice in favoring rewards for merit.[65] Finally, Title VII gives express protection to the benefits that individual work and achievement have attained, again consistently with individual justice. Even where the effect is to perpetuate the effects of past discrimination, § 703(h) ensures the sanctity of seniority systems and thus protects the expectations of incumbent employees, presumably innocent of their employers' discriminatory acts.

---

[61] See, *e.g.*, Arizona Governing Comm. v. Norris, 103 S.Ct. 3492 (1983).

[62] In United Steelworkers v. Weber, 443 U.S. 193, 202 (1979) (quoting 110 Cong. Rec. 6548 (1964) (remarks of Sen. Humphrey)), the Supreme Court termed this "Congress' primary concern in enacting the prohibition against racial discrimination in Title VII of the Civil Rights Act of 1964."

[63] See McDonald v. Santa Fe Trail Transp. Co., 427 U.S. 273, 280 (1976) (holding that Title VII forbids discriminatory treatment of whites). When opponents of the statute protested that it would establish a requirement of quota hiring, supporters of Title VII not only gave repeated assurances that it would not, but also drafted and introduced the amendment that became Section 706(j), 42 U.S.C. 2000e–2j, which provides that "[n]othing contained in (Title VII) shall be interpreted to require any employer . . . to grant preferential treatment to any individual or to any group" because of racial imbalances in the employer's work force.

[64] Title VII imposes no general obligation of fairness in hiring and firing, and the use of aptitude tests as employment criteria was specifically approved. See Chamallas, *Evolving Conceptions of Equality under Title VII: Disparate Impact Theory and the Demise of the Bottom Line Principle*, 31 UCLA L. REV. 305, 379 (1983).

[65] The principal proponents of Title VII argued that a ban on racial hiring would prod employers to make employment decision on the basis of talents, not prejudice or stereotypes, and thus to achieve the economic benefits of a more efficient work force. See Chamallas, note 64 *supra*, at 306. In a particular context it of course is possible that merit traits will correlate sufficiently well with race that a rational, wealth-maximizing employer would find it economically efficient to engage in racial hiring. See Jencks, *Discrimination and Thomas Sowell*, 30 NEW YORK REV. BOOKS, 33, 37–38 (March 3, 1983). Title VII reflects a judgment that racial hiring should not be permitted even in such cases.

Conceived as a framework for interpreting Title VII, the Model of Individual Justice dominated the early jurisprudence under the statute.[66] Where employers made race a basis for employment decisions, as had been the norm in much of the economy, Title VII struck quickly and powerfully at this illegally "disparate treatment." Nor has time shown the Model of Individual Justice to be obsolescent. Today, more than twenty years after the enactment of Title VII, the Model of Individual Justice continues to protect an ideal of individualized treatment that prohibits employers from acting on race- or gender-based animus, or even on true generalizations about classes defined by race or gender.[67]

It was within the Model of Individual Justice that the Supreme Court decided *Stotts*. The district court had forbidden the disproportionate layoff of blacks, and the Supreme Court construed its injunction as either mandating or at least authorizing the dismissal of more senior whites.[68] So interpreted, the order posed a threat to the seniority interests of "innocent" incumbents—a threat offensive to the Model of Individual Justice and, the Court held, to Title VII's § 703(h). Even more expressive of the Model of Individual Justice, however, was the *Stotts* Court's broader pronouncement that the policy of the Title VII was "to provide make-whole relief only to those who have been actual victims of illegal discrimination."[69] On this view of Title VII, only the individually identified victims of discrimination should be entitled to the benefits of a judicial remedy; and no individual white, innocent of personal wrongdoing, should be dispreferred as an incident of race-conscious relief.

The Model of Individual Justice supplies a context in which this view is rooted in morality and economics as well as sources of

---

[66] But *cf.* Blumrosen, *Strangers in Paradise: Griggs v. Duke Power Co. and the Concept of Employment Discrimination*, 71 MICH. L. REV. 59, 70–71 & n.46, 74 (1972).

[67] Even now its implications are occasionally controversial. For example, actuarial tables show that women have a longer life expectancy than men. See City of Los Angeles Dep't of Water and Power v. Manhart, 435 U.S. 702, 704 (1978). Despite strong economic arguments for a contrary result, the Supreme Court has held that Title VII requires individualized treatment and therefore forbids an employer to take account of this difference in fixing either employee contributions, see *id.*, or employee benefits under employee-funded retirement schemes, see Arizona Governing Comm. v. Norris, 103 S.Ct. 3492 (1983). Actuarial tables based on racial differences would warrant a similar condemnation. *Id.* at 3498.

[68] See note 16 *supra*.

[69] 104 S.Ct. at 2589.

positive law. But Justice White's reasoning on the broad issue of permissible remedies—largely composed of excerpts from the 1964 legislative history[70]—is bereft of moral, philosophical, economic, or policy discussion. The paucity of argument is disappointing, not least because it gives no clue as to why the issue of remedial quotas has preoccupied so many judges, lawyers, and scholars, or how it could be that the courts of appeals are unanimous in their approval of quota remedies.

It also fails to reckon with two factors that have changed since the moral consensus of 1964 behind the Model of Individual Justice. First, there has emerged a coherent, powerful, and jurisprudentially plausible alternative. Briefly sketched by Justice Blackmun in dissent, the starting point for the competing position is that the role of civil rights law is not just to compensate individual victims of specific acts of discrimination, but to provide race-conscious relief to undo or prevent the classwide effects of racial injustice.

The second changed factor has been the emergence of powerful critiques, directed to the practical and philosophical merits of the Model of Individual Justice. One criticism is that it misconceives the deep structure of race discrimination, and thus renders the fundamental problem incapable of solution. The Model of Individual Justice imagines, as its paradigmatic wrong, an employer consciously making a racially based employment decision, reflecting either racial animus or a racial stereotype.[71] The standard remedy would involve a prohibitory injunction against the perpetrator, together with compensation to the individual victim for the wrong done to him, with the cost borne directly by the wrongdoer and not, for example, by an innocent employee. It can be argued, however, that the problems of employment discrimination are as often institutional as individual, inhering in "institutionalized societal practices and policies, such as testing procedures, subjective selection standards, race and sex-role stereotypes, and seniority rules"[72]

[70] See *id.* at 2588–90.

[71] The framers of Title VII had similar expectations. See S. Rep. No. 415, 92nd Cong., 1st Sess. (1971), at 5, quoted in part with approval in Franks v. Bowman Transp. Co., 424 U.S. 747, 765 n.21 (1976).

[72] Belton, *Discrimination and Affirmative Action: An Analysis of Competing Theories of Equality and Weber*, 59 N.C. L. REV. 531, 545 (1981). See Freeman, *Legitimizing Racial Discrimination through Antidiscrimination Law: a Critical Review of Supreme Court Doctrine*, 62 MINN. L. REV. 1049, 1052–53 (1978).

that have the effect of excluding disproportionate numbers of blacks from desirable jobs. The problem is partly one of costs and incentives: victimized individuals may not seek remedies for the injuries that they suffer; the costs of a lawsuit may be too high, the wrongs too difficult to prove. But also troublesome is the Model of Individual Justice's definition of discrimination: the problem may not be racial animus but racial effect; not intent to exclude individuals but practices that keep out blacks as a group; not willful decisions but continued application of criteria, often unjustified by business needs, that have a racially differential impact. If this diagnosis is correct, race discrimination may not be eliminatable without pervasive systemic reform, unattainable within the conceptual apparatus and remedial limitations that the Model of Individual Justice prescribes.

A related challenge to the Model of Individual Justice addresses its philosophical foundations. The Model of Individual Justice, with its conceptions of equal treatment and equality of opportunity, accepts individuals as it finds them upon their entry into the labor market. Their entitlements, at least in the employment market, are a function of their currently demonstrable aptitudes. But current talents and abilities correlate closely with educational and cultural background; the lone individual does not stand independent of history as he or she confronts the meritocratic world. Moreover, it surely is no coincidence that groups traditionally victimized by discrimination, especially blacks, not only suffer economic disadvantage but are able to demonstrate disproportionately few of the qualities and aptitudes most favored by employers.[73] If current disabilities are traceable to past wrongs, it is possible to argue that historical injustices to disadvantaged groups are not irrelevant to the demands of justice in the current day. More specifically, arguments have emerged for a theory of employment discrimination that makes allowances and prescribes corrections for the unhappy historical legacy.

B. THE MODEL OF GROUP JUSTICE

The Model of Group Justice interprets the leading civil rights laws, including the Fourteenth Amendment, as intended primarily

---

[73] See Griggs v. Duke Power Co., 401 U.S. 424, 430 (1971).

to protect and advance the interests of historically disadvantaged groups, especially blacks.[74] This model emerges less from philosophical abstraction than from perceptions of historical and sociological fact. American blacks were first subjected to slavery, then relegated to segregation and poverty.[75] And, the Model of Group Justice emphasizes, cultures of poverty and ignorance perpetuate themselves through the generations. The deprivations of grandfathers and grandmothers thus are visited on fathers and mothers, sons and daughters.[76]

Consistent with its group orientation, the Model of Group Justice holds that employment practices that have a racially disparate impact should be at least presumptively illegal.[77] Nor would this model limit the scope of the remedy to compensation of direct victims of the legal wrong. Regarding race-based wrongs as harming all members of the stigmatized group, the Model of Group Justice affirms the appropriateness of group-benefiting quota remedies.[78]

Although seldom reflected explicitly in the initial legislative history of Title VII, the Model of Group Justice accords with what was clearly one of Congress's predominant purposes: to open em-

---

[74] Judicial opinions reflecting the principles of the Model of Group Justice, and suggesting the elements we have used to construct it, include *Weber*, 443 U.S. at 202–07 (1979); *Bakke*, 438 U.S. at 363, 369 (1978) (opinion of Brennan, White, Marshall, and Blackmun, J.J., concurring in part and dissenting in part); *id.* at 387–402 (opinion of Marshall, J. concurring in part and dissenting in part); Fullilove v. Klutznick, 448 U.S. 448, 517–28 (1979) (concurring opinion of Marshall, J.) Griggs v. Duke Power Co., 401 U.S. 424 (1971). Among the commentators, see, *e.g.*, Belton, note 72 *supra;* Blumrosen, *The Group Interest Concept, Employment Discrimination, and Legislative Intent: The Fallacy of Connecticut v. Teal*, 20 HARV. J. LEG. 99 (1983); Fiss, *Groups and the Equal Protection Clause*, 5 PHIL. & PUB. AFF. 107 (1976); Freeman, note 72 *supra*.

[75] See *Bakke*, 438 U.S. at 387–94 (Marshall, J., concurring in part and dissenting in part). See generally WOODWARD, THE STRANGE CAREER OF JIM CROW (3d ed. 1974).

[76] Linking current social problems with historical injustices, proponents of affirmative action and race-conscious remedies sometimes have emphasized the relevance of the Thirteenth Amendment, the constitutional provision abolishing slavery and investing Congress with enforcement power. See, *e.g.*, Williams v. City of New Orleans, 34 Fair Empl. Prac. Cas. 1009, 1028–31 (5th Cir. 1984) (*en banc*) (Wisdom, J., dissenting).

[77] See, *e.g.*, Belton, note 72 *supra*, at 538–552; Blumrosen, note 74 *supra*, at 99–103.

[78] A representative discussion of the constitutional limits of group remedies appears in the concurring and dissenting opinion that Justice Brennan, White, Marshall, and Blackmun jointly authored in *Bakke*, 438 U.S. at 356–62 (1978). In the private employment context, Justice Brennan's opinion for the Court in *Weber*, 443 U.S. 193 (1979), which is written from a group justice perspective, would demand a predicate of past discrimination in the affected job categories and would impose some limits on the extent and duration of affirmative action preferences. See *id.* at 208–09.

ployment opportunities that previously had been closed to blacks and other minorities.[79] As a jurisprudential construct, the group justice model rose to prominence in the late 1960s and early 1970s, when impatience mounted with persisting conditions of black economic inequality.[80] Today it is possible to identify at least two types of group-based theory, one weak and one strong, which appear to be supported by divergent rationales. But it is the strong version that lies at the heart of current debate.

The weaker of the group-based approaches attempts to justify only "disparate impact" theory, a theory of Title VII employment discrimination approved specifically by the Supreme Court in *Griggs v. Duke Power Co.*[81] Disparate impact theory does not require a plaintiff to establish that an employer had any intention to discriminate. Instead, the plaintiff need only show that an employment test or practice, neutral on its face, excludes from employment opportunities a disproportionate number of minority applicants. Once a showing of disparate impact has been made, the burden shifts to the employer to demonstrate that its practice is justified by "business necessity."[82]

Champions of disparate impact theory have sometimes portrayed it as supplementing rather than supplanting the Model of Individual Justice. On this interpretation, discriminatory impact has its moral and theoretical force as evidence of intentional, race-based decision making.[83] Because of "the unique difficulties of dealing with discriminatory intent or motive,"[84] concerns of practicality and convenience may justify findings of unlawfulness predicated on group impact alone. But the animating purpose remains that of uprooting intentional discrimination against discrete individuals; the ideal to be advanced is not equality of achievement for blacks as

---

[79] See, *e.g.*, 443 U.S. 193, 204–05 (1979); Belton, note 72 *supra*, at 539 & n.30; Blumrosen, note 74 *supra*, at 122–23.

[80] For a report of this phenomenon and a partial endorsement, see Fiss, *The Fate of an Idea Whose Time Has Come: Antidiscrimination Law in the Second Decade after Brown v. Board of Education*, 41 U. CHI. L. REV. 742, 765–70 (1974).

[81] 401 U.S. 424 (1971).

[82] Dothard v. Rawlinson, 433 U.S. 321, 332 n.14 (1977); Griggs v. Duke Power Co., 401 U.S. 424, 431 (1971).

[83] See, *e.g.*, International Bhd. of Teamsters v. United States, 431 U.S. 324, 339–40 & n.20 (1977); Brest, note 5 *supra*, at 26–31.

[84] *Id.* at 26.

compared with whites, but equality of opportunity for individual blacks who are harmed by discriminatory practices.[85] Disparate impact lawsuits thus may be brought by individual blacks.[86] And the theory seemingly accords with the meritocratic values of the Model of Individual Justice.[87]

Whatever certain proponents may argue, however, two difficulties inhere in this essentially individualistic justification for group-based findings of liability. First, under disparate impact theory, proof of nondiscriminatory intent does not excuse an employer from liability.[88] Accordingly, an irreducible conceptual as well as practical divergence separates the disparate impact theory from the disparate treatment paradigm of the Model of Individual Justice.[89]

Second, disparate impact analysis rejects the principle of color blindness. It puts group concepts and statistics inevitably at the center of litigation.[90] It also gives rise to a racial distinction within the law: although blacks and minorities can sue on disparate impact

---

[85] *Cf. Griggs*, 401 U.S. at 431.

[86] See Mitchell v. Board of Trustees, 599 F.2d 582, 584, 584–85 (4th Cir. 1979); Spurlock v. United Airlines, Inc., 475 F.2d 216, 218 (10th Cir. 1972).

[87] By requiring that employment tests with racially disparate impact "must measure the person for the job and not the person in the abstract," 401 U.S. at 436, *Griggs* may have aspired to "transform the theory of meritocracy into reality." Belton, note 72 *supra*, at 545.

[88] See *Griggs*, 401 U.S. at 432.

[89] From one perspective this might not appear a significant movement: the employer's liability rests on a close analogue to negligence, which imputes fault based on failure to take reasonable steps to avoid a disparate impact. In fact, the shift to a negligence-type theory entails an enormous departure from the Model of Individual Justice's conception of equality of opportunity and, more importantly, from its principles of autonomy and fairness. The leading disparate impact case, *Griggs*, is illustrative. Embracing disparate impact theory, the Supreme Court reasoned in *Griggs* that black applicants for employment had suffered the disadvantages of inferior public education and accordingly that it was unfair to allow the employer to judge blacks on the basis of tests of general knowledge and education. Although the Court did not acknowledge it, this line of analysis essentially abandoned the traditional conception of equal opportunity associated with the Model of Individual Justice, which uses as its starting point the person as he enters the labor market. Further, by precluding the employer's using unvalidated but widely utilized tests, the Court effectively imposed on the employer an obligation to compensate for past societal discrimination, especially in the schools. The individualistic premises of the Model of Individual Justice would regard it as unfair to burden an employer on the basis of past wrongs committed not by him but by third parties.

[90] Not only does the plaintiff establish a prima facie case by showing that an employment test or practice has a disproportionately exclusionary impact on the group, but if an employer then wants to defend a test, it may need to engage in "differential validation"—that is, show that the test is as good a predictor of job performance for blacks, as a group, as it is for whites as a separate group. See Albemarle Paper Co. v. Moody, 422 U.S. 405, 435 (1975).

theories, white males cannot.[91] Finally, and perhaps of greatest practical significance, the threat of disparate impact liability creates a powerful incentive for employers to engage in quota hiring.[92] The group implications of disparate impact theory therefore cannot be avoided. Yet the weaker version of the Model of Group Justice offers no adequate rationale for regarding the group as a relevant entity entitled to a remedial quota or preference.[93]

The stronger, more straightforward version of the group justice model holds that the group is an independently relevant entity, not merely a construct invoked to prove individual discrimination. The nub of the theory is that blacks, and possibly other minorities, should be regarded for some purposes as an entity, and that the entity should be conceived as having a moral and legal status of its own. With the group thus identified as a morally relevant concept, the wrongs of racial discrimination are regarded as wrongs to the group, not merely to individuals, and the group (as well as its individual members) is held entitled to a remedy.[94] The most influential expositor of a group theory, Owen Fiss,[95] has identified two conditions that must be satisfied for a group to assert morally compelling claims to group justice. First, there must be a longstanding practice, whether social or legal, that makes it both possible and commonplace to "talk about the group without reference to the particular individuals who happen to be its members at any one moment."[96] Second, Fiss imposes a demand of psychological inter-

---

[91] Whenever the Supreme Court has validated disparate impact analysis the case has involved either minorities or women. Chamallas, note 64 *supra*, at 366 & n.299. See also U.S. COMM'N ON CIVIL RIGHTS, AFFIRMATIVE ACTION IN THE 1980s: DISMANTLING THE PROCESS OF DISCRIMINATION 17 n.20 (1981). But see Weisbord v. Michigan State Univ. 495 F. Supp. 1347 (W.D. Mich. 1980).

[92] See Blumrosen, note 74 *supra*, at 101–02. The incentive arises because the validation of tests—the alternative to quotas if disparate impact liability is to be avoided—has proved so difficult. See Meltzer, note 56 *supra*, at 430.

[93] Because judicial remedies for disparate impact violations commonly have taken the form of racial hiring quotas, it might seem arguable that the weaker group approach cannot justify its own remedial prescriptions. But while the weaker group theory provides no strong justification for quota remedies, neither does its logic seem to require them. Quotas—the central interest of *Stotts* and a large issue in the future of antidiscrimination law—thus seem inevitably to implicate a second, stronger version of the Model of Group Justice.

[94] See, *e.g.*, *Bakke*, 438 U.S. at 387–402 (opinion of Marshall, J., concurring in part and dissenting in part); Bayles, *Reparations to Wronged Groups*, 33 ANALYSIS 17 (1973); Taylor, *Reverse Discrimination and Compensatory Justice*, 33 ANALYSIS 185 (1973).

[95] See Fiss, note 74 *supra*.

[96] *Id*. at 148.

dependence. The members of the group must so associate with the group—and, as members of the group, with each other—that the "identity and well-being" of individual members is "linked" with their perceptions of the status and well-being of the group as a whole.[97]

Even if the validity of the group concept is conceded, it still might be objected that the most frequently prescribed remedy, a racial quota, cannot be justified. Remedial justice, at least traditionally understood, has typically prescribed compensation from a wrongdoer to a specific victim.[98] Departing from this paradigm, quota remedies frequently result in the disadvantaging of white males, personally innocent of any racial wrongs. And this, arguably, is unfair. To answer this objection, the Model of Group Justice must rely on a concept of "past" or "societal" discrimination.[99] Asserting that past societal discrimination has constituted blacks as a perpetual underclass, the model must contend that racial preferences are necessary to remedy historical wrongs, long antedating the triggering statutory violation, that are taxable less to the guilty employer than to the society as a whole.

This argument appears to create a kind of symmetry within the Model of Group Justice: if widespread acts of racism have created a legacy of poverty and disadvantage, then the remedial obligation—as well as the remedial entitlement—seems to have at least a group dimension. But the appearance is deceiving. Although they constitute a racial class, whites do not satisfy the conditions of historical labeling and psychological interdependence necessary to constitute them as a "group" in the relevant sense.[100] The burdens of affirmative action thus must be recognized to fall less on a group than on discrete individuals, such as the white males who are disadvantaged by employment preferences for minorities.[101] The claims of

---

[97] *Id.* at 148–49.

[98] See, *e.g.*, ARISTOTLE, NICHOMACHEAN ETHICS 405 (McKeon ed. 1947).

[99] See Fiss, note 80 *supra*, at 769–70.

[100] See text accompanying notes 95–96 *supra*.

[101] Not surprisingly, therefore, group justice arguments characteristically blur the concept of remedial and distributive justice. While the argument for racial preferences often is cast in remedial terms, see, *e.g.*, Bayles, note 94 *supra*, quota remedies do not effect specific restitution from wrongdoer to victim. Rather, an employer's conviction of wrongdoing provides the occasion for undertaking an enterprise of redistribution—the according of preferences to blacks or other minorities who otherwise would not receive them. But this redistribution is not justified on the theory that an individual black deserves the preference as a matter of

blacks to group justice simply are conceived as sufficiently compelling to justify the imposition of burdens on individual dispreferred whites.[102]

Despite the generally individualistic tenor of American jurisprudence,[103] by the late 1970s important themes in civil rights law resonated increasingly well with the Model of Group Justice. In *Griggs*,[104] the Supreme Court found that Title VII's general prohibition of race discrimination was broad enough to sustain a disparate impact theory, which is rooted in group-based concepts.[105] Moreover, the general remedial provision of Title VII is entirely open textured in its authorization to the federal courts to order such relief as they may deem appropriate, and the courts of appeals are unanimous in finding there a warrant for remedial quotas.[106] Acting outside of Title VII, the executive branch had strengthened Executive Order 11246 to establish numerical targets and timetables that must be satisfied by employers which have contracts with the federal government.[107] And in a series of cases the Executive Order has received the judicial imprimatur of federal courts of appeals.[108] Too, when Congress adopted the 1972 amendments to Title VII, it appeared to endorse the group-based legal developments proliferating in both the judicial and executive branches.[109] An analysis ac-

---

distributive justice—the term "distributive justice" traditionally has applied to burdens and benefits distributed by political authorities, based on the personal merit, needs, or achievements of the recipient. See, *e.g.*, FEINBERG, SOCIAL PHILOSOPHY 107 (1973). It is supported as made appropriate by past discrimination against blacks as a group.

[102] Rejected are arguments by the dispreferred that to lose a job is to pay more than their fair share of any group-based program of racial preferences.

[103] See, *e.g.*, Horwitz, *The Jurisprudence of Brown and the Dilemmas of Liberalism*, 14 HARV. C.R.-C.L. L. REV. 599, 606–10 (1979).

[104] 401 U.S. 424 (1971).

[105] See text accompanying notes 81–93 *supra*.

[106] For a collection of cases, see *Stotts*, 104 S.Ct. at 2606 n.10 (Blackmun, J., dissenting). Essentially ignoring these cases and their rationales, the *Stotts* majority seemed to suggest that remedial quotas were barred by the plain language of Section 706(g), 42 U.S.C. 2000e-5(g) (1982) (which it quoted in a footnote, 104 S.Ct. 2589 n.12). Compare 104 S.Ct. at 2608 (Blackmun, J., dissenting).

[107] See note 47 *supra*.

[108] See, *e.g.*, Contractors Ass'n v. Schultz, 442 F.2d 159 (3d Cir.), *cert. denied*, 404 U.S. 854 (1971).

[109] Committee reports in both the House and the Senate included language generally supportive of disparate impact theory, see S. Rep. No. 415, 92d Cong., 2d Sess. 5 (1971); H.R. Rep. No. 238, 92d Cong., 2d Sess. 68–69 (1972), and the House report referred to *Griggs* with specific approbation. See *id.* at 5 n.1.

companying the final bill stated that "it was assumed that the present case law as developed by the courts would continue to govern the applicability and construction of Title VII."[110] In addition, both the House and the Senate rejected amendments that would have precluded the use of race-conscious measures under the Executive Order or the 1964 Civil Rights Act.[111]

Finally, at the end of the 1970s, the Supreme Court itself adopted a group-based approach—consistent with and supporting surrounding legal developments—when it addressed the lawfulness of voluntary affirmative action programs. In *United Steel Workers v. Weber*,[112] the Court upheld an affirmative action quota that reserved half the slots in an employee training program for black applicants. Justice Brennan's opinion for the Court stressed the purpose of Title VII to improve "the plight of the Negro in our economy."[113] Despite Title VII's recurrent references to the individual, the majority found the statute's economic aspiration, defined in group terms, to be controlling. While *Weber* presented only a statutory question, *Fullilove v. Klutznick*[114] affirmed the constitutionality of a congressionally mandated quota system reserving fixed percentages of government contracts for minority businesses. Although the direct beneficiaries were not themselves proved victims, the Court apparently found it sufficient that minorities as a group had suffered past discrimination, and that Congress had enacted the quotas to eradicate the continuing legacy of group prejudice.[115]

Justice Blackmun's *Stotts* dissent embodied an appeal to the

---

[110] 118 CONG. REC. 7166 (1972).

[111] Ordinarily the Supreme Court will not place much weight on the views of a later Congress in interpreting the meaning of a provision adopted by an earlier Congress, and in International Bhd. of Teamsters v. United States, 431 U.S. 324, 354 n.39 (1977), the Supreme Court found the 1964 legislative history controlling in reaching a decision about the scope of the seniority provision, § 703(h). But powerful arguments supported a contrary conclusion even in that context. See *id.* at 390–94 (Marshall, J., dissenting). Moreover, it is entirely unclear that the Teamsters holding or logic should extend to an interpretation of § 706(g), the general remedial provision, which was itself rewritten and broadened in 1972 by the 92d Congress.

[112] 443 U.S. 193 (1979).

[113] *Id.* at 202 (quoting 110 CONG. REC. 6548 (1964) (remarks of Sen. Humphrey)).

[114] 448 U.S. 448 (1980).

[115] Although there was no majority opinion in the case, the two opinions that were each joined by three of the Justices composing the six-member majority are in accord on this point. See *id.* at 472–89 (opinion of Burger, C.J., joined by White and Powell, J.J.); *id.* at 517–19 (opinion of Marshall, J., joined by Brennan and Blackmun, J.J.).

Model of Group Justice in the layoff context. Carefully developing a distinction between "individual relief and race-conscious class relief,"[116] Justice Blackmun noted with apparent approbation that "the Courts of Appeals are unanimously of the view that race-conscious affirmative relief can be 'appropriate' " under Title VII.[117] Justice Blackmun did not attempt to justify quotas in the traditional terms of remedial justice, which restores to a specific victim that which a specific wrongdoer has taken from him. Instead, the dissent portrayed race-conscious remedies as attempting a kind of class-based redistribution, noting that "[t]he distinguishing feature of race-conscious relief is that no individual member of the disadvantaged class has a claim to it, and individual beneficiaries need not show that they were themselves victims of the discrimination for which relief was granted."[118] Having argued at length that the *Stotts* case was moot,[119] the dissent appropriately satisfied itself with sketching positions rather than resolving issues. But Justice Blackmun even provided a Model of Group Justice rationale for departing from precedents that had protected seniority systems against restructuring by remedial orders. The earlier cases, Justice Blackmun argued, had dealt with claims to individual relief. Because the issue of classwide relief had not been expressly presented in the Court's leading case on seniority remedies, Justice Blackmun found that the prior decision had "little relevance"[120] for the *Stotts* issue, and he considered the Court free to entertain a group justice approach even to class-based remedies upsetting settled seniority rights.

C. CONFLICT OR COEXISTENCE?

Framed as alternatives, as they were in *Stotts*, the Model of Individual Justice and the Model of Group Justice pose for decision a morally and legally wrenching choice.[121] Group-focused preferences commend themselves as necessary to improve the economic status of minority groups and possibly to eliminate divisive and

[116] 104 S.Ct. at 2605 (Blackmun, J., dissenting).

[117] *Id.* at 2606.

[118] *Id.*

[119] See *id.* at 2596–2600.

[120] *Id.* at 2608.

[121] *Cf.* Calabresi, *Bakke as Pseudo-Tragedy*, 28 CATH. U. L. REV. 427 (1979).

debilitating structures of racial caste.[122] To this end the Model of Individual Justice simply seems not merely inadequate in an instrumental sense, but also morally inadequate to the special case of racialism in American history.

On the other hand, there loom two large issues of fairness. First, affirmative discrimination is impossible to defend within the traditional categories of distributive justice or corrective justice.[123] A question therefore arises whether, even in principle, a program of group-based preferences can be justified. Second, "benign" racial preferences are not costless. Preferential employment remedies typically result in the exclusion from employment opportunities of a class of persons, most often white males, who themselves may be innocent of any race-based wrongdoing.[124] Moreover, this excluded class may comprise the relatively least advantaged whites, who may have enjoyed no personal advantages traceable to past racial injustices.

In *Firefighters v. Stotts*, the Supreme Court tipped strongly in the direction of the Model of Individual Justice—a movement entailing important sacrifices, so long as the issue is framed as between the familiarly contending perspectives. But it is as unlikely as it would be undesirable that *Stotts* reflected an ultimate legal choice. Not cited in *Stotts* was the *Weber* case,[125] infused with the Model of Group Justice, in which the Supreme Court found Title VII to authorize voluntary hiring quotas by private employers. *Stotts* made no reference to Executive Order 11246. And the *Stotts* rationale, focused on remedies, leaves untouched the group logic embedded in disparate-impact theories of employment discrimination.

After *Stotts* as before, the Model of Individual Justice and the Model of Group Justice are in a relation of as yet unrationalized conflict. Each of the models possesses substantial normative power and jurisprudential plausibility, and each has at times commended itself to nearly every Justice of the Supreme Court.

---

[122] See, *e.g.*, Fiss, note 74 *supra*, at 151.

[123] See note 101 *supra*. It may be especially problematic that the beneficiaries frequently will be those least likely to have suffered the effects of race-based injustice. See GOLDMAN, JUSTICE AND REVERSE DISCRIMINATION 90–91 (1979).

[124] The burden tends to fall on young white males just entering the job market, rather than on those who may have been parties to past injustices in the employment market. See *id.* at 114–15.

[125] United Steelworkers v. Weber, 443 U.S. 193 (1979).

Debate generally has focused on which of these models ought to be preferred. A more fruitful inquiry may be whether there is some third alternative, which would avoid the need for a tragic election and achieve at least a partial reconciliation at the level of values.

IV. The Model of Social Justice

Issues of racial justice can be viewed as subsuming at least two questions. One involves the required affirmative predicates for programs of affirmative action and race-conscious remedies—the conditions that must be satisfied to justify even in principle a program of race-conscious redistribution. Another involves the fairness of cost allocation. Programs of affirmative discrimination entail costs, and many impose those costs directly on particular "dispreferred" individuals.

Although there are two questions,[126] the Models of Individual Justice and of Group Justice each allow but one mode of response. The Model of Individual Justice answers both questions from an individualistic perspective: only those personally harmed by illegal discrimination should be entitled to a remedy, and the costs should not be borne by persons individually innocent of wrongdoing. The Model of Group Justice, viewing discrimination as a wrong against a group, favors group remedies and does not shrink from imposing the costs on "innocent" individual whites.

The law undoubtedly has unfolded less symmetrically. But it does exhibit at least hints of a pattern, traceable along the divide between the two questions that we have distinguished. In cases defining Title VII violations and establishing the necessary predicates for voluntary affirmative action, the Supreme Court very often has reached the results commended by the Model of Group Justice. Group logic underlies the disparate impact theory endorsed in *Griggs*.[127] And while *Griggs* may not logically justify quota remedies, lower courts have regarded them as the natural remedial com-

[126] The distinction between the two questions undoubtedly can be blurred or even collapsed; it is possible to frame only the single question whether a particular program of affirmative discrimination, involving its specific benefits and costs, ought to be implemented. For us, however, the relevant issues are exposed more clearly and helpfully when the two questions are separated: attention is focused first on the arguments supporting affirmative action, then on the costs, in a way that systematically develops the relevant concerns.

[127] See text accompanying notes 82–93 *supra*.

plement to a group-based theory of liability.[128] Even more striking are cases in which the Supreme Court has upheld voluntary racial quotas. In both *Weber* and *Fullilove*, past societal discrimination, defined wholly in group terms, established a sufficient predicate for a quota "remedy." Neither individual wrongdoing nor individual victimization was required.

The Supreme Court has tended to respond differently when an issue of cost allocation to innocents has lain on the surface of a lawsuit. In such cases the Supreme Court, often in the language of equity jurisprudence,[129] recurrently has expressed concern about fairness to individuals. Presenting such a burdening-of-innocents question, *Stotts* follows the line of prior seniority holdings: because of potential harm to senior incumbents, *Teamsters v. United States*[130] held that competitive seniority—potentially disadvantageous to incumbent whites—could be awarded only to the proved victims of unlawful discrimination.[131] And the seniority cases by no means sound an anomalous theme. Even when plaintiffs have sought only financial relief, unrelated to any seniority system, two cases arising from discrimination in the management of employee pension plans have weighed the interests of innocents in prescribing that relief should be prospective only.[132] Precisely because retroactive awards might jeopardize the interests of innocent pensioners, the Court found that damage relief would offend the equitable spirit of Title VII. Upholding voluntary affirmative action, *Weber* conditioned its approval on a finding that the plan under review did not "unnecessarily trammel the interests of white employees."[133] And constitutional cases reflect similar sensitivity to the burdens accompanying race conscious remedies and affirmative action. Most notably, Jus-

[128] See note 106 *supra*.

[129] See, *e.g.*, International Bhd. of Teamsters v. United States, 431 U.S. 324, 374–75 (1977); Franks v. Bowman Transp. Co., Inc., 424 U.S. 747, 777 (1976).

[130] 431 U.S. 324 (1977).

[131] Even in the case of proved victims entitled to take their "rightful places" in the seniority ladder, the lower courts generally have held that no white incumbent can be directly "bumped" from his job to create a position for the victim. Instead the victims must await the development of future vacancies. See, *e.g.*, Patterson v. American Tobacco Co., 535 F.2d 257, 267 (4th Cir. 1976); Local 189, United Papermakers and Paperworkers v. United States, 416 F.2d 980, 988 (5th Cir. 1969).

[132] See Los Angeles Dep't of Water & Power v. Mahnart, 435 U.S. 702, 722–23 (1978); Arizona Governing Comm. v. Norris, 103 S.Ct. 3492, 3509–10 (1983).

[133] 443 U.S. 193, 208 (1979).

tice Powell's demand for individualized consideration of innocent whites defined the Court's position in the famous *Bakke* case.[134]

Although this pattern can be traced at the level of results, Supreme Court jurisprudence has not expressly distinguished between our two questions—one involving the necessary affirmative predicates for racial preferences, the other defining the permissible limits on cost-allocations. But if the Court's holdings support our distinction, the unfolding law would appear to embody a set of moral beliefs not coherently explicable within either the Model of Group Justice or the Model of Individual Justice. It is our aspiration—independent of arguments about the meaning of Supreme Court decisions—to explain why these questions should be addressed separately, and to develop a theory that locates our intuitions in a moral and legal structure. The gist of our theory, which we term the Model of Social Justice, is this:

Pervasive historical racism has marked blacks as a class that still suffers economic, cultural, and social disadvantages. Against this background, strong arguments frequently support "rectification"—the elimination from economic and social institutions of the presumptive incidents of past discrimination, including racial skewings in the distribution of wealth, jobs, power, and opportunities. Rectification expresses a moral rejection, not only of willful, individual wrongs, but of the pervasive systematic discrimination that has left blacks as a class in a status of economic deprivation. Though this undertaking could be justified in terms of social policy, it also reflects a moral stance opposing racial stratification traceable to past wrongs. Attempting to break the historic connection between race and life prospects in American society, rectification attacks both the psychological and economic bases of minority deprivation. Race-conscious remedies help alleviate the sense of rejection and futility left by a system of racial caste, thus encouraging the development of black talents. Too, affirmative discrimination advances the values associated with a broader and more attractive conception of equality of opportunity, which does not take as given the talents of people as they enter the labor market. Assuming a significant correlation between minority status and current deprivation, rectification extends preferences to the most talented minority applicants. It aspires to locate them close to where they would have

[134] Regents of the Univ. of California v. Bakke, 435 U.S. 265, 317, 318 (1978).

been situated but for educational and cultural disadvantages that may be a legacy of historic racism. Often the triggering incident for a program of rectification will be the statutory violation of a particular employer. But the deep, underlying wrongs are social and historical, more than those of a contemporary law violator. In prescribing rectification largely on the basis of past, societal wrongs, our model views issues of racial justice as ones of social justice.[135]

On the other hand, we do not adopt the justifications for racial preferences offered by the Model of Group Justice, nor do we accept its views as to the scope of appropriate remedies. Selecting the justifiable beneficiaries of affirmative discrimination raises significant issues, both at the group and individual level. Furthermore, our model acknowledges that questions of cost allocation raise issues of fairness.[136] The wrongs of racial discrimination often having been social and legal, we believe that, where feasible, the costs should be spread broadly across relevant segments of the economy or the political community.[137] But widespread cost sharing will not always be possible in the labor market, the particular concern of this article. Where cost spreading would be difficult to achieve consistently with the ordinary practices of American government, we assume that the costs of affirmative discrimination—as of any other social policy—may be assigned to identifiable classes of citizens.[138] The mandatory draft in wartime provides a relevant if extreme example of socially imposed individual burdens. We also assume, however, that the moral dubiousness of an assignment of costs will increase with the burden imposed on particular individuals. In fact, outside the most exigent circumstances, some individual sacrifices are too large to be demanded. Thus, beyond

[135] We use the term "justice" in a loose sense. We do not claim that the particular programs commended by our model represent the single and perfect solution commended by principles of natural right. Using the term "social justice" somewhat more colloquially, we mean only to imply that our proposals do not offend anyone's moral rights, and that they are themselves supported by moral and policy arguments that we find convincing.

[136] We do not understand fairness to require that persons could be taxed only with those obligations that result from their individually voluntary acts, such as individual wrongdoing. It is in the nature of national communities that the moral obligations of one historical generation can be passed on to another, much as the national debt can.

[137] For a classic discussion of the possibilities of cost spreading in another context, see CALABRESI, THE COSTS OF ACCIDENTS (1970).

[138] See Sedler, *Racial Preferences and the Constitution: The Societal Interest in the Equal Protection Objective*, 26 WAYNE ST. L. REV. 1227, 1240–45 (1980).

the implicit restraints of our positive justification for affirmative discrimination, considerations of fairness in cost assignment will impose limits on the circumstances in which racial preferences ought to be allowed. The arguments for racial preferences therefore need to be stated clearly and, what is more, linked to their specific contexts of application. Only in particular contexts can the costs of racial quotas—the burdens that they impose on nonbeneficiaries—be weighed with precision, and thus only in context can the full range of concerns—encompassing both benefits and costs—be assessed.[139]

A. THE CIRCUMSTANCES OF RACIAL JUSTICE

America's history has given meaning to race.[140] Uprooted from their ancestral homes and transported in chains to American shores, blacks were sold into a condition of slavery endorsed by a Constitution that promised freedom to everyone else.[141] After that "peculiar institution" was abolished, most of the southern states enacted Jim Crow laws—legislation not merely keeping the freedman in "his place" but "constantly pushing the Negro further down."[142] Ultimately many American blacks undertook a second long trek, this time to northern cities, there to be met by a pattern of social and economic exclusion that largely confined them to living in ghettos.[143]

Past racial injustices have left to the present an appalling legacy.

---

[139] By using the language of "costs" and "benefits" we do not mean to imply that our framework is "utilitarian" in the sense of, *e.g.*, BENTHAM, THE PRINCIPLES OF MORALS AND LEGISLATION (1789). Utilitarianism in this sense views a political or moral decision as correct only if that decision maximizes the average level of satisfaction or pleasure within some relevant community. Although not blind to considerations of pain, pleasure, and utility, we assume that moral principles may have a value not reducible to such currency, and that conflicts of values therefore cannot always be resolved by application of a Benthamite calculus.

[140] See, *e.g.*, Wasserstrom, *Racism, Sexism, and Preferential Treatment: An Approach to the Topics*, 24 UCLA L. REV. 581, 584–87 (1977).

[141] Although the Framers did not explicitly use the words "race" or "slavery," several provisions of the original Constitution implicitly recognize and sanction the legal existence of slavery. *E.g.*, United States Constitution, Art. I, § 9, cl. 1, which forbade Congress to forbid "Importation of such Persons" (before 1808), and Art. IV, § 2, cl. 3, which prevented states from altering the status of any fugitive "held to Service or Labour" in another state, and compelled delivery of fugitives on demand.

[142] See WOODWARD, THE STRANGE CAREER OF JIM CROW 93 (1957).

[143] See, *e.g.*, WILSON, THE DECLINING SIGNIFICANCE OF RACE 62–87 (2d ed. 1980).

The average income of black families is still only slightly more than half that of whites.[144] Black unemployment rates are consistently double those of whites,[145] and while black women have overtaken white women in earnings from work, the black male still earns only two-thirds as much as his white counterpart.[146] These indices of economic deprivation are both cause and effect of a profound dislocation of the black family structure, exhibited in the dramatic growth in single-parent, female-headed households.[147] Nor are the effects of racial injustice measurable solely in poverty statistics. To invoke Wasserstrom's telling comparison:[148]

> Race does not function in our culture as does eye color. Eye color is an irrelevant category; . . . it is not an important cultural fact. . . . It is important to see that race is not like that at all. . . . In our culture to be nonwhite—and especially to be black—is to be treated and seen as a member of a group that is different from and inferior to the group of standard, fully developed white males. . . . That is simply part of the awful truth of our cultural and social history, and a significant feature of the social reality of our culture today.

The impulse to affirmative action and race-conscious remedies has arisen in this economic and social context. In the 1964 Civil Rights Act, Congress expressed the view that racial subordination is morally wrong. At that time the primary engine for correction was the antidiscrimination principle. Within a few years, however,

---

[144] The ratio of median black to white family income, which was 58 percent in 1966, shortly after Title VII came into force, and reached as high as 65 percent in 1975, had dropped all the way back to 55 percent in 1982, in the valley of an economic recession. See CURRENT POPULATION REPORT, note 2 *supra*, at 135.

[145] This ratio of black to white unemployment rates has held from the time Title VII came into force (when it was 8.1 percent black unemployment to 4.1 percent white in 1965) until more recently (13.1 percent vs. 6.3 percent in 1980), in good times (6.4 percent vs. 3.1 percent in 1969) and bad (17.3 percent vs. 8.6 percent in 1982). See ECONOMIC REPORT OF THE PRESIDENT, note 2 *supra*. And these unemployment rates disguise the underlying fact that more and more discouraged blacks have dropped out of the labor market. By mid-1982, the black male nonparticipation rate was up to 28 percent from 17 percent in 1960. As a result, the actual employment rate of black males was only 55 percent, compared with 69 percent for whites. See CENTER FOR THE STUDY OF SOCIAL POLICY, A DREAM DEFERRED: THE ECONOMIC STATUS OF BLACK AMERICANS 19 (1983).

[146] See CURRENT POPULATION REPORT, note 2 *supra*, at 166.

[147] By the early eighties, the number of single-parent, female-headed families was 40 percent for blacks vs. 12 percent for whites. The children of these families accounted for the bulk of black children living in poverty. See Jencks, note 65 *supra*, at 35.

[148] Wasserstrom, note 140 *supra*, at 586–87 (footnote omitted).

there had emerged in judicial,[149] executive,[150] and legislative action[151] an additional policy of affirmative discrimination for blacks, born out of a desire to achieve tangible economic effects. In contrast with the antidiscrimination principle, affirmative discrimination aspired not only to forbid future race-based wrongs but to eradicate the identifiable residues—traceable in racially skewed distributions of wealth, jobs, and education—of past, legally sanctioned injustices.

Prescribing the award of preferences on group-based racial grounds, affirmative discrimination reflected from its inception a departure from the principles more generally prevalent in American law and morality.[152] Nor could this practice be justified within the traditional categories of justice. Affirmative discrimination is not corrective in the classic sense. The immediate beneficiaries are not the actual victims of particular wrongs, and the people on whom the burden is imposed are usually not the perpetrators of those wrongs. Similarly, affirmative discrimination is not often justified as expressing ultimate principles of distributive justice. Long-term commitment to race-based principles would give race a moral significance unjustifiably exalted beyond that attached to other relevant factors, including personal need, effort, achievement, and talent.

If affirmative discrimination is to be supported, the justification must be extraordinary, linked to the unique features of American

---

[149] The most important developments included Griggs v. Duke Power Co., 401 U.S. 424 (1971), in which the Supreme Court expanded the concept of discrimination, and the early cases in the courts of appeals approving quota remedies for Title VII violations, see, *e.g.*, United States v. Ironworkers Local No. 86, 443 F.2d 544 (9th Cir. 1971).

[150] The Office of Federal Contract Compliance had begun as early as 1965 to establish special, geographically targeted programs to assure minority representation in firms doing business with the federal government under Executive Order 11246. The best known of these, the so-called Philadelphia Plan, required bidders for construction projects to establish numerical goals for minority utilization. The Philadelphia Plan was upheld against constitutional challenge in Contractors Assn. of Eastern Pennsylvania v. Schultz, 442 F.2d 159 (3d Cir.), *cert. denied.* 404 U.S. 854 (1971).

[151] See notes 109–11 *supra* and accompanying text.

[152] Among other indications, public opinion polls consistently have registered strong majority support for special programs to assist blacks, but also a strong preference for the merit principle as opposed to racial quotas in hiring. See, *e.g.*, AFFIRMATIVE ACTION AND EQUAL PROTECTION: HEARINGS BEFORE THE SUBCOMMITTEE ON THE CONSTITUTION OF THE SENATE JUDICIARY COMMITTEE ON S.J. RES. 41, 97th Cong., 1st Sess. 939, at 939–52, 1050–51 (1981).

racial history. For us, the justification begins with the intuitive judgment that it is appropriate to afford blacks, as a group, strong positive assistance to eradicate the group-based effects of history.[153] From that starting point, we locate the justification for affirmative discrimination in the conjunction of three factors. We cannot, here, prove all the empirical assumptions on which we rely. Our position is only that it has been and remains as morally and intellectually reasonable to act on these assumptions as on any others.[154]

The first material factor is the history of group-based subordination, aided and abetted by government and by law. The injustices were spread over a long span of time.[155] The experience of blacks differs both quantitatively and qualitatively from that of most if not all national groups in the immigrant generation. Moreover, the implication of the law, within an institutional heritage that shapes a na-

---

[153] By terming the judgment intuitive, we mean only to suggest that the decison as to right and wrong with which we are concerned has not yet been located within or rationalized by any coherent legal or moral theory. See HAMPSHIRE, TWO THEORIES OF MORALITY 6 (1977). By beginning the process of moral reasoning with an intuition as to morally correct behavior, we do not suggest that the starting point is infallible, or that it is not subject to correction after argument and reflection. We do assume, however, that a moral intuition is an appropriate starting point in a moral argument. First, if intuitions can be explained by reference to general moral principles, then it becomes possible to engage in a "two-way traffic by which intuitions are modified by reflection on the general principles that explain them, and the general principles are qualified by the particular cases that do not fit under them." *Id.* at 5. Second, the movement from intuitions to explanatory principles brings into view the possibility of a further testing of the principles themselves—an evaluation of their conformity with a general way of life that can be affirmed as desirable or good. This notion of a "way of life" is vague, and probably has to be. We are concerned with a social ideal, but not a social ideal of the utopian society. In evaluating principles, we therefore mean to acknowledge and accommodate many of the habits, values, institutions, and assumptions that give shape to the society in which we live. As much as any critic, we wish that moral theory could offer an Archimedean perspective on moral issues. But when we are prepared to universalize our moral prescriptions as assertions of first-order moral truths, we are aware that we begin our reflections located in time, place, and culture, and acknowledge a second-order awareness of the cultural influences affecting us.

[154] Rationalizing an intuitive judgment, we seek an explanation of how the intuition might be correct, both in terms of the moral principles that explain it and the empirical propositions needed to show that the moral principles in fact apply. In dealing with empirical questions, our method of initially accepting possible explanations is similar to that commended in NOZICK, PHILOSOPHICAL EXPLANATIONS 8–24 (1981). We are open to evidence concerning the truth of the empirical propositions on which we rely, and we must be prepared to abandon positions ultimately shown to depend on false premises. But we are prepared to act initially on empirical assumptions supported by some evidence, or even plausible hypotheses, even in the absence of "proof." Another way of putting it is to say that we reject the argument that the proponents of affirmative discrimination must prove all disputed empirical assumptions before they are justified in going forward.

[155] See generally WOODWARD, note 75 *supra*, at 81–95.

tional community defined by a shared sense of continuity with the American past, establishes a dimension of social responsibility.[156]

Second, historical wrongs against blacks have had an enduring impact, measurable now in economic and social disparities between racial groups. American blacks are more likely than whites to start life, and to enter the employment market, from a background of low family income and single-parent homes, with little cultural or intellectual stimulation in the family or the neighborhood.[157] All of these factors tend to reduce prospects for educational and cultural advancement.

Third, in at least two respects blacks constitute a group, appropriately treated as such in programs of affirmative discrimination. One stems from the social meaning of blackness. In the labor market, employers have tended to appraise blacks through the lens of unfavorable racial stereotypes,[158] thus depressing the economic prospects even of middle-class blacks.[159] In this context, benefits afforded to one black offer a potential spillover benefit to others. Requiring the hiring of blacks in previously all-white jobs or firms, so that they can be seen as performing capably, may be important in opening doors through which others can follow.[160] Moreover, fuller representation of blacks in positions of responsibility pro-

---

[156] For detailed estimates of the dimensions of these relationships, see JENCKS, WHO GETS AHEAD? THE DETERMINANTS OF ECONOMIC SUCCESS IN AMERICA (1979).

[157] See notes 144–48 *supra* and accompanying text.

[158] See text accompanying note 148 *supra*.

[159] Econometric research has documented some of the barriers that racism has raised against black prospects at all levels of American life. Examining data from the 1962 Survey of Occupational Change in Generation for black and white males, Duncan, *Inheritance of Poverty or Inheritance of Race*, in MOYNIHAN (ed.), ON UNDERSTANDING POVERTY 85 (1968), found that if one compared blacks and whites from homes where family heads had the same levels of education and jobs and where each of the individuals had received the same amount of education and scored the same on intelligence tests, the black worker would receive on average one-quarter less income than the white. In effect, this was the price of being black in America. Fifteen years later, Freeman, *Black Economic Progress after 1964: Who Has Gained and Why?* in ROSEN (ed.), STUDIES IN LABOR MARKETS 247 (1981), confirmed these findings in his analysis of the 1966 National Longitudinal Survey of older blacks and whites (ages 45–59), whose socioeconomic status was largely determined by their experience in the labor market before the Civil Rights Act of 1964 became effective in 1965. Freeman found that differences in region, parental occupation, and personal schooling accounted for only half the black/white disparity in occupational status and earnings. *Id.* at 266–67.

[160] For this purpose, sociological studies suggest that more than a "token" presence of minorities may be needed. Isolated minority workers tend to be the subject of unusually exacting critical scrutiny. When they seek success through exceptionally hard work, they may suffer disabling hostility and resentment from members of the dominant group.

vides some assurance against a reversion to reliance on stereotypes. Second, for many if not most blacks, social and historical experiences have made blackness an important element of self-identity.[161] For this reason, individual perceptions of status, respect, and security may depend on the status and well-being of blacks as a group.[162] As a result, preferences to individual blacks do not constitute mere windfalls to individual beneficiaries. Their aggregate effect—breaking the link between race and economic, cultural, and social status—may advance the aspirations, confidence and self-esteem of other group members.

Implicit in the second and third of these arguments is an acknowledgment of contingency. However true our assumptions may once have been or may be now, the social reality itself could change. In this sense our Model of Social Justice mirrors a familiar belief embedded in the unfolding pattern of civil rights law: that affirmative discrimination is justified by special facts of historical context, to which the historical categories of distributive and remedial justice seem morally inadequate, and that it should be viewed as a short-term response to current exigencies, not as embodying an ultimate vision of the good society.[163]

B. PREFERENCES AND FAIRNESS

The Model of Social Justice assumes that programs of racial preference—even prior to considerations of fairness in cost allocation—are not inherently unjust. Important arguments to the contrary therefore need to be met. These include objections that affirmative discrimination stands on the same moral plane with racial quotas based on bias and that racial preferences abridge the moral rights either of employers or of dispreferred individuals.

1. Quotas and Racial Stigma

The Model of Individual Justice assumes that race is a morally impermissible basis for the assignment of burdens or the award of

[161] See, *e.g.*, Wasserstrom, note 140 *supra*, at 585–87 & n.12.

[162] See, *e.g.*, Fiss, note 74 *supra*, at 148–56.

[163] Undoubtedly there is a danger that racial classifications teach the relevance of race, and that they foster race-based hostility and resentment. Although this concern is not to be dismissed, our view is that the balance of considerations support limitations on the scope and duration of affirmative discrimination, not its outright prohibition.

benefits.[164] Stated in strong form, this view holds that people have a moral right to the benefits of color blindness[165] and that affirmative discrimination must therefore be condemned. There is no doubt that this view resonates with widely shared moral sentiments.[166] But it is important, in considering this view, to be clear about its basis.

One version of the argument appeals to universal ideals of justice or to natural law. But this position lacks the surrounding moral structure that would be necessary to support it. Distinctions on the basis of personal characteristics other than race, even immutable ones, generally are not thought to violate moral rights. If the question is pressed why race should be treated differently, the answer seems to be founded not in natural law but in conventional social meanings. As a matter of social fact, racial distinctions have had a clear meaning, involving the assertion of moral inferiority,[167] and that meaning has been deemed singularly wrong and pernicious.

Once the objection is rooted in social meanings and understandings, however, there is a clear distinction between racial quotas based on exclusionary animus and those, motivated by hatred toward none, that undertake not to stigmatize or exclude any group but to compensate for past social injustices.[168] To say that stigmatizing racial classifications are morally impermissible does not entail that noninsulting distinctions must be forbidden also. Indeed, explanation of the difference suggests that the principle applicable to stigmatizing or insulting quotas should not apply to preferences that aspire only to rectification.

Even after the distinction between two kinds of preferences is established, there remains a further basis for argument. As a matter of social understanding, color blindness stands within a cluster of related values, including those associated with merit, efficiency, and autonomy.[169] Acceptance of race as a basis for distribution of

---

[164] See, *e.g.*, BICKEL, note 53 *supra*, at 133.

[165] For a clear statement, though not an endorsement, of this position, see DWORKIN, TAKING RIGHTS SERIOUSLY 225 (1977).

[166] See note 152 *supra*.

[167] See, *e.g.*, Wasserstrom, note 140 *supra*, at 584–87.

[168] See DWORKIN, note 165 *supra*, at 223–39; Marshall, *A Comment on the Nondiscrimination Principle in a "Nation of Minorities,"* 93 YALE L.J. 1006, 1011–12 (1984).

[169] See Fallon, note 56 *supra*, at 834–40.

jobs and other benefits might threaten all these values. For the response to this argument, the objector will need to wait. To arguments that other values give rise to moral rights against affirmative discrimination, we shall respond below. Here we claim only that affirmative discrimination offends no right not to be morally derogated on account of race.

2. Racial Preferences and Moral Rights

Opponents sometimes argue that affirmative action and race-conscious remedies violate moral rights held by "dispreferred" whites to achieve whatever benefits their talents and efforts otherwise would bring them.[170] This argument requires one of two assumptions. The first is that people have moral rights—for reasons related to merit, but not uniquely dependent on it—to any job that a freely operating labor market (regulated only by the antidiscrimination principle) would allot them. Alternatively, the argument might assume that there is a moral right to have jobs distributed on the basis of merit itself.

The argument is stronger if premised on the moral sanctity of a free labor market. This position would draw support from the personal autonomy argument for freedom of contract, and it would be buttressed by the widely shared notion that it is desirable to reward individual effort and productivity, as a free market will tend to do. Moreover, there is no doubting the central role of the market as an engine of distribution—and, the argument would run, of distributive justice—in the American economy. Beyond the subsistence provisions of various welfare programs, and a few specific restraints such as the antidiscrimination principle, the sum of freely made economic decisions—decisions to buy and sell, hire and fire, work and invest, give and bequeath—defines the principal features of the economic, and, many would argue, the "just" landscape.[171]

It is not enough, however, to show that the market does in fact

[170] See, *e.g.*, BICKEL, note 53 *supra*, at 133–34. Under this argument it also might be wrong to deny employers the right to contract with the most meritorious applicant for a job.

[171] For a celebrated elaboration of a libertarian conception of distributive justice, see NOZICK, ANARCHY, STATE, AND UTOPIA (1974). Reduced to a maxim, Nozick's theory of distributive justice holds: "From each according to what he chooses to do, to each according to what he makes for himself (perhaps with the contracted aid of others) and what others choose to do for him and choose to give him of what they've been given previously (under this maxim) and haven't yet expended or transferred." *Id.* at 160.

have a large role in determining distributions of jobs and other opportunities. To succeed, the argument needs a moral theory that shows the justness of the market itself, such that redistributive intervention is forbidden. This is harder to establish. The concept of merit will not bear the moral weight of demonstrating that justice requires an unalloyed free market. First, merit itself cannot be adequately identified objectively as a standard by which the market could be tested. Although there has been some historical consistency in the traits that society has valued, merit is a concept intrinsically bound up with human interests, desires and purposes that are subject to change.[172] For example, at one time a society might place a high value on the ability to split rails with an axe or to do addition without a computer. In other eras these capacities may count for little. As a result, merit is not a concept external to the market, but, on the contrary, one more often defined within it: merit consists of those talents for which the market is willing to pay. A concept frequently defined by the market, merit cannot provide an independent justification for adherence to market principles.

Second, even within a market—with "merit" defined in terms of ability to satisfy existing societal desires and tastes—there is only an attenuated connection between the principles of "market freedom" and of "rewards to merit." On the whole, the market can be expected to sort people into the jobs for which they are best suited by their relative talents and productivity. If so, it will lure the ablest people into the most important jobs, help to maximize the productive output of the society, and reward people for their personal talents and achievements. But these are the expected byproducts of a market, not its governing rules. No legal compulsion demands that talent and effort be rewarded. Nepotism seems a relatively common practice. And other reasons may cause merit to go unnoticed or unrewarded.

If it is to be established at all, the moral inviolability of the market—and the justification for the outcomes that it produces—would need to be justified morally by what Robert Nozick has termed an "historical" or "entitlement" theory of distributive jus-

[172] See Fallon, note 56 *supra*, at 823–25.

tice.[173] In contrast with "patterned" or "substantive" theories,[174] an entitlement theory tests the justice of distributive shares—including wealth, jobs, and opportunities—mostly by the process through which the distribution occurs. An entitlement theory posits as its ultimate, justifying value respect for the free, individual choices through which the market functions.[175] Any interference with the natural process of free exchange—including employment decisions providing rewards to merit—is presumptively illegitimate.

Even within an entitlement theory, however, process and liberty do not alone account for patterns of economic distribution. As people begin to exercise autonomy, some are endowed with enormous material and educational advantages, others with none. Entitlement theories lodge no per se objection against unequal starting points; liberty upsets any patterns that a free society might attempt to impose. But, even if it is not required to demonstrate affirmatively that the original distribution is just, if it is to establish that free market choices cannot fairly be interfered with, an entitlement theory must at least require that the structure of starting points not have been reached unjustly.[176] In the absence of just acquisitions, it would be unfair to permit people to exploit assets that confer competitive advantages in the pursuit of scarce opportunities and resources. For example, it would be unfair to allow a thief or the recipient of stolen funds to exploit the stolen wealth to purchase scarce goods in competition with other potential buyers. The unfairness would be measurable not only by its effect on the initial victim of theft, but on his heirs and on others subsequently subjected to a competitive disadvantage.

---

[173] See NOZICK, note 171 *supra*, at 149–82.

[174] See *id.* at 155–60. Nozick defines principles of distributive justice as "patterned" if they provide that distributive shares should depend on substantive criteria of desert, such as "moral merit" or "usefulness to society." See *id.* at 156.

[175] Nozick's objection to patterned or substantive theories is that liberty upsets patterns. See *id.* at 160–62.

[176] Nozick defines a distribution as just "if it arises from another just distribution by legitimate means." *Id.* at 151. This formulation presupposes justice in the original acquisition of holdings. *Id.* at 150. Where past injustices have occurred, Nozick recognizes the need for a theory of rectification of injustice in holdings. *Id.* at 152. He does not, however, attempt to provide any theory of rectification that would answer such questions as "How far back must one go in wiping clean the slate of historical injustices?" *Id.*

The most conspicuous asset in a market economy is financial wealth. But similarly important are personal assets such as the testable intelligence and various occupational skills that an individual brings to the labor market. Talents and abilities may seem conceptually difficult to separate from the person possessing them.[177] But premarket experiences, including education and nurture, importantly influence aptitude and employability.[178] Analogously to the transfer of wealth, with which they are correlated if not causally linked, educational and cultural advantages, most visibly manifest in measurable aptitudes, are subject to charges of unjust acquisitions at the beginning of an historical chain.[179]

In the context of American history, past racial injustices have permeated the existing structure of economic and educational advantages that are crucial in the market's apportionments of jobs and material benefits. As passed through the generations, unjust acquisitions continue to give rise to comparative advantages—measurable in disparities between racial groups—in a competitive economic and social community. Citing past racial injustices, many of them having the sanction of law, a group-based argument therefore succeeds at least in showing that an historical theory of distributive justice, even within its own terms, could not establish the necessary predicates to demonstrate the justice of market allocations of jobs.[180] In other words, an entitlement theory cannot establish the

[177] See *id.* at 214–31; SANDEL, LIBERALISM AND THE LIMITS OF JUSTICE 77–95 (1982).

[178] See generally JENCKS, note 156 *supra.*

[179] We can imagine, for example, that a thief steals a sum of money, half of which he hides and half of which he spends on education. The education, as much as the money saved, may be traced back to roots in an unjust acquisition. The immediate difference between the hidden money and the education is that the money retains a tangible status, independent of the thief, while the education is now literally inseparable from the thief himself. He has been transformed by his education; it helps to constitute him as he now is. Because this is so, the unjust acquisition of education could not be rectified by taking the thief's education away from him, or by restoring him to the intellectual state that he would have had "but for" his unjust acquisition. But it may be possible, and morally appropriate, to impose limitations on the thief's capacity to "exploit" his educationally fostered talents by, for example, denying him a job or by placing a special tax on his income.

[180] The argument is sometimes made that past injustices have only a relative brief "half-life," after which their effects and significance should be regarded as morally dissipated. Fried, *Is Liberty Possible?* in TANNER LECTURES ON HUMAN VALUES (1982), at 103; *cf.* Sher, *Ancient Wrongs and Modern Rights,* 10 PHIL. & PUB. AFF. 3 (1980). The premise for this argument seems to be that anyone's present circumstances result from some combination of material advantage and of personal character and effort, and that the latter factors progressively overwhelm the significance of past wrongs. If the claim is empirical, its accuracy is dubious with respect to black Americans. Nearly universal discrimination against blacks,

injustice of the intervention into the market that is commended by the Model of Social Justice.[181]

Once the argument for the justice of market distributions is shown to be problematic, it becomes difficult to argue from the second assumption, that people have a moral right to employment or other rewards based on their measurable intelligence or talents or similar merit characteristics. As argued above, merit cannot be identified independently of societal tastes, values, and preferences, such as those that the market reflects. Although society may wish to encourage employment decisions based on traditional merit traits, a person has no moral right to have employers make their decisions on the basis, for example, of measurable intelligence.[182] If employers began instead to favor congeniality, or to hire athletic heroes or military veterans, a rejected applicant would have no valid claim of injustice.

The claim of injustice is no stronger where society, to serve legitimate purposes, makes a political decision to change its structure of opportunities and rewards. For example the nation may decide to give preferences to veterans, in order to recognize the sacrifices that they made for their country.[183] Or a community may decide to give local residents a preference in work projects being funded out of local taxes.[184] Or a poverty program may allot jobs to

---

spread over a long period of time, seems not only to have caused direct economic deprivation but also to have transformed many of the victims' behaviors in self-defeating ways. See Jencks, note 65 *supra*. If the argument is moral, it must rely on harsh and contentious principles that would threaten to trivialize a historical theory of distributive justice; after a few generations, it would justify nearly any structure or advantage and disadvantage.

[181] In contrast to arguments that undertake to trace the individualized consequences of historical deprivations, our argument aspires only to show that the existing structure of distributions is tainted at its foundations by historically unjust acquisitions. In other words, justice does not forbid group-based redistributive policies. This is a group-based argument, and group arguments for corrective justice generally have been thought susceptible to the objection that only individuals are entitled to compensation for past injustices. But this objection does not defeat, because it does not address, our argument that the society's existing structure of distributive starting points, tainted at base by historical injustices, cannot be defended on grounds of distributive justice, and that group-based redistributive programs—justified on other grounds of morality and social policy—therefore ought not to be held impermissible.

[182] See DWORKIN, note 165 *supra*, at 225.

[183] See Koelfgen v. Jackson, 355 F. Supp. 243 (D. Minn. 1972), *aff'd. mem.*, 410 U.S. 976 (1973); *cf.* Personnel Adm'n of Mass. v. Feeney, 442 U.S. 256 (1979).

[184] See White v. Massachusetts Council of Constn. Employers, Inc., 103 S.Ct. 1042 (1983); but *cf.* United Trade Council of Camden v. Mayer and Council, 104 S.Ct. 1020 (1984).

the poorest candidates, not the most deserving. Each of these policies may have the effect of excluding the applicant who otherwise would be regarded as the most able. But none offends any individual right to have only traditional merit characteristics count in awarding jobs. If the defeated applicant has a compelling argument, it must be that he has been dispreferred for reasons that are themselves morally impermissible.

C. THE MODEL OF SOCIAL JUSTICE: WHO BENEFITS?

So far we have asserted a positive case for affirmative discrimination, tied closely to the special status of blacks in American history. We have also rejected three familiar arguments that justice forbids intervention into the market to achieve redistribution along group lines. But an important question left open involves the relationship between our positive and our negative arguments.

From one perspective, the negative arguments may seem to prove unsettlingly more than do the positive ones. If interference with a largely meritocratic labor market cannot be defeated by the arguments considered, have we introduced a regime in which any group-based redistribution whatsoever must be held morally permissible? The answer is no. First, despite our abstract arguments against the moral inviolability of traditional merit criteria and of the labor market, conventional moral norms would hold it unfair to impose excessive costs of rectification on particular individuals, based on a predicate of social instead of individual wrongdoing. We accept limitations arising from this concern. Second, our negative arguments merely show that particular appeals to "justice" fail to demonstrate the moral necessity of the status quo. The negative arguments do not mandate particular redistributions, and, more important, they do not deny that other moral considerations impose limits on the scope of defensible changes. Fairness requires that like cases should be treated alike and that discriminations should be based on morally relevant differences. To the extent that redistribution is mandated by the government, the basis for the prescribed allocations would need to satisfy a standard of moral relevance.[185] Similarly, within the private sector, the normally governing value scheme holds that race and certain other group-based

[185] Goldman, note 123 *supra*, at 23.

characteristics represent impermissible criteria for the distribution of jobs. Even if there is no "right" to be hired on the basis of particular talents, other moral concerns—especially to respect expectations that the society has fostered and to honor values to which it generally remains committed—demand a presumption against group-based allocations of employment opportunities.[186] Under what circumstances then are group-based preferences appropriate in the labor market?

In addressing this question, we assume throughout that racial or ethnic preferences would require a modification of selection processes linked to merit or to the ability to perform a particular job. But this assumption will not always be correct, and the bounds of its validity define an important limitation of our argument. There are contexts in which racial or minority status may enhance a person's ability to fulfill a particular function in employment. For example, a black policeman may win the trust of ghetto residents more easily and therefore perform more successfully than a white; a teacher from a minority background may communicate more successfully with, and provide greater inspiration to, minority students. In such contexts, because racial or ethnic background is relevant to job performance, it serves the same function as more traditional indicia of merit and would seem compatible with distribution on the basis of talent and productivity.[187] This, however, is not the type of racial preference with which we are concerned here. Our arguments address the more typical and more problematic case in which group characteristics presumptively provide no valid measure of individual capability.[188]

---

[186] *Cf.* Dreyfuss & Lawrence, The Bakke Case: The Politics of Inequality 96 (1979) ("In a society in which men and women expect to succeed by hard work and to better themselves by making themselves better, it is no trivial moral wrong to proceed systematically to defeat this expectation") (quoting Alexander Bickel).

[187] Race is most likely to be relevant in this sense when a job involves the performance of a service, and the recipients of that service are more comfortable with, or possess greater confidence in, members of some groups than of others. A difficulty about allowing the assimilation of race to more traditional merit traits, even in these contexts, is that some whites may be more comfortable with, or otherwise prefer to be served by, other whites. In response to such attitudes by the white majority, a traditional function of merit criteria has been to affirm the moral and economic irrelevance of racial and similar criteria as indicia of individual talent and productivity. See Fallon, note 56 *supra*, at 837.

[188] Racial or ethnic background is likely to enhance the ability to perform a job only in a relatively narrow range of contexts. It has little if any relevance to the firefighting positions involved in *Stotts*, for example. Where applicable, our justifications for affirmative discrimi-

1. The Justification of Group Selection

Framed initially as an expression of the antidiscrimination principle, Title VII extended its protections broadly, forbidding any discrimination based on race, sex, or national origin. So construed, the statute reflected a moral judgment that group-based bias and animus have no rightful place in the labor market. In the years since 1964, however, Congress, the executive branch, and the courts have moved increasingly from the individualistic values associated with the antidiscrimination principle to a group conception of equality of opportunity, expressed in various forms and programs of affirmative discrimination.

Superimposed on the original structure of Title VII, the group approach to employment discrimination has tended to extend its affirmative preferences as broadly as the antidiscrimination principle establishes prohibitions against prejudiced wrongdoing. It is far from clear, however, that all groups protected by the antidiscrimination principle should receive the benefits of group-based affirmative discrimination. It is possible, of course, to imagine a societal transition from free market and meritocratic principles to a group-based conception of distributive justice, with jobs allotted on proportional bases. But this approach, requiring a general restructuring of the labor market, would also represent a sharp departure from traditional practice and values, which hold race irrelevant to nearly all moral questions and prescribe respect for individual autonomy, talents, and efforts. Indeed, the strongest arguments for affirmative discrimination generally have acknowledged as much. Instead of proffering a general defense of racialism as a theory of distributive justice, they have built upon the intuition that the historical circumstances of black Americans define a morally special case. Consistently with the intuition of moral uniqueness, an extraordinary justification, going beyond that needed to earn the protection of the antidiscrimination principle, should be required before a group qualifies for affirmative discrimination.

The appropriate requirements cannot be defined by any process of logical deduction. Our justification for affirmative action for

---

nation sweep more broadly. It is possible, however, that an argument founded on the relevance of race to a particular job might justify preference for a nonblack minority applicant who would not qualify for a racial preference within the terms of the argument that we develop.

blacks began with a moral intuition of appropriateness, supported by three arguments. Some clarity may be gained if those arguments are restated as conditions for affirmative discrimination: (i) there has been an historic pattern of legally sanctioned, group-based discrimination; (ii) the legacy of historical discrimination includes a current condition of group disadvantage, resulting in social problems at least partly remediable through affirmative discrimination; and (iii) social and psychological factors give current meaning to the group as more than an arbitrary collection of individuals.

Reflecting an effort to explain and justify the moral intuition that affirmative discrimination represents an appropriate response to historical discrimination against American blacks, these conditions can be used to test the arguments for affirmative discrimination advanced on behalf of other groups. If their application to other cases should yield consequences that seem jarring or intolerable, then the original justifications might need to be modified or abandoned, or the initial intuition possibly reconsidered. In point of fact, however, these conditions do not call for affirmative discrimination of unsettling breadth. When any of these conditions is not satisfied, the case for affirmative discrimination seems to us to be significantly weaker.

a) Japanese and Chinese Americans. Is it justifiable for the advantages of affirmative discrimination to be denied to Japanese and Chinese Americans, racial groups that did suffer from severe and officially sanctioned discrimination in the United States? Historical treatment of these groups has included many wrongs, some of them within the domain of government responsibility. Where the direct victims can be identified, corrective justice would make reparations appropriate. But the argument for group-based affirmative discrimination in the job market is much weaker. Were such programs implemented, the beneficiaries would tend to be the children and grandchildren of those most directly harmed by governmentally perpetrated or sanctioned injustices. And, happily, historical wrongs have not measurably reduced the life prospects of Japanese and Chinese Americans of this generation.[189] In the absence of

[189] As of 1970, adult Japanese males earned 104 percent of what white males earned, while the Chinese earned 106 percent. When one controls for the influence of age, residence and schooling, however, the earnings ratios were essentially the same. See Chiswick, *An Analysis of the Earnings and Employment of Asian-American Men*, 1 J. LAB. ECON. 197 (1983).

continuing group deprivation, affirmative discrimination does not seem warranted.

b) Other racial and ethnic groups. Blacks are not the only ethnic group at the lower levels of the economic spectrum. There are Hispanic and Asian groups that may rank even below blacks in current achievements.[190] Some of them exhibit a strong sense of group identity and interdependence. Despite arguments in favor of affirmative discrimination, there is a material difference between these cases and that of American blacks, who suffered centuries of discrimination within the United States, sanctioned if not abetted by government. Successive waves of immigrant groups have come to this country, often predominantly impoverished when they entered, though commonly better off here than in the nations that they left.[191] Upon arrival, newcomers should have access to the array of public programs and services generally available to the poor in this country. They also should enjoy full protection against invidious discrimination based on race, nationality, or religion. But group-based preferences in the job market represent extraordinary action, burdensome to employers and especially to dispreferred individuals. Because their interests are inevitably affected, more should be required to justify affirmative discrimination than present group disadvantage and psychological interdependence.

Who besides blacks should receive the benefits of affirmative action?[192] This is a difficult and important question, the complexity of which we have only tried to suggest. Our effort has been to identify, regrettably only to leave, a set of moral, empirical, and jurisprudential issues that deserve more careful treatment. Ideally, inquiry would proceed at two levels. One would ask whether other groups—for example, Hispanics—or possibly "subgroups"—for example, Chicanos as a subcategory of Hispanics—satisfy all three of the conditions that we framed initially to rationalize special treatment for American blacks.[193] The other line of analysis would

---

[190] See Jencks, note 65 *supra*, at 34.

[191] See generally SOWELL, ETHNIC AMERICA (1981).

[192] We assume that North American Indians also would satisfy the conditions set out above. See Morton v. Mancari, 417 U.S. 535 (1974).

[193] Hispanics represented 6.4 percent of all U.S. residents in 1980 (vs. the 11.7 percent black share), and male Hispanics earned 76 percent of what white males earned in 1975 (vs. 73 percent for blacks), with Chicanos (who were 60 percent of all Hispanics) earning slightly less than the overall Hispanic average. See McManus, Gould, & Welsh, *Earnings of Hispanic*

further test the adequacy of the three conditions themselves to describe and to guide moral and legal choice. Treated as individually necessary to justify affirmative discrimination, the three conditions could yield results that would seem too objectionable to be countenanced. Without close inspection of individual cases, however, we are inclined to believe that a persuasive case for any racial or ethnic group's claim to affirmative discrimination would need to satisfy all of the three conditions.

c) The poor. A somewhat different issue involves claims on behalf of the poor. Invoking the ideal of equality of opportunity for people who encounter the obstacles of a deprived social, economic, or family environment, a familiar argument holds that the benefits of affirmative discrimination—if extended at all—should be based on poverty,[194] not race. Blacks suffer disproportionately more from these conditions than do whites. But because there are more poor whites than there are poor blacks, more whites presumably are denied the opportunity to develop and exercise talents to the fullest. And it is unfair, the argument continues, to deny the white poor the special help afforded to blacks.

Under the conditions that we have identified, it is not morally arbitrary to conclude that affirmative discrimination for blacks finds support in special interests and justifications that are not equally compelling in the case of the poor. Racial injustices have stigmatized blacks as a group, even those who are reasonably well off, in a way that has not happened to the poor. There also is a

---

Men: The Role of English Language Proficiency, J. LAB. ECON. 101, 107–09 (1983). Moreover, at least some of the distinctive ethnic communities within the overall Hispanic population appear to have been the target of sustained discrimination. (For an illuminating review of the relevant history in the case of Chicanos, see Lopez, *Undocumented Mexican Migration: In Search of a Just Immigration Law and Policy*, 28 UCLA L. REV. 615, 641–72 (1981).) However, when one takes account of their relative age, residence, and education, the current disparities in the earnings of Hispanics disappear (although they remain in the case of blacks). See Shapiro, *Wage Differentials among Black, Hispanic and White Young Men*, 37 INDUS. & LAB. REL. REV. 570 (1984). McManus *et al.*, *supra*, at 117–19, therefore conclude that the major obstacle faced by Hispanics is English language deficiency. In justifying affirmative discrimination for any or all Hispanic groups, a central issue is whether current lack of success in the labor market should be viewed as a legacy of discrimination or as a natural feature of their rate of immigration and assimilation. Interestingly, employment preferences for Hispanics under Executive Order 11246 appear not to have produced any significant gains in Hispanic employment (by contrast with the sharp improvement it has worked for blacks). See LEONARD, note 47 *supra*, at 127.

[194] See, *e.g.*, FISHKIN, JUSTICE, EQUAL OPPORTUNITY, AND THE FAMILY 86 (1983); GOLDMAN, note 123 *supra*, at 170–200.

unique contemporary need to surmount racial prejudice and to address race-linked social alienation. Accordingly, the logic of the case for racial preferences for blacks does not require—under the principle of like treatment for like cases—affirmative discrimination for the poor.

It is a further question, however, whether our argument would forbid affirmative discrimination to alleviate the obstacles of poverty in the labor market. We think not.[195] Affirmative discrimination for the poor differs from programs of racial preference in at least two relevant respects. First, in light of their history, racial preferences deserve to be regarded as suspect. This is not to say that affirmative discrimination should never be approved; we have argued precisely the contrary. But racial preferences should be tested against a more stringent standard than those based on other factors.

Second, unlike racial preferences, affirmative discrimination for the poor can be justified in individual terms, without reference to group concepts. If poverty is viewed as a barrier to equality of opportunity, then the purpose of providing equal opportunity justifies a preference for all (or nearly all) individual beneficiaries. There is no need to defend, in group terms, a preference for someone who could not be characterized as individually deserving within the morally legitimate purposes of the program. It is a special problem of racial preferences that they may visit their benefits on persons who seem little disadvantaged by past racial injustice.[196]

2. The Selection of Individual Beneficiaries

While the justifications for affirmative action relate to the situations of blacks as a group, preferences in the labor market confer their benefits on black individuals. Whatever group benefits may ensue, they are attenuated. One form of criticism, which any justification for affirmative discrimination must meet, focuses on the

[195] Like preferences based on race, affirmative discrimination for the poor would defeat expectations that hiring will be based on presently demonstrable merit. But these expectations are neither universally respected nor morally inviolable. See notes 170–84 *supra* and accompanying text.

[196] Although the expectations of dispreferred persons may be defeated in either case, it is a weaker expectation that hiring will be based on "pure merit" than that hiring cannot be based on race. See Fallon, note 56 *supra*, at 837.

situations of individual beneficiaries. The distributional difficulty arises from the nature of the labor market. The bigger and better employers tend to be the major targets of government policies—including disparate impact theory under Title VII and the strictures of Executive Order 11246—that virtually require affirmative discrimination. Since these employers are likely to prefer and bid for the best qualified blacks to fill the higher-ranking jobs,[197] the concern is that an excessive share of the benefits will be concentrated on the more advantaged blacks,[198] from whom the historical burden of race is now largely removed.[199] This is not to deny that blacks on average still suffer much more from the obstacles to advancement presented by poverty and family structure.[200] The point of the argument, rather, is that a sharp economic divide appears to have opened up within the black community, such that it is no longer appropriate to treat blacks as an undifferentiated group.[201] We can no longer be confident, this criticism asserts, that

---

[197] Both LEONARD, note 48 *supra*, at 131–34, and Smith and Welsh, note 47 *supra*, at 281–83, found that the employment impact of the Executive Order among professionals and managers was more than double that felt by black workers overall, with essentially no impact on the demand for black laborers or service workers. An intriguing aspect of these trends is that the differential impact of affirmative discrimination comes in spite of the fact that federal judges have taken a much less aggressive approach toward "upper-level jobs" under Title VII. See Bartholet, *Application of Title VII to Jobs in High Places*, 95 HARV. L. REV. 945 (1982).

[198] See, *e.g.*, FISHKIN, note 194 *supra*, at 92. There is substantial evidence of this trend. For example, the differential in black/white earnings of male college graduates shot up from 59 in 1965 to 84 in 1979, whereas the rate for black high school graduates made only modest improvement, from 67 to 74 in that same period. See Jencks, note 65 *supra*, at 36. Indeed, by the early seventies, the young (twenty-five to twenty-nine) black male college graduate (the person who came into the labor market under the umbrella of Title VII and the Executive Order) actually earned more (1.09) than his white counterpart, as also did the black, college-educated couple with both husband and wife working, regardless of age. See SOWELL, CIVIL RIGHTS: RHETORIC OR REALITY 80 (1982).

[199] Econometric analysis of these statistical trends shows that for young blacks, pre-labor-market characteristics have essentially the same influence as they have for whites on hourly earnings (.17 vs. .16) and occupational status (.20 vs. .23). See Freeman, note 159 *supra*, at 266–67. This is not to deny that black youths suffer disproportionately more from a disadvantaged background. But when one controls for the latter variables, there is very little difference between the achievement of young blacks and that of whites in occupational status and weekly earnings, and drastically less than is true of the older blacks whose prospects were largely fixed before Title VII and Executive Order 11246 came into force (.03 vs. .15 variance in occupational position and .03 vs. .32 in weekly earnings). *Ibid.*

[200] Freeman found that, on average, black male youths were considerably worse off than their white counterparts in parental years of schooling (7.9 vs. 10.5), parental median income (7.7 vs. 8.5), and in female-headed homes (40 percent vs. 12 percent). See *id.* at 257.

[201] One tangible index is to be found in the difference between the share of black income going to the upper 40 percent of black families and that going to the bottom 40 percent. This

the benefits of affirmative discrimination will eventually trickle down to the poor black in the urban ghetto,[202] the very black whose interests are so often invoked to justify racial preferences in the first place.

This is a substantial objection, but ultimately it is not persuasive. First of all, at the time the seeds of affirmative discrimination were sown in the late 1960s and early 1970s,[203] it was clear and demonstrable that the bare fact of race, independent of poverty and family background, was a major barrier to black achievement. This powerful index of entrenched racism affected blacks of all economic classes. Against the background of historical discrimination, not yet purged from the economy, there existed ample justification for a vigorous governmental effort to break down the unfavorable link between blackness and life prospects for the black middle and working classes—even if that effort would not necessarily suffice at the lowest levels to elevate the black ghetto classes from abject poverty. The effort that was undertaken took the form of affirmative discrimination in the employment market, a policy that the Supreme Court tacitly ratified in *Weber*. And, viewed from one perspective, affirmative discrimination has been remarkably successful. Now, class variables such as poverty and education explain better than race the occupational and income status of blacks and whites alike. It is far from clear, however, what this evidence "proves." Though often cited in arguments against affirmative discrimination, it surely does not show that programs of racial preference should be condemned as unjustified at their inception. If the assertion is that affirmative discrimination now benefits the "wrong" blacks, the argument must instead be that affirmative discrimination has done its work and should therefore be dismantled, possibly to be replaced by more carefully targeted programs.

---

differential has widened considerably from 1964 (when it was 69 to 15) to 1982 (when it was 72 to 13). The disparity is now significantly greater among blacks than it is among whites where the comparable ratio was 66 to 17 in 1982. See CURRENT POPULATION REPORT, note 2 *supra*, at 47–48.

[202] For a provocative discussion of this issue, and of possible alternative policies, see WILSON, note 43 *supra*, at 144–54; see also MURRAY, LOSING GROUND (1984).

[203] This roughly was the period of *Griggs*, the early court of appeals decisions prescribing quota remedies for Title VII violations, and Congress's seeming approval of both the emerging case law and Executive Order 11246 when it enacted the 1972 amendments to Title VII. See notes 104–11 *supra* and accompanying text.

As to this position, the evidence is not yet strong enough to be persuasive. At most, recent statistics establish that race no longer has a significant influence on the occupational status and hourly earnings of young, employed blacks. Even with respect to these figures, however, there remains a sharp dispute among labor economists,[204] and we are some distance from a final verdict. It is also significant that the statistical trends underlying this debate involve the achievements and relative positions of black workers under the umbrella of Executive Order 11246 and other incentives to affirmative discrimination.[205] Certainly there is no guarantee that current patterns would continue if such support were suddenly removed. Finally, we are not persuaded that class divisions have eroded what we have called the group status of the black community. Recent voting patterns, for example, suggest a widely shared black interest in the success of black candidacies. Similarly in the employment market, the achievements of some blacks may lift the aspirations of others, or may combat group-based alienation and despair associated with systems of racial caste.[206]

Our position does not purport to embody ultimate truths. It is accepted that affirmative discrimination is justifiable only as a temporary corrective device.[207] Its termination should be signaled either by the elimination of the identifiable residues of past discrimination or by the failure of affirmative discrimination as a rational corrector. Candidly, however, our position is to insist on a positive showing that American blacks are no longer held back by the color of their skin.

---

[204] Compare Freeman, note 159 *supra*, and Jud & Walker, *Racial Differences in the Returns to Schooling and Experience among Prime-Age Males*, 17 J. HUM. RESOURCES 622 (1982); Brown, *Black-White Earnings Ratios since the Civil Rights Act of 1964: The Importance of Labor Market Dropouts*, 1984 Q. J. ECON. 33; with Butler and Heckman, *The Goverment's Impact on the Labor Market Status of Black Americans: A Critical Review*, in HAUSMAN *et al.* (eds.), EQUAL RIGHTS AND INDUSTRIAL RELATIONS 235 (1977); Lazear, *The Narrowing of Black-White Differentials Is Illusory*, 69 AM. ECON. REV. 553 (1979); and Shapiro, note 193 *supra*. However this particular debate is resolved, there remains a clear link between being black and being unemployed, with unemployment statistics causing a considerable difference in annual earnings. Freeman found that while the influence of race on annual earnings is far greater for older black males (.34), there still remains a substantial effect for young blacks (.12), more than he was able to locate for occupational position (.04) and weekly earnings (.03). See Freeman, note 159 *supra*.

[205] See note 48 *supra*.

[206] See Fiss, note 74 *supra*.

[207] See, *e.g.*, Steelworkers v. Weber, 443 U.S. 193, 208 (1979); Regents of the University of California v. Bakke, 438 U.S. 265, 403 (1978) (separate opinion of Blackmun, J.).

V. The Model of Social Justice: Who Pays?

Even if affirmative discrimination can be justified in principle, there remains within our Model of Social Justice the further question what burdens reasonably may be imposed on individual whites. There would be no serious problem if the costs of affirmative discrimination could be discharged collectively: for example, by raising money through the general tax system to be used as reparations, as has been suggested for the mistreatment of Japanese-Americans during World War II. But affirmative discrimination is seldom paid for in this way. Employment preferences to blacks most often come at the expense of individual whites, who lose jobs that otherwise would be theirs.

In *Stotts* the Supreme Court confronted the problem of assessing burdens in the context of seniority layoffs. This is a singularly difficult situation. Layoffs can undoubtedly pose a serious threat to the maintenance, let alone the momentum, of black progress achieved through recruitment and hiring. But the remedy usually endorsed by the Model of Group Justice—the layoff of senior whites to preserve current levels of black employment within an employer's work force—exacts enormous costs from displaced white workers, who have often invested the most productive years of their lives in attaining the security normally associated with seniority. Moreover, as a matter of both industrial practice and of positive law under Title VII's § 703(h), the importance of seniority is pervasively acknowledged and respected. In light of these factors, insofar as *Stotts* barred the federal courts from simply evicting innocent senior whites to preserve the jobs of junior blacks, its holding ought to be approved.

But affirmative discrimination does not ordinarily require the displacement of white incumbents from their jobs. Even in situations such as that in *Stotts*, the sole choice may not be between laying off junior blacks or senior whites. Alternative possibilities include concentration of the burden on the employer, whose statutory violations provided the predicate for judicial action, or distributing the burden across wider segments of the work force or the community. More importantly, there are compelling differences between racial preferences that result in seniority layoffs and those that operate at the level of initial hiring. This distinction between layoff and hiring preferences was actually reflected in Title VII case law until the early 1980s,[208] and it is supported by persuasive arguments of policy and public morality. Despite the Supreme Court's contrary dictum in *Stotts*, the rationale that best justifies its holding as to seniority layoffs does not imply that affirmative discrimination is inappropriate at the hiring stage.

A. SENIORITY SYSTEMS AND LAYOFFS

The importance of seniority—the seemingly mundane fact of length of service with a particular employer—is recognized in both industrial practice and in federal law. The vast majority of union contracts stipulate that seniority is the most important factor in deciding which workers are to be laid off.[209] And while management is much less likely to tie its hands through a written policy in nonunion employment, the actual practice even in nonunion firms reveals seniority to be far the most prominent factor in layoff decisions.[210] Unilateral adoption of this policy by nonunion firms shows that the institution of seniority reflects values widely shared by employers and workers alike. Congress echoed these popular sentiments when it inserted explicit protection of seniority systems into § 703(h) of Title VII, a provision that the Supreme Court has

[208] Compare the cases collected by Justice Blackmun in *Stotts*, 104 S.Ct. at 2606 n.10, upholding hiring preferences, with, *e.g.*, Chance v. Board of Examiners, 534 F.2d 993 (2d Cir. 1976); Jersey Central Power & Light Co. v. Electrical Workers, 508 F.2d 687 (3rd Cir. 1975); Watkins v. United Steelworkers, 516 F.2d 41 (5th Cir. 1975); and Waters v. Wisconsin Steelworks of International Harvester, 502 F.2d 1309 (7th Cir. 1974), all rejecting racial preferences in layoffs precipitated by the recession of the middle 1970s. Not until the recession of the early 1980s did several of the courts of appeals change direction and mandate layoff quotas overriding seniority rights, most commonly in cases involving public employers. See, *e.g.*, Oliver v. Kalamazoo Bd. of Educ. (6th Cir. 1983); Boston Chapter NAACP v. Beecher, 679 F.2d 965 (1st Cir. 1982); Stotts v. Memphis Fire Dept., 679 F.2d 541 (6th Cir. 1982); and Brown v. Neeb, 6434 F.2d 551 (6th Cir. 1981) (Toledo); Morgan v. O'Bryant, 671 F.2d 23 (1st Cir. 1982) (Boston); Arthur v. Nyquist, 712 F.2d 816 (2d Cir. 1983) (Buffalo). *Cf.* Tangren v. Wackenhut Serv., 658 F.2d 705 (9th Cir. 1981) (upholding voluntary affirmative discrimination in layoffs). For illuminating scholarly discussions of layoffs under Title VII, see Summers & Love, *Work Sharing as an Alternative to Layoffs by Seniority: Title VII Remedies in a Depression*, 124 U. PA. L. REV. 893 (1976); Edwards, *Race Discrimination in Employment: What Price Equality?* 1976 UNIV. ILL. L. FORUM 572 (1976); Poplin, *Fair Employment in a Depressed Economy: The Layoff Problem*, 23 UCLA L. REV. 177 (1975).

[209] A recent review of union contracts found that three-quarters of all collective agreements, including 90 percent of those in manufacturing, singled out seniority as the dominant factor in layoffs. See FREEMAN & MEDOFF, WHAT DO UNIONS DO? (1984).

[210] In one recent study, 86 percent of the surveyed nonunion firms made seniority the dominant factor in layoffs, and 42 percent even responded that they would never lay off a senior employee and keep the junior. See Abraham & Medoff, *Length of Service and Layoffs within Union and Nonunion Work Groups*, INDUS. & LAB. REL. REV. 87 (1984).

expansively and vigorously implemented.[211] The Justices, however, have never sought to explain why seniority rights are so important as a matter of sound policy or moral principle that § 703(h) warrants the expansive interpretation that it has received. The question for us is why seniority—in the layoff context—might deserve to be accorded such respect.

1. Seniority and Equity

Perhaps the most common rationale for the use of seniority[212] is that it furnishes an objective, "bright line" rule—length of service with the firm—that protects employees from arbitrariness and favoritism by lower echelon supervisors[213] and relieves management from having to make and defend contentious judgments about the relative qualifications of employees. But this argument will not suffice as a reason to override affirmative action for blacks. A number of criteria could serve the values of objectivity and nonarbitrariness: in particular, the creation of dual seniority systems—one for blacks and one for whites. Approved by the federal courts in Memphis and Boston, this approach has the added virtue of preserving the benefits of affirmative discrimination.

Another familiar argument holds that length of service with a firm is a fairly reliable rule-of-thumb index of workers' relative productivity, reflecting the degree of training and experience in a particular job. If this were true, one could understand why, when a layoff looms, even nonunion firms voluntarily choose to retain their senior workers.[214] But this argument fails to accord with the

[211] See, *e.g.*, International Bhd. of Teamsters v. United States 431 U.S. 324 (1977) (reversing the unanimous view of the courts of appeals that an existing seniority system that perpetuated the effects of past discrimination could not be said to be "bona fide" within the meaning of S.703(h)); American Tobacco Co. v. Patterson, 456 U.S. 63 (1982) (extending the Teamsters ruling to post-1965 seniority systems); California Brewers Ass'n v. Bryant, 444 U S. 598 (1980).

[212] See Cooper and Sobol, *Seniority and Testing under Fair Employment Laws*, 82 HARV. L. REV. 1589, 1604–05 (1969).

[213] Reliance on objective criteria may be especially important to blacks, because racial prejudice more easily infects subjective evaluation processes. See Bartholet, note 197 *supra*. Significantly, the relative situation of black workers is improved more than that of whites under collective bargaining, not simply in terms of compensation, see Holzer, *Unions and the Labor Market Status of Whites and Minority Youth*, 35 INDUS. & LAB. REL. REV. 392 (1982), but also in terms of tenure and advancement in employment with the firm. See Leigh, *Unions and Nonwage Racial Discrimination*, 32 INDUS. & LAB. REL. REV. 439 (1979).

[214] See Parsons, *Specific Human Capital: An Application to Quit Rates and Layoff Rates*, 80 J. POL. ECON. 1120 (1972).

facts.[215] Recent research shows that younger employees are relatively more productive than those with longer service, especially in light of the increasing cost of compensating more senior employees who typically receive salary increments and enjoy higher-cost fringe benefits based on length of service.[216]

Happily, however, this fact—that the standard compensation package in modern employment is tilted in favor of senior employees even though performance and productivity eventually decline with length of service—suggests a subtler but more powerful explanation. Employers are not irrational in adopting seniority rules, nor are employees irrational in welcoming them. From the employer's perspective, this compensation arrangement enhances productivity by reducing turnover within its work force and reinforcing the employees' commitment to a career with the firm.[217] By the same token, the employee has an interest in attaining the security afforded by the implicit promise of gradual upward progress in earnings, as well as in achieving the stability in his personal life associated with secure employment.

Seniority is the glue that holds together this mutually beneficial arrangement for stable career employment. To the worker, seniority guarantees that his employer, having obtained the benefit of a higher performance/compensation ratio during the early years of employment, will not replace its older employees when that ratio becomes unfavorable. At the same time, a strong commitment to seniority serves the long-run interest of employers, by allowing them to make credible promises of de facto tenure to their newer employees[218] in order to obtain their consent to an overall compensation package.

[215] See Cornfield, *Seniority, Human Capital, and Layoffs: A Case Study*, 21 INDUS. REL. 352 (1982).

[216] See Medoff & Abraham, *Experience, Performance and Earnings*, 95 Q. J. ECON. 703 (1980); Medoff & Abraham, *Are Those Paid More Really More Productive? The Case of Experience*, 16 J. HUM. RESOURCES 186 (1982).

[217] Career employment reduces the cost of hiring and training replacements, see OKUN, PRICES AND QUANTITIES 49–80 (1981); it is conducive to the kind of cohesive teamwork essential in a social system of production, see WILLIAMSON, MARKETS AND HIERARCHIES 57–81 (1979); and it enhances the confidence of experienced employees in transmitting their lore to new workers without being concerned about endangering their own personal prospects. See THUROW, DANGEROUS CURRENTS 196–214 (1983). As a result, a system of stable career employment is much more productive than a casual, at-will relationship—a lesson from the Japanese experience.

[218] The promise is subject, of course, to exceptions allowing dismissal for personal misconduct or especially poor performance.

Once a seniority regime is established, an employee working under it knows that in return for staying (rather than accepting or even looking for better jobs elsewhere), he is improving his relative ranking in the system. In a real sense, the added seniority credit for each period worked represents an intangible but crucial aspect of the return on the employee's labor (albeit one he cannot "spend" but rather must invest with the firm). At a certain point, the worker achieves the equivalent of tenure, because he knows that he is sufficiently high on the seniority list to be protected against nearly any risk of permanent job loss.[219] At that point, the rights and expectations surrounding seniority make up what is probably the most valuable capital asset that the worker "owns," worth even more than the current equity in his home.

Although less subject to quantification, a set of psychological concerns also supports the employee's interest in seniority. In American society, a job helps to define who a person is: not merely what the person does at work, but how he thinks of himself and the purposes of his life. As a worker invests the most productive years of his life in a particular job or a particular firm, the stable, continuing employment may play an increasing role in self-definition.

It is true that the traumatic features of a layoff—both economic and psychological—cannot be measured solely by their impact on senior whites. In layoffs where affirmative discrimination is also of concern, less senior black workers also face financial and emotional losses, and their well-being should not be ignored. Under some circumstances a partial accommodation, in which no one loses a job entirely, will be feasible. Sometimes, however, a clear choice must be made, and the question then concerns the appropriate content of the governing legal rule. Three arguments support the choice for seniority. First, whatever the interests of a junior black, the otherwise protected rights of a senior white provide a measure of the sacrifice that a layoff would demand of him to advance the policies of affirmative discrimination. And the burden may be very large indeed. Second, even if the relevant questions are seen as compara-

---

[219] Seniority protection may not be as strong against short-term layoffs, due to shutdowns for maintenance or retooling. Nor is it an absolute guarantee against economic disaster, involving an employer's bankruptcy, the closing of a plant, or the relocation of operations. Nevertheless, by committing a certain part of his working life to one firm, the employee can insure himself against most of the vicissitudes that might affect his job security.

tive—calling for a weighing of the relative stakes of senior white and junior black—seniority probably provides the best available measure. More subjective standards would be impracticable. Finally, seniority defines the best "bright-line" rule for layoff cases of the most serious kind. Seniority layoff cases exhibit two important dimensions, one involving the degree to which integration is threatened if junior blacks are laid off, the other concerning the severity of the invasion of seniority rights if whites instead are displaced. In a case such as *Stotts*, which involved the layoff of only a handful of firefighters, and for a brief period, with the affected persons actually having been hired on the same day, no large sacrifice of values is required. Little is at stake, with respect either to the benefits of integration or the losses of seniority and security. Were this the paradigm case, it would seem nearly a matter of moral indifference what rule was followed. Similarly, important questions of civil rights policy are seldom likely to arise in cases involving long-term layoff choices between relatively senior white and relatively senior black employees. Choices such as this generally will occur only in radically shrinking firms or industries, where affirmative discrimination promises few important social benefits. The true moral dilemma arises when there is a forced choice between a serious setback to integration on the one hand and severe invasion of seniority rights on the other. That is why we have regularly recurred to the situation in Boston.

Consider what affirmative discrimination implies in a serious long-term layoff, such as occurred in the Boston school system. Observing that "there is nothing magical about seniority,"[220] the court of appeals effectively took this "asset" away from hundreds of senior white teachers, all of whom had been hired after intentional discrimination by the school board had ended, and gave the benefits to recently hired black teachers, who had not committed much of their lives to teaching in the Boston schools and probably enjoyed substantial mobility in the early stages of their careers.[221] In the light of the nature and operation of seniority systems in the real world of employment, this judicial evisceration of seniority rights imposed a severe burden that could not reasonably be as-

---

[220] Morgan v. O'Bryant, 671 F.2d 23 (1st Cir. 1982).

[221] This mobility is enhanced by widespread programs of affirmative discrimination in hiring, which are encouraged by both Title VII and the Executive Order.

signed to only a few white workers[222] to rectify historic injustices by American society as a whole.[223]

2. Alternatives to Layoffs

If it is held inequitable to require a senior white worker to give up his job in order to rectify societal injustices, a gap may emerge in the structure of programs of affirmative discrimination. But part of the dilemma may arise from the question who—as between senior white and junior black—is to be selected for a layoff. Perhaps the inquiry should be recast as whether there need be any layoff at all.

One avenue of inquiry would focus on the employer rather than senior white workers, as the appropriate candidate to bear the cost of affirmative discrimination. In *Stotts*, for example, the district judge might have forbidden the layoff of blacks but without authorizing the layoff of senior whites. The employer then would have had either to retain the senior whites in their jobs, or, if he dismissed them, pay compensation for any loss of earnings suffered as a result.[224]

This "full payroll" approach[225] has conspicuous advantages. It offers the benefits of affirmative discrimination without burdening innocent whites with the loss of their job. It also assigns the costs to a legal wrongdoer, thereby creating incentives to future lawful be-

[222] Some measure of the burden can be gained by realizing that the expected value to the worker of seniority may exceed the actual value of such tangible assets as his home or accumulated pension benefits. Presumably no one would suggest taking a white teacher's home or pension benefits, either to fund a program of affirmative discrimination or to promote racial equality in post retirement income.

[223] The argument in the text is that the seniority rights of white workers are entitled to protection in a layoff as a matter of sound policy supported by moral principle, independent of whether this was the specific intent of Congress when it enacted Title VII. As such, the argument has force even beyond the context of judicial orders for violations of Title VII or other statutes requiring the federal courts to frame remedies for employment discrimination. It also should apply to "voluntary" private affirmative discrimination, such as was upheld in Steelworkers v. Weber, 443 U.S. 193 (1979). The Court in *Weber* was careful to note that the specific program involved did not "unnecessarily trammel the rights of white employees." Our argument suggests that a voluntary program that deprived whites of substantial seniority rights in a layoff context would violate the interests of whites in a way that ought not to be allowed. But see Tangren v. Wackenhut Services, 658 F.2d 705 (9th Cir. 1981); Wygant v. Jackson Bd. of Educ., 36 Fair Empl. Prac. Cas. 153 (6th Cir. 1984).

[224] The Supreme Court essentially took this approach in *W. R. Grace*, discussed note 23 *supra*.

[225] The label comes from Burke and Chase, *Resolving the Seniority/Minority Layoffs Conflicts: An Employer-targeted Approach*, 13 HARV. C.R.-C.L. L. REV. 81 (1978).

havior. Regrettably, however, the full payroll strategy has significant limitations. One problem is the limited availability of funds. The full payroll approach requires the employer to pay both the senior white and junior black workers. Yet presumably it is the financial difficulty of maintaining an undiminished work force that inspires layoffs in the first place. This financial concern will not always be compelling. In some cases, it may be both feasible and equitable to force a firm to absorb the costs necessary to avoid sliding backward into a segregated work force. Inevitably, though, there will be many situations in which a judicial order forbidding a firm to reduce its labor costs would simply endanger the future viability of the entire enterprise, including all the jobs that it sustains.

Public employers pose a different set of problems. Even where a public employer has scheduled layoffs, the need for public services—for example, fire protection—often will not have diminished. Further, while taxpayer resistance may have decreased the funds immediately available to support those services, financial shortages would not obviate the obligation of public bodies to obey constitutionally valid judicial orders. Therefore, at least prior to *Stotts*, a federal judge might have thought it both equitable in result and supportable under Title VII to meet threatened layoffs by imposing the costs of affirmative discrimination on the public employer.[226] At the same time, however, judicial orders affecting budgetary priorities present a host of problems, involving both the constitutional and the practical competence of the judicial branch.[227] All in all, this is an area where judicial restraint ought to be exercised.

Another alternative to layoffs would seek accommodation of conflicting values through work sharing.[228] The logic of this approach is simple. If an employer experiences a drop in demand and revenues, it need not adjust by paring the number of employees in its

---

[226] The general remedial provision of Title VII, section 703(h), invests the district courts with broad remedial discretion in fashioning appropriate relief. See note 106 *supra*, and accompanying text.

[227] See, *e.g.*, Frug, *The Judicial Power of the Purse*, 125 U. PA. L. REV. 715 (1978).

[228] For a detailed and insightful analysis of this option, see Summers and Love, note 208 *supra*.

work force. Instead it could cut the hours of all its employees.[229] Because this would produce no drop in the number of people employed, many of the benefits of affirmative discrimination would be retained. And the price is spread across the entire complement of employees, not concentrated on a few senior whites who would be deprived entirely of their seniority rights.[230]

From the employer's perspective, work sharing could often be an attractive alternative to the normal layoff. Although there may be additional costs in maintaining fringe benefits,[231] these costs are overshadowed by the employer's ability to retain experienced workers whom it has recruited and trained,[232] and, more important, by significant savings in assessments for unemployment insurance.[233] For many employees, however, this solution may appear less desirable. Unemployment benefits are generally not payable if employees suffer only a reduction in the hours that they work. Yet many workers come to rely on all the earnings that they receive from their regular employment schedule. If there is to be no more than a marginal decrease in the work week, employees may be able

---

[229] For example, instead of cutting the number of workers by one-fifth, it could retain all of its employees but reduce the hours of each by the same proportion, *e.g.*, from forty to thirty-two hours a week.

[230] Under this approach a share of the burden is appropriately borne by older whites, who may have reaped some advantage from the employers' earlier invidious discrimination, and also by the most junior blacks, who may have reaped the benefit of later affirmative discrimination. A variant of the work-sharing approach would respond to financial difficulties by prescribing that all workers simply accept a proportionate cut in pay in order to fund the "full payroll" approach. But this variant would confer a windfall on the employer (or its consumers, shareholders, or taxpayers). Under work sharing, the employees at least get the benefit of some additional leisure as a trade-off for having to accept lower weekly earnings.

[231] While most fringe benefits, such as pension contributions, are wage-related and thus will decline automatically with the hours worked, other benefits, such as employer-paid health insurance, are paid for on a per capita basis, and thus would not decline under work sharing as they would with layoffs. However, empirical research indicates that this additional cost is just a tiny part of the overall wage bill, which is likely to be outweighed by other savings to the employer. See Reid, *U-I Assisted Work Sharing as an Alternative to Layoffs: The Canadian Experience*, 35 INDUS. & LAB. REL. REV. 319, 323 (1982).

[232] Although laid-off employees typically have rights of recall before new workers are hired, they will be under pressure to find other jobs in the interim, and some will therefore not be available for recall. The loss to the employer of this valuable "human capital" has been estimated to be greater than the additional cost in per capita fringe benefits created by work sharing. See Reid, note 231 *supra*.

[233] In most states, levies upon individual firms are influenced by the degree to which their own workers can and do draw on unemployment benefits. See Summers & Love, note 208 *supra*, at 929. Work sharing often will spare the employer higher assessments, because unemployment insurance benefits are not payable when employees suffer only a reduction in their number of hours worked.

to adjust reasonably well, taking into account the effects on after-tax income under a progressive tax system.[234] But if there is to be a substantial cut in paid hours, the result will be a real burden to families that have grown dependent on a certain level of income in every paycheck.

The function of unemployment insurance cannot be overlooked. In a dynamic economy, in which movement and adaptation are expected to occur, it is the role of unemployment insurance to shift much of the economic burden arising from work shrinkages in small economic units to a larger state or national pool financed by a payroll tax. In this social and institutional context, seniority rules ordinarily supply the criterion for deciding which workers are to retain their jobs with regular income and which are to depend on unemployment insurance while looking for other employment. The use of work sharing instead significantly reduces the total income received by the unit of employees immediately affected, as compared with the total income that would be realized from the aggregate of wages and unemployment insurance benefits. For this reason, and because work sharing also confers a windfall on the employer whose potential unemployment insurance assessments will be reduced, judicial imposition of this remedy is likely to be received even less enthusiastically than would a forthright layoff out of seniority order.

The current design of unemployment insurance is not, of course, unalterable. Moreover, there is a strong policy argument for removing artificial economic disincentives to the use of work sharing, rather than layoffs, as the means through which firms and their employees adjust to changes in market demand. Unemployment insurance systems in Europe, in Canada, and most recently in California have been revised to provide benefits in situations where all the employees in a work unit lose some hours of work, not only where some lose their jobs entirely.[235] If such a change were to be

[234] *Stotts* was a likely candidate for work sharing. The Memphis Fire Department ended up reducing its staff by only twenty-four firefighters, less than 2 percent of the 1,500-person department, or the equivalent of a reduction of less than one hour of work a week (assuming an average cycle of forty hours a week).

[235] Another alternative to layoffs in order of seniority was explored recently in Vulcan Pioneers v. New Jersey Department of Civil Service, 34 Fair Empl. Prac. Cas. 1239 (D.N.J. 1984). Having overridden the seniority rights of white firefighters in a layoff in order to retain a black presence within the fire departments, the federal district court characterized its own action as effecting a "taking" of the property rights of the senior whites, for which the

accomplished nationally, work sharing often might be the ideal way to secure the benefits of affirmative discrimination in a recession.

We should not be unduly optimistic, however, about the promise of work sharing in those situations in which racial integration is most seriously threatened. This technique is sensible mainly in cases of a relatively small reduction in available work, where the downturn is likely to be sufficiently brief so that most of the laid off employees will not likely find work elsewhere. Yet these are precisely the cases that pose no serious threat to black employment progress. *Stotts* is a good example. As Memphis's budgetary situation improved, the City's seniority system would have triggered a recall to work of all the laid-off blacks and thus a restoration of black representation within the fire department. The real threat to racial integration occurs when there is a major contraction in the business and work available in particular firms or industries (e.g., the auto and steel industries), or occupations (e.g., teaching), and the decline is likely to be long lived, if not permanent. In such settings, neither the "full payroll" nor the work-sharing alternatives to layoffs is a panacea,[236] and the social justice model implies that, however important the policies supporting affirmative discrimination, it would be misguided and inequitable to eviscerate the hard-earned seniority rights of innocent white workers.

B. HIRING PREFERENCES

Many in the civil rights movement view seniority as a major obstacle in the quest for racial justice in employment. They assume that blacks, who have only recently received fair opportunities in much of the labor market, do not have much seniority relative to white workers, and accordingly that blacks will inevitably suffer

federal government, as the author of Title VII, was responsible to provide compensation. Whatever its legal footing (after *Stotts* came down, the district court reversed its own ruling, see 35 Fair Empl. Prac. Cas. 25), the court's initial ruling is resonant with our social justice approach, insofar as it rejects the potentially large and unfair burden associated with the evisceration of seniority rights. But while the federal government might appear better able to provide needed funds than financially straitened municipalities, it is not clear why federal taxpayers—and especially those who live in similarly impoverished municipalities to which they already pay taxes—should be made to provide this form of financial assistance to a city wishing to engage in layoffs.

[236] See Best & Mattesich, *Short-Time Compensation Systems in California and Europe*, MONTHLY LAB. REV., July 1980, at 13.

disproportionately under the "last-hired, first-fired" principle.[237] This assumption was certainly valid well beyond the 1960s, when effective civil rights policies first were put in place. But today, two decades after the enactment of Title VII and the implementation of affirmative discrimination under Executive Order 11246, the situation has changed. On average, black workers now have accumulated seniority roughly equal to that of whites.[238] This is an important development. Not subject to undermining by latent prejudice or racial stereotypes, the practice of seniority is now as valuable to black workers as it is to whites.

Appreciation of the facts about seniority encourages a shift of attention from race-based layoffs to affirmative discrimination in hiring. The enlistment of black workers not only puts them in jobs but also places them on the seniority ladder. There they accumulate service with a firm, establish rights of recall during temporary layoffs, and eventually secure the kind of tenure that may insulate them from job loss even if the employer must institute a severe, long-term layoff.

The view that racial preferences were appropriate in hiring but not in layoffs until recently represented a consensus reflected in judicial, executive, and congressional action throughout the 1970s. Since then, this consensus has suffered erosion from both sides: prior to *Stotts*, several courts of appeals had prescribed race-based layoff preferences, and in *Stotts* itself the Supreme Court suggested that quota hiring remedies might be impermissible in Title VII lawsuits.

The earlier law reflected our intuitive judgment that affirmative discrimination in hiring was quite a different matter from racial quotas in the context of layoffs. But the question remains whether there is a principled rationale for this distinction. We have argued

---

[237] See, *e.g.*, U.S. Commission on Civil Rights, Last Hired First Fired: Layoffs and Civil Rights (1977).

[238] The May 1979 Current Population Survey asked a representative national sample of 29,000 workers how many years they had worked for their current employer. In the work force as a whole, blacks had accumulated 6.8 years of service vs. 6.6 for whites. In the public sector, blacks led whites by 8.1–7.9 years. Among schoolteachers and police officers, the relative positions were the same. There was insufficient response by blacks to provide an average for firefighters, but other minorities (predominantly Hispanics in this sample) outpaced white firefighters in length of service, and these other minorities trailed blacks in just about every other category. (We are grateful to James Medoff and Alan Krueger for extracting these data from the CPS tapes for us.)

that even as vital a policy as helping blacks overcome the legacy of racial oppression does not justify imposing on innocent whites the burden entailed by the denial of seniority rights in a long-term layoff. Why then does a comparable judgment not hold true in the context of entry-level hiring?

Material differences between layoffs and hiring exist along two dimensions. One involves the defeat of socially fostered expectations. The incumbent white in a layoff context seeks to enforce an explicit or implicit contractual right that he has earned with his labor. Having invested his energies and his aspirations in a firm, he feels—and it is desirable both economically and morally that he should feel—entitled to the security that seniority is designed to provide. Quite different is the situation of the first-time job applicant. He has no individual right to have the selection made in accordance with any particular set of criteria.[239] Undoubtedly there is a general expectation that relative competence ought to be taken into account. But private employers are not required to conduct purely meritocratic hiring competitions, and the community, by law, familiarly establishes nonmerit hiring preferences in a variety of ways and for a variety of reasons.[240] Established to help purge the legacy of historic racism, affirmative discrimination can be fitted into the existing fabric of departures from meritocratic standards.

The same distinction obtains along the dimension of tangible impact. In the layoff context, the senior white loses a currently held job in which he may have invested a good part of his working life (thus foreclosing a variety of other options). By contrast, the unsuccessful applicant for a new job suffers essentially the same loss as anyone else who fails to get a desired position, whatever the selection criteria used, whatever the employer's or the community's aim in designing the process. We do not mean to trivialize the sense of grievance that may be felt by dispreferred whites; nor do we deny that the unsuccessful applicant suffers a palpable economic loss. But the burden of losing an unheld job is not so large that a morally decent community, determined to rectify the legacy of racism, could not reasonably impose that burden on some individual community members. At issue is not the gratuitous infliction of suffer-

[239] See notes 170–82 *supra* and accompanying text.

[240] See notes 183–84 *supra* and accompanying text.

ing but a question of appropriate distribution. Absent a policy of affirmative discrimination, there will be many blacks who experience the same disappointment of nonselection. At least some of their losses will occur because sufficient steps were not taken to overcome inherited disadvantages and the unfair head start enjoyed by some white competitors.[241]

C. OTHER ISSUES

The operation of a labor market consists of more than just initial hiring and eventual termination, whether by indefinite layoff or otherwise. In between occurs a continual process of transfers, upgrading, and promotions.[242] Positive action both by private firms and by government is important at this intermediate stage: the goal of affirmative discrimination is not simply to get blacks anywhere inside the firm, possibly in dead-end jobs, but to insure that they have a fair chance at the more attractive and more important positions. How should one assess the burden that affirmative discrimination here might impose on individual whites? On the one hand, promotion resembles hiring in the sense that the dispreferred white does not lose an existing job, but merely fails to progress to a more attractive position. On the other hand, because seniority does play a significant role in promotion decisions, overriding that criterion can produce the same sense of grievance about the denial of an earned right as it does in the layoff setting.[243] We concede that we cannot here sort out the competing considerations and indicate precisely where to strike the balance. Our Model of Social Justice at least clarifies the agenda of issues.

---

[241] There is a further aspect to the evaluation of hiring quotas, involving the adoption by courts of rather ambitious short-term hiring targets (*e.g.*, one black for one white in an area where the black share of the available labor force may be 20 percent or even less). While we note this as a pertinent problem for a fully worked-out theory of affirmative discrimination in employment, see Williams v. City of New Orleans, 34 Fair Empl. Prac. Cas. 1009, 1015–18 (5th Cir. 1984) (*en banc*) (plurality opinion), we are not able to address it here.

[242] United Steelworkers v. Weber, 443 U.S. 193 (1979), the case in which the Supreme Court explicitly approved of affirmative discrimination in employment (albeit, through private voluntary action), involved a program under which employees would be trained for and then promoted to the skilled trades position at Kaiser Steel.

[243] ABRAHAM & MEDOFF, YEARS OF SERVICE AND PROBABILITY OF PROMOTION (Nat. Bur. Econ. Research, November 1983), found that while a substantial majority of firms reported that seniority was a relevant factor in their promotion decisions, it was considerably less important for promotions than it was in layoffs. See note 209 *supra*.

VI. Conclusion

Sometimes, "No answer is what the wrong question begets."[244] On other occasions, a conclusion does emerge, however misbegotten and misguided. *Memphis Firefighters v. Stotts* fits the second category. Conceiving the question before it as requiring a selection between the Model of Individual Justice and the Model of Group Justice, the Supreme Court opted for the individual justice approach. The result was an apparent sacrifice of the values supporting affirmative discrimination.

The issues surrounding affirmative discrimination are better expressed in two questions than, as the *Stotts* Court apparently believed, in one. The first question involves the necessary justifications, in principle, for programs of affirmative discrimination aimed to rectify past, group-based injustices. The second, which assumes that a justification exists, concerns issues of fairness in cost allocation, and more particularly, the reasonableness of placing the burden on particular, dispreferred individuals.

Although the *Stotts* Court's formulation of the question for decision was wanting, its holding as to seniority layoffs was correct. There are important differences between race-based hiring preferences and racial quotas that eviscerate seniority rights. The latter, when causing senior whites to be evicted from their jobs, impose an excessive burden on the displaced individuals. By comparison, because hiring quotas exact a lesser cost, preferences at the entry level ought to be upheld.

Fortunately, the objectionable aspects of *Stotts* fairly can be characterized as dicta. The broader issues—including the permissibility of race-based hiring preferences in the job market—remain open for reconsideration.

---

[244] Ely, *The Supreme Court 1977 Term—Foreword: On Discovering Fundamental Values*, 92 Harv. L. Rev. 5 (1978), quoting Bickel, The Least Dangerous Branch 103 (1962).

Part II
Liberal Perspectives

[4]

VOLUME 95 JANUARY 1982 NUMBER 3

HARVARD LAW REVIEW

THE EMPTY IDEA OF EQUALITY

*Peter Westen**

The principle of equality — that likes should be treated alike — has been a fixture of Western thought for thousands of years. In this Article, Professor Westen argues that the endurance of the principle is due to the fact that it is empty of content. For the principle to have meaning, it must incorporate some external values that determine which persons and treatments are alike, but once these external values are found, the principle of equality is superfluous. Worse, equality tends to cause confusion and logical errors. Consequently, Professor Westen concludes, the rhetoric of equality should be abandoned.

EQUALITY is commonly perceived to differ from rights and liberties. Rights are diverse; equality is singular. Rights are complicated; equality is simple. Rights are noncomparative in nature, having their source and their justification in a person's individual well-being; equality is comparative, deriving its source and its limits from the treatment of others. Rights are concerned with absolute deprivation; equality is concerned with relative deprivation. Rights mean variety, creativity, differentiation; equality means uniformity. Rights are individualistic; equality is social. Or so it is said.[1]

---

* Professor of Law, University of Michigan. Harvard University, B.A., 1964; University of California, Berkeley, J.D., 1968.

This Article is based on a paper presented at a Michigan Faculty Seminar on February 6, 1980. I would like to thank my colleagues at the Michigan Law School for their insight and encouragement. I am especially grateful to my friends and colleagues here and elsewhere for reading and commenting upon earlier drafts of the Article: Bruce Ackerman, Vince Blasi, Paul Brest, Owen Fiss, Dede Freedman, Charles Fried, Kenneth Karst, Tom Green, Diane Lehman, Jeffrey Lehman, Dustin Ordway, Ted St. Antoine, Joe Sax, Phil Soper, Paul Stephan, David Westin, Christina Whitman, and my brother, Tracy Westen. I owe a very special debt of thanks to W.T. Jones and Don Regan for initiating an extraordinary correspondence with me on the idea of equality. To spare them possible embarrassment, I should say that they all disagreed with some or all of the Article. I would also like to thank the John Simon Guggenheim Memorial Foundation for its financial support.

[1] *See* J. FEINBERG, SOCIAL PHILOSOPHY 98–119 (1973) (rights are noncomparative in nature, while equality is comparative); A. FLEW, THE POLITICS OF PROCRUSTES 29 (1981) ("To the extent that you are indeed an authentic egalitarian you are committed to saying that what various persons are to hold is to be determined primarily by reference to what other people have, rather than by reference to what those persons

These perceived differences are reflected in a certain ebb and flow between the ideal of equality, on one hand, and the ideal of rights and liberties, on the other. When the framers of the United States Constitution came to define the relationship between the central government and the people, they spoke in a bill of rights; when the victors of the Civil War reconstructed the relationship between the people and the states three-quarters of a century later, they spoke in the language of "equality."[2] Fifty years ago equality was dismissed as a legal argument of "last resort,"[3] one to be eschewed until all available "rights" had been tried and rejected; today equality is becoming the argument of first choice, one that threatens to swallow "rights" that once ranked far above it.[4]

---

themselves both are or are not, and have or have not done."); S. LAKOFF, EQUALITY IN POLITICAL PHILOSOPHY 6 (1964) ("*Formally* there is one idea of equality . . . ."); Feinberg, *Noncomparative Justice*, 83 PHIL. REV. 297, 310 (1974) (noncomparative principles are "irreducibly diverse," while comparative principles always share the same "form"); Lucas, *Against Equality Again*, 52 PHIL. 255, 271 (1977) ("[J]ustice is not equality . . . . Justice is much more complicated than equality."); Nisbet, *The New Despotism*, COMMENTARY, June 1975, at 31, 40 (liberty means "differentiation," "variety," and "creativity," while equality means "uniformity"); Raphael, *Tensions Between the Goals of Equality and Freedom*, in 2 EQUALITY & FREEDOM 543, 553 (G. Dorsey ed. 1977) (freedom is an individual value, while equality is a social value); Wright, *Judicial Review and the Equal Protection Clause*, 15 HARV. C.R.-C.L. L. REV. 1, 17–18 (1980) (equality speaks in "relative" not "absolute" terms).

[2] *Compare* Handlin, *The Quest for Equality*, 1979 WASH. U.L.Q. 35, 35 ("The concept of equality entered only tangentially into the Constitution as ratified in 1789. This was not a subject that greatly concerned either the framers of that document or the people who ratified it."), *and* W. ADAMS, THE FIRST AMERICAN CONSTITUTIONS 176 (1980) ("[T]he majority of the states did not formally acknowledge the principle of equality in their first constitutional documents in the years following Independence."), *with* J. POLE, THE PURSUIT OF EQUALITY IN AMERICAN HISTORY 148–76 (1978) (the reconstruction amendments were centrally concerned with the idea of equality).

[3] Buck v. Bell, 274 U.S. 200, 208 (1927) (Holmes, J.).

[4]

> What we are witnessing now is a shift, not as yet decisive but significant, of the center of gravity from the Due Process Clause to the Equal Protection Clause of [the Fourteenth] Amendment. It is highly probable that to the next generation the Equal Protection Clause will be, in constitutional and political interpretation, what the Due Process Clause was in the past.

Commager, *Equal Protection as an Instrument of Revolution*, in CONSTITUTIONAL GOVERNMENT IN AMERICA 467 (1980); *see* Kurland, *The Supreme Court, 1963 Term — Foreword: Equal in Origin and Equal in Title to the Legislative and Executive Branches of the Government*, 78 HARV. L. REV. 143, 144 (1964). *Compare* Karst, *The Supreme Court, 1976 Term — Foreword: Equal Citizenship Under the Fourteenth Amendment*, 91 HARV. L. REV. 1, 4, 26–33 (1977) (arguing that the equal protection clause of the 14th amendment provides constitutional basis for the rights of "citizenship" that have previously been treated as separate entitlements), *with* Perry, *Modern Equal Protection: A Conceptualization and Appraisal*, 79 COLUM. L. REV. 1023, 1024, 1074–81 (1979) (arguing that fundamental rights cases are "not really *equal protection* doctrine at all").

The juxtaposition of "rights" and "equality" also has led to a perceived tension between them.[5] Equality is sometimes said to be flourishing at the expense of rights, just as rights are sometimes said to be flourishing at the expense of equality.[6] Each is also said to be more important than the other. Thus, rights are often said to be the source of equality, while equality is often said to be the root or source of all rights.[7]

I believe that this contrasting of rights and equality is fundamentally misconceived. It is based on a misunderstanding, both in law and in morals, about the role of equality in ethical discourse. To avoid possible misunderstanding, let me emphasize what I mean by equality and rights. By "equality" I mean the proposition in law and morals that "people who are alike should be treated alike"[8] and its correlative, that

---

[5] *See* E. BARKER, PRINCIPLES OF SOCIAL & POLITICAL THEORY 159 (1951); D. PHILLIPS, EQUALITY, JUSTICE AND RECTIFICATION 70–75 (1979); Baechler, *Liberty, Property, and Equality*, 22 NOMOS: PROPERTY 269 (1980) (equality is a menace to liberty in that, if one attempts to achieve equality, liberty will perish); Mazor, *The Exhaustion of the Ideals of Freedom and Equality in the United States*, in 1 EQUALITY & FREEDOM, *supra* note 1, at 175, 177; McLean, *Liberty, Equality and the Pareto Principle: A Comment on Weale*, 40 ANALYSIS 212 (1980) (liberalism cannot be coherently reconciled with egalitarianism); Nagel, *Issues Regarding Tensions Between Goals of Equality and Freedom*, in 2 EQUALITY & FREEDOM, *supra* note 1, at 603, 610 n.1; Nisbet, *supra* note 1, at 32; Raphael, *supra* note 1, at 553.

[6] For authority that equality is flourishing today, see 2 F. HAYEK, LAW, LEGISLATION AND LIBERTY 80–85 (1976); *cf.* Nisbet, *The Pursuit of Equality*, PUB. INTEREST, Spring 1974, at 103, 116–18 (equality flourishing among philosophers). For the view that rights are flourishing today at the expense of equality, see P. GREEN, THE PURSUIT OF INEQUALITY 166, 262 (1981); M. LEWIS, THE CULTURE OF INEQUALITY 4–17, 126–31 (1978).

[7] For the view that rights and liberties are more basic than equality, see Beck, *Liberty and Equality*, 10 IDEALISTIC STUD. 24, 36 (1980) (liberty is "more basic" than equality); Machan, *Equality's Dependence on Liberty*, in 2 EQUALITY & FREEDOM, *supra* note 1, at 663, 664–65; Raphael, *supra* note 1, at 555 ("Freedom appears to be a greater value than equality."). For the contrary view, i.e., that equality is the source of all rights and liberties, see R. DWORKIN, TAKING RIGHTS SERIOUSLY 273–74 (1977); Rawls, *Justice As Fairness*, 67 PHIL. REV. 164, 165–66 (1958). *But cf.* Hart, *Between Utility and Rights*, 79 COLUM. L. REV. 828, 845–46 (1979) (criticizing Dworkin's view that all liberties derive from the principle of equality).

[8] It is sometimes said that, instead of one basic idea of equality, there are really numerous distinct ideas of equality. *See, e.g.*, P. POLYVIOU, THE EQUAL PROTECTION OF THE LAWS 1–5, 7–24 (1980) (three basic kinds of equality); D. RAE, EQUALITIES 133 (1981) (at least 108 kinds of equality); A. ROSS, ON LAW AND JUSTICE 270–72 (1959) (five kinds of equality); Mortimore, *An Ideal of Equality*, 77 MIND 222, 225–26 (1968) (seven kinds of equality); *cf.* W. FRANKENA, *Some Beliefs about Justice*, in PERSPECTIVES ON MORALITY 93, 96–97 (1976) (five kinds of distributive justice); C. PERELMAN, THE IDEA OF JUSTICE AND THE PROBLEM OF ARGUMENT 6–7 (J. Petrie trans. 1963) (six kinds of distributive justice); N. RESCHER, DISTRIBUTIVE JUSTICE 73 (1966) (seven kinds of distributive justice). In reality, however, the foregoing kinds of equality are merely substantive variations on the common, formal principle that "likes should be treated alike." Thus, to say that goods should be distributed accord-

"people who are unalike should be treated unalike."[9] Equality thus includes all statements to the effect that the reason one person should be treated in a certain way is that he is "like" or "equal to" or "similar to" or "identical to" or "the same as" another who receives such treatment.[10] "Rights," by contrast, means all claims that can justly be made by or on behalf of an individual or group of individuals to some condition or power[11] — except claims that "people who are alike be treated alike." The right may be a "liberty," "prerogative," "privi-

---

ing to merit, or needs, or works, or wants is simply to say that the substantive criterion that defines the respect in which all people are alike is merit, or needs, or works, or wants. In that sense, it is a mistake to believe that the various kinds of equality can be enumerated as a multiple and yet finite list. On one hand, there are as many substantive versions of equality as there are substantive notions of right and entitlement by which persons can be said to be "alike" or "unalike"; on the other hand, there is only one formal idea of equality — that "likes should be treated alike." *See* S. LAKOFF, *supra* note 1, at 6 ("*Formally* there is one idea of equality; *substantively* there are many."). One idea of equality that does not take the form that "likes should be treated alike" is the so-called "presumption of equality" — namely, the proposition that everyone should be treated alike unless there is a good reason for treating them differently. For an argument that the "presumption of equality" is not only incompatible with the idea that "likes should be treated alike," but is incoherent in its premises, see *infra* pp. 569–77.

[9] Although the proposition that "likes should be treated alike" is sometimes said to have nothing to do with the proposition that "unlikes should be treated unalike," *see* A. FLEW, *supra* note 1, at 36; Honoré, *Social Justice*, 8 MCGILL L.J. 77, 83 (1962), it can be shown that one logically entails the other. *See* Note, *Equal Protection: A Closer Look at Closer Scrutiny*, 76 MICH. L. REV. 771, 781 n.34 (1978); *see also* sources cited *infra* note 123.

[10] Although some authorities distinguish between the terms "like," "similar," "equal," "identical," and "the same," *see, e.g.*, Adler & Hutchins, *The Idea of Equality*, in THE GREAT IDEAS TODAY 1968, at 303, 321–22 (M. Adler & R. Hutchins eds. 1968); Bedau, *Egalitarianism and the Idea of Equality*, 9 NOMOS: EQUALITY 3, 4–13 (1967); Menne, *Identity, Equality, Similarity: A Logico-Philosophical Investigation*, 4 RATIO 50 (1962), unless I explicitly indicate otherwise, I shall assume that these terms are interchangeable for purposes of the proposition that "equals should be treated equally."

[11] I take my definition of "right" from M. GINSBERG, ON JUSTICE IN SOCIETY 74 (1965). I am not wedded to Ginsberg's particular wording. For alternatives that I would consider equally satisfactory, see J. FEINBERG, *The Nature and Value of Rights*, in RIGHTS, JUSTICE, AND THE BOUNDS OF LIBERTY 143, 155 (1980) ("To have a right is to have a claim against someone whose recognition as valid is called for by some set of governing rules or moral principles."); Gewirth, *The Basis and Content of Human Rights*, 23 NOMOS: HUMAN RIGHTS 119, 120 (1967) ("A person's rights are what belong to him as his due, what he is entitled to, hence what he can rightly demand of others."), *reprinted in* 13 GA. L. REV. 1142, 1150 (1979); Hart, *Bentham On Legal Rights*, in OXFORD ESSAYS IN JURISPRUDENCE (Second Series) 170, 197 (A. Simpson ed. 1973) (referring to "legal right" as "a legally protected choice"); McCloskey, *Rights — Some Conceptual Issues*, 54 AUSTRALASIAN J. PHIL. 99, 99 (1976) (rights are "entitlements to do, have, enjoy, or have done").

lege," "power," "exemption," or "immunity."[12] The right may have its source in law or morals or custom;[13] it may be comparative or noncomparative;[14] it may consist of a principle or

---

[12] Wesley Hohfeld found it useful to divide "rights" into four subcategories: "claims" (or "rights"), "privileges" (or "liberties"), "powers," and "immunities." *See* W. HOHFELD, FUNDAMENTAL LEGAL CONCEPTIONS 35–63 (W. Cook ed. 1964) (1st ed. 1919). I use the term "right" in what Hohfeld (disparagingly) called its "generic" sense, namely to denote "any sort of legal advantage, whether claim, privilege, power, or immunity." *Id.* at 42, 71; *see also* People v. Dikeman, 7 How. Pr. 124, 130 (N.Y. Sup. Ct. 1852) (Strong, J.) ("The word 'right' is defined by lexicographers to denote, among other things, property, interest, *power*, *prerogative*, immunity, *privilege* (*Walker*'s *Dict.* word 'Right'). In law it is most frequently applied to property in its restricted sense, but it is often used to designate *power*, *prerogative*, and *privilege* . . . .") (emphasis in original), *quoted in* W. HOHFELD, *supra*, at 36–37; Hart, *supra* note 11, at 173 (Bentham used "rights" to refer generally to "claim-rights," "liberties," "privileges," and "powers.").

While Hohfeld's subcategories highlight distinctions and relationships that one might otherwise overlook, *see* Brady, *Law, Language and Logic: The Legal Philosophy of Wesley Newcomb Hohfeld*, 8 TRANSACTIONS CHARLES S. PEIRCE SOC'Y 246 (1972); Perry, *A Paradigm of Philosophy: Hohfeld on Legal Rights*, 14 AM. PHIL. Q. 41 (1977), the subcategories are not useful for purposes of distinguishing the "generic" denotation of "right" from the propositions that "likes should be treated alike" and "unalikes should be treated unalike." Thus, although some would distinguish between "rights" (or "claims") on one hand and "privileges" (or "liberties") on the other, *see, e.g.*, Hart, *Are There Any Natural Rights?*, in HUMAN RIGHTS 61, 64–65 (A. Melden ed. 1970); Hart, *supra* note 11, at 171, 173–78, 179–82; Williams, *The Concept of Legal Liberty*, 56 COLUM. L. REV. 1129 (1956), the legal distinction is essentially between a claim to action by the state or to action or nonaction by private persons, on one hand, and a claim to nonaction by the state, on the other hand. *See* W. BUCKLAND, SOME REFLECTIONS ON JURISPRUDENCE 92–96 (1945); H. Hart & A. Sacks, The Legal Process 147–48 (tent. ed. 1958) (unpublished manuscript in Harvard Law School Library). Similarly, while some would distinguish between "rights" and "powers," *see, e.g.*, H.L.A. HART, THE CONCEPT OF LAW 26–41 (1961), the distinction is essentially between unconditional claims and conditional or contingent claims. *See* J. LUCAS, THE PRINCIPLES OF POLITICS 157 n.1 (1966); Cohen, Book Review, 71 MIND 395, 405–06 (1962) (reviewing H.L.A. HART, *supra*). Finally, while some have criticized the distinction between "rights" and "liberties," on one hand, and "immunities," on the other, *see* J. STONE, LEGAL SYSTEM AND LAWYERS' REASONING 147, 157 & nn.74–75, 161 n.93 (1964), the distinction (if any) seems to be between nonconstitutional claims and constitutional claims. *See* Hart, *supra* note 11, at 198–200.

[13] The source of the right depends on the purpose for which it is being asserted. For purposes of constitutional law, the right must have its source in the Constitution; for purposes of domestic law, it must have its source in a statute or doctrine of common law; for purposes of morals, it must have its source in an agreed-upon or authoritative set of moral premises. *See* J. FEINBERG, *supra* note 11, at 154. For a description of the various moral principles that are commonly asserted to support rights, see Gewirth, *supra* note 11, at 1144.

[14] A "comparative" right is a right of a person that is "determinable *only* by reference to his relations to other persons," while a "noncomparative" right is one that can be "determined independently of that of other people." Feinberg, *Noncomparative Justice*, 83 PHIL. REV. 297, 298 (1974); *see also* Browne, *Nonegalitarian Justice*, 56 AUSTRALASIAN J. PHIL. 48, 49–50 (1978) (adopting Feinberg's terminology).

a policy;[15] it may be absolute or defeasible.[16] The only claims that do *not* qualify as "rights" are claims that "likes should be treated alike."

I try in this Article to establish two propositions: (1) that statements of equality logically entail (and necessarily collapse into) simpler statements of rights; and (2) that the additional step of transforming simple statements of rights into statements of equality not only involves unnecessary work but also engenders profound conceptual confusion. Equality, therefore, is an idea that should be banished from moral and legal discourse as an explanatory norm.

The Article proceeds in three Parts. Part I seeks to demonstrate that: (1) the proposition "people who are alike should be treated alike" is tautological; (2) the entitlements people mistakenly attribute to the idea of equality all derive from external substantive rights; and (3) the idea of equality is logically indistinguishable from the standard formula of distributive justice — that is, that "every person should be given his due." Part II analyzes the three paradigmatic forms of equal protection cases in American constitutional law to show that formulating them in terms of "equality" is entirely superfluous. Part III then argues that the confusion caused by analyzing problems in terms of equality outweighs the purely rhetorical benefits.

I. EQUALITY IN MORALS

The study of equality begins with Plato and Aristotle, the first to proclaim that likes should be treated alike and to give equality its prominence in law and morals. Aristotle, building on the work of Plato,[17] said two things about equality that have dominated Western thought ever since:

[15] Ronald Dworkin confines the term "rights" to what he calls "principles" (as opposed to mere "policies"). *See* R. DWORKIN, *supra* note 7, at 22–31, 90–100, 180–82, 191, 227, 273. One of the distinguishing features of Dworkinian "rights," so defined, is their capacity to "trump" mere "policies." *See* Regan, *Glosses on Dworkin: Rights, Principles, and Policies*, 76 MICH. L. REV. 1213, 1214–34 (1978). I shall not use the term "right" in any such specialized sense.

[16] For the distinction between "absolute" and "prima facie" rights, see J. FEINBERG, *Voluntary Euthanasia and the Inalienable Right to Life*, in RIGHTS, JUSTICE, AND THE BOUNDS OF LIBERTY 221, 225–27 (1980). For a further taxonomy of rights, including distinctions between in personam and in rem rights, positive and negative rights, and active and passive rights, see J. FEINBERG, *supra* note 1, at 59–60.

[17] PLATO, GORGIAS 507E–508A (B. Jowett trans. 1892); PLATO, LAWS VI.757 (B. Jowett trans. 1892); PLATO, PHAEDO 74 (B. Jowett trans. 1892); PLATO, THE REPUBLIC VIII.558 (B. Jowett trans. 1892); *see* M. GINSBERG, *supra* note 11, at 66, 80–81; P. POLYVIOU, *supra* note 8, at 7 ("[E]quality invariably begin[s] with the principle of Aristotle that equality consists of treating equals equally and unequals unequally.") (footnote omitted). For the Pythagorean notion of equality, see Guthrie, *Pythagoras and Pythagoreanism*, in 7 ENCYCLOPEDIA OF PHILOSOPHY 37, 38 (1967).

(1) Equality in morals means this: things that are alike should be treated alike, while things that are unalike should be treated unalike in proportion to their unalikeness.[18]

(2) Equality and justice are synonomous: to be just is to be equal, to be unjust is to be unequal.[19]

These propositions raise two questions for discussion. First, what is the connection between the fact that two things are alike and the moral inference that they should be treated alike? Second, what is the justification for equating justice and equality?

A. The Connection Between Being Alike and Being Entitled to Be Treated Alike

The proposition that "likes should be treated alike" is said to be a universal moral truth — a truth that can "be intuitively known with perfect clearness and certainty."[20] Why? What is the connection between the fact that people are alike and the normative conclusion that they ought to be treated alike? How can one move from an "is" to an "ought"?

The answer can be found in the component parts of the equality formula. The formula "people who are alike should be treated alike" involves two components: (1) a determination that two people are alike; and (2) a moral judgment that they ought to be treated alike. The determinative component is the first. Once one determines that two people are alike for purposes of the equality principle, one knows how they ought to be treated. To understand why this is so — that is, to understand how (1) works — one must understand what kind of

---

[18] ARISTOTLE, ETHICA NICOMACHEA V.3.1131a–1131b (W. Ross trans. 1925); *see also* ARISTOTLE, METAPHYSICA I.5.1055b–1056b (W. Ross trans. 2d ed. 1928). *See generally* W. HARDIE, ARISTOTLE'S ETHICAL THEORY 189 (2d ed. 1980); H. KELSEN, *Aristotle's Doctrine of Justice*, in WHAT IS JUSTICE? 110, 127–28 (1957); K. MARC-WOGAU, *Aristotle's Theory of Corrective Justice and Reciprocity*, in PHILOSOPHICAL ESSAYS 21 (1967).

[19] ARISTOTLE, ETHICA EUDEMIA VII.9.1241b (W. Ross ed. 1925); ARISTOTLE, ETHICA NICOMACHEA V.3.1131a–1131b (W. Ross trans. 1925); ARISTOTLE, POLITICS III.9.1280a, III.12.1282b–1283a, V.1.1301a–1301b (B. Jowett trans. 1921).

[20] C. PERELMAN, *supra* note 8, at 12 ("To everyone the idea of justice inevitably suggests the notion of a certain equality. From Plato and Aristotle, through St. Thomas Aquinas, down to the jurists, moralists and philosophers of our own day runs a thread of universal agreement on this point."); H. SIDGWICK, THE METHODS OF ETHICS 380 (7th ed. 1907); Frankena, *supra* note 8, at 94 ("[T]here is one principle of distributive justice on which there seems to be general agreement, namely, that like cases or individuals are to be dealt with in the same way or treated alike, or that similar cases are to be treated similarly."); *see also* ARISTOTLE, ETHICA NICOMACHEA V.3.1131a–1131b (W. Ross trans. 1925) (relationship between equality and justice is self-evident: "If, then, the unjust is unequal, the just is equal, as all men suppose it to be, even apart from argument.").

determination (1) is. One must know precisely what it means to say for purposes of equality that two persons are alike.

First, "people who are alike" might mean people who are alike in every respect. The trouble is that no two people are alike in every respect. The only things that are completely alike in every respect are immaterial symbols and forms, such as ideal numbers and geometric figures, which are not themselves the subject of morals.[21]

Second, "people who are alike" may mean people, who, though not alike in every respect, are alike in some respects. Unfortunately, while the previous definition excludes every person in the world, the present definition includes every person and thing because all people and things are alike in some respect; and one is left with the morally absurd proposition that "all people and things should be treated alike."[22]

Third, "people who are alike" may refer to people who are *morally* alike in a certain respect. The latter interpretation successfully avoids the philosophical hurdle of deriving an "ought" from an "is."[23] It starts with a normative determi-

---

[21] *See* C. PERELMAN, JUSTICE, LAW AND ARGUMENT 35 (1980) (referring to the Leibnizian principle of the identity of the indiscernibles, i.e., that no two identical beings exist); Bedau, *supra* note 10, at 8 (referring to "the Leibnizian principle that things the same in every respect are the same thing"); Tammelo, *Equality as the Core of Justice*, 52 ARCHIV FÜR RECHTS UND SOZIALPHILOSOPHIE 135, 138 (1966) ("equality between two entities can be asserted only in the realm of formal entities"). Plato's discussion of equality in *Phaedo* is enigmatic:

> "Did we not see equalities of material things, such as pieces of wood and stones, and gather from them the idea of an equality which is different from them? For you will acknowledge that there is a difference? Or look at the matter in another way: — Do not the same pieces of wood or stones appear at one time equal, and at another time unequal?"
> "That is certain."
> "But are real equals ever equal? or is the idea of equality the same as of inequality?"
> "Impossible, Socrates."
> "Then these (so-called) equals are not the same with the idea of equality?"

PLATO, PHAEDO 74 (B. Jowett trans. 1892). For analyses, see Allen, *Forms and Standards*, 9 PHIL. Q. 164 (1959); Haynes, *The Form Equality, as a Set of Equals*: Phaedo *74b–c*, 9 PHRONESIS 17 (1964).

[22] "[T]he attempt to conceive [of] . . . a society [in which all persons are treated equally in every respect] faces [the same] number of formidable obstacles, so much so that it must lead one to wonder if it really is a coherent notion." J. REES, EQUALITY 98 (1971); *see* J. FEINBERG, *supra* note 1, at 100–02; J. LUCAS, *supra* note 12, at 244–45; *see also* Berlin, *Equality as an Ideal*, in JUSTICE AND SOCIAL POLICY 128, 137 (F. Olafson ed. 1961) (describing a world of "absolute" equality as "perhaps [an] absurd ideal").

[23] Oppenheim, *The Concept of Equality*, in 5 INTERNATIONAL ENCYCLOPEDIA OF SOCIAL SCIENCES 102, 107 (1968) ("[N]ormative principles cannot be derived from factual generalizations; neither equality nor inequality of characteristics entails the desirability of either egalitarian or inegalitarian treatment."); *see also* D. LLOYD, INTRODUCTION TO JURISPRUDENCE 87 (3d ed. 1972) ("The idea of equality or non-

nation that two people are alike in a morally significant respect and moves to a normative conclusion that the two should be treated alike. Instead of deriving an "ought" from an "is," it derives an "ought" from an "ought." However, categories of morally alike objects do not exist in nature; moral alikeness is established only when people define categories.[24] To say that people are morally alike is therefore to articulate a moral standard of treatment — a standard or rule specifying certain treatment for certain people[25] — by reference to which they are, and thus are to be treated, alike.[26]

Now that we understand what it means to be alike, it should be easy to understand what it means to be treated alike. Oddly enough, some commentators take it to mean that if a moral standard prescribes some uniform treatment for all members of a class (for instance, that all Rhodes Scholars shall receive fellowships to Magdalen College, Oxford), equal treatment is achieved by either uniformly granting or uniformly denying that treatment to all members of the class.[27] Thus,

---

discrimination is essentially a value-judgment which cannot be derived from any assertions or speculations regarding the nature of man."). *But see* A. WEALE, EQUALITY AND SOCIAL POLICY 20 (1978) (implying that equality is a formula by which one can infer an "ought" from an "is").

[24] *See* Tussman & tenBroek, *The Equal Protection of the Laws*, 37 CALIF. L. REV. 341, 346 (1949).

[25] It is possible to have norms that are purely definitional, but they are not relevant to the discussion here.

[26] *See* Montague, *Comparative and Non-comparative Justice*, 30 PHIL. Q. 131, 135 (1980) (notion of "'relevant similarity' [in the proposition that people relevantly similar should be treated similarly] . . . concerns features that require or call for treatment of a certain kind"). Gillespie argues that the proposition "people who are alike should be treated alike" is not a universal truth but rather applies only in cases in which the actor otherwise has a duty to such "persons." *See* Gillespie, *On Treating Like Cases Differently*, 25 PHIL. Q. 151, 154–55 (1975). He says so, however, because of the way he chooses to define the phrase "people who are alike." By "people who are alike" he means people who are morally alike in some respect — but not in respect of being morally entitled to similar treatment. Consequently, he is obliged to import an additional notion of duty of treatment toward such persons as a deus ex machina to make sense of the notion that "likes should be treated alike." The deus ex machina can be avoided altogether if "people who are alike" is defined to mean "people who are entitled to be treated alike in a certain respect." While Gillespie appears to have in mind something different from the latter definition of "people who are alike," it is difficult to identify precisely what such a different definition would be.

[27] *See* G. DEL VECCHIO, JUSTICE 86 n.3 (1952); J. LUCAS, ON JUSTICE 171–72 (1980) (implying that it would be "equal" to take laborers who are entitled to be paid by the hour and pay them all per capita); Del Vecchio, *Equality and Inequality in Relation to Justice*, 11 NAT. L.F. 36, 46 (1966); Feinberg, *supra* note 1, at 312 (suggesting that it would be equal to take persons who are alike entitled to be free and enslave them all); Frankena, *The Concept of Social Justice*, in SOCIAL JUSTICE 1, 17 (R. Brandt ed. 1962) (suggesting that it would be equal to "boil . . . in oil" all persons who are alike entitled to a "certain minimum level of welfare"); Vlastos,

they would say, although it would not be just to deny all Rhodes Scholars fellowships, it would be equal.

This interpretation of like treatment, whatever else it may be, is certainly not empty. On the contrary, it instructs people to do what they would otherwise know they should not do — that is, to give people who are "alike" by one standard the treatment that is alike by that standard or by its converse. The real trouble with the concept is not that it is empty, but that it is patently absurd.[28] Indeed, it is so preposterous a moral proposition that, if it were what equality really meant, no one would give it a moment's thought. To say "likes should be treated alike" is to make an "ought" statement — a statement of what people are morally enjoined to do. Yet if the statement directs people in countless cases to do what they concededly ought not to do (for instance, either award *or* deny fellowships to Rhodes Scholars), the statement itself cannot be true. Hence, if "likes should be treated alike" is to be taken seriously as a moral proposition — if it is to be accepted as true or just or lasting (as Aristotle and all the proposition's subsequent students have taken it to be) — "like treatment" cannot plausibly carry the foregoing meaning.[29]

As the reader may have noticed, a more natural view of "like treatment" is suggested by the way "people who are alike" was interpreted. Just as no categories of "like" people

Justice and Equality, in SOCIAL JUSTICE, *supra*, at 31, 62 (suggesting that it would be equal to prohibit all persons who are alike entitled to read *Doctor Zhivago* from reading it).

[28] It is morally contradictory to say that people who are alike entitled to certain treatment should therefore either receive the treatment to which they are entitled or not receive it. This is not to deny, however, that rules sometimes take the form, "everyone in class *A* shall either receive *X* or not receive *X*." Take Rhodes Scholars again. Cecil Rhodes, in establishing a scholarship trust, could have instructed the trustees to give all Rhodes Scholars either scholarships to Magdalen College or not, whichever the trustees in their discretion preferred. If the trust instrument so provided, Rhodes Scholars could legally and justly be treated accordingly; that is, it would be just and legal to give all Rhodes Scholars either scholarships to Magdalen College or not. If the latter treatment is just and legal, however, it is not because "likes should be treated alike." It is because the substantive rule of treatment by which Rhodes Scholars are defined to be alike — in this case, the trust instrument — itself prescribes the latter treatment.

[29]

> [I]t is hardly likely that anyone would want to see all men treated alike in every respect. We should not wish rheumatic patients to be treated like diabetics. Equals . . . ought to be treated alike in the respect in which they are equal; but there may be other respects in which they differ . . . which justify differences in treatment. Men who make identical tax returns ought to be taxed alike, but if they suffer from different ailments they should be treated with different medicines.

S. BENN & R. PETERS, THE PRINCIPLES OF POLITICAL THOUGHT 124 (1959); *see also* J. LUCAS, *supra* note 12, at 244–45.

exist in nature, neither do categories of "like" treatment exist; treatments can be alike only in reference to some moral rule. Thus, to say that people who are morally alike in a certain respect "should be treated alike" means that they should be treated in accord with the moral rule by which they are determined to be alike. Hence "likes should be treated alike" means that people for whom a certain treatment is prescribed by a standard should all be given the treatment prescribed by the standard. Or, more simply, people who by a rule should be treated alike should by the rule be treated alike.

So there it is: equality is entirely "[c]ircular."[30] It tells us to treat like people alike; but when we ask who "like people" are, we are told they are "people who should be treated alike." Equality is an empty vessel with no substantive moral content of its own.[31] Without moral standards, equality remains meaningless, a formula that can have nothing to say about how we should act. With such standards, equality becomes superfluous, a formula that can do nothing but repeat what we already know. As Bernard Williams observed, "when the statement of equality ceases to claim more than is warranted, it rather rapidly reaches the point where it claims less than is interesting."[32]

The recognition that equality is tautological explains several things. It explains why people who are alike should therefore be treated alike; why equality expresses a universal moral truth; why equality is taken to be a "law of thought";[33] and why this one aspect of Aristotle's moral views remains indisputable today, as it was 2,500 years ago. Equality is an undeniable and unchangeable moral truth because it is a sim-

---

[30] "[A]s soon as any weight is put on this principle it seems to collapse into the shattering triviality that cases are alike, morally or in any other respect, unless they are different." Locke, *The Trivializability of Universalizability*, 77 PHIL. REV. 25, 25 (1968); *see* Recasens-Siches, *Dignity, Liberty and Equality*, in 1 EQUALITY & FREEDOM, *supra* note 1, at 3, 17 ("[H]uman beings should be treated unequally as to the diversities that in justice should be taken into account. This . . . principle . . . theoretically is obvious . . . ."); *see also infra* note 141.

[31] Equality is not alone in its emptiness. For the argument that freedom, too, is a formal concept with no substantive content apart from the variables inserted to give it meaning, see MacCallum, *Negative and Positive Freedom*, 76 PHIL. REV. 312 (1967).

[32] Williams, *The Idea of Equality*, in PHILOSOPHY, POLITICS AND SOCIETY 110, 111 (P. Laslett & W. Runciman eds. 1962).

[33] H. KELSEN, *supra* note 18, at 134; *see also* M. GINSBERG, *supra* note 11, at 80 ("The second principle, namely, that like cases should be treated in like manner . . . is an axiom of all rational ethics . . . ."); Feinberg, *supra* note 1, at 319 ("[T]he principle that relevantly similar cases should be treated in similar ways . . . is a principle of reason . . . ."); *infra* note 37.

ple tautology. This should come as no surprise; as an a priori moral truth, equality could scarcely be anything else.

B. The Connection Between Equality and Rights

1. Equality As Derivative of Rights. — Relationships of equality (and inequality) are derivative, secondary relationships; they are logically posterior, not anterior, to rights. To say that two persons are the same in a certain respect is to presuppose a rule[34] — a prescribed standard for treating them — that both fully satisfy. Before such a rule is established, no standard of comparison exists. After such a rule is established, equality between them is a "logical consequence"[35] of the established rule. They are then "equal" in respect of the rule because that is what equal means: "Equally" means "'according to one and the same rule.'"[36] They are also then entitled to equal treatment under the rule because that is what possessing a rule means: "To conform to a rule is (tautologically) to apply it to the cases to which it applies."[37] To say

---

[34] Gewirth, *Political Justice*, in SOCIAL JUSTICE, *supra* note 27, at 119, 124 ("[E]quality is involved in the very idea of rules . . . .").

[35] C. PERELMAN, *supra* note 8, at 38 ("Equality of treatment is merely a logical consequence of the fact of keeping to [a] rule."); Berlin, *supra* note 22, at 132.

[36] Flathman, *Equality and Generalization, A Formal Analysis*, 9 NOMOS: EQUALITY 38, 45 (1967) (quoting the *Oxford English Dictionary*). Honoré offers a more extended discussion:

> The notion of conformity to rule can be made to yield the notion that like cases should be treated alike. If we think of those species of rule that prescribe that certain people be treated in a certain way when certain conditions are fulfilled, the demand that such rules should be observed entails the demand that cases falling within the conditions mentioned should be treated in the way prescribed in the rule, that is that people who are alike in the relevant respect should be treated alike. This, then involves the principle "*treat like cases alike.*"

Honoré, *supra* note 9, at 82; *see also* A. ROSS, *supra* note 8, at 273 ("[E]quality . . . simply means the correct application of a general rule . . . ."); Beck, *Liberty and Equality*, 10 IDEALISTIC STUD. 24, 28 (1980) (some commentators "would ground equal treatment in the very nature of a rule governed social practice"); Flathman, *supra*, at 38 ("To treat people equally is to treat them in the same way. To treat people in the same way is to treat them according to a rule.").

[37] Browne, *The Presumption of Equality*, 53 AUSTRALASIAN J. PHIL. 46, 51 (1975). According to one writer:

> All rational moral theories have an element of formal equality because formal equality is inherent in the notion of rationality. If characteristic x is a sufficient reason to treat individual *A* in a particular manner, then it is a sufficient reason to treat *B* in the same manner unless some relevant distinction between *A* and *B* can be adduced to block this inference.

W. GALSTON, JUSTICE AND THE HUMAN GOOD 133 (1980); *see* Adler & Hutchins, *supra* note 10, at 340 ("It does not seem especially helpful to speak of the rule being applied equally when nothing more is meant than that it is being applied."); *see also* M. GINSBERG, *supra* note 11, at 80 (Equality "is an axiom of all rational ethics and is implicit in the notion of a norm or law of action as such."); J. LUCAS, *supra* note

that two people are "equal" and entitled to be treated "equally" is to say that they both fully satisfy the criteria of a governing rule of treatment. It says nothing at all about the content or wisdom of the governing rule.

It might be thought that, while relationships of equality logically follow substantive definitions of right, equality may also precede definitions of right. Thus, it might be thought that a substantive right of persons to be treated with human respect is itself a product of an antecedent judgment that all persons are equal.[38] That is not so. To see why, consider how one would go about deciding whether monstrously deformed neonates or human embryos or stroke victims in irreversible comas should be treated as "persons" for purposes of the right to respect. In trying to make the decision, one gets nowhere by intoning that all persons are equal, because the very question is whether the three candidates are indeed "persons" within the meaning of the rule.[39] Nor does it do any good to say that likes should be treated alike, because the very question is whether the three candidates are indeed alike for purposes of human respect. Rather, one must first identify the trait that entitles anyone to be treated with respect and then ascertain empirically whether the trait appears in one or more of the three candidates.[40] If the candidates possess the rele-

12, at 246 (Equality is "none other than the weak principle of universalisability, the principle of rationality . . . ."); Freund, *The Philosophy of Equality*, 1979 WASH. U.L.Q. 11, 14 (equality "a premise of rational thought").

[38] *See* Hofstadter, *The Career Open to Personality*, in ASPECTS OF HUMAN EQUALITY 111, 112–13 (L. Bryson ed. 1956) ("If there is anything that should be called a postulate of equality, it is the principle of the intrinsic dignity of the human being, the infinite worth of the human person.").

[39]

> Do human beings have properties which distinguish them *in general* from (other) animals, and which justify general discrimination in their favour? These are profoundly difficult problems; their solution, however, has nothing to do with *equality*. . . . If an "elitist" preference for human beings over animals *is* justified, then that is . . . because of the particular moral significance of the differentiating properties which people have.

Browne, *supra* note 14, at 58.

[40] The issue of the empirical basis for moral traits has caused some confusion. Some commentators, believing that relationships of equality must be grounded in some verifiable traits, tend to conclude that equality is entirely empirical. *See, e.g.*, A. WEALE, *supra* note 23, at 22. Others, believing that an "ought" cannot be inferred from an "is," tend to conclude that moral notions of equality have no empirical basis. *See, e.g.*, P. SINGER, PRACTICAL ETHICS 15–16 (1979) ("The plain fact is that humans differ, and the differences apply to so many characteristics that the search for a factual basis on which to erect the principle of equality seems hopeless."); Blackstone, *On the Meaning and Justification of the Equality Principle*, 77 ETHICS 239, 239 (1967) ("[T]he primary function of the equality principle in its moral and political contexts is prescriptive, not descriptive, and . . . the quest for some property essential to all men, a property which justifies equality of treatment, is a mistake.").

vant trait, they become "persons" within the meaning of the rule and hence entitled to respect. If they lack the relevant trait, they are not "persons," not equal to persons, and not to be treated like persons for purposes of the rule.[41]

2. Equality and Uniform Administration of Rules. — Some commentators have argued that, while equality cannot by itself supply the content of any rule, it is nonetheless a "principle of crucial importance"[42] in the administration of rules: once a rule has been formulated, they say, equality comes into play as a "central"[43] and "necessary"[44] element of justice, ensuring

---

In fact, both contending camps are correct. Statements of moral and legal equality do have an empirical base, because otherwise one would have no way of distinguishing those creatures who are equal from those who are not. *See* Reck, *The Metaphysics of Equality*, 34 NEW SCHOLASTICISM 327, 335–37 (1960). Yet at the same time, statements of moral or legal equality also presuppose a normative element. *See* Raphael, *Equity and Equality*, 21 PHIL. 118, 122 (1946) ("The considerations which are 'relevant' to a claim for inequality are *moral* considerations, they are special moral claims."). In short, statements of equality presuppose the presence of empirical traits that we decide ought to carry certain moral consequences:

> [The modern classical philosophers] did indeed assert the axiom of equality as a statement of a factual truth about human beings . . . . More recent philosophers have given these classical writers a hard time; not because the critics are against equality, but on the general ground that those theories attempted to derive moral principles from purely factual arguments, doing a kind of illegitimate logical glide from the "is" to the "ought." But this kind of criticism often does its own kind of logical glide, from the correct statement that moral judgments cannot be deduced from factual ones, to the false conclusion that these two kinds of judgments are logically unrelated to each other. Factual premises alone are not sufficient for moral conclusions, it is true; but they are remarkably necessary.

D. HAWKINS, THE SCIENCE AND ETHICS OF EQUALITY 11–12 (1977).

[41] Suppose, for example, that the framers of a rule differ about whether citizenship should be a prerequisite for voting. Those who advocate a requirement of citizenship will argue that their proposed rule treats people equally because it treats people alike who are alike (i.e., citizens), and treats people unalike who are unalike (i.e., all aliens). By the same token, however, those who oppose a requirement of citizenship will argue that their rule treats people equally by treating people alike who are essentially alike (i.e., citizens and resident aliens) and treating people unalike who are unalike (i.e., nonresident aliens). *See generally* Rosberg, *Aliens and Equal Protection: Why Not the Right to Vote?*, 75 MICH. L. REV. 1092 (1977) (discussing disenfranchisement of aliens and arguing in favor of their right to vote). Needless to say, the foregoing dispute is not between equality and inequality, but between competing versions of equality. When parties disagree about whether people are substantially alike, however, the disagreement cannot be resolved by enjoining them to treat like people alike. The parties cannot know whether citizens and aliens are alike or unalike until they first agree on the substantive relevance of citizenship to voting. Once they agree on the substantive relevance of citizenship, they do not need to be told who is alike and who is unalike, or who should be treated alike and who should be treated unalike, because by then they already know.

[42] J. LUCAS, *supra* note 12, at 246.

[43] H.L.A. HART, *supra* note 12, at 155.

[44] Frankena, *supra* note 8, at 94.

that the rule is applied consistently and "impartial[ly]"[45] to all cases that are "alike" under the rule.[46] Such statements erroneously imply that equality imposes some substantive requirement of consistency apart from the substance of the rule itself. It is true that rules should be applied equally, consistently, and impartially, if by "equally," "consistently," and "impartially" one means the tautological proposition that the rule should be applied in all cases to which the terms of the rule dictate that it be applied. But it is wrong to think that, once a rule is applied in accord with its own terms, equality has something additional to say about the scope of the rule — something that is not already inherent in the substantive terms of the rule itself.[47] To say that a rule should be applied "equally" or "consistently" or "uniformly" means simply that the rule should be applied to the cases to which it applies.[48]

3. Equality and Comparative Rights. — It is sometimes said that two very different sorts of rules are at work in equality and rights cases. Equality differs from rights, it is said, because equality presupposes comparison,[49] while rights do not. Substantive rights, such as the right of free speech and the right to counsel, can be described without reference to a person's relationship to other rightsholders. To decide whether a person's speech rights are violated, one juxtaposes the state's general duty of behavior against the state's particular treatment of the person to determine whether the state treats the person in accord with its prescribed duty. Equality, in contrast, is comparative in nature; it involves "comparative

---

[45] M. SINGER, GENERALIZATION IN ETHICS 49 (1961).

[46] *See* M. GINSBERG, *supra* note 11, at 7 (Once one identifies the substantive content of rules, "it is necessary . . . to examine them in the light of the formal principle of equality, the aim being to exclude every form of discrimination not justified by relevant differences."); C. PERELMAN, *supra* note 21, at 38 (arguing that by producing "predictability and security," equality "permits the coherent and stable functioning of a juridical order").

[47] Browne, *supra* note 14, at 58–59.

[48]

> [T]he resultant "consistency" in my moral behavior is no more than the spelling out of what it means for an act to be prohibited or required; it has nothing to do with consistency *per se*. There is, instead, only the consistency that results from my taking seriously the idea that an act is morally prohibited or morally required.

Gillespie, *supra* note 26, at 157.

[49] Joel Feinberg, for example, seems to assume that the proposition "likes should be treated alike" is uniquely concerned with entitlements that can be determined only by reference to the treatment of others. *See* J. FEINBERG, *supra* note 1, at 98–117; Feinberg, *supra* note 1; *see also* R. FULLINWIDER, THE REVERSE DISCRIMINATION CONTROVERSY 223 (1980) (equality is essentially "comparative"); Karst, *supra* note 4, at 40 (equality is concerned with "relative" deprivation); Wright, *supra* note 1, at 17–18.

rights,"[50] rights that cannot be assessed without ascertaining a person's relationship to others. In more precise terms, the contrast is between "noncomparative rights" on one hand and equality on the other; equality and comparative rights are taken to be identical.

This equation of comparative rights and equality is fundamentally misconceived. For one thing, some rights entail comparison without any suggestion of equality. Consider, for example, the right of secured creditors to absolute preference over unsecured creditors; or the right of veterans of foreign wars or physically handicapped persons or women or members of racial minorities to preferential treatment of certain kinds over other groups; or the right of certain applicants for competitive positions to be selected on the basis of relative exam scores. In each case, to determine whether the claimant's substantive rights are satisfied one must first ascertain his relationship to others.

Conversely, just as rights can be comparative, claims of equality can be noncomparative in nature. Again, it all depends on the content of the particular right that substantiates the equality claim. Consider such equality claims as the right of persons qua persons not to be tortured or their right to basic economic subsistence.[51] To decide whether a person has been tortured or denied basic subsistence, one need not know how anyone else has been treated. One can assess each person's claim solely by reference to the particulars of his treatment, without the necessity of referring to others.

Why, then, do people think comparative rights have some special relationship to the principle of equality? It may stem from a tendency to confuse comparisons for purposes of equality with comparisons for purposes of comparative rights. Statements of equality (or inequality) entail comparisons of two things or persons by reference to some external criterion that specifies the relevant respect in which they are the same or different.[52] To say that an apple is "like" or "equal to" an

---

[50] For the distinction between "comparative" and "noncomparative" rights, see *supra* note 14.

[51] *See, e.g.*, R. FULLINWIDER, *supra* note 49, at 221–22 (discussing the right to be free from torture as a right of equality); Michelman, *The Supreme Court, 1968 Term — Foreword: On Protecting the Poor Through the Fourteenth Amendment*, 83 HARV. L. REV. 7 (1969).

[52] To speak of "equals" is to presuppose the existence of two or more persons or things that are identical in a relevant respect. *See* Browne, *supra* note 14, at 51 ("Equality is a relational attribute which holds between any two individuals in respect to any attribute which they have in common."); Menne, *supra* note 10, at 51 ("'equal' presupposes two objects").

orange means that, despite their many differences, they each possess the feature or features that are relevant to an external criterion, whether those features be weight, surface area, or sugar content; to say that they are "unequal" means that they do not share the relevant feature, whether it be color, taste, or juice content. This analysis also holds for ethical and legal statements of equality, the only difference being that, instead of testing the persons or things by a descriptive standard for determining which of them *are* the same, one tests them by a moral or legal standard for deciding which of them should be treated the same.[53] In each case, however, the comparison for purposes of equality simply spells out what it means to have tested both subjects by the controlling standard of relevance.

Comparisons for purposes of comparative rights differ from the foregoing comparison in two respects. First, instead of comparing two persons to determine whether they both do (or do not) satisfy an external criterion, one compares them in order to make a quantitative assessment about how much, if any, they differ in relation to one another. Second, instead of comparing them after having tested each by the criteria of an external standard of treatment, one compares them before applying the standard. Consequently, the two sorts of comparisons differ both in type and in time. For purposes of equality, one first decides how each person, separately, is to be treated under the controlling moral or legal standard, and then compares the respective treatments to see if the treatments are (or are not) the same. For purposes of comparative rights, one first compares the two persons to see how much (if at all) they differ from each other, and then decides how each is to be treated under the controlling standard of treatment. Equality and comparative rights both involve comparison, but comparisons for purposes of equality have no necessary connection either to comparative rights as such or to the comparisons entailed by such rights.[54]

To illustrate, consider the right of blacks under present affirmative action programs to preferential admission to graduate school. The right is comparative because it cannot be enforced for a person without first ascertaining his relationship to others; the affirmative action preference may be enough to advance a given black applicant past one competing white applicant but not past another. The right can also be stated in terms of equality, because it contains standards for distin-

[53] *See supra* pp. 544–45.

[54] *See* Browne, *supra* note 14, at 51, 57–59; Carr, *The Concept of Formal Justice*, 39 PHIL. STUD. 211, 217–22 (1981).

guishing "like" from "unalike" and for allocating treatment to each; admissions standards determine some applicants to be alike (those who are admitted, with or without an affirmative action preference) and others to be unalike (those not admitted). Yet the quantitative comparisons entailed in seeking to apply the right to putative rightsholders have nothing to do with the comparisons of "equality" and "inequality" entailed in describing persons who have already been ascertained to be rightsholders. One cannot know whether blacks have been denied their measure of preferential admission without first assessing the quantitative relationship between their credentials and the credentials of competing candidates; the quantitative comparison logically precedes the determination of their rights (or the correlative determination that their rights have been violated). In contrast, one cannot know which blacks are "like" or "equal to" which whites for purposes of admission until one first determines their respective rights under the affirmative action policy; the comparison of "like" to "like" in respect of admission logically follows the determination of everyone's admissions rights.

It might be argued that, while comparative rights as a whole may not sound in equality, certain comparative rights necessarily do, namely "conditional" rights that entitle a rightholder to whatever benefits other persons enjoy. The privileges and immunities clause of article IV of the Constitution is a conditional right of that kind: although the clause does not require a state to give sister-state citizens any particular entitlements, the clause does require a state to give sister-state citizens whatever benefits of a certain kind it grants its *own* citizens.[55] The privileges and immunities clause derives its substance from equality (so the argument goes) because its

---

[55] "The Citizens of each State shall be entitled to all Privileges and Immunities of Citizens of the several States." U.S. CONST. art. IV, § 2, cl. 1; *see* Toomer v. Witsell, 334 U.S. 385, 395 (1948) ("It [the privileges and immunities clause] was designed to insure to a citizen of State A who ventures into State B the same privileges which the citizens of State B enjoy.").

It bears emphasizing, however, that despite its sweeping language article IV does not grant sister-state citizens *all* the privileges of in-state citizens, but rather grants them only privileges the denial of which would violate the interests article IV was designed to protect. *See* Baldwin v. Fish & Game Comm'n, 436 U.S. 371, 383 (1978); Varat, *State "Citizenship" and Interstate Equality*, 48 U. CHI. L. REV. 487, 516–19 (1981). This point is a reminder that the "equality" that obtains between in-state and out-of-state citizens does not derive from some direct comparison of the two, but is rather a logical consequence of their relationship in light of an external rule serving particular substantive ends.

beneficiaries have no independent rights at all — only the right to be treated equally to others.[56]

In reality, conditional rights are indistinguishable from other comparative rights for equality purposes. The sole distinguishing characteristic of conditional rights is that, while treatments for each person are quantitatively proportional under other comparative rights, treatments for each person are quantitatively identical under conditional rights. The latter feature is a contingency, however, with no moral significance for purposes of equality.[57] First of all, every moral or legal rule provides for quantitatively identical treatment among persons who are quantitatively identical with regard to the relevant criteria of the rule.[58] Second, a rule can treat certain persons on a quantitatively identical basis without at the same time being comparative in nature.[59] Third, no moral inference can be drawn from the mere fact that a rule proceeds on a per capita basis; per capita treatment is as likely to be unjust as just, depending upon the subject of the treatment, the class of persons being treated, the reasons for their treatment, and the standards for determining the justice of treatments.[60] In short, conditional rights have no greater logical claim to the language of "equality" than any other comparative right, and rights that treat people on a per capita basis have no greater moral claim to equality than rights that treat people on proportional grounds.[61]

---

[56] *See, e.g.*, J. Ely, Democracy and Distrust 23, 90–91, 193 n.45 (1980) (describing article IV as an "equality" provision).

[57]

> [T]he relational attribute of equality is not identical with, but is just one instance of, the relational attribute of proportionality. It is true that the two relations of equality and inequality exhaust the field between them; but unless it is already presupposed that *equality* has some special significance, the designation of all other proportionalities as 'inequalities' is tendentious and unjustified.

Browne, *supra* note 14, at 52 (emphasis in original).

[58] Berlin, *supra* note 22, at 132.

[59] Consider, for example, the right of widows and widowers under the Social Security Act, 42 U.S.C. § 402(i) (1976), to receive a $255 burial allotment promptly upon the death of an insured individual. The statute provides quantitatively identical treatment for all beneficiaries, yet a beneficiary's right to the $255 allotment can be fully ascertained without reference to how other beneficiaries are, or may be, treated.

[60] *See supra* note 29.

[61] Consider, for example, the question whether blacks have a constitutional right to be treated with the same dignity as whites. A constitutional rule that *prohibits* a state from according blacks less dignity than whites can be described in terms of "equality": on the premise that blacks are "equal" to whites with respect to the dignity they deserve, the rule treats blacks and whites alike by constitutionally requiring a state to give blacks whatever dignity the state chooses to extend to whites. By the

To conclude, any noncomparative right — such as the claim of persons to basic economic subsistence or their right not to be tortured — can be stated either indirectly in terms of equality or directly as a right.[62] The same is true of any comparative right, such as the claim of blacks to preferential admission. The distinction, therefore, is not between equality and some contrary notion of substantive justice, but between rights that cannot be determined independently of a person's relationship to others and rights that can. Moreover, the comparison entailed in rights that cannot be determined independently of a person's relation to others differs from the comparison entailed by framing rights in terms of equality.

C. *The Connection Between Equality and Justice*

"Justice" means "giving every person his due."[63] What then is the relationship between "giving persons their due" and "treating like persons alike"? Are the two formulas equivalent, as Aristotle thought them to be?[64] Or are they two separate (although related) principles, as others think them to be?[65] Can something be just and yet unequal? Or, alternatively, can something be equal and yet unjust?

The answers, once again, can be found in the structure of the two moral propositions. The idea of justice, like the idea of equality, is entirely formal.[66] It requires that persons be

---

same token, however, a contrary rule that *allows* a state to treat blacks with less dignity than whites can also be described in terms of equality: on the premise that blacks and whites are alike in respect of their need (or lack of need) for constitutional protection of "dignity," the latter rule treats blacks and whites alike by leaving the treatment of both to the discretion of the state. Because the conditional rule and its opposite can both be described in terms of equality, it follows that neither can have an essential relationship to the idea of equality.

[62] *Compare* Nagel, *Commentary: The Meaning of Equality*, 1979 WASH. U.L.Q. 25 (discussing the right to basic economic subsistence in terms of "equality"), *with* Michelman, *Welfare Rights in a Constitutional Democracy*, 1979 WASH. U.L.Q. 659 (discussing the same in terms of "rights"); *compare* Vlastos, *supra* note 27, at 47–51 (discussing the entitlement to be free from pain in terms of "equality"), *with* Lucas, *Against Equality*, 40 PHIL. 296, 298 (1965) (discussing same in terms of entitlements).

[63] *See* Browne, *supra* note 14, at 49 (referring to the "fundamental axiom, which is definitive of the concept of justice . . . that each person must be rendered his due").

[64] ARISTOTLE, ETHICA NICHOMACHEA V.3.1131a (W. Ross trans. 1925).

[65] *See, e.g.*, Beck, *supra* note 7, at 28 ("equality" a "component" of "justice"); Bedau, *supra* note 10, at 18 ("The concept of justice involves that of equality."); Brandt, *Preface* to SOCIAL JUSTICE, *supra* note 27, at v, v (equality and justice "have a close relation").

[66] *See* H. KELSEN, *supra* note 18, at 135–36 (the formula "'To every one His due'" is an "empty tautology"). For examples of other "formal" moral norms, see Perelman, *What the Philosopher May Learn From the Study of Law*, 11 NAT. L.F. 1, 12 (1966).

given their due but does not itself define what is their "due." To render justice meaningful, one must look beyond the proposition that every person should be given his due to the substantive moral or legal standards that determine what is one's "due."

One way to decide whether the two concepts are interchangeable is to determine whether each can be reduced linguistically to a statement of the other. Consider first the idea of justice:

> (1) To "give persons their due" entails giving them the treatment they deserve;
>
> (2) To give persons the treatment they deserve entails treating them in accordance with moral rules;
>
> (3) To treat persons in accord with moral rules entails: (a) determining whether they possess those criteria determined to be morally significant by the rules; and (b) according those who possess the criteria the treatment prescribed by the rules, while not according such treatment to those who do not possess the criteria;
>
> (4) To accord those who possess the criteria the treatment prescribed by the rules, while not according that treatment to those who do not possess the criteria, entails treating alike those who are alike in the morally significant respects while treating unalike those who are unalike in the morally significant respects; and
>
> (5) To treat alike those who are alike in the morally significant respects while treating unalike those who are unalike in the morally significant respects entails "treating likes alike" and "treating unlikes unalike."

In short, to say that "every person should be given his due" means "persons who are alike should be treated alike" and "persons who are unalike should be treated unalike."

Just as justice can be reduced to equality, equality can be reduced to a statement of justice; one simply reverses the sequence of steps set forth in the previous paragraph. After all, to say that two people are "alike" and hence must be treated alike is to presuppose substantive principles of right and wrong, principles that render it "right" to treat them alike and "wrong" to treat them unalike. To speak of right and wrong regarding the treatment of people is to define what is "due" them under the circumstances. That is why philosophers from the time of Aristotle to the present have said that treating people equally means "giving every person his due."[67]

67

What, then, roughly does it mean to "act unjustly"? Roughly, it seems that "act unjustly" means the same as "treat persons unequally . . . ."

Claims that treatment can be simultaneously just and unequal, or equal but unjust, are grounded in simple self-contradiction. Consider, for example, the sentencing of armed robbers under a statute that requires a mandatory three-year prison sentence for all armed robbers. It might be said that sentencing some robbers to three years while sentencing one to probation because of a unique physical hardship would be just but unequal; conversely, sentencing them all to four years would be equal but unjust.[68] Such moral judgments can only be maintained, however, by asserting one set of substantive standards in the name of justice while simultaneously asserting a contrary set in the name of equality. In the probation case, for example, either the mandatory-sentence statute is the society's sole legal standard for sentencing armed robbers or the society has a supplemental standard (whether constitutional or statutory) prescribing probation in cases of unique physical hardship. If the mandatory-sentence statute is the society's sole legal standard, as a matter of law it cannot be just for society to violate its statute by treating one robber differently from the others. If, on the other hand, a supplemental legal standard renders it just to take that robber's unique physical hardship into account, the very same standard also renders it equal in law to treat him differently from the others because of his unique differences. In short, the probationary sentence may be just (and equal) or unjust (and unequal), but it cannot be just and unequal without suffering self-contradiction.

One recalls the phrase in stone over the entrance to the United States Supreme Court: "Equal Justice Under Law." Would the phrase mean less if it said "Justice Under Law"? Or "Equality Under Law"? Is anything gained, then, by using four words instead of three — anything, that is, besides redundancy and obfuscation?[69]

> . . . It also implies that injustice is essentially unequal treatment, thereby conforming with a tradition that holds that equity is essentially a matter of equality. Moreover, the phrase "treat unequally in matters involving allocations of good and bad things" is so general as to permit application in widely different sorts of context; it permits us to accept an ancient adage that "justice is giving every man his due."

R. Brandt, Ethical Theory 410 (1959).

[68] *See, e.g.*, Feinberg, *supra* note 1, at 309–16.

[69] An inquiry into the relationship between justice and equality may cast light on one of the conundrums in American constitutional law. Many courts and commentators have been troubled by the relationship between the due process clause of the fifth amendment (applicable only to the federal government) and the equal protection clause of the 14th amendment (applicable only to the states). On one hand, they are reluctant to conclude that the federal government under the "due process" clause may treat people unequally in ways that the states under the "equal protection" clause may not. *See* Bolling v. Sharpe, 347 U.S. 497, 500 (1954) ("In view of our decision that

II. Equality in Law

The primary source of equality analysis in American constitutional law is the equal protection clause of the fourteenth amendment.[70] Unlike most constitutional provisions, which govern specific and limited instances of state action, the equal protection clause is all-encompassing; it governs all state action. State regulations are commonly placed in one of three categories for purposes of equal protection analysis: (1) regulations affecting the exercise of "fundamental rights"; (2) regulations classifying people on the basis of criteria that are constitutionally "suspect"; and (3) all remaining regulations. It is unnecessary to decide whether the three categories are genuinely distinct or whether their respective levels of scrutiny

the Constitution prohibits the states from maintaining racially segregated public schools, it would be unthinkable that the same Constitution would impose a lesser duty on the Federal Government."); *see also* Karst, *The Fifth Amendment's Guarantee of Equal Protection*, 55 N.C.L. Rev. 541, 552–58 (1977). On the other hand, some of them are uneasy about reading "equal protection" into a provision of the fifth amendment that speaks not of treating people equally but of giving people their "due." *See* J. Ely, *supra* note 56, at 32 (calling it "gibberish both syntactically and historically" to read equal protection into the due process clause of the fifth amendment); Alexander, *Modern Equal Protection Theories: A Metatheoretical Taxonomy and Critique*, 42 Ohio St. L.J. 3, 57 n.179 (1981) (describing the Supreme Court's fifth amendment equal protection doctrine as "kinky"). The answer is that the paradox itself may be specious: there is no necessary tension between the constitutional language of substantive "due process" and the constitutional language of "equal protection," because "giving every person his due" means "treating like persons alike." There is no necessary difference between a national constitution that contains a substantive due process clause (and omits an equal protection clause) and a national constitution that contains an equal protection clause (and omits a due process clause). That is why the Supreme Court's substantive due process jurisprudence can mirror its equal protection jurisprudence without doing violence to the language of the text. *See, e.g.*, Jones v. Helms, 101 S. Ct. 2434 (1981); *id.* at 2443 (White, J., concurring); Weinberger v. Wiesenfeld, 420 U.S. 636, 638 n.2 (1975) (fifth amendment equal protection "has always been precisely the same as" 14th amendment equal protection); Jackson v. Indiana, 406 U.S. 715 (1972); Loving v. Virginia, 388 U.S. 1 (1967); *see also* Perry, *supra* note 4, at 1077 n.280 (conceding that the conceptual difference between "due process" and "equal protection" does not necessarily lead to a difference in outcomes); *cf.* Harris v. McRae, 448 U.S. 297 (1980) (upholding a federal statute as a matter of both fifth amendment "due process" and fifth amendment "equal protection"). *Compare* Zablocki v. Redhail, 434 U.S. 374, 383–91 (1978) (invalidating a state statute on equal protection grounds), *with id.* at 391–96 (Stewart, J., concurring) (same on due process grounds); *compare* San Antonio Indep. School Dist. v. Rodriguez, 411 U.S. 1 (1973) (upholding a state statute on equal protection grounds), *with id.* at 59–62 (Stewart, J., concurring) (same on due process grounds); *compare* Boddie v. Connecticut, 401 U.S. 371 (1971) (invalidating a state statute on due process grounds), *with id.* at 383–86 (Douglas, J., concurring) (same on equal protection grounds). "Justice" and "equality" are merely alternative formulations of whatever one's substantive notions of right or wrong happen to be.

[70] "No State shall . . . deny to any person within its jurisdiction the equal protection of the laws." U.S. Const. amend. XIV, § 1.

are appropriate. My purpose here is to demonstrate that, regardless of the categories and levels of scrutiny, equality analysis logically collapses into rights analysis and that analyzing legal problems in terms of equality is essentially redundant.

All legal regulation involves classification.[71] Every state law is thus subject to scrutiny under the fourteenth amendment as a potential violation of constitutional equality — as a violation of, among other things, the constitutional norm that "likes be treated alike." In order to decide whether a state classification treats differently people who are constitutionally deemed to be "alike," however, we must first possess a constitutional standard for distinguishing those people who are alike from those who are not. We cannot find such standards in the formula that "likes should be treated alike," because the equality formula *presupposes* anterior constitutional standards for ascertaining "likeness" and "unalikeness."[72] Yet once we ascertain the anterior constitutional standards (as we must do anyway), our substantive work is complete, and the additional and self-evident step of stating our conclusion in terms of "equals" or "unequals" is entirely superfluous.[73]

A. Fundamental Rights

Any equal protection case can be invoked to illustrate the superfluousness of equality. But the "fundamental rights" cases[74] may serve as a congenial introduction because com-

---

[71] *See* J. WILSON, EQUALITY 121 (1966) ("[I]n framing a rule, we have *ipso facto* accepted certain characteristics as relevant and others as irrelevant."); Tussman & tenBroek, *supra* note 24, at 343–44.

[72]

> The principle that persons who are alike in the relevant respects must be treated alike, while persons who are unalike in the relevant respects must be treated unalike and in direct proportion to the differences between them is formal in the defined sense, since it fails completely to specify which respects are relevant.

J. FEINBERG, *supra* note 1, at 100; *see* H.L.A. HART, *supra* note 12, at 155; C. PERELMAN, *supra* note 8, at 36, 82; A. ROSS, *supra* note 8, at 270, 272; Browne, *supra* note 14, at 53; Honoré, *supra* note 9, at 83 ("The principle of treating like cases alike is . . . an empty, though as we shall see not a merely formal one, until we know in what respect the cases are supposed to be like or unlike."); Sandalow, *Racial Preferences in Higher Education: Political Responsibility and the Judicial Role*, 42 U. CHI. L. REV. 653, 655 (1975).

[73] *See* Browne, *supra* note 14, at 53–55 (substantive standards that define when people are "alike" and when "unalike" are not only necessary to give meaning to the proposition that "likes should be treated alike," but also in themselves sufficient); Carr, *supra* note 54, at 212–14 (same); Montague, *supra* note 26, at 136–37 (same).

[74] The line of cases takes its name from Skinner v. Oklahoma, 316 U.S. 535, 541 (1942).

mentators have recognized that statements of "equality" regarding fundamental rights invariably reduce to statements about "rights." Consider, for example, the decision in *Carey v. Brown*.[75] The plaintiffs in *Carey* engaged in peaceful picketing on the sidewalk in front of the home of Chicago's mayor in order to protest the mayor's busing policies. The plaintiffs were arrested and prosecuted under a state statute that prohibited the picketing of private residences except "the peaceful picketing of a place of employment involved in a labor dispute."[76] The Supreme Court held that, by treating labor picketers differently from political picketers, the statute denied the plaintiffs equal protection of the laws.[77]

Retracing the Court's reasoning unmasks *Carey* as a first amendment decision masquerading in the form of equality. The Court reasoned as follows: (1) by classifying picketers on the basis of the content of their message, the Illinois statute makes labor picketers unlike other picketers; (2) the first amendment protects persons engaged in peaceful picketing on public sidewalks for political purposes;[78] (3) when the state classifies speech so that it prohibits expression presumptively protected by the first amendment, courts must "carefully scrutinize[]" the state's "justifications" to ensure that the legislation is "finely tailored to serve substantial state interests";[79] (4) the state of Illinois cannot justify the statute by asserting a special interest or preference for labor speech, because by first amendment standards "social" and "political" speech are at least as valuable as labor speech;[80] (5) the state cannot justify the statute by asserting an interest in the absolute privacy of residential neighborhoods, because the statute itself permits inroads on such privacy for the purpose of some peaceful picketing;[81] (6) the state advances no other interests that are sufficient under the first amendment to justify prohibiting peaceful political picketing;[82] (7) because the state has no constitutionally sufficient reason for distinguishing political picketing in residential neighborhoods from labor picketing, the statute denies the plaintiffs equal protection by treating them differently from persons who are constitutionally the same.[83]

---

[75] 447 U.S. 455 (1980).

[76] *Id.* at 457.

[77] *Id.* at 459 n.2.

[78] *Id.* at 460.

[79] *Id.* at 461–62.

[80] *Id.* at 466.

[81] *Id.* at 462, 464–65.

[82] *Id.* at 467–69.

[83] *Id.* at 458–59 & n.2, 471.

The *Carey* decision is a paradigm of equality reasoning: the first and the last steps, those that place the decision in the context of equality, are entirely superfluous. The Court starts in step (1) by stating the case in terms of the formula that "likes should be treated alike," and reverts to the equality formula in step (7) by restating in terms of "likes" the consequences that logically flow from the intervening steps. But the substance of the decision to invalidate the Illinois statute derives entirely from the first amendment analysis, steps (2) through (6), not from the equal protection clause. As Justice Stewart emphasized in his concurring opinion and as others have argued, cases like *Carey* can be decided directly on first amendment grounds without any reference to the idea that "likes should be treated alike."[84]

To be sure, *Carey* does not specify whether the plaintiffs' constitutional right to picket is comparative (that is, a right to engage in only as much picketing as the state granted labor pickets) or noncomparative (that is, a right to engage in a political picketing without regard to whether the state allows others to picket). The Court did not decide between the two formulations of the right in *Carey* because both sufficed to invalidate the statute at hand. Whether comparative or noncomparative, however, the right must inevitably draw its content from first amendment notions of free speech.[85]

---

[84] *See id.* at 471–72 (Stewart, J., concurring); *see also* Perry, *supra* note 4, at 1076 (analyzing Police Dep't v. Mosley, 408 U.S. 92 (1972), entirely in first amendment terms, rather than on equal protection grounds); Stone, *Restrictions of Speech Because of Its Content: The Peculiar Case of Subject-Matter Restrictions*, 46 U. CHI. L. REV. 81, 86–88 (1978) (same); Comment, *Equal But Inadequate Protection: A Look at* Mosley *and* Grayned, 8 HARV. C.R.-C.L. L. REV. 469 (1973) (arguing that *Mosley* should have been decided either on first amendment or on overbreadth grounds so that the state could not later prohibit *all* picketing). For the proposition that fundamental rights cases should be decided as rights cases, see San Antonio Indep. School Dist. v. Rodriguez, 411 U.S. 1, 59–62 (1973) (Stewart, J., concurring); Barrett, *Judicial Supervision of Legislative Classifications — A More Modest Role for Equal Protection?*, 1976 B.Y.U. L. REV. 89, 108–21; Lupu, *Untangling the Strands of the Fourteenth Amendment*, 77 MICH. L. REV. 981, 1060–75 (1979).

[85] 447 U.S. at 459 n.2 ("Because we find the present statute defective on equal protection principles, we likewise do not consider whether a statute barring all residential picketing regardless of its subject matter would violate the First and Fourteenth Amendments."). For discussion of whether the right of picketers is comparative or noncomparative, see Karst, *Equality as a Central Principle in the First Amendment*, 43 U. CHI. L. REV. 20, 38, 40–41 (1975). For the difference between "comparative" and "noncomparative" rights, see *supra* note 14.

The two rights derive from very different first amendment premises. A comparative right to picket derives from the substantive premise that, although the government is not prohibited from limiting the quantity of the messages to which people may be exposed, it may not skew the content of those messages by allowing some speakers but not others to be heard. *See* Metromedia, Inc. v. City of San Diego, 101

This analysis of *Carey* suggests not only that fundamental rights cases *can* be decided by direct reference to the underlying substantive right, but also that, ultimately, they *must* be so decided.[86] Regardless whether one takes the extra step of placing an argument in the form of equality, one must always analyze the underlying right. The equal protection clause provides that, *if* political picketing is "like" labor picketing for constitutional purposes, the state must treat them alike. But the idea that likes should be treated alike does not — and cannot — have anything to say about whether political picketing is like labor picketing for constitutional purposes. To determine that, one must look to the purposes and scope of the right of free speech. Even if one is disposed to frame constitutional values in terms of equality, therefore, one cannot avoid the task of identifying and assessing the substantive constitutional rights that determine when people are "alike" and when "unalike."

The right to vote is another example. It does not matter, the defender of equality jurisprudence will argue, how many votes or fractions of votes any single person possesses, provided that his electoral "voice" is the same as everyone else's. The right to vote is taken to derive from and be governed by an anterior principle of equality; to say that a person has a right to vote means that he has an equal voice in electoral matters with anyone and everyone else.

Such an argument entirely misunderstands and obscures the nature of the right to vote. For one thing, the right to

---

S. Ct. 2882, 2895–96 (1981) (plurality opinion); Stone, *supra* note 84, at 100–03. A noncomparative right to picket derives from the substantive premise that the first amendment does restrain the government from limiting the quantity of messages people may hear, absent good reasons for restricting those messages. *See Metromedia*, 101 S. Ct. at 2900 (Brennan, J., concurring in the judgment); Grayned v. City of Rockford, 408 U.S. 104 (1972), *discussed in* Shiffrin, *Government Speech*, 27 U.C.L.A. L. REV. 565, 574–77 (1980). It follows from the latter right that at least as long as Illinois' standards and values regarding residential privacy remain unchanged — that is, as long as the permissibility of labor picketing demonstrates that the state places less than absolute weight on the value of residential privacy — it must allow some amount of residential picketing for political purposes, even if it were otherwise disposed to prohibit all residential picketing. *See* Karst, *supra*, at 40–41.

86

> [A]n explicit rule of constitutional equality, such as the equal protection clause of the Fourteenth Amendment, does not *add* anything distinct from and independent of the other rights (to liberty, security, due process, etc.) already enumerated in or implied by other provisions of the constitution. Since these other constitutional rights apply to all citizens, their form already entails their equal application. The explicit principle of constitutional equality serves only a rhetorical purpose, reminding us of the nature of other constitutional principles.

R. FULLINWIDER, *supra* note 49, at 223.

vote does not require that every person — or indeed every eligible voter — possess an equal voice.[87] The way votes are allocated by any rule of law or morals depends entirely on the substantive standards underlying the rule. Thus, the Constitution allocates votes for Senators in inverse proportion to the population of voters' respective states,[88] while some states allocate votes in special purpose districts in proportion to the amount of real property that landowners hold.[89]

Furthermore, even when every person's vote equals everyone else's, the equality between them is purely derivative: it is an inevitable and uninteresting consequence of the particular substantive right at issue. For example, the right of corporate shareholders to vote in proportion to their company ownership follows logically from the rule that every share carries an equal vote and that every shareholder possesses a total vote equal to every other shareholder owning the same number of shares. The relationship of equality between shares and shareholders is simply a "logically necessary"[90] consequence of the right at issue.

B. Suspect Classifications

So far, so good. However, I am not the first person to argue that equal protection cases involving fundamental rights collapse into simple rights cases — commentators have been making the point for some time.[91] Yet strangely enough, some commentators simultaneously deny that the same is true of equal protection cases involving "suspect"[92] classifications based on race, sex, and so forth. Suspect classification cases, they say, are "true equality cases" that cannot be collapsed

---

[87] The notion of an "equal voice" is itself fundamentally ambiguous, because it does not assign the "precise criteria for determining" the basis of suffrage. *See* Still, *Political Equality and Election Systems*, 91 ETHICS 375, 377 (1981) (discussing the various, distinct substantive standards of suffrage that are imprecisely gathered under the notion of "equality" of suffrage).

[88] U.S. CONST. art. I, § 3, cl. 1; *id.* amend. XVII.

[89] *See* Ball v. James, 101 S. Ct. 1811 (1981).

[90] Flathman, *supra* note 36, at 45 ("[E]quality is a significant normative criterion only in a *derivative* sense."); *id.* at 51; *see* H. KELSEN, *supra* note 18, at 127–28; Adler & Hutchins, *supra* note 10, at 303 ("There has always been a suspicion . . . that equality as applied to things human is at best a derivative idea . . . and . . . that carrying it over into social and political discussion may be to some extent illicit, confusing, and metaphorical in no helpful way."); *see also* Browne, *supra* note 14, at 52 (equality a "consequential property").

[91] *See* sources cited *supra* note 84.

[92] The "suspect" classification cases take their name from Korematsu v. United States, 323 U.S. 214, 216 (1944).

into rights cases and cannot be separated from the "textual embrace [of] equality."[93]

It is emphatically true that the equal protection clause has legal and moral substance,[94] substance as significant and enduring as any norm of our society.[95] The framers of the fourteenth amendment, having triumphed in war against slavery, enacted the equal protection clause to radically transform national notions of racial justice.[96] It would be a mistake, however, to think that these notions of racial justice have anything in particular to do with the idea that likes should be treated alike. They are independent rights, identical in their logic to first amendment rights of speech and religion. Like rights of speech and religion, rights of race and sex can be stated without reference to "likes" or "equals." Indeed, not only *can* they be so stated, they *must* be so stated, because they provide the standards by which people are rendered "alike" or "unalike."

The point can be illustrated by considering *Sweatt v. Painter*.[97] Mr. Sweatt, a black applicant to law school, challenged the constitutionality of a state statute that barred blacks from attending the state's all-white law school. How does one go about deciding whether the statute denied Sweatt equal protection of the laws? How does one decide whether the statute treated him differently from people who were constitutionally the same?

---

[93] Lupu, *supra* note 84, at 985; *see* R. FULLINWIDER, *supra* note 49, at 222–23, 236–37; Lupu, *supra* note 84, at 1073 ("Cases presenting issues of forbidden classifications [are] true equality cases."); *id.* at 1001 n.98 ("[S]ubstantive due process, in contrast, speaks to substantive liberties, without direct regard to the inequality in their distribution."); *cf.* Perry, *supra* note 4, at 1083 ("[N]either constitutional doctrine regarding alienage-based classifications nor the fundamental-rights and fundamental-interests strands of 'equal protection' doctrine can fairly be understood to implement the principle of equal protection; both doctrines, therefore, ought to be conceptualized in other than equal protection terms.").

[94] Karst, *supra* note 4, at 1. *But cf.* Lupu, *supra* note 84, at 1054 ("Equal protection has no 'substance' in the sense in which I have employed the term.").

[95] *See* J. ELY, *supra* note 56, at 30–32; Karst, *supra* note 4, at 4 ("Equality, as an abstraction, may be value-neutral, but the fourteenth amendment is not.").

[96] The equal protection clause of the 14th amendment, ratified in 1868, reversed the Supreme Court's 11-year-old decision in Dred Scott v. Sandford, 60 U.S. (19 How.) 393 (1857), in which the Court held that "the negro African race" was regarded by the framers of the Constitution as "beings of an inferior order, and altogether unfit to associate with the white race, either in social or political relations; and so far inferior, that they had no rights which the white man was bound to respect." *Id.* at 406–07. The constitutional process by which the 14th amendment's revolutionary norms of racial justice were adopted and ratified were so intrusive and coercive that some have even questioned the amendment's validity. *See* James, *Is the Fourteenth Amendment Constitutional?*, SOC. SCI., Winter 1975, at 3.

[97] 339 U.S. 629 (1950).

Needless to say, it does no good at all to ponder the axiom that "likes should be treated alike." As with every person,[98] Sweatt was like his white counterparts in some respects and unlike them in others: like them in his professional aspirations and academic credentials, unlike them in his skin color. It might be argued that race and skin color are simply irrelevant constitutionally to the way people should be treated.[99] The trouble is that race and skin color *are* sometimes relevant to the way people should be treated. They are relevant to public physicians in deciding whether to test for race-specific diseases like sickle cell anemia and Tay-Sachs disease; to Public Broadcasting System directors and make-up artists in staging color-specific performances like *Othello* or *Roots*;[100] to public employers and university admissions officers in implementing race-specific affirmative action programs.

The real question, therefore, was whether Sweatt's race would be allowed to make a constitutional difference between Sweatt and his white coapplicants. That is not a question, however, that equality can answer, for a constitutional requirement that likes be treated alike cannot itself distinguish constitutionally relevant differences from constitutionally irrelevant ones.[101] To argue that race or skin color should not constitutionally be allowed to matter in Sweatt's particular case, one must show that excluding blacks from law school on the basis of race causes them a kind of injury not caused in cases in which using race is conceded to be acceptable — an injury, furthermore, from which the Constitution gives them a right to be free.[102] Such a prohibition cannot be found in

---

[98] *See* Lucas, *Vive la Différence*, 53 PHIL. 363, 363 (1978) ("Men are all alike, and . . . [m]en are all different."); Sandalow, *supra* note 72, at 655 ("All individuals are similar in some respects and different in others.").

[99] Professor Perry seems to make this argument. *See* Perry, *supra* note 4, at 1051; *cf. id.* at 1056 (legitimacy of birth); *id.* at 1061 (alienage).

[100] *See* Lucas, *supra* note 62, at 301 ("It is irrelevant to a man's right to own property or to travel in buses that his skin is of a certain colour, though not, presumably, to his being employed as an actor in the part of Iago.").

[101] *See* A. ROSS, *supra* note 8, at 270. H.L.A. Hart argues:

> [T]hough "Treat like cases alike and different cases differently" is a central element in the idea of justice, it is by itself incomplete and, until supplemented, cannot afford any determinate guide to conduct. This is so because any set of human beings will resemble each other in some respects and differ from each other in others and, until it is established what resemblance and differences are relevant, "Treat like cases alike" must remain an empty form.

H.L.A. HART, *supra* note 12, at 155.

[102] This discussion is based on a particular conception of the substantive content of the equal protection clause. That conception is chosen for illustrative purposes only. I do not mean to enter the ongoing debate over what the equal protection clause means, *see infra* pp. 567–68, but only to demonstrate what it cannot usefully be thought to mean.

a constitutional requirement that likes be treated alike, because until black applicants are shown to suffer constitutional injury by being denied admission to an all-white school, they cannot be said to be constitutionally "like" their white counterparts for admissions purposes. The constitutional prohibition, if any, must originate in a substantive idea of the kinds of wrongs from which a person has a right to be free.

Having ascertained Sweatt's substantive rights, we can say that the state treated Sweatt "unequally" by treating him differently from persons who, we now know, were the "same." Once notions of racial desert are articulated, they can always be formulated in the derivative language of equality — as they are now formulated in terms of the equal protection clause.[103] The same is also true of substantive due process: once a standard of desert is defined — whether it concerns speech, religion, privacy, punishment, or reproduction — it can always be stated in the conclusory terms of giving a person his "due."[104] But stating entitlements in terms of treating "equals equally" (or in terms of giving a person his "due") does not and logically cannot alter the content the entitlements would otherwise possess. It can do nothing but incorporate the entitlements by reference.

Significantly, the courts thus far have failed to identify the precise sort of injury that the substance of the equal protection clause is designed to prohibit, a failure that may itself result from the fact that the clause is stated in the language of equality.[105] The substance of equal protection is variously stated to include the right of "cumulative[ly] disadvantage[d]" racial minorities not to be further "degraded" or "stigmatized" as racially inferior;[106] the right of a person not to be treated as "morally inferior"[107] by virtue of his race; the right of a

---

[103] *See* Rostker v. Goldberg, 101 S. Ct. 2646, 2659 (1981) ("The Constitution requires that Congress treat similarly situated persons similarly . . . ."); F.S. Royster Guano Co. v. Virginia, 253 U.S. 412, 415 (1920) (equal protection clause requires that "all persons similarly circumstanced shall be treated alike"), *quoted in* San Antonio Indep. School Dist. v. Rodriguez, 411 U.S. 1, 89 (1973) (Marshall, J., dissenting); *cf.* Michael M. v. Superior Court, 101 S. Ct. 1200, 1204 (1981) (plurality opinion) ("[T]he Equal Protection Clause does not 'demand that a statute necessarily apply equally to all persons' or require 'things which are different in fact . . . to be treated in law as though they were the same' . . . .") (quoting Rinaldi v. Yaeger, 384 U.S. 305, 309 (1966)).

[104] *See* Graham, *Procedure to Substance — Extra-Judicial Rise of Due Process*, 40 CALIF. L. REV. 483, 488 (1952) (suggesting that the due process clause constitutionalizes the formal notion that persons should be given their "due").

[105] *See infra* pp. 580–81.

[106] *See* Brest, *The Supreme Court, 1975 Term — Foreword: In Defense of the Antidiscrimination Principle*, 90 HARV. L. REV. 1, 8–11 (1976).

[107] *See* Perry, *supra* note 4, at 1030, 1083.

person not to be denied opportunity because of "an immutable characteristic determined solely by the accident of birth," which bears "no relation to ability to perform or contribute to society";[108] the "right to be treated by the organized society as a respected, responsible, and participating member";[109] and the right to be treated "with the same respect and concern as anyone else."[110] Whatever the particular substance of equal protection turns out to be, however, it is — and must be — a claim that does not rely on the axiom that likes be treated alike,[111] a maxim that cannot of itself have anything to say about *Sweatt* one way or the other.

In conclusion, fundamental rights cases and suspect classification cases involve different substantive rights, but their logic is the same: each comes clothed in the form of equality, yet each finds its substance in an underlying entitlement that can and must be worked out without reference to the general notion that likes should be treated alike. Equal protection cases involving classifications based on speech exhibit the following logic:

> (1) Persons who are alike should be treated alike;
> (2) The state shall not deny persons the right of free speech;
> (3) Persons who are treated differently from others solely by virtue of regulations that violate their right of free speech are necessarily "like" the others and hence must be treated alike.

Equal protection cases involving classifications based on race exhibit a similar logic:

> (1) Persons who are alike should be treated alike;
> (2) The state shall not deny persons the right to be free from racial injury;
> (3) Persons who are treated differently from others solely by virtue of regulations that violate their right to be free from racial injury are necessarily "like" the others and hence must be treated alike.

Steps (1) and (3) place the constitutional issue in the form of equality, yet all the substantive work is done in step (2). Like

[108] *See* Frontiero v. Richardson, 411 U.S. 677, 686 (1973) (plurality opinion of Brennan, J.).

[109] *See* Karst, *supra* note 4, at 4.

[110] R. DWORKIN, *supra* note 7, at 227; *accord* O'Fallon, *Adjudication and Contested Concepts: The Case of Equal Protection*, 54 N.Y.U. L. REV. 19, 34 (1979).

[111] *Cf.* L. TRIBE, AMERICAN CONSTITUTIONAL LAW § 16-1, at 991 (1978) ("Equality makes non-circular commands and imposes non-empty constraints only to the degree that we are willing to posit substantive ideals to guide collective choice.").

equal protection cases involving speech, equal protection cases involving race must be resolved by reference to step (2).

C. Rational Basis

All other state regulations — that is, all regulations containing classifications that involve neither fundamental interests nor suspect traits — fall into a third and residual category for equal protection purposes. This third category differs functionally from the other two only with regard to the level of judicial scrutiny it triggers. Thus, although courts are said to use "strict"[112] (and sometimes "intermediate"[113]) scrutiny to analyze classifications affecting fundamental interests or based on suspect traits, they review all remaining regulations by the less demanding standard of simple "rationality":[114] such classifications are valid as long as they are "'rationally related to furthering a legitimate state interest.'"[115]

Ironically, while rationality review is an uncelebrated[116] and often criticized[117] aspect of constitutional equality, it is

---

[112]

> The basic framework of analysis of such [an equal protection clause] claim is well settled: "We must decide, first, whether [state legislation] operates to the disadvantage of some suspect class or impinges upon a fundamental right explicitly or implicitly protected by the Constitution, thereby requiring strict judicial scrutiny."

Maher v. Roe, 432 U.S. 464, 470 (1977) (quoting San Antonio Indep. School Dist. v. Rodriguez, 411 U.S. 1, 17 (1973)).

[113] *See* Harris v. McRae, 448 U.S. 297, 342 & n.3 (1980) (Marshall, J., dissenting); L. TRIBE, *supra* note 111, § 16-25, at 1065–66 (discussing Craig v. Boren, 429 U.S. 190 (1976)); Note, *Equal Protection and Due Process: Contrasting Methods of Review Under Fourteenth Amendment Doctrine*, 14 HARV. C.R.-C.L. L. REV. 529, 541–45 (1979).

[114] *See* Barrett, *The Rational Basis Standard for Equal Protection Review of Ordinary Legislative Classifications*, 68 KY. L.J. 845, 856–66 (1980); Bennett, *"Mere" Rationality In Constitutional Law: Judicial Review and Democratic Theory*, 67 CALIF. L. REV. 1049, 1051 (1979) (the rationality requirement may simply be a "shorthand for judicial deference to [the] political process"); Gunther, *The Supreme Court, 1971 Term — Foreword: In Search of Evolving Doctrine on a Changing Court: A Model For a Newer Equal Protection*, 86 HARV. L. REV. 1, 19–21 (1972); Perry, *supra* note 4, at 1073–74; Note, *State Economic Substantive Due Process: A Proposed Approach*, 88 YALE L.J. 1487, 1497–99 (1979). *See generally* Barrett, *supra* (analysis and criticism of use of rationality test).

[115] Vance v. Bradley, 440 U.S. 93, 97 (1979) (quoting Massachusetts Bd. of Retirement v. Murgia, 427 U.S. 307, 312 (1976)); *see* Parham v. Hughes, 441 U.S. 347, 351–52 (1979) (plurality opinion).

[116] *See* Bennett, *supra* note 114, at 1050 ("most attention" nowadays is directed toward areas of equal protection other than "mere rationality" analysis).

[117] Commentators generally agree that rationality analysis presupposes the existence of a constitutional standard or values for assessing the validity of legislative ends. *See* L. TRIBE, *supra* note 111, § 16-2, at 995; Baker, *Neutrality, Process, and Rationality: Flawed Interpretations of Equal Protection*, 58 TEX. L. REV. 1029, 1039

for some commentators the truest embodiment of what equality really means. Their argument proceeds as follows: (1) equality requires that people who are alike should be treated alike; (2) all people are in some sense alike; (3) therefore, equality entails a "presumption" that all people be treated the same unless society advances some justification for treating them differently.[118] As Isaiah Berlin puts it:

> The assumption is that equality needs no reasons, only inequality does so; that uniformity, regularity, similarity, symmetry . . . need not be specially accounted for, whereas differences, unsystematic behaviour, change in conduct, need explanation and, as a rule, justification. If I have a cake and there are ten persons among whom I wish to divide it, then if I give exactly one tenth to each, this will not . . . call for justification; whereas if I depart from this principle of equal division I am expected to produce a special reason.[119]

(1980); Linde, *Due Process of Lawmaking*, 55 NEB. L. REV. 197, 212 (1976); Mashaw, *Constitutional Deregulation: Notes Toward A Public, Public Law*, 54 TULANE L. REV. 849, 866 (1980); Sandalow, *supra* note 72, at 659–60; Note, *supra* note 9, at 798; Note, *supra* note 114, at 1491; Note, *Legislative Purpose, Rationality, and Equal Protection*, 82 YALE L.J. 123, 128 (1972). The controversies about rationality analysis, therefore, are really disputes about the constitutional invalidity — and degree of invalidity — of certain legislative ends. *Compare* Mashaw, *supra*, at 866–76 (arguing that legislation is unconstitutional if directed solely toward "private" — as opposed to "public" — ends), *with* Linde, *supra*, at 223, 250 n.148 (arguing that special interest legislation is not unconstitutional as long as political compromise is acknowledged to be a legitimate end); *compare* Bennett, *supra* note 114, at 1058–59 (legislation is unconstitutional unless the legitimate end it serves was the legislature's actual purpose), *with* Note, *supra* note 9, at 810–13 (legislation is not unconstitutional if the legitimate end it serves was not in fact the legislature's purpose).

118

> The . . . principle [that the concept of justice involves that of equality] may be called the *presumption of equality*. Again, Aristotle was the first to imply that social inequalities, not equalities, are in need of some justification, and that inequalities for which no adequate reason can be given are unjustified. As Leslie Stephen phrased it more explicitly, "There should always be a sufficient reason for any difference in our treatment of our fellows." If this is so, then we cannot need any "sufficient reason" for treating people equally. Hence, we may say: . . . [s]ocial equalities need no special justification, whereas social inequalities always do.

Bedau, *supra* note 10, at 19 (quoting Stephen, *Social Inequality*, 1 ETHICS 267, 268 (1891)) (footnotes omitted) (emphasis in original); *see* Browne, *supra* note 37, at 46 ("In the absence of reasons for treating people unequally, they should be treated equally.").

For commentators who derive the so-called "presumption of equality" from the proposition that "likes should be treated alike," see S. BENN & R. PETERS, *supra* note 29, at 124–28; A. GEWIRTH, REASON AND MORALITY 186 (1978); Blackstone, *supra* note 40, at 240; Evans, *Equality, Ambiguity and Public Choice*, 14 CREIGHTON L. REV. 1385, 1386 (1981); Flathman, *supra* note 36, at 55; Frankena, *supra* note 27, at 10–13; Rawls, *supra* note 7, at 165–66; Spaemann, *Remarks on the Problem of Equality*, 87 ETHICS 363, 364 (1977); Wasserstrom, *Rights, Human Rights, and Racial Discrimination*, 61 J. PHIL. 628, 634–37 (1964).

119 Berlin, *supra* note 22, at 131.

This argument can also be incorporated into the constitutional notion of equal protection. Thus, if the equal protection clause embodies the idea that likes should be treated alike and if that idea truly entails a rebuttable presumption in favor of treating all persons alike, it therefore follows that the equal protection clause contains a rebuttable presumption in favor of treating people alike — a presumption rebuttable only by a showing of "rational" reasons for treating people differently.[120] In short, so the argument goes, any person who wishes to challenge a state regulation that treats him differently from others may invoke the equal protection clause and, by doing so, place the burden on the state to show rational grounds for treating him differently.

The so-called "presumption" of equality raises two separate problems: (1) the rebuttable presumption in favor of treating people alike is neither logically derivable from nor consistent with the idea that "likes should be treated alike"; and (2) the presumption of equality is essentially meaningless.

The first problem is that none of the plausible interpretations of the presumption of equality can be derived logically from the idea of equality. If the proposition that "all people are in some sense alike" means that all people are *morally* alike in all relevant respects (and if that is a coherent thing to say), it does not follow that all people should be treated alike until rational reasons are given for treating them differently. After all, if persons who are alike should be treated alike and if all persons are morally alike, it follows that all persons should *always* be treated alike; if all persons are truly alike in every moral respect, there could never by any reason — much less any rational reason — for treating them differently. The command to "treat likes alike" is absolute, while the presumption of equality is a lesser prima facie command, a command rebuttable by a showing of "rational reasons" for treating people differently. One cannot derive a prima facie command from an absolute command.[121] If, on the other hand, "all people are in some sense alike" means that all persons are

---

120

> It is unnecessary to say that the "equal protection of the laws" required by the 14th Amendment does not prevent the states from resorting to classification for the purposes of legislation. Numerous and familiar decisions of this court establish that they have a wide range of discretion in that regard. But the classification must be reasonable, not arbitrary, and must rest upon *some ground of difference* having a fair and substantial relation to the object of the legislation, so that all persons similarly circumstanced shall be treated alike.

F.S. Royster Guano Co. v. Virginia, 253 U.S. 412, 415 (1920) (emphasis added); *see supra* note 115.

121 *See* J. FEINBERG, *supra* note 1, at 100–02.

empirically and morally alike in certain significant respects, it does not follow that the state has an obligation to treat them alike in *all* respects.[122] On the contrary, if all people are alike in some particular respect, the most that follows is that all people must be treated alike in the particular respect — and in that respect alone — in which they are alike.

Of course, it could be that people are alike in only certain respects but that the presumption functions as a procedural rule for reaching correct decisions in the face of uncertainty about particular cases. A presumption of equality in that event would have to be based on one of two assumptions. First, we might assume ignorance of whether the respects in which people are morally alike are more numerous or more significant than the respects in which they are unalike. Yet in that case, a presumption of equality would be logically inconsistent with the idea that likes should be treated alike. The presumption expresses a *preference* for treating people "alike" as opposed to "unalike." The idea of equality, in contrast, expresses no preference for "like" treatment as opposed to "unlike" treatment. In requiring that likes be treated alike, it necessarily also requires that unlike be treated unalike.[123] This is so because to say that two people are "alike" for purposes of claiming certain treatment means that they both possess whatever quality or qualities are prescribed for that treatment by existing rules, and thus are both entitled to the treatment; and to say that two people are "unalike" means that one of them *lacks* a quality prescribed by rules for that treatment, and thus is not entitled to the treatment.[124] The very rules of treatment

---

[122] "[I]t no more follows that things equal to one another in one respect *are* (or cannot be) equal in yet other respects, any more than it follows that things equal to one another in one respect *ought* to be equal in that (or some further) respect." Bedau, *supra* note 10, at 8.

[123] *See* H.L.A. HART, *supra* note 12, at 155; E. WOLGAST, EQUALITY AND THE RIGHTS OF WOMEN 22 (1980); Frankena, *supra* note 27, at 9; Note, *supra* note 9, at 781 n.34.

[124] A.M. Honoré, although agreeing that adhering to a rule requires that "likes should be treated alike," denies that such adherence entails the corollary that "unlikes should be treated unalike." Honoré, *supra* note 9, at 84. Honoré observes that a rule that all adult males shall be allowed to vote (and thus shall be treated "alike" in that respect) does not necessarily mean that adult females shall *not* be allowed to vote (or that they shall be treated "unalike" in that respect). *Id.* at 83.

Honoré errs in confusing the equality engendered by individual rules with the equality that results when rules are taken in the aggregate. Taken by themselves, individual rules do logically require that persons who are "unlike" by reference to an individual rule be treated unalike under that rule. Thus, the rule of a society that entitles adult males to vote operates by itself to entitle adult males to vote and does not operate by itself to entitle adult females to vote. With respect to the substance of the rule itself, therefore, adult females are different from males and must be treated

that render some people "alike" (and thus require they be treated alike) logically render other people "unalike" (and require they be treated unalike).[125] As far as equality is concerned, therefore, when one is ignorant as to whether people are likely to be alike in morally significant respects, a presumption in favor of treating people alike is as unjustified as a presumption in favor of treating them *un*alike; each presumption creates an unjustified risk that it will deny people the treatment to which they are actually entitled.[126]

---

differently. Nothing in the rule itself, however, and nothing in the idea of equality precludes the society from enacting an independent rule that entitles adult females to vote. If the society adopts such a rule and if the two rules are read together, then the aggregate new rule is that adult males and adult females shall be allowed to vote. By the same token, the aggregate standard that now defines "likes" and "unlikes" by reference to the rule is no longer all adult males alone or all adult females alone, but all adults: as far as the combined rules themselves are concerned, all adults are "alike" with respect to voting and shall be treated alike in that respect, and all minors are "unlike" adults with respect to voting and shall be treated unlike them in that respect. Regardless of whether one talks about individual rules alone or aggregate rules alone, "likes should be treated alike" logically entails that "unlikes should be treated unalike," because the two propositions are correlative aspects of all rules (and sets of rules).

[125] "[A]ny rule which allots 'equal shares to equals' implicitly not only allots 'unequal shares to unequals' but also allots them 'in proportion to their inequality.'" Oppenheim, *The Concept of Equality*, in 5 INTERNATIONAL ENCYCLOPEDIA OF THE SOCIAL SCIENCES 103 (1968).

The equivalence of "likes should be treated alike" and its analogue, "unalikes should be treated unalike," inheres in their semantics. Assume, for example, that a society believes that food should be distributed to needy people in proportion to their body weight, with the heavier people receiving more food and the lighter people receiving proportionately less. Assume, too, that *X* weighs twice as much as *A* or *B*. An "equal" distribution under the rule can be described in one of two ways. One can say that *A* and *B* should be treated "alike" by being given like quantities of food and that *X* should be treated "unalike" by being given a double quantity of food. Alternatively, one can say that *all* three persons should be treated "alike" by being given food in proportion to their body weight. Each of the foregoing formulations — the one that employs "likes should be treated alike" in conjunction with "unalikes should be treated unalike," and the one that employs solely "likes should be treated alike" — suffices entirely as a statement of the rule; they are alternative statements of the very same thing. The only difference lies in the level of generality at which the governing standard of treatment is stated — the standard that defines "like" treatment for purposes of the rule. A legal regime that uses "likes should be treated alike" in conjunction with "unlikes should be treated unalike" is therefore logically indistinguishable from a regime that uses "likes should be treated alike" alone.

[126]

> It is important to appreciate that the Aristotelian formula [that likes should be treated alike] does not state a *presumption* at all. We are not to presume either equality or inequality, but are directed to treat equally those who are equal, and to treat unequally those who are unequal.
>
> . . . .
>
> . . . The crucial point is that if we are concerned to justify our treatment of other people . . . then equal and unequal treatments are on the same footing. There is no *a priori* reason for singling out one of them as peculiarly preferred. . . . We should say, not that there is an *a priori* principle which demands

The same procedural rule, however, could be based on a second assumption. The presumption of equality could express a judgment that people are alike in more morally significant respects than they are unalike. Put another way, the presumption could be that, in instances of uncertainty, there is greater moral danger in treating persons unalike than in treating them alike. Such a presumption, however, cannot be derived from the general proposition that likes should be treated alike. Instead, it would have to derive from particular experience that distinctions between persons are either *usually* unjustified or sufficiently grave to outweigh the harm of *usually* doing the opposite.[127] Because the principle that "likes should be treated alike" does not itself entail the idea that people are alike in more morally significant respects than they are unalike, any presumption of the latter kind must derive its substance from outside the idea of equality.

The second, and more serious, problem with the presump-

> of us that we should presume equality, but that the only reasonable thing to do is not to presume at all. It is true that there is no reason for treating *A* and *B* differently. It is also true that there is no reason for treating *A* and *B* the same. What is *not* true is that the proposition that there is no reason for treating them differently entails the proposition that there is a reason for not treating them differently.

Browne, *supra* note 37, at 47, 52 (emphasis in original); *see* J. FEINBERG, *supra* note 1, at 100–02; J. LUCAS, *supra* note 27, at 173–75; Hare, *Justice and Equality*, 6 DIALECTICS & HUMANISM, Autumn 1979, at 17, 18–19.

[127] The point may be clearer when one considers a more narrowly drawn presumption. One can imagine a rule that men and women ought to be treated alike unless there are good reasons for treating them differently — meaning that neither sex as a whole ought to be denied advantages enjoyed by the other based on sexual stereotypes, unless the reasons for doing so outweigh the injury done by slighting persons on the basis of sexual stereotyping. The rule against making sexual distinctions, however, does not derive from any general presumption against making distinctions; it derives from specific experience with the usual consequences of distinctions of a particular kind. As Joel Feinberg puts it: "The presumption in favor of equal treatment holds [only] when the individuals involved are [already] believed, assumed, or expected to be equal in the relevant respects . . . ." J. FEINBERG, *supra* note 1, at 101.

To be sure, one can reformulate the "presumption of equality" as a rule that (1) when categorical distinctions between persons are found usually to cause unjustified injury to one class or the other (or both), or (2) when categorical distinctions between persons are found to cause injuries that are worse than the harm of usually drawing no distinctions, (3) then the actor should presumptively treat the two classes as a single class unless his reasons for categorically distinguishing between them outweigh any resulting injury. The trouble with this reformulated rule is that, though it may be morally plausible, it is entirely derivative; it does not tell us anything we do not already know. It tells us that, when facial distinctions of a certain kind are found to be usually unjustified, we should usually refrain from making them; and that, when such distinctions are shown to be justified for reasons of a certain kind, we may then make them for reasons of that certain kind.

tion of equality is that it is totally indeterminate.[128] For one thing, just as the presumption of equality itself contains no standards for distinguishing "like" from "unlike" objects, neither can it distinguish "like" from "unlike" treatments.[129] Furthermore, because every rule treats people alike in some respects and unalike in others,[130] the presumption cannot fill its "core function"[131] of distinguishing rules that require justification from those that do not. Finally, even if the presumption could definitely identify rules requiring justification, the presumption itself contains no standards for distinguishing "good" from "bad" reasons for treating people unalike, and so it cannot tell an actor when the presumption is rebutted. For all three reasons, the presumption remains meaningless as a moral norm.

To illustrate, consider *Morey v. Doud*,[132] a case involving

---

[128] *But see* B. ACKERMAN, SOCIAL JUSTICE IN THE LIBERAL STATE 16, 37–58 (1980) (implying that the presumption of equality is an intelligible and important political norm); D. HAWKINS, *supra* note 40, at 10 (same); Graham, *Liberty and Equality*, 74 MIND 59, 64 (1965) (same); Spaemann, *supra* note 118, at 364 (same).

[129] "We can only call two things similar in virtue of some rule or criterion of similarity. Thus whether two objects are the same colour depends on what we count as 'the same colour' . . . ." J. WILSON, *supra* note 71, at 41; *see supra* p. 545 & note 24.

The point can be illustrated by considering a rule that requires that every person be given one pound of bread each day. Such a rule treats persons alike by reference to distribution of bread per capita, but it treats them unalike by reference to distribution of bread by body weight, by need, by age, or by achievement. As one author has put it, "[s]imply to say that it is right to treat two people equally rather than unequally is meaningless . . . since to treat two people equally in one respect will always be to treat them unequally in others." *Developments in the Law — Equal Protection*, 82 HARV. L. REV. 1065, 1164 (1969) (footnote omitted). Anatole France expressed the thought more quotably: "The law in its majestic equality forbids the rich as well as the poor to sleep under bridges, to beg in the streets, and to steal bread." A. FRANCE, LE LYS ROUGE (1894), *quoted in* J. BARTLETT, FAMILIAR QUOTATIONS 802a (14th rev. ed. 1968).

[130] *See supra* pp. 545–47 & note 129.

[131] *See* J. LUCAS, *supra* note 27, at 173 ("bulldozing power" of the presumption of equality disappears unless it can separate those cases that require justification from those that do not). To be sure, one can "read into" the presumption a standard of treatment that renders the presumption sensible. Thus, the presumption can be taken to mean that, in the absence of good reasons for treating people otherwise, people should be treated "alike" by reference to the standard by which they should be treated. This reading of the presumption renders it morally plausible, but it does so only by reducing it to a tautology. That is, it instructs the actor to treat persons alike by reference to the rule by which they should be treated unless he has good reasons for treating them in accord with some other rule, "good" being defined by the standards that determine when the first rule yields to the second. One receives nothing from such a presumption that one has not already put there oneself.

[132] 354 U.S. 457 (1957), *overruled by* City of New Orleans v. Dukes, 427 U.S. 297 (1976).

a state statute that classified all money-order issuers for purposes of inspection and bonding by placing them in one of two categories; one category consisted solely of American Express by name, the other category of all other companies. The plaintiff, who did not enjoy the exemption granted to American Express, challenged the classification on the ground that it denied him equal protection of the law. His argument seemed to be that, if the statute had granted the exemption to both the plaintiff and American Express (or had denied the exemption to both), it would have treated them "alike" and hence would have needed no justification; but because the statute granted the benefit to one company and not the other, it treated them "unalike," and hence required rational justification.[133] The obvious difficulty was that the Court had no way of knowing whether the statute treated the two companies alike or unalike without first identifying the rule by which the companies' conduct should be governed. If the appropriate rule was that every company that lacked the size, assets, and lobbying power of American Express ought to be bonded, then by that standard the companies were treated *alike*; if the appropriate rule was that every money order issuer ought to be bonded, then the companies were treated *unalike*. Because the presumption of equality contains no standards for choosing between the two rules, it could not tell the Court whether the statute treated the two companies alike or unalike and hence whether the statute required rational justification. Moreover, since the presumption contains no standards for distinguishing "good" reasons from "bad" reasons for treating companies unalike, it could not tell the Court whether the unalike treatment (if any) was justified or unjustified.

What does all this mean for rationality review under the equal protection clause? It means that rationality review cannot be justified or defended as a distinctive attribute of equality. That is not to say that the state may enact regulatory classifications that are "rationally unrelated" to "legitimate state interest[s]."[134] The pros and cons of rationality review are matters of substantive constitutional value that must be decided on their own merits.[135] The point is that, if rationality review has merit, it is not because the state is constitutionally obliged to have rational reasons for treating people "unalike" (as opposed to "alike") but because the state is obliged to have rational and legitimate reason for *every* way in which it treats

[133] Brief for Appellee at 13–18, Morey v. Doud, 354 U.S. 457 (1957) (No. 475).

[134] *See supra* note 115.

[135] *See supra* note 117; *infra* note 136.

people.[136] Whatever merit rationality review has must ultimately derive not from notions of equality but from notions of substantive due process.[137]

III. The Confusions of Equality

I have argued thus far that equality is an entirely formal concept: it is a "form" for stating moral and legal propositions whose substance originates elsewhere, a "form"[138] of discourse

---

[136] *See* Hare, *supra* note 126, at 19.

Ultimately, of course, "rationality" review is itself a *formal* standard: it instructs the courts to strike down regulations containing classifications that are not "rationally related" to "legitimate" state ends, but it does not itself set forth substantive standards for determining what means are "rational" or what ends "legitimate." To give substance to rationality review, one must incorporate by reference and from elsewhere substantive standards for determining rationality and legitimacy. *See* Note, *supra* note 9, at 813–56. In doing so, one may discover that the Constitution prescribes more than one such standard. In the last analysis, therefore, rationality review requires one to identify a substantive constitutional standard (or standards) and to weigh that standard (or standards) against competing legislative policies. Before one has identified such standards, one has no way of knowing whether two persons are "alike" or "unalike." After one has identified such standards and weighed them against competing policies, one has no further need for the propositions that "likes should be treated alike" because one has already determined how to treat the respective parties.

[137] *See* Sandalow, *supra* note 72, at 658. Similarly, whatever merit equality has derives from notions of justice:

> If it is said that the demand for equality must not be taken in a formal sense, but that the decisive factor is whether the limitation takes place according to distinctive marks which are "well founded," "reasonable" or "just," this means that the idea of equality vanishes, to be replaced by a reference to what is considered "just" according to a subjective and emotional opinion.

A. Ross, *supra* note 8, at 288.

Thus far I have argued that the "presumption" of equality does not dictate "rationality" review. I should add that the idea of equality does not dictate "rationality" either. Equality requires that an actor treat likes alike and unlikes unalike. It does not require that he explain or justify his action, or that he give reasons for finding his actions to be in accord with the maxims of equality:

> Thus, the application of the nonpresumptivist principle [that likes should be treated alike] does not rest solely on what can and cannot be *shown*. What justifies difference of treatment in the case of the nonpresumptivist principle is that there *is* an actual (relevant) difference between the individuals involved (whether or not this distinction can be shown), whereas what justifies difference of treatment in the case of the [presumption of equality] is being able to *show* grounds for distinction (whether or not this distinction actually exists).

Katzner, *Presumptivist and Nonpresumptivist Principles of Formal Justice*, 81 Ethics 253, 255 (1971) (emphasis added).

[138]

> A formal principle of justice . . . "contains a completely unspecified variable whereas [substantive] principles constitute different ways of replacing the variable by a constant." The principle that persons who are alike in the relevant respect must be treated alike, while persons who are unalike in the relevant respect must be treated unalike and in direct proportion to the differences

with no substantive content of its own.[139] Yet some commentators take the position that, as a form of legal argument, equality may facilitate analysis of legal problems. Although they concede that equality is an "empty"[140] and "[c]ircular"[141] idea and that to find any meaning in the equal protection

> between them is formal in the defined sense, since it fails completely to specify which respects are relevant.

J. FEINBERG, *supra* note 1, at 100 (quoting L. Katzner, An Analysis of the Concept of Justice 2 (1968) (unpublished Ph.D. dissertation)). For further description of the terms, "formal" and "formalism," see C. PERELMAN, *supra* note 8, at 11–29, 36; Locke, *supra* note 30; Perelman, *supra* note 66, at 10–11.

Unfortunately, some commentators purport to adhere to the conventional distinction between "formal" and "substantive" equality yet simultaneously smuggle implicit notions of substantive justice into their descriptions of "formal" equality. Thus, some commentators describe the so-called "presumption of equality," *see supra* note 127, as a principle of "formal" equality, *see, e.g.*, S. BENN & R. PETERS, *supra* note 29, at 126–28; P. POLYVIOU, *supra* note 8, at 7-8, even though the "presumption" clearly has substantive effect. *See* W. GALSTON, *supra* note 37, at 143–45. Other commentators use "formal equality" to describe a judicial system that is "impartial" in the sense of being "no respecter of persons," *see, e.g.*, B. ACKERMAN, *supra* note 128, at 18; J. LUCAS, *supra* note 12, at 253; Hare, *supra* note 126, at 24, yet the prohibition on paying "respect" to "persons" is itself a substantive limitation on the power of government — a limitation having its source in controvertible notions of right and wrong. Still other commentators use "formal" equality to refer to the proposition that everybody counts for one and nobody counts for more than one, *see, e.g.*, R. HARE, FREEDOM AND REASON 118 (1963), even though the latter is not a logical consequence of the proposition that "likes should be treated alike." *See* W. GALSTON, *supra* note 37, at 144–45. Finally, some commentators use "formal" equality to refer to the requirement that persons be equal "before the law," meaning that the "grounds for deciding between two persons should be only those laid down [in advance] by law," even though such a requirement of "legality" has definite substantive components. *See* J. LUCAS, *supra* note 12, at 253 (distinguishing "equality before the law" from "formal equality").

[139] Flathman, *supra* note 36, at 38, 40; *see* C. PERELMAN, *supra* note 8, at 11–29, 36–87; A. ROSS, *supra* note 8, at 270–75; Hart, *Introduction* to C. PERELMAN, *supra* note 8, at vii; Sandalow, *supra* note 72, at 655.

[140]

> First attempts at defining equality invariably begin with the principle of Aristotle that equality consists in treating equals equally and unequals unequally. . . . It has often been observed that such statements are empty of substance. They do not contain any suggestion as to how to identify people who are equals or unequals, nor do they provide any yardstick by which appropriate criteria of relevance can either be identified or developed.

P. POLYVIOU, *supra* note 8, at 7 (footnote omitted); *accord* Honoré, *supra* note 9, at 83 ("The principle of treating like cases alike is . . . an empty . . . one . . . ."). Professor Ely notes that "the content of the Equal Protection Clause — the answer to the question of what inequalities are tolerable under what circumstances — will not be found anywhere in its terms." J. ELY, *supra* note 56, at 32; *accord* J. REES, *supra* note 22, at 95–96; Carr, *supra* note 54, at 211–12; Fiss, *Groups and the Equal Protection Clause*, in EQUALITY AND PREFERENTIAL TREATMENT 84, 85 (M. Cohen, T. Nagel & T. Scanlon eds. 1977). *But cf.* Perry, *supra* note 4, at 1082 ("[I]t is important to understand that equal protection is not an indeterminate, vacuous principle.").

[141] L. TRIBE, *supra* note 111, § 16-1, at 991.

clause one must posit "substantive ideals"[142] having nothing to do with the principle of equality, these commentators argue for its continued use on the grounds that equality "serves a distinctive function,"[143] that it is "more protective" of persons than are substantive rights,[144] and that as "a model — a way of looking at constitutional issues generally"[145] — it "offer[s] alluring alternatives for constitutional arguments."[146]

I believe that these commentators are mistaken about both the distinctiveness of equality and its usefulness. As a source of entitlements, equality cannot produce substantive results unattainable under other forms of analysis, because, as we have already seen, equality has no substantive content of its own. As a form of analysis, equality confuses far more than it clarifies,[147] for at least four reasons: (1) by masquerading as an independent norm, equality conceals the real nature of the substantive rights it incorporates by reference; (2) by framing a person's entitlements in terms of his equivalence to others, equality misleadingly suggests that one person's rights vis-a-vis another's are identical in all contexts; (3) by encouraging use of monolithic levels of judicial scrutiny undifferentiated by the importance of the underlying right, equality erroneously suggests that all questions of equality are to be scrutinized under a single (or sometimes, a two-tier) standard of justification; and (4) by emphasizing that some issues of equality entail dual

---

[142] *Id.*; *see also id.* § 11-1, at 566 ("[I]t has been possible to give content to [the equal protection clause] only through controversial substantive judgments."). Professor Tribe's recent article on constitutional theory elaborated on this distinction:

> Any constitutional distinction between laws burdening homosexuals and laws burdening exhibitionists, between laws burdening Catholics and laws burdening pickpockets, must depend on a substantive theory of which groups are exercising fundamental rights and which are not . . . . [T]he idea of blacks or women as properly segregated beings can be rejected *only* by finding a constitutional basis for concluding that, in our society, such hierarchical visions are substantively out of bounds, at least as a justification for government action. And such a finding would in turn entail a theory of unenumerated substantive rights.

Tribe, *The Puzzling Persistence of Process-Based Constitutional Theories*, 89 YALE L.J. 1063, 1076 (1980) (footnotes omitted) (emphasis in original).

[143] Perry, *supra* note 4, at 1083–84.

[144] Karst, *supra* note 85, at 67.

[145] L. TRIBE, *supra* note 111, § 16-1, at 992.

[146] *Id.* § 11-1, at 565; *see also id.* § 16-1, at 991 (describing the "Model of Equal Protection" as a "crucial but independent variable," to be distinguished from the "Model of Preferred Rights").

[147] I do not mean to suggest that all "formal" concepts are useless. Some formal concepts are quite handy, even indispensible. *See, e.g.*, Ross, *Tû-Tû*, 70 HARV. L. REV. 812, 817–19 (1958) (arguing that, although "rights" have no semantic meaning except as rhetorical devices for connecting descriptive and prescriptive statements, "rights" are nonetheless quite useful for purposes of "presentation").

remedies, equality erroneously implies that it entails uniquely flexible remedies.

A. The Fallacy of the Independent Norm

The principle of equality is taken by some people to be an independent norm — a norm comparable to rights and liberties of speech, conscience, and religion. Such a perception conceals the need to look outside equality for substantive rights to give the principle content. The resulting confusion is evident in the way courts and commentators talk about the content of the equal protection clause of the fourteenth amendment. One member of the Supreme Court goes so far as to say that "the Equal Protection Clause confers no substantive rights and creates no substantive liberties."[148] A commentator recently has argued that the equal protection clause "cannot and should not bear a substantive content."[149] Another has asserted that the substantive meaning of the equal protection clause can "be profitably approached *through the meaning of equality itself*."[150]

Moreover, because equality camouflages rights under a formula that makes no explicit reference to the substantive rights it incorporates from elsewhere, equality "blind[s]" us not only to the existence of such rights but to their specific substantive content also.[151] Constitutional rights, even relatively specific

---

[148] San Antonio Indep. School Dist. v. Rodriguez, 411 U.S. 1, 59 (1973) (Stewart, J., concurring); *cf.* Harris v. McRae, 448 U.S. 297, 322 (1980) (Stewart, J.) ("The guarantee of equal protection under the Fifth Amendment is not a source of substantive rights or liberties . . . ."). To be fair to Justice Stewart, he may have used "substantive rights" to refer to noncomparative rights.

[149] Lupu, *supra* note 84, at 985; *see also id.* at 1054 ("Equal protection has no 'substance' in the sense in which I have employed the term."); *cf.* Wright, *supra* note 1, at 19 (since deciding whether official action accords equal treatment "involves few basic policy choices," judges tend to do it well).

[150] Wilkinson, *The Supreme Court, The Equal Protection Clause, and the Three Faces of Constitutional Equality*, 61 VA. L. REV. 945, 946 (1975) (emphasis added).

[151] Carr, *supra* note 54, at 223 (equality "serves only to blind us to the actual workings and character of the practice of doing justice"); Karst, *supra* note 4, at 1; Sandalow, *supra* note 72, at 660–61 ("Although the Supreme Court has in recent years frequently invoked the equal protection clause to invalidate legislation, it has not carefully considered the problem of justifying the material principles upon which those decisions rest."); *see also* Browne, *supra* note 14, at 53 (equality "is a wholly trivial implication of some more basic facts, whose real significance it *distorts* and *obscures*") (emphasis added). For an illustration of the extent to which equality disguises underlying substantive arguments, see Kamisar, *Has the Court Left the Attorney General Behind? — The Bazelon-Katzenbach Letters on Poverty, Equality and the Administration of Criminal Justice*, 54 KY. L.J. 464, 482 (1966) (suggesting that the Attorney General was using "equality" as a mask for surreptitiously reasserting substantive claims that the Supreme Court had already directly rejected).

freedoms such as those of speech and religion, are already difficult enough to identify and assess. It only compounds the problem to subsume them under the "catchall"[152] proposition that "likes should be treated alike," a formula that is capable of incorporating any substantive right by reference.[153]

This is not to say that equality necessarily distorts the analysis of underlying substantive rights. As long as we keep an eye on the substance of the underlying right, the language of equality can be used to state and analyze any right. The point, rather, is that equality produces unnecessary confusion, because it does circuitously what could be done directly.[154]

B. The Fallacy of Equivalences

As a form for analyzing problems, equality is a search for equivalences. Unfortunately, by justifying particular moral and legal conclusions on the ground that one individual is "equal to" another, equality tends to mislead people into assuming that such persons are generally equal for moral and legal purposes. As a result, foolish mistakes are made in the assessment of moral and legal standards, mistakes that would not occur if focus remained on the substantive rights that inform the notions of equality.

To illustrate the fallacy of equivalences, consider the relationship between a program that excludes blacks from a law

---

[152] Perry, *supra* note 4, at 1077.

[153] *See* H. KELSEN, *supra* note 18, at 127; C. PERELMAN, *supra* note 21, at 10–11, 22 (equality "can be reconciled with the most varied philosophies and codes of law"); A. ROSS, *supra* note 8, at 273 ("It is plain that this formal demand [for equality] never can justify any claim that one rule is to be preferred for another one."); Berlin, *supra* note 22, at 130 ("[*A*]*ny* kind of behavior can be safely subsumed under the general rule enjoining equal treatment . . . .") (emphasis in original); Browne, *supra* note 14, at 54 ("*every* distribution" can be characterized by relations of equality and inequality) (emphasis in original).

[154] Justice Stewart, discussing equal protection cases involving fundamental rights, put it well:

> The Court is understandably reluctant to rely on substantive due process. . . . But to embrace the essence of that doctrine under the guise of equal protection serves no purpose but obfuscation. "[C]ouched in slogans and ringing phrases," the Court's equal protection doctrine shifts the focus of the judicial inquiry away from its proper concerns, which include "the nature of the individual interest affected, the extent to which it is affected, the rationality of the connection between legislative means and purpose, the existence of alternative means for effectuating the purpose, and the degree of confidence we may have that the statute reflects the legislative concern for the purpose that would legitimately support the means chosen." . . .
>
> To conceal this appropriate inquiry invites mechanical or thoughtless application of misfocused doctrine.

Zablocki v. Redhail, 434 U.S. 374, 395–96 (1978) (Stewart, J., concurring in the judgment) (quoting Williams v. Illinois, 395 U.S. 235, 260 (1970) (Harlan, J., concurring in the result)).

assume that what makes for equality in mathematics also makes for equality in law and morals.[161]

C. The Fallacy of Equal Scrutiny

Some constitutional rights are acknowledged to be more important than others and hence to trigger higher degrees of judicial scrutiny when they are abridged.[162] The constitutional right to disseminate sexually explicit messages is not as strong as the right to disseminate political messages and thus is subject to a lesser degree of judicial scrutiny;[163] a person's fifth and fourteenth amendment rights to procedural due process in civil cases are not as strong as his sixth amendment right to a fair trial in criminal cases;[164] the right to divorce appears to be not as strong as the right to marry;[165] the right of a woman to abort a fetus may not be as strong as her right to carry the child to term.[166] The weaker the constitutional interest, the

---

[161] *See, e.g.*, H. KELSEN, *supra* note 153, at 128 (describing the principle that "likes should be treated alike" as a "mathematical formulation"); Stone, *Equal Protection and the Search for Justice*, 22 ARIZ. L. REV. 1, 2 (1980) ("Partially because of its kinship to mathematics, equality seems to have a definite meaning in a sense in which notions of 'justice' or even 'fairness' do not."). *But see* S. BENN & R. PETERS, *supra* note 29, at 130 ("[I]n the end, doing justice calls for decision-making, not calculation: we have to *decide* what is relevant, and what consequences ought to follow — and though we decide according to rules, we are still doing something different from arithmetic.") (emphasis in original).

[162] *See* Vlandis v. Kline, 412 U.S. 441, 458–59 (1973) (White, J., concurring in the judgment); San Antonio Indep. School Dist. v. Rodriguez, 411 U.S. 1, 98–99 (1973) (Marshall, J., dissenting); *cf.* Martin & Nickel, *Recent Work on the Concept of Rights*, 17 AMER. PHIL. Q. 165, 172 n.14 (1980) ("The relative weights of rights has been established to some extent within U.S. constitutional law through the idea of 'preferred freedom.'"); Sartorius, *Dworkin On Rights and Utilitarianism*, 1981 UTAH L. REV. 263, 265 ("[Dworkin's] claim that principles have a dimension of weight which rules do not, conjoined with his view that principles reflect rights, suggests that some rights are weightier than others and that in cases of conflict the weightiest right ought to prevail."). *But see* J. FEINBERG, *supra* note 1, at 66; *cf.* Lupu, *supra* note 84, at 1014 & n.160 (government obligated to remain neutral when individual forced to choose between two constitutionally significant alternatives).

[163] Young v. American Mini Theatres, Inc., 427 U.S. 50, 70 (1976) (plurality opinion) ("[S]ociety's interest in protecting [sexually explicit] . . . expression is of a wholly different, and lesser, magnitude than the interest in untrammeled political debate . . . ."). A similar distinction exists between commercial and noncommercial speech. *See* Metromedia, Inc. v. City of San Diego, 101 S. Ct. 2882, 2895 (1981) (plurality opinion) ("[O]ur recent . . . speech cases have consistently accorded noncommercial speech a greater degree of protection than commercial speech.").

[164] *See* Gagnon v. Scarpelli, 411 U.S. 778, 783–91 (1973); Morrissey v. Brewer, 408 U.S. 471, 480–82, 484–90 (1972).

[165] *See Developments in the Law — The Constitution and The Family*, 93 HARV. L. REV. 1156, 1310–11 (1980).

[166] *See* Harris v. McRae, 448 U.S. 297, 336 n.6 (1980) (Brennan, J., dissenting); Maher v. Roe, 432 U.S. 464, 477 (1977); *see also* Regents of the Univ. of Cal. v.

less strict the degree of scrutiny by which courts test competing state interests; the stronger the constitutional interest, the stricter the degree of scrutiny.

The variety among constitutional rights is well understood. Unfortunately, people tend to lose sight of these variations when they analyze the same rights under what they view as the monolithic ideal of the equal protection clause.[167] As a consequence, people who analyze constitutional problems in terms of equality tend to give different weight to certain constitutional rights than they would if they analyzed the rights directly.

To illustrate, consider whether a state may enact zoning regulations to prohibit bookstores selling sexually explicit material from locating within one mile of one another. If one analyzes the issue in terms of rights, one would attribute to the right to disseminate sexually explicit literature the appropriate weight — and hence the proper degree of scrutiny — that the right itself is deemed to deserve. If one proceeds under the rubric of equality, in contrast, one tends to force the evaluation into crude levels of scrutiny that are unrelated to the precise weight that the right to disseminate sexually explicit literature properly deserves. Thus, one might conclude that the zoning regulation classifies persons on the basis of their exercise of a "fundamental right" and that the regulation is therefore subject to the strictest degree of judicial scrutiny.[168] As a conse-

Bakke, 438 U.S. 265, 355–59 (1978) (opinion of Brennan, White, Marshall, and Blackmun, JJ., concurring in the judgment in part and dissenting in part) (stating that the right of a person not to be disadvantaged solely on the basis of race is not as strong as his right not to be stigmatized as racially inferior); Gregg v. Georgia, 428 U.S. 153, 188–95 (1976) (opinion of Stewart, Powell, and Stevens, JJ.) (implying that a person's sixth amendment right to a trial in a noncapital case is not as rigorous as his sixth and eighth amendment right to a criminal trial in a capital case); Y. KAMISAR, W. LAFAVE, & J. ISRAEL, MODERN CRIMINAL PROCEDURE 80–81, 165 (5th ed. 1980) (suggesting that a person's sixth amendment right to represent himself in criminal proceedings is not as rigorous as his sixth amendment right to be represented by counsel).

[167] *See* Craig v. Boren, 429 U.S. 190, 211–12 (1976) (Stevens, J., concurring) ("There is only one Equal Protection Clause. . . . It does not direct the courts to apply one standard of review in some cases and a different standard in other cases."); *see also* Baker, *supra* note 117, at 1038 (noting "the strangeness of the notion that a court should use different levels of scrutiny to judge the constitutionality of government practices"); *supra* notes 112 & 113.

[168] For an illustration of such reasoning, see American Mini Theatres, Inc. v. Gribbs, 518 F.2d 1014, 1019–20 (6th Cir. 1975), *rev'd sub nom.* Young v. American Mini Theatres, Inc., 427 U.S. 50 (1976); Note, *Zoning, Adult Movie Theatres and the First Amendment: An Approach to* Young v. American Mini Theatres, Inc., 5 HOFSTRA L. REV. 379, 402–10 (1977). For the general tendency to require delicate "balancing" with respect to rights and liberties while requiring procrustean levels of scrutiny with respect to equal protection, see Note, *supra* note 113, at 547, 566–69.

quence, one would give the right to disseminate sexually explicit literature the same weight that one would give the right to disseminate political literature, without any reference to whether one truly believe that sexually explicit literature deserves the same protection as political literature. One ends up treating political and sexually explicit literature the same — not because one has previously determined them to possess equivalent weights, but because one has been misled by the unitary formula of equality into thinking that all rights are created equal.

Significantly, the same kind of confusion also occurs in suspect classification cases. In the area of sex discrimination, for example, assume that, while men and women both have a constitutional right not to be disadvantaged solely on account of sex, the right of men to be free from such discrimination is somewhat weaker than the comparably worded but constitutionally stronger right of women.[169] If we analyze a statute that discriminates against men in terms of these two rights, we take account of the differences between them. If we analyze the statute as an abridgement of equality, however, we might be inclined to subject it to the single form of scrutiny — whether "strict" or "intermediate"[170] — that all forms of sex discrimination are thought to deserve. By forcing all constitutional claims into categorical levels of scrutiny, equality may distort the variety of standards that are ordinarily thought to govern the resolution of substantive claims.[171]

There are two ways to escape from the fallacy of thinking that all equality cases are subject to procrustean levels of scrutiny. One is to retain equality as a form of argument while rejecting the notion that equality entails levels of scrutiny peculiar to itself. Thus, as some authorities have suggested, instead of analyzing all equality problems under single-tiered (or two-tiered or three-tiered) scrutiny, one would incorporate by reference whatever scrutiny is otherwise deemed to be entailed by the substantive right at issue.[172] The other way is

---

[169] *See* Craig v. Boren, 429 U.S. 190, 217–20 (1976) (Rehnquist, J., dissenting).

[170] *See supra* notes 105, 106, 112 & 113.

[171] The underlying right will not necessarily be distorted; existing equal protection doctrine can accommodate different rights within a single level of scrutiny by assigning different weights to the different interests served by the challenged classifications. For example, a court could simultaneously strike down a state college admissions policy favoring men on the ground that it did not bear a close relation to a substantial state policy, and uphold an admissions policy favoring women on the ground that it did bear a sufficiently close relation to such a policy. The point is simply that the present three-tiered system of scrutiny may lead to error, not that it must do so.

[172] *See* Karst, *supra* note 4, at 2 ("level of judicial scrutiny" should be "commensurate with the degree of suspectness of legislative classifications and the degree of

simpler and safer still: eschew equality altogether and proceed directly in terms of the underlying claim of right.[173]

D. The Fallacy of Fungible Remedies

The common factor in these confusions, the premise that equality has irreducible content of its own, is particularly pronounced in the notion that equality provides a richer and more flexible array of remedies than do rights. The advocates of this view hold that, when a legislative burden violates one person's rights, the only legislative response that can remedy the violation is to remove the burden altogether. In contrast, when a legislative burden denies one person equal treatment vis-a-vis another, the denial can be remedied by any legislative response that results in treating them the same. The principle of equality is presumably indifferent to whether the legislature responds by removing the burden from him or by extending it to everyone. Consequently, since equality envisages a wider range of legislative responses and therefore intrudes less into the democratic process, equality is the preferable form of analysis.[174]

This argument, usually attributed to Justice Robert Jackson,[175] is flawed for several reasons. For one thing, even if equality has substantive content, it does not follow that a court is justified in choosing an equality analysis (and rejecting the consequences of a rights analysis) simply because the court

---

importance of the interests invaded by legislation"); Wilkinson, *supra* note 150, at 954.

[173] Note, *supra* note 113, at 537–41, 548–54, 561–65.

[174] *See* L. TRIBE, *supra* note 111, § 16-1, at 991; Ely, *Toward a Representation-Reinforcing Mode of Judicial Review*, 37 MD. L. REV. 451, 463 (1978); Gunther, *supra* note 114, at 43; Karst, *supra* note 85, at 38; Lupu, *supra* note 84, at 1017–19; Comment, *supra* note 84, at 476–77.

[175]

> The burden should rest heavily upon one who would persuade us to use the due process clause to strike down a substantive law or ordinance. Even its provident use against municipal regulations frequently disables all government — state, municipal and federal — from dealing with the conduct in question because the requirement of due process is also applicable to State and Federal Governments. Invalidation of a statute or an ordinance on due process grounds leaves ungoverned and ungovernable conduct which many people find objectionable.
>
> Invocation of the equal protection clause, on the other hand, does not disable any governmental body from dealing with the subject at hand. It merely means that the prohibition or regulation must have a broader impact. . . . The framers of the Constitution knew . . . that there is no more effective practical guaranty against arbitrary and unreasonable government than to require that the principles of law which officials would impose upon a minority must be imposed generally.

Railway Express Agency, Inc. v. New York, 336 U.S. 106, 112 (1949) (Jackson, J., concurring).

prefers the remedies of equality to the remedies of rights. If the substance of equality and rights differs, a court must enforce not whichever norm it prefers but whichever norm the entitled party demands. If, on the other hand, a court is free to choose between the norms, it can only be because there are no substantive differences between them. In short, Justice Jackson cannot have it both ways — either a court is free to choose between equality and rights, in which event the two cannot entail different remedies, or equality and rights do entail different remedies, in which event courts are not free to choose at will between them.

More serious problems arise from the starting assumption that, while rights entail single remedies, equality can be satisfied by any remedy that treats both parties the same. First of all, rights do not necessarily entail single remedies. Rights entail as many remedies (and as few) as suffice to redress the violation of the interests they safeguard. Assume, for example, that the state proposes to construct and maintain a public forum for the discussion of political views but plans to exclude the views of the Libertarian Party. The appropriate remedy for this apparent violation of the Libertarian Party's right of free speech depends entirely on the nature of the right being violated. If the right being violated is the right to insist that the state remain neutral regarding the content of political speech, one of two remedies would be appropriate: either ordering the state to permit the Libertarian Party to participate in the forum without regard to the content of its speech or prohibiting the state from inviting any other political spokesman to participate in the forum. If, instead, the right being violated is the affirmative right to insist that the state maintain public forums for the expression of political views, different alternative remedies would be appropriate: either ordering the state to open the forum to the Libertarian Party to express its views or ordering the state to make some other forum available for that purpose.[176] In either event, the nature of the alter-

[176] *See supra* note 85. To say, however, that two people are "alike" for purposes of a given rule does not mean that a repeal of the rule would affect both parties to the same extent. Assume, for example, that a state enacts a statute that treats pornographers and politicians "alike" with respect to speech by allowing both to sell books without a license. Although both are "alike" for purposes of the existing statutory rule, they are not both alike with respect to a repealer of the rule. While the state may repeal the law with respect to pornographers (and thus require pornographers to obtain a license for selling their books), it may not do so with respect to politicians, because the first amendment gives politicians an independent right to sell their books without a license. In other words, given a repeal of the state statute that treated pornographers and politicians alike, they are left with a residual constitutional rule that treats them differently.

native remedies depends on the nature of the underlying right. In either event, too, the alternative remedies remain constant, regardless of whether one uses an equality or a rights analysis.[177]

A second flaw in the starting assumption is that equality does not necessarily entail choice among remedies. Equality entails as many remedies (and as few) as the underlying substantive rights it subsumes. Some issues of equality (like some rights) necessarily require particular remedies. Assume, for example, that a state discriminates between men and women by requiring parental support of male children until the age of twenty-one while requiring parental support of female children only until the age of eighteen, and that a twenty-year-old woman demonstrates that the statute violates equal protection by disadvantaging her vis-a-vis her male counterparts solely on the basis of sex. If a court is persuaded that equality claims necessarily entail freedom to choose between two remedies, it might feel at liberty to choose between extending financial support to all women until the age of twenty-one or terminating support for males at the age of eighteen, whichever the court believes the legislature would prefer.[178] In reality, however, the latter remedy does not fully redress the woman's injury. The woman is complaining not only about future discrimination during the remaining year until she becomes twenty-one, but also about past discrimination during the two years of her life since the age of eighteen. A court does not compensate past injury by prohibiting continuing, future injury. The only remedy that repairs her past injury — and thus treats her the "same" as her male counterparts — is to order retrospective financial relief for the two years during which she was disadvantaged vis-a-vis males.[179] Her equality claim entails a single compensatory remedy, because under these circumstances the underlying substantive right (that is, the right not to be disadvantaged solely on the basis of sex) demands that remedy.[180] Once again, the confusion about

---

[177] *See* Alexander, *supra* note 69, at 67. It should be noted that one form of right entails only a single remedy: a noncomparative "negative" right, one that forbids the state to limit some category of private action. For example, a law penalizing the practice of Catholicism would not suffer multiple remedies; the only remedy would be for the law to be struck down.

[178] *See, e.g.*, Wengler v. Druggists Mut. Ins. Co., 446 U.S. 142, 152–53 (1980).

[179] *See* Ginsburg, *Some Thoughts on Judicial Authority to Repair Unconstitutional Legislation*, 28 CLEV. ST. L. REV. 301, 319, 322–24 (1979).

[180] The need to include a particular compensatory element in the remedial package obviously depends on the retrospective nature of the relief sought; for example, if the law in question had yet to take effect and declaratory or injunctive relief were sought,

This may explain why the proponents of the equal rights amendment (ERA) drafted it in the language of equality. The ERA states: "Equality of rights under the law shall not be denied . . . on account of sex." The ERA would mean the same thing if it simply said: "Rights under the law shall not be denied . . . on account of sex." Why then did the ERA's proponents draft it in the tautological language of equality? Perhaps it is because their adversaries do not perceive the tautology and, not perceiving it, are placed in the uncomfortable position of having to argue against equality.[193]

Another good example of the distortion created by equality arguments is the dispute in *Reynolds v. Sims*[194] over whether representatives for state legislatures should be apportioned strictly on the basis of population. Chief Justice Warren, advocating the substantive principle of "one person, one vote," chose to frame his position as an argument for "equality."[195] He reasoned (1) that the fourteenth amendment guarantees every person "equal protection";[196] (2) that "the concept of equal protection" means that persons who are "the same"[197] should be treated the same; and (3) that all voters within a state are the same "regardless of where they live."[198] Since steps (1) and (2) were undeniably true, they tended to mask the controversial substantive value concealed in the equality language of step (3). As a consequence, Justice Harlan, writing for the dissenters, was placed on the defensive. Unable to deny that the fourteenth amendment guarantees equality, or that equality means treating "equals" equally, Justice Harlan found himself in the unhappy position of having to argue against equality. Thus, the best he could do was to argue lamely that, while the fourteenth amendment guarantees equality, it does not guarantee "full equality"[199] with respect to voting.

Justice Harlan's mistake in *Reynolds* was to assume that, once the majority stated its position as an argument *for* equality, he had to state his position as an argument *against* equality.[200] In fact, although one party to a dispute may argue in

---

193 "[T]he assertion that everyone has equal rights seems to come to no more than the assertion that everyone has such rights as he has. In the expression 'equal rights' the word 'equal' occurs vacuously." Wollheim, *Equality and Equal Rights*, in JUSTICE AND SOCIAL POLICY 111, 116 (F. Olafson ed. 1961).

194 377 U.S. 533 (1964).

195 *Id.* at 558, 560–61.

196 *Id.* at 565.

197 *Id.*

198 *Id.*

199 *Id.* at 607 (Harlan, J., dissenting).

200 For another example of arguing against equality, see Bork, *The Impossibility*

favor of treating likes alike, his opponent can argue just as well in favor of treating unlikes unalike.[201] Thus, just as the *Reynolds* majority advocated "one person, one vote" in terms of equality, Justice Harlan could have opposed it as forcefully in terms of equality.[202] Just as the majority argued that votes should be weighted equally in proportion to each voter's share of the total number of votes cast in the state in which he resided,[203] Justice Harlan could have argued that votes should be weighted equally in proportion to each voters' share of the total number of votes cast in the legislative district in which he resided. By countering the majority's argument for equality with an opposing argument for equality, Justice Harlan would have forced the Court to realize that the case could not be resolved in those terms.[204] Instead, he allowed the majority to claim equality by default and thus to pretend that the ancient and undeniable truth that likes should be treated alike was really on the majority's side rather than on his.[205]

---

of Finding Welfare Rights in the Constitution, 1979 WASH. U.L.Q. 695, 701 ("Equality is not the only value in society; we must balance degrees of it against other values.").

[201] *See* D. RAE, *supra* note 8, at 19 ("The question is not 'Whether equality?' but *Which* equality?"); Benn, *supra* note 192, at 41 ("Equality . . . usually . . . means getting rid of one system of distinctions and replacing it with another."); Karst, *Equality and Community: Lessons From the Civil Rights Era*, 56 NOTRE DAME LAW. 183, 191 (1981) ("The achievement of one form of equality necessarily implies the imposition of corresponding inequalities."); Lucas, *supra* note 1, at 261 ("If we set out to establish equality in one respect, we shall thereby establish some other inequality in another respect."); Mortimore, *supra* note 8, at 222 ("In practice, egalitarians have been concerned merely to replace one type of discrimination by another . . . ."); *supra* note 153.

[202] For a brilliant demonstration of this point, see Flathman, *supra* note 36, at 40–51.

[203] This formulation of the majority's rule would call for representatives to be elected at large in statewide elections. Equally acceptable to the majority was a scheme in which each vote would be weighted equally in proportion to each voter's share of the total number of votes cast in his legislative district, with the size of all districts in the state uniformly being the total number of persons in the state divided by the number of representatives to be elected.

[204] *See* Flathman, *supra* note 36, at 43 ("Inasmuch as he is choosing between competing equalities, he has, again if only tacitly, turned to some principle other than equality to make that choice, that is, to decide what is right."); *cf.* J. POLE, *supra* note 2, at 358 (essential political question today is "to determine . . . preferences not between equality and inequality but between one concept of equality and another").

[205] Each side in the *DeFunis* controversy could state its legal position in terms of equality, *see* D. RAE, *supra* note 8, at 4–5; Stone, *supra* note 161, at 11; Winter, *Changing Concepts of Equality: From Equality Before the Law To the Welfare State*, 1979 WASH. U.L.Q. 741, 747–48, because equality by itself is empty. Marco DeFunis would argue that he is constitutionally "equal" to his black counterparts because treating him differently would cause him constitutional injury — that is, it would deprive him of benefits solely on the basis of race. The University of Washington

Equality will cease to mystify — and cease to skew moral and political discourse — when people come to realize that it is an empty form having no substantive content of its own.[206] That will occur as soon as people realize that every moral and legal argument can be framed in the form of an argument for equality. People then will answer arguments for equality by making counterarguments for equality. Or simpler still, they will see that they can do without equality altogether.

Law School, on the other hand, would argue that DeFunis is *not* equal to his black counterparts because (1) admitting him would not serve the purposes of affirmative action, and (2) treating him differently does not cause him constitutional injury, that is, does not stigmatize him as racially inferior.

206

> But from the very fact that the definition of formal justice does not in the least prejudge our judgments of value, we shall find all the less difficulty in reaching agreement on this definition, since when it is presented in this way, the idea of justice loses at once much of its attraction and nearly the whole of its emotive meaning.

C. PERELMAN, *supra* note 8, at 28.

[5]

Liberals and Unlawful Discrimination

JOHN GARDNER*

I

Contemporary liberal theory faces substantial difficulties in containing its doctrines of political legitimacy. Liberalism is committed by definition to making claims about the limits of governmental authority, and a theoretical investigation of these claims must provide good reasons for drawing the limits at one point rather than another.[1] Such investigations are regularly impeded—even frustrated—by the indeterminacy of the concepts in terms of which they are conducted.

The most familiar concept associated with liberal theories of legitimacy is that of 'harm'. Liberals invariably rely upon their 'harm principle' to delimit at least one kind of state action—the attaching of sanctions to behaviour. Plainly, this principle cannot extend to justify the prohibition of all conduct which disadvantages others, for such an extensive standard would subsume much of the personal freedom which the principle purports to protect. If it is to help us ascertain one of the boundaries of legitimacy, the understanding of 'harm' which is appealed to in the harm principle must have intelligible limits. The process of discerning these limits is laborious and eventually frustrating, because in fact we properly understand the concept of 'harm' in a way that is context-relative. While in one context the description 'harm' only extends to physical injuries, in another we might include intense irritations, demoralizations, emotional manipulations and so on.[2] Responding to this conceptual elasticity, a liberal could attempt to provide a rigid definition of 'harm', but the process of definition eliminates some of the important reflective appeal and subtlety of the harm principle, and introduces the different and inappropriate context-relativity of some further set of defining terms. We cannot usefully transcend the fluidity of our understanding by stipulation.[3]

The other significant concept at the core of contemporary liberal theories of legitimacy is that of 'distributive justice'. Many liberals accept that a further reason for legislative activity, apart from the harm principle, is to effect some redistribution of advantage among citizens. Here the profound difficulties include that of

* Fellow of All Souls College, Oxford. I am grateful to Jerry Cohen, Tony Honoré, Niki Lacey, Christopher McCrudden, Stephen Mulhall and Alan Summers for their careful reading and helpful remarks. I am also indebted to Tom Dimitroff and Ruth Yaffe, for instructive discussion of Raz's work, and to the participants in the 1986–7 Oxford BCL seminar on Comparative Human Rights, for educating and provoking me in relation to all the issues raised here.

[1] See Thomas Nagel, 'Moral Conflicts and Political Legitimacy', *Philosophy and Public Affairs* 16 (1987), 215.

[2] Compare Timothy O'Hagan, *The End of Law?*, (Oxford 1984), 108–111.

[3] See Joel Feinberg's *Harm to Others*, (New York 1984), 65: 'we are forced to refine our analysis by stipulation since [such] vagueness cannot be tolerated in a concept that is to be put to such important normative uses.' In fact, Feinberg's stipulations, in so far as they add anything at all, merely jeopardize the plausibility of the harm principle.

 Oxford Journal of Legal Studies Vol. 9, No. 1

isolating the relevant disadvantages, and that of containing the legitimate government responses to them, without straying too far from our ordinary understanding of what justice involves.[4] Some liberals have, of course, offered detailed proposals for the implementation of liberal distributive programmes. However, the result here is usually as difficult to accept as are stipulated definitions of harm. As we define the limits in more and more detail, we lose once again the important and powerful context-relativity of our intuitive views about justice itself, and we engage some new conceptual indeterminacies instead. We end up with ideals of distributive justice which are in some respects overinclusive, in others underinclusive.[5]

Liberals differ, of course, as to the extensiveness and force to be accorded to these two legitimacy doctrines. Some liberal theorists do not admit the legitimacy of redistributive activity by the state at all, limiting legitimacy to the prevention of harms. In such accounts, redistribution is commonly defined as a form of 'coercion', a rhetoric which makes distributive justice appear illiberal by definition.[6] Less extreme arguments, aiming to elude the accusation of overextensive state power, are inclined to avoid reducing all governmental activity to the terminology of 'coercion', and stress instead the important *differences* between the harm principle and distributive justice as legitimacy doctrines. On this approach, the methods available to governments in response to harms and injustices respectively are distinct and specific. Citizens are then not simply coerced indiscriminately: they are subject to that form of regulation which is appropriate to each of the state's roles as protector and as provider. The range of permitted state actions is narrowly tailored to correlative legitimate state functions.

For those who subscribe to this popular moderate style of liberalism, it immediately matters whether we classify some social event, circumstance or practice as an injustice or as a harm. It matters because appropriate governmental response differs accordingly. The harm principle operates, under specified conditions of liability, to implicate individual members of society. Citizens may be held personally responsible for those harms that take place under their control, and may be subjected to enforced treatment of some kind in the light of their personal blameworthiness. By contrast, the injustice of a distribution is attributed to no one but the society as a whole. Although the appropriate response may be to require some or all to contribute in some way to the process of redistribution, and legislative provisions may be used to secure this contribution, disadvantage and its correction are perceived as areas of collective, not individual, responsibility.

But some important matters of governmental concern are difficult to bring either squarely within the harm principle or squarely within the concerns of distributive justice. One problem case of this sort involves the legitimacy of legislation prohibiting discrimination on grounds of race, gender or religion. There is a major problem here about just who can legitimately be prohibited from adopting

[4] An influential perspective on the context-relativity of justice is Michael Walzer's. See especially his *Spheres of Justice*, (New York 1983). For a different view of the problem, see James Griffin, *Well-being*, (Oxford 1986), ch 13.

[5] For some instances, see Michael Sandel, *Liberalism and the Limits of Justice*, (Cambridge 1982), 32–5.

[6] The tactic is used by Robert Nozick in *Anarchy, State and Utopia*, (New York 1974).

discriminatory practices, and on what grounds. Liberals find it relatively easy to explain why the *state itself* should follow certain sensitive employment or education policies: the liberal state is ordinarily required to pursue policies which secure 'equal respect' for its citizens, and some kinds of 'discrimination' clearly deny 'equal respect' in the relevant sense.[7] On the other hand, it is seriously problematic for liberals to explain the basis upon which *citizens* may be required to abstain from discriminating against *each other*, and the fact that there seem to be some hints of harm and some hints of distributive injustice at stake in discriminatory behaviour leads to internecine dispute about the proper basis of regulation. Plainly, liberals cannot merely recite the incantation of 'equal respect' here. Requiring *citizens* to adopt a policy of equal respect would be wholly inconsistent with any commitment to allowing their personal preferences and projects to prevail, for such a policy would stipulate that personal preferences be excluded from every social practice, and would eclipse all spheres of individual judgment. It follows that the liberal state cannot properly require us to desist from discriminating merely because, by discriminating, we fail to treat fellow citizens with equal respect. Liberals must offer some further argument, one which shows that eliminating discrimination among citizens *inter se* falls within a legitimate area of state activity, that an accepted legitimacy doctrine applies.

The United Kingdom's and the United States' extensive legislation about discrimination requires that we conform to certain non-discriminatory standards in our dealings with our employees, our customers, our pupils, our tenants. Among the most vociferous supporters of this sort of legislation are many whose arguments are distinctively liberal.[8] But unless these liberal theorists can bring the prohibition of the various types of discrimination at stake here squarely within one or other of the liberal doctrines of legitimacy, we are entitled to suspect that their support for the legislation is disingenuous or mistaken. We can properly enquire why anyone committed to personal autonomy should sincerely endorse legislation which interferes so comprehensively with the pursuit of our own social preferences.

II

A rudimentary reply to this sceptical enquiry is neatly provided by the relevant legal provisions themselves.

In the structure of United Kingdom and United States discrimination law there are two concepts of unlawful discrimination. Looking at the two concepts as they are defined in our British legislation, we can see that these are not just two ways of doing the same thing. What is remarkable is that each seems, at any rate superficially, to fall within a different legitimacy doctrine. Recall that there are two doctrines of legitimacy (the harm principle and distributive justice) which authorize two distinct sorts of governmental response (attribution of individual

[7] Ronald Dworkin, 'Liberalism', reprinted in his *A Matter of Principle*, (Cambridge, Mass. 1985), especially 191 ff. (Theorists disagree, of course, about what 'equal respect' requires.)

[8] One example: Ronald Dworkin endorses the application of the United States Civil Rights Act 1964 to cases of race discrimination by private employers. See his 'How to Read the Civil Rights Act' in *A Matter of Principle*, above n 7.

responsibility and attribution of collective responsibility). Of the two concepts of unlawful discrimination, one bears the hallmarks of a harm, while the other seems to reflect a structure of perceived distributive injustice.

The first variety of unlawful discrimination is known in the United Kingdom as 'direct discrimination'. Someone discriminates directly, for instance, if he treats a woman 'less favourably' than he would a man 'on grounds of her sex'.[9] The definitional elements of this activity approximate in a number of ways to the definitional elements of a conventional harm-based tort. For instance, direct discrimination is reminiscent both of crimes and of conventional torts in requiring an element of culpability for there to be liability: the discrimination must be intentional, gender must influence some decision process.[10] And as with ordinary culpability requirements, the finding of intention depends upon the wrongdoer's decision and not upon his motives: if gender influenced the decision, it is irrelevant that benign 'chivalry' or 'courtesy' brought gender into play.[11] Again, 'direct discrimination' approximates to the traditional model of a harm-based tort by requiring a nexus of wrongdoing between the complainant and the defendant. As with assault or defamation, a compensatory claim arises out of a specific relation between two agents, and the principles for the assessment of compensation are, broadly, carried over from the law of tort.[12]

Given these similarities between direct discrimination and more conventional crimes and torts, it is hardly surprising that theorists frequently opt for the ready assumptions that direct discrimination is unlawful because it is harmful, and that state prohibition of intentional acts of discrimination is legitimate by virtue of the harm principle.[13]

If we move now to the second variety of discrimination in the United Kingdom legislation, we find a remarkable structural correlation with the legitimacy doctrine based on distributive justice. 'Indirect discrimination' was transposed into the British legislation from the American judicial theory of 'disparate impact'. Someone discriminates indirectly, for example, if he applies some unjustifiable 'requirement or condition' to a woman, with which she cannot comply, and with which, additionally, statistically fewer women than men can comply.[14] The statutory formulation suggests that the issue at stake is the relative social advantage or disadvantage of certain social groups: evidence of statistical inability to comply shows merely the relative positions of two social groups (in this case women and

[9] Sex Discrimination Act 1975, s 1(1)(a). An equivalent provision is s 1(1)(a) of the Race Relations Act 1976. See also Fair Employment (Northern Ireland) Act 1976 s 16(2); (United States) Civil Rights Act 1964, Title VII.

[10] Compare Gerald McGinley, 'Judicial Approaches to Sex Discrimination in the United States and the United Kingdom—A Comparative Study', (1986) 49 *Modern Law Review* 413 at 420.

[11] *Gill and Coote* v *El Vinos Co* [1983] QB 425.

[12] *Skyrail Oceanic* v *Coleman* [1981] ICR 864.

[13] Consider, for example, Jeremy Waldron's assumptions in his 'Indirect Discrimination', or Sandra Marshall's approach in her 'Reversing Discrimination'—both in Guest and Milne (eds), *Equality and Discrimination: Essays in Freedom and Justice*, (*ARSP* Beiheft 21), (Stuttgart 1985).

[14] Sex Discrimination Act 1975, s 1(1)(b). See similarly, Race Relations Act 1976, s1(1)(b). For the United States equivalent, see *Griggs* v *Duke Power* 401 US 424 (1971). In the Northern Ireland legislation against religious and political discrimination there is a revealingly named provision on 'equality of opportunity', which has been interpreted so as to be roughly equivalent to the indirect discrimination provisions: see Fair Employment (Northern Ireland) Act 1976, s 3.

men) in competition for certain opportunities—it reveals 'institutional' disadvantage.[15] Moreover, the fact that otherwise indirectly discriminatory processes may be 'justified' indicates that what is at stake is not a harm, but a redistributive goal which must be balanced against some other interests which citizens are at liberty to pursue. Finally, although indirect discrimination is actionable as a tort, no damages are available if the alleged discriminator can show that he had no intention to discriminate by his practice.[16] This indicates that indirect discrimination does not, in the absence of intention, involve the nexus of wrongdoing involved in direct discrimination, and that distributive justice, as opposed to harm, is what is at stake here. Unlike the direct discriminator, it appears that the indirect discriminator is not marked off as a wrongdoer, but is implicated in our collective responsibility for social injustices.

Since there are these several points of contact with redistributive activities, there is obviously a temptation for liberals to propose distributive justice as the rationale of the indirect discrimination model in our legislation, and to portray the relevant rules of law as legitimate on account of their distributional sensitivity and redistributive effect. The goal of redistribution therefore produces an attractive explanation of the Anglo-American jurisprudence of indirect discrimination.[17]

So the liberal theorist is assisted in the task of explaining why our legislation is legitimate by the striking symmetry between, on the one hand, the two liberal legitimacy principles and, on the other, the two varieties of discrimination impugned by law. Direct discrimination seems to have a close association with harm; the state's proper interest in pursuing distributive justice seems to inform the law of indirect discrimination.

Is this enough? So far, the semblance of correlation remains precarious, because we have to discover what the relevant harm in direct discrimination is, and we have to question whether our existing law of indirect discrimination constitutes an acceptable variety of governmental response to distributive injustice. The two concepts of unlawful discrimination are not yet securely legitimate for liberals.

III

1. When we try to view direct discrimination as necessarily involving harm, the serious obstacle is to explain what the harm in question actually *is*. An attempt has been made by Paul Brest, who constructed an important and sustained argument in favour of the 'antidiscrimination principle' as an American constitutional doctrine.[18] Some of his arguments can apply only to the state's self-regulation; but he includes a useful set of suggestions about the harmfulness of direct discrimination.

[15] See generally Christopher McCrudden, 'Institutional Discrimination' (1982) 2 *OJLS* 303.

[16] Sex Discrimination Act 1975 s 66(3).

[17] For example, Christopher McCrudden, 'Changing Notions of Discrimination' in Guest and Milne (eds), *Equality and Discrimination: Essays in Freedom and Justice*, n 13 above; similarly, Richard Fallon and Paul Weiler, '*Firefighters* v *Stotts:* Conflicting Models of Racial Justice', [1984] *Supreme Court Review* 1.

[18] Paul Brest, 'In Defence of the Antidiscrimination Principle', (1976) 90 *Harvard Law Review* 1.

Brest proposes three 'harms which may result from race-dependent decisions.'[19] The first of these—and, as Brest points out, it seems obvious—'is the denial of the opportunity to secure a desired benefit.'[20] This is a good card for liberals to play; for clearly denial of opportunities is a detriment of some kind, and it is an essential element of direct discrimination that some opportunity should have been denied. However, it is not at all clear how this sort of detriment satisfies the requirements of the harm principle. We would not say that an applicant was 'harmed' in any relevant sense if she was rejected because underqualified; nor if she was passed over when I compiled the guest list for my dinner party. At any rate, any attempt to regulate these 'denials of opportunity' would appear to even the most faint-hearted liberal to be an illegitimate state activity. The point is that the harm principle does not respond to just any disappointment or rejection, but requires something further; and to plead denial of opportunity *by itself* simply does not go far enough to be convincing.[21]

We can look, perhaps, to Brest's second suggestion as a source of the necessary 'something further'. He claims:

> Decisions based on assumptions of intrinsic worth and selective indifference inflict psychological injury by stigmatizing their victims as inferior.[22]

There is an ambiguity in Brest's discussion of this proposal: is it the 'psychological injury' which counts as the relevant harm, or is it the stigmatization? Brest's repeated references to 'stigmatic harm' suggest the latter, but we should consider both possibilities. If the harm of direct discrimination is supposed to be the 'psychological injury' it inflicts, then the Anglo-American definition of direct discrimination is fatally overinclusive. Direct discrimination clearly remains unlawful whether or not its victim suffers an emotional response, and indeed whether its victim realizes the discrimination has happened or not; it follows that the unlawfulness of discrimination extends beyond the incidence of any 'psychological injury'. Stigma, of course, is different. We can be said to have stigmatized somebody without their knowledge, and it might be this 'harm' which direct discrimination targets. Once again, though, it is difficult to see how stigmatization without more could suffice. I stigmatize a colleague if I truthfully point out his deficiencies, but the liberal state would not treat this as a relevant harm. Once again, direct discrimination, if it is harmful, must be a special case of stigmatization, must be stigmatization-*plus*.

Brest's third proposal, that direct discrimination generates particularly pervasive injury, is seriously question-begging, because it fails to reveal what the 'injury' in question is. Nevertheless, the 'pervasiveness' proposal steers us in the right direction. Brest correctly implies that we must view unlawful direct discrimination

[19] Ibid, 8.

[20] Ibid.

[21] Feinberg attempts to supply 'something further' for such cases. He suggests that the 'harm principle' employs a 'strict and narrow sense' of harm, which includes only 'wrongful' harms. Despite Feinberg's protestations to the contrary, this refinement seems only to restate the question. See *Harm to Others*, n 3 above, 109–114.

[22] 'In Defence of the Antidiscrimination Principle', above n 18, 8.

in a way that discloses its cumulative aspect, and we should not expect to isolate a harm out of context. However, Brest is wrong to use language which suggests that the accumulation is primarily quantitative. It is not the large *amount* of stigmatization or denied opportunity which brings discrimination within the harm principle, but the *quality* of the stigmatization and rejection. We respond, in our classification of harms, to the cultural context of our subject-matter. Taking this line, there seem to be two broad ways in which cultural context might allow intentional acts of discrimination to count as harms.

The first of these ways points to a strong relationship between stigma and denied opportunity on the one side, and their historical significance as instruments of wholesale disenfranchisement and disadvantage on the other. We might say that, in the classification of ethnic groups as unworthy, or women as inferior, a set of momentous and enduring collective disadvantages has been inflicted upon the ethnic groups in question and upon women; and that our willingness to treat continuing disparate treatment as a harm is a product of its close historical association with distributional injustice.[23] This may be close to what Brest had in mind when he pointed to the 'pervasiveness' of injury.

The other way of isolating a harm involves pointing out a rather weaker relationship between stigma, denial of opportunities and the historical facts of disadvantage. In this weaker connection, we have developed an historically-informed view that race- and gender-dependent decisions are *unfair*, and this claimed *unfairness* is sufficient to turn stigmatization and denial of opportunities into harms of the required sort. A distinct part of Brest's argument in support of the 'antidiscrimination principle' proposes that race-dependent decisions are 'procedurally unfair'.[24] Brest actually suggests that the 'unfairness' of discrimination could be an *independent* reason for supporting the antidiscrimination principle, but it seems clear that the unfairness of some activity could not be enough on its own to justify the prohibition of that activity among the citizens of a liberal state. Still, a history of subjugation might produce such a radical conception of unfairness that we could allow the harm principle to extend to those present activities which simulate the pattern of familiar historical outrages. In this way a particular notion of harmful unfairness becomes part of our cultural sensibilities, embedded in our social education.

A crucial difference between these two methods of isolating a relevant 'harm' should be noted. If we trace a strong link between a history of disadvantage and our present view that intentional discrimination is harmful, we can only really include discrimination which compounds that disadvantage among the activities which we count as harmful. If we make the strong connection, then the only sort of discrimination which falls within the harm principle is discrimination against certain sorts of people—primarily blacks and women. It would then be difficult to see the exclusion of a white male from some opportunity as a relevant 'harm', and

[23] For an argument expressly adopting this approach, see Dworkin's 'Bakke's Case: Are Quotas Unfair?' in his *A Matter of Principle*, above n 7.

[24] 'In Defence of the Antidiscrimination Principle', above n 18, 6.

our present legal provision would be irresponsible in so treating it. If, on the other hand, we trace the rather weaker link between disadvantage and harm, through the mediating principle of 'unfairness', then we perceive the whole business of taking race or gender into account as a harm. Then we can treat any exclusion which has race or gender among its reasons as a harm within the harm principle. If we say, as United Kingdom law does, that we can discriminate unlawfully against white males just as we can against blacks and women, then I think we must be perceiving discrimination in this last way, perceiving it to be harmful as a result of the conception of *unfairness* generated by its cultural associations with subordination and disadvantage.

But there is a serious risk to liberalism here, a risk that the unfairness itself may start to count as an independent legitimacy principle which justifies the legislation, without reference to the harm or its historical origins. By shifting the focus of 'harm' from womanhood or blackness (specifically) to gender or race (generally), the liberal risks slipping into the very alien ideology of meritocracy—the idea that selecting applicants on the basis only of their qualifications is not only a *sensible* or *rational* thing for employers to do, but also an *obligatory* thing for them to do.[25] Once the 'unfairness' takes over from the harm in this way, we risk identifying the wrongness of sexual subjugation or slavery with the failure of those invidious and enduring historical traditions to be perfectly meritocratic, and we start, illiberally, to treat all non-meritocratic preferences as being on all fours with slavery. So in the liberal tradition, the harmful unfairness must instead be narrowly tied to the degradation suffered by those whose race or gender have been devalued, and the cultural meanings which race and gender have, on that account, assumed for us.

Whether or not they take the risky option of mobilizing unfairness as a way of reinforcing harm, it should be clear by now that liberals cannot hope to provide any *definition* of harm which would transcend the overarching dependence of the harm principle upon social context. Brest's attempt to catalogue independent harms is unenlightening largely because it presupposes (in the manner of many liberal arguments) that 'harm' is a context-independent notion. To persuade us that direct discrimination falls within the harm principle, liberal accounts must admit from the outset that we use the harm principle, and other liberal doctrines, as *gnomons* for our dynamic cultural values. Both strong and weak associations between the identification of harms and the recognition of historical oppression are influential in British and American social values. If liberals are willing to admit this, and to treat harms as culturally delimited, then they need not hesitate to acknowledge the vital and flexible relationship between history and legitimacy.

2. We can turn now to consider the law of indirect discrimination and its aptness as a cure for distributive injustice. As will emerge, it is far from obvious that a liberal theory of distributive justice should permit anyone to enforce a claim for some

25 A tension between liberalism and meritocracy can be seen, for instance, in Alan Goldman, 'The Justification of Equal Opportunity' in Paul, Miller, Paul and Ahrens (eds), *Equal Opportunity*, (Oxford 1987).

opportunity on certain terms from another citizen; yet this sort of claim is precisely what the law of indirect discrimination sanctions.

Moderate liberal theories of distributive justice have been correctly characterized as involving 'end-state principles'.[26] According to such principles, 'all that needs to be looked at, in judging the justice of a distribution, is who ends up with what.'[27] When liberals entrust governments with the function of *re*distribution, they demand that advantages be redistributed so that the resulting arrangement (or end-state) be more just than the arrangement which preceded the redistribution. For example, a system of progressive income or expenditure taxation might well be a liberal solution to radical disadvantage. Such a system is calculated to ensure that the relatively well-off subscribe to the advancement of the relatively badly-off. In this way, the redirection of wealth by state taxation is always from more advantaged citizens to less advantaged citizens, so that the distribution of wealth afterwards is altogether more just than it was beforehand.[28]

When liberals cite distributive justice as a legitimacy principle, they mean it to authorize the correction of existing patterns of advantage and disadvantage *exclusively*. They do not mean the principle to respond to information of certain other kinds about the various citizens involved, such as their past conduct or their personal responsibility for the existing patterns. To respond to such further factors would be to go beyond a response to the injustice of particular states of affairs, and to engage instead in a consideration of how, and by whose agency, they arose.[29]

Now, Christopher McCrudden has suggested that the law of indirect discrimination bears the distinguishing marks of a liberal redistributive technique.[30] He views the indirect discrimination provisions as simply 'requiring that the interests of blacks and women be adequately taken into account by employers in choosing means, ends and goals.'[31] While the idea of 'adequacy' here is not elaborated, the argument seems to be that the aim of precluding statistically disadvantaging practices is the 'frankly redistributive' one of ensuring continual adjustment of relative advantages as between the members of distinct social groups. Here McCrudden correctly identifies both an existing distributive injustice, and a respect in which the indirect discrimination technique is indeed an end-state approach to alleviating the injustice: we want a better distribution tomorrow than we have today.

Nevertheless, as McCrudden realizes, his analysis requires us to endorse an apparently serious departure from the orthodoxy of the redistributive taxation or end-state model. An employer who is selecting from a group of applicants is required, for instance, to ensure that his selection criteria do not proportionately and unjustifiably disadvantage Asian applicants. He is under a duty to distribute

26 Nozick, *Anarchy, State, and Utopia*, above n 6, 153–5 and 198–204. Nozick applies his analysis specifically to the liberal distributive programme in John Rawls' *A Theory of Justice* (Cambridge, Mass. 1971).

27 *Anarchy, State, and Utopia*, 154.

28 Rawls, *A Theory of Justice*, above n 26, 277–80, offers detailed proposals for redistributive taxation of this kind and gives it the central role in the state's implementation of distributive justice.

29 A distinction of this kind is at the core of Rawls' argument. See ibid, 314–15.

30 McCrudden, 'Changing Notions of Discrimination', above n 17, 86 ff.

31 Ibid, 87.

certain opportunities according to legally specified criteria. But he is under this duty not on account of his own relative advantages, but on account of his status as prospective employer. The incidence of this duty is *prima facie* arbitrary from the point of view of the employer's ability to contribute: it therefore seems to be arbitrary from the point of view of distributive justice. As Jeremy Waldron has expressed it, replying to McCrudden's argument:

> [I]n the case of *indirect* discrimination, the wrongness of the employers' actions is nothing more than that they are not doing their bit to promote racial or sexual equality; it seems odd, then, to respond to *that* by requiring them to do *more* than their fair share.[32]

While the duty to contribute to a system of progressive taxation is sensitive only to the existing distribution of advantages, including the advantages of the person contributing, the duty not to 'discriminate indirectly' seems to be imposed on citizens in a way that is partly arbitrary from the point of view of relative advantage. Employers, in other words, seem to be required by the state to do more than that which is entailed by their ordinary share of collective responsibility for disadvantage.

McCrudden obliquely identifies one respect in which regard for the employer's own interests is indeed provided for in the legislation, by virtue of the test for the 'justifiability' of an indirectly discriminatory practice. In United Kingdom law, the question of the justifiability of the defendant's selection process is answered principally from the defendant's perspective. The emergent test of justifiability requires 'the party applying the discriminatory condition to prove it to be justifiable in all the circumstances on balancing its discriminatory effect against the discriminator's need for it. But that need is what is reasonably needed by the party who applies the condition.'[33] The urgency of the 'need' which the employer must show has recently been increased by virtue of the application of European Economic Community directives,[34] but in principle the function of the test is still founded in sensitivity to the employer's circumstances. A severe but functionally equivalent 'business necessity' test has been adopted in the United States.[35] Employers are, on this account, not required to take on burdens wholly disproportionate to their means, and the duty is, in this respect, somewhat like a tax.

This, however, is hardly enough to make the provision conform to an end-state model of distributive justice. Certainly, the legislation provides for the recognition of the employer's own interests; however, the recognition falls far short of ensuring that the relative contribution of employers is proportionate only to their relative material advantage. From the point of view of redistribution, it is at first sight irrelevant that some citizen came to be involved in a transaction of some sort with another citizen, such as considering her for employment; but from the point of view of indirect discrimination, such a transaction is the very fact which must be proved to ground a cause of action.

[32] 'Indirect Discrimination', above n 13, 98.

[33] *Ojutiku* v *Manpower Services Commission* [1982] ICR 661, per Stephenson LJ.

[34] *Bilka Kaufhaus GmbH* v *Weber von Harz* [1986] IRLR 317. But contrast *Hampson* v. *Department of Education and Science* [1988] IRLR 86, where *Ojutiku* is favoured.

[35] Eg *Albemarle Paper Co* v *Moody* 422 US 405 (1975).

In our search for an explanation here, McCrudden's dispute with Waldron gives us a starting point, because the dispute seems to revolve around conflicting understandings of the role of employers in liberal social practice. Unlike Waldron, McCrudden properly recognizes a correlation between certain institutional practices and the incidence of distributional advantage and disadvantage. This recognition can be elaborated and used to generate a liberal case for the legitimacy of the indirect discrimination provisions which explains specifically their application to the institution of employment with non-state employers.[36]

At least two factors about the employment relationship give it a special institutional role in our culture. Firstly, whether or not I am employed, and in what capacity, plays in our culture an absolutely decisive role in the relative advantages which I may enjoy throughout my life; secondly, the formation and preservation of the employment relation involves a peculiarly large amount of control for one of the parties (the employer). For these two reasons, a relationship which seems to be arbitrary from the point of view of distributive justice turns out to have deep institutional associations with it. The employer finds himself in a special privileged position in the distributive mechanics of society, which makes him, for every individual employee or applicant, every bit as strong and as peremptory a distributive agency as the state itself.[37] It is natural for liberals to find themselves, in their reflective responses, taking this cultural fact seriously, and to respond by treating the employment relation as involving near-governmental responsibility. The duty not to discriminate indirectly can be characterized, then, as a responsibility upon those who, like a government, determine some of the society's most important distributions.

In this description, the 'end-state' characteristics of the employer's duty not to operate indirectly discriminatory systems re-emerge. Market-based institutional factors which feature prominently in the social structure of the liberal state impede the effectiveness of orthodox governmental redistribution, because they allow for the constant re-emergence of disadvantage. To impose direct contributory duties on those *predominantly* in control of such institutional factors is simply to interpret their social roles as those of *agents* of redistribution rather than merely those of *subscribers*. By adding a justifiability criterion, the law remains aware that in some cases the agency role could require disproportionate and crippling personal contribution. So the agency role does not eclipse altogether the subscriber role. When the employer's social significance is recognized, requiring him not to discriminate indirectly is merely a proper response to current patterns of advantage and disadvantage, coupled with an understanding of the distribution of effective social power. The provisions, so understood, conform to a model of distributive justice which a liberal can consistently endorse. A moderate liberal finds himself, as before, moulding his social theory to its cultural and institutional context.

[36] Comparable arguments relating to other institutional arrangements might, of course, be attempted. For a claim that citizens' responsibilities here are wide-ranging, see Standing Advisory Commission on Human Rights, *Religious and Political Discrimination and Equality of Opportunity in Northern Ireland—Report on Fair Employment*, (London 1987), 45.

[37] On the general importance of this social fact, see Hugh Collins, 'Against Abstentionism in Labour Law' in Eekelaar and Bell (eds), *Oxford Essays in Jurisprudence (Third Series)*, (Oxford 1987), especially 92–4.

IV

If the liberal who supports the discrimination legislation envisages an analysis of the sort just outlined, then we have no grounds for doubting his sincerity and consistency. The moderate liberal's two legitimacy principles extend, on this contextual interpretation, to authorize the prohibition of both kinds of discrimination, direct and indirect.

Nevertheless, we should remain profoundly wary of some features of the argument. Direct discrimination has indeed been classified as harmful, but the harmfulness emerges (in one way or another) from the historical scale of disadvantage and exclusion involved in certain practices. Meanwhile, the law of indirect discrimination has been approved (at least as far as employment decisions are concerned) as a redistributive technique, but only because we recognize a special responsibility among employers which emerges from their present and enduring institutional control. In this process of apparent mutual reinforcement, the concept of harm is made sensitive, *inter alia*, to radical distributional imbalances; while a powerful idea of quasi-governmental responsibility is annexed to distributive justice in the law of indirect discrimination. In their indeterminacy, the concepts of harm and distributive justice have grown together, each informed by some social relations which are ordinarily associated with the other.

Central applications of the harm principle (such as imprisonment for murder) are, of course, relatively remote from ordinary applications of the principle of distributive justice (such as progressive taxation). Where applications are this remote, conflicting governmental responses to a single social situation are unlikely to arise. But in the present context, the remoteness is sacrificed. Instances arise where a single practice is viewed as involving part harm, part distributive injustice, so that the liberal state seems at first to have two different grounds for responding. Yet since the two different grounds of response entail (as we have seen) different *modes* of response, this ambiguous legitimacy is not merely an inconsequential nicety. Each mode of response requires its own appropriate structure of legal rules and a distinct set of social institutions, and this is to the exclusion of other possibilities. The indeterminacy of his concepts leads the liberal into an arena where they appear to be mutually antagonistic. I would like to point to two instances of this in the context of discrimination law.

The first is revealed in a pair of British cases concerning the interpretation of our provisions about indirect discrimination. In *Steel* v *Union of Post Office Workers*[38] the Post Office operated a practice whereby vacant postal walks were allocated according to seniority within the organization. The seniority system was such that those who had been temporary workers but had become permanent workers were not entitled to count their time as temporary workers towards their seniority rating. Since women had, until 1975, been precluded from acquiring permanent status, the allocation practice excluded a proportionately higher number of female

[38] [1978] 1 WLR 64.

than male employees. The Employment Appeal Tribunal held the practice to be indirectly discriminatory, and remitted the case to the Industrial Tribunal on the issue of 'justifiability', suggesting that the Post Office would have to satisfy a heavy burden of proof to show justifiability. The Appeal Tribunal also pointed out, in passing, that the case was an illustration of one way in which the law of indirect discrimination could be effectively used to eradicate the effects of past *direct* discrimination.

In *Ojutiku* v *Manpower Services Commission*[39] the Court of Appeal came to consider another case where past direct discrimination seemed to have handicapped the applicant. It was alleged that intentional race discrimination in the employment market had prevented the applicant from obtaining the experience which the respondent Commission required of him as a condition of paying him an allowance. The Court held that, even if past direct discrimination were proved, the Commission was entitled to claim justifiability. According to the Court of Appeal, the *Steel* case, suggesting the existence of a heavy burden to prove justifiability, was to be restricted to cases where the *respondent himself* had been shown to have directly discriminated in the past.

The distinction drawn by the Court of Appeal between the innocent respondent and the respondent whose past directly discriminatory practices have themselves been impugned is based on considerations which emerge from the harm principle. It is appropriate, according to these considerations, that the employer's individual responsibility for past harms determines his present obligations. We may contrast the principle underlying this distinction with the principle, also referred to in *Ojutiku*,[40] that the respondent's present economic needs determine the availability to him of the justifiability defence. The latter criterion is only compatible with a purely redistributive programme.

The courts, if they represent a liberal state, very properly treat past harmful wrongdoing as a ground for response: in this case they treat it as a ground for penalizing a respondent's chances of successfully defending associated litigation. But in this instance the penalizing of the past offender is antagonistic to the redistributive principles underlying the litigation, for it seems to involve redistributive taxation based not on ability to contribute but on past wrongdoing. As has been argued, liberal theories of distributive justice must treat this arrangement as illegitimate, because it cannot cohere with any end-state theory.

A second example of this sort of antagonism between liberal principles causes much theoretical controversy, but arises primarily in American rather than British cases. In the United States, unlike the United Kingdom, some important interpretations of the general law against discrimination have permitted degrees of 'positive discrimination' in favour of underrepresented groups. That is, the direct discrimination model has been held from time to time not to preclude the offering of certain additional opportunities to blacks and women.

[39] Above n 33.
[40] Text at n 33 above.

If the United States Civil Rights Act 1964 does indeed permit some positive discrimination, on what principle does it do so? The leading case of *United Steelworkers* v *Weber*[41] provides the most remembered proposition. The defendant's own workforce suffered from a serious racial imbalance as compared with the balance in the local working population. He provided an enhanced recruitment and promotion plan for black applicants. The Supreme Court, in an action under the Civil Rights Act, accepted that an employer could institute a voluntary affirmative action plan, within certain limits, for the purpose only of 'breaking down old patterns of racial segregation and hierarchy'.[42]

Some subsequent cases have followed *Weber* by interpreting the Court's words to mean that the purpose of voluntary affirmative action plans is to break down earlier patterns of *disadvantage*.[43] On this view, such plans are voluntary contributions to the state's legitimate redistributive programme, and the legality of *some* positive discrimination is treated as a natural concomitant of the prohibition on *indirect* discrimination—what the Supreme Court calls 'disparate impact'. Since this branch of the law of discrimination is largely about redistribution, voluntary contributions to the programme seem, within certain bounds, to be unimpeachable.

But an alternative interpretation of *Weber* treats the Court's words as referring directly to an employer's *own* past patterns of segregation. On this account, affirmative action plans are voluntary extensions of the *direct* discrimination principle ('disparate treatment'), not of the indirect discrimination principle. An employer may adopt such a plan only as a method of admitting and atoning for past discriminatory practices for which he is personally responsible; he may not simply take it upon himself to become an agent of redistribution. He may discriminate positively because he has inflicted past harms, not because redistribution is a pressing social goal. One commentator calls this the 'sins of discrimination' approach:[44] we can find evidence of its influence in a number of cases under the Civil Rights Act.[45]

These two approaches to positive discrimination are like the two mutually antagonistic dicta on the issue of 'justifiability' under the British legislation. An employer who has previously discriminated directly will find his new affirmative practice easier to justify in law, just as he might find his negative practice more difficult to justify. But this example is even more striking than the British one: there is a prohibition on redistributive activity except in response to past harms. This has led some commentators to suggest that the employer is not really being penalized, but is being permitted to pay some kind of reparation to his past victims through their successors, or some kind of reparation for his generally odious contribution to racial underprivilege.[46] Yet these peculiar views bring in a whole

[41] 443 US 193 (1978).

[42] Ibid, 209.

[43] For instance, *Johnson* v *Santa Clara Transportation Agency* 107 SCt 1442 (1987).

[44] Kathleen Sullivan, 'Sins of Discrimination', (1986) 100 *Harvard Law Review* 78.

[45] See, for example, *Firefighters* v *Stotts* 104 SCt 2576 (1984).

[46] For two variations on the compensatory way of arguing, see Judith Jarvis Thomson, 'Preferential Hiring', *Philosophy and Public Affairs* 2 (1973), 364; and George Sher, 'Justifying Reverse Discrimination in Employment', *Philosophy and Public Affairs* 4 (1975), 159.

host of new problems about who is being compensated, and for what, and they merely serve to reinforce the point that past wrongdoing is being viewed as the issue.[47] Once again, the understandable instinct to treat past direct discrimination as a proper subject for disapprobation is in conflict with the moderate liberal view which treats positive discrimination as simply a redistributive activity. Neither principle can legitimately countenance the application of the other.

So the context-relativity of the two liberal legitimacy doctrines turns out to be both blessing and curse. It is a blessing in so far as liberals can explain their responses to the two concepts of discrimination by reference to extended notions of harm and of distributive justice, extended notions which are sensitive to peculiarities of cultural context. But the relativity is also a curse, because it throws the liberal end-state redistributive programme and the idea of personal responsibility for harms together into one melting-pot. Sometimes, as in the instances I have mentioned, the two legitimacy principles are both implicated in one set of facts, and each ends up controverting the legitimacy of the other.

V

One interpretation of these difficult cases portrays them as no more than symptoms of factional conflict within liberalism. For instance (it could be claimed), more 'right-wing' liberals would instinctively insist on a largely harm-based account of positive and indirect discrimination so as to resist the egalitarian pull of redistributive techniques.[48]

Yet the pattern I have charted does not merely reveal battle-lines within the liberal tradition. It also seems to illustrate some important respects in which the whole conceptual armoury of political liberalism is inescapably blunt. Far from emphasizing the flexibility of liberalism, the context-relativity of its legitimacy principles serves to highlight a remarkable intransigence in liberal thought. We may present this, for present purposes, as a contrast between the discontinuity of liberal method and the continuity of the social concerns to which it is claimed to apply.

As I have already suggested, our reflective understanding of 'harm' has grown to accommodate the historical flux of social life; meanwhile, our concept of distributive justice responds to the changing structure of cultural institutions. These developments reflect the subtle complexities of social practice. And the special instances I have pointed to, where one social practice seems to implicate both of the concepts under scrutiny here, harm *and* distributive justice, are illustrations of the *continuity* of social practice, its non-susceptibility to definitive classification. When we have difficulties deciding whether positive discrimination is a compensatory technique or a redistributive technique, this is because the practice is not simply

[47] On the coherence of the reparation arguments, see eg Robert Simon, 'Preferential Hiring: A Reply to Judith Jarvis Thomson', *Philosophy and Public Affairs* 3 (1974), 312.

[48] See Owen Fiss, 'Groups and the Equal Protection Clause', *Philosophy and Public Affairs* 5 (1976), 107. Part 1 of his essay deals with the 'right-wing' liberal's resistance to egalitarian justifications.

one or other of these things, but must be understood in terms of both of them, and in a way which precludes their severance from one another.

We have seen that liberals are sometimes sensitive to the fluidity and complexity of our cultural understandings. They are willing to develop an interpretation of the meaning harm has for us, rather than merely stipulating a definition; and they properly perceive the changing power relations of our post-industrial culture as supplementing the redistributive responsibilities of some citizens. Liberals who accept these shifts of social meaning see social theory as necessarily implicating social practice.

Yet, at the same time, since the moderate liberal theory of distributive justice treats it as an end-state principle, and the moderate liberal view of the harm principle associates it with past harmful actions and state responses to culpability, there is no point at which the two principles could be said to be joined, to be continuous. Given a single practice which could be a harm, or could be an injustice, there is no single state response which is a legitimate application of the harm principle *and* a legitimate implementation of distributive justice. So, as we saw with positive discrimination and with the problem of justifiability, an application of the liberal harm principle will be incoherent and arbitrary from the perspective of liberal distributive justice, because it will look to past behaviour; meanwhile, redistribution will not cohere with the harm principle, because it will look only to the justness of end-states, ignoring how they came about. The two principles are radically discontinuous.[49]

Many liberals seem to believe quite unquestioningly that we can extend indefinitely the coverage or application of an argument (responding to changes in social meaning) while leaving the nature of the argument intact: rather as if one could change indefinitely the rules of chess while leaving the game the same. So, in general, the fact that there are new, previously undiscovered harms in ever-more-complex social matrices is not thought to alter the fundamental truth of the harm principle and the legitimacy which it produces. And the fact that ever-changing distributive relations and changing social significances distort our previous social roles is not thought, in itself, to be a good reason to change our idea of what it is we are looking for when we try to find a principle of distributive justice. When, owing to this gradual indefinite conceptual extension, we find both harm and injustice at once, the orthodox principles conflict instead of converging. Far from reflecting in any thoroughgoing way the dynamics of culture, the structure of the resulting social theory is static and intransigent.

It is, of course, true of theoretical principles *in general* that their articulation renders them irreversibly discontinuous with each other. We cannot articulate critical standards without numbing them perceptibly to the intricacy of that to which they apply, that which they reflect. This is not, of course, a good argument against the making of social theory generally. Social theory can challenge our

[49] Thus liberals often struggle to sever the complex motivations for the social practice of positive discrimination, and to argue that one 'justification', such as redistribution, should prevail: eg Christopher McCrudden, 'Rethinking Positive Action', (1986) 15 *Industrial Law Journal* 219.

ordinary understandings, and is itself a vital part of the culture which it reflects.[50] Still, social theorists must recall that there is 'a pre-theoretical understanding of what is going on among the members of a society, which is formulated in the descriptions of self and other which are involved in the institutions and practices of that society.'[51]

This is precisely why the continuity of culture is a good reason for mistrusting the *radical* discontinuity which we have discovered in the two liberal social principles under scrutiny, the harm principle and distributive justice. The development of our pre-theoretical concept of harm is not just the annexation of new instances onto a settled doctrine, but instead the evolution of the whole doctrine, the emergence of new principle. What we have in true social practice is not an old harm principle supplemented from time to time, but at each time a new harm principle. Meanwhile, the liberal arguments I have charted are attempts at annexation: extensions to the list of harms but the same old harm principle, more redistributive agencies but the same old constraints on redistribution. This static, discontinuous set of responses in the face of organic evolution is merely dogmatism.

Taylor reminds us, writing of distributive justice, that we should 'defend our views about [it] in relation to our actual culture and history; and that will make it at least somewhat harder to espouse dogmatically one principle in utter blindness to the relative claims of the others.'[52] The peculiarity of most contemporary liberalism is its *selective* implementation of this injunction, its zeal to preserve traditional formalistic dogma concerning the characterization of its principles, while responding opportunistically to culture and history in the extension of those principles to new circumstance.

VI

Could one be a liberal without making this mistake? For many liberals, the prospect is no doubt perplexing. How could one remove the core distinctions of liberal thought but remain a liberal?

The possibility has been explored by Joseph Raz.[53] In Raz's argument the close relation between liberal political principles and 'public culture' is expressly recognized. Constitutional rights, for example, are treated as worthy of protection by virtue of the contribution that their protection makes to the promotion and protection of a certain public culture, and our being autonomous agents is predicated upon and defined by our situation in an autonomy-enhancing community. For Raz, our liberal culture fosters a particular ideal of autonomous agency, and we can view the legitimacy of the state as depending primarily upon its pursuit of that ideal. We can therefore identify a single legitimacy doctrine within

50 See Michael Walzer, *Interpretation and Social Criticism*, (Cambridge, Mass. 1987), eg 30.

51 Charles Taylor, 'Social Theory as Practice', reprinted in his *Philosophy and the Human Sciences: Philosophical Papers* 2, (Cambridge 1985), 93.

52 Taylor, 'The Nature and Scope of Distributive Justice' in ibid, 317.

53 Raz, *The Morality of Freedom*, (Oxford 1986).

our culture, which associates the state with the protection and promotion of a particular conception of valuable freedom. Instead of proposing the two conventional doctrines, the harm principle and distributive justice, as the theoretical foundation of political argument, Raz advocates a single and continuous principle which 'calls for the creation of conditions of valuable autonomy through the pursuit of perfectionist policies.'[54] This is not a 'neutral' principle which excludes particular views about the moral value of certain ways of life, but is 'a perfectionist doctrine which holds the state to be duty-bound to promote the good life. It stops at coercion and manipulation only where their use would not promote the ability of people to have a good life but frustrate or diminish it.'[55]

This shift of focus to the unitary ideal of autonomy, and away from the distinct legitimacy doctrines associated with harm and distributive justice, affects in two major ways the relationship between liberalism and the legitimacy of legislation against discrimination.

1. Firstly, the orthodox liberal principles are subsumed and consolidated. When we support a particular view of what valuable autonomy requires, we implicate an understanding of what harms citizens must be protected against *as well as* an understanding of what opportunities and provisions must be secured for them. Pursuing autonomy involves social action of both these varieties. So, reinterpreting the liberal tradition, Raz suggests that the harm principle does indeed set the boundaries of the use of state power, but that the harm principle is a wide harm principle: it allows governments 'to use coercion both in order to stop people from actions which would diminish people's autonomy and in order to force them to take actions which are required to improve people's options and opportunities.'[56] So understood, distributive justice is not a principle which *competes* with the harm principle, but is rather a concomitant of it. 'Sometimes failing to improve the situation of another is harming him.'[57] There is, on this account, no distinction between end-state principles and culpability-based principles in our new criterion of legitimacy. The 'harm principle' and 'distributive justice' are not discontinuous principles but are subsumed within a single, continuous wide principle which authorizes the state to impose upon us the morality of autonomy.[58]

When we become more culture-specific, we can see what role freedom from discrimination plays in the United Kingdom government's protective role. On one hand, the right not to suffer intentional discrimination 'is meant to foster a public culture which enables people to take pride in their identity as members of . . . groups.'[59] Those who do not enjoy such pride in identity are deprived of a component of valuable autonomy as we understand it, are harmed in the wide

[54] Ibid, 426.
[55] Ibid.
[56] Ibid, 416; see further Raz, 'Autonomy, Toleration and the Harm Principle' in Gavison (ed), *Issues in Contemporary Legal Philosophy*, (Oxford 1987).
[57] *The Morality of Freedom*, above n 53, 416.
[58] Ibid, 415.
[59] Ibid, 254.

sense. Meanwhile, the rules governing indirect discrimination provide another example of a legitimate implementation of our ideal of autonomy: 'The government has an obligation to create an environment providing individuals with an adequate range of options *and the opportunities to choose them*.'[60] Securing (rather than merely permitting) access to opportunities is a governmental task; and an employer who fails to provide opportunities to a woman, because his criterion of selection disadvantages women, harms her in the sense required by the wide harm principle—he fails to enhance her opportunities in the way that respect for her autonomous agency requires. Individual responsibility for harms is not contrasted with collective responsibility for injustices. We are all involved in a participative enterprise of protecting autonomy, an enterprise which carries with it obligations of mutual life-enhancement. The tension between the harm principle and distributive justice is entirely relaxed.

2. While the first aspect of Raz's project is largely a restatement of orthodox moderate liberal attitudes to protection and provision, it is closely tied to a second, more distinctive commitment to a creative role for the state, which is a further concomitant of the high value placed upon autonomy.

According to Raz, the state must *promote* a particular ideal of the autonomous self, an agent who finds his autonomy defined by his commitments and his participation as much as by his gradually emerging individuality. The state can be overtly partisan in its encouragement of toleration and competitive pluralism, and of forms of life which cohere with these ideals,[61] and may legitimately provide and prefer institutional arrangements which contribute to this process of social creation.

In order to understand completely the role of legislation against discrimination in our culture, it is necessary to appreciate the creative power which governments in participative democracies necessarily enjoy. The application of forms of institutional control is as much an alteration of the future value-structure of society as it is a response to specific social ills, and the full importance of the discrimination legislation is only understood when its reconstitutive functions are recognized. We can see these functions, for example, in the English case of *Mandla* v *Dowell Lee*.[62] A Sikh boy sought admission to an independent school but the headmaster refused to admit him unless he removed his turban when at school. To have done this would have offended against the boy's faith, and the boy's parents claimed that there had been unlawful indirect discrimination contrary to the Race Relations Act 1976. The school argued in defence that the turban could not be worn because the school's policy was to minimize the external differences between persons, to discourage fashion-competition and (ironically) to present a Christian image to outsiders.

[60] Ibid, 418. My emphasis.
[61] Ibid, 395–9, 401–7.
[62] [1983] 2 AC 548.

The question before the House of Lords was one of justification, and the House took the view that the school's practice was not, on balance, justifiable. Here, of course, the unarticulated focus of argument was not upon the economic interests of the discriminator (as it frequently is in employment cases), but upon the school's privilege to pursue its ideals. So the question was at base a thoroughly ideological one, namely whether the school's ideals could properly be permitted to eclipse the boy's self-identity, which was so closely tied to his wearing the turban. A harm-based argument might be constructed to deal with this problem, for the attack on the boy's religious integrity might well be viewed as a reason for deciding against the school. But an equally significant implication of the resolution of the *Mandla* case was its potential reformative effect on the value-structure of our social institutions: what sort of culture are we pursuing?

We can only speculate about the importance of this aspect of the case to the House of Lords. But the question's political importance is plain. For Raz, we are pursuing a culture in which the value of personal autonomy is understood to be the core value. Since the value of personal autonomy requires a culture of toleration and competitive pluralism, one of the reasons for precluding certain institutional structures in our society is that they fail to contribute to the pursuit of ideals of toleration and competitive pluralism. A significant feature of the resolution of the *Mandla* case would accordingly be an inquiry whether precluding the wearing of turbans at school enhanced or retarded the pursuit of a commitment to autonomy. If a commitment to total uniformity at school could indeed be perceived to be the best way to contribute to education in toleration, then arguments against deviation might well be seen as sympathetic to the emergence of a culture of autonomy. In fact, though, the arguments voiced by the school in *Mandla* made it plain that the culture it envisaged itself to be promoting was associated with a significantly less pluralistic value-structure. It follows that the school's practice was culturally invidious; we have a further reason for condemning the school's practice, associated with the attack on the *boy's* autonomy, but grounded in the pursuit of *a culture* of autonomy.

Many discrimination cases involve judicial choices which, like those in *Mandla*, influence the structure of future social values, and the legislation itself seems to envisage the sort of broad cultural impact which Raz's theory (unlike orthodox liberal doctrine) recognizes and addresses. As a recent report very properly urges, discrimination legislation is necessarily concerned with a 'forward looking' approach, (literally) 'making a better society in the future'.[63] This concern is consistent with and entailed by the legitimate aims of the creative, perfectionist liberal state.

However, this second dimension of Raz's enterprise, that which recognizes the creative state, draws attention to an apparent problem in his theory. It seems at first that the indeterminacy of the liberal concepts of harm and injustice is seriously compounded by Raz's references to autonomy, and that if indeterminacy is a

[63] Standing Advisory Commission on Human Rights, *Religious and Political Discrimination and Equality of Opportunity in Northern Ireland*, above n 36, 43.

problem for orthodox liberals (as I suggested it is), then it is *a fortiori* an obstacle to the pursuit of Raz's ideal. The meaning of 'autonomy', after all, remains the locus of substantial controversy, and the creative role of the state seems at first only to compound the problem of selecting from among numerous competing views of freedom.[64] At first sight, Raz is committed to an ideal which can only be given meaning by stipulation.

In fact, though, Raz pursues his commitment to the elaboration of a public culture to its conclusion. The creative function ascribed to government by Raz is far from arbitrarily creative. The conception of autonomy which the state is to promote is not invented or revealed, but is already defined in our existing cultural institutions, and is part of our shared heritage. The authority of government is not associated with creation as invention, imposition or stipulation; rather it is associated with creation as a product of interpretation, the creation of a culture which is as close as possible to that pluralistic and tolerant culture which it already understands itself, collectively, to be.

The idea of autonomy is not, therefore, one which requires unfettered personal choice, but is instead the repository of shared cultural values.[65] The liberalism at stake here involves 'a recognition that autonomous persons, capable of self-creation, are not themselves self-created'.[66] The movement envisaged is towards the recognition of a shared dimension in our self-understandings, or 'communitarianism'[67]—an implementation in a liberal culture of the truth that 'we need to see social theory as practice in order to understand what its validation amounts to.'[68] Conceptual indeterminacy is, on this approach, comfortably alleviated by the referability of the concept of autonomy to an existing cultural understanding.

Where orthodox liberalism sees legitimacy as something to be delimited by relatively narrow constraints, Raz's perfectionist doctrine sees state authority as a participative project, the implementation of our pre-theoretical self-understanding. It suffers from no discontinuity, and renders the traditional and troublesome bifurcation of doctrine, into the harm principle and the principle of distributive justice, entirely redundant. The discrimination legislation, with its two methods of enforcement, consists of two methods with a single end in view, namely the enhancement of the valuable autonomy of citizens and the implementation of the ideals of their shared culture. That culture is, on Raz's interpretation, one of competitive pluralism and mutual toleration; but also one of participation and unavoidable commitment. The wholesale exclusion or marginalization of women, religious groups and racial minorities is, of course, inconsistent with the pursuit of such a culture.

[64] See eg Charles Taylor, 'What's wrong with negative liberty?' reprinted in his *Philosophy and the Human Sciences*, above n 51.

[65] See Raz, *The Morality of Freedom*, above n 53, 410.

[66] Michael Walzer, 'The Imperfectionist', *The New Republic*, December 7 1987, 30.

[67] Contrast Christopher McCrudden's doubts about the relationship between discrimination legislation and 'communitarian' argument: 'Community and Discrimination' in Eekelaar and Bell (eds), *Oxford Essays in Jurisprudence (Third Series)*, above n 37.

[68] Charles Taylor, 'Social Theory as Practice', above n 51, 115.

VII

I have explored the difficulties of state legitimacy in contemporary liberal thought by reference to a single institutional construct which many liberals have aspired to call their own, namely the Anglo-American legislation against discrimination. The exercise has been intended both to add credibility to this aspiration, and to point to some persistent difficulties in the orthodox articulation of it.

One strength of recent liberal thought—even in its more orthodox forms—has been its responsiveness to the development of social practice, and liberals who endorse the discrimination legislation have very properly allowed themselves to see the identification of harms and injustices as a function of context, institution and history. The correlative weakness has been their general failure to extend this sensitivity to a point where it requires complete reappraisal and re-identification of the two orthodox legitimacy doctrines themselves, rather than just their extension to new circumstances. This weakness is most evident where the doctrines are at odds, where they have ceased, by reason of extension, to occupy logically separate space, but continue to claim their separateness. When this is so, the fixity of the principles makes them mutually antagonistic.

However, it is possible to remain within the important tradition which respects the autonomy of persons without clinging hopelessly to old doctrines. Indeed, if Raz is correct, the tradition in our culture which respects individual autonomy does so because it takes a particular view of what valuable autonomy amounts to. The law of discrimination sits comfortably in this non-individualistic theory of autonomy, according to which the state has its own project of providing the conditions of valuable flourishing for its citizens. In this theory, prohibiting both sorts of discrimination is merely a central and straightforward example of the state's legitimate role.

Part III
Left Perspectives

[6]

Legitimizing Racial Discrimination Through Antidiscrimination Law: A Critical Review of Supreme Court Doctrine†

Alan David Freeman*

> if it will kindly be considered that while it is in our interest as tormentors to remain where we are as victims our urge is to move on
>
> —Samuel Beckett, *How It Is*

THE LAW: *"Black Americans, rejoice! Racial discrimination has now become illegal."*

BLACK AMERICANS: *"Great, we who have no jobs want them. We who have lousy jobs want better ones. We whose kids go to black schools want to choose integrated schools if we think that would be better for our kids, or want enough money to make our own schools work. We want political power roughly proportionate to our population. And many of us want houses in the suburbs."*

THE LAW: *"You can't have any of those things. You can't assert your claim against society in general, but only against a named discriminator, and you've got to show that you are an individual victim of that discrimination and that you were intentionally discriminated against.[1] And be sure to demonstrate how that discrimination caused your problem,[2] for any remedy*

---

* Professor of Law, University of Minnesota Law School. I wish to express my gratitude to the Law Alumni Association of the University of Minnesota for its generous support of the research leading to this Article. The views expressed in the Article are, of course, mine alone.

I am most grateful to Peter Gabel, Duncan Kennedy, Karl Klare, Mark Tushnet, and everyone associated with the Conference on Critical Legal Studies, without whose emotional and intellectual support neither this Article nor its forthcoming sequel ever would have left its author's head.

I also wish to thank Mike Becker, Morris Clark, Marcia Gelpe, and Erich Russell for their helpful comments and willingness to take the time to help; all of the students who have taken my course in Civil Rights over the past five years for proving through this Article that teaching and scholarship can be the same enterprise; Jeff Ring, whose thought-provoking research got this project moving at the outset; and the editors and staff of the *Minnesota Law Review* for their patience and support.

1. *See, e.g.*, Village of Arlington Heights v. Metropolitan Hous. Dev. Corp., 429 U.S. 252, 264-65 (1977); Washington v. Davis, 426 U.S. 229, 239-42 (1976).

2. *See, e.g.*, Pasadena City Bd. of Educ. v. Spangler, 427 U.S. 424, 430 (1976); Rizzo v. Goode, 423 U.S. 362, 371-73 (1976); Warth v. Seldin, 422 U.S. 490, 497, 502 (1975).

> *must be coextensive with the violation.*[3] *Be careful your claim does not impinge on some other cherished American value, like local autonomy of the suburbs,*[4] *or previously distributed vested rights,*[5] *or selection on the basis of merit.*[6] *Most important, do not demand any remedy involving racial balance or proportionality; to recognize such claims would be racist."*[7]

This Article, along with a sequel that will follow, attempts, through a discussion of Supreme Court decisions over a period of some 25 years, to account for the dissonance in this dialogue, for as surely as the law has outlawed racial discrimination, it has affirmed that Black Americans can be without jobs, have their children in all-black, poorly funded schools, have no opportunities for decent housing, and have very little political power, without any violation of antidiscrimination law.[8] The purpose of the discussion is descriptive

---

3. *See* Milliken v. Bradley, 418 U.S. 717, 744-45 (1974); Swann v. Charlotte-Mecklenburg Bd. of Educ., 402 U.S. 1, 16 (1971).

4. *See* Milliken v. Bradley, 418 U.S. 717, 745 (1974); *id.* at 766-68 (White, J., dissenting); San Antonio Independent School Dist. v. Rodriguez, 411 U.S. 1, 47-55 (1973); *id.* at 63-65 (White, J., dissenting).

5. *See* International Bhd. of Teamsters v. United States, 431 U.S. 324, 352-54 (1977).

6. *See* Washington v. Davis, 426 U.S. 229 (1976).

7. *See* Swain v. Alabama, 380 U.S. 202, 203, 208 (1965); Hughes v. Superior Court, 339 U.S. 460 (1950); Bakke v. Regents of the Univ. of Cal., 18 Cal. 3d 34, 61-62, 553 P.2d 1152, 1171, 132 Cal. Rptr. 680, 699 (1976), *aff'd in part, rev'd in part,* 98 S. Ct. 2733 (1978). *See also* Beer v. United States, 425 U.S. 130, 139-43 (1976).

8. For the purpose of this Article, antidiscrimination law is federal constitutional and statutory law, as expounded or interpreted by the United States Supreme Court, defining the conduct to be treated as racial discrimination. I regard this body of law as the best evidence of the current prevailing or official national moral consensus on the subject of racial discrimination. With respect to the inclusion of both constitutional and statutory law, one would have supposed, until recently, that federal statutes shared with the Constitution the same substantive notion of racial discrimination, with the role of the statutes being to add those violators otherwise immune from constitutional coverage because of the state-action doctrine. That there has been a substantive divergence is part of the story to be told in this Article. *See* text accompanying notes 275-76 *infra.*

I should also add that the almost exclusive emphasis of this Article is on racial discrimination, with the principal model that of black-white relations in the United States. To the extent that other forms of discrimination overlap with the model, this Article speaks to them. My belief in the necessity of emphasizing the concrete and historical suggests that other problems of discrimination demand separate scrutiny in their own particular contexts. It seems, for example, that, when compared to race, sex discrimination is in some respects a more tractable problem (where all the law has to do is strike down an irrational and inaccurate factual generalization based on gender) and in other respects more intractable (as in the as yet incomplete task of developing a dominant moral consensus in the face of still widely held cultural assumptions that support sex-stereotypic modes of thought and behavior). *Compare* Reed v. Reed, 404 U.S. 71 (1971), *with* Dothard v. Rawlinson, 433 U.S. 321 (1977), *and* General Elec. Co. v. Gilbert, 429 U.S. 125 (1976). *See generally* Wasserstrom, *Racism, Sexism, and Preferential Treatment: An Approach to the Topics,* 24 U.C.L.A. L. Rev. 581, 587-94,

and explanatory, *not* prescriptive or normative. The Article is not a doctrinal brief; no attempt will be made to reconcile new arguments with existing case law or find instances for optimism in the interstices of depressing Supreme Court opinions. Nor will there be any discussion of issues internal to the legal system, such as the apportionment of tasks between courts and legislatures, federal and state courts, or higher and lower courts.[9] Those issues are simply irrelevant to an author seeking to observe and report on evolution of legal doctrine rather than to participate in its manipulation.

While all of the Supreme Court opinions to be discussed are, of course, technical assertions of legal doctrine, and can be analyzed as such, they are also an evolving statement of acceptable public morality. In their latter role, the opinions not only reflect dominant societal moral positions,[10] but also serve as part of the process of forming or crystallizing such positions. Given a view that law serves largely to legitimize the existing social structure and, especially, class relationships within that structure, the ultimate constraints are outside the legal system.[11] But if law is to serve its legitimation function, those ultimate constraints must yield up just enough autonomy to the legal system to make its operations credible for those whose allegiance it seeks as well as those whose self-interest it rationalizes.

The sequel to this Article will deal more explicitly with the relationship between antidiscrimination law and the outside social struc-

605-15 (1977); *see also* B. BABCOCK, A. FREEDMAN, E. NORTON, & S. ROSS, SEX DISCRIMINATION AND THE LAW 89-92 (1973); S. FIRESTONE, THE DIALECTIC OF SEX 118-41 (1970); Easton, *Feminism and the Contemporary Family*, SOCIALIST REV., May-June 1978, at 11; Lasch, *The Flight from Feeling: Sociopsychology of Sexual Conflict*, MARXIST PERSPECTIVES, Spring 1978, at 74.

9. Such nonsubstantive issues as federalism or institutional competence are, for me, never neutral and never severed from a particular substantive position or at least from a world view with heavy substantive implications. For a characterization, with respect to these issues, of the internal workings of judicial decisionmaking that roughly corresponds to my own view, see Kennedy, *Form and Substance in Private Law Adjudication*, 89 HARV. L. REV. 1685, 1760-66 (1976).

10. *See* S. SCHEINGOLD, THE POLITICS OF RIGHTS 13-79 (1974); Tushnet, *A Marxist Analysis of American Law*, MARXIST PERSPECTIVES, Spring 1978, at 96, 97-101.

11. *See, e.g.*, C. BOGGS, GRAMSCI'S MARXISM 36-54 (1976); E. GENOVESE, ROLL, JORDAN, ROLL 35-49 (1972); A. GOULDNER, THE COMING CRISIS OF WESTERN SOCIOLOGY 266-77 (1970); J. HABERMAS, LEGITIMATION CRISIS 86-88, 98-102 (paperback ed. T. McCarthy trans. 1975); D. HAY, P. LINEBAUGH, J. RULE, E.P. THOMPSON, & C. WINSLOW, ALBION'S FATAL TREE 17 (1975); K. MARX & F. ENGELS, THE GERMAN IDEOLOGY 26-27, 28-29, 39-43, 60-62 (paperback ed. R. Pascal 1963); THE OPEN MARXISM OF ANTONIO GRAMSCI 35-44 (C. Marzani trans. & ed. 1957); R. UNGER, LAW IN MODERN SOCIETY 196 216 (1976); R. WOLFF, THE POVERTY OF LIBERALISM 150-61 (1968); Balbus, *Commodity Form and Legal Form: An Essay on the "Relative Autonomy" of the Law*, 11 LAW & SOC'Y REV. 571 (1977); Fraser, *The Legal Theory We Need Now*, SOCIALIST REV., July-October 1978, at 147; Klare, *Judicial Deradicalization of the Wagner Act and the Origins of Modern Legal Consciousness, 1937-1941*, 62 MINN. L. REV. 265 (1978); Wood, *The Marxian Critique of Justice*, 1 PHILOSOPHY & PUB. AFF. 244 (1972); Gabel, Book

ture. For the present, the emphasis is on the workings of the legal system within its sphere of limited autonomy. The discussion is premised upon the lack, even within that sphere, of any objective criteria to which one might appeal to justify particular substantive decisions. Neither formal criteria nor more substantive "shared values" emerge to resolve the underlying value-conflicts in these cases.[12] The supposedly shared values that are asserted always turn out, even when presented sincerely, to be attempts to rationalize self-interest through appeal to universal criteria. The lengthy discussion of Supreme Court opinions that follows is intended to be, among other things, a testament to the manipulability of legal doctrine.

The major emphasis, however, is on how the process of legitimation works through that manipulation of doctrine. The doctrine cannot legitimize unless it is convincing, but it cannot be convincing in the context of antidiscrimination law unless it holds out a promise of liberation. Simultaneously, the doctrine must refrain from delivering on the promise if it is to serve its function of *merely* legitimizing. And finally, the doctrine must occasionally offer at least illusions of reconciliation and resolution, lest it collapse in obvious self-contradiction.[13]

I. THE PERPETRATOR PERSPECTIVE

The concept of "racial discrimination" may be approached from the perspective of either its victim or its perpetrator. From the victim's perspective, racial discrimination describes those conditions of actual social existence as a member of a perpetual underclass. This perspective includes both the objective conditions of life—lack of jobs, lack of money, lack of housing[14]—and the consciousness asso-

Review, 91 HARV. L. REV. 302 (1977) (R. DWORKIN, TAKING RIGHTS SERIOUSLY).

12. *See* R. UNGER, KNOWLEDGE AND POLITICS 88-103, 151-56 (1975); Kennedy, *supra* note 9; *cf.* Heller, *The Importance of Normative Decisionmaking: The Limitations of Legal Economics as a Basis for a Liberal Jurisprudence—As Illustrated by the Regulation of Vacation Home Development,* 1976 WIS. L. REV. 385, 469-500 (describing the inadequacy of economic analysis of law). *See also* Wright, *Professor Bickel, The Scholarly Tradition and the Supreme Court,* 84 HARV. L. REV. 769 (1971).

13. While limiting the presentation to antidiscrimination law, I am willing to speculate that the principal techniques described, especially the victim-perpetrator dichotomy and the remedy-violation relationship, are not peculiar to antidiscrimination law, but, rather, typical of other ostensible law reform efforts.

14. *See, e.g.,* F. PIVEN & R. CLOWARD, POOR PEOPLE'S MOVEMENTS 181-263 (1977); RACE AND POVERTY (J. Kain ed. 1969); THE BURDEN OF RACE (G. Osofsky ed. 1967); U.S. COMM'N ON CIVIL RIGHTS, LAST HIRED, FIRST FIRED: LAYOFFS AND CIVIL RIGHTS (1977); U.S. COMM'N ON CIVIL RIGHTS, TWENTY YEARS AFTER BROWN: EQUAL OPPORTUNITY IN HOUSING (1975); U.S. COMM'N ON CIVIL RIGHTS, TWENTY YEARS AFTER BROWN: EQUALITY OF ECONOMIC OPPORTUNITY (1975); U.S. COMM'N ON CIVIL RIGHTS, TWENTY YEARS AFTER BROWN: EQUALITY OF EDUCATIONAL OPPORTUNITY (1975); S. WILLHELM, WHO NEEDS THE NEGRO? 123-76 (1970); Drake, *The Social and Economic Status of the Negro in the United States,* in SOCIAL INEQUALITY 297 (paperback ed. A. Beteille 1969); Was-

ciated with those objective conditions—lack of choice and lack of human individuality in being forever perceived as a member of a group rather than as an individual.[15] The perpetrator perspective sees racial discrimination not as conditions, but as actions, or series of actions, inflicted on the victim by the perpetrator. The focus is more on what particular perpetrators have done or are doing to some victims than it is on the overall life situation of the victim class.

The victim, or "condition,"[16] conception of racial discrimination suggests that the problem will not be solved until the conditions associated with it have been eliminated. To remedy the condition of racial discrimination would demand affirmative efforts to change the condition. The remedial dimension of the perpetrator perspective, however, is negative. The task is merely to neutralize the inappropriate conduct of the perpetrator.

In its core concept of the "violation," antidiscrimination law is hopelessly embedded in the perpetrator perspective. Its central tenet, the "antidiscrimination principle," is the prohibition of race-

---

serstrom, *supra* note 8, at 584-87. *See also* Greer, *Racial Employment Discrimination in the Gary Works, 1906-1974*, in SOCIAL CLASS IN THE CONTEMPORARY UNITED STATES 29-73 (G. Erickson & H. Schwartz eds. 1977).

15. *See, e.g.*, J. BALDWIN, NOTES OF A NATIVE SON 71-95 (paperback ed. 1964); C. BROWN, MANCHILD IN THE PROMISED LAND (1965); F. DOUGLASS, MY BONDAGE AND MY FREEDOM (New York 1855); W.E.B. DUBOIS, SOULS OF BLACK FOLK (1903); F. FANON, BLACK SKIN WHITE MASKS (1967); W. GRIER & P. COBBS, BLACK RAGE (1968); INSTITUTIONAL RACISM IN AMERICA (paperback ed. L. Knowles & K. Prewitt 1969); R. WRIGHT, BLACK BOY (paperback ed. 1951); Yerby, *The Thunder of God*, in WRITERS IN REVOLT 203 (paperback ed. J. Conroy & C. Johnson 1973).

16. I concede an irony in, but nevertheless will adhere to, my use of "victim perspective." If the real point of the victim perspective is to talk about conditions rather than practices, why talk about victims? Both are true. In the context of race, "victim" means a current member of the group that was historically victimized by actual perpetrators or a class of perpetrators. Victims are people who continue to experience life as a member of that group and continue to experience conditions that are actually or ostensibly tied to the historical experience of actual oppression or victimization, whether or not individual perpetrators, or their specific successors in interest, can be identified now. The victim perspective is intended to describe the expectations of an actual human being who is a current member of the historical victim class—expectations created by an official change of moral stance toward members of the victim group. Those expectations, I suggest, include changes in conditions.

The perpetrator perspective, on the other hand, is the stance of the legal system, or legal ideology, as a third entity subjecting all of contemporary society to its gaze. To the extent the ideology is received, that view also becomes the view of members of the victim group, nonperpetrator members of the nonvictim group, and perpetrator members of the nonvictim group.

For a related dichotomy between the "consumer" and the "imperial" perspectives, which has some overlap with mine and probably affected my choice of phrases, see E. CAHN, *Law in the Consumer Perspective*, in CONFRONTING INJUSTICE 15 (L. Cahn ed. 1966).

dependent decisions that disadvantage members of minority groups,[17] and its principal task has been to select from the maze of human behaviors those particular practices that violate the principle, outlaw the identified practices, and neutralize their specific effects. Antidiscrimination law has thus been ultimately indifferent to the condition of the victim; its demands are satisfied if it can be said that the "violation" has been remedied.

The perpetrator perspective presupposes a world composed of atomistic individuals[18] whose actions are outside of and apart from the social fabric and without historical continuity. From this perspective, the law views racial discrimination not as a social phenomenon, but merely as the misguided conduct of particular actors.[19] It is a world where, but for the conduct of these misguided ones, the system of equality of opportunity would work to provide a distribution of the good things in life without racial disparities and where deprivations that did correlate with race would be "deserved" by those deprived on grounds of insufficient "merit." It is a world where such things as "vested rights," "objective selection systems," and "adventitious decisions" (all of which serve to prevent victims from experiencing any change in conditions) are matters of fate, having nothing to do with the problem of racial discrimination.[20]

Central to the perpetrator perspective are the twin notions of "fault" and "causation." Under the fault idea, the task of antidiscrimination law is to separate from the masses of society those blameworthy individuals who are violating the otherwise shared norm. The fault idea is reflected in the assertion that only "intentional" discrim-

---

17. The best summary and explanation is Brest, *The Supreme Court, 1975 Term—Foreword: In Defense of the Antidiscrimination Principle,* 90 HARV. L. REV. 1 (1976).

18. *See id.* at 49-52.

19. *See* Kiltgaard, *Institutionalized Racism: An Analytic Approach,* in RACIAL CONFLICT, DISCRIMINATION, & POWER 9 (W. Barclay, K. Kumar, & R. Simms eds. 1976).

20. *See* Brest, *supra* note 17, at 36-48, 53.

> I believe that an individual's moral claim to compensation loses force as the nature, extent, and consequences of the wrongs inflicted become harder to identify and as the wrongs recede into the past. . . .
>
> Indeed, as claims to compensation based on the past injustices of human institutions become attenuated, they begin to compete with claims based on the vagaries of fate, and thus become indistinguishable from demands for greater distributive justice among all individuals. . . .
>
> The poor nonpreferred white and the black beneficiary of a preferential program are like two children raised as brothers in an impoverished household. It is later discovered that one . . . is . . . the heir to a small fortune . . . . All parties concerned would regard the occurrence as a windfall, and certainly not based on desert. So too is a preference premised on a greater probability that the minority's situation is the result of past injury.

Id. at 42-43.

ination violates the antidiscrimination principle.[21] In its pure form, intentional discrimination is conduct accompanied by a purposeful desire to produce discriminatory results.[22] One can thus evade responsibility for ostensibly discriminatory conduct by showing that the action was taken for a good reason,[23] or for no reason at all.[24]

The fault concept gives rise to a complacency about one's own moral status; it creates a class of "innocents," who need not feel any personal responsibility for the conditions associated with discrimination, and who therefore feel great resentment when called upon to bear any burdens in connection with remedying violations. This resentment accounts for much of the ferocity surrounding the debate about so-called "reverse" discrimination,[25] for being called on to bear burdens ordinarily imposed only upon the guilty involves an apparently unjustified stigmatization of those led by the fault notion to believe in their own innocence.

---

21. *See, e.g.*, Village of Arlington Heights v. Metropolitan Hous. Dev. Corp., 429 U.S. 252, 264-65 (1977); Washington v. Davis, 426 U.S. 229, 239-42 (1976); Milliken v. Bradley, 418 U.S. 717, 737 (1974); Keyes v. School Dist. No. 1, 413 U.S. 189, 208 (1973).

On the ideology of fault, see Pashukanis, *The General Theory of Law and Marxism*, in SOVIET LEGAL PHILOSOPHY 111, 216-21 (H. Babb trans. 1951). The fault notion as applied to racial discrimination today is, I believe, related to the assumption of 1950's liberals that such discrimination was largely a Southern problem. I can recall distinctly the response of my own naively liberal consciousness, as I was sitting in a fifth grade classroom at an all-white elementary school in New York City in 1954, to the announcement that the Supreme Court had outlawed racial segregation in schools: the Law is now going to make those bad Southerners behave; the land of opportunity is just around the corner.

22. *See* Village of Arlington Heights v. Metropolitan Hous. Dev. Corp., 429 U.S. 252, 264-65 (1977); Washington v. Davis, 426 U.S. 229, 239-42 (1976). These cases emphasize that both an act and an intent are necessary to effect intentional discrimination.

23. *See* Palmer v. Thompson, 403 U.S. 217, 225 (1971) (public swimming pools closed for the good reason that they "could not be operated safely and economically on an integrated basis"); Swain v. Alabama, 380 U.S. 202, 221 (1965) (intent of a jury selection system that operated to exclude blacks from petit juries was selection of an "impartial and qualified" jury).

24. This situation arises in cases involving inherently nonrational decisions, such as where to draw district boundary lines. Absent proof that the lines were drawn with intent to discriminate on account of race, the districts are valid regardless of effect. *See, e.g.*, Wright v. Rockefeller, 376 U.S. 52 (1964) (no violation absent proof of intentional discrimination despite proof that four contiguous and irregularly shaped congressional districts ranged in black population from 86.3% (highest) to 5.1% (lowest)).

25. *See, e.g.*, N. GLAZER, AFFIRMATIVE DISCRIMINATION: ETHNIC INEQUALITY AND PUBLIC POLICY (1975); I. KRAFT, DEFUNIS V. ODEGAARD: RACE, MERIT, AND THE FOURTEENTH AMENDMENT (1976); MINORITY ADMISSIONS SUMMER PROJECT, AFFIRMATIVE ACTION IN CRISIS (1977); R. O'NEIL, DISCRIMINATING AGAINST DISCRIMINATION (1975); REVERSE DISCRIMINATION (B. Gross ed. 1977); *Discrimination in Higher Education: A Debate on Faculty Employment*, CIV. RIGHTS DIG., Spring 1975, at 3-21; Dworkin, *Why Bakke Has No Case*, N.Y. REV. BOOKS, November 10, 1977, at 11.

Operating along with fault, the causation requirement serves to distinguish from the totality of conditions that a victim perceives to be associated with discrimination those that the law will address.[26] These dual requirements place on the victim the nearly impossible burden of isolating the particular conditions of discrimination produced by and mechanically linked to the behavior of an identified blameworthy perpetrator, regardless of whether other conditions of discrimination, caused by other perpetrators, would have to be remedied for the outcome of the case to make any difference at all.[27] The causation principle makes it clear that some objective instances of discrimination are to be regarded as mere accidents, or "caused," if at all, by the behavior of ancestral demons whose responsibility cannot follow their successors in interest over time. The causation principle also operates to place beyond the law discriminatory conduct (action taken with a purpose to discriminate under the fault principle) that is not linked to any discernible "discriminatory effect."[28]

The perpetrator perspective has been and still is the only formal conception of a violation in antidiscrimination law. Strict adherence to that form, however, would have made even illusory progress in the quest for racial justice impossible. The challenge for the law, therefore, was to develop, through the usual legal techniques of verbal manipulation, ways of breaking out of the formal constraints of the perpetrator perspective while maintaining ostensible adherence to

26. For an attempt to build an entire theory on a civil rights version of proximate cause, see Eisenberg, *Disproportionate Impact and Illicit Motive: Theories of Constitutional Adjudication*, 52 N.Y.U. L. REV. 36, 42-99 (1977).

27. *See* International Bhd. of Teamsters v. United States, 431 U.S. 324, 354-55 (1977); Milliken v. Bradley, 418 U.S. 717, 738-45 (1974).

> As applied here, the remedy for unquestioned violations of the equal protection rights of Detroit's Negroes . . . must be totally confined to the limits of the school district and may not reach into adjoining or surrounding districts unless and until it is proved there has been some sort of "interdistrict violation" . . . .
>
> . . . The core of my disagreement [with the Court] is that deliberate acts of segregation and their consequences will go unremedied, not because a remedy would be infeasible or unreasonable . . . , but because an effective remedy would cause what the Court considers to be undue administrative inconvenience to the State.

Id. at 763 (White, J., dissenting).

28. *See* Palmer v. Thompson, 403 U.S. 217, 225 (1971) ("Here the record indicates only that Jackson once ran segregated public swimming pools and that no public pools are now maintained by the city. . . . It shows no state action affecting blacks differently from whites."); Evans v. Abney, 396 U.S. 435, 445 (1970) ("Here the effect of the Georgia decision eliminated all discrimination against Negroes in the park by eliminating the park itself, and the termination of the park was a loss shared equally by the white and Negro citizens of Macon . . . .").

the form itself. This was done by separating violation from remedy, and doing through remedy what was inappropriate in cases involving only identification of violations. But since one of the principal tenets of the perpetrator perspective is that remedy and violation must be coextensive, it was necessary to state that tenet and violate it at the same time, no mean task even for masters of verbal gamesmanship. For a while, the remedial doctrines seemingly undermined the hegemony of the perpetrator form, threatening to replace it with a victim perspective. In the end, however, form triumphed, and the perpetrator perspective, always dominant in identifying violations, was firmly reasserted in the context of remedies as well.

The next three parts of this Article will trace these doctrinal developments through the major Supreme Court cases and congressional enactments that comprise modern antidiscrimination law.

II. 1954-1965: THE ERA OF UNCERTAINTY, OR THE JURISPRUDENCE OF VIOLATIONS

In the first era of modern antidiscrimination law, commencing with the Supreme Court's decision in *Brown v. Board of Education* (*Brown I*),[29] there was little occasion to consider the limits of the perpetrator perspective. For the most part, the Court concerned itself with identifying violations rather than remedying them and was therefore able to remain within the perpetrator perspective tradition of merely declaring the illegality of specific practices.[30] Although it was obvious that school desegregation was going to require something more than a statement of illegality, the Court in its subsequent opinion in *Brown v. Board of Education* (*Brown II*)[31] chose to relegate the problem to lower courts, leaving ambiguous the scope of the remedial obligation.

The *Brown I* opinion offers no clear statement of the perpetrator perspective, however, containing within its inscrutable text a number of possible antidiscrimination principles that "explain" the result in the case. These in turn are linked to various "meanings" of the equal protection clause[32] and to conceptions of reality even more abstract

29. 347 U.S. 483 (1954).

30. For the most part, of course, there was no such tradition, since the separate-but-equal doctrine of Plessy v. Ferguson, 163 U.S. 537 (1896), and its progeny served to place much blatant discrimination beyond any declaration of illegality. Nevertheless, to the extent that there was antidiscrimination law, it was exclusively concerned with identifying and outlawing discrete practices. *See, e.g.*, Terry v. Adams, 345 U.S. 461, 470 (1953); Shelley v. Kraemer, 334 U.S. 1, 20 (1948); Smith v. Allwright, 321 U.S. 649, 663-64 (1944); Buchanan v. Warley, 245 U.S. 60, 82 (1917); Strauder v. West Virginia, 100 U.S. 303, 309 (1880).

31. 349 U.S. 294 (1955).

32. The "equal protection clause," as used herein, includes, of course, the equal

and ahistorical than the modern perpetrator perspective—meanings and conceptions that still occasionally insinuate themselves into arguments such as the debate about so-called "reverse" discrimination.[33]

A. The Equal Protection Clause

There are at least three different "meanings" that one can ascribe to the equal protection clause, each of which appears to explain a particular kind of controversy under that clause. The first, the "means-oriented" approach, regards the clause as nothing more than a judicial check on legislative mistakes. Under this view, the judicial role is to articulate permissible levels of overinclusion or underinclusion in legislative classifications and send back to the legislature those statutes that have exceeded the allowable tolerances. In its pure form, the principle is perfectly abstract, concerned only with questions of neatness;[34] inasmuch as it serves to check technique rather than goal, it is utterly value-neutral. It is, therefore, a principle suited to the demands of a formalistic, positivist jurisprudence that purports to separate rule application from questions of value.[35]

There is some question, however, whether the principle ever has been, or ever could be, applied in its pure form. On the one hand, the degree of overinclusion or underinclusion that will be tolerated necessarily varies with the subject matter of the legislation. This problem gives rise to the necessity of separating the occasions for "strict"

---

protection dimension of the due process clause of the fifth amendment. *See* Bolling v. Sharpe, 347 U.S. 497 (1954).

33. *See, e.g.*, notes 70-78 *infra* and accompanying text (discussing the color-blind explanation of *Brown I*).

34. *See, e.g.*, Gunther, *The Supreme Court, 1971 Term—Foreword: In Search of Evolving Doctrine on a Changing Court: A Model for a Newer Equal Protection*, 86 Harv. L. Rev. 1, 20-24 (1972). "The [means-oriented] model of modest interventionism would have the courts do more than they have done for the last generation to assure rationality of means without unduly impinging on legislative prerogatives regarding ends." *Id.* at 23. *See also* Fiss, *Groups and the Equal Protection Clause*, 5 Philosophy & Pub. Aff. 107, 107-11, 120 (1976); Tussman & tenBroek, *The Equal Protection of the Laws*, 37 Calif. L. Rev. 341, 344-53 (1949) (discussing the principle of "reasonable classification").

35. *Cf.* Heller, *supra* note 12, at 388:

> [M]uch of the current attraction of law to economics seems to lie in the hope of finding a technocratic, value free, nondiscretionary method to resolve social problems. Such a quest for purely procedural justice reflects the influence of liberal social theory which, for historical reasons, is committed to the positivist principle that it is not possible to philosophically compare the merits of competing normative propositions. Contemporary jurisprudence, which has evolved in the liberal period, has drawn back from explicit consideration of the moral and distributional choices which must be made to provide the necessary legal structure for innovative types of conflict.

scrutiny from those demanding only "minimal" scrutiny. Since any legislative generalization is likely to fall if subjected to strict scrutiny, the choice between these alternatives takes on a highly substantive content with the judgment involved in that choice becoming the key decision.[36] Alternatively, the technique of means scrutiny may be employed as a cover for condemnation of an inappropriate purpose or for the creation or extension of a new substantive right.[37]

In either event, the means-oriented technique by itself is a procedural abstraction having nothing in particular to do with racial discrimination. Its application to racial discrimination cases depends on value choices external to questions of means alone. And even where means-oriented review is employed to confirm an implicit value choice about racial discrimination, the employment of this ostensibly value-neutral technique will have the effect of representing the problem of racial discrimination as an ahistorical abstraction removed from the actual setting that gave rise to the implicit value choice for intervention. Moreover, given its preoccupation with the validity of previously chosen means, this version of equal protection is wholly negative in outlook and therefore does not easily lend itself to remedying conditions associated with racial discrimination.

A second meaning of equal protection, which has on occasion produced affirmative remedies for conditions rather than just negative invalidation of practices, is the "fundamental right" rationale. This approach has arisen largely as a way for the Supreme Court to evade self-created limitations on judicial review while seeming to adhere to ground rules such as those offered by the famous footnote in *United States v. Carolene Products Co.*[38] Given a choice between

36. *Compare, e.g.*, Geduldig v. Aiello, 417 U.S. 484, 494-95 (1974), *and* Goesart v. Cleary, 335 U.S. 464, 466-67 (1948), *with* Califano v. Goldfarb, 430 U.S. 199, 206-07 (1977), Frontiero v. Richardson, 411 U.S. 677, 682-88 (1973) (plurality opinion), *and* Reed v. Reed, 404 U.S. 71, 74-77 (1971).

37. *See, e.g.*, Eisenstadt v. Baird, 405 U.S. 438, 448-49, 452-53 (1972) (means analysis obscures extension of the substantive right of privacy); Harper v. Virginia Bd. of Elections, 383 U.S. 663, 666-67 (1966) (means analysis obscures extension of substantive voting rights). *See also* Skinner v. Oklahoma, 316 U.S. 535, 541-42 (1942).

38. 304 U.S. 144, 152 n.4 (1938) (citations omitted):

> There may be narrower scope for operation of the presumption of constitutionality when legislation appears on its face to be within a specific prohibition of the Constitution, such as those of the first ten amendments, which are deemed equally specific when held to be embraced within the Fourteenth. . . .
>
> It is unnecessary to consider now whether legislation which restricts those political processes which can ordinarily be expected to bring about repeal of undesirable legislation, is to be subjected to more exacting judicial scrutiny under the general prohibitions of the Fourteenth Amendment than are most other types of legislation. . . .
>
> Nor need we inquire whether similar considerations enter into the review

inventing a new constitutional right explicitly[39] and inventing a new constitutional right by pretending simply to enforce the text of the equal protection clause, the Court has on occasion used the fundamental right doctrine to do the latter.[40] Indeed, in its heyday, the fundamental right doctrine seemed to be the vehicle by which the Court would usher in an era of distributive justice.[41] Now that the smoke has cleared, however, all that happened was the affirmation of some formal, procedural rights.[42] Explicitly rejected as fundamental were those rights having more to do with the substantive conditions of life: education,[43] housing,[44] welfare payments,[45] the right to obtain an abortion[46] (as opposed to the right not to be prevented from going out and paying for one[47]), and even the right to the blessings of federal bankruptcy law.[48]

> of statutes directed at particular religious, . . . or national, . . . or racial minorities . . . : whether prejudice against discrete and insular minorities may be a special condition, which tends seriously to curtail the operation of those political processes ordinarily to be relied upon to protect minorities, and which may call for a correspondingly more searching judicial inquiry.

39. *See, e.g.*, Griswold v. Connecticut, 381 U.S. 479 (1965) (creating a substantive right to privacy).

40. *See, e.g.*, Eisenstadt v. Baird, 405 U.S. 438, 448-49, 452-53 (1972) (extension of substantive right of privacy obscured by equal protection analytic framework); Shapiro v. Thompson, 394 U.S. 618, 627, 630-31 (1969) (extension of substantive right to travel obscured by equal protection analytic framework); Harper v. Virginia Bd. of Elections, 383 U.S. 663, 666-67 (1966) (extension of substantive right to vote obscured by equal protection analytic framework).

41. For an eloquent presentation of this view, see Michelman, *The Supreme Court, 1968 Term—Foreword: On Protecting the Poor Through the Fourteenth Amendment*, 83 HARV. L. REV. 7 (1969). For some, there are instances for continuing hope to be found in even the most depressing of recent opinions. *See* Tribe, *Unraveling* National League of Cities: *The New Federalism and Affirmative Rights to Essential Government Services*, 90 HARV. L. REV. 1065 (1977).

The Warren Court's opinions certainly offered a basis for optimism and nearly implied that the fundamental right notion would be extended to substance. For example, Kramer v. Union Free School Dist., 395 U.S. 621 (1969), was trivial in its ostensible role as a voting case, but in its emphasis on the importance of education seemed to promise the opposite of what was finally decided in San Antonio Independent School Dist. v. Rodriguez, 411 U.S. 1 (1973). Similarly, Shapiro v. Thompson, 394 U.S. 618 (1969), while credible as a travel case, gains much greater force if regarded as the prelude to a contrary decision in Dandridge v. Williams, 397 U.S. 471 (1970).

42. *See, e.g.*, Boddie v. Connecticut, 401 U.S. 371 (1971); Harper v. Virginia Bd. of Elections, 383 U.S. 663 (1966); Gideon v. Wainwright, 372 U.S. 335 (1963).

43. *See* Milliken v. Bradley, 418 U.S. 717 (1974); San Antonio Independent School Dist. v. Rodriguez, 411 U.S. 1 (1973).

44. *See* Lindsey v. Normet, 405 U.S. 56 (1972); James v. Valtierra, 402 U.S. 137 (1971).

45. *See* Dandridge v. Williams, 397 U.S. 471 (1970).

46. *See* Maher v. Roe, 432 U.S. 464 (1977); Poelker v. Doe, 432 U.S. 519 (1977).

47. *See* Roe v. Wade, 410 U.S. 113 (1973); Doe v. Bolton, 410 U.S. 179 (1973).

48. *See* United States v. Kras, 409 U.S. 434 (1973).

There is no necessary relation between the fundamental right concept and racial discrimination, since the doctrine is principally concerned with the fundamentality of the abstract right involved—a concern that is ostensibly neutral with respect to the race of the claimants. In fact, however, since racial minorities bear so disproportionately the burdens of economic class in the United States, any claim for substantive distributive justice is in essence a claim on behalf of those minorities. For practical reasons alone, the rejection of those claims forms part of the history of antidiscrimination law.

The fundamental right litigation also forms part of, or at least helps one to understand, the doctrinal, as well as the practical, history of antidiscrimination law. For one thing, many of the same decisions that denied fundamental right claims also refused to characterize the problems involved as ones of actual racial discrimination.[49] The Court accomplished that rejection by employing the narrow conception of violation associated with the perpetrator perspective. In addition, even apart from whether the cases should have been treated as racial discrimination cases, to have recognized substantive fundamental rights would have been tantamount to recognizing affirmative claims, a practice associated with the victim perspective. By rejecting such claims, the law, when directly confronted with the victim perspective, explicitly rejected it. Thus, what starts out as a victim perspective claim about the results of racial discrimination is transformed into a complaint about not racial but economic injustice, and then denied in those recast terms. The net effect is that the victim of racial discrimination must persevere until the utopian day when everyone is entitled to distributive justice.[50]

The third meaning of equal protection is the oldest one, and the one that speaks directly to discrimination against black people in the setting of American history. This meaning may be found in the tradition that regards the overwhelming goal of the Civil War amendments to be "the freedom of the slave race, the security and firm establishment of that freedom, and the protection of the newly-made freeman and citizen from the oppressions of those who had formerly exercised unlimited dominion over him."[51] Under this conception, the particular target of the equal protection clause is "discrimination against the negroes as a class, or on account of their race":[52]

49. *See* San Antonio Independent School Dist. v. Rodriguez, 411 U.S. 1, 35-37, 57 (1973) (no fundamental right to education); Jefferson v. Hackney, 406 U.S. 535, 547-49 (1972) (by implication) (no fundamental right to obtain welfare benefits); James v. Valtierra, 402 U.S. 137, 140-41 (1971) (by implication) (no fundamental right to housing).

50. *See* Brest, *supra* note 17, at 5, 42-43, 52-53.

51. Slaughterhouse Cases, 83 U.S. (16 Wall.) 36, 71 (1873).

52. *Id.* at 81.

> The words of the amendment . . . contain a necessary implication of a positive immunity, or right, most valuable to the colored race, — the right to exemption from unfriendly legislation against them distinctively as colored, — exemption from legal discriminations, implying inferiority in civil society, lessening the security of their enjoyment of the rights which others enjoy, and discriminations which are steps towards reducing them to the condition of a subject race.[53]

This version of equal protection is one that I prefer to call "substantive equal protection" to emphasize both its centrality in relation to the other versions of equal protection and its clear focus on ends and purposes, and not just means or legislative rationality. Of the three versions of equal protection, this is the only one that, in employing phrases like "oppressions," "implying inferiority," or "condition of a subject race," speaks to the concrete historical situation of black people in the United States.[54]

To identify a separate principle of equal protection directly concerned with racial discrimination is hardly to give it content, however. In fact, substantive equal protection might be regarded as the source of such divergent formulations as Tussman and tenBroek's "discriminatory legislation,"[55] *Carolene Products*' "discrete and insular minorities,"[56] Owen Fiss' "group-disadvantaging principle,"[57] and

53. Strauder v. West Virginia, 100 U.S. 303, 307-08 (1880).

54. This is not to suggest that no other oppressed group can claim the benefit of substantive equal protection, but only that any such claim must be premised on a similarity between that group's condition and the basic model of white oppression of blacks.

55. *See* Tussman & tenBroek, *supra* note 34, at 356-61.

56. 304 U.S. at 152 n.4. The text of the *Carolene Products* footnote appears in note 38 *supra*. *See generally* Ely, *The Constitutionality of Reverse Racial Discrimination*, 41 U. CHI. L. REV. 723, 729-32 (1974).

57. *See* Fiss, *supra* note 34. Fiss purports to articulate a new conception of equal protection, which he calls the "group-disadvantaging principle." Although the article is ambiguous, and may well do more, Fiss seems to describe as a new principle of antidiscrimination law one that is difficult to distinguish from the modern perpetrator perspective version of substantive equal protection. For one thing, he sets up the narrow means-oriented view as the existing principle against which his new one is to be measured, *see id.* at 107-12, noting, but seemingly discarding, the traditional substantive content of equal protection, *see id.* at 110 n.2, 112, 117 n.14. By going against the easy target, Fiss does not have to go further and discuss competing substantive notions of equal protection. The extent to which his principle might go beyond the perpetrator perspective remains unclear. His discussion is limited to antidiscrimination law under the equal protection clause, rather than antidiscrimination law generally. Under that doctrine, the state is the only perpetrator. Fiss makes it clear that he would limit the application of his principle to practices or action by the state, and he rejects the notion of affirmative claims. *See id.* at 168-70. On the critical question of whether particular practices produce "status-harms" and thereby violate his principle, it is uncertain whether some notion of intent accompanying the practice is relevant or not. *See id.* at 153-59.

Paul Brest's "antidiscrimination principle."[58] Although occasionally threatened by the means-oriented principle, which, in some of its manifestations, tries to consume and supplant substantive equal protection,[59] it is the latter that forms the basis of modern antidiscrimination law and tells us which instances of racial discrimination are to be deemed violations.[60]

A great deal of the confusion surrounding these three separate principles of equal protection stems from their frequent appearance together in individual cases. Given the ambiguity of Supreme Court opinions, it may be nearly impossible to discover in any particular case which principle is the controlling one, or whether it is some, or all. In *Harper v. Virginia State Board of Elections,*[61] for example, the Court struck down as violative of the equal protection clause a Virginia statute requiring payment of an annual tax of $1.50 as a precondition to eligibility for voting. Using means-oriented language, the Court noted that wealth was "not germane to one's ability to participate intelligently in the electoral process, that it was a "capricious or irrelevant factor."[62] This approach makes perfect sense if one assumes that the purpose of the poll tax was to classify potential voters into two categories: those interested in the election (worthwhile voters) and those not interested in the election (worthless voters), with willingness to pay the tax the measure of sufficient interest. It is obvious that the taxpayer category is both overinclusive and underinclusive as a measure of voter interest, since it will include some people who pay the tax just because it is due, regardless of how they feel about voting, while it will exclude others who really care about voting but who cannot afford to pay the tax. The classification thus fails to fit the purpose, and the legislation is not rational.

One problem is that if, as Justice Black did in his *Harper* dissent,[63] one merely adds another purpose to the analysis of the tax—that of collecting revenue—it is hard to say why it is irrational to use the privilege of voting to coerce payment. In fact, it is difficult to see why that choice is any less rational than attaching bank accounts, or seizing property, or putting people in jail, or denying them

On the other hand, the Fiss article is to be applauded for its careful separation of substantive equal protection from the other equal protection principles, its placement of that notion in its specific historical context, and its admonition to refrain from interpreting the equal protection clause as if its implicit classless individualistic society already existed. *See id.* at 147-50.

58. *See* Brest, *supra* note 17.

59. *See* notes 70-78 *infra* and accompanying text.

60. *See* text accompanying notes 90-94 *infra*.

61. 383 U.S. 663 (1966).

62. *Id.* at 668.

63. *See id.* at 674.

the right to drive automobiles. All this suggests that the case had more to do with the fact that voting was involved than with a mere question of rationality. This view also finds support in the majority opinion, which cites a fundamental right precedent for the proposition that " 'the opportunity for equal participation by all voters in the election of state legislators' is required."[64] This version is bolstered by hindsight, since the Court did go on to develop a substantive jurisprudence of voting as a fundamental right, spelling out in subsequent cases that the right to vote in a general election[65] could not be conditioned on anything other than age, minimal residence, and citizenship.[66]

A third explanation of *Harper* concerns the employment of the poll tax as an administrative device for disenfranchising black people in the South. The Court made no more than passing reference to what would be a substantive equal protection view of the case, merely observing in a footnote that while the " 'Virginia poll tax was born of a desire to disenfranchise the Negro' . . . we do not stop to determine whether on this record the Virginia tax in its modern setting serves the same end."[67] In the next footnote, however, the Court neutrally catalogued the states still using poll taxes as prerequisites to voter eligibility, which, in addition to Virginia, just happened to be Alabama, Texas, and Mississippi.[68]

Having identified these various "meanings" of equal protection, this Article will now return to the more specific context of racial discrimination cases to illustrate how these alternative views may be

64. *Id.* at 670 (quoting Reynolds v. Sims, 377 U.S. 533, 566 (1964)).

65. The Court has distinguished the right to vote in general elections from the right to vote in special elections dealing with issues of particular interest to a limited class of people. *Compare* City of Phoenix v. Kolodziejski, 399 U.S. 204, 206, 215 (1970) (holding unconstitutional as a violation of equal protection an Arizona constitutional and statutory scheme that restricted voting in an election to approve issuance of general obligation bonds to those who paid tax on real property), *and* Kramer v. Union Free School Dist., 395 U.S. 621, 622, 633 (1969) (holding unconstitutional as a violation of equal protection a New York statute that restricted voting in school district elections to those who either owned or leased taxable real property within the district or were parents or had custody of children enrolled in the local public schools), *with* Salyer Land Co. v. Tulare Lake Basin Water Sewage Dist., 410 U.S. 719, 720-21, 725, 734-35 (1973) (holding that a California statute restricting voting in water storage district elections to landowners did not violate equal protection since the water storage district was " 'a special-purpose unit of government assigned the performance of functions affecting definable groups of constituents more than other constituents.' ") (quoting Avery v. Midland County, 390 U.S. 474, 483-84 (1968)).

66. *See, e.g.*, Dunn v. Blumstein, 405 U.S. 330 (1972).

67. Harper v. Virginia Bd. of Elections, 383 U.S. 663, 666 n.3 (1966) (quoting Harman v. Forssenius, 380 U.S. 528, 543 (1965)).

68. *See id.* at 666 n.4.

linked to the development of antidiscrimination doctrine. The illustrative case is *Brown I.*

B. *Brown v. Board of Education*[69]

There are a number of different ways of looking at the *Brown* case, all of which permeate the subsequent evolution of antidiscrimination law. I shall discuss five such: the color-blind constitution theory; the equality of educational opportunity theory; the white oppression of blacks theory; the freedom of association theory; and the integrated society theory.

1. *Color-Blind Constitution*

To explain *Brown* by invoking the slogan that the "Constitution is color-blind"[70] reflects the means-oriented view of the equal protection clause. On this view, what was wrong with school segregation was that government was employing an irrational classification—race. This approach, however, does not explain why it was irrational to classify people by race if the purpose was to prevent blacks and whites from going to school together. How else could one rationally achieve segregation by race in public schools? One answer is that the purpose itself is illegitimate, that it is no business of government to seek to segregate by race in public schools. If that is the answer, however, the color-blind constitution theory is not a means-oriented approach at all, but rather one that collapses into substantive equal protection. If that is the case, however, one must consider not legislative rationality, but, as I suggested above, particular relationships between blacks and whites in the context of American history.

A ploy that avoids the quick collapse into substantive equal protection is to bootstrap the means-oriented principle into its own substantive principle. This is done by starting with the means-oriented assumption that racial classifications are almost always unrelated to *any* valid governmental purpose (purpose here being the wholly abstract world of possible purposes). Since such classifications are likely to be irrational, they should be treated as "suspect," and subjected to "strict scrutiny," which they will survive only if found to satisfy a "compelling governmental interest."[71] If the degree of scrutiny is so

69. 347 U.S. 483 (1954).

70. The color-blind theory was first given explicit voice in 1896: "Our Constitution is color-blind, and neither knows nor tolerates classes among citizens." Plessy v. Ferguson, 163 U.S. 537, 559 (1896) (Harlan, J., dissenting); *see* Posner, *The DeFunis Case and The Constitutionality of Preferential Treatment of Racial Minorities*, 1974 SUP. CT. REV. 1, 21-26; *Developments in the Law—Equal Protection*, 82 HARV. L. REV. 1065, 1088-89 (1969) [hereinafter cited as *Developments—Equal Protection*].

71. *See Developments—Equal Protection*, *supra* note 70, at 1088-90.

strict and the possibility of a sufficiently compelling governmental interest so remote that the rule operates as a virtual per se rule, we then seem to have a means-oriented principle that explains the *Brown* case.

The problem with this second formulation of the color-blind theory is that it still contains a substantive assumption: racial classifications are almost always unrelated to any valid governmental purpose. As an abstract matter, this is hardly intuitively obvious.[72] One could easily envision a society where racial or other ethnic classifications are unrelated to any pattern of oppression or domination of one group by another and, in fact, promote feelings of group identity.[73] Thus, the initial assumption cannot be made except in the context of a particular historical situation, and the source of the assumption that underlies the color-blind theory can easily be found in American history by taking a brief glance at relationships between whites and blacks. Accordingly, the color-blind theory must originate in a notion of substantive equal protection.

Despite this fact, the color-blind theory has tended to become a reified abstraction, to gain a life of its own, and finally to turn back on its origins. Thus, a pure form of the color-blind theory would outlaw any use of racial classifications, no matter what the context, thereby providing easy answers to questions like whether a black community can refuse to participate in an integration plan[74] or whether black students at a public university can establish their own housing units from which whites are excluded. The answers remain easy only so long as the theory remains divorced from its origins in the actuality of black-white relations. By abstracting racial discrimination into a myth-world where all problems of race or ethnicity are fungible, the color-blind theory turns around and denies concrete demands of blacks with the argument that to yield to such demands would be impossible since every other ethnic group would be entitled to make the same demand.[75]

72. Consider, for example, Paul Brest's illuminating hypothetical: "How should a court treat a school principal's decision, based solely on aesthetics, to have black and white students sit on opposite sides of the stage at the graduation ceremony?" P. BREST, PROCESSES OF CONSTITUTIONAL DECISIONMAKING 489 (1975). The validity of this hypothetical seems no more difficult a question than the validity of school segregation in general. Both require a look at the concrete historical setting to figure out who is doing what to whom at whose behest. *Compare* Fiss, *supra* note 34, at 116-17.

73. *See* Wasserstrom, *supra* note 8, at 603-15.

74. Consider, for example, Derrick Bell's hypothetical on this issue, in D. BELL, RACE, RACISM AND AMERICAN LAW 572-73 (1973).

75. *See* Swain v. Alabama, 380 U.S. 202, 208 (1965); Hughes v. Superior Court, 339 U.S. 460, 464 (1950).

> The reservation of a proportion of the law school class for members of selected minority groups is fraught with . . . dangers, for one must immedi-

The color-blind theory has never become the law; the Supreme Court has in fact explicitly upheld the remedial use of racial classifications on a number of occasions.[76] Nevertheless, the theory does share certain features with something that is part of the law—the perpetrator perspective. Among these features is the emphasis on negating specific invalid practices rather than affirmatively remedying conditions, with a consequent inability to deal with ostensibly neutral practices.[77] In addition, the color-blind theory exerts an insistent pressure on antidiscrimination law to produce special justifications for deviations from its norm and to limit their duration to facilitate a quick return to the comfortable, abstract world of color-blindness.[78]

2. *Equality of Educational Opportunity*

Brown can also be viewed as a case concerned with equality of educational opportunity. This approach corresponds with the fundamental right concept of equal protection. Under this view, *Brown* did not merely outlaw segregation in public schools; it also guaranteed that black children would have an affirmative right to a quality of education comparable to that received by white children. The Court in its opinion stressed the importance of education, calling it the "very foundation of good citizenship,"[79] and "a principal instrument in awakening the child to cultural values, in preparing him for later

---

> ately determine which groups are to receive such favored treatment and which are to be excluded . . . . [F]irst the schools, and then the courts, will be buffeted with the competing claims.
>
> . . . .
>
> Nor . . . will the problem be solved if next year the Law School included only Japanese and Chinese, for the Norwegians and Swedes, Poles and Italians, Puerto Ricans and Hungarians, and all other groups which form this diverse Nation would have just complaints.

DeFunis v. Odegaard, 416 U.S. 312, 338, 340 (1974) (Douglas, J., dissenting).

But one should not underestimate the force of ideology. Consider the actual "ethnicity" movement that has emerged in recent years through which such demands are actually being asserted. *See, e.g.*, ETHNICITY (N. Glazer & D. Moynihan eds. 1975); THE REDISCOVERY OF ETHNICITY (paperback ed. S. TeSelle 1974); Stein & Hill, *The Limits of Ethnicity*, 46 AM. SCHOLAR 181 (1977).

76. *See, e.g.*, United Jewish Organizations v. Carey, 430 U.S. 144 (1977); Wright v. Council of Emporia, 407 U.S. 451 (1972); Swann v. Charlotte-Mecklenburg Bd. of Educ., 402 U.S. 1 (1971). *See also* Monroe v. Board of Comm'rs, 391 U.S. 450 (1968).

77. For a discussion of how antidiscrimination law has dealt with ostensibly neutral practices, see text accompanying note 132 *infra*; notes 180-203 *infra* and accompanying text.

78. *See* Brest, *supra* note 17, at 15; Fiss, *supra* note 34, at 129-35; Sandalow, *Racial Preferences in Higher Education: Political Responsibility and the Judicial Role*, 42 U. CHI. L. REV. 653, 675-81 (1975).

79. 347 U.S. at 493.

professional training, and in helping him to adjust normally to his environment."[80] The Court added that where a state undertakes to provide public education, it "is a right which must be made available to all on equal terms."[81]

By way of hindsight, the case stood for both more and less than a guarantee of equal educational quality. It came to stand for more insofar as its holding was quickly extended to other forms of state-imposed segregation.[82] But it stood for a great deal less insofar as black children today have neither an affirmative right to receive an integrated education[83] nor a right to equality of resources for their schools,[84] which, ironically, was a litigable claim under the regime of de jure segregation.[85] While there is no way to prove "objectively" what the opinion in *Brown* meant with respect to a right to educational equality, both a claim for equal resources and a claim for the

80. *Id.*

81. *Id.* This view is also consistent with the litigation strategy of the lawyers in *Brown*, for whom the case was the culmination of years of effort to obtain a quality education for black children, first within the structure of separate-but-equal and then in open confrontation with that structure. *See* R. KLUGER, SIMPLE JUSTICE 3-540 (1975).

82. *See, e.g.*, Gayle v. Browder, 352 U.S. 903, *aff'g per curiam* 142 F. Supp. 707 (M.D. Ala. 1956) (buses); Holmes v. City of Atlanta, 350 U.S. 879, *vacating per curiam* 223 F.2d 93 (5th Cir. 1955) (municipal golf courses); Mayor of Baltimore v. Dawson, 350 U.S. 877, *aff'g per curiam* 220 F.2d 386 (4th Cir. 1955) (public beaches and bathhouses).

83. *See* Pasadena City Bd. of Educ. v. Spangler, 427 U.S. 424, 436-37 (1976); Milliken v. Bradley, 418 U.S. 717, 744-45 (1974). "The suggestion . . . that schools which have a majority of Negro students are not 'desegregated,' whatever the racial makeup of the school district's population and however neutrally the district lines have been drawn and administered, finds no support in our prior cases." *Id.* at 747 n.22.

84. *See* San Antonio Independent School Dist. v. Rodriguez, 411 U.S. 1, 50-51 (1973).

85.
> The inner core of Detroit is now rather solidly black; and the blacks, we know, in many instances are likely to be poorer, just as were the Chicanos in *San Antonio School District* v. *Rodriguez* . . . . By that decision the poorer school districts must pay their own way. It is therefore a foregone conclusion that we have now given the states a formula whereby the poor must pay their own way.
>
> Today's decision, given *Rodriguez*, means that there is no violation of the Equal Protection Clause though the schools are segregated by race and though the black schools are not only "separate" but "inferior."
>
> So far as equal protection is concerned we are now in a dramatic retreat from the 7-1 decision in 1896 that blacks could be segregated in public facilities, provided they received equal treatment.

Milliken v. Bradley, 418 U.S. 717, 759-61 (1974) (Douglas, J., dissenting) (citation and footnotes omitted).

This is not to suggest that black children were better off under the regime of *Plessy*, inasmuch as "separate-but-equal" did not have to be equal. *See* Cumming v. Richmond County Bd. of Educ., 175 U.S. 528 (1899). On the other hand, the irony is underscored by the successful lawsuits demanding equalization in the years immediately prior to *Brown I*. *See* R. KLUGER, *supra* note 81, at 543-81, and cases cited therein.

choice of an integrated education can be supported from the text of the opinion. The Court assumed for its opinion that the black and white schools in the cases under review "have been equalized, or are being equalized, with respect to buildings, curricula, qualifications and salaries of teachers, and other 'tangible' factors."[86] With respect to the fact of integration, the Court quoted a finding of one of the lower courts: " 'Segregation of white and colored children in public schools has a detrimental effect upon the colored children. The impact is greater when it has the sanction of the law; for the policy of separating the races is usually interpreted as denoting the inferiority of the negro group.' "[87] To the extent the text suggests that the detrimental effect, with its attendant denotation of inferiority, would persist even in the absence of state sanction, the case may be read as addressing not the *practice* but the *fact* of racial separation.

For the Court to have recognized affirmative claims to resources or integrated classrooms would have been to adopt explicitly a victim perspective on racial discrimination. Essential to this perspective is the conferral upon the members of the formerly oppressed group a choice that is real and not merely theoretical with respect to conditions over which they had no control under the regime of oppression. Instead, under the perpetrator perspective, the Court recognizes only the right of the black children to attend schools that are not intentionally segregated by the jurisdiction that runs them. This right, it is argued, is all that *Brown* stands for anyway, since all the case did was outlaw de jure segregation. And the famous "social science footnote"[88] of *Brown* is today turned inside-out to make the question of whether integration can be compelled nothing more than a matter of empirical study of educational "outputs."[89]

3. *White Oppression of Blacks*

On this view, the *Brown* case was a straightforward declaration that segregation was unlawful because it was an instance of majoritarian oppression of black people, a mechanism for maintaining

86. 347 U.S. at 492.

87. *Id.* at 494 (quoting "a finding in the Kansas case").

88. *See id.* at 494 n.11.

89. *See, e.g.*, C. Jencks, Inequality 97-106 (1972); Fiss, *School Desegregation: The Uncertain Path of the Law*, 4 Philosophy & Pub. Aff. 3, 36-39 (1974); Kaplan, *Equal Justice in an Unequal World: Equality for the Negro—The Problem of Special Treatment*, 61 Nw. U.L. Rev. 363, 401-04 (1966); Goodman, *De Facto School Segregation: A Constitutional and Empirical Analysis*, 60 Calif. L. Rev. 275, 436-37 (1972); *cf.* Castaneda v. Partida, 430 U.S. 482, 515-16 (1977) (Powell, J., dissenting) (commenting on empirical assumptions underlying jury discrimination law). *But see* Yudof, *Equal Educational Opportunity and the Courts*, 51 Tex. L. Rev. 411, 459-64 (1973). *See generally* School Desegregation (F. Levinsohn & B. Wright eds. 1976).

blacks as a perpetual underclass. This approach, which begins and ends with historical fact instead of trying to find a neutral abstraction from which one can deduce the invalidity of segregation, was eloquently stated by Charles Black in 1960:

> First, the equal protection clause of the fourteenth amendment should be read as saying that the Negro race, as such, is not to be significantly disadvantaged by the laws of the states. Secondly, segregation is a massive intentional disadvantaging of the Negro race, as such, by state law. No subtlety at all. Yet I cannot disabuse myself of the idea that that is really all there is to the segregation cases.[90]

That this was the "explanation" for the "segregation cases" was self-evident to Professor Black on the basis of both American history and his own boyhood experience in Texas.[91] The striking feature of Professor Black's approach is that it makes sense not as the presentation of another "neutral principle" that can be separated from its factual context and given a life of its own,[92] but as a method for taking a hard look at the truth and describing it as one knows it to be. It is the same method that the Supreme Court used, in a more candid opinion than *Brown*, to outlaw Virginia's criminal miscegenation statute:

> There is patently no legitimate overriding purpose independent of invidious racial discrimination which justifies this classification. The fact that Virginia prohibits only interracial marriages involving white persons demonstrates that the racial classifications must stand on their own justification, as measures designed to maintain White Supremacy.[93]

As a method, the white oppression of blacks approach would ask in each case whether the particular conditions complained of, viewed in their social and historical context, are a manifestation of racial oppression. Such an approach would reflect adoption of the victim perspective. It is not an approach congenial to a system of law that wishes to rationalize continued discrimination just as much as it wants to outlaw it.[94] That goal, if it is to be accomplished through a practice that can be convincingly described as "law," requires a gap between social reality and legal intervention, with that gap mediated

90. Black, *The Lawfulness of the Segregation Decisions*, 69 YALE L.J. 421 (1960); *accord*, Cahn, *Jurisprudence*, 30 N.Y.U. L. REV. 150, 159-60 (1955).

91. *See* Black, *supra* note 90, at 424.

92. The penchant for neutral principles is reflected in Fiss, *supra* note 34. The classic is Wechsler, *Toward Neutral Principles of Constitutional Law*, 73 HARV. L. REV. 1 (1959).

93. Loving v. Virginia, 388 U.S. 1, 11 (1967) (footnote omitted).

94. *See* notes 215-23 *infra* and accompanying text.

by an abstract, objective principle against which particular instances of discrimination can be tested and upheld or struck down depending on the results.

Regarded as a principle, Professor Black's formulation is ambiguous, however, and can lead just as easily to a perpetrator perspective. One can argue that he said nothing more than that "Southern" segregation is illegal, that the violation is simply the practice of intentional, de jure segregation. So formulated, the principle does not speak to the problem of remedying that practice, nor does it indicate which other practices or conditions might be regarded as sufficiently similar to "Southern" segregation to be deemed unlawful. That the version of substantive equal protection described by Professor Black is the explanation for *Brown* seems obvious, but it took some years to transform his method into an abstraction, largely under the influence of the color-blind theory.

4. *Freedom of Association*

The "freedom of association" view sees *Brown* not as an equal protection case at all, but as a case dealing with the due process right of people to associate with one another free of state interference.[95] While it is clear that this was not the actual rationale of the *Brown* opinion, as the Court specifically eschewed reliance on any due process theory[96] and later cases specifically rejected the freedom of association viewpoint,[97] it nevertheless seems worth discussing. For one thing, the freedom of association theory may be a more accurate explanation of the limits of *Brown* in its historical context. Second, the freedom of association theory exemplifies the rationalization that serves to legitimize discrimination and therefore provides an early model for the contemporary perpetrator perspective. Third, it is still

95. *See* D. BELL, *supra* note 74, at 452; Wechsler, *supra* note 92, at 34.

96. "[W]e hold that the plaintiffs . . . are, by reason of the segregation complained of, deprived of the equal protection of the laws guaranteed by the Fourteenth Amendment. This disposition makes unnecessary any discussion whether such segregation also violates the due process clause of the Fourteenth Amendment." 347 U.S. at 495 (footnote omitted).

97. The Court rejected the freedom of association interpretation of *Brown I* by holding that school desegregation plans that did no more than allow students free associational choice were constitutionally inadequate. *See* Monroe v. Board of Comm'rs, 391 U.S. 450, 457-58 (1968); Green v. County School Bd., 391 U.S. 430, 440-42 (1968). In *Green*, the Court stressed that the goal of *Brown I* and *Brown II* was the creation of unitary school systems. *See id.* at 436. Desegregation plans that relied purely on associational choice were acceptable only where they offered "real promise of aiding a desegregation program." *Id.* at 440-41. "On the other hand, if there are reasonably available other ways . . . promising speedier and more effective conversion to a unitary, nonracial school system, 'freedom of choice' " was "unacceptable." *Id.* at 441.

a living principle, although one operating in a narrow context, that does serve to explain some contemporary decisions. Finally, the theory shares some significant features with the color-blind theory and further exposes the abstract world view associated with color-blindness.

The freedom of association theory is as much a statement about the right to discriminate as it is about the right not to be discriminated against. All it outlaws is state action. The autonomous individual remains free to discriminate, or not, according to personal preference. Racial discrimination is thus wrenched from its social fabric and becomes a mere question of private, individual taste. This theory serves to explain the few Supreme Court interventions against racial discrimination during the otherwise racist hegemony of *Plessy v. Ferguson.*[98] But it also sheds light on *Brown*, since the ethical norm reflected in national antidiscrimination law at the time of the *Brown* decision was one that recognized the legitimacy of private discrimination. Because of the constraints of the state-action principle, there was nothing illegal, as a matter of *national* law, about blatant and explicit discrimination in employment, housing, or public accommodations, so long as such practices were "private."[99] The freedom of association theory legitimizes that tolerance of racial discrimination by transforming it into a freedom to discriminate. It thus speaks directly to the needs of an era that had not yet fully developed even the perpetrator perspective, inasmuch as only one perpetrator—the state—could be held accountable for racial discrimination.

On its own terms, the theory became moot with the subsequent

98. 163 U.S. 537 (1896).

> [V]oluntary adherence [to a racially restrictive covenant] would constitute individual action only. When, however, the parties cease to rely upon voluntary action to carry out the covenant and the state is asked to step in and give its sanction to the enforcement of the covenant, . . . it becomes not respondent's voluntary choice but the state's choice that she observe the covenant or suffer damages. The action of a state court . . . to sanction the validity of the restrictive covenant . . . constitute[s] state action [violative of the Equal Protection Clause].

Barrows v. Jackson, 346 U.S. 249 (1953); *see* Shelley v. Kraemer, 334 U.S. 1, 19-20 (1948); Buchanan v. Warley, 245 U.S. 60, 80-81 (1917).

99. "[C]ivil rights, such as are guaranteed by the constitution against state aggression, cannot be impaired by the wrongful acts of individuals, unsupported by state authority. . . . The wrongful act of an individual, unsupported by any such authority, is simply a private wrong . . . ." The Civil Rights Cases, 109 U.S. 3, 17 (1883). For a particularly blatant example, see Dorsey v. Stuyvesant Town Corp., 299 N.Y. 512, 542-45, 87 N.E.2d 541, 553-57 (1949) (Fuld, J., dissenting) (exclusion of Negroes from a $90,000,000 housing project occupying some eighteen city blocks and housing some 25,000 people deemed a private action not violative of equal protection, despite significant state involvement with the project), *cert. denied*, 339 U.S. 981 (1950).

demise of the state-action doctrine through legislation[100] and constitutional decisions[101] expanding the list of responsible perpetrators. It serves to explain only those contemporary decisions that do affirm a right to discriminate in the limited areas that are still beyond the reach of the perpetrator principle.[102] But the presence of even those few areas of permissible discrimination does keep alive the idea that racial discrimination is ethically proper, as long as it is restricted to private life.

Where it does apply, the freedom of association theory implies a notion of racial equivalence similar to the color-blind theory's idea that blacks and whites have equal grounds for complaint about instances of racial discrimination. In this sense, the two theories share a world view—the abstract utopia where racial discrimination has never existed and where, ironically, both theories would probably be irrelevant. The only way that discriminations by whites against blacks can become ethically equivalent to discriminations by blacks against whites is to presuppose that there is no actual problem of racial discrimination. It is just like saying today that the principles of freedom of association and color-blindness govern relationships between long- and short-ear-lobed people.[103]

5. *The Integrated Society*

This view is not so much another way of explaining the *Brown* decision as it is an additional perspective from which to regard all of the other theories and explanations. It begins with the assumption that a decision like *Brown*, which merely outlaws a particular practice, nevertheless implies that the practice is being outlawed to achieve a desired end-state where conditions associated with the outlawed practice will no longer be evident. If particular practices are to be outlawed as deviations from a norm, then the norm must in-

100. *See, e.g.*, Civil Rights Act of 1964, 42 U.S.C. §§ 2000a to 2000h-16 (1970). Although formally relying on the commerce clause, the legislation was a practical circumvention of the state-action doctrine insofar as it applied to congressional legislative authority and has been so recognized in more candid later opinions. *Compare* Katzenbach v. McClung, 379 U.S. 294 (1964), *with* Fitzpatrick v. Bitzer, 427 U.S. 445, 453 n.9 (1976).

101. *See, e.g.*, Jones v. Alfred H. Mayer Co., 392 U.S. 409 (1968) (Congress can outlaw private discrimination under the thirteenth amendment, which has no state-action limitation); United States v. Guest, 383 U.S. 745 (1966) (six Justices agreeing that Congress has the power under section 5 of the fourteenth amendment to reach private conspiracies to deprive persons of civil rights); Burton v. Wilmington Parking Auth., 365 U.S. 715 (1961) (state involvement transforms private into public conduct).

102. *See, e.g.*, Moose Lodge No. 107 v. Irvis, 407 U.S. 163 (1972); Civil Rights Act of 1964 § 201(e), 42 U.S.C. § 2000a(e) (1970) (private club exemption from public accommodations statute).

103. *See generally* Wasserstrom, *supra* note 8, at 585-86.

clude within it a vision of society where there would not be such deviations. It should then be possible to test current conditions against the desired end-state to decide whether progress is being made. The end-state usually associated with antidiscrimination law is some version of the "integrated society."[104] This ambiguous phrase, however, contains within it a number of possibilities as to the content of the end-state, the extent to which it has already been achieved, and in whose interest it is to achieve it.

The most complete version of the integrated society can be found in the science-fiction story where it is the year 2200 and everybody is a creamy shade of beige.[105] Race has not only become irrelevant, it has disappeared altogether under the guiding hand of genetic entropy. A second and slightly less extreme version of the utopia posits a society where racial identification is still possible, but no longer relevant to anyone's thinking or generalizations about anyone else. In this world of racial irrelevance, the sensory data employed in making a racial identification would still be available, but would have returned to the domain of other similar human identification data in such a way as to obliterate the cultural concept of race. Race would have become functionally equivalent to eye-color in contemporary society. In a third version of the integrated society, racial identification persists as a cultural unifying force for each group, equivalent to an idealized model of religious tolerance.[106] Each group respects the diverse character of every other group, and there are no patterns of domination or oppression between different groups.

Each of these visions of the future reflects the achievement of a casteless, if not classless, society in which there is no hierarchy of status that corresponds with racial identification. The essential defect in the color-blind theory of racial discrimination is that it presupposes the attainment of one of these futures. It is a doctrine that at the same time declares racial characteristics irrelevant and prevents any affirmative steps to achieve the condition of racial irrelevance. The freedom of association theory, to the extent it is antidiscrimination at all, also presupposes an already existing future, but it is the tolerance model that it contemplates.

These theories are not alone in presupposing the goal that one is supposedly working toward. Suppose one were to visit the future

104. *See id.* at 603-15. Although I stress different aspects of the "future society" concept, I gained much insight from and acknowledge a debt to Richard Wasserstrom for his clarification of the similar dichotomy between "social reality" and "ideal."

105. *See, e.g.*, Brown & Reynolds, *Dark Interlude*, in NIGHTMARES AND GEEZENSTACKS 74 (paperback ed. 1961) (male unirace visitor from the future travels to the South of the 1950's, marries a white woman, and is subsequently murdered by the woman's father after revealing his mixed racial background).

106. *See* Wasserstrom, *supra* note 8, at 604-05.

society of racial irrelevance and discover conditions that in any other society might be regarded as corresponding with a pattern of racial discrimination. Among such conditions might be that one race seems to have a hugely disproportionate share of the worst houses, the most demeaning jobs, and the least control over societal resources. For such conditions to be fair and accepted as legitimate by the disfavored race in future society, they would have to be perceived as produced by accidental, impartial, or neutral phenomena utterly disassociated from any racist practice. Otherwise the future society would fail to meet its claim of racial irrelevance and would not be a future society at all.

Any theory of antidiscrimination law that legitimizes as nondiscriminatory substantial disproportionate burdens borne by one race is effectively claiming that its distributional rules are already the ones that would exist in future society. From the perspective of a victim in present society, where plenty of explicitly racist practices prevail, the predictable and legitimate demand is that those ostensibly neutral rules demonstrate themselves to be the ones that would in fact exist in future society. The legitimacy of the demand is underscored by the fact that those very rules appealed to by the beneficiaries to legitimize the conditions of the victims were created by and are maintained by the dominant race. From the perpetrator perspective, however, those practices not conceded to be racist are held constant; they are presumed consistent with the ethics of future society, and the victims are asked to prove that such is not the case. This is a core difference between the victim and perpetrator perspectives.

A vision of the future also bears on the question of whom attainment of the integrated society benefits. To introduce this issue more precisely, one might ask whether the integrated society is an end in itself, or just a symbolic measure of the actual liberation of an oppressed racial group from the conditions of oppression. To say that the integrated society is an end in itself, apart from the interest of the oppressed group in its own liberation, is basically to say that the goal is in the interest of society at large, or in the interest of the dominant group as well as the oppressed one. It is hardly controversial to contend that integration is for everyone's benefit, or even that it is in some sense for the benefit of the dominant group.[107] Problems arise when interests diverge and the dominant group's desire for integration supersedes the victim group's demand for relief.

Although rarely litigated, this issue did arise in *Otero v. New York City Housing Authority.*[108] The Second Circuit there upheld in

107. *See, e.g.*, Trafficante v. Metropolitan Life Ins. Co., 409 U.S. 205 (1972); *cf.* HEGEL, THE PHENOMENOLOGY OF MIND 228-40 (paperback ed. J. Baillie trans. 1967) (1st ed. Bamberg 1807) (lordship and bondage).

108. 484 F.2d 1122 (2d Cir. 1973).

principle the notion of a benign "integration quota" to be imposed on black residents of a housing project so as to limit their numbers.[109] The purpose of such a quota is to keep the number of black people below the level where, according to social scientists, a "tipping point" will be reached where the white majority, presumably motivated by racism, will leave the area.[110] The net result of this approach is both to keep the black group as a small minority witin the project and to deny the benefit to blacks otherwise eligible for it, all for the sake of producing an "integrated result." In such a situation, it is really unclear whose interests the integrated result serves.

The potential conflict of interest raised by the "integration quota" problem is a powerful metaphor for some of the deeper problems of antidiscrimination law. Such a quota admits a token number of black people to a more desirable condition of existence, thereby illustrating progress toward the integrated society, while making sure they remain outnumbered by the whites so as to be powerless and nonthreatening. And at the same time the deprivation imposed on those blacks who are denied admission is rationalized as being in everybody's interest since an integrated society is the goal to be attained.

C. Post-*Brown* Developments

The remainder of the era of uncertainty offered almost no occasions for resolving any of the ambiguities of *Brown* or exposing the difference between the perpetrator and victim perspectives. Instead, the major task for that era, which put off the question of remedy,[111] was to increase the list of perpetrators against whom antidiscrimination law might be directed. This was accomplished largely through the systematic demolition of the state-action doctrine, a process involving liberal interpretation,[112] partial abolition,[113] judicial[114] and leg-

109. *See id.* at 1134-36.

110. On the subject of "tipping points," see Ackerman, *Integration for Subsidized Housing and the Question of Racial Occupancy Controls*, 26 Stan. L. Rev. 245, 254-60 (1974).

111. *See* Brown v. Board of Educ., 349 U.S. 294, 300-01 (1955).

112. *See, e.g.*, Reitman v. Mulkey, 387 U.S. 369, 376-77 (1969); Griffin v. Maryland, 378 U.S. 130, 133, 136-37 (1964); Burton v. Wilmington Parking Auth., 365 U.S. 715, 723-24 (1961).

113. *See* United States v. Guest, 383 U.S. 745 (1966) (six Justices agreeing that Congress had power under the fourteenth amendment to reach private conspiracies that interfere with constitutional rights).

114. Griffin v. Breckinridge, 403 U.S. 88, 105-07 (1971) (no need to reach state-action issue because the alleged and arguably private violation trenched on the constitutional right to travel); Jones v. Alfred H. Mayer Co., 392 U.S. 409, 438-44 (1968) (no need to reach state-action issue because the private violation was within the purview of congressional power under thirteenth amendment).

islative circumvention,[115] and a great deal of human effort.[116]

On one of the few occasions that the Court did have a chance to elaborate on the emerging antidiscrimination principle, it opted for steadfast adherence to the perpetrator perspective. In *Swain v. Alabama*,[117] a black man in Talladega County, Alabama, who had been convicted of rape and sentenced to death, brought to the Supreme Court a claim of jury discrimination.[118] He offered three facts in support of this claim: first, that while blacks accounted for 26% of the relevant local population, only ten to fifteen percent of the grand and petit jury panels had been black since 1953; second, that in the immediate prosecution, the prosecutor had used his peremptory challenges to exclude all blacks from the jury that tried the defendant; and, third, that no black had ever served on an actual petit jury in a civil or criminal case in the county.

The Supreme Court denied the claim, rationalizing all three facts into irrelevance and invoking much of the doctrine associated with the perpetrator perspective. The Court began by acknowledging that purposeful exclusion of blacks from juries had been unconstitutional since *Strauder v. West Virginia*[119] had been decided in 1880, but then reminded the defendant that "purposeful discrimination may not be assumed or merely asserted. . . . It must be proven . . . ."[120] As for the statistical disparity, the Court concluded: "We cannot say that purposeful discrimination based on race alone is satisfactorily proved by showing that an identifiable group in a community is underrepresented by as much as 10%."[121] Why not? Was it a matter of mere accident or random factors? Perhaps that would be the case in the future color-blind society, but this was Alabama in the 1950's and 1960's.[122]

With respect to the peremptory challenges, the Court found

115. Congressional utilization of the commerce clause power to reach private discriminatory acts was upheld in Katzenbach v. McClung, 379 U.S. 294 (1964), and Heart of Atlanta Motel, Inc. v. United States, 379 U.S. 241 (1964).

> [T]he action of the Congress in the adoption of the [Civil Rights] Act [of 1964] as applied here to a motel which concededly serves interstate travelers is within the power granted it by the Commerce Clause of the Constitution . . . . It may be argued that Congress could have pursued other methods to eliminate the obstructions it found in interstate commerce caused by racial discrimination. But this is a matter of policy . . . .

Id. at 261.

116. *See, e.g.*, 2 T. Emerson, D. Haber, & N. Dorsen, Political and Civil Rights in the United States (1967); R. Kluger, *supra* note 81.

117. 380 U.S. 202 (1965).

118. *See id.* at 203, 205, 210, 222-23.

119. 100 U.S. 303 (1880).

120. 380 U.S. at 205 (citations omitted).

121. *Id.* at 208-09.

122. *See id.* at 203, 205.

merit in Alabama's contention that the practice "affords a suitable and necessary method of securing juries which in fact and in the opinion of the parties are fair and impartial."[123] Again adopting the perspective of future society, the Court justified the actual results of the peremptory challenges in the case before it by deeming those results the product of a fair, neutral, and impartial system of selection. And in typical fashion the Court dragged out the color-blind theory to support this conclusion, approving Alabama's position that "[t]his system, it is said, in and of itself, provides justification for striking any group of otherwise qualified jurors in any given case, whether they be Negroes, Catholics, accountants or those with blue eyes."[124]

On the final claim that no black had ever served on a petit jury in the county, the Court invoked the principle of causation, reasoning that while such proof might support a prima facie case that "the peremptory system is being used to deny the Negro the same right and opportunity to participate in the administration of justice enjoyed by the white population,"[125] in this case the mere fact that no blacks had served on juries was not a prima facie case of anything since there was no showing that the result was directly attributable to the peremptory system.[126]

Thus an affirmative claim for representation directed against a *system* that was obviously denying that representation was neatly transformed into a burdensome and elusive hunt for the particular villains within that system who were "causing" the result. Necessarily, the Court ignored the results of the system and presumed, despite the obvious fact that blacks were not represented, that the system was operating impartially. To answer what was the core of the defendant's claim—that regardless of causes, it was the results that were the problem—the Court again appealed to the color-blind theory:

> But a defendant in a criminal case is not constitutionally entitled to demand a proportionate number of his race on the jury which tries him nor on the venire of jury roll from which petit jurors are drawn. . . . "Obviously the number of races and nationalities appearing in the ancestry of our citizens would make it impossible to meet a requirement of proportional representation."[127]

---

123. *Id.* at 212.

124. *Id.* at 211-12.

125. *Id.* at 224.

126. *See id.*

127. *Id.* at 208 (citations omitted) (quoting Cassell v. Texas, 339 U.S. 282, 286-87 (1950)). On the issue of proportional participation, see Hughes v. Superior Court, 339 U.S. 460 (1950).

Swain points up a deep contradiction in antidiscrimination law that sees no absurdity in legitimizing the precise result that would occur under the regime of de jure exclusion struck down in *Strauder*. Strict adherence to the perpetrator form makes results irrelevant; a concern with results violates the form. For a time, in the next era of antidiscrimination law, the Court violated the form, while pretending not to, to produce some results. In the third and present era, the Court returns to strict adherence, pretending never to have deviated from it, while pretending to have produced some results in the interim.

III. 1965-1974: THE ERA OF CONTRADICTION, OR THE JURISPRUDENCE OF REMEDY

A. An Overview

A growing tension between the concepts of violation and remedy characterized the second era of modern antidiscrimination law. While the form of the law, with one possible exception,[128] remained squarely within the perpetrator perspective, its content began to create expectations associated with the victim perspective. The perpetrator perspective remained the basic model for a violation, without which there could be no occasion for remedy. Given that finding, however, remedial doctrine took over and, in so doing, subtly changed the concept of violation by addressing itself to substantive conditions beyond the scope of the original violation.

One kind of case that gave rise to this development might be termed the "infinite series" problem. Suppose a jurisdiction that had previously been nearly all white in population experienced a sudden wave of black migration into the area, to the point where its population became sixty percent white and forty percent black. Suppose further that, in response to this population change, the jurisdiction redistricted its legislative body so that each of its ten districts had a population that was sixty percent white and forty percent black.[129] Even under the perpetrator perspective, this action would clearly violate an antidiscrimination principle, whether on the basis of evidence of purposeful racial exclusion or simply on the basis of an effect explicable only in terms of discriminatory purpose. Thus we have a

128. *See* Griggs v. Duke Power Co., 401 U.S. 424 (1971), *discussed at* notes 183-203 *infra* and accompanying text. The Court has since moved to contain and weaken *Griggs*. *See* notes 271-98 *infra* and accompanying text.

129. *Cf.* Gomillion v. Lightfoot, 364 U.S. 339, 341 (1960) ("Prior to Act 140 the City of Tuskegee was square in shape; the Act transformed it into a strangely irregular twenty-eight-sided figure . . . . The . . . inevitable effect . . . is to remove from the city all save four or five of its 400 Negro voters while not removing a single white voter or resident.").

traditional "violation." Because the perpetrator perspective refuses to recognize any claims of racial proportionality or for relief from the plain fact of political powerlessness, however, all that can be done with a violation of the type described is to call it one and declare the reapportionment invalid.

Now suppose that the same jurisdiction, perhaps because required by local law,[130] again redistricts, this time coming up with a plan that calls for one district that is 100% black and nine districts that are two-thirds white and one-third black. If there is evidence of purposeful discrimination,[131] a court could again declare the practice a violation and send it back again in the hopes that a clean version of the plan will reappear without any evidence of "purpose." If there is no evidence of purpose, however, how do we decide if the plan itself gives rise to an inference of purposeful discrimination? The perpetrator perspective is powerless. To decide whether the second plan is discriminatory requires a comparison of that plan with a hypothetical state of affairs in a community where race is irrelevant. But that comparison is impossible as an abstract matter since, in a community where race was really irrelevant, neither of the plans described would seem odd; there would be no perceived relationship between race and political power.

In a community where race is relevant, however, the second plan must be compared with a scheme that produces racial proportionality, even if this is done only for the limited purpose of deciding whether the second plan is a violation or not. At the moment when the *condition* of racial political power, with its implicit affirmative claim for such power, becomes relevant, the victim perspective enters into the analysis. Without taking the victim perspective into account, there can never be, in this kind of case, either a finding of violation absent explicit evidence of purpose or any remedy for either the initial or any subsequent violation. But once the question of racial political power becomes relevant in a community that once committed a traditional "violation," it is difficult to see why it is not equally relevant in a community where, although no specific violation has been found, race is relevant, and there is extensive racial discrimination in all areas of life. At this point, what arose as remedy in one

130. *See, e.g.*, Beer v. United States, 425 U.S. 130, 134 (1976), *discussed at* notes 224-35 *infra* and accompanying text.

131. Purposeful discrimination, of course, means something more than either motive on the part of some decisionmakers or one of several explanations for the action. *See* Village of Arlington Heights v. Metropolitan Hous. Dev. Corp., 429 U.S. 252, 265-66 (1977); City of Richmond v. United States, 422 U.S. 358, 373-74 (1975); Palmer v. Thompson, 403 U.S. 217, 224-26 (1971). *See generally* Brest, Palmer v. Thompson: *An Approach to the Problem of Unconstitutional Legislative Motive,* 1971 SUP. CT. REV. 95.

case threatens to define violation in another, unless the new community can be so severed from the society in which both communities exist as to be hurled by semantic fiat into the future society described earlier.

A second kind of problem case is the "no results" situation. Suppose that for many years a community maintained a blatant de jure system of school segregation by race that was finally declared unconstitutional. Further suppose that despite the ruling of unconstitutionality, no remedial efforts occurred or were required for a number of years, with the result that when those efforts were finally undertaken, the resultant school system looked like one that was still substantially segregated. Why? Because the new basis of school assignment, neighborhood, for example, while itself not a manifestation of discriminatory purpose, nevertheless amplified an existing pattern of pervasive discrimination.

The problem here is embarrassment; it is difficult to call these schools "desegregated" because there has been substantially no change since the era of explicit segregation. To cover the embarrassment requires some integrated schools even though, under the perpetrator perspective, there is no affirmative right to have such schools, nor is it the condition of segregation, as opposed to the practice, that is the violation. By going after the conditions, ostensibly to remedy the original violation, the victim perspective is incorporated, and one wonders whether the very same conditions are equally remediable elsewhere regardless of the remote presence of a no longer existent violation.

A third example is the case of the ostensibly neutral and rational practice. Suppose an employer who for years simply refused to hire any black workers at all suddenly, in response to recently enacted antidiscrimination law, adopts an aptitude test for prospective employees that just happens to exclude all black applicants.[132] There is an inescapable inference that the employer is trying to do implicitly what can no longer be done explicitly, but there is no plausible evidentiary link between the prior *practice* and the current one. If one wants either to remedy what looks like a continuation of the earlier violation or avoid the no results dilemma, the neutral practice must be the target of inquiry. At that point, however, the analysis again shifts to the victim perspective, demanding that neutral practices producing conditions of discrimination at the very least justify themselves in terms of their own claims to rationality. Here again the plausible contention arises that the very same practices, as well as a lot of similar ones, should be required to justify themselves wherever they appear.

132. *See* Griggs v. Duke Power Co., 401 U.S. 424, 427-28 (1971).

The patterns illustrated by these typical cases, occurring either singly or in combination, are characteristic of the era of contradiction. The following sections will describe the appearance and operation of these patterns in three substantive areas: voting, education, and employment.

B. Voting

It is not surprising that the contradictions of the perpetrator perspective first began to appear in the area of voting rights. Voting had already passed through the era of merely identifying violations, beginning with the fifteenth amendment itself, which brought racial discrimination in voting explicitly within the perpetrator principle.[133] Although the Court had punctuated its efforts with enormous timelags, it had occasionally even struck down particular practices as unconstitutional.[134] But none of these efforts had resulted in any significant participation of black voters in twentieth-century Southern political life.[135] While a massive litigation offensive persisted well into the 1960's, it was met by continuing frustrations of the "infinite series" variety, which in turn produced a serious "no results" problem.[136] Thus, for voting, something more than repeated outlawry of particular practices was needed if the fifteenth amendment was ever to make any practical difference.

Voting was a sensible starting place for other reasons as well. Lack of results in voting rights has a particularly noxious symbolic effect, given the key role of political participation in sustaining the form of liberal democracy. To deny a substantial racial minority the

133. Section 1. The right of citizens of the United States to vote shall not be denied or abridged by the United States or by any State on account of race, colbr, or previous condition of servitude.

> Section 2. The Congress shall have power to enforce this article by appropriate legislation.

U.S. Const. amend. XV.

134. *See, e.g.*, Louisiana v. United States, 380 U.S. 145, 149-50, 153 (1965) (holding unconstitutional a voting registration device that required the applicant to give a reasonable interpretation of any section of the state or federal constitution read to her or him by the registrar and that had been used to deprive otherwise qualified blacks of the right to vote); Terry v. Adams, 345 U.S. 461, 462, 470 (1953) (holding unconstitutional a private primary election that excluded black voters); Smith v. Allwright, 321 U.S. 634, 656-57, 664 (1944) (holding unconstitutional a state-run primary election where the Democratic party was allowed to exclude black voters); Lane v. Wilson, 307 U.S. 268, 271, 275 (1939) (holding unconstitutional an Oklahoma voter registration scheme that inordinately burdened potential black voters by providing a grandfather clause to protect previously registered white voters while offering a sixty-day, one-time-only chance for otherwise qualified voters to register).

135. *See, e.g.*, U.S. Comm'n on Civil Rights, Voting in Mississippi (1965).

136. *See* South Carolina v. Katzenbach, 383 U.S. 301 (1966); United States v. Duke, 332 F.2d 759 (5th Cir. 1964).

right to vote is, whatever the rationalizations offered to support it,[137] a failure to offer even formal, much less substantive, equality. The conferral of voting rights is not only symbolically useful, but it need not impose any serious systemic costs, since voting will only make a difference, if at all, when translated into effective political power.

Confronted with a massive record of systematic deprivations of the right to vote and the apparent inability of the courts to remedy the problem by outlawing specific practices, Congress chose to make the operative provisions of the Voting Rights Act of 1965[138] depend on the presence of *conditions*, which, though suggestive of actual violations, were not in themselves violations or even causally linked to violations through any process of proof.[139] Thus the basic triggering provisions of the Act depended only on the litigation-proof facts of nonparticipation, or nonregistration, in a presidential election,[140] plus the existence of a "test or device," broadly defined.[141] The second-level triggering provisions leading to the employment of federal registrars similarly depended on straightforward conclusive administrative facts.[142] Thus, however much the intent of the Act was just remedial in the sense of finally dealing with those years of actual violations,[143] the effect of the Act was to create an affirmative right to vote, with the functional violation being the conditions associated with the absence of that right.

Once the affirmative right to vote had been conferred on the vast numbers of previously disenfranchised black people,[144] section 5 of the Act[145] became the most important provision. Under section 5, a triggered jurisdiction must demonstrate that any proposed change in voting practice or procedure will not have the purpose or effect of

137. For example, in Lassiter v. Northampton County Bd. of Elections, 360 U.S. 45, 53 (1959), the Supreme Court upheld the use of a literacy test as a voter registration device. The Court ignored the commonly known fact that such tests were used to exclude black voters: "[T]he ability to read and write likewise has some relation to standards designed to promote intelligent use of the ballot. Literacy and illiteracy are neutral on race, creed, color, and sex . . . ." *Id.* at 51.

138. Pub. L. No. 89-110, §§ 2-19, 79 Stat. 437 (current version at 42 U.S.C. §§ 1973-1973p (Supp. V 1975)).

139. *See id.* § 4 (current version at 42 U.S.C. § 1973b (Supp. V 1975)), *construed in* South Carolina v. Katzenbach, 383 U.S. 301, 327-28 (1966).

140. *See* Voting Rights Act of 1965, Pub. L. No. 89-110, § 4(b), 79 Stat. 437 (current version at 42 U.S.C. § 1973b(b) (Supp. V 1975)).

141. *See id.* § 4(c) (current version at 42 U.S.C. § 1973b(c) (Supp. V 1975)).

142. *See id.* §§ 3, 6 (current version at 42 U.S.C. §§ 1973a, 1973d (Supp. V 1975)).

143. *See* South Carolina v. Katzenbach, 383 U.S. 301, 309 (1966).

144. *See* U.S. COMM'N ON CIVIL RIGHTS, THE VOTING RIGHTS ACT: TEN YEARS LATER (1975).

145. Voting Rights Act of 1965, Pub. L. No. 89-110, § 5, 79 Stat. 437 (current version at 42 U.S.C. § 1973c (Supp. V 1975)).

discriminating on the basis of race or color with respect to voting.[146] In the remedial scheme of the Act, this provision made sense as a way of preventing future violations, since jurisdictions so inclined might otherwise creatively manipulate their voting laws to leave black voters formally enfranchised but practically disenfranchised.[147] Without section 5, endless litigation of the "infinite series" variety might have resulted.

A jurisdiction can effectively neutralize the political power of its black voters by altering its geographic boundaries to change the overall racial composition, by switching from ward to at-large systems to decrease minority power, or simply by gerrymandering districts to maximize the political strength of the white population. The Supreme Court itself had deemed an extreme version of the latter to be a constitutional violation in *Gomillion v. Lightfoot,*[148] decided prior to the enactment of the Voting Rights Act. To have said that section 5 did not apply to these practices would have been to invite their use to achieve renewed discrimination. Thus the Court, even from within the confines of the perpetrator principle, had no choice but to bring all of these practices under the application of section 5.[149]

By bringing geographic manipulation under substantive scrutiny, the Court was compelled to consider explicit issues of racial proportionality in political power. But since the perpetrator perspective, under the guiding influence of the color-blind theory, is indifferent to affirmative claims for racial political power,[150] it was difficult

146. *See id.*

147. *See, e.g.*, Georgia v. United States, 411 U.S. 526 (1973); Perkins v. Matthews, 400 U.S. 379 (1971); Allen v. State Bd. of Elections, 393 U.S. 544 (1969).

148. 364 U.S. 339 (1960).

149. *See, e.g.*, Beer v. United States, 425 U.S. 130 (1976); City of Richmond v. United States, 422 U.S. 358 (1975); Georgia v. United States, 411 U.S. 526 (1973); Perkins v. Matthews, 400 U.S. 379 (1971); Allen v. State Bd. of Elections, 393 U.S. 544 (1969).

150. *See* Whitcomb v. Chavis, 403 U.S. 124, 163 (1971), *rev'g* 305 F. Supp. 1364 (S.D. Ind. 1969).

> The District Court's holding, although on the facts of this case limited to guaranteeing one racial group representation, is not easily contained. It is expressive of the more general proposition that any group with distinctive interests must be represented in legislative halls if it is numerous enough to command at least one seat and represents a majority living in an area sufficiently compact to constitute a single-member district. This approach would make it difficult to reject claims of Democrats, Republicans, or members of any political organization in Marion County who live in what would be safe districts in a single-member district system but who in one year or another, or year after year, are submerged in a one-sided multi-member district vote. There are also union oriented workers, the university community, religious or ethnic groups occupying identifiable areas of our heterogeneous cities and urban areas. Indeed, it would be difficult for a great many, if not most,

to ascertain the substantive validity of such practices. These difficulties became evident in *City of Richmond v. United States,*[151] the Court's first substantive confrontation with geographic manipulation under section 5. The case dealt with the racial impact of Richmond's annexation of a large, predominantly white, suburban area. On that issue, the Court simultaneously applied section 5 to an annexation and made section 5 inapplicable to annexations. In fact, with respect to the annexation issue, the decision is more typical of the third "era," to be discussed below. The importance of *Richmond* for the present discussion, however, is that while legitimizing annexation as a means of diluting minority voting strength, the Court implied a right to proportional political power within any given geographical unit of government.

The only useful sense in which an annexation of territory may be evaluated with respect to its discriminatory impact is in terms of the racial population mix before and after annexation, since all the annexation itself does is add people and territory to an existing jurisdiction. To say that section 5 applies to an annexation, then, would seem to imply an inquiry into the percentage population of the minority race in the expanded jurisdiction to see whether its political power has been diluted. *Richmond*, for example, involved the annexation of 23 square miles of territory with a population of 45,705 whites and 1,557 blacks, which changed the racial mix of the entire city from 52% black and 48% white to 42% black and 58% white.[152] If the annexation were tested as to discriminatory *impact,* it would seem to present a clear violation, since a black majority had been transformed into a black minority. The Court avoided that conclusion only by confusing the issue of the annexation's discriminatory impact with the separate issue of the validity of an at-large system of representation. Thus the Court held that the relegation of the black population to minority political status was not a discriminatory "effect" within the meaning of section 5.[153] This is the sense in which the Court nullified the application of section 5 to annexations, since if the change in racial percentage from majority to minority is not discrimination, then the annexation itself becomes immune from scrutiny on that ground.

At the same time, the Court did require Richmond to switch from at-large representation to a ward system, but regarded as sufficient a plan that gave the black population majorities in four of the

---

multi-member districts to survive analysis under the District Court's view

. . . .

Id. at 156 (footnotes omitted).

151. 422 U.S. 358 (1975).

152. *See id.* at 363.

153. *See id.* at 371.

nine council districts, rejecting a request for control of five districts.[154] Thus, while upholding the basic political effect of the annexation, the reassertion of white political control, the Court guaranteed the black minority a proportional share of political power in the expanded community.[155] That decision would seem to create, despite the perpetrator perspective, an affirmative expectation that the antidiscrimination principle applicable to voting implies a right to proportional political power. That expectation arises quickly if one makes three plausible assumptions about the *Richmond* decision.

The first assumption is that the issue of at-large versus ward representation is separable from the question of annexation. If, as the Court said, an annexation is valid notwithstanding its reversal of majority power, then unless there is a right to proportional representation, it should make no difference whether the black minority can command control of four seats or none in the expanded community. Since the Court required the four-seat guarantee, it thus becomes difficult to differentiate the case of annexation from a case where geography has remained constant but the black community is underrepresented because of gerrymandering or use of at-large representation with a white majority. In all three situations, the evil is precisely the same—underrepresentation of the black community. The cases can only be distinguished by the rather embarrassing "principle" that a black community has a right to be paid off with proportional power if forced to submit to an annexation that dilutes its power, but has no such right if its power is effectively minimized without a boundary change.

The second assumption is that, apart from the question of burden of proof,[156] the standard mandated by section 5—that the particular practice "not have the purpose [or] . . . effect of denying or abridging the right to vote on account of race or color"[157]—is substan-

154. *See id.* at 371-72.

155. *Cf.* City of Petersburg v. United States, 410 U.S. 962, *aff'g mem.* 354 F. Supp. 1021 (D.D.C. 1973) (effect of annexation on black voting power in at-large voting districts). The trial court acceded to the annexation, as was done in *Richmond,* but stated,

> [T]his annexation, insofar as it is a mere boundary change and not an expansion of an at-large system, is not the kind of discriminatory change which Congress sought to prevent; but . . . this annexation can be approved only on the condition that modifications calculated to neutralize to the extent possible any adverse effect upon the political participation of black voters are adopted, i.e., that the [City] shift from an at-large to a ward system of electing its city councilmen.

354 F. Supp. at 1031.

156. Section 5 imposed the burden of proof on the political subdivision seeking to have the practice validated. *See* Voting Rights Act of 1965, Pub. L. No. 89-110, § 5, 79 Stat. 437 (current version at 42 U.S.C. § 1973c (Supp. V 1975)).

157. *Id.*

tively identical to the standard set by the Constitution with respect to the same practice. Under this assumption, the only difference in a jurisdiction not subject to section 5 would be that instead of being able to rely on preclearance review to test the substantive issue, an aggrieved person would have to commence litigation to challenge the practice. And a showing of substantial underrepresentation would presumably be sufficient to make out a prima facie case of discrimination.

The assumption that the standards are the same is rooted in the absence of any rational reason for their being different. Whatever its worth, semantic scrutiny yields no significant difference.[158] Nor does the distinction between remedy and violation suggest a difference if, as common sense would dictate, the notion of remedy refers to the mandatory review part of section 5 rather than its substantive content. The original violation that triggered application of the Voting Rights Act provides little explanatory help, since that violation was merely the occasion for invoking the Act, and there is no pretense of any causal linkage between the practice reviewed under section 5 and the original triggering conditions. To apply different standards would make sense only if it could be said that the kinds of communities subject to section 5 are really ones where race is perceived as more relevant or significant than in those not subject to the statute. The argument would be that even if section 5 creates a right to proportional representation, that right does not pertain in American communities not subject to that law, because in such communities substantial black underrepresentation is hardly indicative of anything. Here again, the argument is essentially that future society already exists, that race is irrelevant. That argument again amounts to no more than a denial of reality.

The third assumption about the *Richmond* opinion, which merely reinforces the other two, is that the Court itself recognized a claim of proportionality not only in what it did, but also in what it said. In rejecting the black community's request for control of five seats in the larger community, the Court said that it could not approve a "requirement that the city allocate to the Negro community in the larger city the voting power or the seats on the city council in excess of its proportion in the new community and thus permanently to underrepresent other elements in the community."[159] The Court's own use of the word "underrepresent" as applied to the white major-

158. Section 5 addresses itself to practices whose "purpose" or "effect" is "denying or abridging the right to vote on account of race or color." *Id.* The fifteenth amendment provides that the right to vote "shall not be denied or abridged on account of race, color, or previous condition of servitude." U.S. CONST. amend. XV.

159. 422 U.S. at 373.

ity implies an expectation of racial proportionality and speaks to a world where race is very relevant to political representation. In the color-blind world, a racial group, black or white, could not be regarded as underrepresented. And as a matter of pure gerrymandering, the enlarged Richmond with its population of 58% white and 42% black, could be districted so as to give as many as seven seats to the black community or as few as none. The color-blind world would be indifferent to either extreme. But the *Richmond* opinion is concerned about white underrepresentation, a concern that is inconsistent with the color-blind model. If the concept of racial underrepresentation is applicable at all, it should be equally applicable to the black community, which should also be able to claim at least proportional representation. But the Court's comment has today become more than a little ironic,[160] since the solicitous concern expressed for the almost-beleaguered white citizens of "greater" Richmond has hardly given rise to a similar concern for claims of black citizens anywhere.[161]

C. Education Prior to *Swann*[162]

For education, the era of contradiction begins with the Supreme Court's decision in *Griffin v. County School Board.*[163] In *Griffin*, the Court faced a thorough and continuous pattern of resistance to its decision in *Brown I.* To avoid compliance with the Court's desegregation mandate, Prince Edward County had closed its schools and facilitated the operation of private segregated schools through a combination of state and local financial aid. The facts of the case make clear that the county intended to maintain a segregated system of public education, attempting to insulate the program from constitutional scrutiny by disguising it in an ostensibly private form. From within the safe confines of the perpetrator perspective, the Court could have simply told the county and state to stop facilitating or supporting segregated public education.[164] Instead, perhaps motivated by the county's recalcitrance, the Court went a step further and told the district court that it "may, if necessary to prevent further racial

160. The Court's concern that the white community might be underrepresented also seems more than a bit racist, especially in light of its indifference, one year later, to a far more severe underrepresentation of blacks. *See* Beer v. United States, 425 U.S. 130 (1976), *discussed at* notes 224-35 *infra* and accompanying text.

161. *See* notes 224-35 *infra* and accompanying text.

162. Swann v. Charlotte-Mecklenburg Bd. of Educ., 402 U.S. 1 (1970). I am greatly indebted to Owen Fiss for the careful and persuasive analysis of *Green, Monroe, Swann, Keyes,* and *Milliken I, discussed at* notes 204-14 & 242-55 *infra* and accompanying text, which he offered in Fiss, *School Desegregation: The Uncertain Path of the Law*, 4 Philosophy & Pub. Aff. 3, 15-35 (1974).

163. 377 U.S. 218 (1964).

164. *See, e.g.*, Norwood v. Harrison, 413 U.S. 455, 463-64 (1973).

discrimination, require the supervisors to exercise the power that is theirs to levy taxes to raise funds adequate to reopen, operate, and maintain without racial discrimination a public school system in Prince Edward County like that operated in other counties in Virginia."[165]

There is a narrow explanation of this curious sentence that is consistent with the perpetrator perspective. The Court might have been saying by way of unstated assumption that so long as public schools remained open throughout the rest of Virginia, any system of private segregated schools in one county would probably be so infected with governmental involvement as to be deemed tantamount to public segregated schools. On this view, to avoid protracted litigation of the infinite series variety with respect to successive forms of "private" segregation, the Court was merely declaring in advance that all such systems would be invalid. While as a logical matter the county could cleanse itself of any violation by having no education whatsoever, either public or private, the Court somehow knew that this alternative would never be chosen and therefore told the county to reopen its public schools.

The sentence nevertheless subtly offered two promises to the black community of Prince Edward County. These promises may be regarded as more or less disingenuous to the extent one ascribes to the Court a secret reason for the sentence, but the promises are there. One is an affirmative right not only to an education, but to an education comparable to that offered throughout Virginia. This view would regard *Griffin* as partially adopting the "equality of educational opportunity" view of *Brown I*,[166] and recognizing that what is important, from the victim's perspective, is not so much whether the violation has been cured but whether the right results are being obtained. The second promise goes to the specifically racial dimension of that education. The Court had not yet suggested, as of 1965, what it might mean to "maintain without racial discrimination a public school system," but the second promise was that whatever that phrase came to mean, the black students of Prince Edward County had an affirmative claim measured by its content.[167] Later cases began to pro-

165. 377 U.S. at 233.

166. *See* notes 79-89 *supra* and accompanying text.

167. *Griffin* can be read to stress purpose more than effect—that a state that has chosen to provide public education cannot cease to provide such services if motivated by hostility to integration, even if, absent such hostility, the services could be terminated. But Palmer v. Thompson, 403 U.S. 217 (1971), casts some doubt on this theory. In *Palmer* it was held that the closing of all municipal swimming pools in the face of an integration order did not violate the constitutional rights of the black plaintiffs. *See id.* at 218-19, 227. At least one commentator has concluded that *Palmer* is inconsistent with *Griffin* in that *Palmer* failed to consider the obvious racist implications of the withdrawal of the service. *See* Brest, *supra* note 17, at 27.

vide that content.

In 1968, the Court decided two cases that began to set standards for the achievement of desegregation and in so doing further widened the gap between the perpetrator perspective and remedies for violation of its norm. In *Green v. County School Board*[168] and *Monroe v. Board of Commissioners*,[169] the Court rejected "freedom of choice" as a sufficient remedy for public school segregation. In terms of the perpetrator perspective, *Green* involved the clearer violation of the two since all the school board had done in that case was to superimpose a system of free choice upon its otherwise unchanged system of segregated schools. Thus the board had in no way ceased to operate the same segregated system that it had always operated, and the burden of opting out of that system was placed upon the students and their families.[170] The Court's rejection of this scheme as constituting neither desegregation nor free choice is hardly surprising.

Monroe was more difficult. There the board had established a new system of geographic zoning to replace the old segregated system. But superimposed on the new system was a scheme of free transfers that permitted students to undo the integrated results of the geographic scheme by reestablishing themselves into a racially concentrated pattern. The Court rejected this scheme as well. Among other things, this decision amounted to a repudiation of the freedom of association theory as applied to public education, under which both black and white students would have had a right to choose not to go to school with the students of the other race. In addition, by focusing its attention on the actual racial percentages in the schools operating under the local plan,[171] the Court partially repudiated the color-blind theory, at least within the narrow context of remedies for de jure segregation. Of even more significance, by emphasizing the degree of actual integration,[172] the Court seemed to be shifting toward a victim perspective, concerned with conditions and results rather than merely with the elimination of offensive practices. Moreover, by directing its remedy not only at the behavior of the school board but also at the private behavior of those whites who chose to leave the integrated schools, the Court seemed to be breaking down the dichotomy between state (or other perpetrator-actor) and the rest of society that is so central to the perpetrator perspective.

Narrowly viewed, both *Green* and *Monroe* were nothing more than cases of remedies for traditional violations. But to the extent the

168. 391 U.S. 430 (1968).
169. 391 U.S. 450 (1968).
170. *See* 391 U.S. at 441-42.
171. *See* 391 U.S. at 453-54.
172. *See id.* at 457.

cases are concerned with, and promise to the black students, an actual condition of integration, they suggest that the absence of integration might be just as remediable in a jurisdiction that had not previously been guilty of de jure segregation. Even apart from this implicit suggestion, the cases must at least stand for the proposition that an established violation will not be deemed remedied until integrated results are achieved. Thus the more the concept of violation could be expanded, the wider the range in which explicit demands for integrated results could be asserted.

The gap between violation and remedy became wider the following year with the decision in *Gaston County v. United States*,[173] an ostensible voting rights case that had more to do with school desegregation. Gaston County, North Carolina, had for many years operated a segregated school system in which the black schools were significantly inferior to the white ones. In March 1966, the county was triggered into the provisions of the Voting Rights Act, which suspended the county's use of a literacy test as a prerequisite to voter eligibility.[174] In August 1966, the county sued to reinstate its literacy test under the provision of the Act that said it could do so if it could prove that the test had not been used during the preceding five years " 'for the purpose or with the effect of denying or abridging the right to vote on account of race or color.' "[175] The Court denied the county's request, on the ground that even a neutrally administered literacy test would serve to perpetuate the effects of the inferior schooling received by the black residents of the county, since the undereducated blacks would more likely fail the test. As the Court said, "It is only reasonable to infer that among black children compelled to endure a segregated and inferior education, fewer will achieve any given degree of literacy than will their better-educated white contemporaries."[176]

Gaston County was the first case to present the problem of the "ostensibly neutral practice." The only practice involved in the case that clearly violated the perpetrator perspective's antidiscrimination principle was the segregated school system. By reaching beyond that violation, under the guise of remedy, to refuse to validate the literacy test, the Court set loose a number of implicit propositions inconsistent with the perpetrator perspective. By using "remedial" law to reach an otherwise valid practice not linked with the original violation, the Court implied that even a neutral governmental practice

173. 395 U.S. 285 (1969).

174. *See id.* at 287.

175. *Id.* (quoting Voting Rights Act of 1965, Pub. L. No. 89-110, § 4(a), 79 Stat. 437 (current version at 42 U.S.C. § 1973b(a) (Supp. V 1975))).

176. *Id.* at 295 (footnote omitted).

may become a violation if it serves to perpetuate the effects of some other discriminatory practice. In this connection, it is significant both that literacy tests, unless suspended by the Voting Rights Act, were still regarded as 1969 as valid techniques for assessing voter eligibility[177] and that the *Gaston County* opinion assumed that school segregation had ceased in the county.[178]

Thus in an important sense the perpetrator whose practice is being outlawed—the 1966-1969 county government—is not the same as the perpetrator whose practice violated antidiscrimination law—the earlier county government that ran the segregated schools. If the effect of one discriminator's activity can serve to invalidate the otherwise valid behavior of a distinct entity, the emphasis seems to shift toward scrutiny of conditions associated with discrimination and away from the particular practices that produce the discrimination. This suggestion is underscored by the Court's own footnote reference to the fact that it was irrelevant whether the present residents of Gaston County had gone to its own segregated schools or to segregated schools in other counties, or even other states.[179]

The footnote is also curiously inconsistent with the Court's characterization of the opinion below, which it was affirming, as premised not on the mere fact that Gaston County had operated segregated schools, "but on substantial evidence that the County deprived its black residents of equal educational opportunities."[180] Since the footnote brings within the opinion all black residents of the county, regardless of where they went to school, it would seem that the substantial evidence was actually irrelevant—either all other segregated schools would be presumed to deny equal educational opportunity, or the evidence of actual inequality was not necessary with respect to Gaston County. Since the footnote speaks more to the fact that some black residents of the county may have gone to school elsewhere than does the text, the practical point of the decision seems to be that where an ostensibly neutral practice operates disproportionately against members of a racial group, which group has been the victim of past discriminatory treatment, that neutral practice cannot be validly applied to members of that group. Viewed this way, there is no longer any strict evidentiary requirement of either causation or victim identification and the neutral practice itself becomes the relevant violation.

177. *See* Oregon v. Mitchell, 400 U.S. 112, 132-34 (1970) (Black, J., announcing the judgment of the Court); *id.* at 144-46 (Douglas, J., concurring in part and dissenting in part); *id.* at 231-32 (Brennan, White, and Marshall, JJ., concurring in part and dissenting in part); *id.* at 282-83 (Stewart, J., joined by Burger, C.J., and Blackmun, J., concurring in part and dissenting in part); South Carolina v. Katzenbach, 383 U.S. 301, 329-31 (1966); Lassiter v. Northampton County Bd. of Elections, 360 U.S. 45, 51-53 (1959).

178. *See* 395 U.S. at 296.

179. *See id.* at 293 n.9.

180. *Id.* at 291.

Although the neutral practice—the literacy test—seems to have been the relevant violation in *Gaston County*, in the sense that the practice was deemed illegal because of its likely effect on the black residents of the county, in another important sense the Court did not regard the literacy test as a violation. The opinion in no way challenges the validity of a literacy test as a device for assuring voter qualification: the test is not required to justify itself.[181] Instead, the test is held constant, and the would-be black voters are regarded as unfortunately incompetent to pass it because of the inferior education they have received in the past.

In any neutral practice case, two basic approaches are possible. Given a practice with disproportionate racial impact, one can focus on the practice, asking whether it serves any useful purpose or whether it is itself a manifestation of discrimination. Alternatively one can focus, as the Court in *Gaston County* did, on the victims of the practice, asking whether they are or have become inferior human beings who need to be relieved from the onerous effects of an otherwise valid procedure. The difference between these approaches is crucial to the distinction between the victim and perpetrator perspectives. The latter is just another version of the assumption that future society is already here; its emphasis on compensation for the ill effects of discrete "other violations" can easily be transformed into a case of inaction justified by blaming the victim.[182] The former approach, on the other hand, amounts to a demand that institutions or practices oppressive in their effects justify themselves as legitimate. *Gaston County* took a small step toward the victim perspective by implicating an otherwise neutral practice in a separate violation, but it would take another case before such a practice was made to justify itself.

D. Employment: The *Griggs* Case

Griggs v. Duke Power Co.,[183] the Court's first substantive decision under title VII of the Civil Rights Act of 1964,[184] is as close as the Court has ever come to formally adopting the victim perspective; it is the centerpiece of the era of contradiction. One tribute to its importance is the amount of effort currently being made to repudiate

181. *See* Lassiter v. Northampton County Bd. of Elections, 360 U.S. 45, 53-54 (1959).

182. *See generally* W. Ryan, Blaming the Victim (paperback ed. 1976); *see also* S. Gould, Ever Since Darwin 243-47 (1977); H. Gutman, The Black Family in Slavery and Freedom, 1750-1925, at xvii-xxii (1976).

183. 401 U.S. 424 (1971).

184. Pub. L. No. 88-352, §§ 701-716, 78 Stat. 241 (current version at 42 U.S.C. §§ 2000e to 2000e-15 (Supp. V 1975)).

it.[185] While the actual decision in *Griggs* may be explained in at least two ways that are consistent with the perpetrator principle, the case seems to go beyond that perspective to the extent that it requires neutral practices to justify themselves, radically alters the concept of "intention" in antidiscrimination cases, and implies a demand for results through affirmative action.

The Court posed the issue in *Griggs* as

> whether an employer is prohibited by the Civil Rights Act of 1964, Title VII, from requiring a high school education or passing of a standardized general intelligence test as a condition of employment in or transfer to jobs when (a) neither standard is shown to be significantly related to successful job performance, (b) both requirements operate to disqualify Negroes at a substantially higher rate than white applicants, and (c) the jobs in question formerly had been filled only by white employees as part of a longstanding practice of giving preference to whites.[186]

A unanimous Court, speaking through Chief Justice Burger, answered that question in the affirmative.

That the case was rooted firmly in the perpetrator perspective may be inferred from the behavior of the employer in the case. Prior to July 1965, the employer had blatantly discriminated against black workers, permitting them to work in only one of its five departments, where the highest paying job paid less than the lowest paying job in any of the other four departments. In 1965, the employer abandoned its policy of explicit discrimination. In the same year, however, the employer added a high school diploma requirement for transfer out of the previously "black" department and a requirement that a person had to "register satisfactory scores on two professionally developed aptitude tests, as well as . . . have a high school education"[187] for placement in any department except the previously "black" one. These newly imposed requirements operated to limit severely the opportunities available to black employees and applicants. Thus, the case posed the problem of the "ostensibly neutral practice" introduced as a substitute for blatant racial discrimination and achieving substantially the same results.

By making its rationale dependent on the prior explicit discrimination the Court could have stayed within the perpetrator perspective. But this would have been somewhat disingenuous. For one thing, the prior discriminatory conduct in *Griggs* was legal when it

185. *See* International Bhd. of Teamsters v. United States, 431 U.S. 324, 348-55 (1977); General Elec. Co. v. Gilbert, 429 U.S. 125, 137-46 (1976); Washington v. Davis, 426 U.S. 229, 238-39, 248-52 (1976).

186. 401 U.S. at 425-26.

187. *Id.* at 427-28.

occurred and could not by itself have given rise to a violation. Moreover, to have made the illegality of the test and diploma requirements dependent upon the prior discrimination would have meant that absent such a history the very same practices would be valid however disproportionate their impact. In any event, the Court chose to sever its rationale from any dependence on the prior discrimination, and in so doing left the perpetrator perspective as explaining, at most, why, but not how, the Court intervened in *Griggs*.

Alternatively, the Court in *Griggs* might have remained closer to, but not clearly within, the perpetrator perspective by straying no further than it had in *Gaston County*. On this view, the tests and diploma requirements were not violations in and of themselves, but only to the extent that they penalized blacks for the inferior educations they had received in segregated schools. Some language in *Griggs* even supports this view: "Basic intelligence must have the means of articulation to manifest itself fairly in a testing process. Because they are Negroes, petitioners have long received inferior education in segregated schools and this Court expressly recognized these differences in *Gaston County v. United States* . . . ."[188] Had this rationale emerged as the dominant one in *Griggs*, the case would have been just another school desegregation case, with the formal violation not the employee selection procedures invalidated but the preexisting system of de jure segregated schools. The *Gaston County* rationale, however, while supportive of the result in *Griggs*, could not be easily transferred to the *Griggs* circumstances.

A straightforward application of *Gaston County* to *Griggs* would have invalidated all test and diploma requirements until the day when black applicants no longer suffered the residual impacts of inferior education. But while the Court was willing to say that all citizens could vote regardless of literacy, they were not equally willing to say that all applicants should be hired, regardless of qualifications.[189] The Court clearly needed a rationale that would describe the instances where tests or other job qualifications could be validly applied even as against black applicants who had suffered inferior educations.[190] To develop such standards, the Court had to take a look

188. *Id.* at 430.

189. [In *Gaston County*], because of the inferior education received by Negroes . . . , this court barred . . . a literacy test for voter registration on the ground that the test would abridge the right to vote indirectly on account of race. Congress did not intend by Title VII, however, to guarantee a job to every person regardless of qualifications.

Id.

190. [Title VII] does not command that any person be hired simply because he was formerly the subject of discrimination . . . . Discriminatory preference for any group, minority or majority, is precisely and only what Congress has proscribed. What is required by Congress is the removal of

at the tests on their merits. Almost inadvertently, then, the opinion switched from blaming the victim to scrutinizing the neutral practices themselves with respect to their claims of rationality. At that point, the background of segregated schools became irrelevant, since standards addressed solely to the merits of the neutral practices limit the issue to whether, under title VII, a particular employee selection procedure that disproportionately excludes black applicants is valid, regardless of the educational experience of the applicants.

Thus, the central rationale of *Griggs* is that selection procedures, even ostensibly neutral ones, that disadvantage minority applicants are not valid unless they can demonstrate themselves to be rational: "The Act proscribes not only overt discrimination but also practices that are fair in form, but discriminatory in operation. The touchstone is business necessity. If an employment practice which operates to exclude Negroes cannot be shown to be related to job performance, the practice is prohibited."[191] The standard of rationality set by the Court seemed to be a tough one, demanding a showing of job-relatedness, the removal of "artificial, arbitrary, and unnecessary barriers,"[192] and standards that "measure the person for the job and not the person in the abstract."[193] In short, the opinion amounts to a demand that the myth of a meritocratic scheme of equality of opportunity be transformed into a reality.

Thus for the first time the Court held that a neutral practice, not purposefully discriminatory, that nevertheless failed to admit blacks to jobs had to justify itself or else be declared invalid. Although the opinion was decided under title VII, its logic did not seem easily confined. The Court even took one general swipe at the workings of meritocracy:

> The facts of this case demonstrate the inadequacy of broad and general testing devices as well as the infirmity of using diplomas or degrees as fixed measures of capability. History is filled with examples of men and women who rendered highly effective performance without the conventional badges of accomplishment in terms of certificates, diplomas, or degrees.[194]

Since the case was concerned not with remedy but with the meaning of "violation" under title VII, it seemed reasonable to conclude that a discriminatory practice under title VII would also be a discrimina-

> artificial, arbitrary, and unnecessary barriers to employment when the barriers operate invidiously to discriminate on the basis of racial or other impermissible classification.

Id. at 430-31.

191. *Id.* at 431.

192. *Id.*

193. *Id.* at 436.

194. *Id.* at 433.

tory practice under the fourteenth amendment in areas not subject to title VII.[195] Read this way, the case becomes a generalized demand that all objective selection procedures under the coverage of some antidiscrimination law be required to justify themselves as consistent with the notion of equality of opportunity. *Griggs* in no way contradicts the meritocratic model, but assumes that it can be made to work, that those who are deserving can be objectively separated from those who are not.[196]

In addition to legitimizing the assertion of an affirmative claim directed at a systemic practice, *Griggs* changed the notion of "intentional" in antidiscrimination law. This aspect of the opinion derives from the Court's severance of its rationale from the prior discriminatory practices of the defendant employer. The opinion makes it clear that "good intent or absence of discriminatory intent does not redeem employment procedures or testing mechanisms that operate as 'built-in headwinds' for minority groups"[197] and that "Congress directed the thrust of the Act to the *consequences* of em-

---

195. Indeed, it is counterintuitive that there should be separate standards for constitutional as opposed to statutory violations.

196. For a similar assumption, see DeFunis v. Odegaard, 416 U.S. 312, 340-41 (1974) (Douglas, J., dissenting). *See also* G. WILLS, NIXON AGONISTES 471-89 (paperback ed. 1971).

Whether that model can fulfill its promise depends largely on the selection criteria employed, a subject to be discussed extensively in the sequel to this Article. On the history and ideology of aptitude testing, see C. KARIER, SHAPING THE AMERICAN EDUCATIONAL STATE 127-232, 275-428 (1975); M. KATZ, CLASS, BUREAUCRACY, AND SCHOOLS 147-94 (2d ed. 1975); M. LAZERSON, ORIGINS OF THE URBAN SCHOOL 179-201 (1971); D. TYACK, THE ONE BEST SYSTEM 204-29 (1974); R. Marks, Testers, Trackers and Trustees: The Ideology of the Intelligence Testing Movement in America 1900-1954 (1972) (unpublished Ph.D. dissertation, University of Illinois at Urbana-Champaign).

On what the tests measure or purport to measure, see E. GHISELLI, THE VALIDITY OF OCCUPATIONAL APTITUDE TESTS (1966); Block & Dworkin, *IQ: Heritability and Inequality* (pts. 1 & 2), 3 PHILOSOPHY & PUB. AFF. 331, 4 PHILOSOPHY & PUB. AFF. 40 (1974); *Brief of Law School Admissions Council as Amicus Curiae in DeFunis v. Odegaard*, in 2 DEFUNIS VERSUS ODEGAARD AND THE UNIVERSITY OF WASHINGTON 695 (A. Ginger ed. 1974); Cooper & Sobol, *Seniority and Testing Under Fair Employment Laws: A General Approach to Objective Criteria of Hiring and Promotion*, 82 HARV. L. REV. 1598, 1637-99 (1969); Funkenstein, *Current Problems in the Verbal and Quantitative Ability Subtests of the Medical College Admission Test*, 40 J. MED. EDUC. 1031 (1965); *Developments in the Law—Employment Discrimination and Title VII of the Civil Rights Act of 1964*, 84 HARV. L. REV. 1109, 1120-40 (1971).

On tests and other measures of ability as legitimizing the existing class structure through the internalization of ability concepts, with attendant psychic stress, see R. SENNETT & J. COBB, THE HIDDEN INJURIES OF CLASS (paperback ed. 1973); Bowles & Gintis, *I.Q. in the U.S. Class Structure*, SOC. POL'Y, November-December 1972 & January-February 1973, at 65-96. For a particularly vivid fictionalized account, see T. DISCH, **334**, at 11-38 (paperback ed. 1974).

197. 401 U.S. at 432.

ployment practices, not simply the motivation."[198] Under the notion of "intention" that emerges from the opinion, then, one is intentionally discriminating if one continues to use a practice or maintains a condition that disadvantages a minority group without being able to justify the rationality of the practice or condition.[199] This idea, too, did not seem easily confined within the employment area to tests alone,[200] nor easily within the employment area at all.[201]

When applied to ostensibly rational practices, the *Griggs* notion of intention merely demands a showing of rationality. When applied to nonrational practices, such as school or voter districting, jurisdictional boundaries, or zoning decisions, all of which are inherently arbitrary,[202] the *Griggs* notion becomes a demand for results and, therefore, an adoption of the victim perspective. If, for example, there are a number of ways to divide a community into districts for school assignment purposes, and the one currently employed produces a great deal of racial concentration in schools, to perpetuate the existing scheme with the knowledge of the racial concentration produced becomes intentional discrimination—unless there is a sufficiently good reason for having chosen that scheme. To follow out the analogy to *Griggs,* such a reason would have to be one that tells the black children, who are confined to schools segregated in fact, why it is *legitimate* that they be so confined. Absent such a reason, the children would have the right to a redistricting that did not produce

198. *Id.* (emphasis in original).

199. Compare Paul Brest's curious footnote, which, whether one agrees or disagrees with its semantic analysis, may be seen as an effort to buttress the perpetrator perspective against the fierce encroachments of the victim perspective on the terrain of intent:

> A common error is to characterize foreseeable segregation as "intentional" and hence de jure by invoking the saw that "an actor intends the foreseeable or foreseen consequences of his conduct." This not only obliterates the conceptual distinction between de jure and de facto but carries a misleading emotive charge. It does not reflect ordinary usage to say that whenever an actor foresees that his conduct will work to someone's detriment, the actor "intends to injure" that person.

P. Brest, *supra* note 72, at 530 n.81. *See also* Note, *Reading the Mind of the School Board: Segregative Intent and the De Facto/De Jure Distinction,* 86 Yale L.J. 317 (1976).

200. *But see* International Bhd. of Teamsters v. United States, 431 U.S. 324, 348-55 (1977) (rejecting application to seniority despite unanimous lower court precedent); General Elec. Co. v. Gilbert, 429 U.S. 125 (1976) (rejecting application to exclusion of pregnancy from employer disability plan).

201. *See* cases cited in Washington v. Davis, 426 U.S. 229, 244 n.12 (1976); *The Supreme Court, 1975 Term,* 90 Harv. L. Rev. 56, 115-16 & nn.16 & 19 (1976).

202. *See* Ely, *Legislative and Administrative Motivation in Constitutional Law,* 79 Yale L.J. 1205, 1231-35 (1970). Ely's characterization of such practices as nonrational leads him to stay with the perpetrator perspective.

racial concentration.

The third outstanding feature of *Griggs* is that it virtually coerces employers (and others affected by its rationale) into adoption of affirmative action programs. The *Griggs* rationale, with its attendant demand for justification, is not even triggered unless the practice complained of produces a disproportionate impact on a minority group. A potential defendant who wishes to avoid litigation, or who wishes to avoid the adoption of different or more cumbersome selection procedures, need only negate the disproportionate impact by adopting different procedures for the minority groups disproportionately excluded. While such an approach in no way legitimizes the original procedure under the rationale of *Griggs,* it does at least neutralize its illegitimacy by offering an alternative. Thus *Griggs* implicitly offers a choice: either make the meritocracy work on its own terms or make up for its flaws through affirmative efforts. That choice also suggests a way of looking at the so-called "reverse" discrimination issue.[203]

E. Education Revisited: *Swann, Wright,* and *Keyes*

In education, the era of contradiction most thoroughly realized itself in three cases decided during the three years following the *Griggs* decision: *Swann v. Charlotte-Mecklenburg Board of Education,*[204] *Wright v. Council of Emporia,*[205] and *Keyes v. School District No. 1.*[206] Each of these cases may be explained by and re-

203. For example, one might justify the adoption of a minority admissions program of the sort at issue in *Bakke* not by claiming to compensate those admitted, or touting the affirmative utilitarian benefits to be gained for society at large, but by simply showing that the existing selection procedure is a prima facie violation under *Griggs* with respect to those disproportionately excluded, that although the procedure cannot be demonstrated to be sufficiently rational, it cannot be replaced without great administrative cost, and that the minority admissions program serves to neutralize for a time the worst effects of an admittedly defective scheme, insofar as that scheme would otherwise operate to exclude those who have been the historical targets of blatant discrimination.

The key to this argument is, of course, the potential applicability of the *Griggs* notion of violation to the existing selection program. Once that potentiality has been neutralized, or greatly reduced, as by limiting the coverage of the *Griggs* rule, or by insisting on a prior adjudication of violation, the argument is easily brushed aside. *See* Regents of the Univ. of Cal. v. Bakke, 98 S. Ct. 2733, 2757-59 & nn.43-45 (1978) (Powell, J., announcing the judgment of the Court). For a discussion of how the Court, two years before the *Bakke* decision, confined the *Griggs* conception of violation, see text accompanying notes 271-87 *infra*. For further discussion of *Bakke*, see note 238 *infra*.

204. 402 U.S. 1 (1971).

205. 407 U.S. 451 (1972).

206. 413 U.S. 189 (1973).

mains formally within the perpetrator perspective, but each, especially when read in light of *Griggs,* creates expectations more consistent with the victim perspective.[207]

All three cases involved explicit findings of de jure segregation. *Swann* and *Wright* involved southern school systems in which the de jure systems were preexisting and remote in time from the actual conditions being litigated;[208] *Keyes* involved a northern city—Denver—where the district court had found de jure segregation in one part of the city. In addition, all three cases involved challenges to neutral practices that operated to produce racially concentrated schools. In *Swann* and *Keyes*, the practice was the neighborhood school; in *Wright*, it was deconsolidation of a combined city-county school system.

In each case, the Court retained formal adherence to the perpetrator perspective by "linking" the current condition under attack to the actual de jure violation. Thus, in *Swann,* while invoking the magic phrase that the "nature of the violation determines the scope of the remedy,"[209] the Court proceeded to show how by inference alone one could conclude either that the prior system of segregation produced segregated neighborhoods, which in turn produced the current condition of segregation, or that the residential segregation led to school siting decisions that continued to produce racial concentration, despite the abolition of de jure segregation.[210] Having linked the current condition to the past violation, the Court was able to conclude that although a prescription of racial balance is not ordinarily within the authority of a federal district court, both an "awareness of the racial composition of the whole school system" and the use of mathematical ratios were appropriate to remedy the current violation.[211]

In *Wright,* the Court could have tied its reasoning to the perpetrator perspective, since the city involved had decided to sever its relationship with the county school system only two weeks after a federal court had ordered pairing of schools. That severance would

207. *See* note 162 *supra.*

208. In *Wright,* the de jure system was less remote in time, inasmuch as the deconsolidation at issue took place only two weeks after the district court in 1969 finally ordered desegregation of the system. Thus, although the Court could have treated the deconsolidation as a present instance of purposeful discrimination, it chose not to rely on that theory of decision. *Cf.* Wright v. Council of Emporia, 442 F.2d 570 (4th Cir. 1971) (focusing on the present conduct but finding no discrimination), *rev'd*, 407 U.S. 451 (1972). In this respect, the case may be viewed as factually analogous to *Griggs* itself. *See* text accompanying notes 186-88 *supra.*

209. 402 U.S. at 16.

210. *See id.* at 20-21.

211. *See id.* at 25.

have changed the racial composition of the system from 66% black and 34% white to 72% black and 28% white (county) and 52% black and 48% white (city). While stressing the factual history and emphasizing that the case involved desegregation rather than lack of racial balance, the Court nevertheless based its decision on the *effect* of deconsolidation: "Thus, we have focused upon the effect—not the purpose or motivation—of a school board's action in determining whether it is a permissible method of dismantling a dual system. The existence of a permissible purpose cannot sustain an action that has an impermissible effect."[212]

In *Keyes,* the Court made a similar effort to tie the condition of segregation to the identified violation. The Court held that proof of a violation with respect to one area of a city, plus racial concentration elsewhere in the system, raised by evidentiary inference (prior similar acts or causal spread) a prima facie case of de jure segregation throughout the system.[213] The school board thereupon became obligated to show that the racial concentration elsewhere was not adventitious, a burden that was not met by a neighborhood school assignment policy.[214]

In all three cases, the Court permitted challenges to neutral practices that produced racial concentration in schools. In none of the cases did the Court demand proof that the original violation caused the challenged racial concentration. In fact, by indulging in causation analysis at least as plausible as that utilized by the Court, one might easily conclude that the real villain in all three cases was discrimination in housing that produced segregated residential patterns. In both *Swann* and *Keyes,* racially concentrated neighborhoods produced the racially concentrated schools; in *Wright,* the relative racial composition of county and city produced the result. Thus regarded, the cases suggest that the de jure segregation merely served as a backdrop for challenges to *conditions* of segregation produced by generalized patterns of discrimination. They further suggest that those same condi-

212. 407 U.S. at 462.

213. *See generally* Fiss, *supra* note 162, at 21-26.

214. 413 U.S. at 208-09. Justices Douglas and Powell, in separate opinions, concurred with the majority on the finding of a violation, but saw no reason to perpetuate the de facto/de jure distinction. *See id.* at 216, 219-20. Justice Powell reasoned that although "some of its language was more expansive," *Brown I*'s holding was "essentially negative," forbidding "state-compelled or authorized segregation of public schools." *Id.* at 220. According to Justice Powell, however, "the concept of state neutrality was transformed into the present constitutional doctrine requiring affirmative action to desegregate school systems" by subsequent decisions. *Id.* at 221. The Powell opinion gains a tongue-in-cheek character, however, when placed in a context with his earlier opinion for the Court in San Antonio Independent School Dist. v. Rodriguez, 411 U.S. 1 (1973), and his subsequent vote with the majority in Milliken v. Bradley, 418 U.S. 717 (1974), *discussed at* notes 242-55 *infra* and accompanying text.

tions should be equally subject to attack wherever they can be ascribed to patterns of discrimination, which would be anywhere other than the future society.

This conclusion gains much greater force from the fact that the three cases followed the decision in *Griggs*, for two aspects of *Griggs* explain the results in *Swann*, *Wright*, and *Keyes* much more convincingly than the formal reasoning used in those opinions. One is the notion that ostensibly neutral practices producing racially disproportionate results must justify themselves or be regarded as violations. Alternatively, by employing the *Griggs* corollary, one might conclude that the "intentional" violation in the three cases was adherence to a practice (the neighborhood schools) or a decision (the deconsolidation) that produced results associated with segregation. Under this view, retention of the practice in the face of its known results becomes a prima facie case of discrimination, again giving rise to a demand for rational justification. Under either approach, the rational justification would have to be one that not only explains the action taken, but also makes the condition of discrimination legitimate. Neither the neighborhood school assignments in *Swann* and *Keyes* nor the deconsolidation in *Wright* satisfied those requirements.

Thus by the end of the era of contradiction the Court, while remaining within the perpetrator perspective, had nevertheless managed to offer to black people expectations of proportional racial political power, a working system of equality of opportunity, if not actual jobs, and integrated schools. In the next era, these expectations were systematically defeated and only the perpetrator perspective was preserved.

IV. 1974-?: THE ERA OF RATIONALIZATION, OR THE JURISPRUDENCE OF CURE

A. An Overview

The typical approach of the era of rationalization is to "declare that the war is over,"[215] to make the problem of racial discrimination go away by announcing that it has been solved. This approach takes many forms. Its simplest and most direct version is the declaration that, despite the discriminatory appearance of current conditions, the actual violation has already been cured,[216] or is being remedied, regardless of whether the remedy prescribed can be expected to alleviate the condition.[217] A more sophisticated approach is to declare

215. Phil Ochs tried unsuccessfully with his song, *The War is Over*, to apply the same technique to the Vietnam War.

216. *See* Pasadena City Bd. of Educ. v. Spangler, 427 U.S. 424, 434-35 (1976).

217. *See* Milliken v. Bradley, 433 U.S. 267 (1977); Milliken v. Bradley, 418 U.S. 717 (1974); *id.* at 767-68 (White, J., dissenting).

that what looks like a violation, based on expectations derived from the era of contradiction, is not a violation at all. This has been accomplished by isolating statutory discrimination from constitutional discrimination to prevent the former from infiltrating the latter[218] and by weakening the previously created statutory standards under the guise of statutory interpretation.[219] The same results have been achieved by renewing insistence on the always manipulable requirement of causation,[220] by emphasizing the form rather than the results of earlier cases,[221] by invoking the purpose-motive distinction to insulate neutral nonrational decisions,[222] or by presuming the rationality of neutral decisions instead of demanding their justification.[223]

Central to the era of rationalization is the pretense—associated with the color-blind theory of racial discrimination—that but for an occasional aberrational practice, future society is already here and functioning. The contradictions implicit in the earlier cases are thus resolved largely by pretending they were never there. This resolution has in turn facilitated a quick and easy return to the comfortable and neat world of the perpetrator perspective. As a result, the actual conditions of racial powerlessness, poverty, and unemployment can be regarded as no more than conditions—not as racial discrimination. Those conditions can then be rationalized by treating them as historical accidents or products of a malevolent fate, or, even worse, by blaming the victims as inadequate to function in the good society. The next few sections will describe, in each of the three substantive areas discussed earlier, the decisions that have brought the era of rationalization into being.

B. Voting

In *Beer v. United States,*[224] the Court finished the job, which began with its treatment of the annexation issue in *Richmond,*[225] of

218. *See* Washington v. Davis, 426 U.S. 229, 238-39 (1976).

219. *See* Dothard v. Rawlinson, 433 U.S. 321, 334-35 (1977); International Bhd. of Teamsters v. United States, 431 U.S. 324, 348-55 (1977); General Elec. Co. v. Gilbert, 429 U.S. 125, 133-36 (1976); Washington v. Davis, 426 U.S. 229, 238-39, 248-52 (1976); Beer v. United States, 425 U.S. 130, 138-42 (1976).

220. *See* Rizzo v. Goode, 423 U.S. 362, 376-77 (1976); Warth v. Seldin, 422 U.S. 490, 502-07 (1975).

221. *Compare* Pasadena City Bd. of Educ. v. Spangler, 427 U.S. 424 (1976), *and* Milliken v. Bradley, 418 U.S. 717 (1974), *with* Keyes v. School Dist. No. 1, 413 U.S. 189 (1973), *and* Swann v. Charlotte-Mecklenburg Bd. of Educ., 402 U.S. 1 (1971).

222. *See* Village of Arlington Heights v. Metropolitan Hous. Dev. Corp., 429 U.S. 252, 265-66 (1977).

223. *See* Washington v. Davis, 426 U.S. 229, 242, 248 (1976); Milliken v. Bradley, 418 U.S. 717, 744-47, 747 n.22 (1974).

224. 425 U.S. 130 (1976).

225. City of Richmond v. United States, 422 U.S. 358 (1975), *discussed at* notes 151-55 *supra* and accompanying text.

destroying the expectations of political power that the Court itself had generated by bringing districting procedures under section 5 of the Voting Rights Act of 1965 and by its own treatment of the districting aspect of *Richmond*. *Beer* was the first case to present a substantive question of section 5's application to legislative redistricting. The City of New Orleans, a jurisdiction subject to section 5, had a population that was 55% white and 45% black, with registered voters 65% white and 35% black.[226] Under the New Orleans districting scheme, there were seven council seats, two of which were elected on an at-large basis. Of the five remaining districts, four had clear white majorities, and black voters comprised 50.2% of the voting population in the fifth district.[227] No black had ever been elected to the city council.

New Orleans was obligated by local law to redistrict itself after the 1970 census. After the Attorney General of the United States rejected a plan that provided for no black electoral majorities in any district, a substitute was offered that provided for a black voting majority of 52.6% in one district.[228] The validity of this plan was the issue in *Beer*, and the Court had to decide whether the plan had the purpose or effect of discriminating on the basis of race within the meaning of section 5. As suggested above, the determination whether a redistricting plan is racially discriminatory seems to demand a test of that plan against a standard of racial proportionality. Under such a test, a black voting population of 35%[229] should control three of seven council seats. A plan that provides a slight majority in one district would seem to fail the test. The Court's response was to rewrite section 5 to change the appropriate inquiry from one about racial discrimination to one about incremental racial discrimination.

The Court's first step was to narrow the scope of its inquiry from the entire new plan to just that portion of the plan involving the five districted seats. Since there had been two at-large seats under the earlier scheme, retaining at-large seats was not a change within the meaning of section 5.[230] Having severed the at-large seats from the case, the Court proceeded to apply the same logic to the five remaining seats, concluding that the concern of section 5 was fulfilled by asking whether the black population was worse off under the new plan than it had been under the old one. Thus rewritten, the concern of section 5 was changed from discrimination to "retrogression."[231]

226. *See* 425 U.S. at 134.

227. *See* Appendix at 621, Beer v. United States, 425 U.S. 130 (1976).

228. *See* 425 U.S. at 136.

229. The actual percentage of black voters had risen to 38.2% in 1974. *See id.* at 142 n.13.

230. *See id.* at 138-39.

231. *See id.* at 141.

The answer to this narrow question was obvious; the district court, in rejecting the plan, had simply misunderstood the statute.[232]

The opinion did not even allude to the "permanent over-representation"[233] of the white community of New Orleans under the approved plan, preferring instead to drag out the color-blind theory to reaffirm that no minority group has any right to proportional representation.[234] The net effect of this decision was to legitimize the status quo by immunizing the preexisting condition of black underrepresentation from statutory or constitutional scrutiny.[235] This implies that the condition of underrepresentation is to be regarded as innocent, fortuitous, unrelated to racial discrimination, and not required to justify itself. It is as if the mighty Voting Rights Act had been set atop a high-heeled shoe, with its awesome force trained upon a tiny, interstitial moment, surrounded by the remainder of a real problem it could no longer touch.

The most recent voting case, *United Jewish Organizations v. Carey*,[236] is a case that, in its relationship to *Beer*, may be characteristic of the era of rationalization: the remedial counterpoint. While *Beer* served to confine the area of legitimate concern by placing a great deal of racial discrimination beyond the concern of the law, *United Jewish Organizations* appears to emphasize the vigorous remedial efforts that will be required, or perhaps tolerated, within that newly-defined area. In *United Jewish Organizations*, the Court upheld a districting plan that self-consciously created 65% nonwhite majorities in enough electoral districts to assure a 35% overall nonwhite population control of 30% of the assembly and senatorial seats in Kings County, New York.[237] In affirming that result, the eight participating Justices produced four opinions containing two statutory rationales, two constitutional rationales, and one dissent, with no more than four Justices agreeing on anything except the result.

The principal illusion created by *United Jewish Organizations* is that the case concerns something significant with respect to racial discrimination. The interplay of rationales and opinions gives the impression of a great intellectual and emotional struggle to find justifications for the employment of powerful remedial devices. The case may come to be seen as an improvisational dress rehearsal for the Court's later performance on the so-called "reverse" discrimination

232. *See id.* at 142.

233. *See* notes 159-61 *supra* and accompanying text.

234. *See* 425 U.S. at 136 n.8.

235. Constitutional voting cases have never made it as far as the era of contradiction, remaining unambiguously imbedded in the perpetrator perspective. *See, e.g.*, Whitcomb v. Chavis, 403 U.S. 124 (1971); Wright v. Rockefeller, 376 U.S. 52 (1964).

236. 430 U.S. 144 (1977).

237. *See id.* at 155-56.

issue in *Regents of the University of California v. Bakke*.[238] And, in this respect, neither *United Jewish Organizations* nor *Bakke* is a very significant case about the real possibilities of remedying racial discrimination. The important cases are the ones that define the violations. For voting rights, *Beer* was the important case, and all that follows must be regarded as confined by and operating within the narrow area of concern left by *Beer*.

From the assortment of opinions in *United Jewish Organizations*, one can infer two main themes of the era of rationalization, both of which are likely to appear in the remedial counterpoint cases. One is the vigorous affirmation of efforts to remedy a violation, with the latter concept having been narrowly defined elsewhere. Two of the "majority" rationales adopt this approach, with their justifications of

238. 98 S. Ct. 2733 (1978). Despite the hoopla surrounding *Bakke* as a media event, the case never promised to be more than a remedial counterpoint inasmuch as the issue was the validity of a *voluntary* affirmative action program. And it turned out to be something less than a remedial counterpoint, although how much less is difficult to predict, given the fragility of the "majority" as well as the juxtaposition in Justice Powell's crucial opinion of reactionary rhetoric with what has been widely received as an implicit invitation to hypocritical practice.

It is interesting in this connection, based on my own experience as both consumer and interviewee at the time, that the media coverage of *Bakke* depicted it as much more of a remedial counterpoint decision than a formal reading would suggest. The public image created was one of a case that had merely outlawed "bad" quotas, while leaving intact the idea of voluntary affirmative action programs that took race into account in admissions decisionmaking. (For an excellent illustration of the persistence of this view, see Footlick & Camper, *New Issues for the Court*, NEWSWEEK, October 9, 1978, at 54, asserting that in *Bakke* the "sharply divided Court struck down a medical-school admissions quota favoring minorities, but upheld the principle of affirmative action.") The formal theory of Justice Powell's opinion is much more hostile to affirmative action programs, invoking the most rigid rhetoric of color-blindness and explicitly rejecting the idea that race may be employed in admissions decisions for reasons having anything to do with securing racial justice or remedying racial discrimination (unless, of course, one has first identified the increasingly elusive "violation"). *See* 98 S. Ct. at 2747-60.

The practical impact of the decision may, however, fit the remedial counterpoint model, by permitting voluntary action to accomplish results not unlike those accomplished under the admissions programs struck down in *Bakke*, while ensuring that strife and cost will precede the achievement of even minimal results. The decision does permit schools to make admissions decisions that take race into account so long as those decisions are part of a "diversity" program (now protected by some quasi-first amendment notion of academic freedom) that is not designed (at least in theory) to promote racial justice and treats race as equivalent to attributes like being a "farm boy from Idaho." *Id.* at 2765 app. Such a program can benefit some minority students if a faculty possesses sufficient will and concern to renew formally its commitment to such results through adoption of an "acceptable" program, tolerate a more complex general admissions process, and risk litigation. And those faculty members who, especially in graduate and professional education, want to further the goals of affirmative action must be willing to pretend to want a "diverse" student body and pretend well enough to earn the protection of Justice Powell's "presumption of legality." *Id.* at 2763 n.53.

the limited use of racial proportionality involved in the case ultimately dependent on the validity and coverage of the Voting Rights Act.[239] The implicit message is one of assurance to white voters generally that, while the remedies upheld look severe, nothing more will be *required* than avoidance of a violation as defined in *Beer*.

The other theme, suggested principally by the constitutional majority rationale joined in by Justices White, Stevens, and Rehnquist is that of voluntary tokenism.[240] The message here is that it is a matter of constitutional indifference if white majorities wish to remedy racial discrimination beyond the extent required by antidiscrimination law.[241] Viewed against the background of the narrowed concept of violation, this approach contains two obnoxious features. First, the possibility of genuine improvement in the condition of the black community is dependent entirely on the benevolence of whites. Thus it becomes unlikely that voluntarism will change very much at all. Second, by relegating significant remedial efforts to the domain of voluntarism, the Court sets up a ferocious ethical debate within the white community. Placing the existing societal institutions and practices beyond the reach of the violation concept tends to legitimize those institutions and practices, making them appear to be the ones that would exist in future society. But color-blindness is the applicable antidiscrimination principle in future society. Thus the battle is joined between those who choose to take seriously the legitimation of existing structures—by mobilizing around the color-blind theory to oppose remedial practices that would not be valid in future society—and those who remain unconvinced that future society has arrived.

C. Education

The era of rationalization began in the same substantive area as modern antidiscrimination law—school desegregation. In *Milliken v.*

239. *See* 430 U.S. at 148-65 (Parts I, II, and III of the opinion of White, J., joined by Blackmun, Brennan, and Stevens, JJ.); *id.* at 168-79 (Brennan, J., concurring in part).

240. *See id.* at 165-68 (White, J., joined by Rehnquist and Stevens, JJ.). The fourth "majority" rationale, that of Justice Stewart, joined by Justice Powell, is also constitutional, but seems to evade the basic issue by misapplying the intent requirement of *Washington v. Davis* to a case that does involve an explicit racial classification. *See id.* at 179-80.

Justice Powell seems to have conceded as much with his quick rejection of the same argument as applied to the *Bakke* case. *See* Regents of the Univ. of Cal. v. Bakke, 98 S. Ct. 2733, 2748 n.27 (1978) (Powell, J., announcing the judgment of the Court).

241. The same message was offered in Swann v. Charlotte-Mecklenburg Bd. of Educ., 402 U.S. 1, 16 (1971). *See generally* Brest, *supra* note 17, at 16-17.

Bradley (*Milliken* I),[242] the Court for the first time applied antidiscrimination law to rationalize a segregated result in a case where a constitutional violation had been found to exist.[243] Despite extensive de jure segregation in the City of Detroit, the Court refused to approve a remedy that would consolidate Detroit schools with those of surrounding suburbs for the purpose of achieving an integrated result. In so holding, the Court rendered irrelevant the district court's conclusion that absent such a remedy, the schools of Detroit would become all-black within a few years.[244] Coupled with the decision a year earlier in *San Antonio Independent School District v. Rodriguez,*[245] which rejected a claim of resource equalization among school districts without regard to ability to pay, the message of *Milliken I* is stark and clear: if whites can find a way to leave the inner city, they may legally insulate their finances and schools from the demands of blacks for racial equality.[246] The only additional requirement for that sense of security is the availability of easily manipulated restrictive land-use practices, which the Court has graciously provided in other cases.[247]

To achieve this result, the Court had to emphasize the form of *Swann* and *Keyes* over their substance, make results irrelevant, refuse to recognize the implications of *Griggs,* and renew its insistence on proof of causation. Citing *Swann,* the Court pointed out that "[t]he controlling principle consistently expounded in our holdings is that the scope of the remedy is determined by the nature and

242. 418 U.S. 717 (1974).

243. The Court had rationalized segregated results before by refusing to find any violation. *See* San Antonio Independent School Dist. v. Rodriguez, 411 U.S. 1, 55 (1973); Jefferson v. Hackney, 406 U.S. 535, 549 (1972); Palmer v. Thompson, 403 U.S. 217, 226-27 (1971); James v. Valtierra, 402 U.S. 137, 143 (1971); Evans v. Abney, 396 U.S. 435, 444 (1970). *Milliken I,* on the other hand, involved an actual violation. *See* 418 U.S. at 738 n.18.

244. 418 U.S. at 735.

245. 411 U.S. 1 (1973).

246. *Milliken I* is typical of a number of Supreme Court cases in recent years, all of which are difficult to reconcile with prior cases in their own narrow doctrinal areas, but which as a group seem consistent and coherent if viewed as designed to insulate and protect the suburbs from the demands or intrusive influences of racial, economic, or political minorities. *See* Village of Arlington Heights v. Metropolitan Hous. Dev. Corp., 429 U.S. 252 (1977); City of Eastlake v. Forest City Enterprises, Inc., 426 U.S. 668 (1976); Hudgens v. NLRB, 424 U.S. 507 (1976); Warth v. Seldin, 422 U.S. 490 (1975); Milliken v. Bradley, 418 U.S. 717 (1974); Lehman v. City of Shaker Heights, 418 U.S. 298 (1974); Village of Belle Terre v. Boraas, 416 U.S. 1 (1974); San Antonio Independent School Dist. v. Rodriguez, 411 U.S. 1 (1973); Lloyd Corp. v. Tanner, 407 U.S. 551 (1972); James v. Valtierra, 402 U.S. 137 (1971).

247. *See* Village of Arlington Heights v. Metropolitan Hous. Dev. Corp., 429 U.S. 252 (1977); City of Eastlake v. Forest City Enterprises, Inc., 426 U.S. 668 (1976); Warth v. Seldin, 422 U.S. 490 (1975); Village of Belle Terre v. Boraas, 416 U.S. 1 (1974); James v. Valtierra, 402 U.S. 137 (1971).

extent of the constitutional violation."[248] The district court's mistake had been in proceeding on the erroneous assumption that "the Detroit schools could not be truly desegregated . . . unless the racial composition of the student body of each school substantially reflected the racial composition of the population of the metropolitan area as a whole."[249] That the district court so assumed is hardly surprising, however, if one reads *Swann* and *Keyes* in light of *Griggs'* concept of intentional violation or its treatment of neutral practices. Even if one takes a narrower view and simply analogizes the neighborhood school policy, which seemed to be the real cause of the segregation in *Swann* and *Keyes,* to the district boundaries in *Milliken,* the district court's assumption again seems sensible.

It is not clear why the Court thought district boundaries were sacrosanct while neighborhood school assignments were not. The Court offered no comparative judgment, merely announcing that the boundary lines were a manifestation of the sacred principle of local autonomy: "No single tradition in public education is more deeply rooted than local control over the operation of schools; local autonomy has long been thought essential both to the maintenance of community concern and support for public schools and to quality of the educational process."[250] But it was not even the principle of local autonomy that the Court was exalting in *Milliken*; it was the precise fact of the district boundaries existing in the Detroit metropolitan area that served to facilitate the operation of virtually all-white suburban schools. The principle of local autonomy may be a fine one as applied to an area of relative equality. In the usual suburb-city context where it is invoked, however, "local autonomy" is a codeword for rationalizing and protecting the prior appropriation of financial resources, environmental amenity, and, in this case, racial homogeneity. In short, it is a principle of vested rights.[251]

Moreover, the local autonomy discussion, although central to the historical meaning of *Milliken I,* was not even relevant to the rationale of the case. Since the Court refused to advance the implicit thrust of *Griggs-Swann-Keyes,* which would have made the conditions of racial concentration produced by the boundary lines at least a prima facie violation, there was no occasion to demand that the boundary lines be justified as either rational or innocently nonrational. The only practice deemed to be a violation at all was the de jure segregation of the City of Detroit. Here, as in the voting cases,

248. 418 U.S. at 744 (citing Swann v. Charlotte-Mecklenburg Bd. of Educ., 402 U.S. 1, 16 (1971)).

249. *Id.* at 740; *see* Fiss, *supra* note 162, at 28.

250. 418 U.S. at 741-42.

251. *See* Freeman, *Give and Take: Distributing Local Environmental Control Through Land-Use Regulation,* 60 MINN. L. REV. 883, 956-58 (1976).

the crucial step toward the result was to narrow the concept of violation. To accomplish that step, the Court had to return to the secure world of the perpetrator perspective:

> Before the boundaries of separate and autonomous school districts may be set aside by consolidating the separate units for remedial purposes or by imposing a cross-district remedy, it must first be shown that there has been a constitutional violation within one district that produces a significant segregative effect in another district. Specifically, it must be shown that racially discriminatory acts of the state or local school districts, or of a single school district have been a substantial cause of inter-district segregation. Thus an inter-district remedy might be in order where the racially discriminatory acts of one or more school districts caused racial segregation in an adjacent district, or where district lines have been deliberately drawn on the basis of race. In such circumstances an interdistrict remedy would be appropriate to eliminate the interdistrict segregation directly caused by the constitutional violation.[252]

Under the strict causation requirements of *Milliken I*,[253] the law does not offer even a feeble presumption that the extensive ghettoization of the City of Detroit in relation to its surrounding suburbs has anything to do with racial discrimination. Having rejected the implications of *Swann* and *Keyes*—that results mattered and that school desegregation remedies would be used to counter the effects of residential segregation—the Court insured that residential racial concentration will be subject to scrutiny, if at all, only in the difficult to litigate and virtually impossible to remedy domain of housing discrimination.[254] Under the combined force of *Rodriguez* and *Milliken*, black city residents are thus worse off in terms of legal theory than they were under the "separate-but-equal" doctrine of pre-*Brown* southern school litigation, where a claim of equivalent resources for black schools was at least legally cognizable.[255] And even if it makes

252. 418 U.S. at 744-45. Justice Stewart, in a concurring opinion, suggested that an interdistrict remedy might be appropriate in other situations as well, such as "purposeful racially discriminatory use of state housing or zoning laws." *Id.* at 755. *See generally* Note, *Interdistrict Desegregation: The Remaining Options*, 28 STAN. L. REV. 521 (1976).

253. These requirements were recently reaffirmed in Dayton Bd. of Educ. v. Brinkman, 433 U.S. 406 (1977).

254. *See* Austin Independent School Dist. v. United States, 429 U.S. 990, 991-95 (1976) (Powell, J., concurring).

255. This is not to suggest that demands for separate but equal educational facilities were met. *See* Gong Lum v. Rice, 275 U.S. 78, 82-84 (1927); Cumming v. Richmond County Bd. of Educ., 175 U.S. 528, 544-45 (1899). *See also* Berea College v. Kentucky, 211 U.S. 45, 46, 53, 58 (1908). Nevertheless, the irony of the posture of present-day victims is, in comparison to a literal reading of the separate but equal doctrine, inescapable. *See* Milliken v. Bradley, 418 U.S. 717, 759-61 (1974) (Douglas, J., dissenting); note 85 *supra*.

sense within the narrow world of the perpetrator perspective to say that school desegregation should not be a remedy for housing discrimination, the effect of *Milliken I* is far worse than neutral with respect to housing. By offering the lure of suburban isolation, the decision invites "white flight," thereby stimulating even greater racial concentration in housing.

That the Supreme Court had become indifferent to results became clear two years after *Milliken I.* In *Pasadena City Board of Education v. Spangler,*[256] the Court completed the task of rationalizing into obscurity the remaining victim perspective implications of *Swann* and *Keyes. Pasadena* involved a single jurisdiction that had been previously adjudged to have maintained segregated schools. The court-ordered remedial plan, which went into effect for the 1970-1971 school year, mandated a set of pupil assignment practices that would ensure that no school in the system had a majority of minority students.[257] The remedial plan produced that result for only one year, however, and by 1974, five of the 32 schools in the system again had black majorities.[258] The Court attributed this change to a "normal pattern of human migration [that] had resulted in some changes in the demographics of Pasadena's residential patterns"[259] and decided that despite the maldistribution in fact, Pasadena had achieved a unitary school system within the meaning of *Swann.*

Whether or not the actual behavior producing the demographic changes in *Pasadena* should be deemed "white flight,"[260] the message of the case on that point is as clear as it was in *Milliken I.* If the only obligation imposed by desegregation is to produce racially balanced schools for a year, intrajurisdictional white flight becomes as attractive an escape as the interjurisdictional variety offered by *Milliken I.* In another sense, however, *Pasadena* was just a logical corollary of *Milliken I.* If the Court had ordered further racial balance in Pasadena's schools, it would likely have accomplished no more than to stimulate further the kind of white flight already legitimized by *Milliken I.*

Pasadena marks the full restoration of the perpetrator perspective in school desegregation cases, with the substance of *Swann* subdued by its form.[261] If it was a concern for lack of results that permit-

256. 427 U.S. 424 (1976).

257. *See id.* at 428.

258. *See id.* at 435.

259. *Id.* at 436.

260. *See id.* at 435.

261. When the District Court's order in this case . . . is measured against what this Court said . . . in *Swann v. Board of Education* . . . regarding the scope of the judicially created relief which might be available to remedy violations of the Fourteenth Amendment, we think the inconsis-

ted the victim perspective to creep into the jurisprudence at all,[262] it is a brazen indifference to results that has facilitated the current doctrinal restoration. Only from the perpetrator perspective does it make sense to say that segregated schools are "caused" by the "badness" of particular actors, that the ephemeral negation of the conditions associated with that "badness" neutralizes the "badness" itself, and that the reappearance of the very same conditions is as irrelevant as if it were to occur in future society.

The remedial counterpoint to *Milliken I* and *Pasadena* appears in *Milliken II*,[263] where the Court upheld a district court order requiring the State of Michigan to pay one-half the support of various remedial programs[264] that the lower court had made a part of its desegregation plan for Detroit. The case exhibits both of the characteristics typical of remedial counterpoint cases—the illusion of vigorous remedial action, the effect of which has been limited to a narrowly defined violation, and the affirmation of voluntary tokenism. The facts of *Milliken II* are so odd, however, that it is unclear which

---

> tency between the two is clear. The District Court's interpretation of the order appears to contemplate the "substantive constitutional right [to a] particular degree of racial balance or mixing" which the Court in *Swann* expressly disapproved. . . . It became apparent, at least by the time of the 1974 hearing, that the District Court viewed this portion of its order not merely as a "starting point in the process of shaping a remedy," which *Swann* indicated would be appropriate, . . . but instead as an "inflexible requirement," . . . to be applied anew each year to the school population within the attendance zone of each school.
>
> The District Court apparently believed it had authority to impose this requirement even though subsequent changes to the racial mix in the Pasadena schools might be caused by factors for which the defendants could not be considered responsible. Whatever may have been the basis for such a belief in 1970, in *Swann* the Court cautioned that "it must be recognized that there are limits" beyond which a court may not go in seeking to dismantle a dual school system. . . . These limits are in part tied to the necessity of establishing that school authorities have in some manner caused unconstitutional segregation, for "[a]bsent a constitutional violation there would be no basis for judicially ordering assignment of students on a racial basis." . . . While the District Court found such a violation in 1970, and while this unappealed finding afforded a basis for its initial requirement that the defendants prepare a plan to remedy such racial segregation, its adoption of the Pasadena Plan in 1970 established a racially neutral system of student assignment in the [district]. Having done that, we think that in enforcing its order so as to require annual readjustment of attendance zones so that there would not be a majority of any minority in any Pasadena public school, the District Court exceeded its authority.

Id. at 433-35 (citations omitted) (quoting Swann v. Charlotte-Mecklenburg Bd. of Educ., 402 U.S. 1, 24, 25, 28 (1971)).

262. *See* text preceding note 132 *supra*.

263. Milliken v. Bradley, 433 U.S. 267 (1977).

264. *See id.* at 288-91.

of these two features predominates. The oddness stems from the lack of adversity in the case: both the Detroit School Board and the State of Michigan favored the remedial programs, and the only issue before the Court was whether the state could be made to contribute.[265]

From the perspective of the school board, the case may be an exercise in voluntary tokenism, with the crucial fact being the school board's willingness to spend more money than would otherwise be required to make up for the effects of past segregation. This view gains further force from the fact that the state defendant also supported some of the special programs on the merits, objecting only to the expense of implementing the order.[266] Thus read, the case stands for nothing more than the proposition that a local government *may* choose to do more than the Constitution requires in remedying school segregation.

The case may also be read, however, as rejecting a claim, at least on the part of the State of Michigan, concerning the propriety of the remedial order apart from the issue of money.[267] Thus interpreted, *Milliken II* stands for the bold proposition that special remedial programs, even expensive ones, may be required to remedy the effects of past segregation. The most striking aspect of this interpretation is the idea that something more than pupil reassignment may be required to undo a past system of segregation. When read together with the prior cases, however, this proposition loses significance. For one thing, the remedial programs may be the only possible remedy in Detroit, since the one aspect of segregation that will not be remedied after *Milliken I* is racial concentration. Pupil reassignment is unlikely to cure segregation in a school system whose students are nearly all black.[268] Second, the obligation to finance special programs would seem in view of *Pasadena* to last only until a court announces that desegregation has been accomplished in Detroit. In this respect, *Milliken II* remains ambiguous, with the ambiguity analogous to the gap between *Swann* and *Pasadena*. One could either insist that the remedial programs be maintained until the actual effects of segregation on Detroit's students are eliminated or neutralized or be ready to abandon the programs as soon as some barely plausible empirical measure of change is offered.

A third feature of *Milliken II* viewed as an instance of remedial vigor is that the compelled state expenditures upheld in *Milliken II*

265. *See id.* at 270-71.

266. *See id.* at 293-94 (Powell, J., concurring).

267. In considering the validity of this alternative reading, compare the opinions of Chief Justice Burger, *id.* at 269-91, Justice Powell, *id.* at 292-98, and Justice Marshall, *id.* at 291-92.

268. *See* Milliken v. Bradley, 418 U.S. 717, 799-802 (1974) (Marshall, J., dissenting); Bradley v. Milliken, 484 F.2d 215, 245 (6th Cir. 1973), *rev'd*, 418 U.S. 717 (1974).

gain significance from the Court's refusal in the 1973 *Rodriguez* case to adopt any generalized principle of statewide resource equalization for school systems.[269] The combined force of *Rodriguez* and *Milliken I* puts the urban school system in the untenable position of being able to claim neither resources of the state or suburbs on any generalized continuing basis nor student access to the actual suburban school systems. Against that background of "separate-but-unequal," the $5,800,000 in state money disputed in *Milliken II* looks significant. In the larger context, however, the money, just like the ward plan in *Richmond*,[270] looks more like a payoff to the black community to gain its quiet acquiescence in the demise of antidiscrimination law.

D. Employment

If *Griggs* was the most important case of the era of contradiction, the only one offering a genuine threat to the hegemony of the perpetrator perspective, then the major task of the era of rationalization must be the obliteration of *Griggs*. And so it is in the area of employment that one finds the case that will likely become the centerpiece of the era of rationalization: *Washington v. Davis*.[271] While not quite obliterating *Griggs*, the Court has so undermined it that it has ceased to be a credible threat. This overall result has been achieved in three discrete steps: *Griggs*' apparent implications for all of antidiscrimination law have been squelched by limiting its doctrine to title VII; its forceful assault on the system of equality of opportunity from within the structure of title VII has been blunted by softening the scrutiny required; and its apparent application to analogous title VII problems has been denied by refusing to extend it to the other major substantive area where it had been applied by the lower courts for some time—seniority. The first two of these steps appear in *Washington v. Davis*; the third required an additional case.[272]

As noted above, *Griggs* was apparently significant for other than title VII cases insofar as it implied that neutral practices producing racially disproportionate results would have to be justified; that, for the purposes of antidiscrimination law, intent would mean no more than voluntary conduct producing racially disproportionate results; and that the best way to avoid or at least defer the impact of the first

269. *See* San Antonio Independent School Dist. v. Rodriguez, 411 U.S. 1, 54-55 (1973). Although there is no general right to resource equalization, *Milliken II* was arguably an instance of partial equalization. This indicates that the *Milliken II* plaintiffs were being paid off, as it were, via the concession of resource equalization, in order to make palatable a solution that may be viewed as no solution at all.

270. *See* text preceding note 156 *supra*.

271. 426 U.S. 229 (1976).

272. *See* International Bhd. of Teamsters v. United States, 431 U.S. 324 (1977), *discussed at* text accompanying notes 289-98 *infra*.

two was to initiate a voluntary affirmative action program.[273] In *Washington v. Davis*, the Court explicitly rejected the first two implications, thereby removing any suggestion of obligation from the third and relegating it to the easier world of voluntary tokenism.

Washington v. Davis involved a test that purported to measure verbal ability, vocabulary, reading, and comprehension. The test was challenged in its role as a criterion for admission to the training program for District of Columbia police officers. Given a failure rate that was four times as high for blacks as for whites, the plaintiffs asserted, in an action commenced before title VII became applicable to governmental employment, that the test was prima facie unconstitutional. The Court held that absent direct or inferential proof that the test was employed with a design to produce racially disproportionate results, the disproportionate failure rate was not itself significant enough to create a prima facie case and that there was no requirement that the test demonstrate any rationality at all.[274] Using an intriguing kind of inside-out reasoning, the Court quickly rebutted the common sense notion that racial discrimination under the fifth or fourteenth amendments meant the same thing as racial discrimination under title VII. Mr. Justice White's terse offering was that "[w]e have never held that the constitutional standard for adjudicating claims of invidious racial discrimination is identical to the standards applicable under Title VII, and we decline to do so today."[275]

To support its position, the Court offered a "parade of horribles" argument that would be embarrassing in a first-year law class: "A [contrary] rule . . . would raise serious questions about, and perhaps invalidate, a whole range of tax, welfare, public service, regulatory, and licensing statutes that may be more burdensome to the poor and to the average black than to the more affluent white."[276] For precedent, the Court turned to cases like *Wright v. Rockefeller*,[277] which involved electoral districting, but failed to explain why a conclusion that an inherently nonrational decision like districting need not be justified in rational terms compels the conclusion that an ostensibly rational practice like testing is equally secure from scrutiny.

Thus, with quiet efficiency[278] the Court eliminated all extra-title

273. *See* notes 194-203 *supra* and accompanying text.

274. *See* 426 U.S. at 244-48.

275. *Id.* at 239.

276. *Id.* at 248 (footnote omitted).

277. 376 U.S. 52 (1964).

278. Compare public awareness of Washington v. Davis, 426 U.S. 229 (1976), with public awareness of the far less significant case of Regents of the Univ. of Cal. v. Bakke, 98 S. Ct. 2733 (1978).

VII implications of *Griggs*. The alternative holding of *Washington v. Davis* went a step further, softening the severe scrutiny thought to be required by *Griggs* to the point where *Griggs* is no longer much of a threat even in title VII cases. *Griggs* itself had never reached the question of degree of rationality demanded from the tests, since the case offered a strong inference of purposeful discrimination and the employer declined to offer any proof concerning the validity of the test.[279] *Griggs* did, however, use strong language in its insistence on job-relatedness, business necessity, and the elimination of "built-in headwinds" to minority employment.[280] In addition, *Griggs* cited with approval the tough stance on job-relatedness taken by the Equal Employment Opportunity Commission (EEOC) and paid homage to the EEOC as deserving of deference in its administrative interpretations of the statute.[281] This strict insistence on proof of job-relatedness seemed doctrinally secure as late as 1975, when the Court in *Albemarle Paper Co. v. Moody*[282] insisted on genuine proof of job-relatedness and again relied on the EEOC guidelines.[283]

In three respects, the Court in *Washington v. Davis* dropped any pretense of strictness with respect to job-relatedness and simultaneously abandoned its posture of deference to the EEOC: the test was ultimately validated by nothing more than intuitive generalization. There may have been evidence that the challenged test correlated with some degree of significance with another test given to trainees at the end of the training program,[284] but there was no evidence that either the entrance test or the final test in any way related to qualities or abilities relevant to being a police officer.[285] In fact, there was no proof that the test given at the end of the training program measured anything taught in that program, even assuming that the program was related to future performance as a police officer. The most that was established was that the test correlated with another test, which in itself is hardly surprising. But that other test may or may not measure something, which something, even if measured, may or may not have anything to do with the job for which the training program is supposed to prepare those who pass the initial test. In this context,

279. *See* Griggs v. Duke Power Co., 401 U.S. 424, 427-28, 432 (1971); notes 186-87 *supra* and accompanying text.

280. 401 U.S. at 431-32.

281. *Id.* at 433-34. The guidelines are set out at *id.* at 433 n.9. *See* 29 C.F.R. §§ 1607.1-.14 (1977).

282. 422 U.S. 405 (1975).

283. *See id.* at 425, 431.

284. *See* 426 U.S. at 251 n.17. But one must go to the court of appeals opinion to see how minimal that significance was. *See* Davis v. Washington, 512 F.2d 956, 962 n.38 (D.C. Cir. 1975), *rev'd*, 426 U.S. 229 (1976).

285. *See* Davis v. Washington, 512 F.2d 956, 963 (D.C. Cir. 1975), *rev'd*, 426 U.S. 229 (1976).

the Court's conclusion, shared with the district court, that "some minimum verbal and communicative skill would be very useful, if not essential, to satisfactory progress in the training regimen"[286] seems little more than an assumption of the desired conclusion.[287]

Thus, while *Griggs* remains good law with respect to title VII cases involving tests and other objective hiring criteria,[288] it has lost a good deal of its force even in those areas. And last Term the Court rejected the unanimous views of eight courts of appeals by refusing to apply the *Griggs* approach to its other major area of application—seniority. In *International Brotherhood of Teamsters v. United States,*[289] the Court conceded that the *Griggs* approach to neutral practices under title VII would serve to invalidate seniority systems that perpetuated the effects of prior racial discrimination even where such discrimination was not proved or provable as a separate violation of the Act.[290] The Justices nevertheless concluded, by a seven-to-two majority, that the qualified exemption clause of section 703(h)[291] insulated such seniority systems from attack as violations in themselves.[292] To reach its result, the Court chose to construe the qualified exemption for seniority contrary to the way it had construed the very similar qualified exemption for tests in *Griggs*. In addition, the Court distinguished as remedy rather than violation its own willingness to uphold awards of retroactive seniority in hiring discrimination cases.[293] That position had been taken just a year earlier in *Franks v. Bowman Transportation Co.,*[294] which turned out to be a remedial counterpoint decided in advance of the case narrowing the violation.[295] The majority relied on the legislative history of the original 1964 Civil Rights Act, which, although seeming to support its position, is difficult to reconcile with equally persuasive arguments

286. 426 U.S. at 250.

287. *See The Supreme Court, 1975 Term,* 90 HARV. L. REV. 56, 122-23 & n.63 (1976). On test validation, see authorities cited note 196 *supra.*

288. *See* Dothard v. Rawlinson, 433 U.S. 321, 328-32 (1977).

289. 431 U.S. 324 (1977).

290. *Id.* at 348-50.

291. 42 U.S.C. § 2000e-2(h) (1970).

292. *See* 431 U.S. at 356-57. *See also* United Air Lines, Inc. v. Evans, 431 U.S. 553, 558-60 (1977).

293. *See* 431 U.S. at 347-56. This separation of remedy issues from violation issues is voiced with even greater force and clarity in United Air Lines, Inc. v. Evans, 431 U.S. 553, 558-60 (1977).

294. 424 U.S. 747 (1976).

295. This same strange juxtaposition of seemingly broad remedy and narrow violation appears in housing discrimination law. *Compare* Hills v. Gautreaux, 425 U.S. 284, 286, 305 (1976) (potentially wide-ranging remedy), *with* Village of Arlington Heights v. Metropolitan Hous. Dev. Corp., 429 U.S. 252, 264-71 (1977) (narrow definition of violation). *See also* Roberts, *The New Segregation,* CORNELL L.F., June 1977, at 2.

based on the legislative history of the 1972 amendment-reenactment of title VII. The latter argument simply presumes some congressional awareness of the numerous and consistent lower court decisions construing section 703(h).[296]

Ultimately, however, the doctrinal intractability of *Teamsters* is irrelevant. The point here is not that *Teamsters* was wrong or that *Griggs* was right. It may even be conceded that as as a purely logical matter *Griggs* could have been decided the other way. The point here is that *Teamsters* is basically inconsistent with *Griggs* and that it amounts to a rigorous reassertion of the perpetrator perspective. To challenge the effects of seniority, which means lay-offs or reduced opportunities for better jobs, it is now necessary, however disproportionate the racial impact, to prove that those suffering the consequences are identifiable victims of post-1965 instances of hiring discrimination. If all you can show is pre-1965 discrimination, however blatant, you have no claim, unlike *Griggs,* where the Court seemed to regard as relevant that the testing scheme was perpetuating the employer's pre-Act discrimination or the effects of years of school segregation.[297] But even for post-1965 hiring discrimination, the effect of *Teamsters* is to place the difficult burdens on the victims, who must identify their perpetrators before being entitled to relief[298] rather than rely on the impact of the seniority system to establish a prima facie case and thereby switch the burden of justifying its results to the defendants. Finally, if the *Griggs* standards continue to be relaxed, it will be that much more difficult to establish the hiring discrimination that is prerequisite to any remedy altering the adverse impact of seniority systems.

V. CONCLUSION

In this Article, I have attempted to describe, with an emphasis on what I have called the "victim perspective," the major developments in antidiscrimination law from the *Brown* case through the present. I do not think the "why" of this development can be an-

296. Until *Teamsters,* the courts of appeals had assumed that title VII did not immunize seniority systems that perpetuated the effects of prior discrimination. *See* International Bhd. of Teamsters v. United States, 431 U.S. 324, 346 n.28 (1977), and cases cited therein. It is altogether rational to assume that Congress was cognizant of and adopted this viewpoint when it amended and reenacted title VII in 1972. Equal Employment Opportunity Act of 1972, Pub. L. No. 92-261, §§ 3-8, 86 Stat. 103 (codified at 42 U.S.C. §§ 2000e to 2000e-17 (Supp. V 1975)). *Teamsters,* however, rejected this interpretation of title VII and overruled, sub silentio, those cases it cited. *Compare* 431 U.S. at 346 n.28, *with id.* at 355-56.

297. *See* Griggs v. Duke Power Co., 401 U.S. 424, 427, 430 (1971).

298. *See* International Bhd. of Teamsters v. United States, 431 U.S. 324, 360-62, 367-71 (1977).

swered with reference to legal doctrine, nor do I think that it is a satisfactory answer merely to invoke the rules that would be appropriate in a future, color-blind society. Despite any implications to the contrary, the preceding pages have not been a critique of the Burger Court, at least not in the sense that I hold that institution responsible for failing to legislate the victim perspective into being. I do believe that the decisions of the era of contradiction created expectations that were subsequently frustrated by Burger Court decisions, but I cannot regard the Court as autonomous and separate from the society that orchestrates it and therefore cannot regard that one institution as the villain of the tale.

In a forthcoming sequel to this Article, I will attempt to explore some of the problems involved in answering the "why" behind the current state of antidiscrimination law and will offer some ways of thinking about antidiscrimination law in the larger context of American society. I will suggest that the developments I have described become more comprehensible when related to class structure in American society, the relationship between problems of race and problems of class, and the special role of the myth of equality of opportunity.

[7]

THE ETHEREAL SCHOLAR: DOES CRITICAL LEGAL STUDIES HAVE WHAT MINORITIES WANT?

*Richard Delgado**

Introduction

What does Critical Legal Studies (CLS) have to offer racial minorities in their quest for social justice? More generally, what legal theory or program best meets the needs and desires of minorities? Any acceptable theory must be radical, or at any rate progressive, one would think, since minorities want to change the world. Although CLS purports to be a radical theory,[1] minorities have not flocked to it. And CLS has not paid much attention to minorities, not placing racial questions on its agenda until this year, ten years after its formation as a legal movement.[2]

This article suggests that the current schism between CLS and minorities results from a fundamental difference between what CLS proposes and what minorities seek in a legal theory. Part I describes what may be called the negative and positive aspects of the CLS program, and explains why they are troublesome for minorities. Part II reveals how a common theme of the CLS critique—the advocacy of informality—ignores the need for structure in containing and eliminating racism. The last section of the article describes what a radical political program must include to serve the interests of minorities, and outlines the social arrangements that could best provide the safe and decent conditions necessary for minorities to flourish.

---

* Professor of Law, University of California, Davis. J.D., University of California, Berkeley (Boalt Hall), 1974.

[1] *See, e.g.*, Hutchinson & Monahan, *Law, Politics and the Critical Legal Scholars: The Unfolding Drama of American Legal Thought*, 36 Stan. L. Rev. 199, 199–202 (1984); Sparer, *Fundamental Human Rights, Legal Entitlements, and the Social Struggle: A Friendly Critique of the Critical Legal Studies Movement*, 36 Stan. L. Rev. 509, 509–10 (1984).

[2] Approximately 40 minority lawyers, law students and law professors, out of a total of approximately 150 people, attended the 1987 annual meeting of the Conference on Critical Legal Studies. (The minority attendance at previous meetings has been much smaller.) The topic of the 1987 annual meeting was race. The program was entitled "The Sounds of Silence: Racism and the Law."

I. CLS Themes—From a Minority Perspective

The CLS program has both negative and positive features. The negative themes include a far-ranging attack on American legal and social institutions,[3] while the positive themes describe an alternative, utopian society.[4] What follows is an analysis of those elements of the CLS negative and positive programs that minorities find unappealing and worrisome.

A. The CLS Negative Program

I admit at the outset that the CLS negative program contains much that is useful for minorities. Its attack on the public/private distinction breaks down the artificial barrier between the public sphere, in which conduct is highly regulated, and the private sphere, in which it is not.[5] The CLS critique of the social order demonstrates that current arrangements and distributions of power are neither necessary nor natural,[6] and that hierarchy irrationally places some at the top while it sacrifices those at the bottom.[7] More generally, CLS challenges and decodes "Eu-

---

[3] Among the targets of the CLS program are legal education, the bar, legal reasoning, rights (including civil rights), precedent, doctrine, hierarchy, meritocracy, the prevailing liberal political vision, and conventional views of labor and the free market. *See, e.g.*, Gordon, *Critical Legal Histories*, 36 Stan. L. Rev. 57 (1984); Hutchinson & Monahan, *The "Rights" Stuff: Roberto Unger and Beyond*, 62 Tex. L. Rev. 1477 (1984); Stick, *Can Nihilism Be Pragmatic?*, 100 Harv. L. Rev. 332 (1986). *See generally* Brosnan, *Serious But Not Critical*, 60 S. Cal. L. Rev. 259 (1986). Admittedly, this article contains a number of generalizations about a body of literature which has more than one strand of thought. Although the description herein may not apply equally to all Critical Legal Scholars, common themes do appear, and I feel I have fairly summarized the field.

[4] *See infra* notes 72–83 and accompanying text; Unger, *The Critical Legal Studies Movement*, 96 Harv. L. Rev. 561 (1983); R. Unger, Knowledge and Politics (1975).

[5] *See, e.g.*, Frug, *The City as a Legal Concept*, 93 Harv. L. Rev. 1057 (1980); Kairys, *Freedom of Speech*, in The Politics of Law: A Progressive Critique 140, 163–65 (D. Kairys ed. 1982); Kairys, *Introduction*, in *id.* at 1, 3; Sparer, *supra* note 1, at 529–31.

[6] *See, e.g.*, Kennedy, *Legal Education as Training for Hierarchy*, in The Politics of Law: A Progressive Critique, *supra* note 5, at 40, 50; Mensch, *The History of Mainstream Legal Thought*, in The Politics of Law: A Progressive Critique, *supra* note 5, at 18.

[7] *See* Kennedy, *supra* note 6; *see also* D. Kennedy, Legal Education and the Reproduction of Hierarchy: A Polemic Against the System (1983); Klare, *Judicial Deradicalization of the Wagner Act and the Origins of Modern Legal Consciousness*, 62 Minn. L. Rev. 265 (1978) (attacking workplace hierarchies and judicial support thereof).

romyths" that rule the lives of minorities and consign us to lowly fates.[8]

At the same time, however, the CLS negative program contains elements that repel and in fact threaten minorities. These elements include: (i) disparagement of legal rules and rights,[9] (ii) rejection of piecemeal change,[10] (iii) idealism,[11] and (iv) use of the concept of false consciousness.[12] Much of CLS scholarship in these areas is either risky, since it asks minorities to give up something of value, or unreliable, because it is based on presuppositions that do not correspond to our experience.[13]

1. The CLS Critique of Legal Rules and Rights

The CLS critique of legal rules and reasoning is well known. Rules, since they are indeterminate and manipulable, can generate practically any result in a given situation.[14] Rules invite the savvy to operate near their borders while the uninitiated remain well inside.[15]

Rights, a special kind of rule, receive particularly harsh criticism from Critical Legal Scholars (Crits).[16] Rights legitimize society's unfair power arrangements, acting like pressure valves

---

[8] *See* Williams, *Taking Rights Aggressively: The Perils and Promise of Critical Legal Theory for Peoples of Color*, Inequal. & the L. J. (forthcoming in 1987) (attacking the Euromyths that whites rule by manifest destiny, being culturally and intellectually superior to third world persons, and that minorities must become westernized in order to gain power and control over their lives).

[9] *See infra* notes 14–22 and accompanying text.

[10] *See infra* notes 38–42 and accompanying text.

[11] *See infra* notes 45–49 and accompanying text.

[12] *See infra* notes 52–63 and accompanying text.

[13] Moreover, the CLS movement may be reaching out to women and minorities now, see *supra* note 2 and accompanying text, in part because it is under attack by the right and needs allies. *See infra* note 35 and accompanying text. Coalition-building may thus serve the temporary interest of all of these groups. *See* Bell, Brown v. Board of Education *and the Interest-Convergence Dilemma*, 93 Harv. L. Rev. 518 (1980).

[14] *See, e.g.*, Frug, *The Ideology of Bureaucracy in American Law*, 97 Harv. L. Rev. 1276, 1292 (1984); Kennedy, *supra* note 6, at 48–49; Kennedy, *Form & Substance in Private Law Adjudication*, 89 Harv. L. Rev. 1685, 1766–74 (1976); Trubek, *Max Weber on Law and the Rise of Capitalism*, 1972 Wis. L. Rev. 720, 748–49 (1972).

[15] *See* Kennedy, *Form & Substance in Private Law Adjudication*, *supra* note 14.

[16] *See generally Symposium: A Critique of Rights*, 62 Tex. L. Rev. 1363 (1984). Among the CLS writers who criticize reliance on rights are: Freeman, *Legitimating Racial Discrimination Through Antidiscrimination Law: A Critical Review of Supreme Court Doctrine*, 62 Minn. L. Rev. 1049 (1978); Hutchinson & Monahan, *supra* note 3, at 1482–83; Klare, *Labor Law as Ideology: Toward a New Historiography of Collective Bargaining Law*, 4 Indus. Rel. L.J. 450, 468–80 (1981); Tushnet, *An Essay on Rights*, 62 Tex. L. Rev. 1363 (1984).

to allow only so much injustice.[17] With much fanfare, the powerful periodically distribute rights as proof that the system is fair and just, and then quietly deny rights through narrow construction, nonenforcement, or delay.[18]

Rights, Crits argue, are never promulgated in genuinely important areas such as economic justice.[19] They protect only ephemeral things, like the right to speak or worship.[20] When even these rights become threatening, they are limited.[21]

For CLS, rights reinforce a soulless, alienating vision of society made up of atomized individuals whose only concern is to protect their own security and property.[22] Crits argue that rights are alienating since they force one to look at oneself and others as isolated rights-bearers ("I got my rights") rather than as interdependent members of a community, and make it impossible for us even to imagine what a nonhierarchical society founded on cooperation and love would be like.

The CLS critique of rights and rules is the most problematic aspect of the CLS program, and provides few answers for minority scholars and lawyers.[23] We know, from frequent and sad experience, that the mere announcement of a legal right means little. We live in the gap between law on the books and law in action. We have no difficulty imagining a better world; for us, eliminating racism would be a good start.

---

[17] *See, e.g.*, Freeman, *Antidiscrimination Law: A Critical Review*, in The Politics of Law: A Progressive Critique, *supra* note 5, at 96, 112–14; Freeman, *supra* note 16; Klare, *The Quest for Industrial Democracy and the Struggle Against Racism: Perspectives from Labor Law and Civil Rights Law*, 61 Or. L. Rev. 157 (1982).

[18] Freeman, *Antidiscrimination Law*, *supra* note 17.

[19] *E.g.*, Kennedy, *supra* note 6, at 49; Kairys, *Freedom of Speech*, *supra* note 5, at 164.

[20] *See* Kennedy, *supra* note 6, at 48–49.

[21] *E.g.*, Kairys, *Freedom of Speech*, *supra* note 5, at 164–65 (freedom of expression is limited when it becomes powerful enough to be threatening, as in the "fighting words" or "clear and present danger" cases).

[22] *See* Gordon, *New Developments in Legal Theory*, in The Politics of Law: A Progressive Critique, *supra* note 5, at 281, 287; Kennedy, *supra* note 6, at 49; Tushnet, *supra* note 16, at 1384. *But see* Singer, *The Player and the Cards: Nihilism and Legal Theory*, 94 Yale L.J. 1, 65–68 (1984) (describing rights-like features of proposed Crit society); Unger, *The Critical Legal Studies Movement*, *supra* note 4, at 597 (drawing distinction between property rights, which tend to make some individuals dependent on others, and political/civil rights, which do not pose this threat).

[23] *See, e.g.*, Williams, *Alchemical Notes: Reconstructing Ideals from Deconstructed Rights*, 22 Harv. C.R.-C.L. L. Rev. 000 (1987); Williams, *supra* note 8; G. Torres, Address at Conference on Critical Legal Studies Annual Meeting (Jan. 7, 1987) (unpublished manuscript on file with Harvard Civil Rights-Civil Liberties Law Review).

Even if rights and rights-talk paralyze us and induce a false sense of security, as CLS scholars maintain, might they not have a comparable effect on public officials, such as the police? Rights do, at times, give pause to those who would otherwise oppress us; without the law's sanction, these individuals would be more likely to express racist sentiments on the job.[24] It is condescending and misguided to assume that the enervating effect of rights talk is experienced by the victims and not the perpetrators of racial mistreatment.

Second, CLS scholars are often hazy about what would provide minorities comparable protection if rights no longer existed.[25] The CLS positive program, or Utopia, discussed below,[26] is both far from adequate and far off in time.

Third, Crits argue that rights separate and alienate the individual from the rest of the human community.[27] This may be so for the hard-working Crits who spend much of their lives in their studies and law offices.[28] For minorities, however, rights serve as a rallying point and bring us closer together.[29] On the other hand, any distance rights place between us and others may be beneficial; there is at least safety in distance.[30]

One explanation for the CLS position on rights may be that the average Crit, a white male teaching at a major law school,

---

[24] *See* G. Allport, The Nature of Prejudice 472 (1954); Delgado, *Words that Wound: A Tort Action for Racial Insults, Epithets and Name-Calling*, 17 Harv. C.R.-C.L. L. Rev. 133, 148–49 (1982); P. van den Berghe, Race and Racism 20–21 (2d ed. 1978) (law's sanction has some effect in discouraging expression of racist sentiments).

[25] *See infra* notes 67–73 and accompanying text (describing CLS' positive program); Brosnan, *supra* note 3, at 264–67 (CLS' critiques of rights lack a theory of justice); *id.* at 268 (describing CLS as politically passive).

[26] *See infra* notes 80–83 and accompanying text.

[27] *See supra* note 22; Sparer, *supra* note 1, at 529–30.

[28] *See* Dalton, *The Clouded Prism*, 22 Harv. C.R.-C.L. L. Rev. 000 (1987) (describing critical scholars, typically white males who spend their lives in books, as being out of touch with the minority experience).

[29] *See generally* D. Bell, Race, Racism and American Law 279–361 (2d ed. 1980) (describing black movement and struggle for civil rights).

[30] *Compare* Kennedy, *The Structure of Blackstone's Commentaries*, 28 Buff. L. Rev. 205, 217 (1979) (we need, but fear, community; observing that a single look from a friend can reduce a victim to misery), *with* Abortion, Moral and Legal Perspectives (J. Garfield & P. Hennessy, eds. 1985) (close—especially sexual—relationships with men are risky and ill-advised because of power disparities between men and women and the oppression of women in society). Minorities run comparable risks. *See, e.g.*, Delgado, *supra* note 24 (minorities frequently subject to slights, rebuffs, and slurs); C. Pierce, Unity in Diversity: Thirty-Three Years of Stress, Solomon Carter Fuller Lectures, American Psychiatric Ass'n Meeting, Washington, D.C. (May 12, 1986) (transcript on file with Harvard Civil Rights-Civil Liberties Law Review) (blacks frequent victims of "microaggressions"). *See generally* A. Higginbotham, In the Matter of Color (1978).

has little use for rights.[31] Those with whom he comes in contact in his daily life—landlords, employers, public authorities—generally treat him with respect and deference. Rarely is he the victim of coercion, revilement, or contempt.[32] In the mind of the average Crit, rights offer relatively little security, while they promote a shrunken, atrophied, and unsatisfying social existence.[33] Rights transform those governed by them into lone, deformed stick figures vulnerable to pressures emanating from large corporations or faceless bureaucracies.[34] Yet, when Crits are treated insensitively or unfairly, or are coerced into giving up something of value—such as an academic appointment in a tenure battle tinged by anti-Crit bias—they have been as quick as anyone to resort to the language of rights.[35] Their behavior in such situations exemplifies the universal tendency of beleaguered persons and groups to revert to rights-talk.

For minorities, however, that rights minimize many forms of coercion is of enormous importance. At the same time, the psychic rewards that Crits believe will result from a rightless interracial "community" are far from our experience. Even if such rewards were achievable, they would necessarily rank lower than simple security on our scale of need. Of course, a utopian community of the sort Crits advocate might provide minorities with both security and psychic satisfaction. As will be shown later, however, that hope is probably vain.[36]

In short, the two groups see rights differently. White CLS members see rights as oppressive, alienating and mystifying. For minorities, they are invigorating cloaks of safety that unite

---

[31] *See generally* Williams, *supra* note 23 (describing differing attitudes of the author and a white male colleague regarding an apartment lease in New York City); Dalton, *supra* note 28; Gabel, *The Phenomenology of Rights-Consciousness and the Pact of the Withdrawn Selves*, 62 Tex. L. Rev. 1563 (1984).

[32] I use "rarely" in a relative sense. *See* Delgado, *supra* note 24, at 135–49 (frequency and severity of race-based harms greatest in minority populations).

[33] *See supra* note 22.

[34] These are the forms of mistreatment most white communitarians seem principally concerned about. *See, e.g.*, Bush, *Between Two Worlds: The Shift from Individual to Group Responsibility in the Law of Causation of Injury*, 34 UCLA L. Rev. (forthcoming in 1987). *See generally* M. Sandel, Liberalism and the Limits of Justice (1982).

[35] For example, when two Crits at an eastern law school were experiencing tenure difficulty, allegedly because of their politics and innovative teaching, CLS members around the country wrote to the university's president, urging him to investigate charges that the law school's personnel procedures were biased and infringed the Crits' rights of academic freedom.

[36] *See infra* notes 75–79 and accompanying text (critique of the CLS positive program).

us in a common bond. Instead of coming to grips with the different function of rights for the two groups, Crits insist that minorities adopt their viewpoint, labeling disagreement on our part false consciousness[37] or a lack of political sophistication.

2. *The CLS Critique of Piecemeal Reform*

Critical scholars reject the idea of piecemeal reform. Incremental change, they argue, merely postpones the wholesale reformation that must occur to create a decent society.[38] Even worse, an unfair social system survives by using piecemeal reform to disguise and legitimize oppression.[39] Those who control the system weaken resistance by pointing to the occasional concession to, or periodic court victory of, a black plaintiff or worker as evidence that the system is fair and just.[40] In fact, Crits believe that teaching the common law or using the case method in law school is a disguised means of preaching incrementalism and thereby maintaining the current power structure.[41] To avoid this, CLS scholars urge law professors to abandon the case method, give up the effort to find rationality and order in the case law, and teach in an unabashedly political fashion.[42]

The CLS critique of piecemeal reform is familiar, imperialistic and wrong. Minorities know from bitter experience that occasional court victories do not mean the Promised Land is at hand.[43] The critique is imperialistic in that it tells minorities and other oppressed peoples how they should interpret events affecting them.[44] A court order directing a housing authority to

---

[37] For an explanation of the term "false consciousness," see *infra* notes 52–63 and accompanying text. *See also* Gabel, *Reification in Legal Reasoning*, 3 Res. in L. & Soc. 25, 25–27 (1980) (defining false consciousness as reification).

[38] *See* Schwartz, *With Gun and Camera Through Darkest CLS-Land*, 36 Stan. L. Rev. 413, 421–23 (1984). *See generally* Brest, *The Fundamental Rights Controversy: The Essential Contradictions of Normative Constitutional Scholarship*, 90 Yale L.J. 1063 (1981).

[39] *See* Gordon, *supra* note 22, at 286. *See also* Freeman, *supra* note 16; Klare, *supra* note 7.

[40] *See* Freeman, *supra* note 16.

[41] *See* Kennedy, *supra* note 6.

[42] *See* D. Kennedy, *supra* note 7; Kennedy, *supra* note 6.

[43] *See, e.g.*, D. Bell, *supra* note 29, at 2–51; *see also* M. Jorrin, Governments of Latin America 120 (1953) (citing slogan, "Hecha la ley, hecha la trampa"—every law generates its own loophole).

[44] *See generally* Delgado, *The Imperial Scholar: Reflections on a Review of Civil Rights Literature*, 132 U. Pa. L. Rev. 561 (1984).

disburse funds for heating in subsidized housing may postpone the revolution, or it may not. In the meantime, the order keeps a number of poor families warm. This may mean more to them than it does to a comfortable academic working in a warm office. It smacks of paternalism to assert that the possibility of revolution later outweighs the certainty of heat now, unless there is evidence for that possibility. The Crits do not offer such evidence.

Indeed, some incremental changes may bring revolutionary changes closer, not push them further away. Not all small reforms induce complacency; some may whet the appetite for further combat. The welfare family may hold a tenants' union meeting in their heated living room. CLS scholars' critique of piecemeal reform often misses these possibilities, and neglects the question of whether total change, when it comes, will be what we want.

3. CLS' Idealism

The CLS program is also idealistic.[45] CLS scholars' idealism transforms social reality into a mental construct.[46] Facts become intelligible only through the categories of thought that we bring to experience. Crits argue that the principal impediments to achieving an ideal society are intellectual. People are imprisoned by a destructive system of mental categories that blocks any vision of a better world.[47] Liberal-capitalist ideology so shackles individuals that they willingly accept a truncated existence and believe it to be the best available. Changing the world requires primarily that we begin to think about it differently.[48] To help break the mental chains and clear the way for the creation of a new and better world, Crits practice "trashing"—a process by which law and social structures are shown

---

[45] I use the word "idealism" in its philosophic sense, whereby explanations of social reality are in the realm of thought or consciousness, rather than in material forces or concrete actions. *See* The Random House Dictionary of the English Language 707 (J. Stein ed. 1971) (definition 5a of "idealism").

[46] *See* Schwartz, *supra* note 38, at 422, 426–28; Gordon, *supra* note 22, at 291.

[47] *See* Gordon, *supra* note 22, at 288–89; Kelman, *Interpretive Construction in the Substantive Criminal Law*, 33 Stan. L. Rev. 591, 671–72 (1981); Kennedy, *Antonio Gramsci and the Legal System*, 6 A.L.S.A. Forum 32 (1982); Kennedy, *Critical Labor Law: A Comment*, 4 Indus. Rel. L.J. 503, 506 (1981).

[48] *See* Gordon, *supra* note 22, at 291 (individuals' principal limitations are their own imagination and thought, but article concedes that, for example, "propensities for evil" and "finite resources" might also play some part in limiting life possibilities of the poor).

to be contingent, inconsistent and irrationally supportive of the status quo without good reason.[49]

CLS scholars' idealism has a familiar ring to minority ears. We cannot help but be reminded of those fundamentalist preachers who have assured us that our lot will only improve once we "see the light" and are "saved."

Are our chains really mental? They may be so for members of privileged groups. They are much less so for minorities. Imagine that the Crits' trashing program succeeded and that all laws were repealed. Would our lot improve? That proposition is open to serious doubt. The forces that hold us back are not largely mental, legal, nor even political. What holds us back is, simply, racism—the myriad of insults, threats, indifference, and other "microaggressions" to which we are continually exposed.[50]

Because the Crits are intellectuals, they assign a large role to reason and ideology. Yet reason and ideology do not explain all evil. Telling an individual that he or she harbors racism will not make it go away; telling a black person that a rebuff was racially motivated will not ease its sting. Racism will not go away simply because Crits show that legalisms are indeterminate, that rights are alienating and legitimizing, and that law is a reflection of the interests of the ruling class. Whatever utility these concepts may have in other settings and in attempting to explain the angst of CLS members,[51] they have limited application in helping to understand, much less cure, racism.

4. The CLS Concept of False Consciousness

The concept of false consciousness is the final aspect of Crit scholarship that minorities find problematic.[52] Workers and

---

[49] *See* Gordon, *supra* note 22, at 289 (thinking one's way through the veil of ideological mystification spun by the dominant culture); Kairys, *Legal Reasoning*, in The Politics of Law: A Progressive Critique, *supra* note 5, at 11–17. *See generally* Kelman, *Trashing*, 36 Stan. L. Rev. 293 (1984).

[50] *See* C. Pierce, *supra* note 30 (describing microaggressions as those "subtle, minor, stunning, automatic assaults . . . by which whites stress blacks unremittingly and keep them on the defensive, as well as in a psychologically reduced condition"); Pettigrew, *New Patterns of Racism: The Different Worlds of 1984 and 1964*, 37 Rutgers L. Rev. 673, 687, 690 (1985).

[51] Rights-based talk may distress white professionals who hunger for a more communitarian, fulfilling lifestyle than is currently attainable within their professional lives and social class.

[52] *See generally* Lukacs, History and Class Consciousness (1968); Freeman, *supra* note 16; Kairys, *Introduction*, *supra* note 5; Kennedy, *Antonio Gramsci and the Legal System*, *supra* note 47.

minorities buy into a system that degrades and oppresses them, and vehemently defend that system with a kind of "false honor."[53] These groups accept their own subordination because they believe that the constitutional system protects their property against takings by the state, and that it elevates their status above that of the lowest class.[54] Thus, oppressed people not only accept the liberal ideology and the mental shackles described in the preceding section, but also embrace it loyally and reject the proffered assistance of revolutionaries.

Some CLS writers even argue that the Framers intended false consciousness to exist. While extolling the virtues of freedom, the Framers set out to achieve ideological hegemony for themselves and their class by providing for separate classes and by protecting the property and prerogatives of employers and slave owners.[55]

False consciousness rationalizes the lowly status of workers, women, minorities and other oppressed groups.[56] According to capitalist-liberal ideology, society consists of individuals who express political preferences through voting and achieve economic results through the marketplace.[57] The system is formally fair; therefore, if one is poor, reviled, hungry, or out of work, it is one's own fault.[58] At the same time, the person who occupies a position of power deserves it. In a meritocratic society, the cream rises to the top. The duty of everyone else is to obey.

Ideologically achieved domination becomes a self-generating spiral. The masses are persuaded that they are of little merit. Demoralized, they take little interest in elections or in the way political and economic life is run.[59] Thus, false consciousness

[53] *See* Gabel & Kennedy, *Roll Over Beethoven*, 36 Stan. L. Rev. 1, 26–27, 33–34 (critique of illusory rights) (1984); Johnson, *Do You Sincerely Want to Be Radical?*, 36 Stan. L. Rev. 247, 255–56 (1984). *See generally* Kennedy, *supra* note 6 (hierarchy sets up artificial and false sense of self); Kennedy, *supra* note 30 (structure of society made possible by consciousness of society); Kennedy, *Form and Substance in Private Law Adjudication*, *supra* note 14.

[54] *See supra* note 52.

[55] Sparer, *supra* note 1, at 537. *See* D. Bell, *supra* note 29, at 16–29. Bell does not subscribe to the Crits' theory of black subordination via false consciousness.

[56] *See* Hyde, *The Concept of Legitimation in the Sociology of Law*, 1983 Wis. L. Rev. 379 (1983); *see also supra* note 52.

[57] *See* Kairys, *Freedom of Speech*, *supra* note 5, at 164; *cf.* Johnson, *supra* note 53, at 255–56.

[58] *See* Freeman, *supra* note 16, at 1075; Klare, *Law-Making as Praxis*, 40 Telos 123, 134 (Summer, 1979).

[59] *See* Pettigrew, *supra* note 50, at 674–75.

blinds them to the alienation, lack of justice, conflict and unfairness inherent in political life.

Civil rights law is subject to particularly scathing criticism. Crits argue that the purpose of civil rights is to reconcile minorities to subordination by convincing us that the system is fair; our lowly status is simply the result of our inferiority.[60] The legal system protects society's investment in the subordination of minorities by assuring everyone that the status quo is inevitable.[61] It accomplishes this by doling out the occasional victory, such as *Brown v. Board of Education*,[62] and by ensuring that most civil rights are formal, rather than substantive.[63]

As with the other elements of the negative program, one should begin by asking whether the concept of false consciousness holds true for minorities. Much of what Crits criticize as false consciousness evinces their distrust of liberal legalisms and the elusive promises of court victories. Most of us have already acquired this distrust; society has provided us with more than adequate tutelage.[64] We know from Derrick Bell[65] and from personal experience not to place too much reliance on liberal attorneys who say they know exactly what we want. We know, indeed we live, the bogus public-private distinction.[66]

Moreover, it is worth questioning the extent to which our current subordination is caused by uncritical absorption of self-defeating ideologies, as opposed to other forces. Much more of our current plight is due to other factors: coercion by the dominant group; exclusion from clubs, networks, information, and needed help at crucial times; microaggressions; and the paralysis and hopelessness caused by the majority culture's denial of our pain and reality. (Who among us has not been asked by a white

---

[60] *See* Kennedy, *Antonio Gramsci and the Legal System, supra* note 47, at 8.

[61] *See supra* note 47 and accompanying text.

[62] 347 U.S. 483 (1954).

[63] *See generally* Freeman, *supra* note 16 (antidiscrimination laws actually perpetuate discrimination through formality).

[64] *See supra* notes 23, 43 and accompanying text; *see generally* Pettigrew, *supra* note 50 (formal condemnation of racism by courts and legislators since 1964 has reduced blatant, violent acts of racism, but other forms persist).

[65] Bell, *Serving Two Masters: Integration Ideals and Client Interests in School Desegration Litigation*, 85 Yale L.J. 470 (1976) (conflicts of interest between minority clients and their lawyers).

[66] *See* Kairys, *Freedom of Speech, supra* note 5, at 163–164.

person, naively or almost incredulously, "Do you really, in this day and age, suffer on account of your race?"[67])

Ultimately, the CLS false-consciousness analysis raises more questions than it answers. If false consciousness exists and is so powerful, why are only minorities and workers afflicted by it, and not white radicals? Is there not something patronizing in diagnosing an intellectual disease that exclusively afflicts persons of color?[68] Is not "false consciousness" an expression, like "incompetent" or "insane," that gives others the authority to treat the victim as if he lacks humanity, autonomy, or will?[69] Is not false consciousness an excuse for white radicals to assert and retain power they would otherwise have to explain and justify? Does not the CLS program create its own false consciousness within the law schools which employ CLS radicals, and ultimately within society at large? Unless coupled with practical action to storm trenches and organize workers, something CLS members have been remarkably slow to do,[70] the CLS reform program allows society to validate myths about free speech and the right to dissent.[71]

B. The CLS Positive Program

Critical Legal Studies, to date, has devoted much less effort to developing a positive program than to criticizing rules and social structures.[72] In general, the Crits' positive aim is to establish a Utopia in which true community would prevail.[73] De-

---

[67] *See* Pettigrew, *supra* note 50, at 690–97 (many whites believe racial problem has been solved, but continue to engage in subtle forms of racism).

[68] *Cf.* Schwartz, *supra* note 38, at 438 (describing elements of paternalism in CLS scholarship).

[69] *Cf.* M. Shapiro & R. Spece, Bioethics and Law: Cases, Materials and Problems 168–73 (1980) (terms like "ill" taken as justifying nonconsensual treatment of those so inflicted, when such treatment would otherwise be intolerable).

[70] *See* Brosnan, *supra* note 3, at 264–68 (CLS politically passive, concentrates on doctrinal and conceptual manipulation at the expense of developing a theory of justice). *See also* Johnson, *supra* note 53, at 281–83 (program for action hazy and platitudinous); *but see* D. Kennedy, *supra* note 7 (proposing concrete reforms to law school structure and operation); Gabel & Harris, *Building Power & Breaking Images*, 11 N.Y.U. Rev. L. & Soc. Change 369 (1982) (urging revolutionary legal activism); Sparer, *supra* note 1, at 565–73 (urging progressive social action).

[71] *See supra* notes 19–21 and accompanying text (CLS criticizes free speech as an ephemeral right).

[72] *See* Sparer, *supra* note 1, at 565–71; Schwartz, *supra* note 38, at 426–28 (theoretical utopianism); *id.* at 448–52 (grotesque and irresponsible proposals).

[73] *See* Brest, *supra* note 38, at 1109; Gabel, *supra* note 37, at 45–46; Kennedy, *Form and Substance in Private Law Adjudication*, *supra* note 14, at 1771.

cisionmaking would be decentralized; rules would be set by small groups such as factory workers, farm workers, and students,[74] and would remain subject to constant renegotiation.[75] Hierarchy would not exist; everyone would be equal.[76] There would be no need for rights—at least not so many as we recognize today. Instead, everyone would share work, goods and responsibilities.[77]

Individuals would benefit from the de-emphasis on individualism in Utopia. In contemporary society, the individual lacks depth and character because of his isolation and lack of commitment to others.[78] He may be free in a formal sense, but he is also stunted and barely human. In a non-hierarchical, nonrepressive society, on the other hand, the human personality would flourish.[79]

The Crits' positive program would poorly serve the needs of minorities. Some radical theoreticians may indeed be lonely. Most minority lawyers and law professors are not: we have each other. We meet, share experiences, recount horror stories, laugh and cry together. Victimization brings us together, building in us a community. It is much more problematic to accept the invitation, if it is that, to join Crits and other whites in mixed-race communities lacking in structure or rules.

Two immediate difficulties confront any serious discussion of incorporating minorities into the utopian communities envisioned by the Crits. First, one must be a self who is fully recognized as a member of a community of selves before one can merge into such a community, and certainly before the lines between self and others can safely begin to blur. How can this

---

[74] *See* Hutchinson & Monahan, *supra* note 1, at 230.

[75] *Id.*; *see also* Kennedy, *supra* note 53, at 1771.

[76] *See, e.g.*, Klare, *supra* note 7 (equality in the workplace); Simon, *The Ideology of Advocacy: Procedural Justice and Professional Ethics*, 1978 Wis. L. Rev. 29, 133 (1978) (equality of lawyer and client).

[77] *See* Abel, *A Socialist Approach to Risk*, 41 Md. L. Rev. 695 (1982) (shared risks among workers and managers); Gabel, Book Review, 91 Harv. L. Rev. 302, 315 (1977) (shared selves—merging of sense of self with sense of others so as to blur lines among persons); Kennedy, *Form and Substance in Private Law Adjudication*, *supra* note 14, at 1771.

[78] *See* Gabel and Kennedy, *supra* note 53, at 46; *cf.* C. Gilligan, In a Different Voice 173 (1983) (identifying in women a morality of connectedness). *See generally* Bush, *supra* note 34.

[79] *See* Unger, *The Critical Legal Studies Movement*, *supra* note 4, at 579–85. *See generally* Bush, *supra* note 34.

happen unless society first recognizes us as coequal members, something it has yet to do?[80]

Second, there are no guarantees that racism would not resurface in the CLS communities. To date, Crits have not articulated a psychological or political theory of the origin of racism or of how it could be eradicated. If racism were to surface in a CLS-style Utopia, there would be no rules, rights, federal statutes, or even courts to counteract it. Even if there were tribunals or people's commissions of some kind, would they be guided by strict scrutiny[81] in examining cases of prejudice? Probably not, since the once-oppressed and politically powerless groups would presumably have been empowered by the egalitarian Utopia. Perhaps these difficulties could be overcome. In the meantime, however, the costs of moving to a utopian society would be borne by minorities, since the dismantling of formal structures would initially lead to an increase in racist behavior.[82]

Ostensibly, the CLS choice of structure for the post-revolutionary community is neutral and based on those arrangements with the greatest potential for humanity. However, that choice is not value-free. Utopian society would empower whites, giving them satisfaction currently denied,[83] and disempower minorities, making life even less secure than it is today. As a black leader is supposed to have said, "Community don't look like me."

II. Informality—The Source of the Trouble

Much of the misfit between the CLS program and the aspirations of minorities is due to the informality of the CLS program.[84] CLS themes and approaches criticize formal struc-

---

[80] On the difficulty of achieving selfhood in a racist society, see, e.g., G. Allport, *supra* note 24, at 142–62; W. Grier & P. Cobbs, Black Rage (1968).

[81] Inability of a group to fend for itself in the political marketplace is a principal justification for applying strict scrutiny under the equal protection clause to state action. *See* San Antonio Indep. School Dist. v. Rodriguez, 411 U.S. 1, 28 (1972); *cf.* United States v. Carolene Products Co., 304 U.S. 144, 152 n.4 (1938).

[82] *Cf.* D. Bell, *supra* note 29, at 29–30, 40–46 (costs of racial remedies always placed on blacks or poor whites); Bell, *Minority Admissions and the Usual Price of Racial Remedies*, 67 Calif. L. Rev. 3 (1979).

[83] *See* G. Torres, *supra* note 23.

[84] For a discussion of formalism and nonformalism in the context of adjudicatory processes, see Delgado, Dunn, Brown, Lee & Hubbert, *Fairness and Formality: Minimizing the Risk of Prejudice in Alternative Dispute Resolution*, 1985 Wis. L. Rev. 1359 (1985).

tures such as rights, rules and bureaucracies, while opting for consciously informal processes that rely on good will, intersubjective understanding and community. The CLS positive and negative programs exemplify this informality; they illustrate the Crits' preference for holistic approaches that sweep everything at once into their scope.[85]

Whatever sense informal, small-scale politics may make for the CLS membership, it is bad news for minorities. Discretionary judgments colored by racism or other forms of prejudice are made possible by replacing rules, guidelines and rights with fluid, informal decisionmaking. In fact, structureless processes affirmatively increase the likelihood of prejudice. CLS theorists have avoided confronting these risks, since CLS lacks a political and psychological theory of racism. CLS theory simply assumes that racism is just another form of class-based oppression, a product of a hierarchal social structure.[86]

The Crits' focus on informality also ignores the influence that rules have on an individual's character and action. A society that enacts rules and provides structures to curb racism announces that racism is unacceptable behavior. By committing ourselves to norms of fairness we become fairer people. By changing the structure, we change the setting in which we act and ultimately change ourselves. If we jettison rules and structures, we risk losing the gains we have made in combatting racism.

The psychological-political analysis that follows explains and illustrates the interaction among rules, conduct and character. I outline the principal social scientific theories of racism and then develop a consensus position which explains the circumstances in which most people are likely to behave in a discriminatory fashion. I apply this view to the highly informal Crit program to demonstrate that the CLS program exposes minorities to an increased risk of prejudicial treatment.

---

[85] *See, e.g., supra* notes 14–22 and accompanying text (rejection of rights in favor of principles, shared love and cooperation); *supra* notes 33–42 and accompanying text (rejection of incremental reform; insistence on global change).

[86] I was unable to locate any CLS articles or books on the psychology of racism. The relatively few treatments of race discuss it in political or class terms. *See, e.g.*, Freeman, *supra* note 16; Hutchinson & Monahan, *supra* note 1, at 227–36 (utopian proposals center almost exclusively on reforming social arrangements to eliminate hierarchy, lessen alienation, and increase community and sharing); *cf.* Pettigrew, *supra* note 50, at 685–86 (current theorists tend to confuse race problems with class struggle).

A. Theories of Race and Racism

Most Americans harbor some degree of racial prejudice.[87] Indeed, individuals rarely come to grips with their racist impulses and bring them completely under control.[88] Most deal with them through a variety of mechanisms: displacement, denial, rationalization, overcompensation and compromise.[89]

Social scientists have developed a number of overlapping theories to explain the origin of prejudice based on race, ethnicity, sex, or other immutable characteristics.[90] The principal approaches are: psychoanalytic theories, which explain prejudice in terms of unconscious forces and deep-seated syndromes, such as the authoritarian personality;[91] socioeconomic theories, which explain prejudice through historical trends, social group clashes and scapegoating;[92] and social-psychological theories, which explain racism by means of social conditioning and in-group/out-group categories.[93] It is likely that each of these theories partly explains the multifaceted aspects of racist behavior.

[87] *See Is the Dream Over?*, Newsweek on Campus, Feb. 1987, at 10, 12 (black students "treated like aliens"; "[t]ales of insults abound"); Friedrich, *Racism on the Rise*, Time, Feb. 2, 1987, at 18, 21 (survey of attitudes); *Racism Flares on Campus*, Time, Dec. 8, 1980, at 28 (changes in national mood; prejudice now considered "acceptable" in some quarters); *Less Tolerance for Cults, Broad Pattern of Prejudice Revealed*, San Francisco Chronicle, Mar. 9, 1987, at 4, col. 3 (reporting results of Gallup poll).

For classic studies of the nature and extent of ethnic prejudice among Americans, see G. Allport, *supra* note 24, at 79–80, 197–202. For a recent study of the more subtle forms of prejudice, see generally Pettigrew, *supra* note 50.

[88] *See* G. Allport, *supra* note 24, at 338; I. Katz, Stigma—A Social Psychological Analysis 97 (1981); Pettigrew, *supra* note 50, at 688–89 (many avoid outward expressions of racism, but without internalizing norms against it).

[89] *See* Delgado, *supra* note 84, at 1384 (discussing the principal psychological methods by which individuals deal with tension between racist impulses and public norms condemning racism); Pettigrew, *supra* note 50, at 690 (discussing avoidance and displacement mechanisms).

[90] Some of these theories are summarized in Delgado, *supra* note 84, at 1375–83. *See generally* P. van den Berghe, *supra* note 24.

[91] For an excellent summary of psychoanalytic theories of racism, see Lawrence, *The Id, The Ego and Equal Protection: Reckoning with Unconscious Racism*, 39 Stan. L. Rev. 317, 331–36 (1987); *see also* G. Allport, *supra* note 24, at 199; T. Adorno, E. Frenkel-Brunswik, D. Levinson & R. Sanford, The Authoritarian Personality (1950); Simpson & Yinger, *The Personality Functions of Prejudice and Discrimination*, in Racial and Cultural Minorities: An Analysis of Prejudice and Discrimination (G. Simpson & J. Yinger 4th ed. 1972).

[92] *See* G. Allport, *supra* note 24, at 224–25 (historical scapegoating); *id.* at 234–38 (unconscious use of racism and scapegoating to maintain group loyalty); J. Kovel, White Racism—A Psychohistory 44 (1984) (psychology of a people a product of historical forces); Delgado, *supra* note 84, at 1378–79; *see also* Handlin, *Prejudice and Capitalist Exploitation*, 6 Commentary 79 (1948) (psychological explanation of racism incomplete; explanation must reach out to include social forces).

[93] *See* G. Allport, *supra* note 24, at 22, 29–47, 139; K. Clark, Prejudice and Your Child 17 (2d ed. 1963); J. Kovel, *supra* note 92, at 132. *See generally* Snyder, *On the*

On the other hand, racism runs counter to the body of public principles that form our national ethos, including fairness, egalitarianism and humanitarianism.[94] The conflict between racist impulses and the American creed causes many people to act inconsistently—fairly and humanely on one occasion, thoughtlessly or with prejudice on another.[95] Racism and racial egalitarianism are thus maintained in equipoise. Americans are influenced by both public and private norms with respect to race.[96] The highly principled public norm exhorts us to treat others in an unprejudiced, evenhanded fashion.[97] The private norms, the standards that guide us during moments of intimacy or familiarity, are much less noble.[98] In private settings, prejudicial behavior and speech are much more likely to appear. The same individual may thus act quite differently on different occasions, depending on whether he sees himself as governed by public or private values.

The "situational specificity"[99] of the racist impulse supplies the best means for its control. Most people suppress their prejudices when environmental features remind them that racism will not be tolerated and that the American creed demands a high standard of conduct. Although there are other theories and approaches to racism,[100] the "confrontation" approach—where prejudice is publicly confronted and discouraged through formal

---

Self Perpetuating Nature of Social Stereotypes, in Cognitive Processes in Stereotyping and Intergroup Behavior 183 (D. Hamilton ed. 1981); Delgado, *supra* note 84, at 1380 (summarizing social-psychological theories of prejudices).

[94] For the classic statement of this view, see G. Myrdal, An American Dilemma: The Negro Problem and Modern Democracy (1962).

[95] *See* I. Katz, *supra* note 88, at 23; P. van den Berghe, *supra* note 24, at 20–21; Delgado, *supra* note 84, at 1384–85; Fairchild & Gurin, *Traditions in the Social-Psychological Analysis of Race Relations*, 21 Am. Behav. 757, 764 (1978).

[96] *See* G. Myrdal, *supra* note 94, at LXXI, 80.

[97] *Id.*

[98] *See supra* notes 87–89 and accompanying text.

[99] *See* I. Katz, *supra* note 88, at 23; J. Kovel, *supra* note 92, at 54–55; Fairchild & Gurin, *supra* note 95, at 764.

[100] The leading contender is the "social contact" theory, which supports much of the push for social integration through, for example, school desegregation. This theory argues that prejudice arises from the individual's mistaken belief that minority group members hold beliefs and values different from one's own. Consequently, the belief may be dispelled through demonstration, via close contact, that it is erroneous. According to the social contact theorists, however, not all kinds of contact reduce discrimination. The contact must be among individuals of equal status and sanctioned by social supports, such as law and custom. *See* G. Allport, *supra* note 24, at 261–81; Delgado, *supra* note 84, at 1382, 1385–86; Simpson & Yinger, *The Reeducation of Prejudice and Discrimination: Changing the Prejudiced Person*, in Racial and Cultural Minorities: An Analysis of Prejudice and Discrimination, *supra* note 91, at 673.

structures—is the most widely accepted means of controlling prejudice in the legal and political literature.[101] The theory is supported by empirical studies of legal decisionmaking, including reviews of alternative dispute resolution and comparisons between the adversarial and inquisitorial modes of presenting evidence.[102]

Little of this will surprise minority readers. We know by a kind of instinct that there are times when our white friends can be trusted and times when they cannot. We know that there are occasions—when the flag is flying, the bands are playing, and public values are foremost in everyone's minds—when we are comparatively safe, and that there are other occasions when we must be careful.

The bottom line is that formal public settings are relatively safe for minorities, while informal private settings present risks. To minimize racism, one should structure settings so that public norms are enforced, and prejudice openly confronted and discouraged. Society should avoid creating intimate, unguided settings where highly charged interracial encounters can take place. It remains to be considered what the confrontation theory, and the formality/informality axis generated by that theory, implies for the CLS program.

B. Applying the Theory of Race to the CLS Program

The confrontation theory helps to explain why the open-ended features of the CLS program worry minority scholars. For example, the CLS positive program, which calls for small communities that function without written agendas, statutes, rules or rights,[103] would allow for discretionary judgments based on racial prejudice, and contain few of the structural features that confront and check racism. The lack of confrontation mech-

---

[101] *See, e.g.*, I. Katz, *supra* note 88, at 16, 109. *See generally* Delgado, *supra* note 84, at 1385–87.

[102] *See generally* Lind, Thibaut and Walker, *A Cross-Cultural Comparison of the Effect of Adversary and Inquisitorial Process on Bias in Legal Decisionmaking*, 62 Va. L. Rev. 271 (1976); Mnookin and Kornhauser, *Bargaining in the Shadow of the Law: The Case of Divorce*, 88 Yale L.J. 950 (1979); Nader, *Disputing Without the Force of Law*, 88 Yale L.J. 998 (1979); Thibaut and Walker, *Discovery and Presentation of Evidence in Adversary and Non-Adversary Proceedings*, 71 Mich. L. Rev. 1129 (1973); Thibaut, Walker, LaTour and Houlden, *Procedural Justice as Fairness*, 26 Stan. L. Rev. 1271 (1974); Thibaut, Walker and Lind, *Adversary Presentation & Bias in Legal Decisionmaking*, 86 Harv. L. Rev. 386 (1972).

[103] *See supra* notes 73–77 and accompanying text.

anisms would likely ensure the invasion of racism into the community.

CLS scholars' rejection of incrementalism also illustrates the dangers of informality. By insisting that everything must change at once, CLS rejects the slow, painstaking process of establishing and refining precedent, replacing that relatively formal process with a mercurial vision of social change with no clear direction and undefined ends.

Similar considerations hold true, although not quite so strongly, for CLS scholars' idealism and their use of the concept of false consciousness. The Crits' emphasis on mental constructs reveals their preference for free-form change over the concrete reform accomplished by litigation, labor activism and community organizing. CLS prefers the broad reach of thought to the measured progression that occurs through new jobs, better housing, court victories and school desegregation.

C. The Laboratory of Daily Life: Applying the Theory of Race to the CLS Organization and Its Mode of Operation

Theories, according to pragmatic philosophy, must be tested by their consequences, and by the ways in which they modify the behavior of their adherents.[104] Thus, one should examine the organizational and personal behavior of the members of the Critical Legal Studies Conference on matters of race in order to determine the possible impact of their theories on minorities, particularly since many members of the Conference believe in the inseparability of politics and daily life.[105] If the Conference's reform program holds promise for minorities, one should find a heightened racial sensitivity among the organization and its members.

An examination of the Conference on racial matters does not yield a clear-cut answer to the question. The organization, as is predictable from its theories and program, is highly informal. There are no bylaws, elections, procedures, officers, membership cards or committees.[106] Annual meetings and summer

---

[104] *See* W. James, Pragmatism, and Four Essays From the Meaning of Truth 133 (1975); *see generally* C. Peirce, *How to Make Our Ideas Clear*, in The Philosophy of Peirce: Selected Writings 23 (J. Buchler ed. 1940).

[105] *See, e.g.*, Boyle, Critical Legal Studies: A Young Person's Guide 18 (1983) (unpublished manuscript on file with Harvard Civil Rights-Civil Liberties Law Review).

[106] *Id.* at 20.

workshops are organized by ad hoc groups who decide that they have something to say. The informality of the structure allows the "white male heavies," most of whom are at Harvard, to wield a disproportionate amount of power.[107] Few women or minorities wield signficant influence.[108]

The record of individual members of the Conference is better than that of the organization itself. At least three of its well-known members wrote powerful and influential articles supporting minority causes.[109] Many Crits welcome minority colleagues on their faculties, and support affirmative action in law school admissions and appointments.[110] Yet few Crits took an active role in the aftermath of an incident in which the competence of a leading black scholar was challenged by students and colleagues.[111] In addition, there have been sporadic reports of racist language and stereotyping in Crits' scholarship,[112] and of rude treatment of minority panelists by Crits.[113] One would conclude that the Conference's record on racial justice matters is good, but not outstanding—perhaps 3.4 on a 4.0 point scale. If racism manifests itself among CLS members, it is frightening to imagine what would occur in a similarly unstructured group with a less progressively-minded membership.

III. Beyond CLS—Toward a Radical Minority Social-Legal Agenda

It is axiomatic that any social reform program that minorities would find appealing would be based on the express need for understanding and coping with racism. It is not enough to

---

[107] *Id.* at 18–28.

[108] *Id.* at 28.

[109] Brest, *The Federal Government's Power to Protect Negroes and Civil Rights Workers Against Privately Inflicted Harm, Part I*, 1 Harv. C.R.-C.L. L. Rev. 2 (1966); Brest, *The Federal Government's Power to Protect Negroes and Civil Rights Workers Against Privately Inflicted Harm, Part II*, 2 Harv. C.R.-C.L. L. Rev. 1 (1966); Freeman, *supra* note 16; Klare, *supra* note 17; *see also* Sparer, *supra* note 1.

[110] Boyle, *supra* note 105, at 18.

[111] *See* Bell, *The Price and Pain of Racial Perspective*, Stan. L. Sch. J., Apr., 1986, at 1, col. 1.

[112] *See* J. Bracamonte, R. Delgado & G. Torres, Statement at the Minority Critique Panel, Critical Legal Studies Annual Meeting (Jan. 1987) (unpublished manuscript on file with Harvard Civil Rights-Civil Liberties Law Review).

[113] *See* N. Gotanda, Statement at the Critical Legal Studies Annual Meeting (Jan. 1987) (on file with Harvard Civil Rights-Civil Liberties Law Review) (describing treatment of minority panelists at an earlier meeting).

subsume racism under some other category, such as class struggle, that fails to understand racism's subtlety and complexity. The program should incorporate some variant of the confrontation approach to containing racism.[114] The new society, and its transitional predecessor, would create structures for detecting and punishing racism and for reminding community members that such conduct will not be tolerated. Because of these structures, such a society would be relatively formal.

Any society consciously designed to promote minority well-being must initially include a strong central authority founded on a healthy skepticism both of human nature and of the possibilities of change through appeals to idealism. Tempering romanticism with watchfulness, it would instead effect change through appeals to citizens' self-interest by arguing that power and resource realignments benefit everyone.[115]

The need for centralized authority stems from the necessity for counter-coercive measures on behalf of minorities. One cannot rely on local authority to redistribute power and physical resources because it is too close to the community and unlikely to upset the status quo. The further authority is from the community, the better.

Our principal worry is not the abuse of corporate or bureaucratic power (CLS' foe), but rather the simple next-door, one-on-one microaggressions by whites.[116] It is a sad truth that, even today, many minorities find success and relative relief from racism only in highly structured, rule-bound environments such as the Army.[117] Group membership may force Crits and other majority-group members to reflect on politics and the nature of the common good, but unless such reflection is accompanied by formal barriers against racism, it is meaningless.

Conclusion

This article asked what minorities would like to see in a legal and political theory, and whether the CLS program

---

[114] *See supra* notes 100–02 and accompanying text.

[115] *Cf.* Bell, *supra* note 82, at 17 (whites permit social remedies only when these coincide with their self-interest).

[116] *See supra* note 50 and accompanying text.

[117] Blacks and other minorities have often found professional advancement in the relatively formal environment of the armed forces. *See* Moskos, *Success Story: Blacks in the Army*, Atlantic Monthly, May 1986, at 64.

matches that vision. The answer is that CLS does not provide what minorities seek.

Although some of the features of the CLS program are attractive to minorities, others increase our vulnerability to oppressive or degrading treatment by the majority. A number of these difficulties arise from CLS scholars' ironic failure to articulate a satisfactory theory of either the genesis or the treatment of racism.

The views of various scholars on racism coalesce to form a "confrontation theory," which describes the best means of confining and combatting racism. Many of the intuitive reservations and fears minorities have about the Crits' program arise from the Crits' desire to eliminate those formal societal structures which, according to the confrontation theory, are needed to curb racist impulses in society. In contrast, the radical social reform program outlined here can provide minorities the protection and security they need to function in a world dominated by persons of a race and heritage different from their own.

This reform program may be a tall order, but it is no taller than the CLS vision of an informal Utopia. Indeed, compared to the Crits' proposed society, it is a great deal more humane, safe and protective for those of us who have been denied humanity, safety and protection for so long.

[8]

VOLUME 101 MAY 1988 NUMBER 7

HARVARD LAW REVIEW

ARTICLES

RACE, REFORM, AND RETRENCHMENT: TRANSFORMATION AND LEGITIMATION IN ANTIDISCRIMINATION LAW

*Kimberlé Williams Crenshaw**

Recent works by neoconservatives and by Critical legal scholars have suggested that civil rights reforms have been an unsuccessful means of achieving racial equality in America. In this Article, Professor Crenshaw considers these critiques and analyzes the continuing role of racism in the subordination of Black Americans. The neoconservative emphasis on formal colorblindness, she argues, fails to recognize the indeterminacy of civil rights laws and the force of lingering racial disparities. The Critical scholars, who emphasize the legitimating role of legal ideology and legal rights rhetoric, are substantially correct, according to Professor Crenshaw, but they fail to appreciate the choices and possibilities available to an oppressed group such as Blacks. The Critics, she suggests, ignore the singular power of racism as a hegemonic force in American society. Blacks have been created as a subordinated "other," and formal reform has merely repackaged racism. Antidiscrimination law, she argues, has largely succeeded in eliminating the symbolic manifestations of racial oppression, but has allowed the perpetuation of material subordination of Blacks. Professor Crenshaw concludes by demonstrating the importance of exposing the racist nature of ostensibly neutral norms, and of devising strategies for change that include the pragmatic use of legal rights.

---

* Acting Professor of Law, University of California at Los Angeles. B.A., Cornell University, 1981; J.D., Harvard Law School, 1984; LL.M., University of Wisconsin, 1985.

Funding for this Article was provided by the University of Wisconsin Law School through the William H. Hastie Fellowship and by a research grant from the Academic Senate of the University of California at Los Angeles. I am unable to express my gratitude to all of the people who provided guidance, assistance, and support during the research and writing of this Article, but I would especially like to thank Dave Trubek, Dirk Hartog, Jim Jones, Bill Clune, The Hon. Shirley S. Abrahamson, Joel Handler, Rick Abel, Christine Littleton, Fran Olsen, Jon Varat, and Susan Prager for their comments and support. Bert Voorhees and Dawn Aberg provided excellent research assistance and will be sorely missed. I must extend very special thanks to Derrick Bell, without whose pathbreaking scholarship on race in law this Article would not have been possible. Finally, I wish to thank four people whose commitment to this project has gone far beyond the call of duty: Judylyn Ryan, Duncan Kennedy, Neil Gotanda, and Marian Crenshaw.

I. INTRODUCTION

IN 1984, President Reagan signed a bill that created the Martin Luther King, Jr. Federal Holiday Commission.[1] The Commission was charged with the responsibility of issuing guidelines for states and localities to follow in preparing their observances of Martin Luther King's birthday. The Commission's task would not be easy. Although King's birthday had come to symbolize the massive social movement that grew out of efforts of African-Americans[2] to end the long history of racial oppression in America, the first official observance of the holiday would take place in the face of at least two disturbing obstacles: first, a constant, if not increasing, socioeconomic disparity between the races,[3] and second, a hostile administration devoted to

---

[1] Act of Aug. 27, 1984, Pub. L. No. 98-399, 98 Stat. 1473. President Reagan's signing is reported at 20 WEEKLY COMP. PRES. DOC. 1192 (Sept. 3, 1984).

[2] I must make several comments at the outset. I shall use "African-American" and "Black" interchangeably. When using "Black," I shall use an upper-case "B" to reflect my view that Blacks, like Asians, Latinos, and other "minorities," constitute a specific cultural group and, as such, require denotation as a proper noun. *See* MacKinnon, *Feminism, Marxism, Method, and the State: An Agenda for Theory*, 7 SIGNS: J. WOMEN IN CULTURE & SOC'Y 515, 516 (1982) (noting that "Black" should not be regarded "as merely a color of skin pigmentation, but as a heritage, an experience, a cultural and personal identity, the meaning of which becomes specifically stigmatic and/or glorious and/or ordinary under specific social conditions"). The naming of Americans of African descent has had political overtones throughout history. *See* W.E.B. DUBOIS, 2 THE SEVENTH SON 12–13 (1971) (arguing that the "N" in Negro was always capitalized until, in defense of slavery, the use of the lower case "n" became the custom in "recognition" of Blacks' status as property; that the usage was defended as a "description of the color of a people;" and that the capitalization of other ethnic and national origin designations made the failure to capitalize "Negro" an insult). "African-American" is now preferred by some because it is both culturally more specific and historically more expansive than the traditional terms that narrowly categorize us as America's "other." *See infra* p. 1385.

A final prefatory remark regards the author's relationship to her subject. One of the conventions of dominant scholarship is the use of "they" or "them" to denote Blacks as a subject group. Implicit in such references is a silent "we" which carries the appearance of objectivity but actually presumes a dominant group perspective. This creates a dilemma for some Black scholars who must either risk self-exclusion by referring to our own cultural group as "they" or adopt a seemingly unscholarly approach to the subject by assuming a "we" identity. I have sometimes succumbed to convention; however, I acknowledge the dilemma in hopes that doing so may somehow bridge the distance created by my occasional use of "them" or "they."

[3] Continuing disparities exist between African-Americans and whites in virtually every measurable category. In 1986, the African-American poverty rate stood at 31%, compared with 11% for whites. *See* Williams, *Urban League Says Blacks Suffered Loss over Decade*, N.Y. Times, Jan. 15, 1988, at A10, col. 1. "[B]lack median income is 57 percent that of whites, a decline of about four percentage points since the early 1970's." Bernstein, *20 Years After the Kerner Report: Three Societies, All Separate*, N.Y. Times, Feb. 29, 1988, at B8, col. 2. Between 1981 and 1985, Black unemployment averaged 17%, compared to 7.3% for whites. *See* NATIONAL URBAN LEAGUE, THE STATE OF BLACK AMERICA 1986, at 15 (1986). In 1986, approximately 44% of all Black children lived in poverty. *See* Lauter & May, *A Saga of Triumph, a Return to Poverty: Black Middle Class Has Grown but Poor Multiply*, L.A. Times, April 2,

changing the path of civil rights reforms that some believe responsible for most of the movement's progress.[4] A focus on the continuing disparities between Blacks and whites might call, not for celebration, but for strident criticism of America's failure to make good on its promise of racial equality. Yet such criticism would overlook the progress that has been made, progress which the holiday itself represents. The Commission apparently resolved this dilemma by calling for a celebration of progress toward racial equality while urging continued commitment to this ideal. This effort to reconcile the celebration of an ideal with conditions that bespeak its continuing denial was given the ironic, but altogether appropriate title "Living the Dream."[5] The "Living the Dream" directive aptly illustrates Professor Derrick

---

1988, § 1, at 16, col. 1. Blacks comprise sixty percent of the urban underclass in the United States. *Id.* at 16, col. 3.

The African-American socioeconomic position in American society has actually declined in the last two decades. Average annual family income for African-Americans dropped 9% from the 1970's to the 1980's. *See* Williams, *supra*, at A10, col. 1. Since 1969, the proportion of Black men between 25 and 55 earning less than $5000 a year rose from 8% to 20%. *See* Lauter & May, *supra*. African-American enrollment in universities and colleges is also on the decline. *See* Williams, *supra*, at A10, col. 2.

The decline in the African-American socioeconomic position has been paralleled by an increase in overt racial hostility. *See generally* U.S. COMM'N ON CIVIL RIGHTS, INTIMIDATION AND VIOLENCE: RACIAL AND RELIGIOUS BIGOTRY IN AMERICA (1983). In addition to well-publicized incidents of racial violence like the Howard Beach attack, *see* Note, *Combatting Racial Violence: A Legislative Proposal*, 101 HARV. L. REV. 1270, 1270 & n.1 (1988); *infra* note 32, and the lynching of Michael Donald, *see Follow-Up on the News: Paying Damages for Lynching*, N.Y. Times, Feb. 21, 1988, § 1, at 45, col. 1, racial unrest has risen dramatically on university campuses. *See* Wilkerson, *Campus Blacks Feel Racism's Nuances*, N.Y. Times, April 17, 1988, § 1, at 1, col. 3.

For a comprehensive analysis of the conditions afflicting the Black urban underclass, see W. WILSON, THE TRULY DISADVANTAGED: THE INNER CITY, THE UNDERCLASS, AND PUBLIC POLICY (1987).

[4] The principal civil rights reforms are the Civil Rights Act of 1964, Pub. L. No. 88-352, 78 Stat. 243 (codified as amended at 42 U.S.C. §§ 2000(e)–2000(h)(6) (1982)); the Voting Rights Act of 1965, Pub. L. No. 89-110, 79 Stat. 437 (codified as amended at 42 U.S.C. §§ 1971–1974 (1982)); U.S. CONST. amends. XIII–XV; 42 U.S.C. §§ 1981, 1983, 1985 (1982); Exec. Order No. 11,246, 3 C.F.R. 339 (1964–1965 comp.); and the Equal Employment Opportunity Commission regulations, 29 C.F.R. §§ 1600–1691 (1987).

See ACLU, IN CONTEMPT OF CONGRESS AND THE COURTS — THE REAGAN CIVIL RIGHTS RECORD (1984); Chambers, *Racial Justice in the 1980's*, 8 CAMPBELL L. REV. 29, 31–34 (1985); Devins, *Closing the Classroom Door to Civil Rights*, 11 HUM. RTS. 26 (1984); Selig, *The Reagan Justice Department and Civil Rights: What Went Wrong*, 1985 U. ILL. L. REV. 785; Wolvovitz & Lobel, *The Enforcement of Civil Rights Statutes: The Reagan Administration's Record*, 9 BLACK L.J. 252 (1986); *see also* Hernandez, Weiss, & Smith, *How Different Is the World of 1984 from the World of 1964?*, 37 RUTGERS L. REV. 755, 757–60 (1985).

Some scholars have been critical of the overall development of civil rights law over the past decade, positing that we have reached the end of the "Second Reconstruction." *See generally* D. BELL, AND WE ARE NOT SAVED (1987); Bell, *The Supreme Court, 1984 Term — Foreword: The Civil Rights Chronicles*, 99 HARV. L. REV. 4 (1985).

[5] MARTIN LUTHER KING, JR. FEDERAL HOLIDAY COMM'N, LIVING THE DREAM (1986).

Bell's observation that "[m]ost Americans, black and white, view the civil rights crusade as a long, slow, but always upward pull that must, given the basic precepts of the country and the commitment of its people to equality and liberty, eventually end in the full enjoyment by blacks of all rights and privileges of citizenship enjoyed by whites."[6]

Commentators on both the Right and the Left,[7] however, have begun to cast doubt upon the continuing vitality of this shopworn theme. The position of the New Right, articulated by members of the Reagan Administration[8] and by neoconservative scholars such as Thomas Sowell,[9] is that the goal of the civil rights movement — the extension of formal equality to all Americans regardless of color — has already been achieved. Therefore, the vision of a continuing struggle under the banner of civil rights is inappropriate.[10] The position of the New Left, presented in the work of scholars associated with the Conference on Critical Legal Studies ("CLS"), also challenges the perception that the civil rights struggle represents a long, steady march toward social transformation.[11] CLS scholars do not significantly disagree with the goal of racial equality, but assert only the basic counterproductivity of seeking that objective through the use of legal rights. Indeed, CLS scholars claim that even engaging in rights discourse is incompatible with a broader strategy of social change. They view the extension of rights, although perhaps energizing political struggle or producing apparent victories in the short run, as ultimately legitimating the very racial inequality and oppression that such extension purports to remedy.[12]

This Article challenges both the New Left and New Right critiques of the civil rights movement. Part II develops the critical indictment of the neoconservative critique. The Right argues that the civil rights community[13] reduces civil rights to mere special-interest

---

[6] D. BELL, RACE, RACISM, AND AMERICAN LAW, § 1.2, at 7 (2d ed. 1981).

[7] I use the terms "Right" and "Left" to contrast opposing views and to offer some idea of the ideological moorings of various critiques of civil rights. I have also followed the lead of others in designating various groups as the "New" Right or the "New" Left. My understanding is that the designation "New" is appropriate given the social and political upheavals of the last two decades which have altered the rhetoric, and indeed the very composition, of traditional political groupings.

[8] *See, e.g.*, Abram, *Affirmative Action: Fair Shakers and Social Engineers*, 99 HARV. L. REV. 1312 (1986); *infra* note 23.

[9] *See infra* pp. 1339–41.

[10] *See generally* Abram, *supra* note 8.

[11] *See infra* pp. 1349–69.

[12] *See* Freeman, *Legitimizing Racial Discrimination Through Antidiscrimination Law: A Critical Review of Supreme Court Doctrine*, 62 MINN. L. REV. 1049 (1978); *infra* pp. 1349–69.

[13] Throughout this Article, I shall use the terms "civil rights community" and "civil rights constituency." The former refers to those who actively engage in political and legal struggle to improve the conditions of racial minorities historically burdened by racism in America. The term "civil rights constituency" refers to those who support the broad objectives of the civil

politics.[14] Because the Right views law and politics as essentially distinct, it presumes that demonstrating that the civil rights vision is essentially political renders it illegitimate. Yet, as is argued below, the neoconservative interpretation of antidiscrimination law reveals assumptions about racism and society that can no more transcend politics than can the civil rights vision. Thus, the neoconservative critique collapses under its own criticism.

The civil rights community, however, must come to terms with the fact that antidiscrimination discourse is fundamentally ambiguous and can accommodate conservative as well as liberal views of race and equality. This dilemma suggests that the civil rights constituency cannot afford to view antidiscrimination doctrine as a permanent pronouncement of society's commitment to ending racial subordination. Rather, antidiscrimination law represents an ongoing ideological struggle in which the occasional winners harness the moral, coercive, consensual power of law. Nonetheless, the victories it offers can be ephemeral and the risks of engagement substantial.

Part III criticizes the CLS attack on civil rights. Critical scholarship clarifies the crisis of antidiscrimination law, identifying the potential costs of engaging in liberal reform discourse. The key flaw in CLS writing on legal ideology and hegemony, however, is that it overlooks the relationship of racism to hegemony. Critical literature focuses primarily on legal consciousness and on consensual domination,[15] leaving coercion and popular consciousness unexamined. Because racism is intimately connected to both coercion and popular consciousness, the Critics' failure to examine them undermines the utility of their critique in analyzing the oppression of Black people and in explaining domination and legitimation in society as a whole.

Part IV expands the CLS perspective to address the role of racism, presenting a somewhat altered vision of society, legitimacy, and racial reform. This expanded critique presents race consciousness as a central ideological and political pillar upholding existing social conditions; race consciousness, I contend, must be taken into account in efforts to understand hegemony and the politics of racial reform. The civil rights movement is recast as a radical challenge to the dominant order even though cooptation has been and remains an ever-present threat to the movement. Finally, a realistic examination of the limited alternatives available to Blacks makes it clear that legal reform was a viable pragmatic strategy for Blacks confronted with the threat of unbridled racism on one hand and co-optation on the other.[16]

---

rights community. Although my analysis focuses on the situation of Black Americans, I leave open the possibility that it may warrant a broader application.

[14] *See infra* pp. 1339–40.

[15] *See infra* pp. 1358–60.

[16] *See infra* pp. 1384–87.

In the course of my analysis, I wish to stress three crucial aspects of the consideration of race in the American legal context. First, racism is a central ideological underpinning of American society. Critical scholars who focus on legal consciousness alone thus fail to address one of the most crucial ideological components of the dominant order. The CLS practice of delegitimating false and constraining ideas[17] must include race consciousness if the accepted objective is to transcend oppressive belief systems. Second, the definitional tension in antidiscrimination law, which attempts to distinguish equality as process from equality as result,[18] is more productively characterized as a conflict between the stated *goals* of antidiscrimination law. Is the goal limited to the mere rejection of white supremacy as a normative vision,[19] or may the goal be expanded to include a societal commitment to the eradication of the substantive conditions of Black subordination?[20] Finally, the Black community must develop and maintain a distinct political consciousness in order to prevail against the co-opting force of legal reform. History has shown that the most valuable political asset of the Black community has been its ability to assert a collective identity and to name its collective political reality. Liberal reform discourse must not be allowed to undermine the Black collective identity.

II. The New Right Attack: Civil Rights as "Politics"

A. The Neoconservative Offensive

The Reagan Administration arrived in Washington in 1981 with an agenda that was profoundly hostile to the civil rights policies of

---

[17] This practice of deconstruction, or, more irreverently, "trashing," is a principal tactic of Critical scholars. *See, e.g.*, Kelman, *Trashing*, 36 STAN. L. REV. 293 (1984); *infra* pp. 1354–56.

[18] *See, e.g.*, Belton, *Discrimination and Affirmative Action: An Analysis of Competing Theories of Equality and* Weber, 59 N.C.L. REV. 531, 539–41 (1981) (characterizing the tension as between means and ends); Freeman, *supra* note 12, at 1052–53 (characterizing the tension as a conflict between "victim" and "perpetrator" perspectives); Fallon & Weiler, Firefighters v. Stotts: *Conflicting Models of Racial Justice*, 1984 SUP. CT. REV. 1 (characterizing the tension as between a model of group justice and a model of individual justice).

[19] When discussed as a normative vision, white supremacy is used to refer to a formal system of racial domination based on the explicit belief that Blacks are inferior and should be subordinated. *See infra* pp. 1372–74.

[20] This characterization is premised on the notion that a society once expressly organized around white supremacist principles does not cease to be a white supremacist society simply by formally rejecting those principles. The society remains white supremacist in its maintenance of the actual distribution of goods and resources, status, and prestige in which whites establish norms which are ideologically self-reflective. The phenomenon is ideological because it is a fantasy, because it is not real. *See infra* pp. 1372–74.

the previous two decades. The principal basis of its hostility was a formalistic, color-blind view of civil rights that had developed in the neoconservative "think tanks" during the 1970's.[21] Neoconservative doctrine singles out race-specific civil rights policies as one of the most significant threats to the democratic political system.[22] Emphasizing the need for strictly color-blind policies, this view calls for the repeal of affirmative action and other race-specific remedial policies, urges an end to class-based remedies, and calls for the Administration to limit remedies to what it calls "actual victims" of discrimination.[23]

A number of early episodes sent a clear message that the Reagan Administration would be inhospitable to the civil rights policies adopted by earlier administrations.[24] For example, the Civil Rights Division of the Justice Department, under Deputy Attorney General William Bradford Reynolds,[25] abruptly changed sides in several cases.[26] Other serious attacks on the civil rights constituency included

---

[21] Prominent among these was the Heritage Foundation. *See, e.g.*, S. BUTLER, M. SANERA & W. WEINROD, MANDATE FOR LEADERSHIP II: CONTINUING THE CONSERVATIVE REVOLUTION (Heritage Foundation) (1984); HERITAGE FOUNDATION, MANDATE FOR LEADERSHIP: POLICY MANAGEMENT IN A CONSERVATIVE ADMINISTRATION (C. Heatherly ed. 1981) (hereinafter HERITAGE FOUNDATION REPORT); HERITAGE FOUNDATION, A MANDATE FOR LEADERSHIP REPORT: THE FIRST YEAR (R. Holwill ed. 1982).

[22] *See* HERITAGE FOUNDATION REPORT, *supra* note 21, at 447–48.

[23] For scholarship generally supportive of this restrictive view, see generally Abram, cited in note 8 above; Cooper, *The Coercive Remedies Paradox*, 9 HARV. J.L. & PUB. POL'Y 77 (1986), which argues for color-blindness in equal protection remedial action and against "victim-blind" remedies; Graglia, *Race-Conscious Remedies*, 9 HARV. J.L. & PUB. POL'Y 83 (1986), which argues that the term "race-conscious remedies" is merely a euphemism for race discrimination; Kristol, *Equal Protection Doctrine: Foundations in Mud*, 9 HARV. J.L. & PUB. POL'Y 35 (1986), which argues that once narrow interpretation is abandoned, there is no principled stopping point; and Schiff, *Reverse Discrimination Re-Defined as Equal Protection: The Orwellian Nightmare in the Enforcement of Civil Rights Laws*, 8 HARV. J. L. & PUB. POL'Y 627 (1985), which argues that Congress intended title VII to mean "equal protection" and not "reverse discrimination." For a critical analysis of affirmative action and the neoconservative view, see Kennedy, *Persuasion and Distrust: A Comment on the Affirmative Action Debate*, 99 HARV. L. REV. 1327 (1986).

[24] *See, e.g.*, Exec. Order No. 11,478, 3 C.F.R. 803 (1966–1970) (establishing the policy of equal opportunity in federal government); Exec. Order No. 11,246, 3 C.F.R. 339 (1964–65 comp.) (establishing nondiscrimination in government employment).

[25] For the views of Deputy Attorney General Reynolds, who directed the implementation of the Reagan civil rights agenda, see Reynolds, *Individualism vs. Group Rights: The Legacy of* Brown, 93 YALE L.J. 995 (1984) [hereinafter Reynolds, *Individualism vs. Group Rights*]; Reynolds, *The Reagan Administration and Civil Rights: Winning the War Against Discrimination*, 1986 U. ILL. L. REV. 1001 [hereinafter Reynolds, *The Reagan Administration and Civil Rights*].

[26] The most notorious was Bob Jones University v. United States, 461 U.S. 574 (1983), in which the Reagan Administration refused to argue a case, initiated by the Justice Department during the previous Administration, that sought to maintain the Internal Revenue Service policy of denying tax-exempt status to schools that discriminated on the basis of race. The Supreme Court denied the Justice Department's request for a dismissal, and appointed a private attorney to argue the case. For a critical analysis of the Administration's conduct in *Bob Jones*, see

Reagan's attempt to fire members of the United States Commission on Civil Rights,[27] the Administration's opposition to the 1982 amendment of the Voting Rights Act,[28] and Reagan's veto of the Civil Rights Restoration Act.[29]

These fervent attempts to change the direction of civil rights law generated speculation that the Reagan Administration was anti-Black[30] and ideologically opposed to civil rights.[31] Yet the Adminis-

---

Selig, cited in note 4 above, at 817–21. A response to the Selig critique of *Bob Jones* appears in Reynolds, *The Reagan Administration and Civil Rights*, cited in note 25 above, at 1011–14.

In Washington v. Seattle School District No. 1, 458 U.S. 457, 471–72 (1982), the Justice Department switched sides to support the constitutionality of an anti-busing initiative. In Plyler v. Doe, 457 U.S. 202 (1982), the Carter Administration had filed a brief as amicus curiae in a suit alleging that Texas had unconstitutionally denied public education to the children of undocumented workers. Although the government had argued this position successfully in the Fifth Circuit, the Reagan Justice Department refused to express any view on the constitutionality of Texas' policy, which the Court subsequently invalidated.

[27] Although the Commission was originally chartered as an independent watchdog agency, Reagan successfully replaced most of its members with persons whose political views reflected his own more restrictive view of civil rights. For a discussion of Reagan's "commission-packing" set against the historical background of the Commission, see Comment, *The Rise and Fall of the United States Commission on Civil Rights*, 22 HARV. C.R.-C.L. L. REV. 449, 476–80 (1987).

[28] Pub. L. No. 97-205, 96 Stat. 131 (1982) (codified at 42 U.S.C. § 1973(b)). The Administration favored a straight extension of the Voting Rights Act of 1965 over the 1982 Amendments' incorporation of a results test in the new section 2(b). The 1982 Amendments provided in part:

> A violation of subsection (a) is established if, based on the totality of circumstances, it is shown that the political processes leading to nomination or election in the State or political subdivision are not equally open to participation by members of a class of citizens protected by subsection (a) in that its members have less opportunity than other members of the electorate to participate in the political process and to elect representatives of their choice. The extent to which members of a protected class have been elected to office in the State or political subdivision is one circumstance which may be considered: *Provided*, That nothing in this section establishes a right to have members of a protected class elected in numbers equal to their proportion in the population.

96 Stat. at 134. For a discussion of the Reagan Administration's role in the passage of the 1982 Amendments, see Boyd & Markman, *The 1982 Amendments to the Voting Rights Act: A Legislative History*, 40 WASH. & LEE L. REV. 1347, 1384–88, 1393–1410 (1983). For a sense of conservative reservations regarding the 1982 Amendments, see the minority views of Senator East as expressed in the Senate Judiciary Committee Reports on the Amendments. *See* S. Rep. No. 417, 97th Cong., 2d Sess., *reprinted in* 1982 U.S. CODE CONG. & ADMIN. NEWS, vol. 2, at 370–410.

[29] *See* Johnson, *Reagan Vetoes Bill That Would Widen Federal Rights Law*, N.Y. Times, March 17, 1988, at A1, col. 6.

[30] Associate Justice Thurgood Marshall recently characterized Reagan as among the Presidents most hostile to the civil rights of Blacks. *See* N.Y. Times, Sept. 9, 1987, at A1, col. 1. Polls show that the vast majority of Black Americans share Marshall's assessment of the Reagan Administration's hostility toward civil rights. *See, e.g.*, *JCPS Survey of Political Attitudes*, FOCUS, Sept. 1984, at 9.

[31] *See* Days, *Turning Back the Clock: The Reagan Administration and Civil Rights*, 19 HARV. C.R.-C.L. L. REV. 309 (1984); *cf.* Selig, *supra* note 4, at 796 (arguing that "[t]he fundamental difference between the Nixon and Reagan administrations in the school desegregation area is that the Nixon administration recognized its responsibility to the rule of law").

tration denied that any racial animus motivated its campaign.[32] Far from viewing themselves as opponents of civil rights, Reagan, Reynolds, and others in the Administration apparently saw themselves as "true" civil rights advocates seeking to restore the original meaning of civil rights.

Neoconservative scholar Thomas Sowell[33] perhaps best articulates the philosophy underlying the New Right policies on race and law. Sowell presents the neoconservative struggle against prevailing civil rights policies as nothing less than an attempt to restore law to its rightful place and to prevent the descent of American society into fascism.[34] Sowell suggests that the growing popularity of white hate groups is evidence of the instability wrought by improvident civil rights policies.[35] To Sowell, the growth of anti-Black sentiment is an understandable reaction to a vision that has threatened to undermine democratic institutions, delegitimize the court system, and demoralize the American people.

The culprit in this epic struggle is a political view which Sowell has dubbed "the civil rights vision."[36] According to Sowell, this view developed as the leaders of the civil rights movement shifted the movement's original focus on equal treatment under the law to a demand for equal results notwithstanding genuine differences in ability, delegitimizing the movement's claim in a democratic society.[37] The civil rights vision has nothing to do with the achievement of civil rights today, according to Sowell, because in reality "the battle for civil rights was fought and won — at great cost — many years ago."[38] Sowell's central criticism is that the visionaries have attempted to infuse the law with their own political interpretation, which Sowell characterizes as separate from and alien to the true meaning of civil rights.[39] He argues that, although these visionaries have struggled

[32] *See, e.g.*, Williams, *Rights Leaders See U.S. Pattern in Queens Attack*, N.Y. Times, Dec. 25, 1986, at 36, col. 3.

[33] Sowell is a Senior Fellow at the Hoover Institution, Stanford University.

[34] *See* T. SOWELL, CIVIL RIGHTS: RHETORIC OR REALITY? 116 (1984).

[35] *See id.* at 90. Sowell observes that "[e]armarked benefits for blacks provide some of these hate groups' strongest appeals to whites." *Id.* Moreover, such appeals are spreading "not only among ignorant southern rednecks but also in more middle class and educated classes across the nation — in short, in places where they never had a foothold before." *Id*; *see also* Williams, *Discrimination and Public Policy*, in 1 SELECTED AFFIRMATIVE ACTION TOPICS IN EMPLOYMENT AND BUSINESS SET-ASIDES: A CONSULTATION/HEARING OF THE UNITED STATES COMMISSION ON CIVIL RIGHTS 9, 18 (March 6–7, 1985) (arguing that affirmative action is "immoral" and builds support for Nazis and the Ku Klux Klan). The Ku Klux Klan, however, has always counted among its members those from middle class and upper class backgrounds. Indeed, some Supreme Court Justices were former Klan members, including Edward Douglas White and Hugo Black.

[36] *See* T. SOWELL, *supra* note 34, at 13–35.

[37] *See id.* at 37–48.

[38] *Id.* at 109.

[39] *See id.* at 109–10 (contrasting Sowell's view of "civil rights" with those of civil rights

and sacrificed in the name of civil rights, they nonetheless merit censure for undermining the stability of American society through their politicization of the law.[40]

Sowell singles out the judiciary for especially harsh criticism.[41] Judges, according to Sowell, have ignored the original understanding of title VII and imposed their own political views instead. "The perversions of the law by federal judges . . . have been especially brazen," Sowell charges.[42] According to Sowell, judges have participated in a process by which "law, plain honesty and democracy itself [have been] sacrificed on the altar of missionary self-righteousness."[43] Sowell cautions that when judges allow law to be overridden by politics, the threat of fascism looms ever large:

> When judges reduce the law to a question of who has the power and whose ox is gored, they can hardly disclaim responsibility, or be

---

advocates). For other examples of this view, see T. EASTLAND & W. BENNETT, COUNTING BY RACE 143–49 (1979), which characterizes the dichotomy between the true and false visions of civil rights as embodying contrasting commitments to "moral" and "numerical" equality, and argues against the "false" commitment to numerical equality on both historical and philosophical grounds; and Williams, cited in note 35 above, at 10, which characterizes this "false" vision of civil rights as the "new civil rights vision."

[40] According to Sowell, "[s]incerity of purpose is not the same as honesty of procedure. Too often they are opposites. Lies and deceptions 'in a good cause' are all too common, and nowhere more so than in political and legal doctrines that falsely sail under the flag of 'civil rights.'" T. SOWELL, *supra* note 34, at 120; *see also* Williams, *supra* note 35, at 10 ("The evolution of the new civil rights movement is an effort by some to impose greater government control as a means to acquire more personal political power and wealth. But another important thrust to the new civil rights results from honest, but incorrect, views of how the world operates.").

[41] Although Sowell is apparently convinced that law is fundamentally separate from politics, he believes that it can be captured by politics. Sowell's position appears to ignore both the critique of law as politics and ethics developed by the Legal Realists, *see, e.g.*, Cohen, *Transcendental Nonsense and the Functional Approach*, 35 COLUM. L. REV. 809 (1935); Cook, *The Logic and Bases of the Conflict of Laws*, 33 YALE L.J. 457 (1924), and the work of European structuralist and post-structuralist philosophical schools showing the general indeterminate "meaning" of texts, *see, e.g.*, J. DERRIDA, OF GRAMMATOLOGY (G. Spivak trans. 1976); V. LEITCH, DECONSTRUCTIVE CRITICISM: AN ADVANCED INTRODUCTION (1983). Both of these approaches have been extended as specific critiques of American legal ideology by Critical legal scholars. For a discussion of the relationship between critical theory, structuralist theory, early post-structuralist theory, and critical legal theory, see Kennedy, *Critical Theory, Structuralism and Contemporary Legal Scholarship*, 21 NEW ENG. L. REV. 209 (1985–86). For a general review of these critiques of legal texts as having a meaning apart from the politics of the interpretive act, see Gordon, *Unfreezing Legal Reality: Critical Approaches to Law*, 15 FLA. ST. U. L. REV. 195 (1987), and Mensch, *The History of Mainstream Legal Thought*, in THE POLITICS OF LAW: A PROGRESSIVE CRITIQUE 18 (D. Kairys ed. 1982).

[42] *See* T. SOWELL, *supra* note 34, at 120. This I also take to be the import of Walter Williams' misleading reference to Thurgood Marshall's remark, "You guys have been practicing discrimination for years. Now it is our turn." Williams, *supra* note 35, at 10 (quoting W DOUGLAS, THE COURT YEARS 1939–1975: THE AUTOBIOGRAPHY OF WILLIAM O. DOUGLAS 149 (1980)).

[43] T. SOWELL, *supra* note 34, at 119.

morally superior, when others respond in kind. We can only hope that the response will not someday undermine our whole concept of law and freedom. Fascism has historically arisen from the utter disillusionment of the people with democratic institutions.[44]

B. A Critique of the Critique: The Indeterminacy of Civil Rights Discourse

Given the seriousness of his accusations, particularly those against the judiciary, one would expect Sowell's proof of subversion to be substantial. His repeated accusations that the true law has been subverted raise expectations that he will eventually identify some determinate, clearly discernible version of that law. Sowell's true law would presumably stand apart from the politics of race, yet control it, without being influenced by inappropriate political factors.[45] Sowell's only "proof" that the law has been subverted, however, rests on his assumption that such subversion is self-evident. In the context of voting, for example, Sowell declares simply: "The right to vote is a civil right. The right to win is not. Equal treatment does not mean equal results."[46]

Sowell fails to substantiate his accusations because he cannot tell us *what* the real law is, or whether it ever existed as he claims. He simply embraces language from antidiscrimination texts, imports his own meaning of its purpose, and ignores contradictory purposes and interpretations. Here Sowell, apparently without realizing it, merely embraces one aspect of a tension that runs throughout antidiscrimination law — the tension between equality as a process and equality as a result.[47]

This basic conflict has given rise to two distinct rhetorical visions in the body of antidiscrimination law — one of which I have termed the expansive view, the other the restrictive view. The expansive view stresses equality as a result, and looks to real consequences for African-Americans. It interprets the objective of antidiscrimination law as the eradication of the substantive conditions of Black subordination and attempts to enlist the institutional power of the courts to further the national goal of eradicating the effects of racial oppression.[48]

---

[44] *Id.*

[45] Sowell relies on neat statements of his formalistic theories, *see, e.g.*, *id.* at 38 ("'Equal opportunity' laws and policies require that individuals be judged on their qualifications as individuals, *without regard* to race, sex, age, etc.") (emphasis in original), but declarations of this kind are decidedly indeterminate in practice. *See infra* note 52.

[46] *Id.* at 109.

[47] *See supra* note 18.

[48] Accordingly, the Supreme Court declared that district courts hold "not merely the power but the duty to render a decree which will so far as possible eliminate the discriminatory effects

The restrictive vision, which exists side by side with this expansive view, treats equality as a process, downplaying the significance of actual outcomes. The primary objective of antidiscrimination law, according to this vision, is to prevent future wrongdoing rather than to redress present manifestations of past injustice. "Wrongdoing," moreover, is seen primarily as isolated actions against individuals rather than as a societal policy against an entire group. Nor does the restrictive view contemplate the courts playing a role in redressing harms from America's racist past,[49] as opposed to merely policing society to eliminate a narrow set of proscribed discriminatory practices. Moreover, even when injustice is found, efforts to redress it must be balanced against, and limited by, competing interests of white workers — even when those interests were actually created by the subordination of Blacks. The innocence of whites weighs more heavily than do the past wrongs committed upon Blacks and the benefits that whites derived from those wrongs.[50] In sum, the restrictive view seeks to proscribe only certain kinds of subordinating acts, and then only when other interests are not overly burdened.[51]

Although the tension between the expansive and restrictive vision is present throughout antidiscrimination law,[52] Sowell dismisses the

---

of the past as well as bar like discrimination in the future." Louisiana v. United States, 380 U.S. 145, 154 (1965).

[49] The Supreme Court stated this viewpoint with stark clarity in United Air Lines v. Evans, 431 U.S. 553, 558 (1977): "A discriminatory act . . . which occurred before the [Civil Rights Act of 1964] was passed . . . may constitute relevant background evidence [regarding present conduct] . . . but separately considered . . . is merely an unfortunate event in history which has no present legal consequences."

[50] This concern has gained special solicitude from the Supreme Court in the context of layoffs. *See* Wygant v. Jackson Bd. of Educ., 476 U.S. 267, 280–84 (1986) (plurality opinion).

[51] Derrick Bell describes this tendency through the following equation: "White Racism v. Justice = White Racism; White Racism v. White Self-Interest = Justice." *See* D. BELL, *supra* note 6, § 1.12, at 41.

[52] The problem of remedying race-neutral practices that perpetuate the effects of past racial subordination policies provides an acute demonstration of how legal reform has failed to resolve conflicts between restrictive and expansive views of discrimination. For example, in opposition to the Civil Rights Act's declared purpose — restoring victims of discrimination "to a position where they would have been were it not for the unlawful discrimination" — § 703(h) provides protection to "bona fide" seniority systems, thereby introducing opposing status quo interests within the very statute committed to bringing about the end of racial subordination. *Compare* Conference Report of the Equal Employment Opportunity Act of 1972, 118 Cong. Rec. 7166, 7168 (March 6, 1972) (stating that the Act would "represent a vital step toward the realization of equal opportunity for millions of Americans") *with* 42 U.S.C. § 2000e-2(h) (1982) ("Notwithstanding any other provision of this subchapter, it shall not be an unlawful employment practice to apply different standards of compensation, or different terms, conditions, or privileges of employment pursuant to a bona fide seniority or merit system."). Protection of bona fide seniority systems was inserted to win labor support for the bill, *see* Chambers & Goldstein, *Title VII at Twenty: The Continuing Challenge*, 1 LAB. LAW. 235, 248 n.66 (1985); W. MURPHY, DISCRIMINATION IN EMPLOYMENT 168 (4th ed. 1979); the definition of bona fide was left unclear and was the subject of repeated litigation. Nevertheless, it was clear from the beginning that this

full complexity of the problem by simply declaring that equal process is completely unrelated to equal results. Yet it is not nearly as clear as Sowell suggests that the right to vote, for instance, has nothing to do with winning; no measure of a process' effectiveness can be wholly

---

protection for seniority systems provided a barrier against the complete remedying of racial inequality. The Supreme Court has resisted efforts to overcome the last hired, first fired problem. *See* Wygant v. Jackson Bd. of Educ., 476 U.S. 267 (1986); Firefighters Local Union No. 1784 v. Stotts, 467 U.S. 561 (1984).

In many cases where § 703(h) was at issue, the question was raised whether facially neutral seniority systems that perpetuated the effects of past discrimination were *bona fide*. This issue arose in situations where employers had completely segregated and subordinated Black workers in company job lines so that the lowest white job paid more than even the highest-ranking Black job. Competitive seniority for all jobs was based on departmental seniority rather than on plant-wide seniority. After 1964, many companies merged their two job progressions; however, the departmental seniority rule still stood. Consequently, the most senior Black workers could not successfully bid for jobs in the previously all-white job progression. Plaintiffs in these cases argued that the seniority systems perpetuated past discrimination against Blacks.

Prior to 1977, at least six circuit courts of appeals held that courts could remedy the effects of past discrimination by requiring that jobs be filled on the basis of plant-wide rather than departmental seniority, and that seniority systems which perpetuated the effects of past discrimination could not be considered "bona fide." *See* United States v. Navajo Freight Lines, 525 F.2d 1318 (9th Cir. 1975); Bowe v. Colgate, Palmolive Co., 489 F.2d 896 (7th Cir. 1973); United States v. N.L. Indus., Inc., 479 F.2d 354 (8th Cir. 1973); Bailey v. American Tobacco Co., 462 F.2d 160 (6th Cir. 1972); United States v. Bethlehem Steel Corp., 446 F.2d 652 (2d Cir. 1971); Jones v. Lee Way Motor Freight, Inc., 431 F.2d 245 (10th Cir. 1970), *cert. denied*, 401 U.S. 954 (1971); Griggs v. Duke Power Co., 420 F.2d 1225 (4th Cir. 1970), *rev'd on other grounds*, 401 U.S. 424 (1971); Local 189, United Papermakers v. United States, 416 F.2d 980 (5th Cir. 1969), *cert. denied*, 397 U.S. 919 (1970). An overwhelming number of commentators agreed. *See, e.g.*, Blumrosen, *Seniority and Equal Employment Opportunity: A Glimmer of Hope*, 23 RUTGERS L. REV. 268 (1969); Fine, *Plant Seniority and Minority Employees: Title VII's Effect on Layoffs*, 47 U. COLO. L. REV. 73 (1975); Gould, *Seniority and the Black Worker: Reflections on* Quarles *and Its Implications*, 47 TEX. L. REV. 1039 (1969); Note, *Title VII, Seniority Discrimination, and the Incumbent Negro*, 80 HARV. L. REV. 1260 (1967).

This view diverged sharply from the approach suggested by unions and employers, who argued that because the Act was intended to apply prospectively, neutral practices that perpetuated the effects of past discrimination were acceptable under § 703(h). Courts, however, failed to extend the logic of their holdings, rejecting as unfair to white workers the theory that restoring Blacks to their rightful places would require employers to grant Blacks the jobs denied them. *See, e.g.*, Quarles v. Philip Morris Inc., 279 F. Supp. 505 (E.D. Va. 1968). Rather than bump whites who had received their jobs because of discrimination, courts merely allowed senior Blacks to compete for the next available vacancies. *See id.* at 520–21.

In 1977, however, the Supreme Court upset even this dubious compromise, holding in International Brotherhood of Teamsters v. United States, 431 U.S. 324 (1977), that Congress intended to protect all facially neutral seniority rights regardless of the discriminatory effect on Black workers. In so holding, the Court rejected the government's contention that no seniority system that perpetuated pre-Act discrimination could be bona fide under § 703(h). *See id.* at 353. *Teamsters* represents a move toward a more restrictive view of discrimination in which the objective of eradicating racial subordination is limited by competing interests. As the various opinions concerning seniority suggest, interpretation of § 703(h) boils down to a choice of which interest will take priority: the achievement of racial equality, or the protection of interests founded in the policies of white supremacy. Simply put, the issue was whether Black hopes of overcoming racial subordination would prevail over, or be defeated by, the status quo.

separated from the purpose for which it was initiated. Sowell implicitly acknowledges that voting is related to some notion of actual representation.[53] Having done so, he cannot completely sever that process from its admitted purpose. Depending on how one views society, democracy, and the historic significance of racial disenfranchisement, the "appropriate" relationship between voting and representation can be defined to require anything from at-large representation to full proportional representation. Sowell's attempt to sever voting from winning merely *raises* the question of process and results; it does not answer it.

As the expansive and restrictive views of antidiscrimination law reveal, there simply is no self-evident interpretation of civil rights inherent in the terms themselves. Instead, specific interpretations proceed largely from the world view of the interpreter.[54] For example, to believe, as Sowell does, that color-blind policies represent the only legitimate and effective means of ensuring a racially equitable society, one would have to assume not only that there is only one "proper role" for law, but also that such a racially equitable society already exists. In this world, once law had performed its "proper" function of assuring equality of process, differences in outcomes between groups would not reflect past discrimination but rather real differences between groups competing for societal rewards.[55] Unimpeded by irrational prejudices against identifiable groups and unfettered by government-imposed preferences, competition would ensure that any group stratification would reflect only the cumulative effects of employers'

---

[53] Sowell spends a great deal of time defending economic, "racially neutral" reasons for statistical inequities in representation. *See* T. SOWELL, *supra* note 34, at 73–90. It is apparent that he does so because one might expect equality of process to lead to equality of result.

[54] There has been a recent explosion of literature on legal texts and their interpretation. *See, e.g.*, *Interpretation Symposium*, 58 S. CAL. L. REV. 1 (1985); *Law and Literature: Symposium*, 60 TEX. L. REV. 373 (1982).

[55] *See* T. SOWELL, *supra* note 34, at 42–48. John Bunzel, then a Senior Research Fellow at the neoconservative Hoover Institution, took exactly this position in his testimony before the U.S. Commission on Civil Rights:

> [T]he most general difficulty with the argument that underutilization/disproportionality equals discrimination is that it conveniently overlooks the fact that there have always been differences of values, orientation, taste, expectation, and the like among the varied groups that compose this or any other country . . . [M]any of the differences of group outlook — differences that have influenced a disproportionate number of Italians to become opera singers, a disproportionate number of Armenians to become truck farmers, and a disproportionate number of Jews to become doctors, college professors, and novelists . . . express prima facie evidence not of discrimination, but, rather, of the vitality of democracy.

2 U.S. COMM'N ON CIVIL RTS., CONSULTATIONS ON THE AFFIRMATIVE ACTION STATEMENT OF THE U.S. COMMISSION ON CIVIL RIGHTS, at 37 (1981). Consider also the statement of Commissioner Horn: "I think one would have to say that underlying much of the discriminatory aspects is a problem . . . — poverty, socioeconomic class, etc. — that *conditions* the response of various individuals and *their inability or ability to take advantages of the opportunities offered.*" *Id.* at 54 (emphasis added).

rational decisions to hire the best workers for the least cost.[56] The deprivations and oppression of the past would somehow be expunged from the present. Only in such a society, where all other societal functions operate in a nondiscriminatory way, would equality of process constitute equality of opportunity.

This belief in color-blindness and equal process, however, would make no sense at all in a society in which identifiable groups had actually been treated differently historically and in which the effects of this difference in treatment continued into the present. If employers were thought to have been influenced by factors other than the actual performance of each job applicant, it would be absurd to rely on their decisions as evidence of true market valuations. Arguments that differences in economic status cannot be redressed, or are legitimate because they reflect cultural rather than racial inferiority, would have to be rejected; cultural disadvantages themselves would be seen as the consequence of historical discrimination.[57] One could not look at outcomes as a fair measure of merit since one would recognize that everyone had not been given an equal start. Because it would be apparent that institutions had embraced discriminatory policies in order to produce disparate results, it would be necessary to rely on results to indicate whether these discriminatory policies have been successfully dismantled.

These two visions of society correspond closely to those held by Sowell and the civil rights visionaries. In each vision, all arguments about what the law *is* are premised upon what the law *should be*, given a particular world view.[58] The conflict is not, as Sowell has suggested, between the true meaning of the law and a bastardized

---

[56] *See* T. SOWELL, *supra* note 34, at 37–60. Walter Williams argues that the real solutions to racial inequalities lie in ending government intervention in the market, such as the imposition of minimum wage laws.

> We overlook the fact that not every discriminatory action reflects dislike of Negroes. For example: certain discrimination may come from the rational behavior of individuals minimizing information costs or confronting real differences in the market, whether that market is free or institutionally constrained. And we often overlook the fact that in a free market economically irrational preferences will impose costs on whoever indulges them. Institutional restraints may render that indulgence costless to the indulger. If they do, the answer is to lift the restraints and reimpose the costs. In other words, to free the market.
>
> When we are formulating policy, we must be careful to distinguish among the three sources of "discrimination" — preference, prejudice, and real differences.

W. WILLIAMS, THE STATE AGAINST BLACKS 27 (1982).

[57] Discrimination based on race would be revealed as a social construct — a fiction — which was nevertheless operative in defining and shaping historically both the distinct culture of the dominated and the ideological constructs devaluing that culture. Recognizing the interrelated historical contingency of culture and race renders any distinction between them meaningless.

[58] For a cogent discussion of this confusion between descriptive and normative claims, see Tushnet, *An Essay on Rights*, 62 TEX. L. REV. 1363, 1371–1382 (1984) (presenting the indeterminacy critique of rights).

version, but between two different interpretations of society. Thus, though they attempt to lay claim to an apolitical perch from which to accuse civil rights visionaries of subverting the law to politics, the neoconservatives as well rely on their own political interpretations to give meaning to their respective concepts of rights and oppression. The crucial point that Sowell overlooks is that law itself does not dictate which of various visions will be adopted as an interpretive base. The choice between various visions and the values that lie within them is not guided by any determinate organizing principle. Consequently, Sowell has no basis from which to argue that color-conscious, result-oriented remedies are political perversions of the law, but that his preference, color-blind, process-oriented remedies are not.

C. The Constituency's Dilemma

The passage of civil rights legislation nurtured the impression that the United States had moved decisively to end the oppression of Blacks. The fanfare surrounding the passage of these Acts,[59] however, created an expectation that the legislation would not and could not fulfill. The law accommodated and obscured contradictions that led to conflict, countervision, and the current vacuousness of antidiscrimination law.

Because antidiscrimination law contains both the expansive and the restrictive view, equality of opportunity can refer to either. This uncertainty means that the societal adoption of racial equality rhetoric does not itself entail a commitment to end racial inequality. Indeed, to the extent that antidiscrimination law is believed to embrace color-blindness, equal opportunity rhetoric constitutes a formidable obstacle to efforts to alleviate conditions of white supremacy. As Alfred Blumrosen observes, "it [is] clear that a 'color-blind' society built upon the subordination of persons of one color [is] a society which [cannot]

---

[59] President Johnson's address to the nation at the signing ceremony was representative of the fanfare that surrounded the passage of the Act:

> I am about to sign into law the Civil Rights Act of 1964. I want to take this occasion to talk to you about what the law means to every American. We believe that all men are created equal. Yet many are denied equal treatment. We believe that all men have certain unalienable rights. Yet many Americans do not enjoy these rights. We believe that all men are entitled to the blessings of liberty. Yet millions are being deprived of those blessings — not because of their own failures, but because of the color of their skin. . . . But it cannot continue. Our Constitution, the foundation of our Republic, forbids it. Morality forbids it. And the law I will sign tonight forbids it. Its purpose is not to punish. Its purpose is not to divide, but to end divisions — divisions which have lasted too long. Its purpose is national, not regional. Its purpose is to promote a more abiding commitment to freedom, a more constant pursuit of justice, and a deeper respect for human dignity. We will achieve these goals because most Americans are law-abiding citizens who want to do what is right.

Address of President Lyndon Johnson, Washington, D.C. (July 2, 1964), *quoted in* C. WHALEN & B. WHALEN, THE LONGEST DEBATE: A LEGISLATIVE HISTORY OF THE 1964 CIVIL RIGHTS ACT 227–28 (1985).

correct that subordination because it [can] never recognize it."[60] In sum, the very terms used to proclaim victory contain within them the seeds of defeat. To demand "equality of opportunity" is to demand nothing specific because "equality of opportunity" has assimilated both the demand and the object against which the demand is made; it is to participate in an abstracted discourse which carries the moral force of the movement as well as the stability of the institutions and interests which the movement opposed.

Society's adoption of the ambivalent rhetoric of equal opportunity law has made it that much more difficult for Black people to name their reality. There is no longer a perpetrator, a clearly identifiable discriminator. Company X can be an equal opportunity employer even though Company X has no Blacks or any other minorities in its employ. Practically speaking, all companies can now be equal opportunity employers by proclamation alone. Society has embraced the rhetoric of equal opportunity without fulfilling its promise; creating a break with the past has formed the basis for the neoconservative claim that present inequities cannot be the result of discriminatory practices because this society no longer discriminates against Blacks.

Equal opportunity law may have also undermined the fragile consensus against white supremacy.[61] To the extent that the objective of racial equality was seen as lifting formal barriers imposed against participation by Blacks, the reforms appear to have succeeded. Today, the claim that equal opportunity does not yet exist for Black America may fall upon deaf ears — ears deafened by repeated declarations that equal opportunity exists.[62] Even Alfred Blumrosen — himself a civil rights visionary — demonstrates how the rhetoric of formal racial equality, by bringing about the collapse of overt obstacles, convinced people that things have changed significantly:

> The public sympathy for the plight of black Americans circa 1965 cannot be recreated, because the condition of black American[s] in

---

[60] A. Blumrosen, Twenty Years of Title VII Law: An Overview 26 (April 18, 1985) (unpublished manuscript on file in the Harvard Law Library).

[61] The decline of the civil rights consensus reflects serious differences about whether the commitment to reject racial discrimination should be extended to include race-conscious affirmative relief. In Regents of the University of California v. Bakke, 438 U.S. 265 (1978), for example, the American Jewish Committee and the Anti-Defamation League of B'nai B'rith — both traditional supporters of civil rights — filed amicus briefs opposing the Davis medical school's affirmative action program.

[62] Polls show that most Americans have adopted the rhetoric of formal racial equality. *See, e.g.*, I. KATZ, STIGMA: A SOCIAL PSYCHOLOGICAL ANALYSIS 14–16 (1981); H. SCHUMAN, C. STEEH & L. BOBO, RACIAL ATTITUDES IN AMERICA: TRENDS AND INTERPRETATIONS 71–138 (1985); Pettigrew, *The Mental Health Impact*, in IMPACTS OF RACISM ON WHITE AMERICANS 97, 114–15 (B. Bowser & R. Hunt eds. 1981). The same respondents, however, expressed anti-Black opinions and attitudes when questions were directed towards specific issues such as housing integration and miscegenation. For a review of literature discussing current racial attitudes, see Pettigrew, *New Patterns of Racism: The Different Worlds of 1984 and 1964*, 37 RUTGERS L. REV. 673, 686–93 (1985).

> 1985 is so much improved, as a result of the 1964 legislation. The success of the Civil Rights Act contained the seeds of its loss of public support. *Racism alone simply will no longer do as an explanation for the current condition of depressed minorities.* The rhetoric of the sixties sounds hollow to Americans of the eighties because it is hollow.[63]

Blumrosen and others may be correct in pointing out that many things have changed under the political, legal, and moral force of the civil rights movement. Formal barriers have constituted a major aspect of the historic subordination of African-Americans and, as I discuss below,[64] the elimination of those barriers was meaningful. Indeed, equal opportunity rhetoric gains its power from the fact that people can point to real changes that accompanied its advent. As the indeterminacy of doctrine reveals,[65] however, what at first appears an unambiguous commitment to antidiscrimination conceals within it many conflicting and contradictory interests. In antidiscrimination law, the conflicting interests actually reinforce existing social arrangements, moderated to the extent necessary to balance the civil rights challenge with the many interests still privileged over it.

The recognition on the part of civil rights advocates that deeper institutional changes are required has come just as the formal changes have begun to convince people that enough has been done.[66] Indeed, recent cases illustrate that the judiciary's commitment to racial equality has waned considerably.[67] These doctrinal and procedural devel-

---

[63] A. Blumrosen, *supra* note 60, at 13 (emphasis added).

[64] *See infra* pp. 1377–79.

[65] *See supra* note 52.

[66] *See* Reeves, *America's Choice: What It Means*, N.Y. Times, Nov. 4, 1984, § 6 (Magazine), at 36, cols. 4–5 (quoting John Seigenthaler, editor of *The Tennessean*: "I think white Americans have reached a consensus on black America. Look, we've done enough for them. If they can make it, fine. If they can't, that's their problem."). Reviewing the results of several opinion surveys, one author has concluded that most white Americans believe that racism can no longer explain the socioeconomic disparity between Blacks and whites and that socioeconomic disparities were largely a result of Blacks' lacking either effort, skills, or the "right values." *See* Kluegel, *"If There Isn't a Problem, You Don't Need a Solution": The Bases of Contemporary Affirmative Action Attitudes*, 28 AM. BEHAV. SCIENTIST 761, 766 (1985). Kluegel further points out that, to the extent whites in this study did acknowledge "some" discrimination in the 1980's, they tended to believe it occurred in roughly equal proportions to preferential treatment. This, combined with other responses, led Kluegel to conclude that the American public believes that Blacks enjoy opportunities that are equal to or greater than those of the average American. *See id.* at 769.

[67] Recent Supreme Court decisions have placed severe limitations on civil rights suits. *See, e.g.*, Firefighters Local Union No. 1784 v. Stotts, 467 U.S. 561 (1984) (precluding race-conscious remedies in layoff cases); Ford Motor Co. v. EEOC, 458 U.S. 219 (1982) (permitting company to toll accrual of backpay by offering the victim only the position previously denied, and not without lost seniority); General Tel. Co. v. Falcon, 457 U.S. 147 (1982) (imposing strict certification requirements in title VII class actions); Kremer v. Chemical Constr. Corp., 456 U.S. 461 (1982) (holding that rejection of a discrimination claim by a state agency may bar plaintiff from pursuing the claim in federal court).

opments, taken along with the overall political climate,[68] indicate that the policy of redressing discrimination no longer has the high priority it once had. As Derrick Bell argues, "At heart, many of the cases seem to reflect an unwillingness that has been evident since *Washington v. Davis* to further expand remedies for discrimination."[69] In discussing what he views as the waning of the commitment to achieve a non-racist society, Bell observes, "Discrimination claims, when they are dramatic enough, and do not greatly threaten majority concerns, are given a sympathetic hearing, but there is a pervasive sense that definite limits have been set on the weight that minority claims receive when balanced against majority interests."[70]

The flagging commitment of the courts and of many whites to fighting discrimination may not be the only deleterious effect of the civil rights reforms. The lasting harm must be measured by the extent to which limited gains hamper efforts of African-Americans to name their reality and to remain capable of engaging in collective action in the future. The danger of adopting equal opportunity rhetoric on its face is that the constituency incorporates legal and philosophical concepts that have an uneven history and an unpredictable trajectory. If the civil rights constituency allows its own political consciousness to be completely replaced by the ambiguous discourse of antidiscrimination law, it will be difficult for it to defend its genuine interests against those whose interests are supported by opposing visions that also lie within the same discourse. The struggle, it seems, is to maintain a contextualized, specified world view that reflects the experience of Blacks.[71] The question remains whether engaging in legal reform precludes this possibility.

III. THE NEW LEFT ATTACK: THE HEGEMONIC FUNCTION OF LEGAL RIGHTS DISCOURSE

Various scholars connected with the Critical Legal Studies movement[72] have offered critical analyses of law and legal reform

---

[68] *See infra* p. 1376.

[69] D. BELL, *supra* note 6, § 9.11.3, at 117 (2d ed. Supp. 1984) (citing Washington v. Davis, 426 U.S. 229 (1976)).

[70] *Id.*

[71] This is essentially Professor Matsuda's "bottom up" argument — that viewing the world through the lives of subordinated minorities provides a distinct perspective on reality. *See* Matsuda, *Looking to the Bottom: Critical Legal Studies and Reparations*, 22 HARV. C.R.-C.L. L. REV. 323 (1987); *see also* B. HOOKS, FEMINIST THEORY FROM MARGIN TO CENTER (1984) (arguing that viewing society and life from the "margin" provides important insights not available to those viewing society from the "center").

[72] This brief summary does not begin to represent a full description of Critical literature. For an introduction to Critical Legal Studies, see, for example, M. KELMAN, A GUIDE TO CRITICAL LEGAL STUDIES (1987); THE POLITICS OF LAW, cited in note 41 above; *Critical Legal*

which provide a broad framework for explaining how legal reforms help mask and legitimate continuing racial inequality. The Critics present law as a series of ideological constructs that operate to support existing social arrangements by convincing people that things are both inevitable and basically fair. Legal reform, therefore, cannot serve as a means for fundamentally restructuring society. This theory, however, is a general one, the utility of which is limited in the context of civil rights by its insufficient attention to racial domination. Removed from the reality of oppression and its overwhelming constraints, the Critics cannot fairly understand the choices the civil rights movement confronted or, still less, recommend solutions to its current problems.

A. The Critical Vision

In broadest terms, Critical scholars have attempted to analyze legal ideology and discourse as a social artifact which operates to recreate and legitimate American society. In order to discover the contingent character of the law, CLS scholars unpack legal doctrine to reveal both its internal inconsistencies (generally by exposing the incoherence of legal arguments) and its external inconsistencies (often by laying bare the inherently paradoxical and political world views imbedded within legal doctrine). Having thus exposed the inadequacies of legal doctrine, CLS scholars go on to examine the political character of the choices that were made in the doctrine's name. This inquiry exposes the ways in which legal ideology has helped create, support, and legitimate America's present class structure.

1. The Role of Legal Ideology. — Critical scholars derive their vision of legal ideology in part from the work of Antonio Gramsci, an Italian neo-Marxist theorist who developed an approach to understanding domination that transcends some of the limitations of traditional Marxist accounts.[73] In examining domination as a combination

Studies Symposium, 36 STAN. L. REV. 1 (1984); Unger, *The Critical Legal Studies Movement*, 96 HARV. L. REV. 561 (1983); Note, *'Round and 'Round the Bramble Bush: From Legal Realism to Critical Legal Scholarship*, 95 HARV. L. REV. 1669 (1982); and Dalton, Book Review, 6 HARV. WOMEN'S L.J. 229 (1983). For a bibliography of Critical scholarship, see Kennedy & Klare, *Bibliography of Critical Legal Studies*, 94 YALE L.J. 461 (1984). Although the scholarship of the conference's members has occasionally been arbitrarily grouped together for collective criticism, *see. e.g.*, Schwartz, *With Gun and Camera Through Darkest CLS-Land*, 36 STAN. L. REV. 413 (1984), the thinking in the movement is far from monolithic. For two insightful discussions of significant tensions in the movement, see Boyle, *The Politics of Reason: Critical Legal Theory and Local Social Thought*, 133 U. PA. L. REV. 685 (1985), and Trubek, *Where the Action Is: Critical Legal Studies and Empiricism*, 36 STAN. L. REV. 575 (1984). For a discussion of the current state of the project, see Gordon, cited in note 41 above.

[73] Traditional Marxist accounts present law as a tool of oppression serving to pacify the working class. *See generally* H. COLLINS, MARXISM AND LAW (1982). The Critics argue that this instrumental view is inadequate because it fails to account for the considerable support that the state and the legal system enjoy from the dominated classes. *See, e.g.*, Gordon, *New*

of both physical coercion and ideological control, Gramsci developed the concept of hegemony, the means by which a system of attitudes and beliefs, permeating both popular consciousness and the ideology of elites, reinforces existing social arrangements and convinces the dominated classes that the existing order is inevitable.[74] After observing the ability of the Italian system to withstand aggressive challenges in the years preceding the ascent of fascism, Gramsci concluded that "when the State trembled a sturdy structure of civil society was at once revealed. The State was only an outer ditch, behind which there stood a powerful system of fortresses and earthworks . . . ."[75]

Some Critical scholars place great emphasis on understanding the "fortifying earthworks" of American society. The concept of hegemony allows Critical scholars to explain the continued legitimacy of American society by revealing how legal consciousness induces people to accept or consent to their own oppression. Legal historian Robert Gordon, for example, declares that one should look not

> only at the undeniably numerous, specific ways in which the legal system functions to screw poor people . . . but rather at all the ways in which the system seems at first glance basically uncontroversial, neutral, acceptable. This is Antonio Gramsci's notion of "hegemony," *i.e.*, that the most effective kind of domination takes place when both the dominant and dominated classes believe that the existing order, with perhaps some marginal changes, is satisfactory, or at least represents the most that anyone could expect, because things pretty much have to be the way they are.[76]

According to Gordon, Gramsci directs our attention to the many thoughts and beliefs that people have adopted that limit their ability "even to *imagine* that life could be different and better."[77]

Although society's structures of thought have been constructed by elites out of a universe of possibilities, people reify these structures and clothe them with the illusion of necessity.[78] Law is an essential

---

Developments in Legal Theory, in THE POLITICS OF LAW, *supra* note 41, at 284–86; Greer, *Antonio Gramsci and "Legal Hegemony,"* in *id.* at 305.

[74] *See generally* A. GRAMSCI, SELECTIONS FROM THE PRISON NOTEBOOKS (Q. Hoare & G. Smith trans. 1971). Gramsci developed his theory after becoming intrigued by the ability of the dominant ideology to contain and dissipate even serious conflicts. Gramsci became convinced that "no regime, regardless of how authoritarian it was, could sustain itself primarily through organized state power; in the long run, its scope of popular support or 'legitimacy' was always bound to contribute to its stability . . . ." C. BOGGS, GRAMSCI'S MARXISM 38 (1976).

[75] A. GRAMSCI, *supra* note 74, at 238.

[76] Gordon, *supra* note 73, at 286 (footnote omitted).

[77] *Id.* at 287 (emphasis in original).

[78] Gordon explains the interlocking social phenomena of reification and legitimation as follows: "Though the structures are built, piece by interlocking piece, with human intentions, people come to 'externalize' them, to attribute to them existence and control over and above human choice [reification]; and, moreover, to believe that these structures must be the way they are [legitimation]." *Id.* at 288.

feature in the illusion of necessity because it embodies and reinforces ideological assumptions about human relations that people accept as natural or even immutable. People act out their lives, mediate conflicts, and even perceive themselves with reference to the law. By accepting the bounds of law and ordering their lives according to its categories and relations, people think that they are confirming reality — the way things must be. Yet by accepting the view of the world implicit in the law, people are also bound by its conceptual limitations. Thus conflict and antagonism are contained: the legitimacy of the entire order is never seriously questioned.

Relating this idea to the limitations of antidiscrimination law, Alan Freeman argues that the legal reforms that grew out of the civil rights movement were severely limited by the ideological constraints embedded within the law[79] and dictated by "needs basic to the preservation of the class structure."[80] These ideological pillars supporting the class structure were simultaneously repositories of racial domination and obstacles to the fundamental reordering of society. For example, Freeman argues that formal equality, combined with the fact that American law does not formally recognize any difference based on wealth, precluded most remedies which would have required the redistribution of wealth.[81] Yet economic exploitation and poverty have been central features of racial domination — poverty is its long-term result. A legal strategy that does not include redistribution of wealth cannot remedy one of the most significant aspects of racial domination. Similarly, the myths of "vested rights" and "equality of opportunity" were necessary to protect the legitimacy of the dominant order and thus constituted insuperable barriers to the quest for significant redistributive reform.[82] Freeman's central argument is that the severe limitations of legal reform were dictated by the legitimating role of legal discourse. If law functions to reinforce a world view that things should be the way they are, then law cannot provide an effective means to challenge the present order.

Some Critics see the destructive role of rights rhetoric as another symptom of the law's legitimating function. Mark Tushnet has offered a four-tiered critique of rights:

---

[79] *See* Freeman, *Antidiscrimination Law: A Critical Review*, in THE POLITICS OF LAW, *supra* note 41, at 96.

[80] *Id.* at 111.

[81] "[F]ormal equality . . . leads easily to evasion of remedial burdens by the rich, since American law sees no formal differences based on wealth . . . . [A] regime of formal equality will ensure that the dislocative impact [of remedying the economic costs of historical discrimination] is disproportionately borne by lower-class whites (not to mention blacks, who are burdened either way)." *Id.* *See* San Antonio Indep. School Dist. v. Rodriguez, 411 U.S. 1 (1973); Lindsey v. Normet, 405 U.S. 56, 74 (1972) ("[T]he Constitution does not provide judicial remedies for every social and economic ill."); Dandridge v. Williams, 397 U.S. 471 (1970).

[82] *See* Freeman, *supra* note 12, at 111–13.

> (1) Once one identifies what counts as a right in a specific setting, it invariably turns out that the right is unstable; significant but relatively small changes in the social setting can make it difficult to sustain the claim that a right remains implicated. (2) The claim that a right is implicated in some settings produces no determinate consequences. (3) The concept of rights falsely converts into an empty abstraction (reifies) real experiences that we ought to value for their own sake. (4) The use of rights in contemporary discourse impedes advances by progressive social forces . . . .[83]

Tushnet's first and second arguments crystallize the doctrinal dilemmas faced by the civil rights community.[84] Antidiscrimination doctrine does not itself provide determinate results. To give rights meaning, people must specify the world; they must create a picture of "what is" that grounds their normative interpretation.

Tushnet's third and fourth arguments spell out pragmatic reasons to approach rights with caution. According to Tushnet, the language of rights undermines efforts to change things by absorbing real demands, experiences, and concerns into a vacuous and indeterminate discourse.[85] The discourse abstracts real experiences and clouds the ability of those who invoke rights rhetoric to think concretely about real confrontations and real circumstances.[86]

According to Tushnet, the danger that arises from being swept into legal rights discourse is that people lose sight of their real objectives. Their visions and thoughts of the possible become trapped within the ideological limitations of the law. Tushnet suggests that, "[i]f we treated experiences of solidarity and individuality as directly relevant to our political discussions, instead of passing them through the filter of the language of rights, we would be in a better position to address the political issues on the appropriate level."[87]

Peter Gabel suggests that the belief in rights and in the state serves a hegemonic function through willed delusion:[88]

---

[83] Tushnet, *supra* note 58, at 1363–64 (footnotes omitted). For a different rendition of the critique of rights which is centered in psychoanalytic theory, see Gabel, *The Phenomenology of Rights-Consciousness and the Pact of the Withdrawn Selves*, 62 TEX. L. REV. 1563 (1984).

[84] *See supra* pp. 1346–49.

[85] *See* Tushnet, *supra* note 58, at 1382–84. Tushnet describes the danger as follows:

> When I march to oppose United States intervention in Central America, I am "exercising a right" to be sure, but I am also, and more importantly, being together with friends, affiliating myself with strangers, with some of whom I disagree profoundly, getting cold, feeling alone in a crowd, and so on. It is a form of alienation or reification to characterize this as an instance of "exercising my rights." The experiences become desiccated when described in that way.

Id. at 1382.

[86] *See id.* at 1384.

[87] *Id.*

[88] This is not to suggest that the scholars discussed in this or any other section view the connections between their work and that of colleagues in the movement in the way that I

> [B]elief in the state is a flight from the immediate alienation of concrete existence into a split-off sphere of people's minds in which they imagine themselves to be a part of an imaginary political community — "citizens of the United States of America." *And it's this collective projection and internalization of an imaginary political authority that is the basis of the legitimation of hierarchy.* It's the mass-psychological foundation of democratic consent.[89]

Hegemony is reinforced through this "state abstraction" because people believe in and react passively to a mere illusion of political consensus.

Gordon, Freeman, Tushnet, and Gabel all assert that these abstractions blind people to the contingent nature of human existence. When people act as if these illusions are real, they actually recreate their own oppressive world moment by moment.

2. *Transformation in the Critical Vision.* — The vision of change that Critical scholars express flows directly from their focus on ideology as the major obstacle that separates the actual from the possible. Because it is ideology that prevents people from conceiving of — and hence from implementing — a freer social condition, the Critics propose the exposure of ideology as the logical first step toward social transformation. Emphasizing how ideology obscures the contingency of human relations, Gordon proposes unearthing conventional thought in order to excavate the potential for change. "[The] point is to unfreeze the world as it appears to common sense as a bunch of more or less objectively determined social relations and to make it appear as . . . it really is: people acting, imagining, rationalizing, justifying."[90] Gabel, too, argues that it is necessary to reveal the ways in which "law is actually constitutive of our social existence."[91] He believes that this can best be achieved by experiencing the character of living through legal ideas, while at the same time critiquing the ways in which these phenomena "appear in our unreflective consciousness."[92] Reflecting his concern that rights discourse misdirects and abstracts our struggle for a better society, Tushnet also advocates ongoing critique, proposing that popular aspirations for change be

---

present them. Categorizing ideas is always tricky business and this is no less true of Critical scholarship than of other varieties of scholarship.

[89] Gabel & Kennedy, *Roll Over Beethoven*, 36 STAN. L. REV. 1, 29 (1984) (emphasis added). In this piece, the authors acknowledge that the critique of rights is itself in danger of becoming reified. *See id.* at 36–37. Elsewhere, Professor Kennedy has advocated "working at the slow transformation of rights rhetoric, at dereifying it, rather than simply junking it." Kennedy, *Critical Labor Law Theory: A Comment*, 4 INDUS. REL. L.J. 503, 506 (1981). "Embedded in the rights notion," Kennedy observes, "is a liberating accomplishment of our culture: the affirmation of free human subjectivity against the constraints of group life, along with the paradoxical countervision of a group life that creates and nurtures individuals capable of freedom." *Id.*

[90] Gordon, *supra* note 73, at 289.

[91] Gabel, *supra* note 83, at 1564.

[92] *See id.*

recast in the language of "solidarity and individuality," rather than in the language of "rights."[93]

Although Alan Freeman does not offer a transformative strategy in his work on antidiscrimination law, he has advocated delegitimation, or "trashing," elsewhere. Explaining the Critical commitment to trashing,[94] Freeman states that:

> The point of delegitimation is to expose possibilities more truly expressing reality, possibilities of fashioning a future that might at least partially realize a substantive notion of justice instead of the abstract, rightsy, traditional, bourgeois notions of justice that generate so much of the contradictory scholarship. One must start by knowing what is going on, by freeing oneself from the mystified delusions embedded in our consciousness by the liberal legal worldview. I am not defending a form of scholarship that simply offers another affirmative presentation; rather, *I am advocating negative, critical activity as the only path* that might lead to a liberated future.[95]

Although the focus of their critiques may differ, the Critics all premise their views of transformative possibility on the necessity of critically engaging dominant ideology. Viewing the structures of legal

---

[93] Tushnet believes that "[t]he language of rights should be abandoned to the very great extent that it takes as a goal the realization of the reified abstraction, 'rights,' rather than the experiences of solidarity and individuality." Tushnet, *supra* note 58, at 1382–83 (footnote omitted); *see also id.* at 1394 (arguing that engaging in rights discourse is politically less useful than demanding that immediate, concrete needs be met now). For an insightful critique of the utility of "needs rhetoric" versus "rights rhetoric," see Williams, *Alchemical Notes: Reconstructing Ideals from Deconstructed Rights*, 22 HARV. C.R.-C.L. L. REV. 401, 412–13 (1987). Professor Williams argues that Tushnet's advocacy of needs rhetoric ignores the fact that "blacks have been describing their needs for generations. [He] overlook[s] a long history of legislation *against* the self-described needs of black people . . . . For blacks, describing needs has been a dismal failure as political activity." *Id.* at 412 (emphasis in original). Indeed, she goes on to argue that the "country's worst historical moments have not been attributable to rights-*assertion*, but to a failure of rights-*commitment*." *Id.* at 424 (emphasis in original).

[94] For other discussions of the merits of "trashing," see Kelman, cited in note 17 above, which alternately defends and advocates trashing and, occasionally, whimsically muses that it would be nice if there were something better to do, and Kennedy, *Cost-Reduction Theory as Legitimation*, 90 YALE L.J. 1275, 1282–83 (1981), which argues that smashing "defense mechanisms" may be an necessary first step in liberating energy that is necessary to utopian speculation. Finally, for a critique of trashing from the perspective of the needs of racial minorities, see Dalton, *The Clouded Prism*, 22 HARV. C.R.-C.L. L. REV. 435, 436 n.4 (1987). Professor Dalton suggests that there are risks of "moving ahead with a positive program before the critique has adequately altered our consciousness." *Id.* He argues, however, that negative critique is not the only path, and that positive programs must be developed simultaneously with the critique. *See id; see also* Matsuda, *supra* note 71, at 362–97 (arguing for reparations as the kind of positive program that might arise out of Critical scholarship, if that scholarship were adequately informed by the experiences and history of people of color).

[95] Freeman, *Truth and Mystification in Legal Scholarship*, 90 YALE L.J. 1229, 1230–31 (1981) (emphasis added) (footnote omitted). In fairness to Freeman, it should be noted that he took this position in discussing the correct "path" for legal scholars, and not for some larger audience which might include the civil rights community.

thought as central to the perception of the world as necessary and the status quo as legitimate, they believe it is crucial to demonstrate the contingency of legal ideology. Once false necessity or contingency is revealed, the Critics suggest, people will be able to remake their world in a different way.

B. A Critique of the Critique: The Problem of Context

The Critics offer an analysis that is useful in understanding the limited transformative potential of antidiscrimination rhetoric. There are difficulties, however, in attempting to use Critical themes and ideas to understand the civil rights movement and to describe what alternatives the civil rights constituency could have pursued, or might now pursue. While Critical scholars claim that their project is concerned with domination, few have made more than a token effort to address racial domination specifically, and their work does not seem grounded in the reality of the racially oppressed.

This deficiency is especially apparent in critiques that relate to racial issues. Critical scholars have criticized mainstream legal ideology for its tendency to portray American society as basically fair, and thereby to legitimate the oppressive policies that have been directed toward racial minorities. Yet Critical scholars do not sufficiently account for the effects or the causes of the oppression that they routinely acknowledge. The result is that Critical literature exhibits the same proclivities of mainstream scholarship — it seldom speaks to or about Black people.

The failure of the Critics to incorporate racism into their analysis also renders their critique of rights and their overall analysis of law in America incomplete. Specifically, this failure leads to an inability to appreciate fully the transformative significance of the civil rights movement in mobilizing Black Americans and generating new demands. Further, the failure to consider the reality of those most oppressed by American institutions means that the Critical account of the hegemonic nature of legal thought overlooks a crucial dimension of American life — the ideological role of racism itself. Gordon, Freeman, Tushnet, and Gabel fail to analyze racism as an ideological pillar upholding American society, or as the principal basis for Black oppression.

The Critics' failure to analyze the hegemonic role of racism also renders their prescriptive analysis unrealistic. In the spirit of Alan Freeman's declaration, Critics often appear to view the trashing of legal ideology "as the only path that might lead to a liberated future."[96]

---

[96] *Id.* at 1231 (footnote omitted).

Yet if trashing is the only path that might lead to a liberated future, Black people are unlikely to make it to the Critics' promised land.[97]

The Critics' commitment to trashing is premised on a notion that people are mystified by liberal legal ideology and consequently cannot remake their world until they see how contingent such ideology is. The Critics' principal error is that their version of domination by consent does not present a realistic picture of racial domination. Coercion explains much more about racial domination than does ideologically induced consent.[98] Black people do not create their oppressive worlds moment to moment but rather are coerced into living in worlds created and maintained by others. Moreover, the ideological source of this coercion is not liberal legal consciousness, but racism. If racism is just as important as, if not more important than, liberal legal ideology in explaining the persistence of white supremacy, then the Critics' single-minded effort to deconstruct liberal legal ideology will be futile.

Finally, in addition to exaggerating the role of liberal legal consciousness and underestimating that of coercion, Critics also disregard the transformative potential that liberalism offers. Although liberal legal ideology may indeed function to mystify, it remains receptive to some aspirations that are central to Black demands, and may also perform an important function in combating the experience of being excluded and oppressed.[99] This receptivity to Black aspirations is crucial given the hostile social world that racism creates. The most troubling aspect of the Critical program, therefore, is that "trashing" rights consciousness may have the unintended consequence of disempowering the racially oppressed while leaving white supremacy basi-

---

[97] As Richard Delgado notes, "CLS scholars' idealism has a familiar ring to minority ears. We cannot help but be reminded of those fundamentalist preachers who have assured us that our lot will only improve once we 'see the light' and are 'saved.'" Delgado, *The Ethereal Scholar: Does Critical Legal Studies Have What Minorities Want?*, 22 HARV. C.R.-C.L. L. REV. 301, 309 (1987).

[98] The term "coercion" is used here to describe all non-consensual forms of domination — that is, all forces external to the individual or group that maintain that individual or group's position in society's hierarchy. As such, it refers to everything from baton-wielding police officers to court injunctions to "White Only" signs. More importantly, it also refers to more subtle forms of exterior domination, such as the institutionalized oppositional dynamic — the vision of "normative whiteness" that pervades current forms of race consciousness. *See infra* Part IV.

[99] The degree to which rights consciousness has been receptive to Black aspirations is probably the most overlooked aspect in the Critique of rights. This may be attributed to Critics' limited understanding of nonmaterial manifestations of racial domination. *See infra* pp. 1360–64. Although Critics argue that rights consciousness only creates an illusion of community that produces alienation, *see, e.g.*, Gabel, *supra* note 83, at 1576–78, this analysis tends to underestimate the extent to which Blacks' exclusion from the illusion creates its own experience of alienation. Thus, although Critics have acknowledged the pragmatic value of rights rhetoric, *see, e.g.*, *id.* at 1597, they have not recognized the legitimacy of Black demands for inclusion in the social illusion and the consequent utility of rights discourse in articulating such demands.

cally untouched. These difficulties are discussed below as they relate to the critiques of Gordon, Freeman, and Tushnet.

1. Gordon: The Underemphasis on Coercion. — Robert Gordon's explanation of ideological domination illustrates how an exclusive focus on consent leaves gaping holes in his reader's understanding of hegemony. Gordon writes that beliefs are "the main constraints upon making social life more bearable."[100] Yet how can others understand the fact that Black people, although unable to bring about a world in which they fully participate, *can* imagine such a world? Clearly, something other than their own structure of thought prevents Blacks from changing their world. This fact suggests that a more complete explanation of domination requires that coercion and consent be considered together.

The coercive power of the state operates to suppress some groups, particularly when there is consensus among others that such coercion is warranted. Racism serves to single out Blacks as one of these groups "worthy" of suppression.[101] Gordon, however, does not offer any way to understand this. If his exclusive focus on ideological domination is to be taken literally, one is left believing that Black Americans are unable to change their world because they accept the dominant ideology and thus cannot imagine an alternative existence. Yet to say that the beliefs of Black Americans have boxed them into a subordinate existence because of what they believe is to ignore the history of coercive racial subordination. Indeed, it would be difficult for Blacks, given the contradiction between American fiction and Black American reality, to believe as much of the American mythology as whites do.[102]

The most significant aspect of Black oppression seems to be what is believed *about* Black Americans, not what Black Americans believe. Black people are boxed in largely because there is a consensus among many whites that the oppression of Blacks is legitimate. This is where consensus and coercion can be understood together: ideology convinces one group that the coercive domination of another is legitimate. It matters little whether the coerced group rejects the dominant ideology

---

[100] Gordon, *supra* note 73, at 291.

[101] Another obvious example of suppression is the extermination campaign waged against Native Americans. The consensus that this suppression was "worthy" is commemorated daily as children and adults alike engage in "cowboy-Indian" imagery with little sensitivity to the genocide that those images represent.

[102] When I say it is difficult for Blacks to believe as much as whites, I do not mean to imply that Black Americans do not accept the ideals of the American fiction. Rather, I am suggesting that Black Americans, more than others, know that the ideals do not describe the present world. As the "contradiction" between ideals and reality diminishes for some classes of oppressed people, however, it becomes easier to accede to the dominant myths. One of the legitimating aspects of reform is that the contradictions, once laid bare, became clothed in the illusion of fairness. The extent that the unique consciousness of some Black people has been undermined by these reforms indicates one of the losses of engaging in reformist rhetoric.

and can offer a competing conception of the world; if they have been labeled "other" by the dominant ideology, they are not heard.[103]

Blacks seem to carry the stigma of "otherness," which effectively precludes their potentially radicalizing influence from penetrating the dominant consciousness.[104] If this is the case, then Blacks will gain little through simply transcending their own belief structures. The challenge for Blacks may be to pursue strategies that confront the beliefs held *about* them by whites. For Blacks, such strategies may take the form of reinforcing some aspects of the dominant ideology in attempts to become participants in the dominant discourse rather than outsiders defined, objectified, and reified by that discourse. In this sense, the civil rights movement might be considered as an attempt to deconstruct the image of "the Negro" in the white mind. By forcing the political system to respond to Black demands, Blacks rejected images of complacency and docility that had been invoked by some whites to dismiss Black demands.[105]

Although Gordon sets out to analyze hegemonic domination, he ends up revealing little about the oppression of those most dominated.[106] This "oversight" probably results from his effort to absorb the *coercive* elements of class rule into the *consensual* elements of ideological hegemony. This, however, is not consistent with Gramsci's view of hegemony.[107] Gramsci explicitly recognized that the two

---

[103] *See infra* pp. 1370–74.

[104] The 1984 Jesse Jackson presidential campaign may serve as a case in point. Most whites dismissed Jackson's positions as simply "special interest" or, more accurately, "pro-Black." To many whites, "pro-Black" translates to "anti-white," even though Jackson's policies might have benefited most whites much more than the policies of the white candidates whom most whites supported. For example, Jackson supported using funds from a reduced military budget to provide employment to the growing number of displaced industrial workers.

For an analysis of the destructive role of racism in contemporary American politics, see the text accompanying notes 169–176.

[105] One of the common complaints of the South's segregationists was that the civil disruptions were caused by "outside agitators." *See, e.g.*, W. WORKMAN, THE CASE FOR THE SOUTH 190–210 (1960). The implication, of course, was that southern Blacks were content before various outsiders stirred them into action.

[106] One must acknowledge that the shortcomings in Gordon's arguments reflect real gaps in the Gramscian thought upon which much of the discussion of hegemony has been based. Gramsci was preoccupied with developing a better approach to understanding domination by consent — a fact which leads many scholars who use his concepts to focus on consent to the virtual exclusion of coercion. Also, Gordon's discussion of the law must be considered in light of the fact that Gramsci himself wrote very little on the law; exactly two pages in the *Prison Notebooks* address law directly. Finally, and most importantly, Gramsci was not concerned with the impact of race and slavery in America, and consequently wrote nothing about it. At least one Gramscian scholar cautions that his narrow understanding of race and slavery undermines some attempts to utilize fully his concepts in the American context. *See* C. BOGGS, *supra* note 74, at 132 n.20.

[107] As Quentin Hoare and Geoffrey Smith, translators and editors of the *Prison Notebooks*, observe:

> The fact that, more than any other great revolutionary Marxist thinker, he concerned himself with the sphere of "civil society" and of "hegemony", in his prison writings,

fundamental types of political control — coercion and hegemonic consensus — were dialectically linked and thus had to be understood together. In Gramsci's view, hegemony consists of "1. the 'spontaneous' consent given by the great masses of the population [and] 2. *The apparatus of state coercive power which 'legally' enforces discipline on those groups who do not 'consent' either actively or passively.*"[108]

An alternative approach more consistent with the dual nature of control would be to discuss, or perhaps suggest, how the coercion of nonconsenting groups may provide an important reinforcement to the creation of consensus among classes that do accept the legitimacy of the dominant order. I have alluded to the possibility that the coercion of Blacks may provide a basis for others to consent to the dominant order. An analysis of hegemony that includes racial subordination suggests that the creation of a clearly visible "other," whose interests are seen as being opposed in every way to the interests of those who identify — by virtue of color and culture — with the dominant class, is a hegemonic tool used to maintain legitimacy. In Part IV, I will discuss this "otherness" as one way of understanding how racism plays a hegemonic role and how legal reform has both transformed and legitimated this dynamic.[109]

2. Freeman: Failure to Analyze Racism as Hegemonic. — Alan Freeman's discussion of antidiscrimination law suffers from a failure to ground the critique in the historical and ideological conditions that brought about antidiscrimination law. This is puzzling, both because Freeman has written more than any other Critical scholar on antidiscrimination law[110] and because he clearly recognizes the uniqueness of racism as a system of domination.[111] Freeman's work pays too little attention to racism's role in legitimating American society and isolating Blacks. He also overlooks one of the consequences of this history of racism: Blacks have succeeded in diminishing this isolation by relying on and deploying the very ideological "presuppositions" that Freeman attempts to delegitimize.

As I have discussed above, Freeman argues that "needs basic to the preservation of the class structure . . . compel[led] rejection" of a developing perspective that would have required an America in which

---

cannot be taken to indicate a neglect of the moment of political society, of force, of domination. On the contrary, his entire record shows that this was not the case, and that his constant preoccupation was to avoid any undialectical separation of "the ethical-political aspect of politics or theory of hegemony and consent" from "the aspect of force and economics."

A. GRAMSCI, *supra* note 74, at 207.

108 *Id.* at 12 (emphasis added).

109 *See infra* pp. 1370–74.

110 *See* Freeman, *supra* note 12; Freeman, *supra* note 79; Freeman, Book Review, *Race & Class: The Dilemma of Liberal Reform*, 90 YALE L.J. 1880 (1980).

111 *See* Freeman, *supra* note 79, at 97.

Blacks were substantively better off, not simply the recipients of formally equal treatment.[112] Oddly, in his account none of the needs that forced this retrenchment is connected to racism, that is, white supremacy and racial stratification.[113] In Freeman's account of the sociopolitical and ideological necessities that underlay the Supreme Court's *Brown* decision,[114] the need to respond to racism and race issues, not the need to deal with class issues, gave birth to antidiscrimination law.[115] Freeman's discussion of the forces that led to retrenchment, however, is couched only in terms of preserving class structure. This failure to discuss the retrenchment in racial terms undermines the force of his analysis, especially in light of the racial character of the subsequent political retrenchment.[116]

Freeman argues that affirmative action and other remedial programs conflicted with beliefs in formal equality, vested rights, and equal opportunity. Thus the preservation of these myths compelled the rejection of these remedies, lest whites and people of color discover that these myths were contingent ideas and thus undermine their beliefs in the legitimacy of American class structure. Indeed, he notes that "[t]he more that civil rights law threatened the 'system' of equality [of] opportunity, which threat was essential to the production of victim-perspective results, the more it threatened to expose and delegitimize the relative situation of lower-class whites."[117]

Freeman implies that the concern that forced the curtailment of affirmative action was the fear that whites would question the legitimacy of the class structure once it was revealed that equal opportunity and vestedness were contingent.[118] Yet a different interpretation suggests that whites were unlikely to question the legitimacy of these conceptions, but rather would question the legitimacy of racial remedies that relied upon a suspension of these myths. Indeed, the fact that these promises had been suspended seemed to make whites believe in and cling to them all the more. Freeman fails to analyze the ways in which whites were on the defensive, not because the promise of vestedness had proven unstable, but because Blacks had been granted some privileges at their expense. The most prevalent threat

---

[112] *See id.* at 111. Freeman notes that what he means by the class structure is "not 'American society' but the particular class relationships characteristic of contemporary American society." *Id.*

[113] *See id.* at 111–14.

[114] Brown v. Bd. of Educ., 347 U.S. 483 (1954).

[115] *See* Freeman, *supra* note 79, at 100–02; *see also* Freeman, *supra* note 12, at 1065–76 (critiquing various explanations of the *Brown* decision).

[116] *See infra* p. 1376.

[117] Freeman, *supra* note 12, at 113.

[118] *See id.* at 111–13; *see also* Freeman, *supra* note 110, at 1894 ("From my perspective, the goal of civil rights law is to offer a credible measure of tangible progress without in any way disturbing class structure generally.").

was not that the ideology would be exposed as fraudulent and that whites would attack the ideology, but that there would be a white backlash against Blacks and against institutions perceived as sympathetic to Black interests.[119] This problem could be rectified — as it has been — by narrowing the focus of antidiscrimination law, thereby sacrificing the interests of Blacks in order to appease the majority.[120]

There was something significant about affirmative action and other civil rights policies that gave rise to a crisis in a way that other more devastating or more common ideological disruptions have not. This suggests that the relatively subordinate status of Blacks serves a stabilizing function in this society. At least one consequence of this "stabilizing" function is that special attention is directed toward the status of Blacks so that ideological deviations arising out of racial issues do not evade popular detection.

The tremendous controversy surrounding the *Bakke* case[121] provides an excellent illustration. Freeman would describe the controversy as arising largely from whites' reaction to suspension of the equal opportunity myth in relation to school admissions. There were other deviations from equal opportunity, however, in the U.C. Davis medical school admissions program that Bakke and other affirmative action opponents could have attacked.[122] Yet advantages granted to others — such as the wealthy — did not appear as presumptively illegitimate as did those granted to minority candidates. The outcry over the specter of "unqualified" minorities being granted privileges over "qualified" whites was not simply a reaction to the suspension of competition per se. Nor was it merely a reaction — as white affirmative action opponents, in particular, would argue — to a fundamental hostility to racial preferences. Racial preferences for whites have existed for years with the tacit and often explicit support of these very opponents. Thus, we must assume either that the adamant disbelievers in racial equality suddenly converted and became racial

---

[119] Some commentators both inside and outside the Democratic Party believe that the crushing defeat suffered by the party in the 1984 presidential election reflects a perception among whites that the party is too sympathetic to Black interests. Whether or not this perception is accurate, it does illustrate the centrality of race in American political analysis. *See infra* p. 1376.

[120] Derrick Bell sees this sacrifice as representing a historical pattern which he calls "The Principle of Involuntary Sacrifice." *See infra* note 176.

[121] Regents of the Univ. of Cal. v. Bakke, 438 U.S. 265 (1978).

[122] *See* G. DREYFUSS & C. LAWRENCE, THE BAKKE CASE 232 (1979) ("For the time being, medical schools would continue to favor the children of the wealthy and exclude thousands of well-qualified applicants of all races. Just a few months before the decision, the *New York Times* had reported on a growing pattern of abuses of the admissions process by wealthy parents attempting to avoid the stiff competition for places. A study by Grace Ziem at Harvard University of the composition of medical students at U.S. universities shows that the percentage of students below the national median income has remained at 12 since 1920.").

equality's high priests, or, more likely, that what really outraged whites about affirmative action was merely that minorities were now getting something at their expense.[123] This race-specific explanation of affirmative action retrenchment is exactly what Freeman's legitimation explanation fails to analyze adequately.

Although we can only speculate why Freeman does not discuss the forced withdrawal of expansive race-reform policies in more racial terms, such an omission is consistent with the assumption that racism is not a central ideological construct of the system. Rejecting what he considers to be the Marxist instrumental view of racism, Freeman declares: "[G]iven the presence of other powerful ideologies that serve to arrest the development of class consciousness, racism seems only marginally necessary, and perhaps superfluous, if regarded from a functional point of view."[124]

This view is further evidenced in Freeman's critique of those who argue that progress in civil rights has advanced class struggle:[125]

> [T]he assault on racism under such circumstances will come to a halt, lest it unleash too much white rage or expose the reality of class relationships. *There is nothing particularly radical about the goal of ending racial discrimination.* The goal would be achieved if non-

---

[123] The irony in the argument that race policies designed to remedy unjust oppression constitute illegitimate "special treatment" has a striking parallel in history. Perhaps this backward argument will eventually be seen in the same light as Justice Bradley's comments in the Civil Rights Cases, 109 U.S. 3 (1883). Even though Blacks at that time were isolated and denied most privileges offered to whites, Bradley argued that it was time for Blacks to stop expecting special treatment and to become ordinary citizens:

> When a man has emerged from slavery, and by the aid of a beneficent legislation has shaken off the inseparable concomitants of that state, there must be some stage in the progress of his elevation when he takes the rank of a mere citizen, and ceases to be the special favorite of the laws . . . .

Id. at 25.

Civil rights advocates argued then and argue now that this is exactly the objective of race reform — to end the special treatment that Blacks receive and to create the conditions that would allow their expectations to approach those of white citizens. Obviously, the issue was not then, and is not now, simply whether Blacks receive "special" treatment — they did in Bradley's day, and they do now. The conflict lies beneath the special treatment tag; the question is what kind of treatment is deemed special and whether that special treatment is legitimate.

[124] Freeman, *supra* note 79, at 108. Lest my comments be misunderstood, I am not arguing that the oppression of Black people can be discussed solely in race terms. Rather, I believe that viewing Black oppression in terms of caste combines an understanding of racism with a class analysis. This Article reflects my concern that class analysis — and now, "hegemony-centered analysis" — overlooks the element of racial oppression that is non-consensual and, to a degree, non-class based. There are significant distinctions between race oppression and class oppression that I think are important in understanding domination. Part IV illustrates the connection between racial oppression and hegemony.

[125] *See id.* at 107–110 (critiquing traditional Marxist treatments of race); *id.* at 110–14 (exploring the ways in which antidiscrimination law may bring about token improvements by "bourgeoisifying" a small number of Blacks who will legitimate and therefore protect the underlying class structure).

> whites were stratified across American society in percentages similar to whites. *The class structure would remain intact.*[126]

What is particularly disconcerting about this analysis is that it appears simply to collapse issues of race into issues of class[127] in only a slightly more sophisticated fashion than do the traditional Marxist accounts of racism that Freeman criticizes so cogently.[128] Freeman's failure to see the attack on white supremacy as radical typifies his failure to critique the ways in which racism operates together with, but differently from, class ideologies central to the maintenance of hegemony. Without such an analysis of racism's role in maintaining hegemony, his explanation simply does not convincingly capture the political realities of racism and the inevitability of white backlash against any serious attempts to dismantle the machinery of white supremacy.

3. Tushnet: The Problem of Pragmatism Without Context. — The problem with Tushnet's critique of rights is perhaps most evident when he rhetorically queries: "Can anyone really think that it helps either in changing society or in understanding how society changes to discuss whether [protestors] were exercising rights protected by the first amendment?"[129] The answer to Tushnet's rhetorical question, given the thrust of his critique is, of course, no. What really matters, says Tushnet, is not whether people are exercising rights, but whether their action is politically effective.[130] If, however, the inquiry is squarely placed within a historical context, the implied disparity between thinking about change in terms of rights and thinking about politically effective action might be diminished. Perhaps the action of the civil rights community was effective, for example, because it raised the novel idea of Blacks exercising rights. Indeed, thinking in terms of rights may have been a radical and liberating activity for Blacks. Tushnet suggests that thinking in terms of rights is incompatible with feelings of solidarity and is not helpful in determining how to be politically effective.[131] The expression of rights, however,

---

[126] Freeman, *supra* note 110, at 1895 (emphasis added).

[127] This "collapse" is revealed if one considers rephrasing Freeman's statement conversely: "There is nothing particularly radical about ending class discrimination. *Incomes* could be equalized, and *racial hierarchy* would remain intact." Racial heirarchy is characterized by the ghettoization of Blacks on the bottom rung of society, but it encompasses much more than class oppression. Consequently, even though relative economic parity might be seen as a radical step toward ending class domination, and would indeed be a tremendous step toward ameliorating conditions in the Black community, equalization alone would not end racial subordination.

[128] *See id.* at 1891–93.

[129] Tushnet, *supra* note 58, at 1370–71.

[130] *See id.* at 1371.

[131] *See id.* ("If . . . action was politically effective, we ought to establish the conditions for its effectiveness, not because these conditions are 'rights' but because politically effective action is important"); *id.* at 1382–83 ("I could not sensibly deny the importance of experiences of

was a central organizing feature of the civil rights movement. Because rights that other Americans took for granted were routinely denied to Black Americans, Blacks' assertion of their "rights" constituted a serious ideological challenge to white supremacy.[132] Their demand was not just for a place in the front of a bus, but for inclusion in the American political imagination. In asserting rights, Blacks defied a system which had long determined that Blacks were not and should not have been included. Whether or not the extension of these rights has ultimately legitimated the subordinate status of Blacks, the use of rights rhetoric was a radical, movement-building act.

Because Tushnet's critique of rights is not sufficiently related to racism, his prescriptive comments are unpersuasive. Tushnet argues that the only circumstance in which rights should be used is when, on pragmatic consideration, they appear useful; he then argues that rights may not be pragmatically useful but instead may actually impede the progress of the "party of humanity":[133]

> [T]here do seem to be substantial pragmatic reasons to think that abandoning the rhetoric of rights would be the better course to pursue for now. People need food and shelter right now, and demanding that those needs be satisfied — whether or not satisfying them can today persuasively be characterized as enforcing a right — strikes me as more likely to succeed than claiming that existing rights to food and shelter must be enforced.[134]

One wonders, however, whether a demand for shelter that does not employ rights rhetoric is likely to succeed in America today. The underlying problem, especially for African-Americans, is the question of how to extract from others that which others are not predisposed to give. As Tushnet has said himself, rights are a way of saying that

---

independence and solidarity. They are central parts of our humanity. But the reification critique claims that treating those experiences as instances of abstract rights mischaracterizes them . . . . The experiences become desiccated . . . . We must insist on preserving real experiences rather than abstracting general rights from those experiences. The language of rights should be abandoned *to the very great extent* that it takes as a goal the realization of the reified abstraction 'rights' rather than the experiences of solidarity and individuality.") (emphasis added).

Tushnet's second comment is actually one of his most intriguing, given the thesis of this Article. Taken in isolation, the passage seems both to recognize the positive process of individuation possible in utilizing rights discourse and to hold open the possibility that rights discourse to some extent might be worth deploying if one were careful to aim such rhetoric at achieving the "real human experiences" of "individuality" and "solidarity." As this Article demonstrates, however, it is precisely these roads which lie largely unexplored by the bulk of Critical literature.

[132] Indeed, Tushnet displayed such an awareness in a history of the civil rights litigation strategy. *See* M. TUSHNET, THE NAACP'S LEGAL STRATEGY AGAINST SEGREGATED EDUCATION, 1925–1950 (1987).

[133] *See* Tushnet, *supra* note 58, at 1386–94.

[134] *Id.* at 1394. It is worth noting that "needs" terminology is no less open to both the indeterminacy and reification critiques than is rights terminology.

a society is what it is, or that it ought to live up to its deepest commitments.[135] This is essentially what all groups of dispossessed people say when they use rights rhetoric. As demonstrated in the civil rights movement, engaging in rights rhetoric can be an attempt to turn society's "institutional logic"[136] against itself — to redeem some of the rhetorical promises and the self-congratulations that seem to thrive in American political discourse.

C. Questioning the Transformative View: Some Doubts About Trashing

The Critics' product is of limited utility to Blacks in its present form. The implications for Blacks of trashing liberal legal ideology are troubling, even though it may be proper to assail belief structures that obscure liberating possibilities. Trashing legal ideology seems to tell us repeatedly what has already been established — that legal discourse is unstable and relatively indeterminate. Furthermore, trashing offers no idea of how to avoid the negative consequences of engaging in reformist discourse or how to work around such consequences. Even if we imagine the wrong world when we think in terms of legal discourse, we must nevertheless exist in a present world where legal protection has at times been a blessing — albeit a mixed one. The fundamental problem is that, although Critics criticize law because it functions to legitimate existing institutional arrangements, it is precisely this legitimating function that has made law receptive to certain demands in this area.

The Critical emphasis on deconstruction as *the* vehicle for liberation leads to the conclusion that engaging in legal discourse should be avoided because it reinforces not only the discourse itself but also the society and the world that it embodies. Yet Critics offer little beyond this observation. Their focus on delegitimating rights rhetoric seems to suggest that, once rights rhetoric has been discarded, there exists a more productive strategy for change, one which does not reinforce existing patterns of domination.

Unfortunately, no such strategy has yet been articulated, and it is difficult to imagine that racial minorities will ever be able to discover one. As Frances Fox Piven and Richard Cloward point out in their

---

135 Tushnet observes:

> The conditions of the society define exactly what kind of rights-talk makes sense, and *the sort of rights-talk that makes sense in turn defines what the society is.* When someone objects to an act as a violation of a right, the ensuing dialogue either involves a claim that the challenged act is inconsistent with some "deeper" commitments that the actor has . . . or deals with what kind of society we ought to have.

Id. at 1370 (emphasis added).

136 *Cf.* F. PIVEN & R. CLOWARD, POOR PEOPLE'S MOVEMENTS 22–23 (1977) (noting that "the opportunities for defiance are structured by features of institutional life").

excellent account of the civil rights movement, popular struggles are a reflection of institutionally determined logic and a challenge to that logic.[137] People can only demand change in ways that reflect the logic of the institutions that they are challenging.[138] Demands for change that do not reflect the institutional logic — that is, demands that do not engage and subsequently reinforce the dominant ideology — will probably be ineffective.[139]

The possibility for ideological change is created through the very process of legitimation, which is triggered by crisis. Powerless people can sometimes trigger such a crisis by challenging an institution internally, that is, by using its own logic against it.[140] Such crisis occurs when powerless people force open and politicize a contradiction between the dominant ideology and their reality. The political conse-

---

[137] *See id.* at 22–25. The observation concerning the inability to bring about change in some non-legitimating fashion does not, of course, rule out the possibility of armed revolution. For most oppressed peoples, however, the costs of such a revolt are often too great. That is, the oppressed cannot realistically hope to overcome the "coercive" components of hegemony. More importantly, it is not clear that such a struggle, although superficially a clear radical challenge to the coercive force of the status quo, would be a lesser reinforcement of the ideology of American society (i.e., the consensual components of hegemony).

[138] Strikes, for example, are a reflection of the logic of the work institution. It only makes sense for employed workers to use strikes as a tactic. Unemployed workers, of course, cannot use the strike to press their grievances.

[139] Reforms necessarily come from an existing repertoire of options. As Piven and Cloward note, "if impoverished southern blacks had demanded land reform, they would probably have still gotten the vote." *Id.* at 33.

[140] Conversely, groups that do not engage the institutional logic are unlikely to create such a crisis; indeed, they are routinely infiltrated, isolated, and destroyed. Compare, for example, the history of the NAACP with that of the Black Panthers. One should not infer from the fact that the Panthers have ceased to exist whereas the NAACP has not that insurgent groups are not essential to reform. Indeed, it is their insurgency that ultimately benefits more moderate groups. Both moderate and radical groups, however, face similar limitations. Although they can create a crisis which forces an institutional response, no oppressed group can control the response. Institutions can respond with either repression or conciliation; often they respond with both. Thus, even enlisting the dominant, legitimating ideology in struggle does not guarantee protection against violent repression.

Indeed, the degree of violence and repression that an oppressed group must endure to wrest even moderate reforms from the dominant class is a measure of its subordinate status in society. Consider, for example, how much real suffering people had to endure during the civil rights movement before even moderate concessions were made. The injustice of racial oppression is succinctly characterized by the fact that thousands of lives were risked, and some lost, to secure for Blacks the most basic rights that whites were routinely granted. *See* H. RAINES, MY SOUL IS RESTED 190–93 (1977) (quoting Willie Bolden, a participant in the struggle for voting rights, as he describes police beatings of marchers occurring inside and around a church in Marion County, resulting in more than twenty hospitalizations and the death of Jimmy Jackson); *id.* at 197–226 (describing "Bloody Sunday," on which mounted Alabama state troopers attempted to thwart a march on Selma, by riding into the crowd, and beating and teargassing the marchers, many of whom were kneeling); J. WILLIAMS, EYES ON THE PRIZE 230–35 (1987) (describing the discovery of the bodies of James Chaney, Andrew Goodman, and Michael Schwerner, civil rights workers executed by Klansmen in June 1964).

quences of maintaining the contradictions may sometimes force an adjustment — an attempt to close the gap or to make things appear fair.[141] Yet, because the adjustment is triggered by the political consequences of the contradiction, circumstances will be adjusted only to the extent necessary to close the apparent contradiction.

This approach to understanding legitimation and change is applicable to the civil rights movement. Because Blacks were challenging their exclusion from political society, the only claims that were likely to achieve recognition were those that reflected American society's institutional logic: legal rights ideology. Articulating their formal demands through legal rights ideology, civil rights protestors exposed a series of contradictions — the most important being the promised privileges of American citizenship and the practice of absolute racial subordination. Rather than using the contradictions to suggest that American citizenship was itself illegitimate or false, civil rights protestors proceeded as if American citizenship were real, and demanded to exercise the "rights" that citizenship entailed. By seeking to restructure reality to reflect American mythology, Blacks relied upon and ultimately benefited from politically inspired efforts to resolve the contradictions by granting formal rights. Although it is the need to maintain legitimacy that presents powerless groups with the opportunity to wrest concessions from the dominant order, it is the very accomplishment of legitimacy that forecloses greater possibilities. In sum, the potential for change is both created and limited by legitimation.

The central issue that the Critics fail to address, then, is how to avoid the "legitimating" effects of reform if engaging in reformist discourse is the only effective way to challenge the legitimacy of the social order. Perhaps the only situation in which powerless people may receive any favorable response is where there is a political or ideological need to restore an image of fairness that has somehow been tarnished. Most efforts to change an oppressive situation are bound to adopt the dominant discourse to some degree.[142] On the other hand, Peter Gabel may well be right in observing that the reforms which come from such demands are likely to transform a given situation only to the extent necessary to legitimate those elements of the situation that "must" remain unchanged.[143] Thus, it might just be

[141] As Piven and Cloward observe, these adjustments often take the form of "new programs that appear to meet the moral demands of the movement, and thus rob it of support without actually yielding much by way of tangible gains." F. PIVEN & R. CLOWARD, *supra* note 136, at 30–31; *see* Gabel, *supra* note 83, at 1591–97. Moreover, governments gain additional leeway for repression once they have achieved the appearance of fairness. *See* F. PIVEN & R. CLOWARD, *supra* note 136, at 31.

[142] This engagement is apparently required of successful efforts at change. *See* F. PIVEN & R. CLOWARD, *supra* note 136, at 1–32.

[143] *See* Gabel, *supra* note 83, at 1591–97 (discussing the means by which state officials

the case that oppression means "being between a rock and a hard place" — that there are risks and dangers involved both in engaging in the dominant discourse *and* in failing to do so. What subordinated people need is an analysis which can inform them how the risks can be minimized, and how the rocks and the very hard places can be negotiated.

IV. THE CONTEXT DEFINED: RACIST IDEOLOGY AND HEGEMONY

The failure of the Critics to consider race in their account of law and legitimacy is not a minor oversight: race consciousness is central not only to the domination of Blacks, but also to whites' acceptance of the legitimacy of hierarchy and to their identity with elite interest. Exposing the centrality of race consciousness is crucial to identifying and delegitimating beliefs that present hierarchy as inevitable and fair. Moreover, exposing the centrality of race consciousness shows how the options of Blacks in American society have been limited, and how the use of rights rhetoric has emancipated Blacks from some manifestations of racial domination.

A realignment of the Critical project to incorporate race consciousness must begin with beliefs about Blacks in American society, and how these beliefs legitimize racial coercion.[144] Thus, this Part examines the deep-rooted problem of racist ideology — or white race consciousness — and suggests how this form of consciousness legitimates prevailing injustices and constrains the development of new solutions that benefit Black Americans.

Racist ideology provides a series of rationalizations that suppress the contradiction between American political ideals and Black existence under white supremacy. Not only does racism legitimate the

---

contain the radicalizing possibilities of social movements via eventual "recognition" of some of the movement's claims).

[144] *See* Lawrence, Book Review, *"Justice" or "Just Us": Racism and the Role of Ideology*, 35 STAN. L. REV. 831 (1983). Professor Lawrence suggests that

> Individuals tend to identify with the socioeconomic order in which they hold privileged positions while at the same time feeling the tension between the harsh realities of that order and their ideal images of themselves within that order. . . . The natural response of the privileged individual confronted with this tension between the real and the ideal is to resolve it by legitimizing the existing structure to himself. This self-mystification manifests itself in his legal arguments, judicial opinions, or theoretical discussions, which in turn become part of a defense mechanism that extends beyond the individual.

Id. at 842–43 (footnote omitted). Lawrence has since applied this approach in the equal protection context, examining the evidence and implications of unconscious racism to critique constitutional theories underlying the intent requirement in equal protection analysis. *See* Lawrence, *The Id, the Ego, and Equal Protection: Reckoning with Unconscious Racism*, 39 STAN. L. REV. 317 (1987). Lawrence proposes a "cultural meaning" test to trigger heightened judicial scrutiny of race-based actions, arguing that principles of due process and antidiscrimination both justify judicial intervention in cases of identified unconscious racial motivation. *See id.* at 355–87.

oppression of Blacks, it also helps to define and privilege membership in the white community, creating a basis for identification with dominant interests. Racism serves a consensus-building hegemonic role by designating Black people as separate, visible "others" to be contrasted in every way with all other social groups.[145] Although not consenting to domination, Black people are seen as legitimate objects of antipathy and coercion by whites. In the first section of this Part, I examine the political and ideological dynamic of white supremacy, which I term the "Politics of Otherness."

In this Part's second section, I sketch the contours of an analysis which suggests that race consciousness legitimates racial oppression.[146] Within this framework, one can better comprehend how the assertion of rights in the context of a formal, legally sanctioned subordination created a radical challenge to the dominant order. In response to this assertion of rights, legal reforms were promulgated that transformed the Black experience by lifting formal barriers that had subordinated all Black people and produced their formal and political designation as "other."

The Critics are correct in observing that, despite these gains, engaging in rights discourse has helped to deradicalize and co-opt the challenge in the current period, in which racial oppression continues to flourish behind the screen of racial equality. Yet only after race ideology itself and the real differences that formal equality made in transforming race ideology are understood can the paradoxical relationship of transformation and legitimation be fully appreciated. Blacks are ultimately presented with a dilemma: liberal reform both transforms and legitimates. Even though legal ideology absorbs, redefines, and limits the language of protest, African-Americans cannot ignore the power of legal ideology to counter some of the most repressive aspects of racial domination.

A. The Hegemonic Role of Racism: Establishing the "Other" in American Ideology

Throughout American history, the subordination of Blacks was rationalized by a series of stereotypes and beliefs that made their conditions appear logical and natural.[147] Historically, white suprem-

---

[145] *See infra* pp. 1370–74.

[146] *See infra* pp. 1377–81.

[147] *See generally* D. DAVIS, THE PROBLEM OF SLAVERY IN THE AGE OF REVOLUTION, 1770–1823 (1975); G. FREDRICKSON, THE BLACK IMAGE IN THE WHITE MIND, 1817 TO 1914 (1971) [hereinafter G. FREDRICKSON, THE BLACK IMAGE]; G. FREDRICKSON, WHITE SUPREMACY: A COMPARATIVE STUDY IN AMERICAN AND SOUTH AFRICAN HISTORY (1981) [hereinafter G. FREDRICKSON, WHITE SUPREMACY]; W. JORDAN, WHITE OVER BLACK: AMERICAN ATTITUDES TOWARD THE NEGRO, 1550–1812 (1968); I. NEWBY, JIM CROW'S DEFENSE: ANTI-NEGRO THOUGHT IN AMERICA 1900–1930 (1968); J. WILLIAMSON, THE CRUCIBLE OF RACE: BLACK/

acy has been premised upon various political,[148] scientific,[149] and religious[150] theories, each of which relies on racial characterizations and stereotypes about Blacks that have coalesced into an extensive legitimating ideology.[151] Today, it is probably not controversial to say that these stereotypes were developed primarily to rationalize the oppression of Blacks. What *is* overlooked, however, is the extent to which these stereotypes serve a hegemonic function by perpetuating a mythology about both Blacks *and* whites even today, reinforcing an illusion of a white community that cuts across ethnic, gender, and class lines.

As presented by Critical scholars, hegemonic rule succeeds to the extent that the ruling class world view establishes the appearance of a unity of interests between the dominant class and the dominated.[152]

WHITE RELATIONS IN THE AMERICAN SOUTH SINCE EMANCIPATION (1984); C. WOODWARD, THE STRANGE CAREER OF JIM CROW (1958).

[148] *See* R. HORSMAN, RACE AND MANIFEST DESTINY: THE ORIGINS OF AMERICAN RACIAL ANGLO-SAXONISM 298–303 (1981) (analyzing Americans' abandonment of the idea of "liberating" various peoples by spreading the American brand of democracy, and subsequent captivation by the notion of Anglo-Saxon superiority and the right to expand limitlessly); *id.* at 158–86 (analyzing the development of "romantic racial nationalism"); *see also* M. CASSITY, LEGACY OF FEAR: AMERICAN RACE RELATIONS TO 1900, at 68 (1985) (critiquing the paternalist arguments for slavery based on beliefs that it improved and civilized Africans).

[149] *See* R. HORSMAN, *supra* note 148, at 43–61, 116–57 (tracing the development and mass dissemination of scientific proof of white superiority); W. JORDAN, *supra* note 147, at 216–65, 482–511 (analyzing the scientific theories prevalent from 1700 to 1755 and from 1783 to 1812). Even Thomas Jefferson, who eloquently proclaimed the inherent equality of mankind, harbored doubts about the equality of the races. Jefferson offered

> as a suspicion only, that the blacks, whether originally a distinct race, or made distinct by time and circumstances, are inferior to the whites in the endowments both of body and mind. It is not against experience to suppose, that different species of the same genus, or varieties of the same species, may possess different qualifications.

T. JEFFERSON, NOTES ON THE STATE OF VIRGINIA 143 (W. Peden ed. 1787, reprinted 1954). For the "modern" Jeffersonian view, see A. JENSEN, EDUCABILITY AND GROUP DIFFERENCES (1973). *But see* F. MORRIS, THE JENSEN HYPOTHESIS: SOCIAL SCIENCE RESEARCH OR SOCIAL SCIENCE RACISM? (1971) (demonstrating the white racist ideology implicit in Jensen's method).

[150] *See, e.g.*, G. FREDRICKSON, THE BLACK IMAGE, *supra* note 147, at 88–89; C. LINCOLN, RACE, RELIGION, AND THE CONTINUING AMERICAN DILEMMA 23–59 (1984).

[151] *See, e.g.*, S. DRAKE, 1 BLACK FOLK: HERE AND THERE 28–30 (1987) (discussing both the content and the context of the development of a negative Black stereotype); J. TURNER, R. SINGLETON & D. MUSICK, OPPRESSION: A SOCIO-HISTORY OF BLACK-WHITE RELATIONS IN AMERICA 11–23, 26–28, 35–38 (1984) (tracing the development of a Black stereotype from the antebellum period to the present day). For a discussion of the historical development of the image of Blacks as "beasts," see G. FREDRICKSON, THE BLACK IMAGE, cited in note 147 above, at 53–58, 275–82. *See generally* G. ALLPORT, THE NATURE OF PREJUDICE 196–99 (1954); J. KOVEL, WHITE RACISM: A PSYCHOHISTORY 51–92 (1970). For a taste of different contexts in which the stereotype grew, see M. CASSITY, cited in note 148 above, at 32–33, 53–54, 62–63 (sexually promiscuous); 48–49 (lazy); 50–52 (morally corrupt and intellectually inferior); 68 ("stupid, immoral, lazy, heathen, docile, sexual and rhythmic creatures").

[152] *See* Gordon, *supra* note 73, at 288 (describing "legal belief structures" as one of the systems of meaning "built by elites who have thought they had some stake in rationalizing their

Throughout American history, racism has identified the interests of subordinated whites with those of society's white elite. Racism does not support the dominant order simply because all whites want to maintain their privilege at the expense of Blacks, or because Blacks sometimes serve as convenient political scapegoats. Instead, the very existence of a clearly subordinated "other" group is contrasted with the norm in a way that reinforces identification with the dominant group. Racism helps create an illusion of unity through the oppositional force of a symbolic "other."[153] The establishment of an "other" creates a bond, a burgeoning common identity of all non-stigmatized parties — whose identity and interests are defined in opposition to the other.[154]

According to the philosophy of Jacques Derrida, a structure of polarized categories is characteristic of Western thought:

---

dominant power positions," which have "the effect of making the social world as it is come to seem natural and inevitable").

[153] The notion of Blacks as a subordinated "other" in Western culture has been a major theme in scholarship exploring the cultural and sociological structure of racism. *See* Trost, *Western Metaphysical Dualism as an Element in Racism*, in CULTURAL BASES OF RACISM AND GROUP OPPRESSION 49 (J. Hodge, D. Struckmann & L. Trost eds. 1975) (arguing that Black and white are seen as paired antinomies, and that there is a hierarchy within the antinomies, with Caucasians and Western culture constituting the preferred or higher antinomy). Frantz Fanon has summarized the attitude of the West toward Blackness as a projection of Western anxiety concerning the "other" in terms of skin color:

> *In Europe, the black man is the symbol of Evil* . . . . The torturer is the black man, Satan is black, one talks of shadow, when one is dirty one is black — whether one is thinking of physical dirtiness or moral dirtiness. It would be astonishing, if the trouble were taken to bring them all together, to see the vast number of expressions that make the black man the equivalent of sin. In Europe, whether concretely or symbolically, the black man stands for the bad side of the character. As long as one cannot understand this fact one is doomed to talk in circles about the "black problem." Blackness, darkness, shadow, shades, night, the labyrinths of the earth, abysmal depths, blacken someone's reputation; and on the other side, the bright look of innocence, the white dove of peace, magical, heavenly light.

F. FANON, BLACK SKINS, WHITE MASKS 188–89 (1967) (emphasis in original); *see* S. GILMAN, DIFFERENCE AND PATHOLOGY: STEREOTYPES OF SEXUALITY, RACE, AND MADNESS 30 (1985) (arguing that the notion that "blacks are the antithesis of the mirage of whiteness, the ideal of European aesthetic values, strikes the reader as an extension of some 'real,' perceived difference to which the qualities of 'good' and 'bad' have been erroneously applied. But the very concept of color is a quality of Otherness, not of reality."); Isaacs, *Blackness and Whiteness*, ENCOUNTER, Aug. 1963, at 8; *see also* W. JORDAN, *supra* note 147 (discussing how 16th and 17th century English writers used the concept that Blacks were the Europeans' polar opposites to establish an elaborate hierarchy to classify other colored people in the world). Others who have used the concept of "otherness" as a framework for examining Black/white relations include C. DEGLER, NEITHER BLACK NOR WHITE: SLAVERY AND RACE RELATIONS IN BRAZIL AND THE UNITED STATES (1971), and Copeland, *The Negro as a Contrast Conception*, in RACE RELATIONS AND THE RACE PROBLEM: A DEFINITION AND AN ANALYSIS 152–79 (E. Thompson ed. 1939). For a general overview of scholarship that further develops and critiques the racial dualism in Western culture, see S. DRAKE, cited in note 151 above, at 75–85.

[154] *See generally* J. KOVEL, *supra* note 151, at 93–105.

> Western thought . . . has always been structured in terms of dichotomies or polarities: good vs. evil, being vs. nothingness, presence vs. absence, truth vs. error, identity vs. difference, mind vs. matter, man vs. woman, soul vs. body, life vs. death, nature vs. culture, speech vs. writing. These polar opposites do not, however, stand as independent and equal entities. The second term in each pair is considered the negative, corrupt, undesirable version of the first, a fall away from it. . . . In other words, the two terms are not simply opposed in their meanings, but are arranged in a hierarchical order which gives the first term *priority* . . . .[155]

Racist ideology replicates this pattern of arranging oppositional categories in a hierarchical order; historically, whites represented the dominant antinomy while Blacks came to be seen as separate and subordinate. This hierarchy is reflected in the chart below. Note how each traditional negative image of Blacks correlates with a counter-image of whites:

Historical Oppositional Dualities

WHITE IMAGES	BLACK IMAGES
Industrious	Lazy
Intelligent	Unintelligent
Moral	Immoral
Knowledgeable	Ignorant
Enabling Culture	Disabling Culture
Law-Abiding	Criminal
Responsible	Shiftless
Virtuous/Pious	Lascivious

The oppositional dynamic symbolized by this chart was created and maintained through an elaborate and systematic process.[156] Laws and customs helped create "races" out of a broad range of human traits. In the process of creating races, the categories came to be filled with meaning — Blacks were characterized one way, whites another. Whites became associated with normatively positive characteristics; Blacks became associated with the subordinate, even aberrational

---

[155] J. DERRIDA, DISSEMINATION viii (B. Johnson trans. 1981) (emphasis in original). Otherness is a corollary to the bipolar conceptualizations that characterize structuralist analysis of Western thought. Some Critical legal scholars have seized these bipolar conceptualizations and used them to explain how doctrine attempts to mediate opposing tendencies in the law. *See, e.g.*, Kennedy, *Form and Substance in Private Law Adjudication*, 89 HARV. L. REV. 1685 (1976).

[156] *See generally* N. Gotanda, Origins of Racial Categorization in Colonial Virginia, 1619–1705 (1980) (unpublished LL.M. thesis, Harvard Law School) (available in the Harvard Law School library) (analyzing the development of racial categories and racist ideology in colonial Virginia).

characteristics. The operation of this dynamic, along with the important political role of racial oppositionalism, can be illustrated through a few brief historical references.

Edmund Morgan provides vivid illustration of how slaveholders from the seventeenth century onward created and politicized racial categories to maintain the support of non-slaveholding whites.[157] Morgan recounts how the planters "lump[ed] Indians, mulattoes, and Negroes in a single slave class," and how these categories became "an essential, if unacknowledged, ingredient of the republican ideology that enabled Virginians to lead the nation."[158] Having accepted a common interest with slaveholders in keeping Blacks subordinated, even whites who had material reasons to object to the dominance over the slaveholding class could challenge the regime only so far. The power of race consciousness convinced whites to support a system that was opposed to their own economic interests. As George Fredrickson put it, "racial privilege could and did serve as a compensation for class disadvantage."[159]

Domination through race consciousness continued throughout the post-Reconstruction period. Historian C. Vann Woodward has argued that the ruling plantocracy was able to undermine the progressive accomplishments of the Populist movement by stirring up anti-Black sentiment among poor white farmers.[160] Racism was articulated as the "broader ground for a new democracy."[161] As racism formed the new base for a broader notion of democracy, class differences were mediated through reference to a racial community of equality.[162] A tragic example of the success of such race-conscious political manipulation is the career of Tom Watson, leader of the progressive Populist movement of the 1890's. Watson, in his attempts to educate the masses of poor farmers about the destructive role of race-based poli-

---

[157] *See* E. MORGAN, AMERICAN SLAVERY — AMERICAN FREEDOM (1975).

[158] *Id.* at 386.

[159] G. FREDRICKSON, WHITE SUPREMACY, *supra* note 147, at 87.

[160] *See* C. WOODWARD, *supra* note 147, at 68–77.

[161] *Id.* at 76. In the words of Southern Progressive Thomas P. Bailey:

> [The] *disenfranchisement of the negroes has been concomitant with the growth of political and social solidarity among the whites.* The more white men recognize sharply their kinship with their fellow whites, and the more democracy in every sense of the term spreads among them, the more the negro is compelled to "keep his place" — a place that is gradually narrowing in the North as well as in the South.

Id. (emphasis in original).

[162] One might argue that the fact that many poor whites were simultaneously disenfranchised cuts against the idea that racist ideology was the glue that organized and held whites together across class lines. In reality, the ability to exclude lower-class whites was achieved politically via racist rhetoric. The need to engage in such rhetoric in order to achieve white political unity led to Populist leader Tom Watson's conversion to white supremacy, which was motivated by his growing belief that true democracy for whites could only be achieved if Blacks were excluded from the political equation.

tics, repeatedly told Black and white audiences, "You are made to hate each other because upon that hatred is rested the keystone of the arch of financial despotism which enslaves you both. You are deceived and blinded that you may not see how this race antagonism perpetuates a monetary system which beggars you both."[163] Yet, by 1906, Watson had joined the movement to disenfranchise Blacks.[164] According to Woodward, Watson had "persuaded himself that only after the Negro was eliminated from politics could Populist principles gain a hearing. In other words, the white men would have to unite before they could divide."[165]

White race consciousness also played a role in the nascent labor movement in the North.[166] Labor historian Herbert Hill has demonstrated that unions of virtually all trades excluded Black workers from their ranks,[167] often entirely barring Black employment in certain fields. Immigrant labor unions were particularly adamant about keeping out Black workers; indeed, it was for the precise purpose of assimilating into the American mainstream that immigrant laborers adopted these exclusionary policies.[168]

---

[163] *See id.* at 44–45.

[164] Woodward traces the cycle of enfranchisement and disenfranchisement of Southern Blacks during and immediately following Reconstruction. He explains that the Black vote increasingly became the swing vote, leading various factions of whites into bitter, even corrupt and violent, competition for it. He particularly argues that white politicians alternately used Blacks as allies and as scapegoats to gain power over other whites. Following the defeat of the Populists, whites from all camps agreed that disenfranchisement of the Blacks was necessary to prevent whites from vying against each other for the Black vote. Thus, white supremacy became the salve that healed the wounds of the bitter conflict, and heralded the new age of democracy in the South. *See id.* at 56–95; *see also* J. FRANKLIN, FROM SLAVERY TO FREEDOM: A HISTORY OF NEGRO AMERICANS 251–67 (5th ed. 1980) (describing the politics of race in the South after Reconstruction).

[165] C. WOODWARD, *supra* note 147, at 73–74.

[166] *See* P. FONER, ORGANIZED LABOR AND THE BLACK WORKER, 1619–1973, at 94–102 (1974); Karson & Radosh, *The American Federation of Labor and the Negro Worker, 1894–1949*, in THE NEGRO AND THE AMERICAN LABOR MOVEMENT 155–87 (J. Jacobson ed. 1968); Hill, *Race and Ethnicity in Organized Labor: The Historical Sources of Resistance to Affirmative Action*, J. INTERGROUP REL., Winter 1984, at 5.

[167] According to Hill,

> Racist ideas and practices in a multitude of forms became a basic characteristic of the most important institution of the working class; labor unions. From the 1880s to the contemporary period, as workers became more union conscious, they also became more race conscious, and as labor organizations became more successful they also intensified their racist practices.

Hill, *supra* note 166, at 5.

[168] "The historical record reveals that the embrace of white supremacy as ideology and as practice was a strategy for assimilation by European working class immigrants, the white ethnics who were to constitute a major part of the membership and leadership of organized labor in the United States." *Id.* at 6.

Even today, unions that are supposed to represent the "consciousness of the working class" often still fail to represent the interests of the Black American worker. For an account of the

The political and ideological role that race consciousness continues to play is suggested by racial polarization in contemporary presidential politics. Several political commentators have suggested that many whites supported Ronald Reagan in the belief that he would correct a perceived policy imbalance that unjustly benefited Blacks,[169] and some argue further that Reagan made a direct racist appeal to white voters.[170] Manning Marable notes, for example, that "[a]ppeals to the 'race consciousness' of white workers were the decisive factor in Reagan's 1984 victory, especially in the South."[171] Reagan received nearly 70% of the white vote whereas 90% of Black voters cast their ballots for Mondale.[172] Similarly, the vast majority of Blacks — 82% — disapproved of Reagan's performance, whereas only 32% of whites did.[173]

Even the Democratic Party, which has traditionally relied on Blacks as its most loyal constituency, has responded to this apparent racial polarization by seeking to distance itself from Black interests.[174] Although it has been argued that the racial polarization demonstrated in the 1984 election does not represent a trend of white defections from the Democratic Party,[175] it is significant that, whatever the cause of the Party's inability to attract white votes, Democratic leaders have expressed a willingness to moderate the Party's stand on key racial issues in attempts to recapture the white vote.[176]

B. *The Role of Race Consciousness in a System of Formal Equality*

The previous section emphasizes the continuity of white race consciousness over the course of American history. This section, by

racist history of the AFL-CIO, see Hill, *The AFL-CIO and the Black Worker: Twenty-Five Years After the Merger*, J. INTERGROUP REL., Sept. 1982, at 5.

[169] *See, e.g.*, M. Marable, Race and Realignment in American Politics (1985) (unpublished manuscript available in Harvard Law School library).

[170] *See, e.g.*, Howell, *Electoral Politics and Racial Polarization*, 101 CHRISTIAN CENTURY 1117 (1984); Wilkins, *Smiling Racism*, 23 THE NATION 437 (Nov. 3, 1984).

[171] M. Marable, *supra* note 169, at 34.

[172] *See Portrait of the Electorate*, N.Y. Times, Nov. 8, 1984, at A19, cols. 8–9.

[173] *See* M. Marable, *supra* note 169, at 17.

[174] *See, e.g.*, *Democrats Sift '84 Rubble, Assess Rebuilding in South*, Wash. Post, Jan. 20, 1985, at A31, cols. 3–4; *Party Looks Inward for Ways to Regain Majority*, N.Y. Times, Nov. 8, 1984, at A24, col. 8; Wicker, *A Party of Access?*, N.Y. Times, Nov. 25, 1984, at E17, col. 1. The party's first response to the 1984 loss was a proposal "to reduce democratic access of Blacks, feminists, and other insurgent social forces inside the party's governing apparatus." M. Marable, *supra* note 169, at 31.

[175] *See, e.g.*, T. FERGUSON & J. ROGERS, RIGHT TURN (1986) (arguing that the "right turn" in 1980 and 1984 was caused not by voter realignment but by a realignment of major investors in the political system).

[176] This effort to minimize Black influence reflects what Derrick Bell has called the principle of "involuntary sacrifice." *See* D. BELL, *supra* note 6, § 1.9, at 29–30. Bell asserts that throughout American history, Black interests have been sacrificed when necessary to reestablish the bonds of the white community, "so that identifiably different groups of whites may settle a dispute and establish or reestablish their relationship." *Id.* at 30.

contrast, focuses on the partial transformation of the functioning of race consciousness that occurred with the transition from Jim Crow to formal equality in race law.

Prior to the civil rights reforms, Blacks were formally subordinated by the state. Blacks experienced being the "other" in two aspects of oppression, which I shall designate as symbolic and material.[177] Symbolic subordination refers to the formal denial of social and political equality to all Blacks, regardless of their accomplishments. Segregation and other forms of social exclusion — separate restrooms, drinking fountains, entrances, parks, cemeteries, and dining facilities — reinforced a racist ideology that Blacks were simply inferior to whites and were therefore not included in the vision of America as a community of equals.

Material subordination, on the other hand, refers to the ways that discrimination and exclusion economically subordinated Blacks to whites and subordinated the life chances of Blacks to those of whites on almost every level. This subordination occurs when Blacks are paid less for the same work, when segregation limits access to decent housing, and where poverty, anxiety, poor health care, and crime create a life expectancy for Blacks that is five to six years shorter than for whites.[178]

Symbolic subordination often created material disadvantage by reinforcing race consciousness in everything from employment to education. In fact, the two are generally not thought of separately: separate facilities were usually inferior facilities, and limited job categorization virtually always brought lower pay and harder work. Despite the pervasiveness of racism, however, there existed even before the civil rights movement a class of Blacks who were educationally, economically, and professionally equal — if not superior — to many whites, and yet these Blacks suffered social and political exclusion as well.[179]

It is also significant that not all separation resulted in inferior institutions. School segregation — although often presented as the epitome of symbolic and material subordination[180] — did not always

---

[177] These two manifestations of racial subordination are not mutually exclusive. In fact, it only makes sense to separate various aspects of racial oppression in this post-civil rights era in order to understand how the movement changed some social norms and reinforced others. Most Blacks probably did not experience or perceive their oppression as reflecting two separate structures.

[178] *See* BUREAU OF THE CENSUS, U.S. DEPT. OF COMMERCE, STATISTICAL ABSTRACT OF THE UNITED STATES 69–71 (107th ed. 1987); *supra* note 3.

[179] *See* J. FRANKLIN, *supra* note 164, at 163–66.

[180] This characterization was the clear motivation of the NAACP's school desegregation strategy. *See generally* R. KLUGER, SIMPLE JUSTICE (1976) (detailing the NAACP's strategy). For an excellent critique of this strategy that discusses some of the paradoxes that attend the simultaneous pursuit of integration and quality education, see Bell, *Serving Two Masters: Integration Ideals and Client Interests in School Desegregation Litigation*, 85 YALE L.J. 470

result in inferior education.[181] It is not separation *per se* that made segregation subordinating, but the fact that it was enforced and supported by state power, and accompanied by the explicit belief in African-American inferiority.[182]

The response to the civil rights movement was the removal of most formal barriers and symbolic manifestations of subordination. Thus, "White Only" notices and other obvious indicators of the societal policy of racial subordination disappeared — at least in the public sphere. The disappearance of these symbols of subordination reflected the acceptance of the rhetoric of formal equality and signaled the demise of the rhetoric of white supremacy as expressing America's normative vision. In other words, it could no longer be said that Blacks were not included as equals in the American political vision.

Removal of these public manifestations of subordination was a significant gain for all Blacks, although some benefited more than others. The eradication of formal barriers meant more to those whose oppression was primarily symbolic than to those who suffered lasting material disadvantage. Yet despite these disparate results, it would be absurd to suggest that no benefits came from these formal reforms, especially in regard to racial policies, such as segregation, that were partly material but largely symbolic. Thus, to say that the reforms were "merely symbolic" is to say a great deal. These legal reforms and the formal extension of "citizenship" were large achievements precisely because much of what characterized Black oppression was symbolic and formal.

Yet the attainment of formal equality is not the end of the story. Racial hierarchy cannot be cured by the move to facial race-neutrality in the laws that structure the economic, political, and social lives of Black people. White race consciousness, in a new form but still virulent, plays an important, perhaps crucial, role in the new regime

---

(1976). For one historical example of the view that the real issue should be education, and not integration, see DuBois, *Does the Negro Need Separate Schools?*, 4 J. NEGRO EDUC. 328 (1935), which is reprinted in W. DUBOIS, cited in note 2 above, at 408.

[181] That there were Black professionals indicates that Black educational achievement was not always inferior. Howard University Law School, for example, is legendary for producing the brilliant Black attorneys who shaped the legal campaign for racial equality, and for producing the first Black Supreme Court Justice. *See* R. KLUGER, *supra* note 180, at 126–31. Thomas Sowell makes much of the fact that students from Washington's Dunbar High excelled in a number of fields. *See* T. SOWELL, BLACK EDUCATION: MYTHS AND TRAGEDIES 282–86 (1972).

[182] Socially, many Blacks lived in a society that was comparable in many ways to that of the white elites. Hardly strangers to debutante balls, country clubs, and vacations abroad, these Blacks lived lives of which many whites only dreamed. Nevertheless, despite their material wealth, upper-middle class Blacks were still members of a subordinated group. Where rights and privileges were distributed on the basis of race, even a distinguished African-American had to take a back seat to each white — no matter how poor, ignorant, or uneducated the white might be. *See generally* E. FRAZIER, BLACK BOURGEOISIE: THE RISE OF A NEW MIDDLE CLASS IN THE UNITED STATES (1957).

that has legitimated the deteriorating day-to-day material conditions of the majority of Blacks.[183]

The end of Jim Crow has been accompanied by the demise of an explicit ideology of white supremacy. The white norm, however, has not disappeared; it has only been submerged in popular consciousness. It continues in an unspoken form as a statement of the positive social norm, legitimating the continuing domination of those who do not meet it. Nor have the negative stereotypes associated with Blacks been eradicated. The rationalizations once used to legitimate Black subordination based on a belief in racial inferiority have now been reemployed to legitimate the domination of Blacks through reference to an assumed cultural inferiority.

Thomas Sowell, for example, suggests that underclass Blacks are economically depressed because they have not adopted the values of hard work and discipline.[184] He further implies that Blacks have not pursued the need to attain skills and marketable education, and have not learned to make the sacrifices necessary for success.[185] Instead, Sowell charges that Blacks view demands for special treatment as a means for achieving what other groups have achieved through hard work and the abandonment of racial politics.[186]

Sowell applies the same stereotypes to the mass of Blacks that white supremacists had applied in the past, but bases these modern stereotypes on notions of "culture" rather than genetics. Sowell characterizes underclass Blacks as victims of self-imposed ignorance, lack of direction, and poor work attitudes. Culture, not race, now accounts for this "otherness." Except for vestigial pockets of historical racism, any possible connection between past racial subordination and the present situation has been severed by the formal repudiation of the old race-conscious policies. The same dualities historically used to legitimate racial subordination in the name of genetic inferiority have now been adopted by Sowell as a means for explaining the subordinated status of Blacks today in terms of cultural inferiority.[187]

---

[183] For examples of this deterioration, see note 3 above.

[184] I take this to be implied by Sowell's opposition to the "civil rights vision," which he shows by challenging the significance of statistical disparities, and by his statements concerning the "way people work." *See* T. SOWELL, *supra* note 34, at 46–47.

[185] *See id.* at 42–46 (illustrating the low levels of educational attainment by Blacks relative to other ethnic and racial groups and arguing that demographic, cultural, and geographic differences among groups strongly affect incomes and occupations).

[186] Sowell recites a predictable and stereotypical litany of ethnic groups that have abandoned political struggle for hard work and achieved success. *See id.* at 29–35. Sowell reduces these complex racial histories into another variant of "otherness."

[187] Sowell exemplifies what may be the worst development of the civil rights movement — that some Blacks who have benefited the most from the formal gestures of equality now identify with those who attempt to affirm the legitimacy of oppressing other Blacks. Clearly, this legitimation and desertion by some Blacks has been politically damaging and may undermine future efforts to organize.

Moreover, Sowell's explanation of the subordinate status of Blacks also illustrates the treatment of the now-unspoken white stereotypes as the positive social norm. His assertion that the *absence* of certain attributes accounts for the continued subordination of Blacks implies that it is the *presence* of these attributes that explains the continued advantage of whites. The only difference between this argument and the older oppositional dynamic is that, whereas the latter explained Black subordination through reference to the ideology of white supremacy, the former explains Black subordination through reference to an unspoken social norm. That norm — although no longer explicitly white supremacist — remains, nonetheless, a white norm. As Martha Minow has pointed out, "[t]he unstated point of comparison is not neutral, but particular, and not inevitable, but only seemingly so when left unstated."[188]

White race consciousness, which includes the modern belief in cultural inferiority, acts to further Black subordination by justifying all the forms of unofficial racial discrimination, injury, and neglect that flourish in a society that is only formally dedicated to equality. In more subtle ways, moreover, white race consciousness reinforces and is reinforced by the myth of equal opportunity that explains and justifies broader class hierarchies.

Race consciousness also reinforces whites' sense that American society is really meritocratic and thus helps prevent them from questioning the basic legitimacy of the free market. Believing both that Blacks are inferior and that the economy impartially rewards the superior over the inferior, whites see that most Blacks are indeed worse off than whites are, which reinforces their sense that the market is operating "fairly and impartially"; those who should logically be on the bottom are on the bottom.[189] This strengthening of whites' belief in the system in turn reinforces their beliefs that Blacks are *indeed* inferior. After all, equal opportunity *is* the rule, and the market *is* an impartial judge; if Blacks are on the bottom, it must reflect their relative inferiority. Racist ideology thus operates in conjunction with the class components of legal ideology to reinforce the status quo, both in terms of class and race.

To bring a fundamental challenge to the way things are, whites would have to question not just their own subordinate status, but also both the economic and the racial myths that justify the status quo. Racism, combined with equal opportunity mythology, provides a rationalization for racial oppression, making it difficult for whites to see the Black situation as illegitimate or unnecessary. If whites believe

---

[188] Minow, *The Supreme Court, 1986 Term — Foreword: Justice Engendered*, 101 HARV. L. REV. 10, 32 (1987).

[189] *See* Kluegel, *supra* note 66, at 774.

that Blacks, because they are unambitious or inferior, get what they deserve, it becomes that much harder to convince whites that something is wrong with the entire system.[190] Similarly, a challenge to the legitimacy of continued racial inequality would force whites to confront myths about equality of opportunity that justify for them whatever measure of economic success they may have attained.

Thus, although Critics have suggested that legal consciousness plays a central role in legitimating hierarchy in America, the otherness dynamic enthroned within the maintenance and perpetuation of white race consciousness seems to be at least as important as legal consciousness in supporting the dominant order. Like legal consciousness, race consciousness makes it difficult — at least for whites — to imagine the world differently. It also creates the desire for identification with privileged elites. By focusing on a distinct, subordinate "other," whites include themselves in the dominant circle — an arena in which most hold no real power, but only their privileged racial identity. Consider the case of a dirt-poor, southern white, shown participating in a Ku Klux Klan rally in the movie *Resurgence*, who declared: "Every morning, I wake up and thank God I'm white."[191] For this person, and for others like him, race consciousness — manifested by his refusal even to associate with Blacks — provides a powerful explanation of why he fails to challenge the current social order.

C. *Rights Discourse as a Challenge to the Oppositional Dynamic*

The oppositional dynamic, premised upon maintaining Blacks as an excluded and subordinated "other," initially created an ideological and political structure of formal inequality against which rights rhetoric proved to be the most effective weapon. Although rights rhetoric may ultimately have absorbed the civil rights challenge and legitimated continued subordination, the otherness dynamic provides a fuller understanding of how the very transformation afforded by legal reform itself has contributed to the ideological and political legitimation of continuing Black subordination.

Rights discourse provided the ideological mechanisms through which the conflicts of federalism, the power of the Presidency, and the legitimacy of the courts could be orchestrated against Jim Crow. Movement leaders used these tactics to force open a conflict between whites that eventually benefited Black people. Casting racial issues in the moral and legal rights rhetoric of the prevailing ideology helped create the political controversy without which the state's coercive function would not have been enlisted to aid Blacks.

---

[190] *See* Kluegel & Smith, *Whites' Beliefs About Blacks' Opportunity*, 47 AM. SOC. REV. 518 (1983).

[191] *Resurgence* (Skylight Pictures–Emancipation Arts Sept. 1981).

Simply critiquing the ideology from without or making demands in language outside the rights discourse would have accomplished little. Rather, Blacks gained by using a powerful combination of direct action, mass protest, and individual acts of resistance, along with appeals to public opinion and the courts couched in the language of the prevailing legal consciousness. The result was a series of ideological and political crises. In these crises, civil rights activists and lawyers induced the federal government to aid Blacks and triggered efforts to legitimate and reinforce the authority of the law in ways that benefited Blacks. Simply insisting that Blacks be integrated or speaking in the language of "needs" would have endangered the lives of those who were already taking risks — and with no reasonable chance of success. President Eisenhower, for example, would not have sent federal troops to Little Rock simply at the behest of protesters demanding that Black schoolchildren receive an equal education. Instead, the successful manipulation of legal rhetoric led to a crisis of federal power that ultimately benefited Blacks.[192]

Some critics of legal reform movements seem to overlook the fact that state power has made a significant difference — sometimes between life and death — in the efforts of Black people to transform their world. Attempts to harness the power of the state through the appropriate rhetorical/legal incantations should be appreciated as intensely powerful and calculated political acts. In the context of white supremacy, engaging in rights discourse should be seen as an act of self-defense. This was particularly true because the state could not assume a position of neutrality regarding Black people once the movement had mobilized people to challenge the system of oppression: either the coercive mechanism of the state had to be used to support white supremacy, or it had to be used to dismantle it. We know now, with hindsight, that it did both.[193]

Blacks did use rights rhetoric to mobilize state power to their benefit against symbolic oppression through formal inequality and, to some extent, against material deprivation in the form of private, informal exclusion of the middle class from jobs and housing. Yet today the same legal reforms play a role in providing an ideological

---

[192] For a detailed account of the crisis that preceded Eisenhower's decision to deploy the 101st Airborne Division in Little Rock, see J. WILLIAMS, cited in note 140 above, at 92–119.

[193] Consider, for example, the possible police responses to students who violated local ordinances by sitting in at segregated lunch counters and demanding service. Government officials could have ordered the students arrested, thereby upholding the segregation policy, or they could have ignored them, which would have incidentally supported the students' efforts. Both tactics were followed throughout the course of the movement. Because officials sometimes had a degree of choice in the matter, and courts had the ultimate power to review the legitimacy of the laws and the officials' actions, Black protesters' use of rights rhetoric can be seen as an effort to defend themselves against arrest or conviction for violating the norms of white supremacy.

framework that makes the present conditions facing underclass Blacks appear fair and reasonable. The eradication of barriers has created a new dilemma for those victims of racial oppression who are not in a position to benefit from the move to formal equality. The race neutrality of the legal system creates the illusion that racism is no longer the primary factor responsible for the condition of the Black underclass; instead, as we have seen, class disparities appear to be the consequence of individual and group merit within a supposed system of equal opportunity. Moreover, the fact that there are Blacks who are economically successful gives credence both to the assertion that opportunities exist,[194] and to the backlash attitude that Blacks have "gotten too far."[195] Psychologically, for Blacks who have not made it, the lack of an explanation for their underclass status may result in self-blame and other self-destructive attitudes.[196]

Another consequence of the formal reforms may be the loss of collectivity among Blacks.[197] The removal of formal barriers created new opportunities for some Blacks that were not shared by various other classes of African-Americans. As Blacks moved into different spheres, the experience of being Black in America became fragmented

---

[194] This is essentially the process described in Freeman, cited in note 79 above, at 110–14.

[195] This phenomenon is undoubtedly exacerbated by periods of economic hardship. It was in this context that the U.S. Commission on Civil Rights commented that some whites "believe that their hard times result from 'reverse discrimination' in employment and a tax burden imposed upon them to support government programs that in their view provide undeserved advantages to minorities." U.S. COMM'N ON CIVIL RIGHTS, *supra* note 3, at 11.

[196] Kristin Bumiller argues that victims of discrimination ultimately fail to "achieve successful resolutions of their problems" for three reasons:

> First, the bonds between the perpetrator and the discrimination victim drive the conflict to self-destructive or explosive reactions. Second, these individuals are guided by an ethic of survival that encourages self-sacrifice rather than action. And third, the potential for legal remedies is diminished by a view of the law that engenders fear of legal intervention. Injured persons reluctantly employ the label of discrimination because they shun the role of the victim, and they fear legal intervention will disrupt the delicate balance of power between themselves and their opponents.

Bumiller, *Victims in the Shadow of the Law: A Critique of the Model of Legal Protection*, 12 SIGNS: J. WOMEN IN CULTURE AND SOC'Y 421, 438 (1987). Note that the last sentence attempts to analyze both the consensual and the coercive components of hegemony.

[197] By "collectivity," I refer to the recognition of common interests and the benefits derived by Blacks of all classes in sharing the burdens of social struggle. The potential for collective struggle is maximized where the grievance is shared by all. It was clear that racial segregation, for example, affected all Blacks. The creation of opportunity for some Blacks — however small the number may be — can obscure the degree to which Blacks have common interests that warrant continual collective struggle. One of the unfortunate consequences of viewing racism solely in terms of economic class is that it may create the impression that there are few common interests that Blacks share across class lines. Although the emergence of a new and outspoken class of Black neoconservatives may confirm this consequence, political opinion surveys indicate that Black political opinions are not so tightly bounded by class lines as those of whites. *See* Gilliam, *Black America: Divided by Class?*, PUBLIC OPINION, Feb.–Mar. 1986, at 53–57.

and multifaceted, and the different contexts presented opportunities to experience racism in different ways.[198] The social, economic, and even residential distance between the various classes may complicate efforts to unite behind issues as a racial group. Although "White Only" signs may have been crude and debilitating, they at least presented a readily discernible target around which to organize. Now, the targets are obscure and diffuse, and this difference may create doubt among some Blacks whether there is enough similarity between their life experiences and those of other Blacks to warrant collective political action.

Formal equality significantly transformed the Black experience in America. With society's embrace of formal equality came the eradication of symbolic domination and the suppression of white supremacy as the norm of society. Future generations of Black Americans would no longer be explicitly regarded as America's second-class citizens. Yet the transformation of the oppositional dynamic — achieved through the suppression of racial norms and stereotypes, and the recasting of racial inferiority into assumptions of cultural inferiority — creates several difficulties for the civil rights constituency. The removal of formal barriers, although symbolically significant to all and materially significant to some, will do little to alter the hierarchical relationship between Blacks and whites until the way in which white race consciousness perpetuates norms that legitimate Black subordination is revealed. This is not to say that white norms alone account for the conditions of the Black underclass. It is instead an acknowledgment that, until the distinct racial nature of class ideology is itself revealed and debunked, nothing can be done about the underlying structural problems that account for the disparities.[199] The narrow focus of racial exclusion — that is, the belief that racial exclusion is illegitimate only where the "White Only" signs are explicit — coupled with strong assumptions about equal opportunity, makes it difficult to move the discussion of racism beyond the societal self-satisfaction engendered by the appearance of neutral norms and formal inclusion.

D. Self-Conscious Ideological Struggle

Rights have been important. They may have legitimated racial inequality, but they have also been the means by which oppressed

---

198 *See* W. WILSON, *supra* note 3, at 7–8.

199 The racial character of the rationalizations that legitimate poverty is exemplified by advocates who seek to educate the American public about the severity of the homelessness problem by revealing that many of the new homeless are white. This does not necessarily indicate that advocates prefer whites over Blacks; instead, it is an acknowledgment that such a problem can easily be disregarded as the result of personal failure if its victims are Black. The vast number of white homeless, however, raises the inescapable inference that something is amiss within America's economic structure.

groups have secured both entry as formal equals into the dominant order and the survival of their movement in the face of private and state repression. The dual role of legal change creates a dilemma for Black reformers. As long as race consciousness thrives, Blacks will often have to rely on rights rhetoric when it is necessary to protect Black interests. The very reforms brought about by appeals to legal ideology, however, seem to undermine the ability to move forward toward a broader vision of racial equality. In the quest for racial justice, winning and losing have been part of the same experience.

The Critics are correct in observing that engaging in rights discourse has helped to deradicalize and co-opt the challenge. Yet they fail to acknowledge the limited range of options presented to Blacks in a context where they were deemed "other," and the unlikelihood that specific demands for inclusion and equality would be heard if articulated in other terms. This abbreviated list of options is itself contingent upon the ideological power of white race consciousness and the continuing role of Black Americans as "other." Future efforts to address racial domination, as well as class hierarchy, must consider the continuing ideology of white race consciousness by uncovering the oppositional dynamic and by chipping away at its premises. Central to this task is revealing the contingency of race and exploring the connection between white race consciousness and the other myths that legitimate both class and race hierarchies. Critics and others whose agendas include challenging hierarchy and legitimation must not overlook the importance of revealing the contingency of race.

Optimally, the deconstruction of white race consciousness might lead to a liberated future for both Blacks and whites. Yet, until whites recognize the hegemonic function of racism and turn their efforts toward neutralizing it, African-American people must develop pragmatic political strategies — self-conscious ideological struggle — to minimize the costs of liberal reform while maximizing its utility. A primary step in engaging in self-conscious ideological struggle must be to transcend the oppositional dynamic in which Blacks are cast simply and solely as whites' subordinate "other."[200]

The dual role that rights have played makes strategizing a difficult task. Black people can afford neither to resign themselves to, nor to attack frontally, the legitimacy and incoherence of the dominant ideology. The subordinate position of Blacks in this society makes it unlikely that African-Americans will realize gains through the kind of direct challenge to the legitimacy of American liberal ideology that is now being waged by Critical scholars. On the other hand, delegiti-

[200] The embrace of the self-definition "African-American" can symbolize the ongoing effort to break free of the subordinate self-identity brought about by exclusive reference to a white norm.

mating race consciousness would be directly relevant to Black needs, and this strategy will sometimes require the pragmatic use of liberal ideology.

This vision is consistent with the views forwarded by theoreticians such as Frances Fox Piven and Richard Cloward, Antonio Gramsci, and Roberto Unger. Piven and Cloward observe that oppressed people sometimes advance by creating ideological and political crisis, but that the form of the crisis-producing challenge must reflect the institutional logic of the system.[201] The use of rights rhetoric during the civil rights movement created such a crisis by presenting and manipulating the dominant ideology in a new and transformative way. Challenges and demands made from outside the institutional logic would have accomplished little because Blacks, as the subordinate "other," were already perceived as being outside the mainstream. The struggle of Blacks, like that of all subordinated groups, is a struggle for inclusion, an attempt to manipulate elements of the dominant ideology to transform the experience of domination. It is a struggle to create a new status quo through the ideological and political tools that are available.

Gramsci called this struggle a "War of Position" and he regarded it as the most appropriate strategy for change in Western societies. According to Gramsci, direct challenges to the dominant class accomplish little if ideology plays such a central role in establishing authority that the legitimacy of the dominant regime is not challenged. Joseph Femia, interpreting Gramsci, states that "the dominant ideology in modern capitalist societies is highly institutionalized and widely internalized. It follows that a concentration on frontal attack, on direct assault against the bourgeois state ('war of movement' or 'war of manoeuvre') can result only in disappointment and defeat."[202] Consequently, the challenge in such societies is to create a counter-hegemony by maneuvering within and expanding the dominant ideology to embrace the potential for change.

Gramsci's vision of ideological struggle is echoed in part by Roberto Unger in his vision of deviationist doctrine. Unger, who represents another strand of the Critical approach, argues that, rather than discarding liberal legal ideology, we should focus and develop its visionary undercurrents:

> [T]he struggle over the form of social life, through deviationist doctrine, creates opportunities for experimental revisions of social life in the direction of the ideals we defend. An implication of our ideas is

---

[201] *See* F. Piven & R. Cloward, *supra* note 136, at 23.

[202] J. Femia, Gramsci's Political Thought: Hegemony, Consciousness, and the Revolutionary Process 51 (1981).

> that the elements of a formative institutional or imaginative structure may be replaced piecemeal rather than only all at once.[203]

Liberal ideology embraces communal and liberating visions along with the legitimating hegemonic visions. Unger, like Gramsci and Piven and Cloward, seems to suggest that the strategy toward meaningful change depends on skillful use of the liberating potential of dominant ideology.

V. Conclusion

For Blacks, the task at hand is to devise ways to wage ideological and political struggle while minimizing the costs of engaging in an inherently legitimating discourse. A clearer understanding of the space we occupy in the American political consciousness is a necessary prerequisite to the development of pragmatic strategies for political and economic survival. In this regard, the most serious challenge for Blacks is to minimize the political and cultural cost of engaging in an inevitably co-optive process in order to secure material benefits. Because our present predicament gives us few options, we must create conditions for the maintenance of a distinct political thought that is informed by the actual conditions of Black people. Unlike the civil rights vision, this new approach should not be defined and thereby limited by the possibilities of dominant political discourse, but should maintain a distinctly progressive outlook that focuses on the needs of the African-American community.

---

[203] Unger, *supra* note 72, at 666.

Part IV
Feminist Perspectives

[9]

JOURNAL OF LAW AND SOCIETY
VOLUME 14, NUMBER 4, WINTER 1987
0263-323X $3.00

Legislation Against Sex Discrimination: Questions from a Feminist Perspective

NICOLA LACEY*

Since the Equal Pay Act was enacted in 1970, Britain has gradually formulated a legislative scheme explicitly aimed at the elimination of certain forms of discrimination.[1] The Sex Discrimination Acts 1975 and 1986 and the Race Relations Act 1986 have resulted. Accession to the European Community has introduced the European standard of equal treatment, prompting developments such as the Equal Pay (Amendment) Regulations 1983, which introduced the concept of equal pay for work of equal value. Indeed, it seems fair to say that protection from unjust discrimination on grounds of sex or race is the area of civil rights which has received the most systematic and innovative legislative attention in Britain over the past two decades. Correspondingly, the technical and strategic problems thrown up by the anti-discrimination legislation and questions about its reform have received much attention.[2]

In this paper, by contrast, I want to raise some more general questions about the underlying basis of principle of the Sex Discrimination Act 1975, specifically from a feminist point of view. For these general questions have, as I shall argue, important implications in terms both of difficulties in using and enforcing the legislation and of our thinking about the proper direction of reform. In arguing from a feminist perspective, I shall not give any detailed account of a particular version of feminist theory. It should be sufficient to my argument to characterise such a theory as one which takes as its starting point the fact of women's subordination and oppression and which thus evaluates anti-discrimination legislation in terms of its actual and potential contribution to the dismantling of such oppression. This is not to say that the project of constructing a detailed theory and working towards a full understanding of the nature of women's oppression is not of fundamental importance. Rather,

**New College, Oxford OX1 3BN, England.*

Earlier versions of this paper were delivered at a meeting of the Industrial Law Society in the autumn of 1986 and at seminars at the universities of Kent, Oxford, and New South Wales, and at Macquarie University and Monash University in the spring of 1987. I should like to thank the participants at all these seminars for their helpful comments.

it is to acknowledge that it is beyond the scope of this article and to affirm that useful feminist critique does not have to await the production of an ultimate 'grand theory'. It will be clear from what I have to say, however, that my own perspective goes beyond that which might be espoused by a liberal feminist whilst falling short of a radical feminist viewpoint, and at many points the argument will doubtless imply or presuppose a particular view of the nature of women's oppression – a view which might be characterised as a socialist feminist approach.

GENERAL DIFFICULTIES WITH BRITISH ANTI-DISCRIMINATION LAW

It will be useful to begin with a concise statement of some of the problems which litigants under the current legislation are generally acknowledged to face – problems which I shall argue look deeper and more intractable from a feminist perspective. First of all, it is widely accepted that plaintiffs bringing discrimination cases encounter grave difficulties of proof. In cases argued under s.1(1)(a) of the Sex Discrimination Act 1975, which allege less favourable treatment on grounds of sex – 'direct' discrimination – it is notoriously difficult to prove the 'ground' of the defendant's action. In many cases it will be possible for the defendant to offer a plausible account of the basis for their treatment of the plaintiff which does not depend on sex or sex-related factors.[3] In cases argued under s.1(1)(b) of the 1975 Act, which allege a requirement or condition which, although applied to members of both sexes, disproportionately and unjustifiably excludes members of one sex to their detriment – 'indirect' discrimination – the plaintiffs face technical difficulties in terms of the identification of relevant pools for comparison, gathering adequate statistics and proving detriment.[4] These difficulties of proof are believed to explain, at least in part, both the small total number of discrimination cases and their low success rate.

Secondly, it is almost universally accepted that the remedies offered to successful plaintiffs under the Sex Discrimination Acts are grievously inadequate. Awards of damages are low, industrial tribunals have no injunctive powers nor any power to award 'front pay' in employment cases, and in cases where indirect discrimination cannot be shown to have been intentional, plaintiffs cannot even claim any damages.[5] Thirdly, it is now recognised that the Equal Opportunities Commission – the administrative agency set up under the 1975 Act with a mixture of investigative, enforcement, advisory, and educational powers – is under-resourced and has inadequate powers properly to fulfil its statutory responsibilities. It is also vulnerable to legal challenge in exercising its investigative powers. Traditional principles of British administrative law tend to be hostile to the Equal Opportunities Commission's combination of functions.[6] Fourthly, doubts are growing about the adequacy of industrial tribunals and county courts as forums for hearing the rare sex discrimination case. Even in the employment area, the number of cases brought is comparatively small, and there is growing evidence of tribunal incompetence in the face of complex and unfamiliar legal provisions.[7] Finally, the unavailability of legal aid for representation before the industrial tribunals, where the vast majority of cases is heard, gives serious cause for concern in view of the complexity of the law and the correlation between legal representation and plaintiff success.[8]

FEMINIST CRITIQUE OF ANTI-DISCRIMINATION LAW

From this brief survey of the most salient problems posed by the current legislation, I now turn to some more general concerns which emerge from a specifically feminist perspective.

1. *The Ideal of Equality*

Starting at the most fundamental level, one obvious set of questions has to do with just what the Sex Discrimination Act 1975 sets out to achieve and the nature of the political commitment from which it proceeded. One way of looking at this question is to understand anti-discrimination law as proceeding from a commitment to the value of equality, which rules out discrimination on certain grounds. Equality, however, is a deeply-contested notion, and several conceptions of equality present themselves as possible candidates to be bases for anti-discrimination law. Perhaps most obviously there is the ideal of formal equality; after all, equality before the law and equal rights – particularly in terms of women's position in the public sphere of paid employment, market transactions, and education – have long been cherished goals of liberal feminism. But the limitations of formal equality as a feminist goal are now widely recognised: it has little bite in view of the disadvantages which women suffer in 'private' areas such as family life, untouched by the sex discrimination legislation. No concept of discrimination which is based exclusively on formal equality can take proper account of aspects of women's different position resulting from prior discrimination and disadvantage in spheres which fall outside the relatively limited ambit of the legislation.[9] Similar limitations surround a second candidate: equality of treatment exclusively on the basis of 'relevant' reasons.[10] Given the history and structure of sex discrimination, merely ruling out sex as a relevant reason for action in certain areas promises little progress in terms of dismantling women's disadvantage. It may even be counter-productive in ruling out sex as a remedially relevant reason in the context, for example, of affirmative action programmes.

It is clear from the content of the Sex Discrimination Act 1975 that neither formal nor relevant reasons for equality formed its exclusive underlying ideal. The concept of indirect discrimination takes on board the idea that women's disadvantage is not solely or even principally the result of individual acts of prejudiced discrimination but of structural discrimination embedded in the practices of social institutions. Practical problems still arise, in that the operation of the test of what prima facie indirect discrimination is *justifiable* is inherently vulnerable to the prejudices of the tribunal and the (often low) importance it gives to sexual equality as a social goal. But it is clear that indirect discrimination moves beyond formal or 'relevant reasons' equality. It aspires towards a more programmatic vision of equality of opportunity – an ideal which is stated in the preamble to the 1975 Act and reflected in the name of the administrative agency which it set up. In effect, the Act uses inequalities of results in certain circumstances as raising prima facie cases of unjust inequality of opportunity, which then have to be justified by the defendant. But what exactly does equality of opportunity mean, how thoroughly is it embedded as the organising principle of the legislation, and does it offer an acceptable goal for feminism?

2. *Equality of Opportunity*

Equality of opportunity represents only one among many of the more programmatic conceptions of equality described and defended in modern political theory. Equality of welfare, results, resources, and consideration of interests, to name but a few, have been energetically and ably defended. Any of these conceptions *might* be easier to extend beyond a liberal world-view or more susceptible of being given a distinctively feminist content than is equality of opportunity.[11] But it is important to analyse the idea of equality of opportunity and to reflect on its status as the chosen stated ideal for current anti-discrimination legislation. And what emerges from such reflection is the clear fact that the idea provided a crucially important campaigning slogan for the legislation, but that, by the same token, it was not discussed or analysed in any open or rigorous way. Had it been, it seems likely that both its ambiguity and its potentially radical implications would have come to the surface and it would have lost its capacity to unite diverse political groups. How many liberal supporters of the current legislation, for example, would have been content to reflect on the implications of a thorough-going commitment to equality of opportunity in terms of socialisation of child-rearing or even genetic engineering? Thus, we should not expect to find that the legislation conforms to a coherent or unitary ideal of equality. We should rather recognise equality of opportunity as a crucial piece of political rhetoric which also provides guiding and limiting principles. These combine in the legislation with an underlying commitment to formal and 'relevant reasons' equality within the public spheres of community activity which form the appropriate focus for political intervention according to liberal theory.

But does equality of opportunity represent an attractive organising ideal for feminists concerned to argue for the reform of anti-discrimination legislation? As we have seen, indirect discrimination uses inequality of impact *in certain very limited circumstances* as a test of prima facie inequality of opportunity. This, of course, implies that in other spheres inequality of impact is *not* an instance of unjust inequality. This is consistent with an equal-opportunity world-view, because the discourse of equality of opportunity presupposes a world inhabited by autonomous individuals making choices. These choices may differ along gender lines, resulting in a very different distribution of jobs or other goods as between women and men. At this point the critical edge of the ideal of equal opportunity is, quite simply, blunt. An equal opportunity principle is inadequate to criticise and transform a world in which the distribution of goods is structured along gender lines. And this relates back to practical problems faced by litigants. Differential treatment and unequal impact, even within the ambit of prima facie discrimination, may be legitimated subconsciously by industrial tribunal members who believe women and men just *do* typically make different choices. Different finishing points are not seen as problematic. In this way the very stereotypes which the legislation is presumably meant to undermine inevitably and invisibly affect the tribunal's reading of legal issues, such as what counts as less favourable or detrimental treatment, or justifiable requirements or conditions.

These difficulties with the ideology underlying the legislation are compounded by its limited scope. Prohibition of differential treatment and unequal impact in a small selection of spheres, all of them within the 'public realm', is unlikely to have any real effect on women's oppression. Attempts to extend the formal market conditions for equal competition between the sexes within an ideology of equal opportunity hardly seems an adequate goal for any really critical feminism. Rather, we must look for a normative basis which provides a real cutting edge against the widespread inequality and injustice which flows from action based on stereotyped assumptions and from the genuinely different socialisation and expectations which still exist between the sexes. For however deplorable we find the fact that gender is still an important factor in the creation and structure of social practices, we cannot ignore it if we are to secure real progress for women.

3. *The Symmetry of Equality Principles*

The logic of the ideal of equal treatment and formal equality which underlies much of the legislation creates another difficulty. Part of this logic is a symmetry – a conception of sex discrimination which encompasses treatment of both men and women – which clearly does not match the nature of the social problem to which, from a feminist perspective, sex discrimination legislation should be addressed. This is the problem of discrimination against and disadvantage of women. An interesting disanalogy is presented by the provisions about sex discrimination on grounds of marital status under s.3 of the 1975 Act. These cover only discrimination against married people. Clearly, the social problem which was seen to exist was one of discrimination by employers against married women. Significantly, the government is now under European pressure to change this provision to make it symmetrical and bring it into line with the principle of equal treatment. If we look at the 1975 Act as a response to a specific set of social problems, we can see that by conceptualising the problem as *sex discrimination* rather than *discrimination against women*, the legislation renders invisible the real social problem and deflects away a social ideal or goal which would identify and address it. And this may have been because the only sources of women's disadvantaged social position that were (and quite probably still are) recognised as a 'social problem' worthy of legal response are those which come within the concept of sex discrimination.

What is more, the result of the compelling logic of the symmetrical principle proscribing direct discrimination is to outlaw any form of reverse discrimination or affirmative action. Even the very moderate practice of choosing the women from a number of equally suitable applicants would be ruled out on a strict approach. Thus, the possibility of determinate, concrete practices designed to secure tangible advances for at least some women are ruled out in favour of an unhappy combination of commitments to rigid equal treatment in a limited sphere and the fluid and intangible goal of equal opportunity. And this ideological framework also renders problematic the accommodation of even the limited provisions which we may currently want to make in recognition of gender difference. For even though issues such as protective legislation of various kinds are recognised as very difficult by feminists and anti-feminists alike, debates about issues such as whether premenstrual tension should act as a mitigating principle in criminal law are rendered much more dangerous to women's interests within the context of subscription to an ideal of formal equality because any accommodation of difference can be represented as 'special pleading'. Such accommodations tend to be seen as acknowledgments of women's special needs and weaknesses, represented principally as questions of sex as a biological category rather than as questions of the socially constructed, mutable category of gender. Such dangers are well illustrated by the fact that 'special features' such as childbearing capacity have on occasion been used to deny women even their formal rights under the Sex Discrimination Act.[12]

4. *The Comparative Aspect*

Further problems from a feminist perspective arise from the fact that the concept of discrimination imports the notion of comparison – of *less* favourable treatment as opposed to purely *un*favourable treatment. Perhaps the most spectacular example of such problems is the history of cases about discrimination on grounds of pregnancy under the British legislation. In the early case of *Turley v. Allders Department Stores Ltd.*[13] the Employment the Appeal Tribunal decided that the logic of comparison ruled out pregnancy discrimination – the reasoning would also pose problems for other 'sex-plus' cases – as direct discrimination under the Sex Discrimination Act. Since men cannot become pregnant, dismissal could not be said to constitute less favourable treatment than would have been accorded to a similarly situated man. It is tempting to dismiss this as the kind of argument that has prompted some feminists to say that if this is 'male' logic then men are welcome to it. But the fact is that the commonsense reasoning behind the later reversal by the

Employment Appeal Tribunal in *Hayes v. Malleable Working Men's Club and Institute*[14] is also threatening to genuine sex equality. In that case it was held that pregnancy discrimination could constitute sex discrimination where the treatment accorded a pregnant woman was less favourable than that accorded a man who, for example, was in a 'similar' position because of ill health. This reasoning reinforces the sexist idea of women as the victims of their hormones and presents an inaccurate and damaging image of pregnant women as genuinely comparable with sick or other abnormally-situated men. Cases like these can sometimes be resolved by being dealt with as cases of indirect discrimination. Then the problem would shift to the issue of justifiability – but this option only exists where the sex-related feature acts as an absolute requirement or condition. The comparative approach also has difficulty in accommodating the notion of sexual harassment – genuinely sexist and disadvantaging behaviour, much of which lacks any truly analogous counterpart in terms of behaviour towards men.

But a deeper problem with the comparative approach underlies these obvious examples. This is that it presupposes (yet suppresses) the idea of a *norm* with which the scrutinised behaviour is compared.[15] In the case of claims brought by women, that norm is the treatment usually accorded to men: thus, in so far as the sex discrimination legislation prescribes equality, it is *equality in terms of a norm set by and for men* – the logic of discrimination allows no challenge to the *general* practices in any area. By definition, sex discrimination cases do not provide a jumping-off point for criticism of general social practices or real debate about what kind of equality is worth having, and with whom. At best, the legislation promises some dismantling of practices restrictive of access to goods and resources which present (that is, male-dominated) culture has determined as valuable. It may go some way towards reducing the overt significance of sex in the allocation of certain goods, but it has no cutting edge against the significance of gender in setting them up as goods in the first place.

5. *Emphasis on Individual Cases and Suitability of the Legal Forum*

Despite the idea of agency enforcement which was introduced in the 1975 Act, the emphasis remains on individual cases as a means of enforcing anti-discrimination law in this country. Quite apart from the problems of proof already discussed, this poses some particularly acute problems from a feminist viewpoint. In the first place, it entails a diversion of attention away from the idea of sexism as a structure or institution – an idea which is crucial to a feminist vision. Indirect discrimination goes some way towards this recognition but it, too, is fitted into the individual framework unmitigated even by the possibility of class actions. Secondly, it seems likely that the general psychological and material barriers to litigation which exist for all those not familiar with the workings of the legal system are, for a number of reasons, particularly strong for women. More subtly, it is also inherent in the approach based on individual cases that the claimant has to prove something *special* or *abnormal*, whereas much institutional discrimination is or is seen as normal, usual behaviour. This may well inhibit tribunals from making findings of discrimination, particularly where they feel there was nothing 'wrong' with the behaviour and hesitate to stigmatise it by finding for the plaintiff.

In view of these and several other more specific features, doubts must arise as to whether the legal forum really represents a useful place in which to attempt to advance arguments for women's liberation, or to seek concrete improvements in the treatment of women in our society. The more specific features relevant to these doubts would include the male domination of the legal forum in terms of its personnel; the male domination of the legal system in terms of the composition of the legislature and powerful interest groups; and the construction of disputes in individual terms and their resolution through a closed system of reasoning. It is hardly surprising that many feminists see the 'equality' legislation as a sop intended to promote false consciousness; it makes women feel things are getting better or enables men to resist women's further claims, whilst actually making no real contribution to the dismantling of sexism in our society. Can such legislation offer more than merely access to male-defined goods for a few relatively privileged women? Such doubts, of course, raise general questions about the efficacy of using law to promote social change against a backcloth of lack of social consensus: is such legislation inevitably ineffective or fraught with hidden agendas? Does persuasive social theory simply rule it out, like genuinely non-racist or anti-capitalist legislation in a racist or capitalist society?[16] Given these general problems and the specific concerns I have identified with respect to the existing legislation, doubts can be cast on whether any committed feminist should spend a significant amount of her political energies campaigning for reforms of anti-discrimination legislation.

A FUTURE FOR ANTI-DISCRIMINATION LEGISLATION?

What lessons, if any, can be learnt from the problems which have been identified by looking at the Sex Discrimination Act 1975 from a feminist perspective? First and foremost, the approach suggests that we should acknowledge the limitations of legislation designed to give individual remedies.[17] From a feminist point of view, primacy should rather be given to action at the policy level such as contract compliance; changes in the practice of education; adequate provision of child care facilities and parental leave; dismantling sexism in rules of property between cohabitees – particularly in terms of proper acknowledgment of women's contributions; revaluation of 'women's' work; reframing of salient aspects of the criminal law – for example, the law of rape; and regulation of enforcement practices in areas such as domestic violence. In other words, the issues basic to the women's movement must take their place at the centre of reform strategy concerning law and its enforcement. We must continue to struggle for a proper emphasis on changes to material conditions which both reflect and consolidate sexism and women's disadvantage by mechanisms we are slowly beginning to understand. And we must campaign for policies which reach a much broader range of women – particularly those such as black women, working-class women, and single mothers – who suffer specific disadvantages and discriminations.

This kind of conclusion re-orders, rather than denies, the value of anti-discrimination legislation. From this point of view, there might still be something to be said for political affirmation of the ideal of gender equality even at a relatively formal level. But, in terms of feminist political principle as a whole, if we are to exploit the ideal of equality our focus must be equality not in terms of opportunity within the liberal model but in terms of welfare, power, resources and goods – including the power to determine what goods are valued. Only by reconstructing the notion of equality can we gradually escape the problem of equality as comparative with a male-defined norm. This project of recapturing normative concepts and reworking them from a feminist perspective has always been one of the most important projects facing feminism. And, given the success of the women's movement in investing concepts such as 'oppression' and 'liberation' with specifically feminist meanings, it would seem unduly pessimistic to abandon the concept of equality, which might offer a powerful, positive feminist ideal. Meanwhile, in liberal societies, there are important strategic advantages to recognising gender equality in general terms as a basic political value.

But is a mere reassessment of the relative importance to be attached to anti-discrimination legislation sufficient? Is the real danger attaching to such legislation simply that it diverts a disproportionate amount of political energy, given its inherent limitations as this response suggests, or does its power to disguise the continuing oppression of women call for some more radical approach? Even those most pessimistic about the status of the current legislation as a reformist sop would, I think, be hard put to argue that it should be dismantled, given the negative symbolic and material effects of doing so. But it does seem worth considering whether we should struggle to reform it in such a way that it at least comes closer to acknowledging the asymmetry of the social phenomenon of sexism. A very modest approach to doing so would be to add exceptions facilitating and indeed requiring affirmative action programmes for women, particularly where, for example, their number in the relevant area is small compared with that in the population or other qualified pool. More radically, we could argue for the abandonment of *formal* equality legislation and the adoption of a specific Act of Parliament prohibiting discrimination against women, thus directly reflecting the social problem which we are addressing. This would be aimed at attaining equality in terms of some more substantive measure, such as resources, in the longer term. This would not, of course, be to imply that discrimination against men on grounds of sex is morally unproblematic, although it certainly does imply that non-discrimination on grounds of sex conceived in formal equality terms is not a moral absolute. But the main thrust of such a strategy would be to acknowledge that sex discrimination against men is not a social phenomenon of the same order, does not involve comparably damaging and oppressive effects as does sex discrimination against women, and that this clear social difference justifies and, indeed, calls for a totally different legal response. The second option is, of course, ruled out in a real world in which Britain belongs to the European Community. Implementation of at least the first option is, I would argue, absolutely necessary if the legislation is to secure any real gains for women.

Furthermore, if we are to minimise both the dangers attaching to the legislation and its limitations, I would argue that we must abandon equality of opportunity as an important underlying principle. The images it conjures up in political and legal discourse are closely associated with a minimal and atomistic libertarian vision which fails to address the factors implicated in women's oppression. The opportunity ideal's presupposition of a world of autonomous individuals starting a race or making free choices has no cutting edge against the argument that men and women are simply running different races. And it poses the real danger of actually serving to legitimate existing differences: inequality of impact or results can just be defined as to do with different 'free' choice – or natural sex difference! Such an approach either forecloses the possibility of changing the social meaning of gender or else is simply unrealisable in a society structured by gender. In the present social context, in so far as we espouse the concept of equality as a valued goal, we would be better advised to aim for a determinate measure of equality of results (as through affirmative action programmes) than to run the risks presented by the manipulable notion of equality of opportunity.

The point of view which I have defended does not address or overcome the problem of society's valuation of goods being male-defined. This problem cannot be resolved until some major feminist victories have been won so that women are at least nearer to having an equal voice and equal power in the process of determining social and political value. The project which I have been engaged in has the limited but important goal of pointing out some problems with existing legislation by employing a feminist perspective and using those problems to argue that anti-discrimination law should be seen as simply one symbolic and moderately functional thread in a web of measures aimed at securing more power for women. This power is a matter of fundamental justice and a means of empowering women ourselves to contribute to the sorts of changes which we as feminists would want to see. I have suggested that we should not abandon the legal arena: in the world as it currently is, citizens sometimes find themselves in courts and other legal forums irrespective of choice, and sometimes legal remedies or defences are their only available weapon. We should neither abandon anti-discrimination legislation just because of its inherent limitations nor regard it as the *only* appropriate *legal* response to women's oppression. Problems such as sexual harassment, property entitlements, and so on, need to be dealt with independently and explicitly. My arguments aim to ensure *at least* that anti-discrimination legislation fulfils a symbolic role and does not generate damaging side-effects in terms of rendering invisible the problems and injustices which are the central concern of feminist theory and practice. The reform of anti-discrimination law *can* form part of a genuinely feminist political strategy, but it cannot be more than a minor part.

NOTES AND REFERENCES

1 Many of the problems which I refer to in this article are also of relevance to the operation of and principles underlying the Race Relations Act 1976. I shall address only the law relating to sex discrimination, since this raises some particular questions for feminists. The further project of considering how sexism and racism relate to each other along with the question of appropriate legal responses is clearly one of central importance to progressive social theory.

2 See, for example, S. Atkins and B. Hoggett, *Women and Law* (1984) pp. 1-62; L. Lustgarten, *Legal Control of Racial Discrimination* (1980); D. Pannick, *Sex Discrimination Law* (1985).

3 For a discussion of some of the technical problems involved in bringing a case of direct sex discrimination, see Pannick, *op. cit.*, n. 2, pp. 25-39.

4 *Id.*, pp. 41-56.

5 *Id.*, pp. 88-90. See also Equal Opportunities Commission, *Legislating for Change?* pp. 25-35.

6 *Id.*, pp. 272-84; see in particular *Commission for Racial Equality v. Amari Plastic Ltd.* [1982] I.C.R. 304; *R. v. Commission for Racial Equality ex parte Hillingdon L.B.C.* [1982] Q.B. 276.

7 See A. Leonard, *Pyrrhic Victories: Successful Sex Discrimination and Equal Pay Cases in the Industrial Tribunals 1980-1984* (H.M.S.O. 1987).

8 *Id.*

9 See, for example, Atkins and Hoggett, *op. cit.*, n. 2, pp. 47-62; K. O'Donovan, *Sexual Divisions in Law* (1985) pp. 1-20, 160-80; F. Olsen, "The Family and the Market: A Study of Ideology and Legal Reform" (1983) 96 *Harvard Law Rev.* p. 1497; F. Olsen, "Statutory Rape: A Feminist Critique of Rights Analysis" (1984) 63 *Texas Law Rev.* p. 387.

10 B. Williams, "The Idea of Equality" in P. Laslett and W. G. Runciman (eds.), *Philosophy, Politics and Society* (1962) p. 110.

11 See, for example, R. Dworkin, "What is Equality? Part 1: Equality of Welfare; Part 2: Equality of Resources" (1981) 10 *Philosophy and Public Affairs* p. 185, p. 283; P. Singer, *Practical Ethics* (1979) pp. 14-47.

12 See, for example, *Page v. Freight Hire (Tank Haulage) Ltd.* [1981] I.C.R. 299, at p. 303.

13 [1980] I.R.L.R. 4.

14 [1985] I.R.L.R. 367.

15 For critical discussion of this aspect of arguments for equality from a feminist perspective see J. Conaghan and L. Chudleigh, "Women in Confinement: Can Labour Law Deliver the Goods?" (1987) 14 *J. Law and Society* p. 133 at pp. 139-140; K. O'Donovan, *op. cit.*, n. 9, pp. 160-80.

16 Cf. Peter Fitzpatrick's discussion of law and racism: "Racism and the Innocence of Law" (1987) 14 *J. Law and Society* p. 119.

17 See L. Lustgarten, "Racial Inequality and the Limits of Law" (1986) 49 *Modern Law Rev.* p. 68.

[10]

MARY E. BECKER

PRINCE CHARMING: ABSTRACT EQUALITY

Most lawyers, scholars, and judges interested in changing the relative status of women and men assume that there is an appropriate general or abstract standard of equality which should be applied by judges. The debate centers on what standard is most appropriate and how to apply it. Throughout the seventies, most participants agreed that formal equality was the most appropriate general standard,[1] though the more flexible disparate impact standard should perhaps be available in some employment cases. Today, these are the two dominant legal standards. The standard of formal equality is applied in constitutional cases under the Equal Protection Clause of the Fourteenth Amendment. And in Title VII cases, involving discrimination in employment, formal equality is augmented by disparate impact, which is available in some cases.

In the eighties, feminists became increasingly critical of these two legal standards.[2] Within the feminist community, a consensus

---

Mary E. Becker is Professor of Law, The University of Chicago Law School.

AUTHOR'S NOTE: I thank Al Alschuler, Walter Blum, Richard Epstein, Mary Ann Glendon, Richard Helmholz, Larry Kramer, Christine Littleton, Michael McConnell, Deborah Rhode, Geoffrey Stone, Cass Sunstein, and Anne Weber for helpful comments on an earlier draft and Paul Bryan, Jeannie Polydoris, William Schwesig, and Charles Ten Brink for research assistance. Research support was provided by the Russell Baker Scholars Fund.

[1] See, *e.g.*, Ginsburg, Sexual Equality under the Fourteenth and Equal Rights Amendments, [1979] Wash. U. L. Q. 161; Ginsburg, Gender and the Constitution, 44 U. Cin. L. Rev. 1 (1975); Ginsburg, Sex and Unequal Protection: Men and Women as Victims, 11 J. Fam. L. 347 (1971); Cole, Stategies of Difference: Litigating for Women's Rights in a Man's World, 2 L. & Inequality 33 (1984); Brown, Emerson, Falk, & Freedman, The Equal Rights Amendment: A Constitutional Basis for Equal Rights for Women, 80 Yale L. J. 871 (1971).

[2] In addition to the sources cited in note 3 *infra*, see Rhode, Justice, Gender, and the Justices, in Women, the Court, and Equality 13, 18–19 (Crites & Hepperle, eds., 1987);

0-226-46440-7/88/1987-0005$01.00

seems to be developing that formal equality is inadequate. Some feminists have proposed alternatives.[3]

This debate has, however, assumed a questionable proposition: that a single general standard of equality should be adopted and applied.[4] Rather than attempting to find one abstract standard to solve women's problems, we should identify objectionable aspects of particular situations and argue for particular changes in the appropriate forum, which will often be the legislature. Any general, or abstract, approach is unlikely to effect much real change without seriously risking worsening the situation of many women, especially ordinary mothers and wives. Three cases from the 1986 Term serve to illustrate these points: *California Federal Savings & Loan Ass'n v. Guerra*,[5] *Johnson v. Transportation Agency*,[6] and *Wimberly v. Labor Commission of Missouri*.[7]

I. Contemporary Legal Standards of Equality

I begin with *Guerra* and *Johnson*. In *Guerra*, the question was the legality of a California statute requiring employers to give workers disabled by childbirth (but not workers otherwise disabled) up to four months unpaid leave. The case arose when Lillian Garland sought to resume working as a receptionist after taking a two-month

Finley, Transcending Equality Theory: A Way Out of the Maternity and the Workplace Debate, 86 Col. L. Rev. 1118 (1986). Other feminists have presented more general critiques of liberalism. See Jaggar, Feminist Politics and Human Nature 27–48, 173–203 (1983); Elshtain, Public Man, Private Woman (1981); Wolgast, Equality and the Rights of Women (1980).

[3]See MacKinnon, Sexual Harassment of Working Women (1979); Littleton, Rethinking Sexual Equality, 75 Calif. L. Rev. 201 (1987); Scales, The Emergence of a Feminist Jurisprudence: An Essay, 95 Yale L. J. 1371 (1986); Kay, Models of Equality, [1985] Univ. Ill. L. Rev. 39; Kay, Equality and Difference: The Case of Pregnancy, 1 Berkeley Women's L. J. 1 (1985); Law, Rethinking Sex and the Constitution, 132 U. Penn. L. Rev. 95 (1984). See also Wolgast, Equality and the Rights of Women (1980) (suggesting some ways in which the standard of equality might be improved but not suggesting any one developed equality standard); Note, 95 Harv. L. Rev. 487 (1981) (similar); Freedman, Sex Equality, Sex Differences, and the Supreme Court, 92 Yale L. J. 913 (1983) (similar).

[4]For a somewhat similar analysis see Krieger & Cooney, The Miller-Wohl Controversy: Equal Treatment, Positive Action and the Meaning of Women's Equality, 13 Golden Gate Univ. L. Rev. 513 (1983).

[5]107 S.Ct. 683 (1987).

[6]107 S.Ct. 1442 (1987).

[7]107 S.Ct. 821 (1987).

leave following the birth of her daughter. Her employer told her that her old job had been filled and that there were no similar positions available. Garland was unable to find another job immediately and, because of her unemployment, she lost her apartment and eventually custody of her daughter.[8] When Garland sought to enforce her statutory right before the California Department of Fair Employment and Housing, her former employer, Cal Fed, brought an action in federal district court seeking a declaration that the California statute was inconsistent with and preempted by Title VII.

The feminist community divided sharply on whether employers should be required to give unpaid leave to workers disabled by pregnancy. NOW, the ACLU's Womens' Rights Project, and a number of other feminist organizations (herinafter NOW et al.), argued against permitting states to require disability leaves only for pregnancy.[9] Other feminist groups argued that such statutes should be permissible despite their violation of formal equality.[10] The Supreme Court agreed, and ruled that the California statute guaranteeing jobs only to women disabled by pregnancy was permissible despite Title VII's ban on sex and pregnancy discrimination.[11]

In *Johnson*, the question was the legality of an affirmative action plan for women in promotions to a position previously held only by men. The Santa Clara County Transit District Board of Supervisors adopted an Affirmative Action Plan for the County Transportation Agency in December 1978. The Plan authorized the Agency to consider sex as one factor in deciding which of several qualified applicants to promote to traditionally male job classifications. A year later,

---

[8]See Garland's Bouquet, Time 14 (January 26, 1987).

[9]See Brief Amici Curiae of the National Organization for Women (and six other signatories); Brief of the American Civil Liberties Union (and four other signatories). Both briefs argued that the Supreme Court should extend the statutory benefit to all workers disabled for four months or less.

[10]See, *e.g.*, Brief Amici Curiae of Coalition for Reproductive Equality in the Workplace; Betty Friedan; International Ladies' Garment Worker's Union, AFL-CIO; 9 to 5; National Association of Working Women; Planned Parenthood Federation of America, Inc., California School Employees Association; American Federation of State, County and Municipal Employees, District Council 36; California Federation of Teachers; Coalition of Labor Union Women, Los Angeles Chapter (and thirty other signatories).

[11]Only Justice Scalia declined to reach the merits of the Title VII issue; his concurrence in the judgment rested on preemption grounds. Chief Justice Rehnquist and Justices White and Powell dissented.

in December of 1979, the Agency announced a road-dispatcher opening. Dispatchers assign road crews, equipment, materials, and maintain records of road maintenance jobs. Twelve employees applied for this promotion, including Paul Johnson and Diane Joyce. Joyce was the first woman ever to be a road maintenance worker. She was the only woman in a force of 110 road maintenance workers at the time of the promotion, and the promotion requirements included at least four years of dispatch or road maintenance work. No woman had previously been road dispatcher, a skilled craft position, nor had any woman ever held any of the 238 skilled craft positions at the Agency. Joyce and six men were certified as eligible for promotion after an interview by a two-person board. This board scored applicants on their interview performance. Johnson received a seventy-five; Joyce a seventy-three. (A score over seventy was required to be deemed eligible for the promotion.)

Thereafter, three agency supervisors conducted a second interview. One of these supervisors had been Joyce's supervisor when she began work as a road maintenance worker. He had issued her coveralls (routinely issued to the men) only after she had ruined her clothes on several occasions, complained several times, and finally filed a grievance. Another member of this panel described Joyce as a "rebel-rousing [*sic*], skirt-wearing person."[12] This member scheduled the interview (apparently deliberately[13]) so as to conflict with Joyce's disaster preparedness class. The three-man panel recommended that Johnson be given the promotion.

James Graebner, the Director of the Agency, was authorized to make the final selection of the new road dispatcher from among those eligible. Graebner, consistent with the recommendation of the Agency's Affirmative Action Coordinator,[14] promoted Joyce. Women's groups unanimously argued that this affirmative action was permissible under Title VII, and the Supreme Court agreed.[15]

---

[12]107 S.Ct. at 1448 n.5.

[13]See *id.* at 1448.

[14]Joyce contacted the County Affirmative Action Officer prior to the second interview because she was understandably worried about receiving a fair review. Under the terms of the Agency's Affirmative Action Plan, the Affirmative Action Coordinator was responsible for keeping the director informed of opportunities for the Agency to accomplish the Plan objectives, which included achieving "a statistically measurable yearly improvement in hiring, training, and promotion of minorities and women throughout the Agency in all major job classifications where they are underrepresented." 107 S.Ct. at 1447.

[15]Rhenquist, C.J., White & Scalia, JJ., dissenting.

A. FORMAL EQUALITY

Both cases were rightly decided. Yet both are inconsistent with the established standard of formal equality. *Johnson* is obviously inconsistent. There, the Court allowed the employer to treat similarly situated women and men differently, by giving women a "thumb on the scale" in promotion decisions.

The inconsistency of *Guerra* (the pregnancy-leave case) and formal equality is more subtle. At first glance, formal equality might seem consistent with the result in *Guerra* (upholding the statute treating workers disabled by pregnancy differently from other workers). This statute does not violate formal equality for sex-based classifications; it classifies on the basis of pregnancy, not on the basis of sex. Title VII was, however, amended specifically to reject this kind of reasoning.[16] As amended, it provides that discrimination on the basis of sex includes discrimination "on the basis of pregnancy, childbirth, or related medical conditions; and women affected by pregnancy, childbirth, or related medical conditions shall be treated the same for all employment-related purposes . . . as other persons not so affected but similar in their ability or inability to work."[17]

The language of the amended statute indicates that Congress considered pregnant women similar to others who were equal in their ability or inability to work. From this perspective, the outcome in *Guerra* is inconsistent with a standard of formal equality for Title VII: similarly situated pregnant women and other individuals are treated differently under the California statute. Only those tem-

[16]In General Electric Co. v. Gilbert, 429 U.S. 125 (1976), the Court had held that Title VII's ban on sex discrimination was not violated by an employer's health plan which covered all medical treatment except treatment related to pregnancy. The Court concluded that a distinction between pregnant and nonpregnant persons was not a distinction on the basis of sex. In response, Congress enacted the Pregnancy Discrimination Act of 1978, which defines sex discrimination to include distinctions based on pregnancy, childbirth, or related medical conditions. According to the reports of both houses on the Pregnancy Discrimination Act, Congress considered the approach in *Gilbert* inconsistent with a proper understanding of Title VII's nondiscrimination mandate. See Amending Title VII, Civil Rights Act of 1964, Sen. Rep. No. 95-331, 95th Cong., 1st Sess. 2–3; Prohibition of Sex Discrimination Based on Pregnancy, H.R. Rep. No. 95-948, 95th Cong., 2d Sess. 2–3 (1978). In Geduldig v. Aiello, 417 U.S. 484 (1974) (challenge to state disability insurance system which specifically excluded pregnancy from list of compensable disabilities), the Supreme Court held that classifications based on pregnancy are not equivalent to classifications based on sex for purposes of equal protection analysis. *Geduldig* remains good law in constitutional cases.

[17]42 U.S.C. 2000e(k).

porarily disabled by pregnancy have any right to a leave of absence; those unable to work for reasons unrelated to pregnancy can be fired.

1. *The inadequacy of formal equality.* These cases illustrate a number of problems with formal equality. First, as the discussion above illustrates, the question of who is similarly situated is hardly susceptible to answer by objective, value-free analysis.[18] There is, for example, a sense in which disabled pregnant workers are similar to other workers disabled for similar periods. From another perspective, it seems strange to consider women and men similarly situated with respect to pregnancy-related disabilities since only women are physically disabled by the onset of parenthood. Which perspective seems appropriate depends on the particular issue and on one's perspective and values.[19] As this example illustrates, formal equality is not capable of discerning discrimination against pregnant people. This, in itself, is a major failing.

As another example of the subjectivity inherent in identifying those similarly situated, consider *Johnson*. Giving Joyce an edge over Johnson at the end of the promotion process is affirmative action only if Johnson and Joyce were similarly situated. If they were not similarly situated, it would not violate formal equality to treat them differently. The notion that they might have been similarly situated is fanciful. Their prior employment experiences were not similar even when they had identical titles. For Joyce, work as the only female road maintenance worker would have involved a constant struggle, including dealing with hazing and harassment. Johnson was one of the boys. It is, however, likely that many male decision makers would neither see what Joyce went through nor appreciate that her unique experiences might be qualifications for promotion. They would be more likely to consider Johnson better qualified because as road dispatcher, Joyce will probably continue to have problems operating in a male world.

[18]See Scales, The Emergence of Feminist Jurisprudence: An Essay, 95 Yale L. J. 1371, 1377 (1986); Minow, The Supreme Court 1986 Term—Foreword: Justice Engendered, 101 Harv. L. Rev. 10, 40–45 (1987).

[19]See General Electric Co. v. Gilbert, 429 U.S. 125; Geduldig v. Aiello, 417 U.S. 484. In other contexts, even prior to Congress' overruling *Gilbert* with the Pregnancy Discrimination Act of 1978, see note 16 *supra*, the Court perceived special treatment of pregnancy as a form of sex discrimination. See Nashville Gas Co. v. Satty, 434 U.S. 136 (1977).

To date, standards have not been developed to identify the appropriate perspective from which to decide whether groups or individuals are similarly situated. Typically, judges simply note, in a conclusory fashion, that A and B are (or are not) similarly situated, as though the point was obvious and noncontroversial.[20] In the absence of appropriate standards, women are not likely to be served well by a formal equality standard applied by predominantly male judges on the basis of their subjective values and perspectives.

Second, under formal equality, women who are perceived to be like men are entitled to be treated like men.[21] This "nondiscrimination" rule is not neutral with respect to sex; it is androcentric.[22] Women cannot use formal equality to challenge workplace rules and practices which fit well with men's life-styles, needs, and experiences but less well with women's. Formal equality is not violated by workplace rules under which—as happened in *Guerra*—a new mother loses her job and custody of her daughter because she was the parent who was pregnant. Similarly, when the next Lillian Garland returns to work at Cal Fed following her statutorily-guaranteed pregnancy leave, her employer can ignore that she is primarily responsible for the care of her daughter. Such results are not sex-neutral. As MacKinnon puts it, "day one of taking gender into account" was the day the job was structured with the expectation that its occupant would have no child care responsibilities.[23]

Let me put the same point in another way. Formal equality uses (or misuses[24]) Aristotle's notion of distributive justice to define equality and discrimination. Aristotle defined distributive justice

[20]For an extreme example of this problem, see Rostker v. Goldberg, 453 U.S. 57 (1981) (upholding registration only of young men for military service because women were not allowed in combat; men and women were not, therefore, similarly situated).

[21]See MacKinnon, Sexual Harassment of Working Women, at 144–46.

[22]For discussions of the chimera of neutrality, see McConnell, Neutrality under the Religion Clauses, 81 Nw. U. L. Rev. 146 (1986); Minow, The Supreme Court 1986 Term—Foreword: Justice Engendered, 101 Harv. L. Rev. 10; Sunstein, Lochner's Legacy, 87 Colum. L. Rev. 873 (1987).

[23]MacKinnon, Feminism Unmodified 37 (1987).

[24]Aristotle also pointed out that it was unjust to treat similarly people who were not similarly situated. See Nichomachean Ethics V(3) at 112 (Ross trans. 1925). The result, under formal equality, is that women are often treated like men though they are not similarly situated. In addition, Aristotle advocated the use of practical, rather than abstract, reason in attempting to identify the good for humans. Nichomachean Ethics I(3) at 2–5.

as treating similarly situated people similarly.[25] Formal equality defines equality as treating similarly situated individuals similarly. Conversely, discrimination is treating differently individuals who are actually similarly situated. But discrimination is not necessarily the opposite of distributive justice. Discrimination and distributive justice might be quite unrelated things. If discrimination encompasses women's experiences of subordination, then there is more to discrimination than treating differently individuals who are similarly situated: "it is not only lies and blindness that have kept women down. It is as much the social creation of differences, and the transformation of differences into social advantages and disadvantages upon which inequality can rationally be predicated."[26]

Discrimination consists of repeatedly turning real or perceived differences into socially constructed disadvantages for women and socially constructed advantages for men. For example, the fact that only women are disabled by pregnancy does not mean that a policy, like Cal Fed's, under which new mothers (but not new fathers) lose their jobs is not discriminatory. Indeed, it is precisely because only women are disabled by pregnancy that a facially neutral policy like Cal Fed's is part of the system which has kept women subordinate to, because economically dependent on, men.[27]

The fact that only women are disabled by pregnancy does not even explain why women lose their jobs because of the onset of parenthood. The actual difference between the ability of women and men to work at the onset of parenthood need not be transformed into this socially created disadvantage for women. Imagine, for example, the socially constructed advantages women could be given as compensation for (and to facilitate) bearing and rearing children. Statutes could give mothers preferences in employment like those given veterans in many states. Large employers could give mothers extended leaves while their children are young, just as they gave

[25] Id., V(3), at 112–14.

[26] MacKinnon, Sexual Harassment of Working Women, at 105.

[27] Although men may sustain as many or more disabilities on the average than women, such disabilities are less likely to lead to parallel male economic dependence on women. Men are likely to sustain more work-related disabilities (because men tend to have more physically hazardous jobs). But work-related disabilities tend to be compensated by workers' compensation systems. Men who sustain them are not, therefore, entirely dependent economically on women. In addition, although social security never affords disability coverage to women temporarily disabled by pregnancy, it often affords disability coverage to workers who sustain other disabilities.

male inductees extended leaves for military service during the draft. Women who care for their children rather than participating full time or at full speed in the wage-labor market could be given social security credits in their own accounts for their contributions to the future rather than having only very contingent claims as their husbands' dependents.[28]

A third major problem is that formal equality is based on a counterfactual assumption; because of this assumption formal equality will, in practice, actually mean inequality. Formal equality assumes that it is possible to ignore an individual's sex. Both common sense and empirical data suggest that we cannot and do not ignore sex in dealing with an individual.[29] Moreover, the empirical data indicate that the routine, unconscious differential treatment of individual women and men tends to dampen ratings of women's competence and potential relative to the ratings of men.[30] To the extent that we cannot treat similarly situated women and men the same, formal equality can mask real, though perhaps unconscious, discrimination.

Johnson illustrates this point. The promotion interviews were conducted entirely by men, who had never promoted a woman to that position before, nor any similar position. One of the interviewers regarded Joyce as a "rebel-rousing [*sic*], skirt-wearing person."[31]

---

[28]Women who care for children (full or part time) could be protected by accounting changes; one need not impose additional taxes on families. During marriage, half of the wages of each spouse could be credited directly to the social security account of the other spouse. See Supplementary Statement by Commissionsers Ball, Keys, Kirkland, Moynihan, and Pepper, from the Report of the National Commission on Social Security Reform, statement (2) at 5–7 (1983).

[29]In addition to the sources cited in note 30 *infra*, see, *e.g.*, Buczek, A Promising Measure of Sex Bias: The Incipendtal Memory Task, 10 Psychology of Women Q. 127 (1986); Schulman & Hoskins, Perceiving the Male Versus the Female Face, 10 Psychology of Women Q. 141 (1986); Deutsch, LeBaron & Fryer, What Is in a Smile, 11 Psychology of Women Q. 341 (1987).

[30]See, *e.g.*, McArthur, Social Judgment Biases in Comparable Worth Analysis, in Comparable Worth: New Directions for Research 53, 55–64 (Hartmann ed. 1985); Gerdes & Garber, Sex Bias in Hiring: Effects of Job Demands and Applicant Competence, 9 Sex Roles 307 (1983); Francesco & Hakel, Gender and Sex as Determinates of Hireability of Applicants for Gender-Typed Jobs, 5 Psychology of Women Q. 747 (1981); Plake, Murphy-Berman, Derscheid, Gerber, Miller, Speth, & Tomes, Access Decisions by Personnel Directors: Subtle Forms of Sex Bias in Hiring, 11 Psych. of Women Q. 255 (1987); Francesco, Gender and Sex as Detriments of Hireability of Applicants for Genders-Typed Jobs, 5 Psychology of Women Q. 747 (1981).

[31]See note 12 *supra*.

Another interviewer had been her first supervisor as a road maintenance worker, the one who issued her work overalls only after she filed a grievance. Those interviews cannot have been precisely equal opportunities for both Joyce and Johnson. In the absence of the affirmative action plan challenged in *Johnson*, it is most unlikely that Joyce would have had a promotion opportunity equal to Johnson's. Yet, after a two-day trial, the District Court found that the Agency had never discriminated on the basis of sex.[32]

A two-day trial could not possibly have afforded a factual basis for concluding that an employer with 238 skilled craft workers and no woman ever in such a position (and one woman out of 110 road maintenance workers) had never discriminated on the basis of sex. Even after the passage of Title VII, women were routinely and overtly excluded from skilled craft positions by both unions and employers. Yet the incredible finding—that the Agency had never discriminated on the basis of sex in hiring skilled craftsmen (as the workers were doubtless originally described)—was not overruled by either reviewing court.

A comparison of *Johnson* and *Steelworkers v. Weber*[33] suggests that systemic discrimination on the basis of sex may be less visible to judges enforcing Title VII than is discrimination on the basis of race. Prior to the affirmative action plan at issue in *Weber*, 1.83 percent (five out of 275) of the skilled craft workers were blacks in Kaiser's plant where *Weber* arose. (Compare zero women out of approximately 238 at the Agency prior to the affirmative action plan at issue in *Johnson*.) In *Weber*, the Court reversed the two lower court decisions holding Kaiser's plan illegal and noted that "[j]udicial findings of exclusion from crafts on racial grounds are so numerous as to make such exclusion a proper subject for judicial notice."[34] Women, too, have been traditionally, explicitly, and routinely excluded from crafts,[35] but—unlike the exclusion of Blacks which was judically noticed in *Weber*—women's exclusion was apparently invisible to all the judges deciding *Johnson*. Justice Scalia relied heavily

[32]See Johnson v. Transportation Agency, Santa Clara County, California, No. C-81-1218-WAI (SJ) (N.D. Calif. July 23, 1982).

[33]443 U.S. 193 (1979).

[34]443 U.S. at 198 n.1.

[35]See generally Falk, Women and Unions: A Historical View, 1 Women's Rights L. Reptr. 54 (1973).

on the district court's finding that the Santa Clara Transportation Agency had never discriminated on the basis of sex and apparently believed it. None of the Justices dismissed the finding as incredible and necessarily lacking a factual basis after a two-day trial.[36] Judges can say no woman was ever discriminated against, but saying it cannot make it true.

Justice Scalia would probably respond that even if road maintenance and skilled craft positions had always been open to women, and even if the agency had advertised for women, it is likely that there would never have been a woman actually interested in either position prior to Joyce. This point brings out another problem with formal equality as a solution to sexual inequality. Systemic discrimination against women is often so effective that no woman will apply for a traditionally male job. Perhaps some women do prefer lower-paying women's jobs. But some may think that the job is only nominally open to them.[37] Others may dread the harassment likely to be experienced in breaking into male jobs, especially blue-collar ones;[38] there is no effective remedy for such harassment. Perhaps women have been socialized not to consider rough outdoor jobs but could be interested with a little encouragement. Formal equality ignores all these problems. As long as the job is open to women, so that there is no discrimination by this decision maker today, formal equality is satisfied. Formal equality is often inconsistent with the only means available for overcoming discrimination, whether by co-workers or by our educational system and socialization practices or by the employer's own practices (past or present, conscious or unconscious): taking "affirmative" steps to encourage and facilitate women's entry into traditionally male spheres.

---

[36]The finding may be partly attributable to collusion between the plaintiff Johnson and the defendant employer. Neither would have wanted to give a court a basis for finding that there had been discrimination against women. The courts upholding the affirmative action plan (the Ninth Circuit and the Supreme Court) could have decided the case without any finding on whether there had ever been discrimination against women. That would seem the more prudent course in the absence of an adequate basis for finding such a fact.

[37]Women often presume that blue collar jobs are not open to them but are interested if information is presented in a form indicating that the employer is interested in hiring women. See Roos & Reskin, Institutional Factors Contributing to Sex Segregation in the Workplace, in Sex Segregation in the Workplace: Trends, Explanations, Remedies 237–38, 241, 245 (Reskin, ed. 1984); Walshok, Blue Collar Women 155–70 (1981).

[38]See, *e.g.*, *id.* at 23, 228–32, 239–40, 259–60.

The "affirmative" action exception to formal equality, both under the Equal Protection Clause of the Fourteenth Amendment and Title VII, alleviates these problems at least a little. In *Johnson*, for example, the Court allowed Joyce's employer to compensate, albeit roughly and indirectly, for the fact that Joyce and Johnson did not have the same opportunities or experiences. "Affirmative" action is troubling because the word "affirmative" implies that, in its absence, women and men would have had equal opportunities. In *Johnson*, "affirmative" conveys the unrealistic notion that had there been no thumb on the scale for Joyce at the very end of the promotion procedure, Johnson and Joyce would have had equal employment opportunities at Santa Clara County's Transportation agency.

Another problem with "affirmative" action is that it is only an exception, a basis for permitting employers to undertake some appropriate but voluntary acts to alleviate the problems faced by women like Joyce. It does not supplement formal equality by offering an alternative model of discrimination for plaintiffs to use in challenging the status quo. Only the disparate impact strand of Title VII offers plaintiff such an alternative.

In sum, formal equality—even with an exception for affirmative action—cannot be expected to transform society by equalizing the status of women and men. In the context of employment, it only opens men's jobs to women on the terms and conditions worked out for men. Further, under formal equality, it is likely that the differences in treatment of women and men will often be invisible to the extent that the differences consist of preferential treatment of men. More specifically, it is likely that a man will appear better qualified when there is no relevant difference between a woman and a man or when the woman is marginally better qualified. And it is likely that a woman's unique qualifications (because of her experiences as a woman) will not be visible, let alone regarded as qualifications.

2. *The case for formal equality, despite its inadequacy.* Despite these flaws, formal equality has an advantage: at least when women are perceived as similar to men, formal equality can be used effectively to challenge rules or requirements expressly restricting entry to privileged male occupations. Throughout the seventies and early eighties, feminists arguing for legal change—either before courts or in pushing for the ERA and other legislative reforms—relied pri-

marily on the concept of formal equality.[39] Because of these efforts, many laws, rules, and practices limiting women's opportunities have been eliminated.[40]

As a result of this experience, a number of feminists continue to insist on strict formal equality.[41] In *Guerra*, NOW et al. filed briefs arguing that California could not require its employers to give unpaid leaves only to women disabled by pregnancy and not to other workers disabled for similar periods. In those briefs, and in the general debate on the issue posed by *Guerra*, these feminists made three major points. First, they argued that "special" treatment of women is dangerous and reinforces traditional sex roles. "Special" treatment has been used to burden as well as to benefit; consider the protectionist legislation of earlier eras. By requiring that pregnant workers be treated like the most similar nonpregnant workers, these feminists would guard against judges' and employers' biases and stereotypes of pregnant women.[42] Maternity leaves (even if nominally for periods of disability) inevitably become child-care leaves. By insisting that parental leaves, if available, are available to both parents, these feminists seek to change the traditional assignment of child care responsibilities primarily to mothers.[43] Second, these feminists have argued that by treating pregnant workers like the most similarly situated nonpregnant workers, we can emphasize what is common about human experience.[44] They argue

---

[39]See, *e.g.*, Ginsburg, Gender and the Constitution, U. Cincinnati L. Rev. 1 (1975); Brief of the American Civil Liberties Union, Amicus Curiae, filed in Orr v. Orr, 440 U.S. 268 (1979); Brown, Emerson, Falk & Freedman, The Equal Rights Amendment: A Constitutional Basis for Equal Rights for Women, 80 Yale L. J. 871 (1971); Cowan, Women's Rights Through Litigation: An Examination of the American Civil Liberties Union Women's Rights Project, 1971–1976, 8 Colum. Human Rights L. Rev. 373 (1976); Mansbrige, Why We Lost the ERA (1986).

[40]See, *e.g.*, Davis v. Passman, 442 U.S. 228 (1979); Phillps v. Martin Marietta Corp., 400 U.S. 542 (1971); Hishon v. King & Spaulding, 457 U.S. 69 (1984).

[41]See, *e.g.*, Williams, Equality's Riddle: Pregnancy & the Equal Treatment/Special Treatment Debate, 13 N.Y.U. Rev. of L. & Social Change 325 (1985); Williams, The Equality Crises: Some Reflections on Culture, Courts, and Feminism, 7 Women's Rights L. Rep. 175 (1983).

[42]See, *e.g.*, Williams, The Equality Crises, *ibid.*, at 196–97; Brief for American Civil Liberties Union, filed in *Guerra*, at 10–35.

[43]Williams, Equality's Riddle, note 41 *supra*, at 353–56; Williams, The Equality Crises, note 41 *supra*, at 195–96.

[44]Williams, Equality's Riddle, note 41 *supra*, at 326; Williams, The Equality Crises, note 41 *supra*, at 196.

that "special" treatment will unnecessarily alienate women and co-workers who actually have common concerns, *e.g.*, adequate leave policies for all disabled workers. Third, these feminists concede that formal equality in itself cannot always effect needed change, but maintain that sex-neutral parental-leave legislation is the best way to achieve such change in law.[45]

3. *The case against formal equality.* There are a number of problems with these arguments. First, NOW et al.'s arguments in *Guerra* are undermined by their own position in *Johnson* (the affirmative action case). Despite their vehement objections to "special" treatment in *Guerra*, in *Johnson* these groups favor "affirmative" action. "Affirmative" action—deliberately giving Joyce a "thumb on the scale" at the end of the decision making process—is as much a form of "special" treatment as is the pregnancy-disability statute at issue in *Guerra*. Affirmative action, perhaps even more than the pregnancy-disability statute at issue in *Guerra*, divides workers from each other and makes men resentful.[46] Yet, in the affirmative action cases, NOW et al. did not consider it so dangerous that it should always be avoided as a solution to women's problems.[47]

Second, the problem with formal equality is not simply that it is incapable of radically changing society or of ensuring that similarly situated women and men are treated similarly. Formal equality has actually hurt many women. Formal equality is likely to help most, and hurt least, professional women who either have no children or who hire other women to care for their children and are able to compete with men on men's terms. These women have tended to control the women's movement. And it is likely to hurt most mothers and wives who are not well-paid professionals.[48]

Despite the failure of the ERA campaign, formal equality has been implemented wholly or partially, directly and indirectly,

---

[45] Williams, Equality's Riddle, note 41 *supra*, at 374–80.

[46] See The Supreme Court Puts the Mike in Diane Joyce's Hands, Giving Feminists a Major Victory, People 49, 53 (April 13, 1987) (quoting Johnson on whether affirmative action should be used in promotion decision: "You should work for what you get, and if you work, you should get it.").

[47] See Brief Amici Curiae for NOW Legal Defense and Education Fund *et al.*, filed in *Johnson*.

[48] See Woloch, Women and the American Experience 384 (1984) (describing criticisms of the ERA movement in the twenties); Rothman, Woman's Proper Place: A History of Changing Ideals and Places, 1870 to the Present, at 160 (1978); Hewlett, A Lesser Life (1986), especially at 202–3.

through legislation and judicial changes in many ways.[49] Because of this trend, women have lost many of the traditional sex-based rules which gave them some measure of financial security and protection. For example, consider the effect on women of the shift from the traditional maternal preference in child custody disputes. During the sixties judges assumed that it was in the best interest of a child of tender years to give custody to its mother.[50] Many jurisdictions have either eliminated this presumption[51] or replaced it with a presumption in favor of joint custody,[52] thus giving a bargaining chip to fathers in negotiations with mothers. Because mothers seem to want custody much more than fathers,[53] the result of giving this bargaining chip to fathers is that mothers who desperately want custody offer economic concessions to settle the custody issue rather than submitting it to a judge.[54]

The gender-neutral custody rules adopted to date have not effected any radical restructuring of parenting roles. Instead, these

---

[49]The ERA would not, necessarily, have to be interpreted as a formal equality standard, see MacKinnon, Excerpts from MacKinnon/Schlafly Debate, 1 L. & Inequality 341, 341 (1983). Nevertheless, the ERA was widely understood as incorporating a formal equality standard. See, *e.g.*, Brown, Emerson, Falk & Freedman, The Equal Rights Amendment, 80 Yale L. J. 871; Ginsburg, Sexual Equality Under the Fourteenth and Equal Rights Amendments, [1979] Wash. U. L. Q. 161.

[50]For a description of the traditional rule, see, e.g., Clark, The Law of Domestic Relations in the United States 17.4 at 584–85 (1968).

[51]See, *e.g.*, Ex Parte Devine, 398 So.2d 686 (1981) (presumption unconstitutional under Supreme Court decisions; court notes presumption has been eliminated in Alaska, Arizona, California, Colorado, Connecticut, Delaware, Georgia, Hawaii, Illinois, Indiana, Iowa, Maine, Massachusetts, Michigan, Nebraska, New York, North Carolina, Ohio, Texas, and Washington and questionable in Kansas, Oregon, Pennsylvania, and Vermont); Legal Rights of Children §6.03 at 236 (Horowitz & Davidson eds. 1984).

[52]See, *e.g.*, West's Ann. Cal. Civ. Code §4600.5 (creating presumption of joint custody on application of either parent); Legal Rights of Children §6.05 at 239–42; Schulman & Pitt, Second Thoughts on Joint Child Custody: Analysis of Legislation and Its Implications for Women and Children, 12 Golden Gate Univ. L. Rev. 539, 545 (1982) (as of March, 1982, 24 states have some form of joint custody statute). Although joint custody can refer to joint physical custody, more often, in practice, it means simply joint legal custody (both parents having the right to make decisions about education, medical care, etc.). See Schulman & Pitt, *id.*, at 542–43. For discussions of problems with joint custody, see, *e.g.*, *ibid.*; Adler & Chambers, The Folly of Joint Custody, 1 Family Advocate 6 (1978).

[53]See, *e.g.*, Weitzman, The Marriage Contract 105–6 & n.* at 105 (1981).

[54]See Schulmann & Pitt, Second Thoughts on Joint Child Custody: Analysis of Legislation and Its Implications for Women and Children, in Joint Custody and Shared Parenting 209 (Folberg, ed. 1984); Scott & Derdeyn, Rethinking Joint Custody, 45 Ohio St. L. J. 455, 478 & n.106 (1981); Pearson & Ring, Judicial Decision-Making in Contested Custody Cases, 21 J. Fam. L. 703, 719 (1982); Neely, The Primary Caretaker Parent Rule: Child Custody and the Dynamics of Greed, 3 Yale L. & Pol. Rev. 168 (1984).

rules may have contributed to the further economic impoverishment of divorced women and their children. The poverty of divorced women and their children (relative to men[55]) is not, of course, entirely attributable to the move away from the maternal presumption. There are no estimates of the effect of movement away from the maternal preference on the post-divorce economic status of women and chidlren. The point is only that notions of formal equality have had a negative economic effect on a group that is not in a good position to bear the cost of social change.

In calculating child or spousal support at the time of divorce, which will typically be paid (if it is paid[56]) by the father to the custodial mother, judges today often assume that the ex-homemaker will find a good-paying job.[57] After all, Title VII and the Equal Pay Act ban wage discrimination; women and men are equal. But full-time female workers continue to earn substantially less than full-time male workers, and a woman who has no recent wage-work experience is likely to have difficulty finding even a decent woman's job. If she is the custodian of small children, as is typically the case when there are small children at the time of the divorce, she cannot enter the workforce unless she either neglects her children or earns a great deal so that she is able to pay for child care. Here, too, treating women and men as though they are equal when, in fact, they are not has worsened the post-divorce economic position of women and children, especially those women (and their children) who are most in need because they are least like men.

Traditionally, during marriage, husbands had a duty to support their wives (and not vice versa). That duty has never been directly

[55]See Weitzman, The Divorce Revolution xii (1985); Espenshade, The Economic Consequences of Divorce, J. of Marriage & Fam. 615 (Aug. 1979); Women's Research & Education Institute, Congressional Caucus for Women, The American Woman: A Report in Depth 78–82 (1987) (citing surveys).

[56]Only 4 million women (out of 8.7 million living with children of absent fathers) were to receive child support from fathers in 1983. Of those due payments, half received (about 2 million) the full amount due. About a quarter (1 million) received nothing and an approximately equal number received a partial payment. See U.S. Bureau of the Census, Child Support and Alimony: 1983, Current Population Reports, Special Studies, Series P-23, No. 141 (July 1985). The New York Times recently reported that the average payment for child support droped 12.4 percent from 1983 to 1985. See Average Child Support Payment Drops by 12%, New York Times, §1, p. 26, Aug. 23, 1987. Because of recent federal legislation, women should be receiving more of what is awarded than in the past. See Child Support Enforcement Amendments of 1984, 98 Stat. 1305 (Aug. 16, 1984).

[57]See, *e.g.*, Weitzman, The Divorce Revolution, at 188–89.

enforceable by wives during marriage,[58] but wives' creditors were sometimes able to enforce the duty.[59] In recent cases, in pursuit of formal equality, some judges have imposed a duty on all women to support their husbands, a duty enforceable by creditors.[60] As a result, a widow who has been a homemaker all her life may find, after her husband's expensive final illness, that she is personally liable for his hospital expenses. Ordinary wives are, however, less likely than their husbands to be economically capable of supporting their spouses, especially at age sixty-five or over when the husband dies. Again, treating women and men as though they are similarly situated when they are not hurts many women.

NOW would respond that sex-neutral legislation is the way to solve these problems. And one can imagine sex-neutral rules that would probably be acceptable solutions to most of these issues. But acceptable sex-neutral rules have not been widely adopted in any of these areas. Consider, for example, the appropriate standard for child custody at divorce. The traditional standard, giving an explicit preference to mothers at least during "tender years," created an explicit distinction on the basis of sex and reinforced traditional stereotypes of mothers as the nurturing parent. This standard is not ideal. Under it, for example, mothers were less likely even to consider whether they actually wanted custody, let alone to decide against custody without guilt, than they would have been under a less loaded standard. A gender-neutral rule could lessen these problems. If the new rule awarded custody to the parent likely to want custody most—for example, to the primary caretaker provided only that she were fit—the gender-neutral rule would not significantly affect the bargaining process. Of the many jurisdictions moving from a maternal preference to a gender-neutral rule, however, very few have adopted a rule preferring the parent who has been primary caretaker.[61] In the real world, there is nothing to ensure that the gender-neutral "solution" to an unnecessarily and inappropriately sex-based classification will not further weaken women's economic position.

---

[58]See, *e.g.*, McGuire v. McGuire, 157 Neb. 226, 59 N.W.2d 336 (1953).

[59]See, *e.g.*, Sharpe Furniture, Inc. v. Buckstaff, 99 Wis.2d 114, 299 N.W.2d 219 (1980).

[60]See, *e.g.*, Jersey Shore Medical Center v. Estate of Baum, 84 N.J.2d 137, 417 A.2d 1003 (1980) (rule to be applied in future cases).

[61]See Garska v. McCoy, 278 S.E.2d 357 (1981). In most jurisdictions, the identity of the primary caretaker is only one of many factors considered; see, *e.g.*, Pusey v. Pusey, Utah. Sup. Ct. No. 20365 (August 18, 1987).

In *Guerra* itself, the choice was not between a sex-based rule giving leave only to women disabled because of pregnancy and the ideal parental-leave rule advocated by NOW when lobbying before Congress. Nor was the choice between a sex-based rule giving leave only to women disabled because of pregnancy and a rule giving all workers leaves for disabilities of up to four months, though in its brief NOW argued that the leave policy be extended to all workers.[62] Instead, the choice was between having no statutorily-guaranteed leave for new parents and having leaves at least for women disabled by pregnancy. In other Western industrialized nations, where parenting leaves of one kind or another have been legally mandated for some time, regulation began in the form of maternity leaves. The trend, however, is to expand the policies to parental leaves.[63] Four jurisdictions in this country have adopted parental leave policies, and two of them began with maternity leave policies.[64] Eleven other jurisdictions have maternity leave policies.[65] These states may, in the future, follow the European trend and extend the benefit to include paternity leave.

A number of the decisions hailed as giant steps for women have hurt rather than helped many women by banning sex-based leg-

[62]NOW might have preferred the extension of the California statute to all workers, but the Supreme Court was not likely to extend that kind of state statute in the way advocated by NOW, despite its alternative holding to that effect in *Guerra*, see note 145 *infra*. In addition, even if the Court had extended the statute, the California legislature would have been free to repeal it. Further, other legislatures could not, in the future, enact maternal-leave statutes unless willing to give short-term disability leaves to all workers.

[63]Seventy- five countries—including every industrialized country except the United States—have some form of maternal or paternal leave. See Kamerman, Kahn & Kingston, Maternity Policies and Working Women 15 & Table 1.3 at 16–22 (1983); Hewlitt, A Lesser Life 96–100 & 167–74 (1986). Sweden adopted the first (and still most generous) parental leave policy in 1975. Id. at 96; International Labor Office, Maternity Benefits in the Eighties: An ILO Global Survey (1964–1984) at 18–22 (1985). As of 1984, five additional countries (Norway, Denmark, Italy, France, and Portugal) within the European Economic Community had adopted some form of paternity leave in addition to maternity leave. *Ibid.*

[64]The four states are Connecticut, Minnesota, Oregon, and Rhode Island. See Pregnancy and Employment: The Complete Handbook on Discrimination, Maternity Leave, and Health and Safety 98, 102, 104–6 (1987). Of these, two began with maternity leave policies—Connecticut and Oregon. See *id.* at 98 & 104. The Connecticut parental leave statute covers only employees. *Id.* at 98.

[65]Five states have statutes guaranteeing maternity leaves: California, Iowa, Massachusetts, Montana, and Tennessee. *Id.* at 96, 100–01, 105. Six states have regulations guaranteeing maternity leaves: Colorado, Hawaii, Illinois, Kansas, New Hampshire, and Washington. See *id.* at 97, 100–01, 103, 105–06.

islative classifications. And some of the Supreme Court cases striking explicitly sex-based classifications as impermissible forms of discrimination seem shockingly irrelevant to discrimination in the real world. *Orr v. Orr*[66] and *Otis v. Otis*[67] illustrate these points.

In *Orr*, the Supreme Court held that state statutes could not constitutionally provide for alimony to be paid by some husbands to some wives. The Court explained that permissible sex-neutral legislation would either deny alimony to both men and women or extend it to both on the same terms. It postulated two reasons for alimony: (i) because the recipient is needy and (ii) because women were discriminated against during marriage. Both purposes could be served by holding individualized hearings, the Court concluded.

Statutes imposing alimony obligations only on some husbands are hardly the linchpin of systemic discrimination on the basis of sex.[68] Far more important, by any measure, are sex-neutral statutes giving employment preferences to veterans[69] and statutes, rules, and practices which result in the ex-husband's receiving the lion's share of the financial security (including old-age security) accumulated during the ordinary marriage.[70] Yet of these policies, formal equality captures only the relatively trivial case of alimony imposed

---

[66]440 U.S. 268 (1979).

[67]299 N.W.2d 114 (Minn. 1980).

[68]. As of 1978, only 14.3 percent of divorced women had been awarded any alimony. See U.S. Bureau of the Census, Current Population Reports, Special Studies, Child Support and Alimony, Series P-23, No. 141, at 4, Table E (July 1985).

[69]Such statutes violate neither the Constitution nor Title VII. See Personnel Administrator of Massachusets v. Feeney, 4422 U.S. 256 (1979) (veterans' preference does not violate Equal Protection Clause though women are effectively excluded from top levels of state government); 42 U.S.C. §2000e-11 (exempting veterans' preference statutes from preemption by Title VII).

[70]The financial security accumulated during the marriage includes the present earning power and future earning potential (to the extent accumulated during the marriage) as well as tangible and intangible pension rights and social security credits. Women who are dependent because of their specialization in domestic production and reproduction are not awarded half of these assets. See, *e.g.*, Umber v. Umber, 591 P.2d 299 (1979) (Social Security Act preempts distribution to wife of part of social security account accumulated in husband's name though both worked in family drug store but social security contributions paid only into husband's account); 42 U.S.C. §402(b) (during life of wage earner, divorced spouse receives, at most, 50 cents for every dollar of benefits he is entitled to receive). When a wife is given a share of a pension, she is sometimes "bought out," *i.e.* given cash or other disposable assets to offset the pension rights given the husband. See, *e.g.*, Weitzman, The Divorce Revolution, at 120–21; In Re Marriage of Gillmore, 29 Cal. 3rd 1, 174 Cal. Rptr. 493, 629 P.2d 1 (1981).

only on men. Such statutes are less than ideal; they reinforce notions that women are dependents because they are women. But they are not of much importance in the systemic subordination of women.[71]

More importantly, *Orr v. Orr* has hurt ordinary mothers and wives. During the last twenty-five years, there has been a decrease in alimony awarded even to full-time long-term homemakers.[72] It is likely that *Orr v. Orr* (and the notion of formal equality which both produced it and was reinforced by it) have contributed to this decline. In *Orr v. Orr,* the Court could imagine only two reasons for awarding alimony: a needy recipient and as compensation for discrimination in marriage. The Court never explains what it means by the latter, rather nebulous, concept.[73] The other reason is need. Need is not, in itself, a very compelling reason for post-divorce payments to an ex-spouse. Far more compelling reasons are ignored entirely by the Court.

Consider *Otis v. Otis*, which was decided a year after *Orr* by the Supreme Court of Minnesota. The Otis marriage had lasted over twenty years. The trial judge ordered the husband (who earned over $120,000 a year as a vice-president of Control Data) to pay his ex-wife alimony for four years (at an average rate of $1,500 per month). Ms. Otis quit her job as an executive secretary when her son was born "in order to fulfill the expected, role of wife and hostess for a rising and successful business executive."[74] She played an important role in her husband's career. For example, before his last promotion, she, too, was interviewed. When the board of directors met in Greece for a week in 1977, she was the official hostess. She had wanted to return to work a number of years previously, but her husband said he was " 'not going to have any wife of mine pound a typewriter.' "[75] When she was awarded only short-term

[71]. See note 70 *supra* and Weitzman, The Divorce Revolution, at 143–45. Even under a statute imposing equivalent obligations on ex-wives and ex-husbands, very few wives are going to be ordered to pay alimony because, *inter alia*, women usually have custody of the children and earn less than ex-husbands.

[72]See *id.* at 143–83 (California).

[73]The Court does suggest that individualized hearings could be held on whether "the institution of marriage did discriminate against" a particular woman but gives no clue as to what a hearing would actually investigate. 440 U.S. at 281. Because of problems of perspective and bias, women might be better off with sex-based rules than with individualized hearings.

[74]299 N.W.2d at 118 (Otis, J., dissenting).

[75]*Ibid.*

alimony, she was forty-five years old and had been out of the workplace for approximately twenty years. The Supreme Court of Minnesota upheld the award of the trial court because, it explained, post-divorce transfer payments are based on need and Ms. Otis should be able to "rehabilitate" herself within four years.

Ms. Otis's need—in and of itself—is the weakest imaginable reason for awarding her post-divorce transfer payments. Her current need reflects her investment in her husband's career, an investment from which he will continue to profit. Her need reflects the reliance loss she sustained by not working in order to raise their son and further her husband's career (and in order to avoid embarrassing him by typing). Having relied so substantially for so long, she cannot now, at forty-five, recover what she would have had had she put her own career first. Her needs should be met because a reasonable term of their arrangement, with its traditional division of labor, is that in exchange for her reliance in engaging exclusively in non-wage domestic production and reproduction and contributing to his career rather than her own, she would receive a reasonable share of the profit brought in by her husband's career and a reasonable share of the financial security accumulated for their old age.[76]

NOW might argue that ideal sex-neutral post-divorce rules can be imagined. There are, of course, other possible approaches besides tying alimony to sex (thus reinforcing stereotypical notions about women's dependency) and ignoring the life-long economic effects of the division of labor within marriage. *Otis v. Otis* is not, however, unusual. Ideal rules have not been developed to replace sex-linked alimony.[77] Instead, judges have stressed the weakest of reasons for ordering one spouse to make post-divorce income transfers to the other spouse.

---

[76]In *Otis*, the court divided approximately equally the property accumulated during the marriage except that it also awarded Mr. Otis all of his vested pension plan. The court does not attach any specific value to that plan.

[77]Ordinary women may also be hurt by discretionary rules—rules requiring judges to find an appropriate basis for awarding alimony in a particular case—rather than alimony awarded on the basis of sex since bias may affect individual decisions. This problem has been ignored by the Supreme Court which seems unable to perceive any cost, other than administrative, associated with individualized hearings. *Cf.* In re Marriage of Hitchcock, 265 N.W.2d 599 (1978) (wife unsuccessfully tries to repudiate divorce settlement reached after trial judge had made statements indicating that he would award her little as her share of husband's business; among other things, the judge compared her "interest in her husband's business to his own wife's interest in his retirement fund should they be divorced" with the implication that neither wife should receive a share of the specified asset).

Orr v. Orr is not, of course, solely responsible for cases like *Otis v. Otis*. *Orr v. Orr* reflects and reinforces notions of formal equality which have eliminated the notion that ex-wives should receive alimony because they are women. Judges, like the Justices in *Orr v. Orr*, have been unable to think of any very good alternative reasons for awarding anyone alimony. Many, probably most judges, like the Justices in *Orr v. Orr* have been unable to come up with anything more compelling than simple need. As a result, alimony (even when awarded) tends to be for relatively short periods of time (typically two to four years) and designed only to allow the ex-wife to become self-supporting. In the past, alimony was more often awarded permanently, *i.e.*, until the ex-wife remarried or either spouse died.[78] This change has not been good for most women, especially women who, like Ms. Orr, were homemakers for twenty years or more. Many women would have been better off if feminists had argued for needed economic rights and greater economic security for women (in recognition of their domestic production and reproduction) rather than for strict formal equality in family law matters.

NOW, or someone else, might argue that women have been hurt just about as much as possible under strict formal equality. They should, therefore, try at least to get its benefits, having paid the price. There are, however, still some sex-specific rules, statutes, and practices. These are still, at least arguably, permissible because we have not yet adopted strict formal equality as the appropriate standard. Further movement towards a formal equality standard would jeopardize such classifications. For example, a few jurisdictions retain a weakened form of the maternal preference;[79] even in those jurisdictions in which it has been formally changed, individual judges continue to use it in actually deciding cases.[80] Public schools still have separate sports programs for girls and women.[81] In many

[78]If alimony is basically a form of expectation-reliance (contract) damages for the needy traditional wife when a marriage breaks up, it should not necessarily terminate entirely with her remarriage. Thus, I do not mean to suggest that traditional rules could not be improved upon.

[79]See, *e.g.*, Pellegrin v. Pellegrin, 478 S.2d 306 (Miss. 1985) (error to award custody to mothers solely on the basis of children's tender years); In Re Marriage of Kershner, 400 So.2d 126 (Fla. 1981) (where all other factors are equal, custody of children of tender years should go to mother (dicta)).

[80]See Weitzman, The Divorce Revolution, at 235–36; Report of the New York Task Force on Women in the Courts 162–65 (1986).

jurisdictions, unwed fathers who have never lived with or supported a child cannot take a newborn away from its mother or interfere with her decision to let the child be adopted.[82] In a few jurisdictions, the obligation of husbands to support their spouses has not been extended to wives.[83] In many jurisdictions, clubs for women only are permissible.[84] All these rules, and others, would be threatened by further movement towards formal equality.[85]

In addition, formal equality has yet to permeate effectively our entire culture. Women can, therefore, be harmed by increased acceptance of formal equality in the surrounding culture. For example, even in the jurisdictions that have formally abolished the maternal custody preference, individual judges deciding individual cases often—consciously or unconsciously—consider mothers the more appropriate custodian for a child of tender years. Similarly, some judges deciding post-divorce economic issues recognize that most women cannot earn as much as men. Despite the fact that courts regard protectionist legislation as preempted by Title VII,[86] some women working in factories continue to enjoy some of the advantages (such as limits on what they can be required to lift) initially implemented through protectionist legislation.[87] Such re-

[81]*Cf.* Vorchheimer v. School District of Philadelphia. 532 F.2d 880 (3rd Cir. 1976) (Equal Protection Clause challenge to "separate-but-equal" public high schools for boys and girls), aff'd by an equally divided court, 430 U.S. 703 (1977)).

[82]See Krause, Child Support in America 139–52 (1981). The trend is, however, *contra*. "Modern" judges tend to equalize the status of new fathers and new mothers despite the obvious disparity between their contributions to, and involvement with, the newborn. See, *e.g.*, Collinsworth v. O'Connell, No. BQ-305 (Fla. 1st Dist. 1987); In re Baby Girl Eason, No. 44709 (Ga. 1987).

[83]See, *e.g.*, Schilling v. Bedford Co. Mem. Hospital, 303 S.E.2d 905 (Va. 1983) (abolishing duty); Marshfield Clinic v. Discher, 314 N.W.2d 326 (Wis. 1982) (retaining traditional doctrine with qualification that wives are ordinarily responsible for their own necessities).

[84]See Rhode, Association and Assimilation, 81 Nw. U. L. Rev. 107, 115 (1986).

[85]Perhaps such distinctions are already unconstitutional. The Supreme Court has not, however, decided cases squarely on these points. It can at least be argued that the Court might allow these distinctions to survivew their middle tier scrutiny applied in sex-discrimination cases.

[86]See, *e.g.*, Rosenfeld v. Southern Pacific Co., 44 F.2d 1219 (1971).

[87]See Hewlett, A Lesser Life, at 202–3; *cf.* Bielby & Baron, Undoing Job Discrimination: Job Integration and Comparable Worth, in Ingredients for Women's Employment Policy 211, 221–22 (Bose & Spitze, eds., 1987) (discussing continuing job segregation by sex; authors stress "the tendency for organizational arrangements to be inert in the absence of profound environmental shocks").

sults might become more tenuous in a world with greater stress on formal equality. As this suggests, the real-world negative effects of formal equality are difficult to see, let alone predict.

In the end, there are two distinct kinds of problems associated with formal equality. One is that formal equality cannot be the basis for implementing the kinds of changes that must be made if the status of women and men is to be equalized. The other is that the limited changes effected by formal equality will often hurt many women, especially ordinary mothers and wives.

Formal equality is dangerous for women in a way in which it is not dangerous for other minority groups. Few, if any, traditional racially explicit classifications ever had either the purpose or overall effect of benefiting a racial minority. There is, for example, no racial analogy to the maternal preference standard in custody disputes, no traditional racial classification which, despite its reinforcement of a stereotype, also gave a racial minority a better bargaining position in negotiations with nonminorities than would race-neutral rules. Because the legal system has protected women better than it has protected other minorities (though not, of course, as well as it has protected men), formal equality is dangerous for women in a unique way.

The trend, throughout law, is strongly towards strict formal equality. There is, at the same time, another legally accepted model of discrimination, a model available for Title VII cases: disparate impact.

B. DISPARATE IMPACT

Under Title VII, a plaintiff can use disparate impact to challenge a practice or requirement that disproportionately disqualifies women from employment opportunities.[88] For example, under Title VII, women can challenge height and weight requirements on the ground that such requirements are likely to disqualify more women than men.

Some feminist students and litigators have argued that disparate impact should be generally available as a basis for challenging dis-

[88]See Griggs v. Duke Power Co., 401 U.S. 424 (1971) (race case).

criminatory policies and practices.[89] There are, however, a number of limitations which prevent disparate impact from being a solution to the problems of formal equality. In order to use disparate impact, one has to have a perspective and some basis for comparison. For example, when disparate impact is used to challenge a height and weight requirement, one looks to see whether more female than male applicants fail to qualify because of the height and weight requirements. One assumes that in the absence of the challenged requirement, women and men would qualify in proportion to their numbers in the applicant pool.[90] One can, therefore, compare the actual pass (or qualifying) rate and the assumed pass rate (*i.e.*, the proportion of women in the pool) to see whether the test or requirement has a disparate impact.

In other settings, there is no single reference for comparison. Even assuming a basis for comparison, often one can imagine many solutions which could be implemented by various defendants. Consider, for example, *Wimberly v. Labor and Industrial Relations Commission*, a third case from the 1986 Term and one factually much like *Guerra* except that it arose in Missouri, which had no statute analogous to California's. Like Garland, Linda Wimberly was not rehired after her pregnancy leave because there were no suitable openings. She filed a claim for unemployment benefits with the Missouri Division of Employment Security. The agency denied her claim because, under Missouri law, unemployment benefits were never available to a claimant who "left his work voluntarily without good cause attributable to his work or his employer." Wimberly challenged the decision, arguing that the Missouri rule violated a federal requirement that states not deny unemployment compensation claims "solely on the basis of pregnancy or termination of pregnancy."[91] The Supreme Court unanimously held that Missouri

[89]See Williams, Equality's Riddle, note 41 *supra*, at 364–65, 372–74; Stone, Comparable Worth in the Wake of AFSCME v. State of Washington, 1 Berkeley Women's L. J. 78 (1986) (arguing for comparable worth as a form of disparate impact); Siegel, Employment Equality Under the Pregnancy Discrimination Act of 1978, 94 Yale L. J. 929 (1985) (arguing for general availability of disparate impact under Pregnancy Discrimination Act); Brief of State of California at 14–21 filed in *Guerra*.

[90]See Dothard v. Rawlinson, 433 U.S. 206 (1977) (height and weight requirements are impermissible because of disparate impact on women; employer must test directly for strength).

[91]This provision applies to states participating in the federal-state unemployment compensation program and is codified at 26 U.S.C. §3304(a)(12) (1982).

law was consistent with the federal requirement since Missouri did not deny claims solely on the ground the employee quit because of pregnancy. Instead, Missouri denied claims like Wimberly's on the more general ground that unemployment compensation was available only to workers who quit their jobs for work-related reasons. But the Missouri law can be viewed as having a disparate impact on pregnant workers relative to other possible policies. Under the Missouri plan workers who lost their jobs because of pregnancy and childbirth are never eligible for unemployment compensation. A policy extending unemployment benefits to all workers—once able to work again—who lost their jobs because of physical disability (lasting up to four months) would not have so negative an impact on new mothers.[92]

No court is likely to recognize a disparate impact claim in this situation;[93] the claim, the remedy, the proper defendant, are all too indeterminate. One solution has just been suggested: to order the Labor and Industrial Relations Commission of Missouri to extend benefits to all workers who lost their jobs because of short-term disabilities lasting four months or less. Alternatively, the Commission could be ordered to extend coverage only to women disabled because of pregnancy or only to individuals who lost their jobs because of a disability lasting two months or less. Or Wimberly's employer could be ordered to reinstate her after her period of disability; that too would eliminate some of the disparate impact of the current Missouri policy. Alternatively, Wimberly's employer could be ordered to give leaves to all workers disabled up to two months (or up to four months or up to six weeks) or to give leaves to all new parents. Indeed, although one can imagine more desirable policies, any disparate impact on pregnant workers would be elim-

[92]One can, of course, imagine other policies which would also be preferable from the perspective of pregnant workers, *e.g.*, a plan which considered all reasonable quits (including pregnancy) as covered by the plan.

[93]Wimberly did not frame her claim in terms of disparate impact. Instead, she argued that the federal provision mandated "preferential teatment for women who leave work because of pregnancy." 107 S.Ct. at 825. Something like disparate impact has, however, been recognized in the context of the Free Exercise Clause. States must extend unemployment benefits to workers who are fired for refusing to work on their Sabbath. See Sherbert v. Verner, 374 U.S. 398 (1963); Hobbie v. Unemployment Appeals Commission of Florida, 107 S.Ct. 1046 (1987).

inated by ordering all Missouri employers to require that every man in Missouri take an (unpaid) paternal leave when his child is born equal to the length of time the mother of his child is disabled by childbirth.

As another example, consider the argument, made by the state of California in its brief in *Guerra*, that the state statute was permissible because an employer's failure to give at least four months disability leave for pregnancy would necessarily have a disparate impact on pregnant workers.[94] The ACLU Women's Project in their amicus brief in *Guerra* responds that "[i]n fact, the average number of days lost from work due to disability, including childbirth and illness during pregnancy, is remarkably similar for men and women workers."[95] The ACLU women's project cites evidence that "men workers experience an average of 4.9 days of work loss due to illness or injury per year while women experience 5.1 days per year."[96] Men lose more days of work from all injuries than women do because, among other things, men tend to work at more dangerous jobs and suffer more job-related disability. In their amicus brief, the California Women Lawyers, et al., respond that this is the wrong comparison. One needs to ask whether disability leaves inadequate for most pregnancies (the average length of pregnancy disability may be six weeks) have a disparate impact on women. The fact that women have an average of only 4.9 days of disability a year and men and average of 5.1 days a year is irrelevant to the question of whether the lack of leaves adequate for most pregnancies has a disparate impact on women.[97]

If the question is whether a no-leave policy has a disparate impact on women, there is a sense in which each of these litigants is right. There is no one perspective from which to judge disparate impact

[94]See Brief of California at 14–21 filed in *Guerra*.

[95]See ACLU *et al.* brief, note 9 *supra*, at 25.

[96]*Id.* at 26.

[97]See Brief of California Women Lawyers, *et al.*, note 10 *supra*, at 12–13. On the other hand, workers who sustain work-related disabilities are less likely (than workers disabled by pregnancy) to lose their jobs. Employers are usually anxious to avoid charges that employees were fired in retaliation for filing a work-related disability claim and are anxious to do everything possible to limit the size of the claim. Both these purposes are served by allowing the worker to return to work at the earliest possible date. Indeed, California prohibits employers from terminating employees because of work-related disabilitites. Cal. Labor Code §132a, cited in Brief of California, filed in *Guerra*, at 18–19 n.16.

on women in this situation.[98] In addition, changes could be made by a number of different entities; disparate impact does not give a court any guidance about who is a proper defendant. At least to date, even supposedly activist judges have not been willing to develop standards for choosing among various policies to be implemented by various defendants.

There is another problem with disparate impact. Like formal equality, disparate impact refers to male performance levels. Women are, at most, entitled to succeed at men's rates.[99] This antidiscrimination rule (like formal equality) has a male reference point; it is not neutral with respect to sex. Disparate impact cannot, for example, afford a basis for challenging promotion requirements designed by and for men as long as women, by dint of whatever efforts are necessary given their typically greater domestic responsibilities[100] and other disadvantages, are nevertheless as successful as men.

Only a few feminists (other than litigators) have argued for a disparate impact standard in contexts outside hiring or promotion requirements.[101] Instead, most feminists disenchanted with contemporary standards of equality have tried to develop alternatives.

II. Feminist Alternatives

For purposes of this discussion, feminist alternatives may be put under three headings: first, Catharine MacKinnon's inequality approach;[102] second, Christine Littleton's acceptance ap-

[98]Because Title VII specifically defines sex discrimination as including discrimination on the basis of pregnancy, perhaps the disparate impact question in this Title VII case should focus on whether a no-leave policy has a disparate impact on pregnant workers rather than women workers. The State of California argued that the appropriate focus was pregnant workers, see Brief of California, at 14–22, especially n.16 at 18–19. The ACLU considered the appropriate focus women workers, not pregnant workers. See ACLU Brief, at 23–35.

[99]*Cf.* MacKinnon, Sexual Harassment, at 145–46 (noting that inequality is buried in standards, such as the height and weight standard at issue in *Dothard*, which was actually average male height and weight).

[100]Even in families in which both spouses work, women are primarily responsible for domestic tasks. See, *e.g.*, Blumstein & Schwartz, American Couples 144–46 (1983); Gilbert, Men in Dual Career Couples: Current Realities and Future Prospects 60–90 (1985); Pleck, Men's Family Work: Three Perspectives and Some New Data, 28 The Family Coordinator 481 (1979).

[101]See sources cited in note 89 *supra*.

[102]See, *e.g.*, MacKinnon, Sexual Harassment, especially at 101–41; MacKinnon, Feminism Unmodified, especially at 32–45.

proach;[103] and third, formal equality with limited special treatment.[104] Some feminists have suggested other approaches to equality in recent years but have not elaborated judicially enforceable standards. Instead, they have primarily attempted to expand the kinds of arguments that might be made to employers and legislators.[105] This discussion is limited to judicially enforceable feminist approaches.[106]

A. THE INEQUALITY APPROACH

The inequality approach, developed by MacKinnon in the seventies, is a powerful and influential model, as well as being, itself, a devastating critique of formal equality. The inequality model begins with the seemingly obvious observation that when we use the word "discrimination," we are referring to "systematic disadvantagement of social groups."[107] As already noted, formal equality assumes that distinctions based on relevant differences are not discriminatory. But systemic discrimination consists primarily of turning differences, real or perceived, into socially constructed disadvantages for women and socially constructed advantages for men.

MacKinnon refuses, therefore, to focus on the rationalizations for distinctions which, however "reasonable," are part of the systemic subordination of women to men. Instead, she focuses on whether a particular practice or rule "participates in the systemic social deprivation of one sex because of sex. The only question for litigation is whether the policy or practice in question integrally

---

[103]Littleton, Reconstructing Sexual Equality, 75 Cal. L. Rev. 201 (1987).

[104]See Kay, Models of Equality, [1985] Univ. Ill. L. Rev. 39; Law, Rethinking Sex and the Constitution, 132 Univ. Pa. L. Rev. 955 (1984); Kay, Equality and Difference: The Case of Pregnancy, 1 Berkeley Women's L. J. 1 (1985); Law, Rethinking Sex and the Constitution, 132 U. Pa. L. Rev. 95 (1984). Ann Scales also advocated this approach in an early article, see Scales, Towards a Feminist Jurisprudence, 56 Ind. L. J. 375 (1981), but in more recent work has advocated MacKinnon's inequality approach. See Scales, The Emergence of Feminist Jurisprudence: An Essay, 95 Yale L. J. 1373 (1986).

[105]Finley, Transcending Equality Theory: A Way out of the Maternity and the Workplace Debate, 86 Col. L. Rev. 1118 (1986); Wolgast, Equality and the Rights of Women (1980).

[106]I do not discuss the "choice" standard advocated by Kirp, Yudof, and Franks in Gender Justice (1986). As Lucinda Finley points out in her review, the choice approach is a reformulation of conventional liberalism. See Finley, Choice and Freedom: Elusive Issues in the Search for Gender Justice, 96 Yale. L. J. 914 (1987).

[107]MacKinnon, Sexual Harassment, at 116.

contributes to the maintenance of an underclass or a deprived position because of gender status."[108]

At least one feminist, Ann Scales, has argued for MacKinnon's inequality standard as a general, judicially enforceable approach to discrimination.[109] Although MacKinnon describes the "question to be litigated" as whether a practice or policy contributes to women's subordinate status, it is unlikely that MacKinnon understands inequality as a general judicially enforceable standard for challenging any practice or policy that contributes to the subordination of women.[110]

Despite Scales's optimism, the inequality approach is not a general solution to the problems raised by formal equality and disparate impact. Typically, a policy or practice contributes to women's subordinate status because of its interaction with other policies, practices, and social mores. Typically, one can imagine many changes to the status quo, implemented by many different entities, which would result in less systematic subordination of women. Inequality's "question to be litigated" does not identify either the appropriate defendant or the appropriate change. Each of the points made in the earlier discussion of disparate impact and pregnancy policies could be made again here.

As an example, consider whether the inequality standard would be violated when a worker disabled by pregnancy is fired. Her employer fires all workers disabled for more than two weeks for reasons that are not work related. Such a policy contributes to the subordination of women, by tending to make them dependent on men after childbirth. But even giving the worker an unpaid leave of absence during pregnancy-related disability tends to contribute to the subordination of women, by tending to make them dependent on men while temporarily disabled by pregnancy. There are a number of ways in which these policies could be changed so as to make

[108] *Id.* at 117.

[109] See Scales, The Emergence of Feminist Jurisprudence: An Essay, note 107 *supra*.

[110] Certainly, MacKinnon has not taken such an approach. In Sexual Harassment of Working Women, she used her inequality approach in arguing that policies of sexual harassment that explicitly treat women and men differently are forms of sex discrimination because they contribute to the inequality of women. But in her attempts to have pornography recognized as a form of sex discrimination, she has used inequality analysis as a basis for arguing for legislative change, rather than as a judicially-enforceable abstract standard of equality capable, in itself, of affording a remedy for such discrimination.

women more independent. Employers could be required to give women leaves for pregnancy-related disabilities with full pay. Alternatively, employers could be required to give women unpaid leaves and state unemployment compensation systems could be changed to give women unemployment compensation during the period of pregnancy-related disability. Or employers could be required to give all new parents a period of paid leave for six months. Alternatively, employers could be required to give new parents six months of unpaid leave and some new state-mandated insurance system could provide financial benefits to parents taking such leaves.

Identifying current policies as contributing to the subordinate status of women simply does not identify a single defendant or one appropriate change. Like disparate impact, inequality as a general standard is simply too indeterminate to expect judges to use it in the foreseeable future.[111]

B. THE ACCEPTANCE STANDARD

Christine Littleton suggests that judges apply equality in terms of an acceptance standard. She identifies men's power to determine what is of value as an essential element of the inequality of the sexes. She proposes to "rescue equality" by "making sex difference not make a difference in equality, by making difference 'costless' (or at least cost less)."[112] In applying an acceptance standard, judges would make difference cost less by equalizing the resources (money, status, and access to decision making) allocated on the basis of "gendered complements."[113]

For example, under Littleton's acceptance standard, comparable worth would be appropriate in disputes about pay because male and female job categories should be paid equally. In other contexts, acceptance would be implemented by "inventing complementary structures containing female norms."[114] For example, an employer with a job-related height requirement (tending disproportionately to disqualify women relative to men) would be required to restruc-

---

[111]For a similar analysis, see Law, Rethinking Sex and the Constitution, 132 Univ. Pa. L. Rev. at 1005–06.

[112]Littleton, Reconstructing Sexual Equality, 75 Cal. L. Rev. at 238–43.

[113]*Id.* at 244, 253

[114]*Id.* at 248.

ture the job (or offer equal job opportunities) to accommodate the disqualified women.[115] In the context of pregnancy, Littleton would require that, in the workplace, "money, status, and opportunity for advancement flow equally to the womb-donating woman and the sperm-donating man."[116] Littleton argues that motherhood and military service could be established as gendered complements; this would mean "requiring the government to pay mothers the same low wages and generous benefits as most soldiers."[117] Littleton suggests that this could "mean encouraging the use of motherhood [like the use of military service today] as an unofficial prerequisite for governmental office."[118]

Littleton's standard adds another level of indeterminancy to disparate impact analysis. In addition to eliminating those policies and practices which have a disparate impact on women in terms of money, status, or access to decision making, judges must initially identify appropriate gendered complements.

Consider a worker who stops working when her first child is born, works on a part-time basis at low-paying jobs intermittently for the next ten years, and then resumes full-time work when her youngest child enters first grade. It is unrealistic to think that judges can or will order changes equalizing her and her husband's (or the average man's?) access to money, status, and decision making. What is the gendered complement for the various stages of her life? Should she receive soldier's pay (what rank?) and benefits until her youngest child is eighteen? Even after the youngest is eighteen, she will probably continue to receive lower wages because she took time off from wage work to care for her children. After twenty years of motherhood, should she be entitled to military retirement benefits? Although Littleton's acceptance standard suggests arguments that might be made to legislatures, it is unrealistic to think that judges will be willing to implement so nebulous a standard.

---

[115] *Id.* at 248 (no remedy would be available under Title VII, as currently interpreted, for the policy described in text because the height requirement is job related).

[116] *Ibid.*

[117] *Id.* at 251.

[118] *Id.* at 251–52 n.260 (by changing media treatment of female political candidates and by establishing preferences for employment similar to those granted veterans).

C. FORMAL EQUALITY WITH LIMITED "SPECIAL" TREATMENT

Through the early eighties, the current feminist movement relied primarily on formal equality in pressing for change both in courts and in other arenas. In recent years, a number of feminists have argued that formal equality should be qualified by allowing for policies treating women differently from men in very limited circumstances centering on the biological fact that only women bear children.[119] These feminists would uphold the California statute challenged in *Guerra*, since women are given "special" treatment only when—on the level of physical reality—they are situated differently from men: they are disabled by pregnancy.

This approach can be criticized both by those who would never permit "special" treatment (other than "affirmative" action) and by those who think "special" treatment in such limited circumstances too narrow a standard. (I have already summarized and responded to the objections of the first group, feminists like Wendy Williams and the leadership of the National Organization of Women, who argue for strict formal equality with no exceptions other than "affirmative" action.) "Special" treatment in such limited circumstances does not go very far towards rectifying the many, and I think devastating, reasons for rejecting formal equality, reasons already discussed in detail. If "special" treatment is permissible only when warranted by physical, biological differences, the standard remains one of formal equality in almost all instances augmented by "special" treatment only in the most narrow of circumstances.

Formal equality augmented by such limited special treatment will not effect nearly enough beneficial change and will often result in change detrimental to most women. Few of the criticisms of formal equality, elaborated above, were limited to the use of formal equality when there is actually a biological difference. Even with

---

[119]See Scales, Toward a Feminist Jurisprudence, 56 Ind. L. J. 375 (women should be regarded as having rights different from men only with respect to sex-specific conditions that are completely unique to women, *i.e.* pregnancy and breast feeding); Law, Rethinking Sex and the Constitution, 132 U. Pa. L. Rev. 955; Kay, Equality and Difference, 1 Berkely Women's L. J. 1 (1985); Kay, Models of Equality, [1985] Ill. L. Rev. 39. In a 1986 article, Scales moved from the limited-special-treatment view to share MacKinnon's dominance approach. See Scales, The Emergence of a Feminist Jurisprudence, 95 Yale L. J. 1371, especially at 1381 n.46.

an exception for biological differences, formal equality affords no basis for challenging rules which structure the work place to fit men's life experiences and needs, but not women's. This limited exception does nothing to correct the male bias inevitable in a standard of formal equality applied mostly by men. It still accepts actual or perceived differences as justifications for further differential treatment. The exception does not help make visible discrimination which is often invisible under a standard of formal equality.

Most importantly, the limited exception for differential treatment based on biological differences will not preclude the use of formal equality though the result may be to further disadvantage many ordinary mothers and wives. True, under this standard, a court would not overrule a statute giving women pregnancy leaves. But courts would continue to strike down the maternal preference in custody and judges would tend increasingly (in a world with greater acceptance of formal equality) to regard fathers as equally appropriate custodians of young children and to regard mothers as equally capable of supporting children financially.

III. An Impossible Dream?

We use equality to refer to a number of things, including both (i) the situation in an ideal (nonsexist) world and (ii) a legal standard to be applied by judges (based either in the Constitution or in a statute such as Title VII). Hopefully, (ii) should be a means to get from this world to the ideal world imagined in (i).

We cannot, today, know what an "ideal" world with equality between the sexes would look like, let alone how best to get there. This is another difference between race and sex. With race, we can at least imagine a world in which Blacks and whites are equal. We can imagine a world in which race is no more important than eye color. We cannot so easily imagine a world in which women and men are equal or in which sex would matter no more than eye color. Most of us would not want to live in a world in which sex was no more important or relevant than eye color. Perhaps equality could occur in a world in which sex still matters, but in different ways from the ways in which it matters in this world. Few of us can imagine what that world might look like.

For those, including myself, who think that whatever it might look like, a reasonably ideal world would look rather different from this one, formal equality must be rejected. Formal equality is not capable of producing enough change in the status quo, and is likely to impose significant costs on those women most in need of change because most unlike men.

Perhaps formal equality's proponents regard harm to some women (especially ordinary mothers and wives) as a justifiable cost of effecting social change. If the economic position of ordinary women (especially after divorce, an ever present danger today) becomes tenuous enough, fewer women will be willing to fulfill traditional roles or (as is often the case) attempt to combine traditional roles and some (often limited) wage work. As a result of greater insecurity, more women will work, even while their children are small, will regard their own jobs as important as their husbands', and will refuse to be primarily responsible for either child care or other domestic duties. Also, if their chances of having post-divorce custody are no greater than their husbands', they will invest less in their children during marriage, thus equalizing fathers' and mothers' investments in raising children.

There are, however, a number of problems with such justifications for formal equality. First, formal equality tends to help most exceptional professional women, with the costs borne by another group. The elite who lead the feminist movement should be reluctant to press for change they consider desirable by imposing its costs on other women.

Second, it is likely that a majority of women would consider this "solution" unacceptable. It is, for example, unlikely that most women would want to be only as involved with children as their husbands. Perhaps this is the result of their socialization, and a form of false consciousness about their own best interests. We should, however, be reluctant to use false consciousness as the basis for ignoring women's desires. One important aspect of women's subordination has been that others have defined who women are and what they want. Feminists have generally stressed the importance of listening to what women say rather than dictating what women should say and feel.

Most women might prefer other means to other ends. True, one way of effecting change is to make traditional roles (even when combined with limited employment) too risky. But one could, instead, improve the position of ordinary women by making women's traditional roles less risky, empowering women by making them less dependent on men. Is "our" goal a world in which there is more respect for and reward of those traits, skills, and contributions traditionally associated with women? Or should we try to discourage these traits, skills, and contributions so that women will be more like men? Feminists today are deeply divided on these issues[120] and, were it possible to ask all women for their views, they too would have vastly different responses. Formal equality should be rejected because it takes one particular approach to a number of complicated questions about which women disagree vehemently.

Third, our young people continue to have different expectations about their futures—and different futures—depending on their sex.[121] As long as we continue producing girls and boys with different expectations, it is fundamentally unfair to treat women, once they are grown, as though they were like men in order to foster change. Change could be more effectively and fairly fostered by changing socialization than by making motherhood, child care, and domestic work riskier through implementation of strict formal equality.

Fourth, if—as feminists have suggested—women tend (more than men) to define themselves in terms of others,[122] it may be very unrealistic to think that women will respond to increased insecurity by taking steps in their own individual self-interest despite harms to the interests of those closest to them. Yet increased risks associated with traditional roles will effect an appropriate level of change only if women act in their individual self interest.

Fifth, making traditional roles more costly as a means of effecting change assumes that women will assess correctly the risk associated

---

[120] There is a great deal of controversy even among those who would identify with the word "feminist" about how and why women are different from men, the causes of any differences, and what changes to the current order are desirable. As Jane Flax has pointed out, "Feminist discourse is full of contradictory and irreconcilable conceptions of the nature of our social relations, of men and women and the worth and character of sterotypcially masculine and feminine activities." Flax, Postmoderism and Gender Relations in Feminist Theory, 12 Signs 621, 638 (1987). See also Gerson, Emerging Social Divisions Among Women: Implications for Welfare State Politics, 15 Politics & Society 213 (1986–87); Rosenfelt & Stacey, Second Thoughts on the Second Wave, 13 Feminist Studies 341 (1987).

[121] See, *e.g.*, Marini, Sex Differences in the Determination of Adolescent Aspirations: A Review of Research, 4 Sex Roles 723 (1978); Marini & Greenberger, Sex Differences in Occupational Aspirations and Expectations, 5 Sociology of Work and Occupations 147 (1978); Lyson, Race and Sex Differences in Sex Role Attitudes of Southern College Students, 10 Psychology of Women Q. 421 (1986); Waite, Haggstrom, & Kanouse, Changes in the Employment Activities of New Parents, 50 Am. Soc. Rev. 263 (1985).

[122] See, *e.g.*, Chodorow, The Reproduction of Mothering (1978).

with traditional roles given the probability of divorce. Although some women, especially remarried women, seem to take the risk of another divorce into account in making decisions about wage-work versus full- or part-time homemaking, many women (especially women who have never been divorced) seem irrationally confident that divorce will not happen to them.

For all these reasons, as well as the reasons stated earlier, formal equality should not be regarded as the solution to women's problems and should not be too rigidly applied in challenges to sex-based classifications. To date, we have not developed any workable and satisfactory general alternative to formal equality, any alternative which judges would be willing to use and which would effect significant change. The remaining question is whether we should continue to seek another general standard for equality, or substitute therefore, as a solution to women's problems.

It is not feasible to prove an abstract negative: that we cannot possibly imagine a workable satisfactory general standard of equality (or substitute therefore) to replace formal equality and to be applied by judges. That may, however, be the case. I suspect it is, at least for the foreseeable future. Any standard capable of effecting real change would have to be based on a notion of both the desired end and of the appropriate means. If we do not know what equality means, we cannot know where we are going nor how to get there. How, then, can we give judges a standard of equality that will ensure our arrival? Women are not a homogenous group with widely-shared beliefs on these issues. Instead, women are a large group of very different people with vastly different interests and concerns. I suspect that for the foreseeable future, any abstract standard capable of effecting real change would implement one subgroups's notion of equality with the risk that other subgroups would bear most of the cost.

IV. Current Standards, Institutional Concerns, and Change

A. The Constitutional Standard

Even if we could imagine a satisfactory general standard capable of effecting real change, we should be hesitant about adopting it as a constitutional standard to be enforced by judges, at least for the foreseeable future. Judges are, and are likely to remain for the foreseeable future, mostly older, relatively conservative males. They are powerful members of the established order. One cannot realistically expect them to use a general abstract standard to implement much real change in the relative status of women and men. More importantly, as the experience with formal equality suggests, one must worry that an abstract standard will be implemented in ways that will hurt women. Harmful decisions are then enshrined as part of constitutional law and difficult to change.

A flexible constitutional standard, allowing a fair amount of leeway to legislatures—rather than a rigid one like formal equality—is, of course, dangerous. Under a flexible standard, a legislature may enact legislation which expressly discriminates between women and men in a way detrimental to women, and the Constitution would afford no reliable basis for striking the statute. But formal equality illustrates that using an abstract standard to overrule legislation creating distinctions between women and men is also dangerous. Under such a standard, courts can replace standards distinguishing between women and men with sex-neutral standards which worsen the position of many women (especially ordinary mothers and wives), because women and men are not similarly situated.

The current constitional standard, although it has gone a ways towards formal equality, is still fairly flexible. I would suggest that it has gone too far already; we should not push for futher movement towards either strict formal equality for sex-based classifications (analogous to the standard for racial classifications) or for any alternative general standard as a constitutional matter.

I do not mean to suggest that feminists should be content with the current constitutional standard. That standard is seriously flawed, and it may be possible to fashion concrete refinements which make it more effective while retaining some flexibility. We should not, however, expect even a refined constitutional standard to solve all, or even many, of women's problems.

For example, MacKinnon suggests one possible refinement to the current constitutional standard. Women might be better off were the current constitutional standard modified so that, instead of permitting express distinctions between women and men based on reasonable differences, express distinctions would be permitted only when they would pass muster under MacKinnon's inequality standard. Judges would decide whether a distinction between women and men was part of the system subordinating women.[123] One could not expect to see any radical restructuring of society with a standard which would only examine express classifications to see if they contribute to the subordination of women. This refinement might, nevertheless, be better than the current standard; it might be less dangerous to entrust the question of whether an express classification contributes to the subordination of women to judges than for judges to continue to uphold express distinctions based on sex whenever supported by a difference perceived as relevant. Thus, for example, were *Johnson* (the affirmative action case) a constitutional challenge to an affirmative action plan designed to increase the number of women in traditionally male jobs, a court could use a refined equal protection standard to uphold it, because such a plan is much more likely to empower women than it is to contribute to their subordination; the alternative to affirmative action is not sex-neutral treatment but invisible discrimination in favor of men.

Other refinements might be possible. For example, it might be possible to expand equal protection coverage of sex discrimination to include other distinctions which are typically part of the systematic subordination of women though not distinctions expressly between the sexes. Thus, for example, a court could recognize pregnant-nonpregnant as a classification as suspect as male-female, since distinctions based on pregnancy have traditionally been used to subordinate women. A statute like that in *Guerra* (requiring disability leaves for only pregnant persons) could then be challenged under the Equal Protection Clause of the Fourteenth Amendment.

Such a statute should, under the refinement suggested above, pass constitutional muster. The statute would be permissible because not part of the systematic subordination of women. Granted, the statute reinforces stereotypical notions connecting mothers, more than fathers, with small infants. And equality may be difficult,

---

[123]Granted, it is not always easy to distinguish benefits (empowerment) from burdens (disempowerment), and women may be hurt if burdens are judged benefits. In addition, as has been noted repeatedly here, often a policy helps some women and hurts others. On the other hand, as the affirmative action cases illustrate well, it is not always impossible to judge that it is likely that a certain policy benefits more women than it hurts. This standard might work out to be much like that proposed by Suzanna Sherry in Selective Judicial Activism in the Equal Protection Context: Democracy, Distrust, and Deconstruction, 73 Georgetown L. J. 89 (1984) (only disfavored classes should be able to bring equal protection challenges).

perhaps impossible, to achieve as long as only women are the primary caretakers of young infants.[124] The stereotype that mothers care for infants remains, nevertheless, overwhelmingly accurate. Ideally, a statute would provide for temporary leave for any new mother or father. But we do not live in an ideal world. We must choose, for the time being in California at least, between letting employers deny all employees short-term disability leaves and requiring that employers give workers disabled by pregnancy up to four months disability leave. Women—who are, after all, the only parents temporarily out of commission because of the onset of parenthood and who are primarily responsible for the care and feeding of newborns in the vast majority of relationships[125]—are less dependent on men under the California statute than they would be under employer policies such as those of Cal Fed. A major part of the systematic subordination of women has consisted of giving them few options other than relying on men for financial security after having children. This statute empowers women by facilitating the combination of motherhood and wage work.

I would not, however, expect even an improved Fourtheenth Amendment standard to offer a remedy whenever women are, in fact, subordinated by a rule, policy, or practice.

B. THE TITLE VII STANDARD: *JOHNSON* AND *GUERRA*

Title VII should also be interpreted as a fairly flexible standard, allowing for some distinctions on the basis of sex in at least some instances, as in both *Johnson* and *Guerra*.

In *Johnson*, the question was whether an employer's voluntary affirmative action plan—which took sex into account in promoting Joyce to a position previously held only by men—was a form of sex discrimination barred by Title VII.[126] Had the Court never

[124]Several feminists have suggested that as long as women are the primary caretakers of young children, we will have difficulty relating to women as individuals. See, *e.g.*, Chodorow, The Reproduction of Mothering (1978); Dinnerstein, The Mermaid and the Minotaur (1976).

[125]See, *e.g.*, Gilbert, Men in Dual Career Couples: The Current Realities and Future Prospects 60–90 (1985); Pleck, Men's Family Work: Three Perspectives and Some New Data, 28 Family Coordinator 481 (1979), reprinted in Work and Family (Voydandor ed. 1984).

[126]Although the defendant was a public employer, Johnson did not use the Fourteenth Amendment to challenge the affirmative action plan. Perhaps he did not use equal protection because, in the context of sex, an equal protection challenge might have been even weaker

decided an affirmative action case, this would have been a difficult question of statutory construction.[127] Justice Brennan was, however, able to rely on *Steelworkers v. Weber*[128] in writing the opinion of the Court upholding Joyce's promotion as a permissible form of affirmative action.

Justice Brennan began by specifying the three *Weber* criteria for a permissible voluntary affirmative action plan. The plan must (i) remedy a " 'manifest imbalance' that reflect[s] underrepresentation of women in 'traditionally segregated job categories' ";[129] (ii) not trammel "the rights of male employees or create[] an absolute bar to their advancement";[130] and (iii) be "intended to *attain* a balanced work force, not to maintain one."[131] Justice Brennan found the first requirement satisfied because women were underrepresented at the Agency in those areas in which " 'women have not been traditionally employed in significant numbers.' "[132] Specifically, he noted that none of the 238 skilled craft positions was held by a woman and that " '[a] plethora of proof is hardly necessary to show that women are generally underrepresented in such positions and that strong social pressures weigh against their participation."[133] (In *Weber*, in contrast, five out of 273 skilled craft positions had been held by Blacks at Kaiser's Gramercy plant prior to the affirmative action plan.[134]) Both Blacks and women have traditionally been excluded from skilled crafts. At the end of the World War II, for example,

than the Title VII challenge. *Cf.* Kahn v. Shevin, 416 U.S. 351 (1974) (upholding Florida statute giving property tax preference to widows but not to widowers). Because he did not challenge the Agency's affirmative action plan on equal protection grounds, the Court did not reach the equal protection standard for permissible affirmative action. See 107 S.Ct. at 1449–50 n.6. That standard might, of course, be different for sex and race.

[127] See Meltzer, The *Weber* Case: The Judicial Abrogation of the Antidiscrimination Standard in Employment, 47 U. Chi. L. Rev. 423 (1980).

[128] 443 U.S. 193 (1979).

[129] 107 S.Ct. at 1452, quoting *Weber*, 443 U.S. at 4383.

[130] *Id.* at 1455.

[131] *Id.* at 1456.

[132] *Id.* at 1453.

[133] *Id.* at 1453 & n.12. Justice Scalia would have interpreted *Weber* as allowing affirmative action only as a remedy for an employer's own past discrimination. See *id.* at 1467. He relied heavily on the district court's finding that the Agency had not discriminated on the basis of sex.

[134] 443 U.S. at 198.

many women were fired from traditionally male—and often skilled—jobs to make room for returning soldiers.

Secondly, Justice Brennan found that the plan did not trammel on the rights of male employees because it did not close any employment opportunities categorically to men and because it set only rather modest goals once fully implemented. True, the initial plan created, as a long-term goal, a workforce in which major job classifications mirrored the available work force. But the plan required the formulation of annual short-term goals in light of a number of factors, such as the number of openings during the coming year and the percentage of women and minorities in the local workforce qualified for the position. At the time Joyce was promoted over Johnson in 1980, no annual goal had been established for skilled craft positions. But, as Justice Brennan noted, the Agency's Plan emphasized "that the long-term goals were not to be taken as guides for actual hiring decisions."[135] Instead, "supervisors were to consider a host of practical factors in seeking to meet affirmative action objectives, including the fact that in some job categories women were not qualified in numbers comparable to their representation in the labor force."[136] Graebner, the person who made the decision to promote Joyce over Johnson, testified: "I tried to look at the whole picture, the combination of her qualifications and Mr. Johnson's qualifications, their test scores, their expertise, their background, affirmative action matters, things like that . . . . I believe it was a combination of all those."[137]

Justice Brennan also noted, though in the margin, that the plan had not, in fact, trammelled the rights of male employees. Of the 111 new skilled craft positions filled at the Agency between 1978 and 1982, "105, or almost 95%, went to men."[138] Indeed, when the Agency first set a numerical goal for hiring women into skilled crafts (for the year 1982) that goal was a modest 5.4% of new hires (three out of 55).[139] Certainly the effort to bring women into skilled

[135] 107 S.Ct. at 1454.

[136] *Ibid.*

[137] Quoted at 107 S.Ct. at 1448. In his dissent, Justice Scalia stresses that Johnson would have received the promotion rather than Joyce but for the affirmative action plan. Sex was therefore the determinative factor in this case. *Id.* at 1468. It is true, of course, that under any affirmative action plan having any effect, some decisions will come out differently because of sex or race.

[138] 107 S.Ct. at 1456.

[139] *Ibid.*

crafts in *Johnson* was much more restrained than the effort at issue in *Weber*, where the employer established a skilled-craft training program and filled half the trainee positions with Blacks.

Finally, Justice Brennan discussed whether the Agency's plan was intended to attain a balanced workforce or to maintain one. The plan did not have any explicit termination date; it could have been better drafted. Justice Brennan refused to invalidate the plan for this reason, however, concluding that the absence of an explicit end date was understandable given the Agency's flexible approach which, as the evidence just cited suggests (given its modest goals), was not expected to yield immediate success. Given the glacial "speed" of the plan—under which only three women were, for example, to be among the fifty-five skilled workers hired in 1982—the failure to specify an end date was irrelevant to anything that might happen during this century and entirely understandable.

Although *Johnson* was a fairly straightforward application of *Weber*, it was the first time that the Supreme Court actually upheld an affirmative action plan in the context of sex. As discussed earlier, however, there is little reason to distinguish between *Johnson* and *Weber* in terms of the need for "affirmative" action if women (like Blacks) are ever to enjoy equal employment opportunity. Women, like Blacks, have traditionally been excluded from the skilled crafts and are likely to be significantly underrepresented in the foreseeable future even with affirmative action.[140]

Guerra does not represent quite as straightforward an application of *Weber*. The California statute gave pregnant workers a permanent preference. The Court nevertheless upheld the California statute on a *Weber*-like rationale. Justice Marshall, speaking for the Court, reasoned that Congress, in requiring that employers treat pregnant workers like other workers similar in their ability to do the job, intended to create a floor below which treatment of pregnant workers could not drop, but that Congress did not intend to create a ceiling above which beneficial treatment could not rise.[141] The Cal-

[140]It is often suggested that women do not want traditionally male skilled-craft jobs. The evidence suggests, however, that women are interested in such jobs if they think that such jobs are actually open to them. See, *e.g.*, Walshok, Blue Collar Women (1981).

[141]The ACLU Women's Project had argued that the California statute, like protectionist legislation in an earlier era, would "reinforce[ ] stereotypical attitudes [towards pregnancy and women's biological nature] which threaten women's employment status in subtle but significant ways." Brief of ACLU Women's Project, *et al.*, at 18 and generally at 11–23. Justice Marshall, speaking for the Court, rejected this argument, noting that "unlike pro-

ifornia statute was therefore permissible because it "promotes equal employment opportunity" which was, after all, Congress' purpose in enacting Title VII.[142]

Although the preference permitted for pregnant workers in *Guerra* is permanent, this extension of *Weber*'s rationale[143] is easily justified in the context of sex. *Weber* allows, in order to achieve equality, some preference as long as a minority group is substantially underrepresented in a position from which it has traditionally been excluded. In general, once a minority group successfully integrates a traditionally closed position, it should (we hope) be possible for members of the minority group to continue to enjoy access for a number of reasons.[144] Women face an additional problem, however. It is not just that some jobs have been formally or informally closed to women. Another access problem (inter alia) is that rules and practices have been structured with the expectation that workers would not be new mothers. This problem is not solved simply by hiring women in appropriate numbers. It can only be solved by changing workplace policies and practices so that it is easier for women to combine wage work and reproduction. *Weber* should, therefore, be extended to allow statutes which guarantee pregnant workers their jobs during pregnancy-related disability.

Guerra and *Johnson* suggest two ways in which Title VII's apparently absolute ban on sex discrimination should be construed so as to permit some distinctions based on sex. Perhaps, in the

tective labor legislation prevalent earlier in this century, [the California statute] does not reflect archaic or stereotypical notions about pregnancy and the abilities of pregnant workers" because it covers only the "period of *actual physical disability*." 107 S.Ct. at 694.

[142]*Ibid.* As an alternative ground for decision, Justice Marshall noted that even if Title VII banned leave policies giving preferential treatment to pregnant workers, California employers could obey both Title VII and the California statute by offering leaves to all workers disabled for up to four months.

[143]This is not to suggest that *Guerra* should be labelled an "affirmative action" case. As discussed earlier, "affirmative" action is misleading. In his opinion, Justice Marshall did not to refer to the California statute as a form of affirmative action. Instead, he stressed that the effect of the California policy was to equalize the situation of working women and men since, "by 'taking pregnancy into account,' California's pregnancy disability leave statute allows women, as well as men, to have families without losing their jobs." 107 S.Ct. at 694. *Cf. id.* at 696 ("preferential treatment") (per Stevens, J.).

[144]For example, those hiring will no longer have unconscious expectations that members of the excluded minority group are uninterested in the position or not competent to hold it. In addition, the "old boy" hiring network should be operating to bring in members of the minority group once they are represented in the job in sufficient numbers.

future, additional refinements will also be suggested for Title VII, refinements which will make it a more effective means to achieving equality between the sexes. *Johnson* and *Guerra* might not be sufficient to promote real equality.

Certainly, as of today, the statute—despite the flexibility afforded by *Guerra* and *Johnson*—is inadequate as the solution to women's problems in achieving equality in the wage-labor market. It does not afford any way to challenge much of what needs to be challenged. For example, the statute (like the Constitution) does not provide a means for women to challenge the use of employment requirements and standards which are well adapted to male life-styles and poorly adapted to female life-styles. Nor does it provide a means of challenging the undervaluation of jobs traditionally performed by women.[145]

C. CHANGE THROUGH THE POLITICAL PROCESS

Since it is unlikely that we will be able to imagine one abstract standard capable of providing an effective means for resolving all such problems, much change in the legal system must occur (if it is to occur at all) as a result of legislative change, often piecemeal legislative change. This "solution" will not, however, be easy.

A responsive political process would seem an ideal forum for resolving women's conflicting visions of equality and how to get there. There are other advantages to legislative forums. One can make all kinds of arguments. Effective arguments need not be traditional arguments. Disparate impact arguments can be effective in this setting and need a label no more esoteric than the simple word "fairness." A legislature can choose which of many policies to modify to effect a desired change. Unlike a court, a legislature can choose the appropriate "defendant." Specific legislative reform—such as changing the social security system so that homemakers receive credits in their own accounts for their contributions (based, perhaps, on their husbands' wages)—is often the only way to effect needed changes. Only a legislature will do the kind of detailed tinkering necessary to implement many of the changes needed if the legal system is to be as responsive to women's needs as it is to

[145] See, *e.g.*, Becker, Barriers Facing Women in the Wage-Labor Market and the Need for Additional Remedies: A Reply to Fischel & Lazear, 53 U. Chi. L. Rev. 934, 942–43 (1986).

men's. Many needed changes simply cannot and will not be ordered by a court pursuant to an abstract standard of equality. A final advantage of the legislative forum is that legislatures can experiment with various approaches more easily than courts. It may not always be apparent whether a certain change would be desirable or not. Or a change, desirable at one time, may become obsolete or undesirable at another. It is easier for legislatures than for courts to take different approaches at different times.

Unfortunately, it is not going to be easy to change the status of women through the legislative process, for two major reasons. The first is that the political process itself is not responsive to women, in part because women are not a homogenous group. A number of factors make it difficult for women to operate as a cohesive political force: women are geographically dispersed; women are members of different classes; women identify with male interests because of relationships that are often only temporary; women are still raised to consider the home (rather than the public arena) their special sphere of interest; women still do not enter politics in proportion to their numbers in the population; women tend (more than men) to define themselves in terms of the interests of others (their husbands and children), and may therefore be less likely than other groups to push for their own interests in the legislative arena; women tend to have less time and money (than men) to spend lobbying; legislatures are still predominantly male enclaves and not, one imagines, much easier for individual women to break into, or to effect change within, than the all-male road maintenance gang on which Joyce worked. In addition, many issues of special concern to women are state-law issues, and many state legislatures are very conservative, even hostile, to "women's lib," a label likely to taint any change designed to equalize the status of women and men.

The second major problem is that even when women succeed in effecting legislative change, the new laws will be more or less general and will typically require judicial implementation. Judges may fail fully to implement the desired change. To some extent, this problem can be avoided by careful drafting and detailed legislative history. But, to be effective, the groups interested in change must continue to monitor the situation after the desired legislation is enacted and, when necessary, begin another round of lobbying for additional legislative reform.

Legislative change, especially piecemeal legislative change, is not a miraculous solution. If, however, for the foreseeable future, it is the only solution to many of women's problems with the current legal structure, surely it is better to face squarely that fact and attempt to implement piecemeal legislative change than to continue to strive to implement some vague and abstract standard of equality which will effect too little good and too much harm.

V. Conclusion

To date, we have not discovered any abstract standard of equality (or substitute therefore) with the potential for real change. Formal equality (with and without limited exceptions when there are biological differences)—the leading contender as the general standard—can effect only limited change. It cannot, for example, ensure that jobs are structured so that female workers and male workers are equally able to combine wage work and parenthood. Nor can it ensure that social security, unemployment compensation, and other safety nets are structured so as to provide for women's financial security as well as they provide for men's. Moreover, women, especially ordinary mothers and wives, have been harmed by the changes effected to date by the movement towards formal equality. Further movement in that direction could bring additional harm. Any other satisfactory and workable general standard to be applied by judges is as yet unimagined and likely to be so for the foreseeable future.

Women do not share a single vision of equality or one view of how to get there from here. Women are not a homogenous group with homogenous values, concerns, and interests. Were the legislative process more responsive to women, it would be a good forum for women to resolve their conflicting interests and visions of equality. Unfortunately, it is unresponsive, and certainly far from ideal. Nevertheless, piecemeal legislative change, especially in the area of economic rights, is likely to be more effective in improving the lives of many women than is the development of any abstract standard of equality.

Part V
Economic and Market-Based Perspectives

[11]

COMMENTARIES

AFFIRMATIVE ACTION: FAIR SHAKERS AND SOCIAL ENGINEERS*

*Morris B. Abram***

I. INTRODUCTION

The civil rights movement has turned away from its original principled campaign for equal justice under law to engage in an open contest for social and economic benefits conferred on the basis of race or other classifications previously thought to be invidious. This essay, written from my perspective as an early participant in the civil rights cause, explains my view that this departure, however desirable to some in the short run, violates the basic principles that hold together our heterogeneous society and secure our civil peace. The civil rights movement, by my lights, should turn its attention back to first principles — the zealous regard for equal opportunity and the promotion of color-blind law and social policy — and away from color-conscious remedies that abandon principle and lead us further from a society free of the bane of racial discrimination.

Between the mid-1940s and the mid-1960s, the civil rights movement grew into a broad coalition united by moral principle and a shared vision of an American society without racial discrimination but with equal opportunity for all. The overarching political goal of this movement was equality — an equality to be reached by the elimination of discriminatory barriers that denied the individual the opportunity to exercise his franchise effectively, to compete for housing and employment, and to use public accommodations. Government, civil rights advocates agreed, was responsible for ensuring that each individual had access to all spheres of public activity — social, economic, and political — regardless of race, sex, or ethnic origin.[1] Because this original vision of the civil rights movement was concerned with equality of *opportunity* and a fair shake for individuals, I will label its advocates "fair shakers."[2]

---

* The authors of these Commentaries have not seen drafts of each other's pieces. The Commentary format is not meant to be a debate, but rather is meant to present different perspectives on current issues of public importance.

** Mr. Abram is a partner in the New York law firm of Paul, Weiss, Rifkind, Wharton & Garrison, and is a commissioner of the United States Commission on Civil Rights. He gratefully acknowledges the assistance of Debra Livingston.

[1] Although in this essay I will speak primarily of racial classifications, my views on the use of invidious distinctions as a basis for social policy also extend to gender and ethnic classifications.

[2] I am indebted to Professor James Blumstein of the Vanderbilt University School of Law for suggesting this term.

The fair shakers were soon challenged, however, by a radically different vision of civil rights. During the late 1960s, the civil rights community began to splinter and, certainly by the mid-1970s, much of its leadership had become preoccupied with equality of *results*.[3] Those who focused on this type of equality attributed socioeconomic or political inequalities between minorities and whites, men and women, the disabled and the unimpaired, to discrimination — past and present. Absent discrimination, these result-oriented leaders claimed, all groups would be represented in the institutions and occupations of society roughly in proportion to their representation in the population. These leaders continue to believe that the only way to measure equality is in terms of such representation, and that it is the government's role to bring about proportional representation in short order. Because this new vision of the civil rights movement requires the attainment of predetermined ends, rather than the abolition of barriers to fair participation, I will call its adherents "social engineers."

My early experience in the civil rights movement now leads me to oppose the social engineers. I joined the civil rights coalition in the late 1940s, first as a citizen and then as a lawyer challenging the Georgia county unit electoral system. That system assigned electoral votes to counties disproportionately, so that in the statewide Democratic primaries — equivalent to general elections — individual votes counted less in more populated counties. Thus, the fewer than 1,900 residents of rural Echols County enjoyed two votes, while the 550,000 residents of Atlanta's Fulton County exercised only six. Proponents of this system — the social engineers of that day — justified the departure from an equal franchise on the ground that Echols County voters needed and deserved 96 times the franchise power of Fulton County voters because the rural voters had neither the benefits of Atlanta's good schools, libraries, health services, and communications systems, nor the massed power of the city's voting blocs.

In fact, the Georgia electoral system was the vehicle through which the racist status quo maintained its power. The social engineers were fully aware that blacks in rural areas were too intimidated to vote. By weighting the virtually all-white rural vote more heavily than the

---

[3] In his 1975 Foreword to the *Harvard Law Review*, Professor Paul Brest describes this erosion of consensus in the civil rights coalition. The article, however, neither addresses nor endorses many of the views herein expressed. *See* Brest, *The Supreme Court, 1975 Term — Foreword: In Defense of the Antidiscrimination Principle*, 90 HARV. L. REV. 1, 2–3 (1976) (describing the erosion of the civil rights coalition). I first heard a black college administrator describe the movement in terms other than the principles of equal opportunity, as formulated by Roy Wilkins, Dr. Martin Luther King, Jr., and Hubert H. Humphrey, in the mid-1970s, during my tenure as Chairman of the United Negro College Fund. As Professor Brest describes it, by this time some members of the civil rights coalition had adopted the "independent goal of assuring that no minority racial group [was] — for any reason — appreciably worse off than the rest of society." *Id.* at 2.

mixed white/black city vote, these segregationists contrived to ensure the election of representatives who favored their views. Ultimately, Georgia liberals, supporting a one-man, one-vote approach on fair shake grounds, successfully overturned this system.[4]

Early in my career, I thus learned to view with suspicion the demand that the historical disadvantage of certain groups be remedied in accordance with a substantive notion of justice — a notion entailing departure from equality before the law. The role of government in securing racial justice, I came to believe, is best limited to vigilant concern with equal opportunity, procedural regularity, and fair treatment of the individual. I have not departed from my original fair shake view, but continue to believe that it is in keeping with our legal and political traditions; that the social engineers' advocacy of result-oriented and color-coded group rights is inconsistent with these traditions and violative of other democratic ideals and principles; and that adherence to the fair shake model is most likely to promote true racial equality and enlightened debate over our conceptions of social justice.

II. FAIR SHAKERS AND SOCIAL ENGINEERS

The fair shake principle is part of a long and respected American legal tradition. It was the force underlying the antislavery amendments to the Constitution,[5] the series of laws passed in the wake of the Civil War that afforded protection of contract and property rights,[6] and the guarantees of equality of opportunity in voting, employment, use of public accommodations, and housing in the mid-1960s.[7] It was

[4] *See* Gray v. Sanders, 372 U.S. 368, 381 (1963) (holding that Georgia's county unit system violated the equal protection clause because it accorded the votes of primary electors in some counties less weight than the votes of electors in other counties).

[5] U.S. CONST. amend. XIII (outlawing slavery); *id.* amend. XIV (guaranteeing equal protection of the laws); *id.* amend. XV (guaranteeing the right to vote and explicitly disfavoring classifications based on race).

[6] Act of May 31, 1870, ch. 114, § 16, 16 Stat. 144 (codified as amended at 42 U.S.C. § 1981 (1982)) (securing the right to contract); Act of Apr. 9, 1866, ch. 31, § 1, 14 Stat. 27 (codified as amended at 42 U.S.C. § 1982 (1982)) (guaranteeing property rights). In addition, 42 U.S.C. § 1983 (1982), originally enacted in 1871, provides legal recourse to individuals deprived of rights under color of state law. Act of Apr. 20, 1871, ch. 22, § 1, 17 Stat. 13 (codified as amended at 42 U.S.C. § 1983 (1982)). *See* Brest, *supra* note 3, at 1 (discussing the "anti-discrimination principle" and civil rights legislation).

[7] *See* Voting Rights Act of 1965, Pub. L. No. 89-110, 79 Stat. 445 (codified as amended at 42 U.S.C. §§ 1971, 1973 to 1973bb-1 (1982)); Civil Rights Act of 1964, Pub. L. No. 88-352, 78 Stat. 243 (codified as amended at 42 U.S.C. § 2000a–2000a-6 (1982)) (public accomodations); Civil Rights Act of 1964, Pub. L. No. 88-352, 78 Stat. 243 (codified as amended at 42 U.S.C. § 2000e–2000e-17 (1982)) (equal employment opportunities); Fair Housing Act of 1968, Pub. L. No. 90-284, Title VIII, 82 Stat. 81 (1968) (codified as amended at 42 U.S.C. §§ 3601–3619, 3631 (1982)). Equality of opportunity was the explicit aim of these provisions. *See* 110 CONG.

in accord with fair shake principles that Congress enacted the Voting Rights Act of 1965[8] to stymie the effort of states such as Georgia to devalue the minority franchise — a form of racial preference for whites.

Although the fair shake principle shaped our civil rights laws, it has, from an early date, been challenged by various forms of social engineering. In 1871, for instance, a black friend wrote to former slave Frederick Douglass, then the most prominent black leader in the country, arguing that blacks deserved government appointments based on their numbers. Douglass replied that "equality of numbers has nothing to do with equality of attainments."[9] In a stunning rebuke to the concept of proportional representation on the basis of race, Douglass wrote:

> The mulattoes, on a solid census basis, ought to have so many offices, the blacks so many, and the whites so many, the Germans so many, the Irish so many, and other classes and nationalities should have offices according to their respective numbers. . . . Upon your statistical principle, the colored people of the United States ought, therefore, not only to hold one-eighth of all the offices in the country, but they should own one-eighth of all the property, and pay one-eighth of all the taxes of the country. Equal in numbers, they should, of course, be equal in everything else. They should constitute one-eighth of the poets, statesmen, scholars, authors, and philosophers of the country.[10]

Because groups — black, white, Hispanic, male, and female — do not necessarily have the same distribution of, among other characteristics, skills, interest, motivation, and age, a fair shake system may not produce proportional representation across occupations and professions, and certainly not at any given time. This uneven distribution, however, is not necessarily the result of discrimination.[11]

REC. 12,723 (1964) (statement of Sen. Humphrey that title VII of the Civil Rights Act of 1964 "does not require an employer to achieve any sort of racial balance in his work force by giving preferential treatment to any individual or group"); *id.* at 8921–22 (statement of Sen. Williams that quota hiring would be just as unlawful as other forms of discrimination). *See also* N. GLAZER, AFFIRMATIVE DISCRIMINATION: ETHNIC INEQUALITY AND PUBLIC POLICY 43–45 (1975) (discussing the equal opportunity impetus behind the Civil Rights Act of 1964).

[8] 42 U.S.C. §§ 1971, 1973–1973bb-1 (1982).

[9] Letter from Frederick Douglass to Major Martin Delany (Aug. 31, 1871), *reprinted in* 4 P. FONER, THE LIFE AND WRITINGS OF FREDERICK DOUGLASS: RECONSTRUCTION AND AFTER 281 (1955).

[10] *Id.* at 280.

[11] Social engineers ignore that it simply takes time for various groups to make their way fully into all sectors of society. For example, as recently as the mid-1960s, few Jews could be found in this country's executive suites. Discrimination is only part of the explanation. Beginning with different kinds of abilities and skills, all the major ethnic groups staked out areas of advancement for themselves (the Italians in construction, for example, the Irish on the police

Thomas Sowell has shown through comparative studies of ethnic group performance that discrimination alone cannot explain these ethnic groups' varying levels of achievement. Groups such as the Japanese, Chinese, and West Indian blacks have fared very well in American society despite racial bias against these groups.[12]

Moreover, although it is true that concern for qualifications has sometimes masked a purposeful intent to exclude individuals on the basis of race or other invidious criteria, the mere fact that some meritocratic devices have the result of excluding proportionally higher numbers of minorities does not in itself demonstrate that minorities are not getting a fair shake. And the fair shake principle, unlike the norm of proportional representation, is perfectly consistent with our meritocratic view of the relevant differences between individuals — a view through which our society rewards the individual for attainment and avoids patronage and spoils systems.

Yet many of those who opposed the use of social engineering to perpetuate segregation now depart from the fair shake model and actively advocate social engineering to achieve proportional representation. They now insist on a presumption that unequal results are due to intentional discrimination.[13] For them, the franchise is not a right to participate equally in the electoral process but a right to the election of a "fair share" of minority representatives.[14] Although no civil rights leader has dared to suggest weighted ballots for blacks, it is now part of civil rights gospel that blacks must not only vote but that we must draw district lines to ensure that blacks are elected. To

---

force and in local politics, Jews in law and medicine). Members of such groups may require several generations to position themselves for more diverse and powerful roles.

Nor does discrimination fully explain the fact that certain groups continue to cluster in certain occupations; other factors, such as age, also influence group performance. The 1970 census revealed that the average age of the Jewish population was 46; the Puerto Rican, 18. *See* T. SOWELL, THE ECONOMICS AND POLITICS OF RACE: AN INTERNATIONAL PERSPECTIVE 190 (1983). Obviously, there will be proportionally more Jewish than Puerto Rican representatives among professionals. By insisting on even rough proportional representation, we may well be working against our own best interests as a society.

[12] *See* T. SOWELL, *supra* note 11.

[13] For example, if test results show minority candidates passing at less than 80 percent of the nonminority passing rate, then the test is presumed discriminatory. *See* Uniform Guidelines on Employee Selection Procedures (1978), 29 C.F.R. § 1607.3 (1984) ("[p]rocedure having adverse impact constitutes discrimination unless justified"); *id.* § 1607.4 (1984) ("A selection ratio for any race . . . which is less than four-fifths of the rate for the group with the highest rate will generally be regarded . . . as evidence of adverse impact . . . ."). These provisions apply to persons subject to title VII of the Civil Rights Act of 1964, 42 U.S.C. § 2000e-2 (1982); Executive Order 11,246, 3 C.F.R. 339 (1964–65), *reprinted in* 42 U.S.C. § 2000e app. at 28–31 (1982) (order of President Johnson calling for "affirmative action"), or other equal employment opportunity requirements of federal law. *See* 29 C.F.R. § 1607.2(D) (1985).

[14] *See* Blumstein, *Defining and Proving Race Discrimination: Perspectives on the Purpose vs. Results Approach from the Voting Rights Act*, 69 VA. L. REV. 633, 650–52 (1983) (discussing the result-oriented view in the voting arena).

my mind, these "piece-of-the-action" concerns[15] depart from the civil rights movement's earlier advocacy of fair participation and return us to the spoils system that the early movement worked so hard to displace.[16]

But today's social engineers, dissatisfied with the results of the fair shake model, invoke a new conception of justice. In their view, justice is less an individual's claim to equality before the law — an idea at the heart of our liberal tradition — than a particular distribution of social, economic, and political power among groups. This new conception of justice necessarily repudiates the ideal of the rule of law — a law that "would treat people equally, but . . . not seek to make them equal."[17] And to achieve this newly announced goal of group justice, the social engineers proclaim that it is necessary to abandon color-blindness.[18]

Judge Damon Keith of the Court of Appeals for the Sixth Circuit has made just such a claim. "[W]e cannot have *representativeness* in America today if we are in any sense of the word *colorblind*," he writes, and "we cannot have *justice* in this country without a strong measure of *representativeness*."[19] A civil rights attorney, commenting on the dismal results achieved by certain minorities on a 1980 federal civil service examination, equates representativeness with justice in a similar fashion. "[S]uppose that 100 whites and 100 blacks applied for 50 jobs. If there were no adverse impact in the examining procedure used to select for these jobs," he suggests, "one would expect to see 25 blacks and 25 whites hired."[20]

These social engineers call their plan for allocating social goods by race "affirmative action." But the term as they use it departs radically from the original intent of affirmative action — to give minorities a fair shake. Executive Order 11,246,[21] for example, far from calling

---

15 *Id.* at 650.

16 Many individual civil rights advocates and civil rights groups, including the Leadership Conference for Civil Rights and the NAACP, have abandoned fair shake objectives in areas other than voting. *See, e.g.*, Belton, *Discrimination and Affirmative Action: An Analysis of Competing Theories of Equality and* Weber, 59 N.C.L. REV. 531, 541 (1981) (discussing a "view of equality" by which "jobs are to be distributed so that the relative economic position of blacks as a group is improved"). *See generally* D. BELL, *Ethnicity and Social Change*, in THE WINDING PASSAGE: ESSAYS AND SOCIOLOGICAL JOURNEYS, 1960–1980, at 184, 188–89 (1980) (discussing redefinition of the value of equality in contemporary political debate).

17 D. BELL, *Liberalism in the Postindustrial Society*, in THE WINDING PASSAGE: ESSAYS AND SOCIOLOGICAL JOURNEYS 1960–1980, at 228, 230–231 (1980) (discussing Hayek).

18 *See, e.g.*, Fiss, *Groups and the Equal Protection Clause*, 5 PHIL. & PUB. AFF. 107, 129–56 (1976) (discussing the limitations of the "antidiscrimination principle" and advocating the "group-disadvantaging principle" in interpretation of the equal protection clause).

19 Keith, *Should Color Blindness and Representativeness Be a Part of American Justice?*, 26 HOW. L.J. 1, 6 (1983) (emphasis in original).

20 Letter from Richard Seymour, Lawyers' Committee for Civil Rights Under Law, to Morris B. Abram (Feb. 13, 1981) (on file at the Harvard Law School Library).

21 3 C.F.R. 339 (1964–65), *reprinted in* 42 U.S.C. § 2000e app. at 28–31 (1983). This order,

the merit system into question, attempted only to eliminate the institutional and informational barriers that stand in the way of the minority individual's ability to compete *equally* with others for jobs and promotions.[22] Vice President Hubert H. Humphrey, who chaired the committee that drafted that order, was a committed fair shaker whose own Equal Employment Opportunity bill of 1964 prescribed affirmative action and at the same time insisted on color-blind equal opportunity.[23]

I believe that the social engineers' result-oriented conception of racial justice is both destructive of true racial equality and potentially harmful to society. Although the social engineers concede that their color-conscious and group-based approach may produce some injustice, they argue that extreme measures are at least temporarily necessary to eliminate discrimination. In my view, however, even the laudable goal of ending racial discrimination cannot justify the adoption of means incompatible with other ends of justice.

Government constantly requires adjustments between ends and means. Crime, for instance, is a problem we desperately need to curb; but not at the expense of due process. We cannot afford to change the character of our society simply in order to achieve desired results more quickly. And, as the following discussion demonstrates, the departure from color-blind decision-making in law and social policy entails a number of serious long-term costs.

The social engineers' approach to affirmative action is without support in our Constitution and civil rights laws. These revisionists would have us read the equal protection clause of the Constitution and the racially neutral language of civil rights legislation so as to grant preferences for groups that they designate as "subjugated." They advance this argument in the face of the plain English of the text and

---

issued in 1965, required government agencies and private contractors to undertake "affirmative action" and "insure that applicants are employed, and that employees are treated during employment, without regard to their race, creed, color, or national origin." For a discussion of the original understanding of affirmative action and its subsequent reinterpretation, see R. MORGAN, DISABLING AMERICA 145–47 (1984).

[22] As Professor William W. Van Alstyne has written:

> This [plan implemented under Exec. Order No. 11,246] is affirmative action (i.e., action of a positive character, discriminating against none, dispreferring no one, involving neither quotas nor queues nor targets nor presumptions of what is the 'right' mix or 'proper' share of each according to race). It has nothing to do with such a philosophy. . . . It seeks the better protection of *each* person from racial discrimination that might otherwise occur, whether in a white-owned enterprise against blacks, in a black-owned enterprise against whites, or whatever. It takes a strong national policy seriously. It is action undertaken consciously (and sometimes at considerable expense) to vindicate more effectively a commitment opposed to racial discrimination in *all* its forms.

U.S. COMM'N ON CIVIL RIGHTS, 1 SELECTED AFFIRMATIVE ACTION TOPICS IN EMPLOYMENT AND BUSINESS SET-ASIDES 180, 182 (1985) (footnote omitted) (testimony of William W. Van Alstyne before the United States Commission on Civil Rights on Mar. 6, 1985).

[23] S. 1937, 88th Cong., 2d Sess. (1964).

a legislative history that contradicts their contentions.[24] As Justice Douglas has observed:

> The Equal Protection Clause commands the elimination of racial barriers, not their creation in order to satisfy our theory as to how society ought to be organized . . . . So far as race is concerned, *any* state-sponsored preference to one race over another . . . is in my view "invidious" and violative of the Equal Protection Clause.[25]

And Professor Alexander Bickel agreed:

> The lesson of the great decisions of the Supreme Court and the lesson of contemporary history have been the same for at least a generation: discrimination on the basis of race is illegal, immoral, unconstitutional, inherently wrong, and destructive of democratic society . . . . Having found support in the Constitution for equality, [proponents of racial preferences] now claim support for inequality under the same Constitution.[26]

Without doing violence to the principles of equality before the law and neutral decisionmaking, we simply cannot interpret our laws to support both color-blindness for some citizens and color-consciousness for others.[27]

One possible, more practical, consequence of this social engineering is the decline of occupational and professional standards. For example, in 1981, the federal civil service exam for over 100 entry-level positions was suspended, because minorities were not passing it in sufficient proportions.[28] In order to make the minority passing rate on the written examination for Foreign Service Officers "relatively similar" to that for nonminorities, the Foreign Service Officers Examination Board simply adds 500 minority "near-passers" to the pool of candidates who actually passed and declares the whole group — "near-passers" and passers alike — qualified to go on to the next stage.[29] Similarly, Department of Labor Revised Order Number 4, providing that "[n]either minority nor female employees should be

---

[24] *See* N. GLAZER, *supra* note 7, at 44–45; R. MORGAN, *supra* note 21, at 144–45. *But see* Hooks, Letter to the Editor, N.Y. Times, Nov. 27, 1985, at A22, col. 3. Hooks argues that the Constitution has never been color-blind, offering as proof its legitimation of slavery. It is a curious irony indeed for a civil rights leader to cite the now thoroughly repudiated compromise on slavery as legal precedent for current proposals.

[25] DeFunis v. Odegaard, 416 U.S. 312, 342 (1972) (Douglas, J., dissenting) (emphasis added).

[26] A. BICKEL, THE MORALITY OF CONSENT 133 (1975).

[27] *See* Cohen, *Naked Racial Preference*, COMMENTARY, Mar. 1986, at 24, 30 (criticizing "group-think" and group preferential systems on the ground that rights inhere not in groups, but in individuals); *cf.* Shelley v. Kraemer, 334 U.S. 1, 22 (1948) ("The rights created by the first section of the Fourteenth Amendment are, by its terms, guaranteed to the individual.").

[28] *See* Luevano v. Campbell, 93 F.R.D. 68, 80–81 (D.D.C. 1981).

[29] Telephone interview with Frontis B. Wiggins, Executive Director, Board of Examiners for the Foreign Service, U.S. Dep't of State (Oct. 10, 1985).

required to possess higher qualifications than those of the lowest qualified incumbent,"[30] creates pressure on government contractors to hire candidates who are not the best available. The social engineers thus defy the existing distribution of skills and abilities — whether naturally present or socially developed — in order to achieve their objective.

Indeed, the social engineers' vision of affirmative action is, for all intents and purposes, a quota system. Though they usually repudiate the idea of "quotas" and insist on characterizing their preferred remedies as "goals and timetables," the effects of numerous enforcement actions and lawsuits brought by government agencies and civil rights groups belie the social engineers' characterization.[31] These actions have effectively transformed goals into quotas by putting the burden on the employer to rebut the presumption of discrimination if the employer fails to meet its minority hiring goals. Failure to meet the goals — even if established solely by reference to population proportionality — raises a presumption of discrimination that the hapless employer can only overturn after great effort, expense, and public embarrassment.

Moreover, even beyond the practical effects of legal presumptions, there is ultimately little theoretical difference between the goals and timetables the social engineers favor, and the quotas they purport to eschew. For to what end are these goals and timetables established if not to be achieved? And what is their basis unless it be that justice requires the allocation of social goods according to race?

Several civil rights policymakers have noted with dismay that, despite their good intentions, affirmative action has degenerated into a spoils system among competing racial and ethnic groups. Thus, Laurence Silberman, President Nixon's Under Secretary of Labor and the legal strategist who transformed the government's contract-compliance affirmative action approach from color-blind to color-conscious, today acknowledges that under Department of Labor Revised Order Number 4, a statistical imbalance is legally tantamount to a finding of discrimination, even without proof of intent.[32] Silberman concedes that the adoption of numerical standards "led ineluctably to the very quotas, guaranteeing equal results, that we initially wished to avoid."[33] And Senator Daniel Patrick Moynihan has wondered in amazement:

---

[30] 41 C.F.R. § 60-2.24(f)(5) (1984) (regulating government prime contractors and subcontractors who meet certain size standards and other criteria).

[31] *See* N. GLAZER, *supra* note 7, at 33-76 (discussing the shift from "equal opportunity" to "statistical parity" in employment).

[32] *See* Silberman, *The Road to Racial Quotas*, Wall St. J., Aug. 11, 1977, at 14, col. 6. Of course, many employers will thus adopt proportional representation as a norm in hiring to avoid litigation. *See* N. GLAZER, *supra* note 7, at 58-59.

[33] Silberman, *supra* note 32. One small company in Kansas, upon failing to meet the

> Who in the executive branch fifteen years ago would have dreamed the day would come when the federal courts would require a census in which all employees and judicial officers be classified by "race/national origin groups" including the sub-group "Arabic" and "Hebrew"? This was just the sort of thing we assumed we were working against.[34]

The social engineers' approach also fails to confront the problem of *who decides* what groups are sufficiently disadvantaged to deserve special treatment. They offer no mechanism for neutral decisionmaking on this critical issue. America is a highly pluralistic and heterogeneous society that has had to expand continuously in order to accommodate different elements; many discrete groups have suffered discrimination here. Consequently, a major problem with addressing discrimination through race-conscious laws is the balancing of historical experiences. How and by whom shall the varying grievances of different groups be weighed and judged in order to decide what varying levels of compensation society should pay?

In the absence of any neutral decisionmaking mechanisms, the attempt to end discrimination through color-conscious remedies must inevitably degenerate into a crude political struggle between groups seeking favored status. Once we have abandoned the principles of fair procedure, equal opportunity, and individual rights in favor of the advancement of a particular group, we have opened wide the door to future abuses of all kinds. Bayard Rustin recently commented upon the charge of discriminatory results that blacks and Hispanics leveled at the New York City police sergeant's exam, an exam members of these groups had helped to devise:[35]

> This approach [of setting aside test scores simply because of disproportionate impact] says to blacks and Hispanics that you don't necessarily have to qualify to be included. Furthermore, if you have enough political pressure in New York City to get away with that, then what's going to happen 20 years from now in California when it is predominantly Hispanic? And then the Hispanics will say "we're

---

Executive Order 11,246 requirement that 12.7% of its truck drivers be minorities and 6.9% of its employees in five job categories be female, was told: "United Bridge Company, Inc. will recruit and hire qualified minorities and females until such time as the required utilization goals have been met. Should no qualified minorities and females be available, the company will document its efforts to meet its goals for the trades." Letter from Betty Robinson, Kansas City Area Director, Office of Federal Contract Compliance Programs, Employment Standards Admin., U.S. Dep't of Labor, to Keith Beach, President, United Bridge Co. (Aug. 12, 1985) (on file at the Harvard Law School Library). Government directives to employers subject to Executive Order 11,246 thus effectively treat statistical goals as presumptive quotas.

[34] Moynihan, *State vs. Academe*, HARPER'S, Dec. 1980, at 31, 32.

[35] New York City has chosen not to base its hiring solely on the test, but to accept quotas, promoting some 200 candidates who failed the examination. *See* N.Y. Times, Nov. 19, 1985, at B3, col. 1.

> very sorry but not enough Hispanics passed the test" so blacks and whites who passed have to go in another line now and wait to get called. Or what's going to happen when women, who far outnumber men in our society, begin to play this game.[36]

Hubert H. Humphrey, one of the pioneers of color-blind affirmative action, sounded a similar cautionary note:

> [O]ur standard of judgment in the last analysis is not some group's power . . . but an *equal* opportunity for *persons*.
>
> Do you want a society that is nothing but an endless power struggle among organized groups? Do you want a society where there is no place for the independent individual? I don't.[37]

What the social engineers fail to perceive is that societies that depart from color-blind, neutral decisionmaking do so at their peril. The history of societies that have adopted this approach in order to reach substantive social goals more quickly has been a history not of liberation but of crippling oppression.[38] As Professor Bickel warned, "[t]he history of the racial quota is a history of subjugation, not beneficence. . . . A quota is a divider of society, a creator of castes, and it is all the worse for its racial base, especially in a society desperately striving for an equality that will make race irrelevant."[39]

Further, the social engineers invite us to view people as statistics; they submerge personality, effort, and character under the blanket concerns of race, sex and ethnicity. In an already divided society, this approach results in a new set of classifications: those who got where they are by merit; those who were leveraged into position by race or gender preferences; those who do not owe their position to such engineering but are viewed as the recipients of preferences by others (and themselves) and are thus stigmatized;[40] and finally those who originally earned their position without any favoritism but were displaced solely because of race, gender or ethnicity. In such a divided system, no one really wins.

Indeed, the social engineers' approach exacerbates divisions within society by implicitly assuming that white males — even the millions who have never finished high school — are the undeserving benefi-

---

[36] *An Interview with Bayard Rustin*, NEW PERSPECTIVES, Winter 1985, at 27, 31.

[37] H. HUMPHREY, BEYOND CIVIL RIGHTS: A NEW DAY FOR EQUALITY 182 (1968) (emphasis in original).

[38] Professor Brest notes that "most societies in which power is formally allocated among racial and national groups are strikingly oppressive, unequal and unstable." *See* Brest, *supra* note 3, at 50.

[39] A. BICKEL, *supra* note 26, at 133.

[40] New York City Police Commissioner Benjamin Ward has asserted that New York City's legally mandated quota system for promotions to police sergeant is "bad for morale," more for black and Hispanic officers than for whites, because "it does make minorities appear to be second-class citizens." N.Y. Times, Nov. 25, 1985, at B3, col. 5.

ciaries of special privileges at the expense of all others.[41] This simplistic division of our complex society into white males and their victims was the hallmark of the United States Commission on Civil Rights when it was dominated by the social engineers. In a 1980 report on affirmative action, the Commission described its view of the American system as one that "now routinely bestows privileges, favors and advantages on white males and imposes disadvantages and penalties on minorities and women."[42] In this view, the civil rights laws are a weapon for wringing from white males the fruits of their exploitation and redistributing these fruits to all other sectors of society. Such an approach is doomed to widen and perpetuate the social divisions it purports to remedy.

Perhaps the most ironic weakness of the social engineers' redistributive approach is that it fails to help those particular members of disadvantaged groups who are most in need of assistance. Blanket orders which blindly benefit groups defined by race, sex or ethnicity — especially when many members of such groups are prospering nicely[43] — are an extremely crude and costly solution for social problems. While civil rights lobbyists frequently bolster their charge of continuing discrimination by pointing to the existence of the black underclass,[44] many of their proposals can hardly have the effect of helping the millions of ghetto teenagers who lack the most basic entry level skills. Indeed, in a recent interview, Harvard sociologist Nathan Glazer indicated that, in his opinion, group-based affirmative action has done "just about nothing" to aid the progress of black Americans.[45]

III. Toward the Future

The civil rights movement has scored resounding victories and worked remarkable changes in American society through its commitment to principles of equal opportunity, fair treatment of the individ-

---

[41] Justice Potter Stewart wrote in refutation of this claim that "[n]o race . . . has a monopoly on social, educational, or economic disadvantage." Fullilove v. Klutznick, 448 U.S. 448, 529–30 (1980) (Stewart, J., dissenting). He also noted that "in 1978, 83.4% of persons over the age of 25 who had not completed high school were 'white,' . . . and in 1977, 79.0% of households with annual incomes of less than $5,000 were 'white.'" *Id.* at 530 n.11 (citations omitted).

[42] U.S. Comm'n on Civil Rights, Affirmative Action in the 1980s: Dismantling the Process of Discrimination 2 (1981).

[43] For example, William R. Beer, a professor of sociology at Brooklyn College, notes that at his school, black West Indian students are taking advantage of racially designed programs even though black West Indians as a group demonstrate a rate of professionalism higher than many other ethnic groups. *See* Beer, *A View from the Trenches*, The New Republic, Nov. 18, 1985, at 17, 17–19.

[44] *See, e.g.*, Hooks, *supra* note 24.

[45] *An Interview with Nathan Glazer*, New Perspectives, Fall 1985, at 27, 28.

ual, and color-blindness. As Bayard Rustin remarked in a recent interview, the period between 1954 and 1968:

> was, perhaps, the most revolutionary period of any country in the world with regard to the achievement of justice for any minority group. In fact, in most of the world during that period, conditions worsened for many minorities. Racism was increasing in England. In the newly independent African countries, tribal hostilities were increasing. Ours was a most unique situation.[46]

The movement, to continue its record of success in uniting the American people behind the moral and legal principles at the heart of our democratic and liberal traditions, should redirect its energies toward eliminating racial discrimination and toward ensuring that *all* Americans, without regard to race, sex or ethnicity, are fairly equipped to compete for individual advancement in every arena.

We have the tools to achieve these goals. We have, for example, strict laws against intentional discrimination. The courts have broad remedial powers to eliminate such discrimination, including the authority to jail recalcitrant violators of the civil rights laws for contempt of court orders. The civil rights movement should press for the use of the courts' powers in a manner consistent with the fair shake principle.[47]

Similarly, despite the mixed record of recent years, we as a society are capable of devising creative social and economic initiatives to aid the truly needy. We can target job training and remedial education programs to all individuals who need them, without regard to race, sex, or ethnicity. In this way we can address past inequities without

---

[46] *An Interview with Bayard Rustin*, *supra* note 36, at 27.

[47] If the purpose of civil rights enforcement litigation is to stop discrimination, it is remarkable to me that civil rights attorneys do not press for jailing and firing discriminators; rather, thay demand goals, timetables, and quotas. Kilgo v. Bowman Transp., Inc., 576 F. Supp. 600 (N.D. Ga. 1984), however, demonstrates what courts can do by enforcing the law without departing from the fair shake principle. In that case, the court found that the defendant had discriminated against women in over-the-road truck hires. The court's order:

> demand[ed] that defendant take aggressive and determined steps to seek out and recruit qualified women as [over-the-road] drivers. Reliance on the 'old-boy' network is no longer acceptable. Those women who applied for positions and those who would have applied had they not been discouraged by the attitude of defendant are entitled to the adoption of a plan that will affirmatively seek out those women who did not have access to these employment opportunities, will actively recruit those overlooked, and will provide remedial action in the form of training and assistance where needed.

Id. at 601. The court retained jurisdiction "in order to keep a close watch on compliance by defendant to ensure that the terms imposed [would] be enforced and obeyed diligently." *Id.* The court refused, however, to impose the goals or quotas sought by the plaintiffs, stating that "[p]referential treatment on the grounds of sex, by means of a quota, is destructive of self respect and merely substitutes one form of discrimination for another." *Id.*; *cf.* *An Interview with Nathan Glazer*, *supra* note 45, at 29 (asserting that problems of group discrimination can be addressed through the law of individual rights).

abandoning the fair shake principle, and we can avoid perpetuating social divisions.

Although the mechanisms for change in our political system are far from perfect, this system has proven itself capable of correcting abuses and injustices with a minimum of violence and without curtailing freedom. The civil rights movement triumphed in this system because it united men and women in a just and principled cause and appealed to conservatives and liberals alike. It was, after all, a Republican President who appointed many of the judges who broke the back of white supremacy in the South.[48] This broad-based support finally created an atmosphere in which all Americans (some more willingly than others, of course) acknowledged the inevitable justice of equality of opportunity.

Unfortunately, a different set of attitudes prevails among many of today's civil rights activists. A large segment of the civil rights lobby has turned from the struggle for equality in civil and political rights to the advocacy of redistribution of economic and social rights. And it has made support for the redistribution of these rights a precondition for being part of the movement; anyone who does not support this redistribution is labeled a racist, a bigot, or even a klansman. Some leaders have tried to read many of the original participants, including myself, out of the civil rights movement. More significantly, they are losing the support of the moderate Americans, both black and white, who sustained the movement from the outset.[49]

This struggle has unfortunately repeated itself within the United States Commission on Civil Rights. The two members of the Commission remaining as holdovers from its social engineering heyday, Mary Frances Berry and Blandina Cardenas Ramirez, have gone so far as to assert that "[c]ivil rights laws were not passed to give civil rights protection to *all* Americans, as the majority of this Commission seems to believe."[50] Their legal analysis is patently false. But Commissioners Berry and Ramirez are right about one thing — the present majority of the Commission, subscribing to the fair shake principle, *does* believe that the civil rights laws and the equal protection clause apply to all Americans. Indeed, the Commission has not retreated from its historic commitment to civil rights objectives, as its critics claim; rather, the Commission has returned to the principles of color-

---

[48] *See generally* J. BASS, UNLIKELY HEROES (1981) (discussing President Eisenhower's appointments to the Court of Appeals for the Fifth Circuit).

[49] *See* Lilla, *What is the Civic Interest?*, THE PUB. INTEREST, Fall 1985, at 64, 76 ("[T]he civil rights movement . . . acquired moral legitimacy in the public eye when it made the case for equality in civic terms (and lost much of it with the social language of redistribution and affirmative action).").

[50] U.S. COMM'N ON CIVIL RIGHTS, TOWARD AN UNDERSTANDING OF *STOTTS* 63 (1985) (statements of Comm'rs Blandina Cardenas Ramirez and Mary Frances Berry).

blindness (including a system of color-blind affirmative action), nondiscrimination, and equality of opportunity — the principles that stand behind our civil rights laws.[51]

The fair shakers maintain that there is a crucial difference between civil and political rights on the one hand and social and economic rights on the other. The American system guarantees civil and political rights — but it does not guarantee those social and economic rights described in the United Nations' Universal Declaration of Human Rights.[52] Guaranteed social and economic rights not only may sharply conflict with civil and political rights, as is the case in many socialist societies, but may also fail to produce high standards of living. Despite its inevitable inequities, the free market system — also a traditional element of American society — has provided most of our citizens with living standards that are among the highest in the world. As fair shakers see it, removing all barriers to the exercise of civil and political rights and to an individual's ability to participate in the free market system is the best possible way to promote justice. In any case, eliminating discrimination and providing a safety net for the truly needy constitute the limits of what the *law* in the American system can do, *if that system is to remain free*.

My participation in the civil rights struggle has shaped my deepest moral and political beliefs. Because the cause of civil rights has meant so much to me, I now feel compelled to register my strong dissent, unpopular though it may be, from what I see as the current direction of the movement. The mantle has now passed to those who believe in enforced equality of results, guaranteed social and economic rights for particular groups, and redistribution of income and jobs. Certainly we can debate ideas such as these in our free society. I ask only that the social engineers be open and candid about their vision for America, and desist from camouflaging their redistributive goals behind the label of "civil rights."[53] Civil rights belong to all Americans; they are too important to be captured by a set of special interest groups.

---

[51] *See id.* at 56–58 (statement of U.S. Comm'n on Civil Rights).

[52] G.A. Res. 217, U.N. Doc. A/810, at 71 (1948). This declaration asserts that "[e]veryone has the right to work, to free choice of employment," and "to just and favourable remuneration ensuring for himself and his family an existence worthy of human dignity." *Id.* at 75.

[53] For example, equal pay for women who do the same or equal work as men is a valid civil rights claim, recognized by law since the enactment of the Equal Pay Act of 1963. But the idea of equal pay for work done by women that is decreed to be of comparable worth to that done by men is a debatable social and economic policy to redistribute income — a concept foreign to the meaning of civil rights as developed in the American tradition. Comparable worth should stand or fall as a political issue, to be decided in political forums, and with regard to the changing social and economic position of women. *See, e.g.*, N.Y. Times, Mar. 19, 1986, at C1, col. 1 (recording "'historic milestone'" that women now hold the majority of professional jobs in the United States (quoting speech of Samuel M. Ehrenhalt, commissioner of New York region of the Bureau of Labor Statistics)).

[12]

EXCHANGE

An Economic Analysis of Sex Discrimination Laws

Richard A. Posner†

There is now a substantial economic literature on discrimination. The literature focuses on racial discrimination but has implications for other forms of discrimination as well, including sex discrimination.[1] There is also a substantial economic literature on the extent and causes of disparities between men and women in wages, employment level, and other measures of professional attainment.[2] At the intersection of the two literatures one finds a number of studies of the economics of sex discrimination in employment.[3] There is also—it goes without saying—an enormous legal literature on sex discrimination law, again focused on employment. But there is relatively little writing on sex discrimination *law* from an eco-

---

† Judge, United States Court of Appeals for the Seventh Circuit; Senior Lecturer, The University of Chicago Law School. The comments of Mary Becker, Dennis Black, John Donohue, Lewis Kaplow, Cass Sunstein, and participants in the law and economics workshop at Harvard Law School, and the research assistance of Seung C. Kim, are gratefully acknowledged.

[1] See my book, Richard A. Posner, *Economic Analysis of Law* ch 27 (Little, Brown, 3d ed 1986), for an introduction to the economics of discrimination with references to some of the leading studies.

[2] See, for example, Gary S. Becker, *Human Capital, Effort, and the Sexual Division of Labor*, 3 J Labor Econ S33 (1985); Victor R. Fuchs, *Women's Quest for Economic Equality* (Harvard, 1988); Morley Gunderson, *Male-Female Wage Differentials and Policy Responses*, 27 J Econ Lit 46 (1989) (a thorough review of the literature); and a particularly accessible, as well as up-to-date, introduction to the literature, *Symposium: Women in the Labor Market*, 3 J Econ Perspectives 3 (1989).

[3] For a recent review of this literature, see Janice Fanning Madden, *The Persistence of Pay Differentials: The Economics of Sex Discrimination*, in Laurie Larwood, Ann H. Stromberg, and Barbara A. Gutek, eds, 1 *Women and Work: An Annual Review* 76 (Sage, 1985); and for an illustrative study see William T. Bielby and James N. Baron, *Sex Segregation Within Occupations*, 76 Am Econ Rev Papers & Proc 43 (May 1986).

nomic standpoint.[4] My objective in this paper is to examine the economic properties of the laws and doctrines relating to sex discrimination in employment. Although I am unable on the basis of existing information and analysis to estimate either the efficiency or the distributive effects of these laws and doctrines, I believe it is a plausible hypothesis—no stronger statement is possible—that sex discrimination law has not increased, and it may even have reduced, the aggregate welfare of women. Underlying this conclusion are four general arguments supported by smatterings of empirical evidence: (1) the sheer variety of practices that cluster together under the law's label "sex discrimination"; (2) the distributive complexities arising from interdependent positive utilities and joint consumption between men and women; (3) the pervasive conflicts of interest between different groups of women (for example, nonworking housewives and unmarried working women); and (4) the probably substantial, and growing, costs of administering sex discrimination laws. Arguments (2) and (3) are related[5] and together help explain why women, despite being a majority of voters, may not have succeeded in obtaining *effective* antidiscrimination legislation.

---

[4] What there is focuses mainly but not exclusively on (1) comparable worth, (2) eliminating sex distinctions in longevity tables used for computing annuities and life insurance premiums, and (3) the use of econometric evidence in sex discrimination litigation. The following list, although by no means complete, is an extensive sample of the literature: Arthur P. Dempster, *Employment Discrimination and Statistical Science*, 3 Stat Sci 149 (1988) (and comments following by other scholars); Robert L. Moore, *Are Male/Female Earnings Differentials Related to Life-Expectancy-Caused Pension Cost Differences?*, 25 Econ Inquiry 389 (1987); Samuel A. Rea, Jr., *The Market Response to the Elimination of Sex-Based Annuities*, 54 S Econ J 55 (1987); Daniel R. Fischel and Edward P. Lazear, *Comparable Worth and Discrimination in Labor Markets*, 53 U Chi L Rev 891 (1986); George E. Johnson and Gary R. Solon, *The Attainment of Pay Equity Between the Sexes by Legal Means: An Economic Analysis*, 20 U Mich J L Ref 183 (1986); Jonathan S. Leonard, *The Impact of Affirmative Action on Employment*, 2 J Labor Econ 439 (1984); Andrea H. Beller, *Occupational Segregation by Sex: Determinants and Changes*, 17 J Human Resources 371 (1982); George J. Benston, *The Economics of Gender Discrimination in Employee Fringe Benefits:* Manhart *Revisited*, 49 U Chi L Rev 489 (1982); Cotton M. Lindsay and Charles A. Shanor, County of Washington v. Gunther*: Economic and Legal Considerations for Resolving Sex-Based Wage Discrimination Cases*, 1 S Ct Econ Rev 185 (1982); Janet C. Hunt and Paul H. Rubin, *The Economics of the Women's Movement*, 35 Pub Choice 287 (1980); Butler D. Shaffer, *Some Economic Considerations in Sex Discrimination Cases*, 26 Labor L J 290 (1975); and Gunderson, 27 J Econ Lit at 53-68 (cited in note 2), and studies cited therein.

[5] This is noted briefly in Hunt and Rubin, 35 Pub Choice at 292-94 (cited in note 4), who find that sex discrimination legislation is more likely to be enacted the lower the marriage rate, since single women tend to gain more from such legislation than married ones.

I. The Legal Background[6]

A complex set of laws regulates sex discrimination in employment; its complexity may be an important reason why more economists have not studied sex discrimination law, as distinct from the phenomenon of sex discrimination. I begin with the federal statutes and judicial interpretation of them. The Equal Pay Act of 1963[7] requires employers to pay their employees the same wages for "equal work" regardless of sex. Equal work is narrowly defined, and unequal pay for equal work is permitted if the employer can show that the inequality is due to something other than the sex of the employees. Title VII of the Civil Rights Act of 1964[8] forbids sex discrimination in employment—in hiring, firing, promotion, and working conditions. Discrimination in pay is also included, so Title VII overlaps with the Equal Pay Act. "Discrimination" as used in Title VII essentially means disadvantage, but the employer can defend against a charge of sex discrimination by showing that the discrimination is necessary to its business. This is the "BFOQ" (bona fide occupational qualification) defense.[9] A standard example is refusing to consider male actors for female acting parts. Finally, Executive Order No 11246, as amended in 1967,[10] forbids discrimination on the basis of sex by federal contractors, under pain of loss of their contracts.

Title VII was amended in 1972 to extend its coverage to public employers and small private employers and to enlarge the powers of the Equal Employment Opportunity Commission (EEOC). In the Pregnancy Discrimination Act of 1978,[11] Congress, repudiating the Supreme Court's decision in *General Electric Co. v Gilbert*,[12] further amended Title VII to forbid discrimination based on pregnancy, with the result that an employer's refusal to classify pregnancy as a disability or to include the medical costs of pregnancy in a health benefits plan for employees is now unlawful discrimination. And the courts have interpreted Title VII discrimination to

---

[6] See generally Charles A. Sullivan, Michael J. Zimmer and Richard F. Richards, 1 *Employment Discrimination* ch 8 (Little, Brown, 2d ed 1988); see also index references to "sex discrimination" in volume 3 of this up-to-date, comprehensive, but one-sided treatise.

[7] 29 USC § 206(d) (1982).

[8] 42 USC § 2000e (1982).

[9] 42 USC § 2000e-2(e) (1982).

[10] Executive Order 11246, 3 CFR 1964-65 Comp 339 (1965), as amended 3 CFR 1966-70 Comp 684 (1967).

[11] 42 USC § 2000e(k) (1982).

[12] 429 US 125 (1976).

include sexual harassment.[13] Although Title VII has been held not to require employers to adopt "comparable worth,"[14] several states have required it of their public employers.[15] California has in addition required its private as well as its public employers to give female workers maternity leave; recently the Supreme Court held that such a requirement does not violate the Pregnancy Discrimination Act.[16]

The Equal Protection and Due Process Clauses have been held to forbid various forms of governmental sex discrimination, both state and federal. For example, the Equal Protection Clause has been interpreted to require the "degendering" of pension plans for public employees and to forbid differentiating spousal pension and fringe benefits on the basis of the employee's sex.[17] It can be taken for granted that laws excluding women from particular occupations, with narrow exceptions such as jobs involving military combat, are unconstitutional, and almost all such laws have in fact been repealed. On the other hand, in the *Feeney* decision the Supreme Court rejected a complaint by women that a state's policy of giving veterans a preference in public employment denied women equal protection because only a minuscule number of women are veterans.[18]

This hasty and oversimplified summary of a complicated legal pattern will make specialists in employment discrimination law wince, but it is sufficient for my economic analysis. Later, however, I shall have to consider a few of the details of the evidentiary and remedial scheme created by Title VII.

II. Some Economics of Sex Discrimination

Before the economic effects of sex discrimination law can be evaluated, one must get a grip on the economics of sex discrimination. This section lists the basic assumptions of the analysis, then examines the causes of sex discrimination, and finally makes a stab at estimating what our labor markets would be like today without any sex discrimination laws.

---

[13] See *Meritor Savings Bank v Vinson*, 477 US 57 (1986).

[14] See, for example, *AFSCME v Washington*, 770 F2d 1401 (9th Cir 1985); *American Nurses Ass'n v Illinois*, 783 F2d 716 (7th Cir 1986).

[15] See, for example, Iowa Code § 602.1401 (1987); and Minn Stat § 471.991-.999 (1984).

[16] See *California Federal Savings & Loan Ass'n v Guerra*, 479 US 272 (1987).

[17] See, for example, *Los Angeles Dept. of Water and Power v Manhart*, 435 US 702 (1978).

[18] See *Personnel Administrator v Feeney*, 442 US 256 (1979).

A. Assumptions

I assume that all people—men and women alike—are rational in the usual economic sense. That is, they consistently act to maximize the excess of their private benefits over their private costs. It is consistent with this model, as we shall see, that some—or, for that matter, many or even most—men are misogynistic, exploitative, or ill-informed. I further assume that even if there is no discrimination against women, women will, on average, invest less than men in human capital, both general and job-specific. The qualification that it is only *on average* that women will invest less is important. The characteristics that are related to productive employment are unevenly distributed within each sex, so that even if the means of the distributions differ, the distributions themselves overlap, with the result that many women invest more in their human capital than many men invest in their own human capital. Nevertheless, the *average* woman expects to take more time out of the work force than the average man to raise children,[19] which makes the expected lifetime earnings of the average woman, and hence return to human capital, lower than those of the average man. The average woman will therefore invest less in her human capital, causing her wage to be lower than the average man's, since a part of every wage is repayment of the worker's investment in human capital.

It is possible that the greater propensity of women than men to take time out of the labor force is itself a product of sex discrimination, but I am skeptical of that proposition—I think child-rearing is an area where nature dominates culture—and I do not accept it for purposes of my analysis. However, I will not try to defend this assumption. It is also possible that the propensity will in time disappear, but again I am skeptical, and for the same reason. Even if it does eventually disappear, there can be little doubt that women's *current* wages are depressed because today's working women did not invest heavily in their human capital when they

[19] It is illustrative that in 1984, women who interrupted their work for more than six months gave "family reasons" as the cause of interruption in 40.7 percent of the cases; men mentioned family reasons in only 0.3 percent of the cases. Sara E. Rix, ed, *The American Woman 1988-89: A Status Report* 379 table 16 (Norton, 1988). In 1986, of all women with children up to the age of six, only a third were employed full time. Id at 375 fig 11. The Bureau of Labor Statistics estimated that in 1985 white males had a "worklife expectancy" at birth of 39.8 years, compared to 29.7 years for white females. U.S. Department of Commerce, Bureau of the Census, *Statistical Abstract of the United States* 364 table 606 (GPO, 108th ed 1988). In 1987, of married persons aged 20-24, 95.7 percent of the men were working outside the home but only 67.4 percent of the women. Id at 373 table 622.

were young. Table 7-3 in the 1987 *Economic Report of the President*[20] shows, for example, that while in 1968 only 27.5 percent of young white women expected to be working when they were 35 years old, in 1985 more than 70 percent of these women *were* working. The table also shows that, by 1979, young women had changed their expectations: almost exactly the same percentage of young women expected to be working at age 35 as were in fact working at that age in 1985. Since women now have more realistic expectations concerning their labor force participation, we can expect them to invest more heavily in their human capital and therefore earn higher wages in the future. Thus, although the fact that the average woman earns substantially less than the average man is often taken to be prima facie evidence of sex discrimination, it is not, and in any case the differential is likely to decline for reasons unrelated to sex discrimination law.

Finally, I assume that men's and women's utility functions are interdependent, and specifically that women derive a benefit from an increase in the income of a husband or other male relative (son, father, brother, etc.), even if no part of the increased income is consumed by the woman. This qualification is necessary because of the importance of joint consumption in the household. Normally if one spouse's income rises, the other spouse will benefit because so much of the consumption in a household is joint. We thus have separate interdependencies: the "pure" interdependency that results from altruism (the satisfaction that most people experience from an increase in the happiness of a close relative), and the interdependency resulting from joint consumption within the household. For simplicity's sake I shall confine my attention to the interdependencies between wife and husband and ignore other relatives.

It is important to note that the interdependencies between spouses often persist after divorce or the death of a spouse. If a widow's or divorcée's standard of living is a function of her husband's income, increases in that income will increase the wife's welfare. This increase will persist even after a woman is widowed, since her standard of living remains tied to her husband's former income; similarly, a divorced woman's standard of living often remains tied to her former husband's current income. Thus the large percentage of women who are unmarried exaggerates the economic independence of women from men. The vast majority of women marry at some time during their lives, and this is all that is neces-

[20] Council of Economic Advisors, *Economic Report of the President* 215 table 7-3 (GPO, 1987).

sary to establish a pervasive economic interdependence between the sexes.[21]

The relationship between majority and minority groups is not characterized by interdependence of either the joint-consumption or altruistic varieties, if only because racial intermarriage remains rare.[22] Interdependence gives the economics of sex discrimination a distinctive cast. To take the extreme case, suppose that all workers were married and that all consumption within the household were joint. Then discrimination against women in the labor force would be compensated for completely in the home, for while wives' wages would be lower than in a nondiscriminatory regime, wives would benefit dollar for dollar from the correspondingly higher wages of their husbands. Of course these assumptions are too strong, and they ignore the fact a woman's earning power may affect her influence over household expenditure decisions,[23] but they point to an important difference between sex discrimination and the other forms of discrimination with which sex discrimination is often, but perhaps facilely, linked.

B. The Meaning and the Causes of Sex Discrimination

To avoid building a normative assessment into the word "discrimination," I shall follow the lead of Title VII and define sex discrimination as treating a woman differently from a man because she is a woman, without worrying at the definitional stage about whether the discrimination is invidious on the one hand, or justified or even beneficent on the other.[24] This definition is more prob-

---

[21] In 1986, of all white women 15 years and older, 20.9 percent had never been married, 56.4 percent were married and living with their husband, 2.7 percent were married but not living with their husband, 11.8 percent were widowed, and 8.2 percent were divorced. Rix, *The American Woman* at 354-55 fig 2 (cited in note 19). For black women, the figures are 36.4 percent, 32.4 percent, 8.9 percent, 11.6 percent, and 10.8 percent, respectively. Id. In 1986, among all women 55-64 years old, only 3.9 percent had never been married. *Statistical Abstract of the United States* at 40 table 49 (cited in note 19). Of course, this figure may decline since fewer women are marrying nowadays. On the changing demographics of American women, see Heidi I. Hartmann, *Changes in Women's Economic and Family Roles in Post-World War II United States*, in Lourdes Benería and Catharine R. Stimpson, eds, *Women, Households, and the Economy* 33 (Rutgers, 1987).

[22] In 1986, out of 51,704,000 married couples in the U.S., only 181,000 (0.35 percent) consisted of a white and a black. *Statistical Abstract of the United States* at 40 table 50 (cited in note 19).

[23] This depends in part, however, on the structure of family and divorce law, which determines the wife's entitlements in her husband's income.

[24] Although there is discrimination against men, I shall ignore it. A more important phenomenon that I do discuss is policy that is designed to combat discrimination against women and has the incidental effect of harming men.

lematic than it may appear to be, because it leaves unresolved the question whether it is discriminatory (in a sense pertinent to public policy) to treat a woman differently because of a characteristic that no men but only some women have, such as the capacity to bear children. The Supreme Court in *Gilbert* held that such differentiation was not discriminatory,[25] but the Court was overruled by Congress. I shall follow Congress's approach and assume that discrimination based on pregnancy is a form of sex discrimination—which is not to say, of course, that it necessarily is inefficient.

When discrimination is defined as broadly as I am defining it, the causes are multifarious. Here are the main ones, in (roughly) descending order of invidiousness. The discussion is confined to employment discrimination, the focus of this paper.

Misogyny. By this I mean an elemental distaste on the part of men for associating with women at work, not founded on any notions of productivity or efficiency. The misogynist, as I am using the word, is not someone misinformed about either the average or individual quality of female employees—he just doesn't like them in the workplace, maybe because he has traditional views of "the woman's place." Misogyny may appear to be a taste like any other, and therefore ethically neutral from an economic standpoint—a given. But this is not so clear. Insofar as it is expressed in hostile behavior, it may be more akin to a taste for assault than to a taste for chocolate ice cream. Perhaps misogyny is in between a harmless taste and an actual externality like rape or theft. But the precise status in economics of misogyny is not important to my analysis. To further complicate the picture I note that a disinclination to associate with women in the workplace need not reflect a dislike of women and could in fact reflect something nearly opposite to dislike—a desire, not necessarily insincere, to protect women from the hardships of the workplace.

Physical or Psychological Aggression. A straightforward case of exploitation, more clearly akin to theft or rape than to misogynistic refusal to accept women workers, is sexual harassment—conduct designed to elicit sexual favors from women against their will. This phenomenon is related to the "conduit" type of discrimination discussed below, because ordinarily it is not the employer himself (more often, itself) who harasses women, but male employees. The employer merely doesn't want to go to the

[25] 429 US at 133-46.

expense of preventing harassment by its employees. More precisely, the required expense would exceed the potential benefit to the employer from not having to compensate female employees for the disutility of being sexually harassed.

Ignorance About the Average Working Woman. A man who is not a misogynist may nevertheless labor under serious misconceptions concerning the abilities of working women. This is especially likely if there are few women in the workplaces with which the man is familiar. This ignorance may be rational, but that is not to say that it is admirable. Indeed, it may be rational for the entire market to be misinformed, because of the well-known externality problems with information. Whom would it pay to develop information about the working qualities of women in general? How would the social benefits of such information be translated into private benefits for the producer of the information? The pioneer in hiring women in a particular segment of the work force may simply be paving the way for his competitors to learn from his mistakes. Notice that in an era of minimum wage (and equal pay) laws, a woman cannot compensate her employer for taking a chance with an unknown quantity by accepting a lower wage. However, the minimum wage is not an important factor in professional and other well-paid employment or in periods such as the present when the minimum wage is far below the average wage.

Monopsony. Married women have high relocation costs when the husband earns more than the wife, as is usually the case. In areas where competition for labor among local employers is weak, these employers may be able to set a monopsonistic wage for female employees, so long as such women represent a large fraction of the female labor force or the employer is able to discriminate among women, paying less to those he believes would have difficulty relocating. Monopsony wage-setting is exploitation of female labor in a straightforward economic sense, although it is less invidious than certain other forms of discrimination because it does not rest on any premise that women are inferior workers to men.

Conduit of Discrimination. In many cases of discrimination the discriminator is merely reflecting the tastes of customers, employees, government agencies, or others with whom the discriminator has a commercial or regulatory relationship. If male employees don't like working with women, or if customers don't like female workers, the employer will perceive these aversions as additional costs of hiring women and will hire fewer of them, or will pay the women a lower wage to compensate the employer for their greater cost.

Statistical Discrimination. Even if employers and their male employees and customers have no discriminatory feelings *and* are perfectly well informed concerning the average characteristics of women in the various types of job, it may be rational for employers to discriminate against women because of the information costs of distinguishing a particular female employee from the average female employee. For example, the average woman may be physically or emotionally less suited for combat than the average man, even though the two distributions overlap. If it is too costly for the Department of Defense to identify women who are as well suited for combat as the minimally qualified male recruit, the Department may rationally, noninvidiously, decide to exclude *all* women from combat jobs.

Differentiation Infinitely Costly. Discussions of statistical discrimination normally assume that, while it would not be efficient to ascertain individual qualifications, it would be *possible* to do so—that is, the cost would not be infinite. But in the case of women, the cost sometimes *would* be infinite, because the uncertainty is inherent and ineradicable. For example, when an employer hires two 21-year-old workers, one male and one female, he knows that the former, being male, has a shorter life expectancy than the latter, but he doesn't know and ordinarily couldn't discover whether *this* female will outlive *this* male. Similarly, he knows that the man is likely to take less sick leave than the woman,[26] but this is just betting on the averages—he doesn't know whether these two workers will track the *average* experience of male and female workers. If differentiations are to be made, they must be made on a statistical basis.

Three things should be noted about my list of the causes of sex discrimination. The first is that it describes a world without sex discrimination laws; for example, we shall see that the problem of "rational ignorance" would be less serious if there were no Equal Pay Act. The second thing to note is the importance of information costs. Half the causes I have identified are based on such costs: ignorance of the average qualities of women workers, statistical discrimination, and inherent uncertainty. Third, only half the causes reflect market failure in a clear economic sense: monopsonistic exploitation of higher relocation costs, aggression against women, and ignorance of the average qualities of women due to

---

[26] In 1985, the average female worker lost six days of work because of illness or injury; the average male, 4.8 days. *Statistical Abstract of the United States* at 105 table 166 (cited in note 19).

information externalities. The other forms of discrimination are, or at least may be, efficient—which does not necessarily make them good from an ethical standpoint. Misogyny, for example, is a morally unattractive trait, but from an economic standpoint it *may* be no different in character from having an aversion to cabbage or rutabaga, though then again it may.

Of the three causes of sex discrimination in employment that clearly reflect a market failure, one has little or no contemporary importance: ignorance of the average qualities of women workers. So many women are employed in so many and diverse fields that few employers can be ignorant any longer concerning women's abilities as workers. The time when the law might have done something to eliminate this information externality is long gone. Another cause, high relocation costs conferring monopsony power on employers, has probably never been very important; I do not recall having seen it mentioned in the literature on female employment. The third cause, sexual harassment in the workplace, probably is largely self-correcting. As more and more women are employed, the employer's self-interest in curbing intrigue and harassment, which lower productivity, grows apace.

I conclude that there is no strong theoretical reason to believe that sex discrimination, even if not prohibited by law, would be a substantial source of inefficiency in American labor markets today. If I am correct, then the costs of administering that law will be largely a deadweight loss, from an economic standpoint. That does not make the law immoral or unjust, but any deadweight losses from law enforcement must be considered in deciding whether a particular law or set of laws furthers the public interest.

C. Discrimination Trends, Ex Law

How much sex discrimination of any sort could we expect today if there were no sex discrimination laws or other pertinent governmental interventions (for example, subsidies for day care)? Some, surely; for we have just seen that some, perhaps most, forms of differential treatment are efficient. But sex discrimination would probably be declining, perhaps steeply, even in the absence of any laws against sex discrimination.

The engine of decline is the increasing participation of women in the work force. No one thinks that discrimination would keep all women from working, any more than racial discrimination keeps blacks from working. The main effect would be to depress the wages women were paid, lower their fringe benefits, and alter the distribution of women among jobs. There would, however, be some effect on the total number of women employed—more so, indeed, than on the number (as distinct from wages and working conditions) of blacks employed. This is because the elasticity of the supply of labor is higher for women than for men, a phenomenon especially pronounced when a higher percentage of women were married and raising children than is the case today. A married woman, especially with children at home, is in an economic sense "employed" in the home, and her household income will be less if she works in the market. Therefore a small reduction in market wages may keep many women out of the labor market, and conversely a small increase in those wages may draw many women into the labor market.

Women began working in large numbers long before sex discrimination in the workplace was widely criticized, let alone prohibited, and certainly long before sex discrimination ceased to be rampant (some believe it is still rampant). The percentage of the labor force that is female has grown steadily since 1947,[27] and the primary causes of this growth could not be anti-discrimination laws. The other causes of the increased female participation in the work force are by now well-known. With the decline in infant and child mortality, with improved techniques of contraception, and with the advent of inexpensive household labor-saving devices, women spent less time pregnant and raising children and doing household chores, so their opportunity costs of working in the market fell. At the same time, work was becoming less strenuous, in part because the entrance of large numbers of women into the work force increased the demand for services, hence for service workers, who do lighter work than industrial workers. So the demand for female workers rose, and hence their wages rose. As their wages rose, the opportunity costs of pregnancy and child raising rose too, reinforcing the trend toward fewer pregnancies. This in turn reduced the benefits of marriage to both men and women. The improvement in female job opportunities also reduced women's dependence on men. For both reasons, marriage rates fell and divorce rates soared: the former trend increased women's incentive to invest in their human capital, because they were working more; the latter increased the pressure on women to work, both as insurance against divorce and to maintain their standard of living after divorce.[28]

[27] See Fuchs, *Women's Quest for Economic Equality* at 12 fig 2.1 (cited in note 2); Rix, *The American Woman* at 366 table 9 (cited in note 19).

[28] See references in note 2; see also Fredricka Pickford Santos, *The Economics of Mari-*

Assuming that the increased female participation in the labor force is largely independent of the laws forbidding sex discrimination, one may ask what effect the increase is likely to have had on the incidence of sex discrimination (still *ex* law). It should reduce that incidence. First, as more women enter the work force, misconceptions concerning the average qualities of female workers should become less common. Of course, if the misconception consisted of exaggerated those qualities, women would be worse off by the elimination of the misconception. But the likelier misconception about a class of people not commonly encountered in the work force is that they are not as good as the existing workers, and this misconception would tend to dissipate with the entry of large numbers of that class into all kinds of jobs.

Second, as more wives and daughters enter the work force, we can expect misogyny to decline. Men who love their wives and daughters and empathize with their wives' and daughters' efforts to find work and to cope with misogynistic coworkers or supervisors are less likely to be misogynists in the workplace than if they lacked this family experience. Third, as more women enter the work force misogynistic employers are placed at a competitive disadvantage: their labor costs are higher than nonmisogynists' because their employment decisions are constrained by misogyny. Fourth, with more and more women workers, sexual harassment becomes more costly. Apart from the impact on productivity noted earlier, a larger fraction of the work force is offended by it, so the total compensating differential that the employer must pay its female employees rises.

As discrimination falls, we can also expect the wage gap between men and women to fall. Another factor working in this direction is the growing value of women's work relative to men's as physical strength becomes a less important labor asset. The declining wage gap among current workers may be masked, however, by an influx of new women workers, since less experienced workers are paid less than more experienced ones.[29] Thus a reduction in discrimination can actually *lower* average female wages, rather than, as one would expect, raise them.

Because economic analysis predicts that sex discrimination

---

tal Status, in Cynthia B. Lloyd, ed, *Sex, Discrimination, and the Division of Labor* 244 (Columbia, 1975).

[29] See James P. Smith and Michael Ward, *Women in the Labor Force and in the Family*, 3 J Econ Perspectives 9 (1989); June O'Neill, *The Trend in the Male-Female Wage Gap in the United States*, 3 J Labor Econ S91 (1985).

would have declined and the wage gap between men and women narrowed since 1963, when the first federal sex discrimination law—the Equal Pay Act—was passed, these trends cannot automatically be attributed, even in part, to law. Law may have had little or even nothing to do with improvements in women's status in the labor force. This suggestion may seem paradoxical: if the law penalizes certain conduct, the economist's "Law of Demand" implies that the conduct will become less frequent. This assumes, however, that the law is effective, and it may not be, for reasons to be examined in the next section.

The effect of sex discrimination laws on discrimination is ultimately an empirical question—and a difficult one. As argued above, discrimination would have declined without those laws—indeed *was* declining, before those laws were enacted—and it is difficult to isolate the effect of one variable from the others pushing in this direction. Victor Fuchs remarks:

> It is easy enough to find particular instances where these laws opened up jobs that were previously closed to women or resulted in a realignment of women's pay scales, but it is difficult to see any major effects on broad trends in women's wages or employment. The Equal Pay laws were passed in 1963 and 1964 [Fuchs is referring to the Equal Pay Act of 1963 and to Title VII], but fifteen years later the women/men wage ratio was unchanged at about 60 percent. It was only in the 1980s that the ratio started to climb, but these were the 'Reagan years'—a period not noted for vigorous enforcement of antidiscrimination and affirmative action legislation. With regard to women's employment, the rate of increase prior to the legislation was as rapid as after the laws were passed.[30]

This is painting with a pretty broad brush; other scholars have found that sex discrimination law *has* helped to break down barriers to the employment of women in traditionally male occupations.[31] Here is Morley Gunderson's cautious summary: "Clearly, the evidence does *not* unambiguously indicate that the EEO [Equal Employment Opportunity] initiatives of Title VII were a resounding success, although there is some evidence of a positive

---

[30] Fuchs, *Women's Quest for Economic Equality* at 27 (cited in note 2).

[31] See, for example, Beller, 17 J Human Resources at 388-90 (cited in note 4); Leonard, 2 J Labor Econ at 459 (cited in note 4); James V. Koch and John F. Chizmar, Jr., *Sex Discrimination and Affirmative Action in Faculty Salaries*, 14 Econ Inquiry 16 (1976). There is, however, contrary evidence besides Fuchs's. See, for example, Smith and Ward, 3 J Econ Perspectives at 15-16 (cited in note 29).

effect on the earnings and occupational position of women. There is also some evidence that the legislation is more effective when it is strictly enforced and when the economy is expanding."[32] There is no evidence of *large* effects[33]—and we shall see that sex discrimination law may not have improved the net *welfare* of women even if it has somewhat reduced the amount of sex discrimination.

Moreover, the costs of administering the sex discrimination laws must be factored into any attempt at an overall evaluation of those laws. No laws are costless to enforce, not even ineffectual ones. The burdens that sex discrimination laws place on the courts are substantial, and are growing even as discrimination is declining. John Donohue and Peter Siegelman have shown in a recent paper that declining discrimination may be associated with a rise rather than (as one might expect) a fall in the number of cases brought, because as more women are employed in better-paying jobs the gains from suit rise, and because women working side by side with men have a benchmark for proving unequal treatment.[34]

III. An Economic Examination of Specific Laws and Doctrines

Having sketched the basic sex discrimination laws and the basic economics of sex discrimination, I am prepared to analyze those laws from an economic standpoint. The highly tentative character of the analysis should be self-evident.

A. Equal Pay Act

At first glance this is the least problematic of the sex discrimination laws. If work is really equal (and the Act has, as I have

---

[32] Gunderson, 27 J Econ Lit at 61 (cited in note 2) (emphasis in original). For a similar appraisal of Executive Order 11246, see id at 63-64. Notice in regard to the last sentence in the quoted passage that the more the government impedes the efficiency of labor markets the less likely the economy is to be expanding.

[33] See also Cynthia B. Lloyd and Beth T. Niemi, *The Economics of Sex Differentials* 304-07 (Columbia, 1979). But there is an exception: Leonard, 2 J Labor Econ at 459 (cited in note 4), found that the executive order had increased the demand for white women by employers subject to the order by 3.5 percent relative to the demand for white men, but the demand for black women by 11 percent relative to the demand for white women. The reason may be that hiring a black woman enables the employer to make progress toward two affirmative action goals at once.

[34] See John J. Donohue and Peter Siegelman, *The Changing Nature of Employment Discrimination Litigation* (Am Bar Found, unpublished April 1989). Their discussion covers racial as well as sexual discrimination, and reaches the same conclusion: as blacks move into higher-paid positions and work in integrated jobs, the net expected gains from filing employment discrimination suits rise.

noted, been narrowly construed in this regard), then it would seem that unequal pay could not be efficient—it must reflect price discrimination. But it is more correct to say that it *may* reflect price discrimination. If the employer is able to pay its female employees a monopsonistic wage because of their high relocation costs, then it is discriminating in the economic (price discrimination) sense. Another possibility, however, is that while the work is nominally equal, the men do it better—are more productive—on average than the women, yet the employer is unable to prove this "factor other than sex" (which, as mentioned above, is a defense under the Act).

A third possibility is that the employer pays its female employees less because the employer's male owners, male managers, or male employees have an aversion to women in the workplace. Then the Act will operate as a tax on misogyny. Such a tax is not objectionable in itself, but we must consider the employer's likely reaction. He (the male pronoun being particularly appropriate in this context) will try to reduce the tax, by hiring fewer female employees, creating working conditions that are not attractive to them, or—the simplest strategy—placing women in jobs where they are doing work that is not equal to men's work. These would not be feasible strategies if Title VII were totally effective, for virtually all the measures that an employer might take to avoid the mandate of the Equal Pay Act would be a form of sex discrimination forbidden in principle by Title VII. Even substituting computers for secretaries might violate Title VII if the employer's motive were to reduce the number of *female* employees. But if we assume, realistically, that the Equal Pay Act is easier to enforce than Title VII, then the Act will result in fewer women being employed even if the average wage of those women who are employed is higher.[35] And the average wage may not be higher if the employer responds to the Act by shifting women to jobs where their

[35] For some evidence that the Act (and its foreign counterparts) has had this effect, see Isabel V. Sawhill, *The Economics of Discrimination Against Women: Some New Findings*, 8 J Human Resources 383, 393-94 (1973); Shaffer, 26 Labor L J at 294 n 10 (cited in note 4); Jacob Mincer, *Intercountry Comparisons of Labor Force Trends and of Related Developments: An Overview*, 3 J Labor Econ S1, S30 (1985); Maureen Pike, *The Employment Response to Equal Pay Legislation*, 37 Oxford Econ Papers 304, 316 (1985). It has even been argued that the covert purpose of the Equal Pay Act was to help men compete with lower-paid women. See Nancy S. Barrett, *Women in the Job Market: Occupations, Earnings, and Career Opportunities*, in Ralph E. Smith, ed, *The Subtle Revolution* 31, 55 (Urban Institute, 1979), citing Jo Freeman, *The Legal Basis of the Sexual Caste System*, 5 Valp U L Rev 213, 226-27 (1971). A comparable effect on blacks was found in a study of state fair-employment laws. See William M. Landes, *The Economics of Fair Employment Laws*, 76 J Pol Econ 507, 544-45 (1968).

work is not equal to men's. In addition, the Act will prevent women from attempting to overcome any information barriers to hiring them that may exist by offering to work for a lower wage than men.

Even if the employer does not try to avoid or evade the Equal Pay Act there may be a disemployment effect. The Act operates as a payroll tax, and the tax is higher the more workers employed. The employer may raise price in an effort to offset the tax, but unless he faces a totally inelastic demand curve—which no seller does—the increase in his price will reduce the demand for his goods, leading him to curtail his output and hence inputs, including labor inputs. He will employ fewer women as well as fewer men.

Another point is that the employer may avoid the Act *unconsciously*. He may simply observe that a department which happens to employ many women now has higher costs and lower profits than it used to, and may decide to reduce the size of the department without knowing or caring *why* its profit margin has fallen. All he needs to know is that his capital will command a higher return in an alternative use.

To the extent that unequal pay reflects differences in productivity that the equal work standard of the Act is insufficiently sensitive to pick up, the Act's distributive consequences are complicated by the interdependencies between men and women noted earlier in this article. If employers must pay a single wage to workers of different average productivity (i.e., men and women), that wage will be lower than that which the more productive workers would command but for the prohibition of "discrimination." So both men (by hypothesis, the more productive group) and their wives will be worse off. By the same token, the husbands of married women whose pay rises as a result of the Equal Pay Act will be better off. But if women are more altruistic on average than men,[36] the increase in men's welfare resulting from an increase in their wives' income will be less than the decrease in women's welfare resulting from a decline in their husbands' income, even if the increase and decrease are identical in dollar terms. In addition, since more married men than married women work, the transfer of welfare to married women will be larger. When this consideration is added to the Equal Pay Act's potential disemployment effect on women, it becomes a plausible speculation (again, no stronger con-

[36] See generally, Carol Gilligan, *In a Different Voice: Psychological Theory and Women's Development* (Harvard, 1982).

clusion is possible) that the Act makes women as a group worse off.

B. Title VII

Two different types of Title VII sex discrimination cases should be distinguished. In a *disparate impact* case, the employee challenges a practice (for example, a height requirement, or a prohibition, as part of an "anti-nepotism" rule, on hiring employees' spouses) that has a disproportionate exclusionary effect on women, though it was not intended to exclude them. Traditionally, such a practice was unlawful unless the employer could show that it was a business necessity; in practice such a showing was difficult to make. Disparate impact litigation has been important in eliminating personnel practices that tended to exclude blacks (i.e., requiring a high-school diploma), but has not been very important in the area of sex discrimination. Most practices challenged under disparate impact theories involve tests and credentials, and these are rarely sex-biased. Recently, the Supreme Court watered down the "business justification" defense and shifted the burden of proof to the plaintiff, so we can expect disparate impact cases to decline.[37]

The other, and more common, type of sex discrimination case is the *disparate treatment* case. This requires proof that the employer intentionally treated the female employee (or applicant) less favorably than it would have treated a similarly situated male employee. The practical difficulties in such litigation are great. First, it is difficult to prove a complex counterfactual (for example, what would have happened if the employee had been male rather than female). Second, it often does not pay the plaintiff to invest in the necessary proof—which involves looking at similarly situated males to show that the plaintiff's inadequacies were not responsible for her being fired or otherwise mistreated.[38] The stakes are small. They consist of backpay minus whatever the plaintiff has earned in a substitute job (for the employee has a duty to mitigate her damages) plus reinstatement. But reinstatement will rarely be sought, since usually the plaintiff will have gotten another job while the litigation was pending and will be reluctant to go back to work for an employer who mistreated her and whom she sued. Finally, bringing an employment suit impairs the plaintiff's earning capac-

[37] *Wards Cove Packing Co., Inc. v Atonio*, 109 S Ct 2115 (1989).

[38] Rarely will an employer fire, or otherwise treat badly, a perfect worker, of whatever race or sex. Discrimination is more apt to be directed against workers who are not, or not much, better than average, and whose complaint is that the employer took a dimmer view of their failings than he would have of a white male's failings.

ity: employers are reluctant to hire people who sue employers![39]

Although the plaintiff's costs in bringing successful sex discrimination litigation under Title VII may well outweigh her gains, there is an important qualification. If class action treatment is possible, as where a large employer is alleged to be discriminating against all or most of its female employees, then plaintiffs will find safety in numbers and it will be feasible for them to develop statistical evidence of discrimination. Yet such evidence often is inconclusive. It usually comes down to an unexplained difference in the wages or number of men and women employed, and it is always possible for the employer to argue that the statistical methodology is insufficiently sensitive to identify all noninvidious explanatory variables.

To the extent that disparate treatment suits do succeed, it is uncertain whether they increase the net welfare of women. Since some forms of unlawful sex discrimination are efficient, Title VII litigation will reduce the efficiency with which employers use labor, and this will result in lower average wages and higher product prices. The direct costs of Title VII litigation—lawyers' fees, executive time, and so forth—will work in the same direction. Full-time housewives will bear a disproportionate share of these costs, since their husbands' wages will fall and the prices they and their husbands pay for goods and services will rise.[40] Conversely, single working women will tend to benefit, except to the extent that employers are reluctant to hire women in the first place out of fear that Title VII will restrict their ability to fire an unsatisfactory female employee without inviting a lawsuit.

C. Comparable Worth

Failure to achieve "comparable worth" has sometimes been challenged under the disparate impact theory of Title VII, but without success. Jobs traditionally dominated by women (the stereotypical examples are nursing and secretarial work) are on average less well paid than jobs traditionally dominated by men, such as truck driving. Proponents of "comparable worth" argue that the disparity reflects sex discrimination and can be eliminated by re-

---

[39] On the reluctance of women for this reason to bring sex-discrimination suits see Kristin Bumiller, *The Civil Rights Society: The Social Construction of Victims* 26 (Johns Hopkins, 1988).

[40] There are fewer full-time housewives today than there used to be, but there are still plenty. In 1985, 23.5 percent of all families had a full-time housewife. Rix, *The American Woman* at 374 table 14 (cited in note 19).

quiring employers to pay wages "objectively" commensurate with the skill, responsibility, and other attributes of each job. The short economic answer is that a competitive labor market will achieve comparable worth; for that is the equilibrium condition of such a market. If a particular job classification happens to be overpaid relative to skill, responsibility, and other considerations that determine the value and cost of a worker's time, workers will flow into the classification, reducing the wage until the excess demand is eliminated. And if the job classification happens to be underpaid, workers will leave for better jobs, causing the wage to rise.

There are, however, three important qualifications to this economic answer; the first two are closely related. First, the equilibrium that results will reflect any systematic wage differences that are due to efficient sex discrimination; and some, maybe most, discrimination is efficient. Second, to the extent that employers "steer" women into traditional women's jobs and men into traditional men's jobs, and this discrimination is not detected and prevented through enforcement of Title VII, competition will not eliminate discrimination based on sex. Finally, public employer labor markets may not be competitive; hiring and firing may be determined by political rather than economic considerations. Thus, requiring public employers to achieve comparable worth is less likely to produce market distortions than requiring private employers to do so.[41]

A deeper objection to making comparable worth mandatory in private markets is that comparable worth neglects important factors that bear on the determination of a competitive wage, such as investment in human capital. Women who because of voluntarily assumed family responsibilities expect to participate only intermittently in the labor market will be attracted to jobs that do not involve as great an investment in human capital, and such jobs will not (and from an economic standpoint) should not pay as well. Also, comparable worth does not take into account the desirability of allowing wages to fluctuate in order to correct temporary imbalances between supply and demand, when a particular labor market is not in equilibrium. Finally, if wages are set on the basis of what is deemed to be comparable worth and, as is likely, the resulting

[41] For evidence in support of these three points see Richard F. Kamalich and Solomon W. Polacheck, *Discrimination: Fact or Fiction? An Examination Using an Alternative Approach*, 49 S Econ J 450 (1982); Bielby and Baron, 76 Am Econ Rev Papers & Proc 43 (cited in note 3); and Elaine Sorensen, *Implementing Comparable Worth: A Survey of Recent Job Evaluation Studies*, 76 Am Econ Rev Papers & Proc 364 (May 1986), respectively.

pattern is not the equilibrium pattern for the labor market in question, entry or exit will occur until the old "discriminatory" pattern is restored. In other words, if women (for whatever reason) prefer "traditionally female" jobs, once the wages in those jobs rise women will enter these occupations in great numbers, driving the wage back down. Hence a commitment to comparable worth implies not merely one-time, but continuous, intervention in competitive wage-setting.

Even if comparable worth were fully achieved, women as a whole might not be better off. Women in the traditional women's jobs would have higher wages, but fewer of them would be employed, because employers would have an increased incentive to substitute capital for these jobs and, to the extent substitution was infeasible, to reduce the scale of the activity in which these women were employed. In general, then, comparable worth can be expected to reduce the employment of women[42] as well as to transfer wealth from childless women to mothers, since the latter are more likely to be attracted to traditional women's jobs, those being the jobs for women who want to balance family and career. In addition, the social costs resulting from so massive a public interference with labor markets would be great and would be borne in significant part by women, as we have seen.

D. Sexual Harassment

When efforts were first made to attack sexual harassment under Title VII they seemed an exotic extension of the statute, in part because of the strange implication that a bisexual harasser couldn't be liable under the Act, since his conduct was sex neutral. However, the case for prohibiting sexual harassment may actually be stronger from an economic standpoint than the case for prohibiting conventional sex discrimination. Sexual harassment, properly defined to exclude mere flirtations and solicitations, is a coercive practice related to such plainly inefficient practices as rape and extortion.[43] Sexual harassment is unlikely, save for the costs of prevention, to be in the employer's interest. While, in principle, grant-

---

[42] For evidence see June O'Neill, Michael Brien, and James Cunningham, *Effects of Comparable Worth Policy: Evidence From Washington State*, 79 Am Econ Rev Papers & Proc 305, 308 (May 1989); Mincer, 3 J Labor Econ at S29-S30 (cited in note 35); see also Johnson and Solon, 20 U Mich J L Ref at 202-03 (cited in note 4); Mark R. Killingsworth, *The Economics of Comparable Worth: Analytical, Empirical, and Policy Questions*, in Heidi I. Hartmann, ed, *Comparable Worth: New Directions for Research* 86 (National Academy, 1985).

[43] See Posner, *Economic Analysis of Law* at 201 (cited in note 1).

ing a "license" to male supervisory employees to harass female employees would enable the employer to pay a lower wage to those male employees, the reduced cost of hiring supervisors is unlikely to offset: (1) the higher wage the employer will have to pay its female employees to compensate them for being exposed to sexual harassment; (2) time lost by employees in harassing or warding off harassment; (3) distortion in promotions; and (4) adverse selection of employees (the employer would be a magnet for male employees wanting to harass females and for female employees desiring to use their wiles to gain advancement). The problem is that, like other antisocial behavior in the workplace (embezzlement, for example), the costs of prevention are high; and this is an argument for public enforcement—depending of course on *its* costs.

The novelty in the legal concept of sexual harassment is that the usual defendant in a Title VII sexual harassment case is not the harassing male employee, but the employer. It is as if banks were the defendants in cases involving embezzlement by bank employees. The proper analogy, however, is to the tort doctrine of respondeat superior. The most efficient method of discouraging sexual harassment may be by creating incentives for the employer to police the conduct of its supervisory employees, and this is done by making the employer liable. Because "employer" is broadly defined in Title VII, the supervisory employee himself can be and sometimes is made a defendant in a Title VII sexual harassment case; so again the analogy to respondeat superior (which is an additional ground of liability, not a defense for the primary tortfeasor) is a close one.

E. Pregnancy Discrimination Act

The requirement that the employer not differentiate among its employees on the basis of pregnancy is analytically the same as a requirement that the employer pay the same retirement benefits to male and female employees despite women's superior longevity, or a requirement that the employer grant maternity leave (in other words, agree to reinstate female employees who take time off to have or take care of their babies). In all three cases, the law compels the employer to ignore a real difference in the average cost of male and female employees. The result is inefficient, but a more interesting point is that it may not benefit women as a whole.[44]

[44] Moreover, unisex longevity tables penalize women buying life insurance, unisex liability insurance premium-setting penalizes women because they are safer drivers than men,

The employer is required in effect to pay them greater fringe benefits than men (since health care for pregnancy is a benefit men do not require). The employer cannot recoup by reducing women's wages—that would violate the Equal Pay Act—but he can minimize his costs by employing fewer women (as by automating secretarial work faster and more completely). To the extent that this succeeds, women will be hurt. To the extent it does not succeed, the employer will experience a rise in his average cost of labor, causing him to reduce the average wage he pays.

Women will lose not only directly, but also indirectly, in their role as the wives of men who will now be paid less. The clearest loser will be a married but childless working woman.[46] Her wage and that of her husband will fall, and she will not recoup the loss in higher fringe benefits, because the additional benefits are of value only to women with children. And even if the aggregate income of the household is higher, women may have less power within the household if their paychecks are smaller. This, however, is pure speculation—it is far from clear that women's consumption within the household depends on the relative size of the woman's paycheck, as distinct from her relative contribution to the full (nonpecuniary as well as pecuniary) income of the household. Housewives will also suffer from the Pregnancy Discrimination Act because their husbands' wages will fall. The point can be generalized: housewives, being economically identified with their husbands, are hurt by efforts to reduce sex discrimination. The clearest beneficiaries of sex-neutral fringe benefits are unmarried working women with many children—a small group.

This analysis, by illustrating the possibility of deep conflicts of interest among women, may help explain why many women are not feminists. Depending on age, marital status, number and age of children, and other factors, women may gain or lose from measures ostensibly designed to eliminate discrimination "against women." Indeed, women are so heterogeneous a group that it is hard to imagine what public policies would benefit them as a group—except

---

and preventing insurers from differentiating among risk groups on the most efficient basis increases the social costs of insurance. These effects illustrate the tendency of sex discrimination law to bring about offsetting redistributions of wealth. Such redistributions are not costless. The only argument for them is that they will contribute to breaking down stereotypes. This is implausible. It is not a stereotype, but a fact, that women live longer than men, have fewer accidents, incur greater medical expenses, and so forth.

[46] There are many women in this category. In 1985, 17.1 percent of all families were childless married couples in which both spouses were working. Rix, *The American Woman* at 374 table 14 (cited in note 19).

policies designed to maximize social wealth by maintaining and strengthening free markets.

F. Equal Protection

The interpretation of the Equal Protection Clause as prohibiting sex discrimination in employment unless the discrimination is justified by an important governmental interest has thus far had little effect. Much of the prohibition overlaps Title VII. Many cases have been brought by men rather than women, although women's groups generally support these cases on the ground that they combat stereotypes harmful to women's aspirations for job equality.[46] Many cases have the usual ambiguous effects. Consider the requirement that spousal benefits under social security programs be equalized regardless of the sex of the spouse, so that a widower is entitled to the same social security death benefit as a widow. If the total benefits payable under social security are assumed to be fixed, the result of this entitlement will be to benefit the better off at the expense of the worse off, since widowers are on average wealthier than widows. The *Feeney* decision,[47] upholding Massachusetts' policy of giving veterans a preference in public employment, illustrates the possibility that the optimal ideology for the women's movement may well be a libertarian one. Veterans' benefits programs, which of course systematically benefit men over women, are redistributive measures that are contrary to the principles of efficiency and limited government.

Conclusion

What has been the net effect of the cascade of laws and lawsuits aimed at eliminating sex discrimination in employment? This is maddeningly difficult to say, but it is possible that women as a whole have not benefited and have in fact suffered. Because of the heterogeneity of women as an economic class and their interdependence with men, laws aimed at combating sex discrimination are more likely to benefit particular groups of women at the expense of other groups rather than women as a whole. And to the extent that the overall effect of the law is to reduce aggregate social welfare because of the allocative and administrative costs of the law,

---

[46] The fact that laws ostensibly discriminating in favor of women may actually harm them suggests that laws ostensibly forbidding discrimination against women may also harm women.

[47] *Personnel Administrator v Feeney*, 442 US 256 (1979).

women as a group are hurt along with men. Sex discrimination has long been on the decline, for reasons unrelated to law, and this makes it all the more likely that the principal effect of public intervention may have been to make women as a group worse off by reducing the efficiency of the economy. The case for ambitious extensions of sex discrimination law—for example in the direction of comparable worth—is therefore weak.

These suggestions should not be surprising, in light of the extensive, and largely negative, economic literature on regulation. There is a tendency to suppose that laws forbidding discrimination are somehow exempt from the critique of regulation. This position is difficult to sustain.

It is possible that the economic costs of sex discrimination law are offset by gains not measured in an economic analysis—gains in self-esteem, for example. But it is not clear that, if the canvass is broadened in this fashion, the picture brightens. For example, if by reducing the wages of men sex discrimination law propels more wives into the job market, with the result that (since they still bear the principal burden of household production) they work harder, have fewer children, and have less stable marriages, it is not clear that they are better off on balance than they were when their husbands had higher wages and they stayed home. The social, like the economic, consequences of sex discrimination law are murky, and not necessarily positive. In any event it is important to know what the sex discrimination laws cost; the price tag for an increase in women's self-esteem, if known, might be thought too high by society.

Name Index

www.ingramcontent.com/pod-product-compliance
Lightning Source LLC
LaVergne TN
LVHW081342011026
849161LV00013BB/2993